The boundaries
of international law

Melland Schill Studies in International Law
Series editor Professor Dominic McGoldrick

The Melland Schill name has a long-established reputation for high standards of scholarship. Each volume in the series addresses major public international law issues and current developments. Many of the Melland Schill volumes have become standard works of reference. Interdisciplinary and accessible, the contributions are vital reading for students, scholars and practitioners of public international law, international organisations, international relations, international politics, international economics and international development.

The boundaries
of international law

A feminist analysis

Hilary Charlesworth
and Christine Chinkin

Juris Publishing

MANCHESTER
1824

Manchester University Press

Published by Manchester University Press
Altrincham Street, Manchester M1 7JA, UK
www.manchesteruniversitypress.co.uk

British Library Cataloguing-in-Publication Data is available

Library of Congress Cataloging-in-Publication Data is available

ISBN 978 0 7190 3739 9 paperback

First published by Manchester University Press in hardback 2000

This edition first published 2016

Printed by Lightning Source

Contents

Contents

Foreword

The law has not always served women well. For centuries, the legal system, shaped and enforced exclusively by men, denied women the attributes of citizenship and personhood, and subordinated them to the decisions of men. Lacking standing, women who fought to overcome their legal disabilities had to enlist the support of fair minded men. Gradually, the most blatant forms of discrimination and disability were removed, so that women could be considered as 'persons', be guardians of their children, exercise the right to vote and enter professions.

Women anticipated that when the main barriers went down, when they were able to take part in making and applying laws, the legal system would deliver equal justice. They turned to the law to protect their interests. But the law remained insensitive to many concerns of women, and did not protect them, for example, as victims of rape and domestic violence.

Feminist legal scholars analysed the law and legal institutions. Their work revealed that the legal system remained permeated by outmoded but nevertheless deeply entrenched attitudes concerning the roles and status of men and women in society. The inherent conservatism of legal institutions, and respect for precedent and established categories, helped to perpetuate the underlying gender bias of the law.

Now, and not before time, feminist scholars have turned their attention to international law. The authors are in the vanguard of the attack on what is indeed a formidable bastion. Their aim is to deconstruct international law, to investigate the ways in which international law has brushed aside the injustices of women's situations around the world, and to 'redraw the boundaries' of international law so that it responds to these injustices.

In mounting their assault, the authors have drawn upon their depth of knowledge of international law and of feminist legal theory and their commitment to equity and justice. By exposing the elements of international law to the clear light of feminist analysis, the authors show that it suffers from defects parallel to those of domestic legal systems. Although in classical theory the subjects of international law (and those most vitally concerned in its content) are states, rather than individuals, international law, as any system of law, is the creation of human beings and its ultimate impact is on individual behaviour. Whatever theory is preferred, whether international law is seen as a manifestation of the universal values of natural law or as derived from state practice, whether it is considered as a neutral set of rules impartially applied or as a process of decision-making, international law is influenced by choices between competing values and by policy considerations. Like all legal systems it is based on values and assumptions about how people should live together in society and how organised communities should relate to each other.

When it is considered that the same individuals and groups who have traditionally controlled laws within the state also determine how the state will act in its relations with other states, it is hardly surprising to find that international law speaks from the perspective of an exclusively male hierarchy of power or that it shows little concern for women, their interests and their special vulnerabilities.

A recurrent theme in this study is that of the absence of women from the processes of international law, starting with the organs of the state, and extending to the make up of international organisations, international courts and tribunals. It is within the power of states to change this; they have international obligations to promote equality of participation. But state action has not gone much further than their many exhortations to each other to take action on this issue. As a consequence, at least until the arrival of scholars like the present authors, women have been denied the opportunity to contribute to the shaping of international law, its goals and its priorities.

The strength of this work is that the authors have used their knowledge of international law to throw new light on its underlying theories and to stimulate new ways of thinking about its traditional concepts. Take, for example, the authors' challenge to the central concept of the sovereign state and the current approach to the legitimacy of states. The recognition of a state allows it to enter the community of nations on equal terms. In theory the concepts of self-determination, and the implied consent of its people, underpin the validity of the state. But, as the authors show, double standards apply in assessing the legitimacy of the state. The entity of Southern Rhodesia and the Bantustans of South Africa were denied recognition because they were founded on racial discrimination. But the systematic exclusion of women from participation in the institutions of government and in decision-making does not have the same consequences. There is no challenge to the legitimacy of a state such as Kuwait, which excludes one half of its population from the right to exercise political rights and to participation in public affairs and discriminates against them in many other ways. Has consistency of principle been replaced by expedience? Will the Palestinian women, whose story is so graphically told here, find that their struggle alongside men for self-determination does not guarantee their right to participate on equal terms in the new entity, or that recognition will not be withheld on that basis?

The entirely unacceptable situation in international law is that the fundamental norms which all states must observe include systematic racial discrimination but not systematic discrimination against women, or even widespread gender-based violence. Women have had to mount a campaign to have violence against women, in all its forms, recognised as an international legal wrong, for which states can be held responsible. Their efforts, described here, show clearly just how states have been complicit or have acquiesced in this kind of abuse, and why the exercise of state power is essential to ensure the right to life and personal security of women and their freedom from cruel and inhuman treatment.

The international law of human rights ought to have a better record than other areas in regard to women's interests, bearing in mind that its central principles are those of equality and non-discrimination. But even when the promotion of universal human rights was made a principal goal of the United Nations Charter, women feared that they would be overlooked. To ensure that their rights were given full attention, they lobbied to have a separate UN body to deal with women's status. Paradoxically, the creation of the Commission on the Status of Women, and the adoption of a separate Convention on the Elimination of All Forms of Discrimination Against Women allowed the other UN human rights institutions and treaty bodies to overlook the gender dimension of their own instruments, and to pay little attention to such issues as violence, sexual abuse and forced prostitution.

There is some good news, however. The past failures of mainstream human rights law to deal adequately with issues of women's rights and with the finer points of discrimination, have been partly offset by recent positive developments. These have been prompted at least in part by the work of feminist scholars and activists.

Some of the treaty bodies are now acting to bridge the gap between women's rights and human rights and to give more attention to issues affecting women. An example of the new approach is the recent work of the Human Rights Committee. Its current draft general comment on article 3 of the International Covenant on Civil and Political Rights involves a comprehensive gender analysis of every provision of the Covenant to identify issues of special relevance to women. The draft incorporates the recent practice of the Committee and addresses some of the concerns raised by the authors. For example, although, as the authors point out, the Committee did not include female infanticide in its general comment on the right to life (article 6), the Committee now raises this issue, as well as prenatal sex selection and abortion of female foetuses, in the reporting process, where relevant to the situation in a particular state. Issues such as restrictions on freedom of movement, forced labour and trafficking, whether in relation to prostitution, domestic service, threats to life from unsafe abortion, compulsory sterilisation, violence and sexual abuse of women are given equivalent treatment. The principle underlying these developments is that for the state to fulfil its obligation to respect and to ensure Covenant rights to women, it must take effective measures to protect them against widespread and systematic threats to their life and personal security.

Other good news, the result of extensive campaigning by women, is that the Committee on the Elimination of Discrimination Against Women has been strengthened by the adoption in October 1999 of an Optional Protocol allowing for the right of petition, and providing for an inquiry procedure; and CEDAW's meeting time has been extended. Successful lobbying by women has also resulted in the project for the international criminal court including rape and sexual violence as violations of the laws of war, as crimes against humanity, and in some cases as war crimes in situations of armed conflict.

These advances by no means displace the central thesis of the authors that women's interests and concerns have played little part in the development of international law. Nor do they put right the many, long standing injustices of the international system in regard to women. Nevertheless, they show that those working for change can achieve practical results.

This feminist analysis of international law is an important contribution to the process of change and to the redressing of past wrongs. If it provokes debate and even dissension, its purpose will be well served. For its objective must be to bring about a change in thinking about the basic concepts and practice of international law and to lead to a new understanding of the limitations of international law, and also of its untapped potential as a force for justice. One can only hope that the authors' insights will provide a fruitful source of inspiration for the future development of international law, and that their brave assault on the bastions of tradition will be rewarded by a gradual moving forward of the boundaries.

Elizabeth Evatt
Member, Human Rights Committee
Sydney
December 1999

Preface

As our children regularly remind us, this book has taken many years to complete. It was conceived in 1991, when Vaughan Lowe, then general editor of the international law series at Manchester University Press, encouraged us to write on the implications of feminist theory for international law. Moves across countries and around the world, babies, deanships, car accidents and other aspects of real life have pushed back our deadlines time and time again. In his *Lives of the English Poets*, Samuel Johnson ponders the question of why it took Alexander Pope five years to complete his translation of Homer's (relatively short) *Iliad*. '[T]he progress of Pope may seem to have been slow', writes Johnson, 'but the distance is commonly very great between actual performances and speculative possibility.' He goes on:

> It is natural to suppose, that as much as had been done to-day may be done tomorrow; but on the morrow some difficulty emerges, or some external impediment obstructs. Indolence, interruption, business, and pleasure, all take their turns of retardation; and every long work is lengthened by a thousand causes that can, and ten thousand that cannot, be recounted. Perhaps no extensive and multifarious performance was ever effected within the term originally fixed in the undertaker's mind. He that runs against Time has an antagonist not subject to casualties.[1]

This book cannot claim the literary qualities of Pope's translation, but it shares its unsuccessful race against time.

Over all these years we have incurred debts to many people and institutions and are pleased to be able to thank them in print at last. We have benefited greatly from the energy and work of research assistants: Jillian Caldwell, Jane Cox, Anna Funder, Urfan Khaliq, Jyoti Larke, Suzanne Leal, Wai Quen, Shaki Sansui, Aaron Shumway, Jane Stratton and Belle

---

[1] S. Johnson, *Lives of the English Poets* (Oxford, Oxford University Press, 1906) 255.

Yang. Cassie Chinkin provided helpful research and organisational assistance. Max Charlesworth and Dianne Otto generously read the manuscript and made many useful comments. Dominic McGoldrick, now the editor of this series, also helped us with comments. Philip Alston, Elizabeth Evatt, Judith Gardam, Michelle Jarvis, Suzanne Karstedt, Anne Orford, Bruno Simma, Cate Steains and Patricia Viseur-Sellers provided valuable information. We were also fortunate to be able to talk to Palestinian women in Gaza in 1993 and Saharawi women in the Western Sahara and London in 1993 about their experiences of struggles for self-determination.

The Law Faculties at the Universities of Melbourne, Sydney, Adelaide, Southampton, the Australian National University, the London School of Economics and the Law Program in the Research School of Social Sciences at the Australian National University supported this research in many different ways. The Frances Lewis Center at Washington and Lee Law School and its Director, Scott Sundby, offered a peaceful haven in the last stages of the book. Colleagues and students at all these different institutions gave us insights, advice and encouragement. We have also benefited from conversations and participation in conferences and workshops with colleagues and friends in academic institutions, non-governmental and inter-governmental organisations around the world. Charles Guest gave tremendous support to this project on many levels throughout its long development. The Australian Research Council provided funding for much of our research and the Oxford Peace Project supported work for chapter eight. We offer our warm thanks to all these people and institutions. In particular we thank Shelley Wright with whom we began this intellectual adventure and who has been consistently generous in her friendship and encouragement.

The book builds on some research that has already been published, although it has been revised and updated. Parts of chapter two draw on H. Charlesworth, 'Feminist critiques of international law and their critics', [1994–5] *Third World Legal Studies* 1 and H. Charlesworth, 'Current trends in international legal theory', in S. Blay, R. Piotrowicz and M. Tsaymenyi eds, *Public International Law: An Australian Perspective* (Melbourne, Oxford University Press, 1997) 251. Parts of chapter four are built on C. Chinkin, 'Reservations and Objections to the Convention on the Elimination of All Forms of Discrimination against Women', in J-P. Gardner ed., *Human Rights as General Norms and a State's Right to Opt Out* (London, British Institute of International and Comparative Law, 1997) 64 and H. Charlesworth and C. Chinkin, 'The gender of jus cogens', 15 *Human Rights Quarterly* (1993) 63. Parts of chapter five draw on H. Charlesworth, 'The sex of the state in international law', in N. Naffine and R. Owens eds, *Sexing the Subject of Law* (Sydney, Law Book Co. Ltd, 1997) 251; H. Charlesworth, 'International human rights law: prospects and problems for Palestinian women', in S. Bowen ed., *Human Rights, Self-Determination and Political Change in the Occupied Palestinian Territories* (The Hague, Kluwer Law International,

1997) 79 and C. Chinkin, 'The potential and pitfalls of the right to self-determination for women', *ibid.* at 93. Chapter six develops H. Charlesworth, 'Transforming the United Men's club: feminist futures for the United Nations', 4 *Transnational Law and Contemporary Problems* (1994) 421. Chapter seven draws on H. Charlesworth, 'What are women's human rights?', in R. Cook ed., *Human Rights of Women: National and International Perspectives* (Philadelphia, University of Pennsylvania Press, 1994) 58 and C. Chinkin, 'Women's human rights: guaranteed by universal standards or discounted by cultural bias?', 5 (2) *Collected Courses of the Academy of European Law* (1997) 11. Chapter eight builds on C. Chinkin, 'Women and peace: militarism and oppression', in K. Mahoney and P. Mahoney eds, *Human Rights in the 21st Century: A Global Challenge* (Dordrecht, Martinus Nijhoff, 1993) 405 and chapter nine on C. Chinkin, 'Rape and sexual abuse of women in international law', 5 *European Journal of International Law* (1994) 326.

In general, the text is up to date to December 1998, although in some cases it has been possible to refer to more recent developments.

H C and C C
Canberra and London
January 2000

Abbreviations

ADR	'alternative' forms of dispute resolution
ANZUS	Pacific Security Treaty between Australia, New Zealand and the United States
ASEAN	Association of South East Asian Nations
CEDAW	Committee on the Elimination of Discrimination Against Women
CERD	Committee on the Elimination of Racial Discrimination
CHR	Commission on Human Rights (UN)
CLS	critical legal studies
CSCE	Conference on Security and Co-operation in Europe
CSW	Commission on the Status of Women (UN)
EC	European Community
ECHR	European Court of Human Rights
ECJ	European Court of Justice
ECOMOG	ECOWAS Monitoring Group
ECOSOC	Economic and Social Council (UN)
ECOWAS	Economic Community of West African States
EU	European Union
FAO	Food and Agriculture Organisation
FRY	Federal Republic of Yugoslavia
GA	General Assembly (UN)
GATT	General Agreement on Tariffs and Trade
GDI	gender-related development index
ICAO	International Civil Aviation Organisation
ICC	International Criminal Court
ICCPR	International Covenant on Civil and Political Rights
ICESCR	International Covenant on Economic, Social and Cultural Rights
ICJ	International Court of Justice
ICTR	International Criminal Tribunal for Rwanda
ICTY	International Criminal Tribunal for Former Yugoslavia
ILC	International Law Commission (UN)

ILO	International Labour Organisation
IMF	International Monetary Fund
IMO	International Maritime Organisation
INSTRAW	International Research and Training Institute for the Advancement of Women
JIU	Joint Inspection Unit (UN)
NATO	North Atlantic Treaty Organisation
NGO	non-governmental organisation
NIEO	New International Economic Order
OAS	Organisation of American States
OAU	Organisation of African Unity
OECD	Organisation for Economic Co-operation and Development
OECS	Organisation of Eastern Caribbean States
OSCE	Organisation for Security and Co-operation in Europe
PCIJ	Permanent Court of International Justice
PLO	Palestine Liberation Organization
SC	Security Council (UN)
UDHR	Universal Declaration of Human Rights
UN	United Nations
UNCC	UN Compensation Commission
UNCITRAL	UN Commission on International Trade Law
UNDP	UN Development Programme
UNFPA	UN Population Fund
UNITA	National Union for the Total Liberation of Angola
UNHCR	UN High Commissioner for Refugees
UNICEF	UN Children's Fund
UNIFEM	UN Development Fund for Women
UNITAR	UN Institute for Training and Research
UNPROFOR	UN Protection Force
UNTAC	UN Transitional Authority in Cambodia
UNWRA	UN Works and Relief Agency
WHO	World Health Organisation
WTO	World Trade Organisation

For
Cassie, Mark, Stephanie and Will

1

Women and the international legal system

Introduction

This book is about why issues of sex and gender matter in international law. Its central argument is that the absence of women in the development of international law has produced a narrow and inadequate jurisprudence that has, among other things, legitimated the unequal position of women around the world rather than challenged it. In this sense, the absence of women in international law is a critical feature of the traditional canon – its boundaries depend upon it. Our aim is to encourage a rethinking of the discipline of international law so that it can offer a more useful framework for international and national justice.

The scope of international law has increased significantly throughout the twentieth century. It now pervades international relations and national political and legal systems. International law is a mechanism for distributing power and resources in the international and national communities. It offers a wide range of normative prescriptions: from regulating coercive behaviour between states, and between states and non-state actors, to the allocation and control of space and territory from Antarctica to the high seas to outer space; from the protection of human rights, the global environment and endangered species to the management of the international system of trade and finance. However, while the international legal system may be broadening in scope, it remains narrow in perspective. Its constraints could be analysed in many different ways, for example from the perspectives of those states that have played little role in its development, or of non-governmental organisations (NGOs), or of individuals that seek access to it. This book examines the boundaries and limits of international law from a critical and feminist perspective. Women form over half the world's population, but their voices, in all their variety, have been thoroughly obscured by and within the international legal order. This book attempts to give expression to some of those voices.

In this opening chapter, we describe, in very broad terms, the conditions of women's lives. The picture that emerges is that the quality of women's lives globally is consistently different from and lesser than men's. We then consider why the international legal order has paid comparatively little attention to the position of women. Finally, we outline the book's general structure and aims.

The categories 'women' and 'female' are contentious when used to make general points, especially in an international context. The use of an undifferentiated classification such as 'women' imposes the appearance of homogeneity that conceals real differences in the lives of women. These include race, ethnicity, indigeneity, religion, class or caste, wealth, familial status, geographic location, education, sexuality and age. In many situations it would be fruitless, as well as inaccurate, to assume that the lives of, for example, a young Afghan woman refugee, a middle-class Canadian housewife and an older Zimbabwean woman agricultural worker are subject to similar pressures and influences. However, because international law claims general, global application and draws no conceptual distinction between its human subjects (nor indeed its primary subjects, states), employing the category 'women' can be a valuable method of highlighting the commonality of the marginalisation of all women in the international legal system.[1] In fact, the international legal system fails all groups of women whatever categorisation is adopted. In this book, we attempt to be specific in using the terms 'women' and 'female' in particular contexts, but we acknowledge that there is inevitably some oversimplification. It is striking that a parallel problem with the use of the categories 'men' or 'male' rarely prompts any question. Men and maleness are assumed to be the norm from which women and femaleness are to be differentiated. Women are construed as the 'other', the deviant from the norm.

We also use a variety of other terms in this book that might be criticised for their generality and lack of specificity. For example, we refer to 'developing' and 'developed' or 'industrialised' states, 'the West', 'the North' and 'the South' (terms that make little geographic sense), 'first world' and 'third world'. Such categories gloss over significant differences between states and the changes that have taken place within and between them. Over thirty years have passed since the decolonisation of many states,[2] especially within Africa, Asia, the Pacific and the Caribbean, and the specificities in their post-colonisation histories cannot be captured by such labels. Nevertheless we employ these broad terms because they are part of the existing vocabulary and concepts of the international legal system that we aim to assess critically from feminist perspectives.

---

[1] For a fuller discussion of this point in the context of the right to food see C. Chinkin and S. Wright, 'The hunger trap: women, food and self-determination', 14 *Michigan Journal of International Law* (1993) 262.

[2] See the Declaration on the Granting of Independence to Colonial Territories and Peoples, GA Res. 1514 (XV), 14 December 1960.

One characteristic that all adult women share is that they have been girls. There is a growing international legal literature on the rights of the child,[3] which occasionally differentiates between girls and boys. Our primary focus is on adult women rather than on girl-children.[4] However, much of our discussion may have relevance to both girls and women: first, because the age of transition from girlhood to womanhood is fluid; second, because womanhood is prematurely imposed upon many girls, for example through sexual abuse, child marriage, trafficking and genital mutilation; and third, because the situation of women has a direct bearing on the situation of girls.

Gender and sex

This book uses the categories of both gender and sex in its analysis of international law. What do they mean and how do they differ? Feminist investigations of different areas of knowledge frequently concentrate upon gender as a category of analysis. The notion of gender captures the ascribed, social nature of distinctions between women and men – the excess cultural baggage associated with biological sex. 'Gender' draws attention to aspects of social relations that are culturally contingent and without foundation in biological necessity. The term also has the advantage of particularly emphasising relationality, that is the connection between definitions of masculinity and femininity,[5] thereby avoiding the implication that only women should be involved in an investigation of gender. Sex, on the other hand, is typically used to refer to biological differences between women and men.

Much theoretical writing about gender assumes that sex is a fixed, immutable characteristic and that it is a given, rather than a contestable category. Indeed, it has been argued that terms such as 'sex' or 'sexual difference' carry with them the resonance of biological determinism and thus should be avoided.[6] Jane Flax has pointed out, however, that the separation of 'gender' and 'sex' in feminist inquiry rests on problematic and culture-specific oppositions such as nature/culture and body/mind.[7] If we attend to the

[3] E.g. G. Van Bueren, *The International Law on the Rights of the Child* (Dordrecht, Martinus Nijhoff, 1995).

[4] See F. Olsen, 'Children's rights: some feminist approaches to the United Nations Convention on the Rights of the Child', 6 *International Journal of Law and the Family* (1992) 192 for a discussion of some of the complexities of feminist attitudes to children's rights.

[5] J. Scott, 'Gender: a useful category of analysis', 91 *American Historical Review* (1986) 1053 at 1054. See also A. Oakley, 'A brief history of gender?', in A. Oakley and J. Mitchell (eds), *Who's Afraid of Feminism? Seeing Through the Backlash* (New York, The New Press, 1997) 29.

[6] J. Scott, above note 5 at 1054.

[7] J. Flax, 'Postmodernism and gender relations in feminist theory', 12 *Signs* (1987) 621 at 635–6.

constitutive role of the law and society in forming the 'naturally' sexed person, the concepts of 'sex' and 'biological difference' can be seen to have constructed, contingent and political elements.[8] The major difference between the notions of 'gender' and 'sex' is in their focus on different elements of dichotomies such as body/mind and nature/culture. Sexing draws attention to body and nature while gendering emphasises mind and culture. The two approaches are in this sense complementary and both are invoked throughout the book. Particular understandings of both gender and sexual differences help construct the 'realities' of international law.

The global position of women

Although its forms differ significantly across societies and cultures, the phenomenon of women's subordination is found worldwide. Throughout the world women are economically, socially, politically, legally and culturally disadvantaged compared with similarly situated men. These disadvantages operate on a number of levels, international, regional, national, local, communal and familial. While these areas can be usefully separated out for the purposes of analysis, they are interconnected and mutually reinforcing. Indeed, as is discussed in chapter 2, the very categories used – 'economics', 'society', 'politics', 'law', 'culture' – are defined by reference to male lives and male experiences. Although many men also suffer forms of oppression that reduce their public autonomy and affect the quality of their lives, it remains true that a category of elite men monopolise all secular, religious, national and international institutional forms of power. This monopoly means that men's interests are defined and accepted as apparently objective and neutral categories, to the ultimate benefit of all men.

One of the consequences of the United Nations (UN) Decade for Women, 1976–85, has been pressure for the generation and analysis of sex-disaggregated data in some significant areas of human activity, although there remain large gaps in the information. The UN Development Programme (UNDP), the UN Division for the Advancement of Women, the UN Development Fund for Women (UNIFEM) and the International Research and Training Institute for the Advancement of Women (INSTRAW) have been particularly active in collecting and analysing this data and making it accessible. The following account draws heavily upon their publications.[9]

---

[8] M. Davies, 'Taking the inside out: sex and gender in the legal subject', in N. Naffine and R. Owens (eds), *Sexing the Subject of Law* (Sydney, Law Book Co. Ltd, 1997) 25.

[9] A number of other UN bodies are active in producing such data in their fields of operation, e.g. the UN Children's Fund (UNICEF), the UN Population Fund (UNFPA) and the World Health Organisation (WHO).

We should acknowledge the limitations of reliance on statistics alone to describe social phenomena. Empirical data, however accurate their collection and collation, reveal only a partial picture of any situation and may obscure the realities of complex social and political ordering. In times of rapid change, especially in economic, social and legal matters, reliance upon such data can be misleading in that it lags behind subsequent developments. Moreover, UN concern with women-specific statistics appears to have peaked in 1995, the year of the Fourth World Conference on Women, held in Beijing. UNDP's 1995 *Human Development Report* contains considerably more sex-disaggregated information than any of its successors,[10] and many statistics have not been updated since. Despite these limitations, we use the available statistics here to provide a context for an analysis of international law that takes women seriously.

On internationally recognised socio-economic indicators, men's quality of life regularly rates better than that of women, whether they live within the industrialised or the developing world. Although women tend to live longer than men, the quality of life for most women is considerably worse and in many areas there is little sign of improvement over time. For example, the ability to earn an independent income is one aspect of life quality. Women's labour force participation rates globally increased only 4 percentage points in the twenty-five years from 1970 to 1995.[11] In 1990, women's share of the adult labour force in the developing world (outside agriculture) varied from 21 per cent in Northern Africa and 25 per cent in Western Asia to 44 per cent in Central Asia.[12] In the industrialised world, women formed 47 per cent of the work force in Eastern Europe and 42 per cent in Western Europe.[13] Occupational segregation within the work force on the basis of sex varies widely. The global percentage of women in administrative and managerial jobs is just over 14 per cent.[14] Industrialised countries have an average of 27.4 per cent, with Canada at 42.2 per cent and Japan, Luxembourg and France at less than 10 per cent.[15] In South Asia, the percentage of women in such positions is 3.1 per cent and in sub-Saharan Africa 10.2 per cent.[16]

Women's average wage rates are consistently lower than men's. Although there is incomplete data, especially on rural and agricultural wages, the average wage for women globally, outside agriculture, is approximately three-quarters

---

[10] UNDP, *Human Development Report* (New York, Oxford University Press, 1995).

[11] UNDP, *Human Development Report* (New York, Oxford University Press, 1998) at 165.

[12] UN, *The World's Women 1995: Trends and Statistics* (New York, UN, 1995) at 109. See also UNDP, *Human Development Report* (New York, Oxford University Press, 1997) at 182–3.

[13] UN, *The World's Women 1995*, above note 12 at 109.

[14] UNDP 1997, above note 12 at 154.

[15] *Ibid.* at 152.

[16] *Ibid.* at 143.

of the average male wage.[17] The ratio varies widely between countries. For example in Tanzania women earn 92 per cent of the average male wage, 75 per cent in the United States, 63 per cent in Canada, 60 per cent in Syria and 42 per cent in Bangladesh.[18] The UNDP has noted that these figures probably underestimate the average disparity because the female–male wage ratio is likely to be lower in the agricultural sector, where many women work.[19]

What causes this significant difference between women's and men's access to income? Part of the problem lies in the fact that the majority of women continue to work in so-called 'female' occupations resulting in the *de facto* segregation and the undervaluation of 'female' work. Occupational evaluations and classifications often depend on gender stereotypes: a typically 'female' job is almost always less well remunerated than a comparable male one.[20] Added to this is women's relative lack of bargaining power through trade union action, cultural and social norms that assign primary parenting duties to women, together with the unavailability of adequate maternity leave and unfounded assumptions about the absenteeism of women workers.[21] Women are also particularly at risk in workplace restructuring in times of economic deterioration. For example, a study of Australian workplaces has shown that 'enterprise bargaining' practices and the introduction of 'flexible' working hours has had a disadvantageous effect on women as compared to men workers.[22] The transition in Central and Eastern Europe from centrally planned to 'market' economies has had a disproportionate impact on women workers: female unemployment rates are higher and women remain unemployed for longer periods than men. Women are the first to be retrenched in 'streamlining' exercises, and employers have cut back on services, such as childcare, which support women's workforce participation.[23]

The UNDP has observed that when paid and unpaid work are combined, women typically work longer hours than men. In a study of thirty-one developing and industrialised countries, women carried 53 per cent of the total burden of work on average in developing countries and 51 per cent in industrialised countries.[24] In rural areas, the total work time of both women

[17] UNDP 1995, above note 10 at 36–7.

[18] *Ibid.* at 36 (table 2.5).

[19] *Ibid.* at 37.

[20] R. Anker, 'Theories of occupational segregation by sex: an overview', 136 *International Labour Review* (1997) 315 at 316.

[21] UNDP 1995, above note 10 at 37.

[22] S. Charlesworth, *Stretching Flexibility: Enterprise Bargaining, Women Workers and Changes to Working Hours* (Sydney, Human Rights and Equal Opportunity Commission, 1996).

[23] UN, *Women in a Changing Global Economy: 1994 World Survey on the Role of Women in Development* (New York, UN, 1995) at 12–13.

[24] UNDP 1995, above note 10 at 88; UNDP 1998, above note 11 at 53.

and men is much longer than in urban areas. The weight of this work falls disproportionately on women who spend an average of 20 per cent more time than men working in rural areas.[25] Further, worldwide the greatest proportion of the work that women do is unpaid, unrecognised as economically productive and largely invisible in national accounts.[26] In developing countries more than three-quarters of men's work time is spent in paid labour and in industrialised countries the proportion is more than two-thirds. By contrast, women worldwide are paid for one-third of their work. The UNDP *Human Development Report* concluded in 1995 that 'men receive the lion's share of income and recognition for their economic contribution – while most of women's work remains unpaid, unrecognized and undervalued'.[27] One reason for inequality in economic recognition and opportunities between women and men is that men typically have much greater access to assets such as land, credit, technology and infrastructure.[28]

In the developing world, women play a major role in agriculture. For example, in many African countries, women form 80 per cent of food producers. Despite this critical contribution, women's work has been relegated to the margins of 'development' programmes, with national and international aid being directed overwhelmingly to men.[29] Thus in Africa, women receive under 10 per cent of credit provided to small farmers and 1 per cent of the total credit to agriculture.[30] Development assistance programmes sometimes target household heads, usually assumed to be men, or provide aid to sectors from which women are excluded. For example, in 1990, of the US$5.8 billion allocation for rural credit by multilateral banks, only 5 per cent reached women.[31] Global economic restructuring, involving transition to market economies, trade liberalisation, the globalisation of markets and the imposition of 'structural adjustment' programmes as a condition for international assistance, may also have a disproportionate effect on women because of their traditional roles.[32] Thus structural adjustment programmes that require the removal of food subsidies affect women particularly because of cultural norms that designate women as providers of food while prioritising the nutrition of boys and men. Deregulation to promote profit

---

[25] UNDP 1995, above note 10 at 92; UNDP 1998, above note 11 at 53.

[26] M. Waring, *Three Masquerades: Essays on Equality, Work and Human Rights* (Sydney, Allen & Unwin, 1996) at 58.

[27] UNDP 1995, above note 10 at 88.

[28] UNDP 1997, above note 12 at 64.

[29] UNDP 1995, above note 10 at 38.

[30] *Ibid.* at 39.

[31] *Ibid.*

[32] Fourth World Conference on Women, Declaration and Platform for Action, 15 September 1995, UN Doc. A/CONF. 177/20, reprinted in 35 *International Legal Materials* (1996) 401 (Beijing Platform for Action), para. 157 notes that more research is required on the impact of globalisation on women's economic status.

and competition may weaken frameworks that protect the conditions of women workers.[33] During a structural adjustment programme in Mexico, for example, the ratio of women's total income to men's dropped from 71 per cent in 1984 to 66 per cent in 1992.[34] Structural adjustment also typically involves reduction of public spending and imposing market objectives on public services such as health and welfare to make them 'cost-effective'.[35] Reduction in spending on health and education as a result of structural adjustment may have a differential impact on women and men because women's gains in these areas are more recent and fragile.

Of the 1.3 billion people estimated by the UNDP to live in poverty in 1995, 70 per cent are female,[36] largely as a result of women's unequal access to paid economic activity and their absence of status and influence within the family and community. Poverty is increasing in both the developing and the developed world,[37] and the proportion of women in poverty is on the rise.[38] Moreover, in many societies women face significant cultural and social disadvantage. Women's cultural and social status are typically linked to their roles as childbearers and child carers rather than their individual capacities. Culture and custom, invariably defined by reference to male perspectives,[39] become vehicles for keeping women out of the male-dominated spheres of public life such as the economy and politics.

There have been considerable improvements in women's access to education and literacy. Between 1970 and 1990, girls' school enrolment and women's literacy increased by almost two-thirds.[40] Female literacy is not directly connected to the wealth of a country. For example, in 1992 the literacy rate in Sri Lanka (whose *per capita* gross national product was US$560) among adult women was 86 per cent, whereas in Saudi Arabia (GNP US$7780) it was 46 per cent.[41] Women's participation in higher education, particularly, has increased dramatically. In 1970 female tertiary enrolment was less than half that of males in developing countries, whereas in 1990 it was 70 per cent.[42]

---

[33] UN, *Women in a Changing Global Economy*, above note 23 at 10–12; UNDP 1997, above note 12 at 88.

[34] UNDP 1995, above note 10 at 40 (box 2.4).

[35] Y. Lee, 'Violence against women: reflections on the past and strategies for the future – an NGO perspective', 19 *Adelaide Law Review* (1997) 45 at 50–1 (discussing how such economic policies perpetuate hardship and violence against women).

[36] UNDP 1995, above note 10 at 36; Beijing Platform for Action, Critical Area of Concern A, Women and Poverty.

[37] UNDP 1997, above note 12 at 3.

[38] UNDP 1995, above note 10 at 36.

[39] A. Rao, 'The politics of gender and culture in international human rights discourse', in J. Peters and A. Wolper (eds), *Women's Rights, Human Rights* (New York, Routledge, 1995) 167.

[40] UNDP 1995, above note 10 at 29–30.

[41] *Ibid.* See also UNDP 1997, above note 12 at 30.

[42] UNDP 1995, above note 10 at 34.

In developed countries, women's participation in tertiary education compared with men's varies from fifty-three women for each 100 men in Switzerland, to sixty-three women for each 100 men in Japan to 113 women to 100 men in France and 153 women to 100 men in Portugal.[43] In developing countries, the figure is the same for women and men – 16 per cent.[44] Despite improvements, women comprise two-thirds of the world's illiterate population of 900 million, with the highest rates in North and sub-Saharan Africa and South Asia, and girls constitute the majority of the 130 million children worldwide without access to primary school.[45] Women and girls in rural areas are at a particular disadvantage. For example, the illiteracy rate for young women in rural areas in Cameroon is four times that of urban areas.[46]

Reliable data on female/male gaps in nutrition and health are harder to obtain and vary from region to region. In developing countries the largest single cause of death among women of childbearing age is complications from pregnancy and childbirth.[47] Indeed, an African woman is 180 times more likely to die from pregnancy and childbirth than a woman in Western Europe.[48] Amartya Sen has argued that women's inferior social status is a direct cause of the fact that there are a hundred million women 'missing' in the world's population.[49] Sen has pointed out that, in conditions of equal nutrition and health care, on average women live slightly longer than men. Using the female:male ratio found in sub-Saharan Africa of 102.2:100,[50] he has calculated that that there should be over a hundred million more women alive: 4.4 million in Latin America, 2.4 million in North Africa, 1.4 million in Iran, 4.3 million in West Asia, 44 million in China, 36.7 million in India, 5.2 million in Pakistan, 3.7 million in Bangladesh and 2.4 million in South East Asia.[51] Sen has contended that these dramatic figures are the result of a web of social customs and practices that discriminate against girls and women. Prominent among them is the societal preference in many communities for male children, which encourages female infanticide and abortion of foetuses

---

[43] UN, *The World's Women 1995*, above note 12 at 93.

[44] UNDP 1997, above note 12 at 22.

[45] UN, *The World's Women 1995*, above note 12 at 89–93. See also UNDP 1995, above note 10 at 34.

[46] UN, *The World's Women 1995*, above note 12 at 89.

[47] G. Santow, 'Social roles and physical health: the case of female disadvantage in poor countries', 40 *Social Sciences and Medicine* (1995) 141. See also UNDP 1997, above note 12 at 3.

[48] UNDP 1995, above note 10 at 36.

[49] A. Sen, 'More than 100 million women are missing', *New York Review of Books*, 20 December 1990, 61.

[50] Sen observed that in the sub-Saharan region of Africa there is great poverty but little evidence of discrimination between women and men with respect to basic health care. He noted that in 1986 the female:male ratio in Western Europe was 105:100 and in North America, 104.7:100. *Ibid.*

[51] See also UN, *The World's Women 1995*, above note 12 at 1–3.

because they are female, and accords priority to the health and nutrition of boys. Other practices that affect women's survival include access to education, the ability to do paid work outside the home thus earning both income and social status, and subjection to violence in the family and community.

Women in many countries are discriminated against by the national legal system. They are disadvantaged in areas such as nationality laws, property rights, including ownership and management of, access to and enjoyment of matrimonial and commercial property, inheritance, marriage, divorce and custody of children, enjoyment of fundamental civil and political rights, lack of participation in and access to law and policy-making, courts and legal remedies, and access to certain types of employment and government benefits.[52] The UNDP has noted that: 'Ironically, what unites countries across many cultural, religious, ideological, political and economic divides is their common cause *against* the equality of women – in their right to travel, marry, divorce, acquire nationality, manage property, seek employment and inherit property.'[53]

Even where 'formal' equality is legally guaranteed in national constitutions or legislation, discrimination exists in both the processes and principles of legal systems. For example, a detailed study of the Australian legal system in 1994 documented the connection between women's unequal social status and their inequality before the law.[54] The report pointed to the social and financial problems women had in gaining access to the legal system, the restrictions on women's contributions to legal and political institutions, and the gendered operation of many (apparently neutral) legal principles, from family law and immigration law to criminal law, social security law and commercial law.

In no country do women have equal political power to men. Political disadvantage ranges from denial of women's right to vote, through to the under-representation and low participation of women in international and national law and decision-making bodies. In 1997, women held an average of 12.9 per cent of the seats in national parliaments.[55] There were wide disparities between countries. The parliaments of Sweden and Norway had around 40 per cent women members, those of Singapore, Korea and Turkey had less than 5 per cent and Kuwait and the United Arab Emirates had none.[56]

---

[52] UN, *The World's Women 1970–90: Trends and Statistics* (New York, UN, 1991) at 72.

[53] UNDP 1995, above note 10 at 43 (emphasis in original).

[54] Australian Law Reform Commission, *Equality before the Law* (parts I and II) (Sydney, Law Reform Commission, 1994). The studies prepared for a Regional Workshop on the Sociolegal Status of Women in Selected Developing Member Countries, Asian Development Bank, Manila 1997, made similar points with respect to Thailand, the Philippines, Indonesia and Malaysia.

[55] UNDP 1997, above note 12 at 154.

[56] *Ibid.* at 152–3.

Overall, there was little difference between developed countries (12.7 per cent) and developing countries (13.6 per cent) in women's participation in parliament.[57]

Many women are treated as economic commodities. Modern forms of slavery include trafficking, forced detention and prostitution and forms of servile marriage. For example, between 1988 and 1992, 286,000 Filipino women went to Japan alone to work in the sex industry. Between 120 and 150 Bengali women are sold into slavery every month.[58] Nearly one million children, most of them girls, are involved in Asia's sex trade, including 300,000 to 400,000 in India, 200,000 to 300,000 in Thailand, 100,000 in the Philippines and Taiwan, 40,000 in Vietnam and 30,000 in Sri Lanka.[59] Sexual slavery is generated by a complex array of factors. Kathleen Barry has argued that 'the conditions of poverty combine with female role socialization to create vulnerability that makes young girls and women susceptible to procurers. Social attitudes that tolerate the abuse and enslavement of women are reinforced by governmental neglect, toleration or even sanction.'[60]

In times of armed conflict, women are particularly vulnerable to slavery. Estimates of the numbers of women from Korea, the Philippines, Indonesia and China abducted or deceived into going to Japan where they were forced to act as 'comfort women' for the duration of World War II, range between 100,000 and 200,000.[61] As has been the case throughout history,[62] women are regularly forced into prostitution, raped and subjected to other forms of sexual abuse in armed conflict. For example, early in the conflict in the former Yugoslavia in 1993 estimates of the number of rapes that had occurred ranged from 12,000 to 20,000.[63] The aftermath of armed conflict also often has particularly deleterious consequences for women. Successful wars of 'liberation' or self-determination, for example, often result in the assertion of a new national identity that may relegate women to a limited, private sphere, as occurred in Algeria in the 1950s[64] and is most evident in the 1990s

---

[57] *Ibid.* at 154.

[58] *Guardian Weekly*, 8 May 1994, 13.

[59] Estimates from End Child Prostitution in Asian Tourism (ECPAT) quoted in *International Herald Tribune*, 14 July 1994, 2. See also Special Rapporteur on Violence against Women, Report on the mission of the Special Rapporteur to Poland on the issue of trafficking and forced prostitution of women (24 May to 1 June 1996) UN Doc. E/CN.4/1997/47 Add. 1., 10 December 1996.

[60] K. Barry, *Female Sexual Slavery* (New York, New York University Press, 1984) at 67.

[61] U. Dolgopol and S. Paranjape, *Comfort Women: An Unfinished Ordeal* (Geneva, International Commission of Jurists, 1995) at 7.

[62] See S. Brownmiller, *Against Our Will: Men, Women and Rape* (London, Secker & Warburg, 1975).

[63] UN, *The World's Women 1995*, above note 12 at 164.

[64] Amina Mama has discussed protests by women at the betrayal of their interests by newly emergent nation states, citing Algeria and Zimbabwe as examples. Her

in Afghanistan. The prolonged fighting in Afghanistan from the mid-1980s produced, in 1997, an uneasy victory for an Islamic fundamentalist group, the Taliban. Strict clothing restrictions on females, removal of female students and teachers from schools and universities, and the confinement of women and girls to the activities of working in the home and shopping have accompanied the Taliban assertion of control.[65]

The most consistent manifestation of the subordinate position of women worldwide is the prevalence of women-specific violence that is either tolerated or even sanctioned by state and community leaders. This violence takes many forms and includes such acts as abortion of foetuses because they are female, female infanticide, sterilisation and compulsory childbearing, inadequate nutrition, wife-murder, assault and rape, 'dowry deaths', practices such as *sati* (where a widow is burned on her husband's funeral pyre) and genital mutilation. The most pervasive type of violence against women reported in all regions of the world is abuse by a husband or partner.[66] Figures on women's violence against their partners indicate that the assaults are less serious and less frequent, and that they are generally in self-defence.[67]

Common to all these expressions of violence is the fact that the victims suffer because of their sex and gender. Womanhood means a particular and universal vulnerability to diverse forms of physical and psychological violence. Radhika Coomaraswamy, the first UN Special Rapporteur on Violence against Women, has identified three distinct, but closely connected, institutions as major sites of violence against women: the family, the community and the state.[68] Women are controlled by all tiers of society, male family and extended family members as well as religious and political leaders within local and national communities. Violence against women is neither random nor circumstantial. Rather it is a structural problem, directly

---

analysis indicates the continuum of gendered violence from colonial times through to the present day. A. Mama, 'Sheroes and villains: conceptualizing colonial and contemporary violence against women in Africa', in M. Alexander and C. Mohanty (eds), *Feminist Genealogies, Colonial Legacies, Democratic Futures* (London, Routledge, 1997) 46.

[65] 'Afghan females vanish under barrage of mullah edicts', *The Weekend Australian*, 5–6 April 1997, 14. See also SC Res. 1214, 8 December 1998 and the report by Dr Kamal Hossain, Special Rapporteur on Afghanistan to the UN Commission on Human Rights, UN Doc. E/CN.4/1999/40, 24 March 1999.

[66] UN, *The World's Women 1995*, above note 12 at 160 (chart 6.13). See also UNDP 1997, above note 12 at 11.

[67] UN, *The World's Women 1995*, above note 12 at 158.

[68] R. Coomaraswamy, 'Of Kali born: women, violence and the law in Sri Lanka', in M. Schuler (ed.), *Freedom from Violence: Women's Strategies From Around the World* (New York, UNIFEM, 1992) 49 at 50. See also Preliminary Report submitted by the Special Rapporteur on Violence against Women, its Causes and Consequences, Ms Radhika Coomaraswamy, in accordance with the Commission on Human Rights Resolution 1994/45, 22 November 1994, UN Doc. E/CN.4/1995/42.

connected to the manifold expressions of imbalance in power between women and men that can be found all around the globe. Violence both results from, and reinforces, women's powerlessness within society. As Margaret Schuler has observed, the dominance of male power 'reduce[s] women to economic and emotional dependency, the property of some male protector.'[69]

Radhika Coomaraswamy has proposed four major reasons for this violence. First, men's views of female sexuality and its role in the social hierarchy make women susceptible to sex-related crimes.[70] Women in particular positions of powerlessness, such as refugees, migrant workers and girl children, are especially vulnerable to sexual violence.[71] Second, a woman's familial relationship to a man or to a group of men makes her vulnerable to types of violence that are 'animated by society's concept of a woman as the property and dependent of a male protector'.[72] Third, violence against women may be directed towards the social group of which she is a member. For example 'to rape a woman is to humiliate her community'.[73] This type of violence is well-illustrated in the conflicts in the former Yugoslavia and Rwanda in the 1990s. Finally, there is a strong connection between militarisation and violence against women. The more general acceptance of armed conflict to resolve international disputes also gives a legitimacy to violent responses to domestic disputes, accentuating violence against women.[74]

Violence, and threats of violence, against women affect their physical and mental health. It has been estimated that gender-based violence poses a health burden to women of a similar magnitude to that caused by tuberculosis or HIV infection.[75] Women may even come to consider violence against them as natural and the prerogative of male family members. For example, in a survey of almost 2000 rural women in two Indian regions, three-quarters of the women regarded wife-beating as a justifiable reaction by a husband.[76] Shireen Jejeebhoy and Rebecca Cook have commented on this: 'Not only is wife-beating seen as a normal part of womanhood but also women are

---

[69] M. Schuler, 'Violence against women: an international perspective', in M. Schuler, above note 68 at 1, 11.

[70] R. Coomaraswamy, 'Of Kali born', above note 68 at 50.

[71] See D. Jang, D. Lee and R. Morello-Frosch, 'Domestic violence in immigrant and refugee communities: responding to the needs of immigrant women', 13 *Response* (no. 4, 1990) 2; Executive Committee of the High Commissioner's Programme, *Note on Certain Aspects of Sexual Violence against Refugee Women*, UN Doc. EC/1993/SCP/CRP 2, 29 April 1993.

[72] R. Coomaraswamy, 'Of Kali born', above note 68 at 50.

[73] *Ibid.*

[74] See also C. Chinkin, 'Women and peace: militarism and oppression', in K. Mahoney and P. Mahoney (eds), *Human Rights in the 21st Century: A Global Challenge* (Dordrecht, Martinus Nijhoff, 1993) 405.

[75] S. Jejeebhoy and R. Cook, 'State accountability for wife beating: the Indian challenge', 349 *The Lancet* (Supplement on Women's Health) (1997) 10 at 11.

[76] *Ibid.*

acutely aware of their limited options, and that socio-economic factors provide them few alternatives to the life of violence.'[77] Women's perception of violence against them by their partners as somehow natural and inevitable has been documented in many other contexts. Indeed UNICEF has noted that women all over the world 'respond to violence by looking first to their own failings, blaming themselves, justifying their attackers, and hiding the marks of their shame, the tears and the bruises from the outside world'.[78]

The picture that emerges of women's lives all around the globe is one of inequality and under-fulfilment. The UNDP has developed a gender-related development index (GDI) which measures gender inequality in three different areas: life expectancy, educational attainment and adjusted real income.[79] In applying its index to 130 countries, the UNDP draws three main conclusions. First, no society treats its women as well as its men, indeed substantial progress in equality is rare. Second, equality between women and men does not depend on a country's income levels. For example Thailand's GDI is higher than Spain's, although the latter has double the real *per capita* income of the former. Third, although there have been some advances in sex equality over the last twenty years, progress has been uneven, with developing countries making more rapid progress than industrialised countries.[80] The world over, women's quality of life is less than men's. This is, we argue, a basic issue of justice and we should expect the international legal system to respond to it.

International legal responses to the position of women

Although women are in a disadvantaged position worldwide, they have not been passive victims of discriminatory structures but have used international fora to air their concerns for the last 150 years. Women were refused the right to participate in the World Anti-Slavery Convention in London in 1840, but they organised outside the formal meetings.[81] International women's groups were established in the late nineteenth and early twentieth centuries with a variety of aims, including equal access to education and training and women's suffrage.[82] In 1915 an International Congress of Women was held in the Hague, attracting over 1500 women to discuss the prevention of war. The Congress resolutions drew a link between the attainment of peace

---

[77] *Ibid.*
[78] UNICEF, *The State of the World's Children* (Oxford, Oxford University Press, 1995) at 26.
[79] UNDP 1995, above note 10 at chapter 3.
[80] *Ibid.* at 75–8. See also UNDP 1997, above note 12 at 39–40.
[81] D. Stienstra, *Women's Movements and International Organizations* (London, Macmillan, 1994) at 47–8.
[82] *Ibid.* at 48–51.

and women's acquisition of equal political rights with men. The Congress also dispatched a group of women envoys to all the belligerent and neutral countries in the ongoing World War to present its proposals to end the conflict and prevent future wars.[83] Women's groups attempted to play some role in the peace settlement negotiations at the end of World War I. They lobbied the national delegations negotiating the establishment of the League of Nations and the International Labour Organisation (ILO), with some success.[84] A provision in the Covenant of the League of Nations that 'all positions under and in connection with the League . . . shall be open to men and women',[85] references to the conditions of women workers[86] and the League's responsibility for supervising agreements on trafficking in women and children[87] were the result of women's deputations to the Paris Peace Conference in 1919, although attempts to include a provision on women's suffrage failed.[88] The inclusion of the principle of equal remuneration for work of equal value in the ILO Constitution was also the product of lobbying by women's groups.[89]

Many international women's groups were formed in the inter-war years and attempted to influence the agenda of the League of Nations.[90] In her work on women in the League of Nations, Carol Miller has described a consistent tension between women's claims for equality of treatment with men and the assertion that women had a distinct contribution to make in international affairs.[91] For example, a British journal, *Women's Leader*, explained in 1929 that:

> it . . . is as humans and as citizens, and not just as women, that women wish to be present at the League . . . but as the world is still suffering from being 'man-made', there are problems which both particularly affect women and also towards the right solution of which women's special experience – accentuated by the 'man-madeness' of the world – can largely contribute.[92]

---

[83] *Ibid.* at 51–5.
[84] J. Connors, 'NGOs and the human rights of women at the United Nations', in P. Willetts (ed.), *The Conscience of the World: The Influence of Non-governmental Organizations in the United Nations System* (Washington DC, Brookings Institution, 1996) 147.
[85] Covenant of the League of Nations, 28 June 1919, 11 Martens (3rd) 323, 225 Parry's TS 195, article 7. On the role of women in the League of Nations see C. Miller, 'Women in international relations: the debate in inter-war Britain', in R. Grant and K. Newland (eds), *Gender and International Relations* (Bloomington, Indiana University Press, 1991) 64 at 65–71.
[86] Covenant of the League of Nations, article 23(a).
[87] *Ibid.*, article 23(c).
[88] D. Stienstra, above note 81 at 55–8.
[89] C. Lubin and A. Winslow, *Social Justice for Women: The International Labor Organization and Women* (Durham, Duke University Press, 1990) at 21–30.
[90] D. Stienstra, above note 81 at 65–7.
[91] C. Miller, above note 85 at 70.
[92] *Women's Leader*, 1 November 1929, quoted in C. Miller, above note 85 at 71.

In 1928, a United States' group, the National Women's Party, drafted an Equal Rights Treaty and tried to persuade the League of Nations and the ILO to adopt it.[93] Although the Treaty was not adopted, it prompted a shift within the ILO from an approach that emphasised protective measures for women workers to one that promoted equal treatment.[94] Women's groups, particularly those from South America, worked hard to ensure that the League's work on codifying the international law on nationality dealt adequately with the nationality of married women.[95] A major League study of the legal status of women around the world was cut short by the League's dissolution.[96] The role that women and women's groups played in the establishment of the UN and subsequently will be discussed in chapter 6.

To date, the longstanding efforts of women's organisations in the international arena have had little effect on the substance and process of international law. The only, limited, exception is in the specialised area of human rights, most particularly the adoption of the Convention on the Elimination of All Forms of Discrimination Against Women in 1979.[97] This contrasts with the phenomenon of racial discrimination. Decolonisation from 1945 onwards ensured that the injustices of racial discrimination and apartheid became linked with nationhood and thus were aired in mainstream international fora, most notably, the UN General Assembly. The prominence of the issue of racial discrimination indeed generated new norms of international law. The clearest examples of this are the right to self-determination from colonial domination and the prohibition of racial discrimination, both of which are often designated *jus cogens* – 'peremptory', or non-negotiable, norms of international law.[98] Despite this formal acknowledgment of the seriousness of race discrimination, the international understanding of its content is limited and essentially confined to a colonial context. Indeed, UN focus on the crime of apartheid has distracted international attention from other complex post-colonial situations such as multiracialism and variations in socio-economic status according to race within states. The international community has typically overlooked manipulation of racial difference by ruling elites to further their own interests until such actions have threatened international peace and security. A further aspect of this narrow understanding

---

[93] S. Whitworth, *Feminism and International Relations* (London, Macmillan, 1994) at 136–8. The Treaty was strongly opposed by another United States' group, the League of Women Voters, because the Treaty would have precluded legislation that gave special protection to women workers.

[94] *Ibid.* at 138.

[95] D. Stienstra, above note 81 at 68–75.

[96] *Ibid.* at 76.

[97] 18 December 1979, 1249 UNTS 13, reprinted in 19 *International Legal Materials* (1980) 33. See further chapter 7.

[98] I. Brownlie, *Principles of Public International Law* (Oxford, Clarendon Press, 5th edn 1998) at 513.

is that the international legal efforts to eradicate racism have had no explicit sex or gender dimension. Indeed, the international focus on racial discrimination and apartheid based on race has often allowed sex discrimination and apartheid based on sex to go unchallenged.[99] The international prohibition of sex discrimination, by contrast, has acknowledged race and colonialism as obstacles to that goal.[100]

Why has the well-documented global situation of women attracted so little attention in international law? There are many answers.[101] In 1979, Helvi Sipila, then UN Assistant Secretary-General for Social Development and Humanitarian Affairs, compared the impact of the decolonisation movement, whereby many developing countries gained independence and international citizenship, with the impact of the attainment of national citizenship by women through acquiring the right to vote and to be elected to public office.[102] She pointed out that: 'The newly independent nations were mostly able to begin restructuring their own countries according to their own political will.' Because of discrimination against women across all areas of activity and the unequal division of labour in the family, she argued that 'women were seldom equipped to take advantage of their new political rights to become active participants in the political process'.[103] The absence of women in national politics may explain to some extent why the primary actors in international law, states, have been reluctant to take effective steps to realise the advancement of women. This reluctance is not challenged by the academic disciplines of international relations and international law.

At a deeper level, the very nature of international law has made dealing with the structural disadvantages of sex and gender difficult. The realities of women's lives do not fit easily into the concepts and categories of international law. In this book we argue that international law is constructed upon particular male assumptions and experiences of life where 'man' is taken to represent the 'human'. The authority of international law has traditionally rested upon its claims to impartiality and objectivity. It is the only legal system that purports to be truly 'universal' in its applicability. Objections to this claim by newly independent states in the aftermath of decolonisation have rested upon

---

[99] In the context of the 'democratisation' of South Africa see F. Ginwala, 'Women and the elephant: the need to redress gender inequality', in S. Bazilli (ed.), *Putting Women on the Agenda* (Johannesburg, Ravan Press, 1991) 62 at 68–73; B. Mabandla, 'Promoting gender equality in South Africa', *ibid.* at 75.

[100] See Preamble to the Convention on the Elimination of All Forms of Discrimination against Women, paras 10 and 11.

[101] See further H. Charlesworth, 'Alienating Oscar? Feminist analysis of international law', in D. Dallmeyer (ed.), *Reconceiving Reality: Women and International Law* (Washington DC, American Society of International Law, 1993) 1.

[102] H. Sipila, 'Introduction', in A. Whittick, *Women into Citizens* (London, The Athenaeum Publishing Co. Ltd, 1979) 1 at 12.

[103] *Ibid.*

international law's Western origins and biases. No states have had an interest in pointing out that international law is also almost entirely man-made and that this too should be recognised as impinging upon its authority and 'universality'.

The approach of this book

In this book we approach international law with a variety of feminist perspectives and techniques to indicate the gendered and sexed nature of its structures, processes and substance. Indeed, like archaeologists digging down into an ancient site, we have used different tools at different stages of the excavation,[104] borrowing from a range of theories described in chapter 2. We tackle this project in a number of well-trodden areas of international law: its sources, treaty law, the notion of statehood and the right to self-determination, the role of international institutions, the law of human rights, the international legal commitment to the peaceful settlement of disputes and the prohibition of the use of force in international relations. We finally consider how women are included in the evolving international criminal system. We focus on these areas because they constitute the cornerstones of traditional international legal doctrine and indeed the major topics of international law text books. The lessons we draw from them, however, are equally applicable to other doctrines of international law. Our academic training is in international law rather than in feminist theory and this book is primarily addressed to those with an interest in international law. We have drawn on the rich literature of feminist theory to study our discipline, but we have not articulated any original feminist theories or methods in the process.

We argue that international law is both built on and operates to reinforce gendered and sexed assumptions. The very choice and categorisation of subject matter deemed appropriate for international regulation reflects male priorities. Feminist analysis can indicate the arbitrariness of the traditional categories of analysis that are rarely questioned by international lawyers. For example why are highly migratory species of sea life regulated by treaty[105]

---

[104] This simile is suggested by N. Naffine, *Law and the Sexes: Explorations in Feminist Jurisprudence* (Sydney, Allen & Unwin, 1990) at 1–2.

[105] UN Convention on the Law of the Sea, 10 December 1982, UN Doc. A/CONF. 62/122, reprinted in 21 *International Legal Materials* (1982) 1261, article 64; Agreement for the Implementation of the Provisions of the United Nations Convention on the Law of the Sea of 10 December 1982, Relating to the Conservation and Management of Straddling Fish Stocks and Highly Migratory Fish Stocks, 4 August 1995, UN Doc. A/CONF.164/37, 8 September 1995, reprinted in 34 *International Legal Materials* (1995) 1542. See D. Herman and D. Cooper, 'Anarchic armadas, Brussels bureaucrats, and the valiant maple leaf: sexuality, governance, and the construction of British nationhood through the Canada-Spain fish war', 17 *Legal Studies* (1997) 415 for an account of gender and sexuality issues in relation to a dispute over straddling stocks.

while the use of breast milk substitutes remains subject to voluntary codes?[106] Why is extra-territorial jurisdiction traditionally invoked against violations of monopoly and competition law but only rarely in cases of trafficking of women and children? Some international lawyers might consider (publicly or privately!) that feminist analysis is an eccentric sideshow, irrelevant to the mainstream of the discipline. Our response is that in reality sex and gender are an integral part of international law in the sense that men and maleness are built into its structure and that to ignore this is to misunderstand the nature of international law.

Of course women are not the only group whose concerns are marginalised in the international legal system. Indigenous peoples, disabled persons, ethnic minorities and other non-state groupings can all claim that they are excluded from the traditional structures of international law, an exclusion that is now in some cases under challenge.[107] Women within these groups may well sense their status as outsiders in a particularly intense way. The intersections of multiple layers of marginalisation and the interrelationship between race, ethnicity and gender in particular has been scrutinised to expose the complex system of dependence and independence between them.[108] Concepts of gender are connected to hierarchies of race and class. While this book offers an explicitly feminist account of international law, we hope that its methods will be of value to other groups outside the boundaries of international law.

Complicating our project are the significant changes in international relations and law in the 1990s. The end of the cold war, marked symbolically by the dismantling of the Berlin Wall in 1989, has had a profound effect on the UN, the central institution in the global legal order. The disintegration of the former Soviet Union and the ensuing reduction in tension within the UN Security Council has allowed the latter to use its powers to ensure 'collective security'[109] (not without controversy), for example after Iraq's invasion of Kuwait (1990) and in cases of internal disarray such as Haiti (1991–94) and Somalia (1992).[110] While the collapse of the Soviet Union and

[106] WHO Code on the International Marketing of Breastmilk Substitutes, 1981 Res. WHA 34.22, Annex WHO Doc. A/34/VR/15.
[107] E.g. Draft Declaration on the Rights of Indigenous Peoples, 26 August 1994, UN Doc. E/CN.4/1995/2, E/CN.4/Sub.2/1994/56, 28 October 1994, reprinted in 34 *International Legal Materials* (1995) 541. On the position of minorities generally see W. McKean, *Equality and Discrimination under International Law* (Oxford, Clarendon Press, 1983). See also Council of Europe Framework Convention for the Protection of National Minorities, 1 February 1995, reprinted in 34 *International Legal Materials* (1995) 351.
[108] E.g. A. McClintock, *Imperial Leather: Race, Gender and Sexuality in the Colonial Context* (New York, Routledge, 1995).
[109] Charter of the UN, 26 June 1945, chapter VII.
[110] For an account of the process by which international military intervention has come to be an accepted response to humanitarian crises see A. Orford, 'Locating the international: military and monetary interventions after the cold war', 38 *Harvard International Law Journal* (1997) 443.

Yugoslavia in the 1990s have created great human suffering and challenges for the international legal order, moves towards further regional integration, particularly in Europe, have also produced new difficulties and tensions. Another major development affecting international law is the phenomenon of globalisation, a term that signifies a variety of tendencies, including the liberalisation of the international economic and trading system. It is also used to describe the changes wrought by technological advances in communications that are often said to have transformed a divided world into a 'global village'. While globalisation may be seen as a process of creating global homogeneity, it has also been accompanied by polarisation and division.[111] International law-making and international dispute resolution are becoming increasingly specialised, with separate regimes and institutions developed for different areas but which also affect each other in diverse ways. Participants in the international legal system have increased beyond states and international governmental institutions to include what is sometimes described as 'international civil society' – individuals, groups of peoples, NGOs, multinational corporations and other entities that have acquired varying degrees of international legal personality.

These developments underlie the suggestion that the international legal order at the end of the millennium is at a 'Grotian moment'.[112] In the seventeenth century, the Dutch international lawyer, Hugo Grotius, provided an account of the transformation of Europe from a feudal order to a community of sovereign states, emphasising the tensions between the old structures and the new political order. In a similar way, the search is now on for a way of understanding the complexities and tensions in international society and for describing a useful, meaningful role for international law within it. This task requires, in Richard Falk's words, 'a special sort of creativity that blends thought and imagination without neglecting to understand obstacles to change'.[113] In this book we suggest that feminist approaches to international law can contribute to the modern Grotian project. They offer ways of recasting the role of international law so that it can transform ideas about justice and order in the international community. International law is often understood as a mechanism to bring 'order' to the 'chaos' of international relations. It draws boundaries around many types of space: territorial, jurisdictional and legal. As we discuss in chapter 2, feminist theories indicate that apparently impermeable boundaries are in reality fluid.

---

[111] C. Sjolander, 'The rhetoric of globalization: what's in a wor(l)d?', 51 *International Journal* (1996) 603.

[112] *Legality of the Threat or Use of Nuclear Weapons* 1996 ICJ Rep. 226 (Adv. Op. 8 July) at 551–2 (diss. op. Judge Weeramantry); B. Boutros-Ghali, 'A Grotian moment', 18 *Fordham International Law Journal* (1995) 1609.

[113] R. Falk, *The End of World Order: Essays on Normative International Relations* (New York, Holmes & Meier, 1983) at 25.

Feminist theories allow us to interrogate the nature of the 'order' and the boundaries sponsored by the international legal system and to seek to undermine the illusory necessity of concepts and rules built on sexed and gendered hierarchies of difference.

Elizabeth Grosz has pointed out that feminist analysis involves an intricate balancing between conceptually inimical forces, a balancing process which is rarely articulated.[114] Feminist theory, Grosz has noted, is both a reaction to 'the overwhelming masculinity of privileged and historically dominant knowledges, acting as a kind of counterweight to the imbalances resulting from the male monopoly of the production and reception of knowledges', and a response to the political goals of feminist struggles.[115] The dual commitments of feminist theory co-exist uneasily. The first requires intellectual rigour (in male terms) in the task of uncovering the hidden gender of areas of knowledge. The second calls for dedication to political change. Feminist scholars are thus often criticised both by the male academy for their lack of 'disinterested' research and 'objective' analysis, and by feminist activists for their participation in privileged, male-structured debates.[116]

This book exemplifies this tension in feminist agendas. Our aims are both academic and political. We want to investigate the ways in which international law has brushed aside the injustices of women's situations around the world and we want to redraw the boundaries of international law so that it responds to these injustices. We will no doubt draw criticism from activists for our focus on legal principles rather than on the battle front. We have already drawn fire from academic theorists for our lack of academic rigour and objectivity[117] and our failure to work within accepted legal doctrine.[118] Others have cautioned against feminist enthusiasm for radical change in our discipline. Thus Martti Koskenniemi has said:

> We can reconceive international law every now and then, but not all the time. Our immediate fears and hopes do not necessarily match to produce the good society ... At some point, we need distance from those fears and hopes – if not objective distance, then at least a partial, consensual, formal distance. That law makes this distance possible (if always only for a moment) is not a defect of law, but its most immediate benefit.[119]

---

[114] E. Grosz, 'A note on essentialism and difference', in S. Gunew (ed.), *Feminist Knowledge: Critique and Construct* (London/New York, Routledge, 1990) 332.

[115] *Ibid.*

[116] *Ibid.*

[117] F. Tesón, 'Feminism and international law: a reply', 33 *Virginia Journal of International Law* (1994) 647.

[118] A. D'Amato, book review of R. Cook (ed.), *Human Rights of Women: National and International Perspectives* (Philadelphia, University of Pennsylvania Press, 1994), 89 *American Journal of International Law* (1995) 840.

[119] M. Koskenniemi, book review of D. Dallmeyer, above note 101, 89 *American Journal of International Law* (1995) 227 at 230.

Koskenniemi thus seems to advocate acceptance of the framework of international law because, flawed as it is, it is some protection from untrammelled subjectivity and political ideology. Our argument here, by contrast, is that international law does not provide even a 'partial, consensual, formal distance' from subjectivity. It is in fact intertwined with a gendered and sexed subjectivity and reinforces a system of male symbols.

Feminist methods encourage reflection on the production of knowledge by feminists. What system of social and cultural relations is involved in writing this book, and on what economic and institutional support does it depend? We have the freedom to speak because we work in universities in wealthy countries and have time to think and write. We can engage in academic work because we have shared the care of our children and households with our partners. More generally we benefit from a particular conjunction of economic and political circumstances on which the opportunity for feminist theorising depends. Rey Chow has pointed out:

> Feminism . . . belongs to a juncture in time when the Western thought's efforts at overcoming itself are still, relatively speaking, supported by a high level of material well-being, intellectual freedom, and personal mobility . . . Even though it often, if not always, speaks the language of oppression and victimization, Western feminism owes its support to the existence of other populations who continue to experience daily exclusions of various kinds, many of which are performed at territorial borders. It is the clear demarcation of such borders which allows us the comfort and security in which to theorize the notion of 'exclusion' itself.[120]

We are conscious that we are able to write about the boundaries of international law because our own lives are made comfortable and secure by other types of boundaries. Inevitably our approach in this book is shaped by our individual identities. In this book we cannot claim to speak for all women, but offer our own particular account of our discipline by casting pebbles into its waters.[121] We hope that it will provoke reflection and debate among all those interested in the future of international law.

[120] R. Chow, 'Violence in the other country: China as crisis, spectacle, and woman', in C. Mohanty, A. Russo and L. Torres (eds), *Third World Women and the Politics of Feminism* (Bloomington, Indiana University Press, 1991) 81 at 98.
[121] The image of pebble-throwing is borrowed from W. Riphagen, 'State responsibility: new theories of inter-state relations', in R. Macdonald and D. Johnston (eds), *The Structure and Process of International Law: Essays in Legal Philosophy, Doctrine and Theory* (Dordrecht, Martinus Nijhoff, 1983) 581 at 624, n. 100.

2

Feminist theories and international law

Introduction

This book uses feminist theories to sustain its claim that the absence of women in international law has distorted the discipline's boundaries. The aim of this chapter is to introduce these theories and to consider their value in understanding international law. As a background to this task, we first discuss the theories that underpin traditional international law and their limited explanatory force with respect to the position of women. We then describe various feminist approaches to law and suggest that no single theory is adequate in the context of international law. We finally consider a number of insights offered by feminist analysis, notably the debates surrounding identity and the distinction drawn between public and private spheres of activity.

Theories of international law

The foundations of modern international law are usually traced by Western international lawyers to the Peace of Westphalia in 1648 at the end of the Thirty Years War.[1] This historical moment is taken to mark the transition from an imperial and ecclesiastical order in which the Emperor and the Pope exercised hierarchical authority over groups and communities to an international society of independent, sovereign national states.[2] In his book *De Jure Belli ac Pacis* published in 1625, Hugo Grotius had articulated the notion of international society, the idea that states form a community and

[1] On the historical development of modern international law see A. Nussbaum, *A Concise History of the Law of Nations* (New York, Macmillan, 2nd edn 1962); A. Cassese, *International Law in a Divided World* (Oxford, Clarendon Press, 1986) at 34–73.

[2] A. Cassese, above note 1 at 34–7.

23

that their conduct with respect to each other was limited by particular rules.[3] Thus the focus of international law was on relations between nation states. However, the *laissez faire* assumptions of international legal doctrine imposed only limited restraints on the activity of states and provided the legal justification for the colonial activities of the European powers. For example, the law afforded colonised peoples little or no status and gave priority to effective occupation and conquest as the basis for acquisition of territory.[4] Slavery and the slave trade were facilitated by the rules upholding the freedom of the high seas and the generally permissive cast of international law.[5] International law, although universal in pretension, is thus built on restricted foundations.[6] The states that contributed to its development and its scholarly exponents have been mainly European, Christian and capitalist,[7] and the discipline has typically represented a narrow range of interests. As David Harris has said, international law was for many generations 'really no more than the Public Law of Europe'.[8]

The ambit of the international legal order has grown significantly since the middle of the twentieth century to include the large number of states that acquired their independence through decolonisation from the European powers, the activities of international intergovernmental institutions and to some extent those of groups and individuals within nation states. International law has also developed restraints upon the use of force between states. Antonio Cassese has described this evolution as a move from a 'Westphalian' order (in which force is the primary, and unregulated, tool of legitimation, states are allowed great freedom of action, and international law-making and enforcement are largely left to individual states), to a 'Charter' order (in which the use of force is controlled,[9] there is a focus on individual and group rights and the acknowledgment of certain fundamental values that fetter state power, and international governmental organisations as distinct

---

[3] For an overview of the work of Grotius see H. Bull, B. Kingsbury and A. Roberts (eds), *Hugo Grotius and International Relations* (Oxford, Oxford University Press, 1990).

[4] A. Cassese, above note 1 at 42–3.

[5] *Ibid.* at 52–4.

[6] A. Anghie, 'Francisco de Vitoria and the colonial origins of international law', 5 *Social & Legal Studies* (1996) 32. See also J. Thomas, 'History and international law in Asia: a time for review?', in R. Macdonald (ed.), *Essays in Honour of Wang Tieya* (Dordrecht, Martinus Nijhoff, 1994) 813.

[7] Cassese has noted evidence that between the sixteenth and eighteenth centuries the states forming the East Indies, Persia, Burma and Siam had relations with the European states on an apparently equal basis. This equality of international status was undermined by the economic progress of Europe after the 'industrial revolution' at the end of the eighteenth century. A. Cassese, above note 1 at 39–40.

[8] D. Harris, *Cases and Materials on International Law* (London, Sweet & Maxwell, 5th edn 1998) at 16.

[9] Charter of the UN, 26 June 1945, article 2(4).

players in the international community are established).[10] A consistent feature of the international legal system, however, remains the absence of any central authority that enjoys exclusive power to create, monitor and implement the law. The efficacy of many principles of international law accordingly depends upon their translation into national legal systems.[11] Despite these shortcomings, the significance of international law is much greater than the extent of its immediate enforcement. It provides a scheme and a vocabulary for the distribution of power and resources in the international community and to an increasing degree within individual states.

International law scholarship has tended to be descriptive and prescriptive, avoiding scrutiny of the assumptions and commitments of the discipline. The lack of any centralised law-making and enforcing authority has meant that theories of international law concentrate on explaining the basis of obligation in the international community.[12] In this section, we describe six different accounts of international law that have had varying degrees of influence on international lawyers. None of these theories of international law has seriously, or even peripherally, addressed the situation of women worldwide.

Natural law

Early accounts of international law based the possibility of a system regulating behaviour between states on enduring, universal commitments of value that constituted a 'law of nature'. Indeed, it has been argued that the initial development of an interstate system of legal principles depended on the universalist premises of natural lawyers. Thus the nineteenth-century British scholar, Sir Henry Maine, described 'the grandest function of the Law of Nature' as 'giving birth to modern International Law'.[13] The attraction of the law of nature as a foundation for an international legal system was enhanced by the absence of international legislative and judicial institutions. In the absence of central authorities, natural law offered a source of directly applicable law to regulate the co-existence of nation states. The content of the law of nature was defined in various ways. According to some scholars it

[10] A. Cassese, above note 1 at 396–400. On the evolution of the concept of 'international community' at the end of the twentieth century see G. Abi-Saab, 'Whither the international community?', 9 *European Journal of International Law* (1998) 248; B. Simma and A. Paulus, 'The "international community": facing the challenge of globalization', *ibid.* at 266.

[11] A. Cassese, above note 1 at 13–22.

[12] E.g. J. Brierly, *The Basis of Obligation in International Law* (Oxford, Clarendon Press, 1958).

[13] H. Maine, *Ancient Law* (London, J. Murray, 1863) at 96, quoted in R. Falk, 'The inadequacy of contemporary theories of international law – gaps in legal thinking', 50 *Virginia Law Review* (1964) 231 at 244–5, n. 32.

was synonymous with divine, religious law while for others it constituted rules developed from right reason.[14] Hugo Grotius considered the law of nature as being composed of general principles of law that could be synthesised from the major systems of jurisprudence.[15]

A significant strand of natural law thinking in modern international law theory has emerged since World War II and has been influential in various practical developments, such as those to define international crimes and to establish jurisdiction over individuals accused of committing them. Fernando Tesón, for example, has argued that the validity of international law rests on 'normative individualism', which makes individuals rather than states the 'primary normative unit' of international law.[16] On this analysis, protection of the rights of individuals is the overarching value on which international law depends and the rights of states are derivative from the rights of individuals within their borders. Membership of the international community is thus contingent on a nation state's observance of the human rights of its population.[17]

How have natural law theories dealt with inequality between women and men? Natural law doctrine, as traditionally formulated in both the national and international contexts, did not question basic inequalities in the social order. Grotius, for example, followed thinkers from Aristotle onwards and justified slavery by reference to the natural law.[18] Modern natural lawyers condemn violations of human rights but rarely comment on the entrenched discrimination against women around the world in these terms. Indeed, Fernando Tesón has described the absence of women in the international legal order as a mere 'statistical underrepresentation' rather than an injustice. Injustice to women, he has argued, would only arise if nation states actively prevented women from participating in international life.[19]

Positivism

Positivism, in its international legal manifestations, developed as a response both to the challenge to state sovereignty posed by natural law and to the perceived failure of natural law theories to articulate objective and reliable

[14] For a general account of natural law theory see J. Harris, *Legal Philosophies* (London, Butterworths, 2nd edn 1997) at 6.

[15] H. Lauterpacht, 'The Grotian tradition in international law', 23 *British Yearbook of International Law* (1946) 1 at 9.

[16] Tesón has based this theoretical account on the work of Immanuel Kant (1724–1804): F. Tesón, 'The Kantian theory of international law', 92 *Columbia Law Review* (1992) 53. See also F. Tesón, *A Philosophy of International Law* (Boulder, Westview, 1998).

[17] F. Tesón, 'The Kantian theory', above note 16 at 69–72.

[18] See H. Lauterpacht, above note 15 at 43.

[19] F. Tesón, 'Feminism and international law: a reply', 33 *Virginia Journal of International Law* (1994) 647 at 652. See generally F. Tesón, *A Philosophy of International Law*, above note 16 at chapter 6.

principles of international conduct. Natural law was seen as open to cynical manipulation by those possessing religious or secular power to support any desired action.[20] Accordingly in the work of theorists such as Richard Zouche (1590–1660) and Cornelius Bynkershoek (1673–1743) international law appeared as a system of restraint based on voluntarism that required states to agree to be bound. In this way consent replaced universal values as the basis of obligation.[21]

International legal positivists regard nation states as the ultimate source of international law – the actual practice of states is the normative foundation of international obligation. Some jurists argue that, given the absence of any centralised law-making authority in the international arena, positivism is the only intellectually coherent approach.[22] The international legal system depends on the generation of totally self-enforcing rules, and prescriptive models of international rules are doomed to failure.[23] Indeed, it has been claimed, the prescriptive effect of international law is 'entirely dependent on the accuracy of the codification of state practice'.[24] The Permanent Court of International Justice (PCIJ) endorsed a positivist understanding of international law in its famous statement in *The Lotus Case* that 'the rules of law binding upon States . . . emanate from their own free will. . . . [R]estrictions upon the independence of States cannot therefore be presumed.'[25] Not surprisingly, positivism has been the favoured theory of international law for most states, whatever their political commitments. The socialist tradition in international legal theory was, for example, firmly positivist in its concern with voluntary agreement to regulation and its emphasis on the role of treaties in international law-making.[26]

Positivists come in various shapes and sizes and nationalities. Some insist on a strict and complete adherence to the principle of consent in international law, deploring attempts to develop notions of majority consent through, for example, the articulation of norms of *jus cogens* that trump the will of

---

[20] R. Falk, above note 13 at 244–5.

[21] *Ibid.* See also J. Stone, *Legal Controls of International Conflict* (Sydney, Maitland Publications, 1954) at 12–13.

[22] E.g. J. Watson, 'State consent and the sources of international law', *Proceedings of the 86th Annual Meeting of the American Society of International Law* (Washington DC, American Society of International Law, 1992) 108.

[23] E.g. J. Watson, 'A realistic jurisprudence of international law', 1980 *The Year Book of World Affairs* 265 at 274–5.

[24] *Ibid.* at 285.

[25] *The Lotus Case* (France v. Turkey) 1927 PCIJ ser. A no. 10 (Judgment of 7 September) at 18.

[26] E.g. V. Tunkin, 'Co-existence and international law', 95 *Recueil des Cours* (1958) 1; R. Mullerson, 'Sources of international law: new tendencies in Soviet thinking', 83 *American Journal of International Law* (1989) 498; G. Danilenko, *Law-Making in the International Community* (United States, Kluwer Academic Publishers, 1993).

individual states.[27] Others have described a gradual movement away from consent to consensus and a 'global will'.[28] Legal positivism has close links to the realist tradition in international relations theory. Realists explain all forms of international behaviour by reference to the national interest of the particular nation states involved. Various schools of realism define the content of 'the national interest' in different ways,[29] but all avoid the articulation of global values as the basis for international decision-making. International law, then, is seen as the product of states' self-interest. Indeed, the realist scholar Hans Morgenthau regarded international law as simply a smokescreen for political policy by powerful states.[30] Such an account of international law cannot explain, however, why international law is regularly obeyed even when it seems to go against states' national interest.[31]

The positivist view of international law as a voluntary system of restraints on states suggests that questions about structural disadvantages within states will rarely emerge as legal issues. Of course, states may agree to prohibit discrimination, as, for example in the Conventions on the Elimination of All Forms of Racial Discrimination (the Race Convention)[32] and All Forms of Discrimination Against Women (the Women's Convention),[33] but a positivist analysis does not require any examination of the legitimacy of global or national power structures that effectively subordinate women.

Liberal international legal theory

The dominant modern Western account of international law is a liberal one. The international order is seen as being based on subjective, sovereign

---

[27] E.g. P. Weil, 'Towards relative normativity in international law?', 77 *American Journal of International Law* (1983) 413. See chapter 4 for a discussion of the concept of *jus cogens*.

[28] R. Falk, above note 13 at 246–7.

[29] See Fernando Tesón's account of 'utilitarian realism' and 'communitarian realism' in 'Realism and Kantianism in international law', *Proceedings of the 86th Annual Meeting of the American Society of International Law* (Washington DC, American Society of International Law, 1992) 113.

[30] H. Morgenthau, *Politics Among Nations: The Struggle for Power and Peace* (New York, Alfred A. Knopf, 5th edn 1973) at 93–4.

[31] The issue of why states comply with international law attracted renewed interest in the 1990s. See e.g. A. Chayes and A. Chayes, *The New Sovereignty: Compliance with International Regulatory Agreements* (Cambridge, Harvard University Press, 1995); T. Franck, *The Power of Legitimacy among Nations* (New York, Oxford University Press, 1990); T. Franck, *Fairness in International Law and Institutions* (New York, Oxford University Press, 1995); H. Koh, 'Review essay: why do nations obey international law?', 106 *Yale Law Journal* (1997) 2599.

[32] 21 December 1965, 660 UNTS 195, reprinted in 5 *International Legal Materials* (1966) 352.

[33] 18 December 1979, 1249 UNTS 13, reprinted in 19 *International Legal Materials* (1980) 33.

consent, just as a national order is based on a social contract negotiated by individuals. The state is a member of the international community similar to the individual being a member of a national or local community.[34] The main difference, as Gerry Simpson has pointed out, is that in international law the requirement of consent is taken literally, while it has been replaced by the notion of representation in liberal democratic theory in national contexts.[35] The 'democratic' liberalism espoused by international lawyers such as Thomas Franck is based on two levels of consent: the consent of states to principles of international law and the consent of a state's citizens as the basis of legitimacy of the state.[36]

Liberalism too has its critics. It is claimed to be a procedural, rather than substantive, political theory, with sovereign autonomy as its only commitment of value in the international context.[37] In this vein, Louis Henkin has said that international law 'is designed to further each state's realisation of its own notion of the Good'.[38] How does the international community then resolve disputes between two sovereign entities which each invoke freedom of action? In theory, the reconciliation is accomplished by the liberal notion of the rule of law. The promise of the rule of law is neutral application of abstract principles, created through the popular will. But the very notion of an 'objective' legal order seems to conflict with the liberal rejection of all but subjective, sovereign, values. A significant tension thus exists between the individualistic, sovereign-based nature of international society and the communitarian justification for a legal system. As a result, in the international arena, the rule of law can only deliver rather indeterminate solutions to disputes between sovereigns. Martti Koskenniemi has pointed out: 'Arguments from legal principles are countered with arguments from equally legal counter-principles. Rules are countered with exceptions, sovereignty with sovereignty.'[39] International law thus becomes 'singularly useless as a means for justifying or criticizing international behaviour'.[40]

---

[34] See J. Rawls, 'The law of peoples', in S. Shute and S. Hurley (eds), *On Human Rights: The Oxford Amnesty Lectures* (New York, Basic Books, 1993) 41; A.-M. Slaughter, 'International law in a world of liberal states', 6 *European Journal of International Law* (1995) 503.

[35] G. Simpson, 'Imagined consent: democratic liberalism in international legal theory', 15 *Australian Yearbook of International Law* (1994) 103.

[36] T. Franck, 'The emerging right to democratic governance', 86 *American Journal of International Law* (1992) 46. See the useful discussion of Franck's approach in G. Simpson, above note 35 at 118–20. See also J. Crawford, 'Democracy and international law', 64 *British Yearbook of International Law* (1993) 113.

[37] M. Koskenniemi, *From Apology to Utopia: The Structure of International Legal Argument* (Helsinki, Finnish Lawyers' Publishing Co., 1989) at 64.

[38] L. Henkin, 'Law and politics in international relations', 44 *Journal of International Affairs* (1990) 186.

[39] M. Koskenniemi, above note 37 at 485.

[40] *Ibid.* at 48.

The liberal account of international law has elements of both the natural law and positivist traditions, co-existing in uneasy tension. Martti Koskenniemi has described these as an 'ascending', individualistic, apologetic (positivist) strand and a 'descending' communitarian, utopian (natural law) strand:

> The ascending strand [in international law] legitimizes political order by reference to individual ends. The existence of natural values is denied. Individuals can be constrained only to prevent 'harm to others'. But any constraint seems a violation of individual freedom as what counts as 'harm' can only be subjectively determined. The descending strand fares no better. It assumes that a set of fundamental rights or a natural distinction between public and private spheres exist to guarantee that liberty is not violated. But this blocks any collective action as the content of those freedoms . . . can be justifiably established only by reference to individuals' views thereof.[41]

The liberal account of international law rests on a series of distinctions between the 'public' and the 'private' that has long played a central part in Western legal and political philosophy. Divisions between the *polis* or public realm and the *oikos* or private sphere of home and family were made in ancient Greek thought.[42] The two spheres were in a symbiotic position: men were able to participate as equals in the public realm only because they were supported by the work of wives and slaves in the private realm.[43] John Locke (1632–1704), one of the most influential architects of liberal thought, drew distinctions between reason and passion, knowledge and desire, mind and body. The first of each of these dualisms was associated with the 'public' sphere of rationality, order and political authority; the latter with a 'private' sphere of subjectivity and desire.[44] Liberal uses of public/private dichotomies are complex. First, there is great debate as to where precisely the boundary between the two spheres lies. Indeed the boundary is constantly shifting in response to economic and social developments such as national 'privatisation' policies and globalisation. Second, notions of public and private are often used in quite different ways from those identified by Locke. Locke distinguished a private, domestic world inhabited by women from that of public civil society, the world of politics and men. In modern liberalism the purely domestic sphere is largely ignored as an area of concern and '[t]he separation between private and public is . . . re-established as a division *within* civil society itself, within the world of men.'[45] Thus

---

[41] *Ibid.* at 66–7.

[42] M. Thornton, 'The cartography of public and private', in M. Thornton (ed.), *Public and Private: Feminist Legal Debates* (Melbourne, Oxford University Press, 1995) 2.

[43] *Ibid.* at 2–3.

[44] J. Locke, *Two Treatises of Government* (J. Harrison and P. Laslett (eds), Oxford, Oxford University Press, 1965).

[45] C. Pateman, 'Feminist critiques of the public/private dichotomy', in S. Benn and G. Gaus (eds), *Public and Private in Social Life* (London, Croom Helm, 1983) 281 at 285.

references to a dichotomy between the public and private can refer to the distinction between politics on the one hand and economic and social life on the other, or between state and civil society. Another important function of the dichotomy in liberal jurisprudence is to demarcate areas appropriate for legal regulation from those that come within the sphere of individual autonomy.

Distinctions between spheres of public and private define the scope of international law. One such distinction is between public international law (the law traditionally governing the relations between nation states) and private international law (the rules applicable to jurisdictional and other conflicts between national legal systems). International law operates in the most public of all public worlds, that of nation states and intergovernmental organisations. Thus the UN Charter makes the (public) province of international law distinct from the (private) sphere of domestic jurisdiction;[46] the acquisition of statehood or international personality confers 'public' status on an entity with consequences for jurisdiction, representation and ownership;[47] the law of state responsibility sorts out (public) actions for which the state is accountable from those 'private' ones for which it does not have to answer internationally.[48] Even international human rights law, which is regarded as radically challenging the traditional distinction between international and domestic concerns, targets 'public', state-sanctioned violations rather than those that have no apparent direct connection to the state. Another manifestation of a public/private distinction in international law is the line drawn between law and other forms of private knowledge, such as social and humanitarian considerations and morality.[49] Public/private distinctions in the international sphere often differ from those in national contexts. For example, NGOs are often considered part of the 'private' within the international legal arenas and part of the 'public' in domestic fora. However, their location at the intersection between the public and private spheres illustrates the changing boundaries of international law. Their penetration of international public arenas and impact upon policy and law-making contrasts with their lack of accountability except under domestic regulation.[50]

What insights has liberal international legal theory provided to understand the situations of women globally? Liberalism asserts that it pays equal

---

[46] UN Charter, article 2(7) provides: 'Nothing contained in the present Charter shall authorize the United Nations to intervene in matters which are essentially within the domestic jurisdiction of any state or shall require the Members to submit such matters to settlement under the present Charter.'

[47] M. Koskenniemi, above note 37 at 126.

[48] See chapter 5.

[49] E.g. *South West Africa Cases*, Second Phase (Ethiopia & Liberia v. South Africa) 1966 ICJ Rep. 4 (Judgment of 18 July); *Western Sahara Case* 1975 ICJ Rep. 12 (Adv. Op. 16 October) at 69 (sep. op. Judge Gros): 'economics, sociology and human geography are not law'.

[50] See further chapters 3 and 4.

concern and respect to all individuals and because of this lays particular claim to the qualities of objectivity, abstractness and neutrality. The liberal idea of equality, however, is limited to procedural rather than to substantive equality. Formally, it requires equal treatment of people or states, but without reference to their actual situation. Consequently liberal equality is a very blunt tool when dealing with cases of long-term, structural disadvantage and inequality both as between states and within them. Moreover, as we shall argue below, the continued separation and opposition of public and private domains in liberal theory and practice has engendered consequences in the international arena.

The 'New Haven' school

Since the 1940s, a number of scholars connected with the Yale Law School in New Haven, Connecticut, have developed a distinctive understanding of the international legal order, building on some of the insights of the American legal realists of the 1920s and 30s.[51] The influence of the New Haven school has extended far beyond New Haven.[52] The New Haven approach rejects the idea that international law is a system of neutral rules and seeks to develop a 'policy science' of international law, focusing on the processes by which legal decisions and policies are made. It assesses international law rules by their capacity to enhance human dignity and its jurisprudence is concerned with making policy choices and decisions based upon a prescribed set of values, rather than with locating the source of obligation in international law.[53] It offers a 'scientific', objective, method for the articulation and application of policies about international activity. International law is regarded as the product of an authoritative decision-making process rather than a discrete body of rules.[54] The concepts of 'decision' and 'decision-making' are very broad, extending from the making of law, to its application, to its reception in economic and social life.[55] The method of analysis promoted by the New Haven school requires, first, the clarification of the standpoint of the observer (for example, through acknowledgment of the observer's position in a hierarchy) to allow disengagement and objectivity;

---

[51] A comprehensive elaboration of the New Haven school's approach is found in H. Lasswell and M. McDougal, *Jurisprudence for a Free Society: Studies in Law, Science, and Policy* (New Haven, New Haven Press, 1992).

[52] E.g. B. Chimni, *International Law and World Order: A Critique of Contemporary Approaches* (New Delhi, Sage Publications, 1993); R. Higgins, *Problems and Process: International Law and How We Use It* (Oxford, Clarendon Press, 1994).

[53] M. Reisman, 'The view from the New Haven school of international law', *Proceedings of the 86th Annual Meeting of the American Society of International Law* (Washington DC, American Society of International Law, 1992) 118.

[54] H. Lasswell and M. McDougal, above note 51, vol. 1 at 24–5.

[55] M. Reisman, above note 53 at 120.

second, consciousness of the conceptual categories used by an observer to analyse particular situations; and third, an understanding of the processes used to influence particular outcomes.[56]

The New Haven school rejects natural law theories of the international legal order because of the inherent manipulability of natural law and because natural law relies on the assertion of subjective values that resist empirical validation. New Haven scholars also disavow positivist approaches because of their formalism, the absence of attention to process and their lack of commitment to the central value of human dignity.[57] At the same time, the New Haven approach combines some elements (and disadvantages) of both the classical theories of international law. There are natural law tendencies because the authority of the decision-making process rests on a normative foundation: the promotion of human dignity. And there are traces of positivism in the concern of the New Haven theorists to generate a systematic, practically testable response to policy problems that can specify the components of the policies that decision-makers must rely upon. The combination of naturalism and positivism in the 'policy science' approach is captured in its description by Richard Falk as 'empirical knowledge analyzed by reference to purposive outcome'.[58]

In turn, critics of the New Haven school point to its own manipulability and subjectivity through its dependence on a notion of human dignity and attention to contextual factors.[59] The tendency of applications of the New Haven method by its adherents to justify United States foreign policy, especially during the cold war,[60] has also undermined its claims to impartial, scientific inquiry. However, the New Haven school offers a number of insights that are consistent with feminist analysis. Its concern with the need for self-consciousness about the observer's perspective, developed to reduce bias, accords with feminist interest in identity politics, although, strikingly, the New Haven school does not in fact recognise gender or sex as an observer perspective. The fundamental principle of human dignity and the notion of international communitarianism that animates the New Haven school's approach is consistent with feminist agendas. Although one of the early major studies on sex discrimination within the international arena was

[56] *Ibid.*
[57] R. Falk, 'Casting the spell: the New Haven school of international law', 104 *Yale Law Journal* (1995) 1991.
[58] *Ibid.* at 1992.
[59] E.g. O. Young, 'International law and social science: the contributions of Myres S. McDougal', 66 *American Journal of International Law* (1972) 60; G. Dorsey, 'The McDougal-Lasswell proposal to build a world public order', 82 *American Journal of International Law* (1988) 41; R. Falk, 'Casting the spell', above note 57.
[60] E.g. M. McDougal and N Schlei, 'The hydrogen bomb tests in perspective: lawful measures for security', 64 *Yale Law Journal* (1955) 648. For an opposing view see E. Margolis, 'The hydrogen bomb experiments and international law', 64 *Yale Law Journal* (1955) 629.

produced by McDougal and Chen in 1975,[61] the New Haven *oeuvre* exhibits no concern with the exclusion of women from the province of authoritative decision-making, nor with the male characteristics of the human being whose dignity is so essential.

'Newstream' theories

The post-modern trend in late-twentieth-century scholarship is reflected in the work of the 'newstream'[62] of international law theorists who have translated the techniques of the United States-based critical legal studies (CLS) movement onto the international plane.[63] Since the late 1970s, critical legal scholars have challenged a view of the law as rational, objective and principled by exposing the indeterminacy of and contradictions inherent in legal rules. The function of legal systems in legitimating the political, social and economic *status quo* have been examined and the notion of the 'false necessity' or essential contingency of legal systems and legal truths developed in a wide variety of contexts.[64] A unifying theme in much CLS scholarship is the coincidence of law and politics and the futility of liberal attempts to carve out a separate and distinct sphere for legal truth.

The newstream of international law scholars develops this critique of liberalism in international law in a great variety of ways. Anthony Carty has described one aspect of newstream inquiries:

> The crucial question is simply whether a positive system of universal international law actually exists, or whether particular States and their representative legal scholars merely appeal to such positivist discourse so as to impose a particularist language upon others *as if it were a universally accepted legal discourse*. So post-modernism is concerned with unearthing difference, heterogeneity and conflict *as reality* in place of *fictional* representations of universality and consensus.[65]

In his analysis of the apparently logical contradiction in the liberal account of the international legal order referred to above, Koskenniemi has argued

[61] M. McDougal and L. Chen, 'Human rights of women and world public order: the outlawing of sex-based discrimination', 69 *American Journal of International Law* (1975) 497.

[62] This term was first used in D. Kennedy's 'A new stream of international law scholarship', 7 *Wisconsin International Law Journal* (1988) 1. For a useful overview of the 'newstream' approach see D. Cass, 'Navigating the Newstream: recent critical scholarship in international law', 65 *Nordic Journal of International Law* (1996) 341.

[63] See N. Purvis, 'Critical legal studies in public international law', 32 *Harvard International Law Journal* (1991) 81.

[64] See G. Simpson and H. Charlesworth, 'Objecting to objectivity: the radical challenge to legal liberalism', in R. Hunter, R. Ingleby and R. Johnstone (eds), *Thinking About Law* (Sydney, Allen & Unwin, 1995) 86 at 100–4.

[65] A. Carty, 'Critical international law: recent trends in the theory of international law', 2 *European Journal of International Law* (1991) 66 (emphasis in original).

that international law cannot live up to its truly neutral, objective promise and in fact is premised on a number of substantive political values. The major problem identified by critics such as Koskenniemi is not that international legal argument is basically highly political and value-laden, but rather that international law achieves its authority precisely by denying its true nature, thus pre-empting debate about the nature and desirability of the values it inculcates. It arbitrarily restricts the range of argumentative possibilities open to international lawyers.[66]

Many of the newstream techniques and insights are important in understanding the relationship of international law to women. As we shall see, some feminist approaches to international law share the newstream concern with the political and contingent nature of liberal legal argument and the law's role in reifying and justifying social, political and economic inequalities. Once we can uncover the unstated political commitments of the present international legal order, we are able to re-imagine it. However, the newstream, just as the mainstream, has displayed little interest in the situation of women. To some extent this is because the newstream is itself rather vague in its normative visions of the international community. Martti Koskenniemi, for example, has referred to an essentially contextual, experiential justice that requires assessing the legal and political issues in a dispute or conflict and proposing tentative, *ad hoc* solutions. This form of justice is based on only two global principles: the exclusion of imperialism and of totalitarianism.[67] The task of the critical enterprise in international law is regarded as simply exposing the political nature of legal argument and expanding its discourse, reminding international lawyers of '[their] painful task of living and choosing in the midst of political conflict'.[68] Koskenniemi has argued that international lawyers should view their professional integrity as a demand not for '"rigorous" legal-technical analysis' but rather 'as a commitment to reaching the most just solution in the particular disputes which he is faced with'.[69] This will involve going beyond legal argument, to 'sociological enquiries into causal relationships and political enquiry into acceptable forms of containing power . . . so as to grasp . . . issues [of international concern] closer to what is significant in them'.[70] Anthony Carty has echoed this: 'It is not the ambition of the critical international lawyer to substitute another pseudo-impartial legal order, but to facilitate the development of the process of inter-state/inter-cultural dialogue and understanding which *may* allow a coming together, however temporary and fragile.'[71] This type of critical approach, built on limited explicit substantive commitments, cannot deal adequately

[66] M. Koskenniemi, above note 37 at 485.
[67] *Ibid.* at 496–7.
[68] *Ibid.* at 501.
[69] *Ibid.* at 496.
[70] *Ibid.* at 485.
[71] A. Carty, above note 65 at 67 (emphasis in original).

with the complex forms of structural disadvantage encountered by women all over the world. Post-colonial theory and critical race theory, however, offer many useful insights and techniques to deal with the multiplicity of global difference.[72]

'Southern' theories of international law

Jurists from the South have made a sustained critique of the international legal order in which their states have emerged as full members on achieving independent status. They have contested the inevitability or universality of particular international law principles by pointing to the Western origins, orientation and cultural bias of such rules.[73] They have argued that many international legal principles, such as the laws relating to the acquisition of territory, diplomatic protection for aliens abroad and compensation for expropriation of property interests, were devised to justify colonial confiscation and appropriation and they have suggested that the participation by states of the South in the further development of international law will lead to a new international legal order.[74] For example, the Tunisian jurist, and former President of the International Court of Justice (ICJ), Mohammed Bedjaoui, has written: 'Like a mastodon crushing the interests of the Third World countries, while the latter attempt with great difficulty to shift it, traditional international law "is, as a whole, the embodiment of situations of predominance of the strong over the weak".'[75]

A major focus for critical analysis has been aspects of the international economic system, which led in the 1970s to a campaign within the UN for a 'New International Economic Order' (NIEO).[76] The campaign aimed to achieve economic, as well as political, independence for states of the South through amplifying a right for peoples and nations to economic self-determination, development and permanent control of their natural resources, while prohibiting interference in a nation's economic affairs, and outlawing

---

[72] See D. Otto, 'Subalternity and international law: the problems of global community and the incommensurability of difference', 5 *Social & Legal Studies* (1996) 337; T. Morrison (ed.), *Race-ing Justice, En-gendering Power* (New York, Pantheon Books, 1992); L. Gandhi, *Postcolonial Theory* (Sydney, Allen & Unwin, 1998).

[73] E.g. F. Snyder and S. Sathirathai, *Third World Attitudes Towards International Law: An Introduction* (Dordrecht, Martinus Nijhoff, 1987); T. Elias, *New Horizons in International Law* (Dordrecht, Martinus Nijhoff, 2nd rev. edn 1992); M. Shahabuddeen, 'Developing countries and the idea of international law', in R. Macdonald, above note 6 at 721.

[74] M. Bedjaoui, *Towards a New International Economic Order* (New York, Holmes & Meier, 1979) at 11–12.

[75] *Ibid.* at 63 (footnote omitted).

[76] See especially the Declaration on the Establishment of a New International Economic Order, GA Res. 3201 (S–VI), 1 May 1974; Charter of Economic Rights and Duties of States, GA Res. 3281 (XXIX), 12 December 1974.

all forms of coercion in international economic matters.[77] The NIEO also involved positive obligations, such as technology transfer. Although in the 1990s it appears that these claims have had little impact on the substance of international law,[78] the tensions still continue, as is illustrated by the debate over the negotiations within the Organisation for Economic Cooperation and Development (OECD) for a Multilateral Agreement on Investment.[79]

Another challenge by jurists from the South has been to the international law-making process, especially with respect to customary international law. Some have argued that, as Southern states did not participate in the development of international law, they should not necessarily be bound by it.[80] This is also sometimes said to be why the South for many years resisted compulsory systems of international adjudication,[81] although in the 1990s Southern states participated actively in such regimes. The UN General Assembly has been favoured as a law-making forum by the South precisely because after the mid-1960s the latter had the numbers to control the former's decisions and the Security Council veto was not available. Since the end of the cold war, however, the diversity of interests of developing states, especially in economic, environmental and resources matters, has become more evident, and formal groupings of developing states such as the Non-Aligned Movement less significant. In turn the preference for 'hard' or 'soft' forms of law-making[82] has become more contextualised, and no automatic alliances can be assumed. In general, however, jurists from the South have not questioned key elements of the traditional legal order, particularly its commitment to state sovereignty.[83] Indeed, state sovereignty has been emphasised as a bulwark against perceived Western neo-colonialism and the broadening scope of international regulation, for example in human rights law and international environmental law.

[77] M. Bedjaoui, above note 74 at 87.
[78] S. Chatterjee, 'The Charter of Economic Rights and Duties of States: an evaluation after fifteen years', 40 *International and Comparative Law Quarterly* (1990) 669. The renegotiation of Part XI of the UN Convention on the Law of the Sea, 10 December 1982, UN Doc. A/CONF. 62/122, reprinted in 21 *International Legal Materials* (1982) 1261, by the Agreement relating to the Implementation of Part XI of the Convention, GA Res. 48/263, 28 July 1994, reprinted in 33 *International Legal Materials* (1994) 1311 before the Convention entered into force in 1994, illustrates the non-acceptance of many of the principles of the NIEO and their effective replacement by market principles.
[79] See D. Rowen, 'Meet the new world government', *The Guardian*, 13 February 1998.
[80] See discussion in L. Henkin, *How Nations Behave: Law and Foreign Policy* (New York, Columbia University Press, 2nd edn 1979) at 121–3, 360, n. 6.
[81] M. Bedjaoui, above note 74 at 102. Compare M. Shahabuddeen, above note 73 at 728–30.
[82] See chapters 3 and 4.
[83] Compare A. Anghie, 'Finding the peripheries: sovereignty and colonialism in nineteenth-century international law', 40 *Harvard International Law Journal* (1999) 1.

It has been argued that there are conceptual links between the critiques of the South and feminist analyses of international law.[84] In practice, however, Southern critiques are as blind to issues of sex and gender as are other approaches to international law. Southern and feminist critiques may share a questioning of Northern 'scientific' objectivity as reflected in international law, but the former generally preserve the basic concepts of the international legal order and seek recognition of economic disparity between states and preferential treatment in overcoming it. Southern theories about international law tend to focus on power imbalances *between* states and have little concern with power differentials *within* them. The oppression of women, if considered at all, is generally linked with colonialism and the achievement of self-determination is seen as the appropriate remedy.

Feminist theories of law

We have argued that the theories of international law outlined above are inadequate, albeit in different ways, to an understanding of and a response to the situation of women globally. We turn now to feminist theories to see what they might contribute to our understanding of international law and the global inequality of women. The Western theories with which we commence are diverse, but they all tend to be concerned with the silencing of women and the failure of traditional systems of knowledge to accommodate women's experiences. Feminist theories can be presented in different ways. For example, Sandra Harding has proposed a tripartite categorisation of feminist theories: empiricism, standpoint theories and post-modernism.[85] Another typology of feminist theories draws a distinction between 'liberal', 'cultural' and 'radical' feminisms. We use both of these descriptive schemes to provide an introduction to the theories upon which we draw in this book, although, as with our discussion of international legal theories, the categories are greatly simplified. It should be stressed that many feminist scholars do not fit neatly into any of the categories we use and, indeed, that the categories overlap in some respects.

Liberal feminism

Liberal feminists typically accept the language and aims of the existing domestic legal order, couching many of their arguments in terms of individual

[84] E.g. I. Gunning, 'Modernizing customary international law: the challenge of human rights', 31 *Virginia Journal of International Law* (1991) 211 at 217–18. See H. Charlesworth, C. Chinkin and S. Wright, 'Feminist approaches to international law', 85 *American Journal of International Law* (1991) 613 at 616–18.
[85] S. Harding, *The Science Question in Feminism* (Ithaca, Cornell University Press, 1986) at 24–9.

rights. They insist that the law fulfil its promise of objective regulation upon which principled decision-making is based. They work for reform of the law, dismantling legal barriers to women being treated like men in the public sphere, and criticise any legal recognition of 'natural' differences between women and men. Their primary goal is to achieve equality of treatment between women and men in public areas such as political participation and representation, and equal access to and equality within paid employment, market services and education.

The approach of insisting that women and men be treated similarly falters when women and men are not in the same position either because of physical difference or because of structural disadvantage. Feminists have debated whether the ability to become pregnant should be legally acknowledged as a difference between women and men or regarded as a merely temporary 'disability'.[86] This controversy has had practical consequences through its distortion of decision-making, for example in the context of industrial relations.[87] More fundamentally, the 'similar treatment' theme in liberal feminism requires women to conform to a male-defined world. In dealing with individual cases of discrimination rather than structural inequality, anti-discrimination law can at most solve a limited number of discrete problems without addressing their underlying causes. The principle of equal treatment, Nicola Lacey has said, is 'inadequate to criticise and transform a world in which the distribution of goods is structured along gender lines'.[88] It assumes 'a world of autonomous individuals starting a race or making free choices [that] has no cutting edge against the fact that men and women are simply running different races'.[89] The promise of equality as 'sameness' to men only gives women access to a world already constituted by men and with the parameters determined by them.[90]

Some versions of liberal feminism go beyond demands for formal equality and are concerned primarily with equality of opportunity and of outcome. This may require prohibition of indirect discrimination and use of affirmative action techniques, but these measures are regarded as temporary methods to counteract inaccurate views that, given the same opportunities, women cannot perform exactly like men.[91] In other words, 'special' treatment is seen

[86] E.g. W. Williams, 'Equality's riddle: pregnancy and the equal treatment/special treatment debate', 13 *New York University Review of Law and Social Change* (1985) 325; L. Finley, 'Transcending equality theory: a way out of the maternity and workplace debate', 86 *Columbia Law Review* (1986) 1118.

[87] E.g. in the context of the European Community (EC) see C. Barnard, *EC Employment Law* (Chichester, Chancery Law Publishing, 1996) at 204–6.

[88] N. Lacey, 'Legislation against sex discrimination: questions from a feminist perspective', 14 *Journal of Law and Society* (1987) 411 at 415.

[89] *Ibid.* at 420.

[90] C. Dalton, 'Where we stand: observations on the situation of feminist legal thought', 3 *Berkeley Women's Law Journal* (1987–88) 1 at 5.

[91] F. Olsen, 'Feminism and critical legal theory: an American perspective', 18 *International Journal of the Sociology of Law* (1990) 199 at 203.

as promoting an ultimately neutral outcome. Apart from this limited acknowledgment of the need for structural change to achieve equality, liberal
feminists do not generally regard the legal system itself as contributing to
the inferior position of women. They assume that the law is ultimately
rational, impartial and capable of achieving justice if it allows proper individual choice. Liberal feminism and the epistemology of feminist empiricism
described by Sandra Harding sometimes overlap in the sense that sexism is
regarded as a bias that can be eliminated by more rational inquiry. Because
scholarly knowledge has almost completely been generated by men observ-
ing other men, liberal feminists may question its objectivity and authority.
However, they see male-centredness as a methodological bias in all disciplines which, once identified, can be eradicated. To adapt Sandra Harding's
words, on this view, bad law is the problem, not law-as-usual.[92]

Cultural feminism

Cultural feminism is concerned with the identification and rehabilitation of
qualities and perspectives identified as particular to women. Epistemologically, it is a 'standpoint' theory in that it emphasises the importance
of knowledge based upon experience and asserts that women's subjugated
position allows them to formulate more complete and accurate accounts
of nature and social life – 'morally and scientifically preferable' to those
produced by men.[93] The work of the American psychologist, Carol Gilligan,
has been very influential in Western legal feminism. Gilligan's research into
modes of moral decision-making and problem-solving by girls and boys
found differences between them.[94] She identified a 'different' voice that based
decisions on the values of caring and connection in contrast to a style of
decision-making based on abstract logic. The former is culturally associated
with women and the latter with men. Gilligan pointed out that the psychological literature generally rated the masculine pattern as more mature and
developed.[95] The hypothesis drawn by some feminist lawyers from Gilligan's
research is that, just as traditional psychological theories have privileged a
male perspective and marginalised women's voices, so too law privileges a
male view of the universe and that law is part of the structure of male
domination. The hierarchical organisation of law, its adversarial format and
its aim of the abstract resolution of competing rights, make the law an
intensely patriarchal institution. Law thus represents a very limited aspect

[92] S. Harding, above note 85 at 25.
[93] *Ibid.*
[94] C. Gilligan, *In a Different Voice: Psychological Theory and Women's Development* (Cambridge, Harvard University Press, 1982).
[95] *Ibid.* at 9–18. See further C. Gilligan, 'Getting civilized', in A. Oakley and
J. Mitchell (eds), *Who's Afraid of Feminism? Seeing through the Backlash* (New York,
The New Press, 1997) 13.

of human experience. The language and imagery of the law underscore its male-ness: it lays claim to rationality, objectivity and abstractness, characteristics traditionally associated with men, and is defined in contrast to emotion, subjectivity and contextualised thinking – the province of women.[96] For legal feminists who are concerned with the fundamentally male orientation of law, traditional forms of legal reform are of limited utility. Indeed the language of 'equal rights' and 'equal opportunities' and the strat-egies of litigation, advocacy and lobbying tacitly reinforce the basic organ-isation of society.[97] Some feminist jurists have tried to devise methods of introducing a different, women's voice into national legal processes. For example, they have questioned the adversarial model of justice that assumes that the right resolution of legal disputes emerges from a contest between two parties, judged by a neutral decision-maker.[98] Some have proposed a model of feminist justice in which the decision-maker goes beyond adjudic-ating on the cases presented by the parties and acts creatively to avoid a win/lose situation.[99] Mediation and conciliation have been explored as altern-atives to litigation and it has been argued that women judges could bring a 'new humanity' to the decision-making process.[100]

Nevertheless, celebrating the differences between feminine and masculine modes of reasoning in the legal system is not without problems. Indeed Gilligan's work has been referred to as a potential 'Uncle Tom's Cabin' for feminist legal theory.[101] Cultural feminist approaches have been controver-sial because of the implication that women are 'naturally' endowed with certain characteristics.[102] Carol Smart, for example, has warned that the acceptance of a distinctive 'women's voice' 'slides uncomfortably and ex-ceedingly quickly into socio-biologism which merely puts women back in

---

[96] F. Olsen, above note 91 at 199–201. Compare K. Bartlett, 'Feminist legal methods', 103 *Harvard Law Review* (1990) 829 at 856–8 (arguing that there is no sharp dichotomy between abstract and contextualised reasoning in either legal or feminist method).

[97] D. Polan, 'Toward a theory of law and patriarchy', in D. Kairys (ed.), *The Politics of Law* (New York, Pantheon, 1982) 294 at 300.

[98] E.g. L. Henderson, 'Legality and empathy', 85 *Michigan Law Review* (1987) 1574.

[99] E.g. C. Menkel-Meadow, 'Portia in a different voice: speculations on a woman's lawyering process', 1 *Berkeley Women's Law Journal* (1985) 39; C. Menkel-Meadow, 'The trouble with the adversary system in a postmodern, multicultural world', 38 *William and Mary Law Review* (1996) 5 at 6. See further chapter 9.

[100] C. Menkel-Meadow, The trouble with the adversary system', above note 99 at 42–3; B. Wilson, 'Will women judges really make a difference?', 28 *Osgoode Hall Law Journal* (1990) 507.

[101] A. Scales, 'The emergence of feminist jurisprudence: an essay', 95 *Yale Law Journal* (1986) 1373 at 1381.

[102] Gilligan herself has not endorsed this implication. She has attributed the difference in 'masculine' and 'feminine' voices primarily to gendered child-rearing practices: C. Gilligan, above note 94 at 171.

their place'.[103] No challenge is offered to the mainstream legal system by a 'different voice' appearing in various isolated areas of the law and neither is there any guarantee that the women's voice would be equally valued or respected. It might indeed impose further burdens on women.[104] Feminist scholars have pointed out the risk that 'feminine' methods of dispute resolution such as mediation between parties in an unequal position with respect to skills, information and power can in fact perpetuate inequality.[105] Some versions of cultural feminism also beg the question of the cause of the difference between gendered modes of reasoning. Catharine MacKinnon has questioned the authenticity of the feminine voice described by Carol Gilligan. The 'feminine', MacKinnon has argued, is defined by a patriarchal culture: 'For women to affirm difference, when difference means dominance, as it does with gender, means to affirm the qualities and characteristics of powerlessness . . . When you are powerless, you don't just speak differently. A lot, you don't speak.'[106] 'Take your foot off our necks,' MacKinnon has said, 'then we will hear in what tongue women speak.'[107]

Radical feminism

Radical feminism explains women's inequality as the product of domination of women by men – inequality is presented as political and sexual in nature. Radical feminism is epistemologically a standpoint theory, although its exponents define women's standpoint in a different way from that of cultural feminists. Qualities such as caring and conciliation have been foisted on women, radical feminists contend, by the structure of patriarchal societies and are based on a male view of personhood. Catharine MacKinnon has been a consistent exponent of this approach. She has argued that the common failing of theories associating equality with equal treatment or with different treatment is that they implicitly accept a male yardstick: women are either the same as or different from a male norm.[108] MacKinnon views social relations between women and men as organised in a way 'that men may dominate and women must submit'.[109] The law, she has said, keeps women 'out and down'[110] by preserving a hierarchical system based on gender and sex. MacKinnon

---

[103] C. Smart, *Feminism and the Power of Law* (London, Routledge, 1989) at 75.

[104] See B. Stark, 'The "other" half of the international bill of rights as a postmodern feminist text', in D. Dallmeyer (ed.), *Reconceiving Reality: Women and International Law* (Washington DC, American Society of International Law, 1993) 19 at 27–31.

[105] H. Astor and C. Chinkin, *Dispute Resolution in Australia* (Sydney, Butterworths, 1993) chapter 5.

[106] C. MacKinnon, *Feminism Unmodified: Discourses on Life and Law* (Cambridge, Harvard University Press, 1987) at 39.

[107] *Ibid.* at 45.

[108] *Ibid.* at 34.

[109] *Ibid.* at 3.

[110] *Ibid.* at 205.

has described an alternative legal analysis of inequality for which the central question is whether the policy or practice in question contributes to the maintenance of a deprived position because of gender or sex.[111] In other words, the law should support freedom from systematic subordination because of sex rather than freedom to be treated without regard to sex.

MacKinnon's 'dominance' approach is not always easily applied because many of the relationships of subordination sanctioned by the law are so deeply ingrained that they appear quite natural. It involves looking 'for that which we have been trained not to see . . . [identifying] the invisible'.[112] If the issue of inequality is understood as one of domination and subordination, sex discrimination laws that promise equal treatment are of limited utility. Catharine MacKinnon has worked instead for an expansion of the ambit of the law and the use of legal strategies such as litigation to cover traditionally legally unrecognised harms of particular concern to women such as sexual harassment[113] and pornography.[114] She has argued that the feminist project in law should be to make the law recognise the real injuries women suffer.[115] In this way relations between women and men can be, slowly, transformed.

Catharine MacKinnon's theories about law and inequality have been controversial both inside and outside the feminist community. Critics have wondered how MacKinnon can identify an 'authentic' women's voice in a world she describes as utterly dominated by men.[116] MacKinnon's work has also been read as being dogmatic[117] and as endorsing an essentialist position without regard to other influences such as race, class or sexuality.[118] Carol Smart has argued that MacKinnon concedes too much authority to law.[119] Although MacKinnon urges changing the values of the law through a comprehensive theory of equality, she nevertheless has accorded it considerable power, preserving its place in the hierarchy of male structures.

Radical feminism has paid attention to the public/private dichotomies that feature in liberal thought. As described by liberal theorists, distinctions between public and private realms operate generally and neutrally with

---

[111] *Ibid.* at 40–5.

[112] A. Scales, above note 101 at 1393.

[113] C. MacKinnon, *Sexual Harassment of Working Women* (New Haven, Yale University Press, 1979).

[114] C. MacKinnon, *Feminism Unmodified*, above note 106 at 127–213; C. MacKinnon, *Only Words* (London, Harper Collins, 1995).

[115] C. MacKinnon, *Feminism Unmodified*, above note 106 at 104.

[116] E.g. C. Smart, above note 103 at 75–7.

[117] E.g. M. Walters, 'American gothic: feminism, melodrama and the backlash', in A. Oakley and J. Mitchell, above note 95 at 56.

[118] E.g. A. Harris, 'Race and essentialism in feminist legal theory', 42 *Stanford Law Review* (1990) 580 at 590–601. Note MacKinnon's spirited defence of her position in 'From practice to theory, or what is a white woman anyway?', 4 *Yale Journal of Law and Feminism* (1991) 13.

[119] C. Smart, above note 103 at 81, 88–9.

respect to individuals. Their central role in liberalism is the preservation of individual freedom through non-regulation of the 'private'.[120] A feminist response to these claims is that public/private distinctions in fact often operate both to obscure and to legitimate men's domination of women. In Western society women are regularly associated with the private, minimally regulated sphere of home, hearth and family. The public sphere of workplace, law, economics, politics, intellectual and cultural life is regarded largely as the province of men, although the increasing numbers and proportion of women in the 'public' workforce make this linkage more complex. Scholars have connected the continuing Western identification of women and the domestic sphere with the separation of production from the household and the 'privatisation' of the family in the eighteenth century together with the growth of capitalism and deeply held beliefs about gender.[121] Public/private dichotomies have thus become a 'metaphor for the social patterning of gender, a description of sociological practice, and a category grounded in experience'.[122] Feminist scholars have pointed out that the gendered character of liberal public/private distinctions effectively supports and reinforces the disadvantaged position of women. Some legal theorists, such as Catharine MacKinnon, associating the 'public' with the state, government and law and the family with the 'private', have argued for greater public regulation of the private sphere of home and family.[123] Others, such as Frances Olsen, have pointed out that whether or not the state formally intervenes in the private, the former nevertheless exercises great influence over the latter.[124]

Post-modern feminism

Post-modern feminism is sceptical of modernist, universal theoretical explanations of the oppression of women and embraces 'the fractured identities . . . [of] modern life'.[125] Thus, Carol Smart and others have questioned whether the construction of 'Grand Feminist Theory' is useful in achieving equality between the sexes because such endeavours do not capture the contextualised and partial nature of our knowledge.[126] Smart has contended that we should avoid general, abstract theories and focus instead on the realities of women's

[120] K. O'Donovan, *Sexual Divisions in Law* (London, Weidenfeld & Nicholson, 1985) at 7–8.

[121] C. Pateman, above note 45 at 286.

[122] E. Garmanikow and J. Purvis, 'Introduction', in E. Garmanikow, D. Morgan, J. Purvis and D. Taylorson (eds), *The Public and the Private* (Aldershot, Gower, 1983) 1 at 5.

[123] C. MacKinnon, *Towards a Feminist Theory of the State* (Cambridge, Harvard University Press, 1989) at 187–90.

[124] F. Olsen, 'The myth of state intervention in the family', 18 *University of Michigan Journal of Law Reform* (1985) 835.

[125] S. Harding, above note 85 at 24–9.

[126] C. Smart, above note 103 at 70–2.

lives, studying the inconsistencies and contradictions in legal regulation.[127] The law, she has pointed out, does not operate in a monolithic way to oppress women and advantage men. There are many different voices and experiences and realities unreflected in the law and '[b]y giving up the goal of telling "one true story," ... [we can] embrace instead the permanent partiality of feminist inquiry.'[128] Post-modern feminism is concerned with the specific operation of the law and the particular contexts of women. This approach emphasises the utility of action at the micro-political level rather than the uncertain path of law reform. It may be more useful, Carol Smart has said, to be a feminist journalist than a feminist lawyer.[129]

Post-modern feminists have paid particular attention to language and the way that it filters our experiences and understanding. They have been concerned with the way the law constitutes identities, such as 'masculinity' and 'femininity'. Analysis of legal texts can show how gender is constructed and reconstructed in discourse. This point is made by Mary Joe Frug: 'The postmodern position locating human experience as inescapably within language suggests that feminists should not overlook the constructive function of legal language as a critical frontier for feminist reforms ... Legal discourse should be recognized as a site of political struggle over sex differences.'[130] Post-modern feminists have also been particularly concerned with the issue of essentialism, which is discussed further below. They have encouraged the development of a 'politics of identity', which challenges the universal concept of self found in legal doctrines. They have promoted the notion of plurality and multiple viewpoints and emphasised the importance of contextual judgment.[131] Post-modern feminism therefore resists the idea that there is a single analysis of, or solution to, the law's involvement in inequality between women and men.

Some feminist activists and scholars are wary of post-modernism, finding that its emphasis on localised narratives produces too weak a discourse to respond to the global structures of continued oppression of women. Attempts have been made to sharpen post-modernism's political edge by devising a 'pragmatic' feminist version. Margaret Radin, for example, has argued that feminists should accept that a range of approaches is appropriate in feminist legal analysis and that 'situated judgment', rather than theory, will tell us which is the most appropriate at any time.[132] In a similar vein, Donna Haraway has spoken of 'situated knowledges' which can lead

---

[127] *Ibid.* at 68–9.

[128] S. Harding, above note 85 at 194.

[129] C. Smart, 'Feminist jurisprudence' (talk at La Trobe University, Melbourne, 2 December 1987).

[130] M. J. Frug, 'A postmodern feminist legal manifesto (an unfinished draft)', 105 *Harvard Law Review* (1992) 1045 at 1046.

[131] See G. Minda, *Postmodern Legal Movements: Law and Jurisprudence at the Century's End* (New York, New York University Press, 1995) at 141–7.

[132] M. Radin, 'The pragmatist and the feminist', 63 *Southern California Law Review* (1990) 1699 at 1718–19.

to shared conversations on methodology, producing fuller accounts of the world than that provided by a single perspective.[133]

Third world feminisms

Feminist arguments and campaigns have not been restricted to women from the North,[134] although inevitably the histories and priorities of feminist movements have been very different elsewhere.[135] The term 'third world feminisms' is used here to refer to the approaches developed by women in the South and women of colour in the North. These approaches have taken many different forms, responding to particular historical contexts and in many cases are based on a long history of often violent nationalist struggle. Geraldine Heng has identified three major influences on third world feminist theories and strategies.[136] First, they have been shaped by their connection with nationalist movements, 'a complicated relationship of sympathy and support, mutual use and mutual cooperation, and unacknowledged contestatory tension'.[137] Second, feminism in the third world is influenced by the role of the state in women's lives, particularly its often interventionist and authoritarian nature that may channel feminist activity into informal networks and alliances.[138] Third, feminism has adapted to the third world ambivalence about modernity. While the technological and economic aspects of modernity may be embraced as essential to development, its cultural baggage is often rejected. Feminism can thus be represented by nationalists as 'the subversive figure, at once of a destabilizing modernity and of a presumptuous Western imperialism'.[139]

Many third world feminists have become increasingly critical of the attempted wholesale application of Western feminist theories to their communities and societies and in particular the liberal feminist emphasis on the removal of sex discrimination. They have argued that, while gender and class underpin the oppression of women in the West, third world women

[133] D. Haraway, 'Situated knowledges: *The Science Question in Feminism* and the privilege of partial accounts of the perspective', 14 *Feminist Studies* (1988) 575 at 580.

[134] There are significant differences among feminists in the North. For an account of differences in the positions of women, the articulation of feminist agendas and activities both within Europe and between Europe and the United States see A. Oakley and J. Mitchell, 'Introduction to the American Edition', in A. Oakley and J. Mitchell, above note 95 at xix. See also N. Walter, *The New Feminism* (London, Virago, 2nd edn 1999).

[135] For an overview of post-communist feminisms see P. Watson, '(Anti) feminism after Communism', in A. Oakley and J. Mitchell, above note 95 at 144.

[136] G. Heng, ' "A great way to fly": nationalism, the state, and the varieties of third-world feminism', in M. Alexander and C. Mohanty (eds), *Feminist Genealogies, Colonial Legacies, Democratic Futures* (New York, Routledge, 1997) 30.

[137] *Ibid.* at 31.

[138] *Ibid.* at 33.

[139] *Ibid.* at 34.

also have to cope with oppression based on race and imperialism.[140] Tensions between first and third world feminists on issues of substance and strategy have been evident in the international arena. For example, there has been criticism of first world feminist focus on issues such as access to contraception and abortion without an appreciation of the way that the politics of contraception have operated in the third world and against poor women of colour in the West.[141] Third world feminists have also criticised the implicit comparisons drawn in some Western feminist work between the first and third world: 'defining third world women in terms of their "problems" or their "achievements" in relation to an imagined free white liberal democracy effectively removes them (and the "liberal democracy") from history, freezing them in time and space'.[142] This criticism of the attribution of a fixed set of characteristics to women based on their geography or culture has meant that third world feminists have been prominent in debates about the methodology of essentialism, which is discussed more fully below. They have emphasised the importance of specific, local accounts of the lives of women.

While early feminist movements in the developing world were typically associated with nationalist struggles, more recently they have focused on the eradication of poverty as a primary goal for women. Because of this, at the international level, they have been concerned with the ways in which the global economy perpetuates poverty and how the economic success of 'developed' nations rests to a considerable degree on the exploitation of the 'developing' world that is supported by the institutions and structures of international law. For example, 'free trade zones' established in developing countries to encourage investment by multinational corporations depend upon a cheap and unregulated workforce. As Cheryl Johnson-Odim has observed:

> In 'underdeveloped' societies it is not just a question of internal redistribution of resources, but of their generation and control; not just equal opportunity between men and women, but the creation of opportunity itself; not only the position of women in society, but the position of the societies in which Third World women find themselves.[143]

While the evidence suggests that women are particularly disadvantaged in the lopsided international economic system,[144] third world feminists have argued that feminism must have a broader agenda than the eradication of

---

[140] C. Johnson-Odim, 'Common themes, different contexts', in C. Mohanty, A. Russo and L. Torres (eds), *Third World Women and the Politics of Feminism* (Bloomington, Indiana University Press, 1991) 314.

[141] *Ibid.* at 323.

[142] C. Mohanty, 'Cartographies of struggle: third world women and the politics of feminism', in C. Mohanty, A. Russo and L. Torres, above note 140 at 1, 7.

[143] C. Johnson-Odim, above note 140 at 320.

[144] Fourth World Conference on Women, Declaration and Platform for Action, 15 September 1995, UN Doc. A/CONF. 177/20, reprinted in 35 *International Legal Materials* (1996) 401 (Beijing Platform for Action), paras 18, 157.

oppression based on sex or gender.[145] It must pay attention to the complex interaction of gender, race, class, colonialism and global capitalism. On this analysis, first world women cannot assert a world sisterhood unified in interest and must acknowledge their partnership in, and the benefits that their societies reap from, the oppression of the third world.[146]

Can there be any basis for shared feminist approaches to the international position of women? Third world feminists have argued that this is possible if there is recognition of the role of racism and economic exploitation in the position of most of the world's women.[147] They have been concerned with 'multiple, fluid structures of domination which intersect to locate women differently at particular historical conjunctures'[148] rather than 'a notion of universal patriarchy operating in a transhistorical way to subordinate all women'.[149] Third world feminisms, then, demand a much more intricate study of the forms and intersections of systems of oppression than is proposed by most first world feminisms.

Using feminist theories in international law

What can feminist theories add to our understanding of international law? As the following chapters explain, women are on the margins of the international legal system. Their participation in the development of international legal principles is minimal and the international legal order appears impervious to the realities of women's lives. Although a specialised area of 'women's human rights law' is evolving,[150] and occasionally women are acknowledged in 'mainstream' international law, by and large, whenever women come into focus at all in international law, they are viewed in a very limited way, chiefly as victims, particularly as mothers, or potential mothers, and accordingly in need of protection.[151] An example of this is found in the Platform for Action adopted by the Fourth World Conference on Women held in Beijing in 1995. Debate in Beijing about what might constitute 'balanced and

[145] See R. Chow, 'Violence in the other country: China as crisis, spectacle, and woman', in C. Mohanty, A. Russo and L. Torres, above note 140 at 81.

[146] See bell hooks' argument that: 'The vision of sisterhood evoked by women liberationists was based on the idea of common oppression – a false and corrupt platform disguising and mystifying the true nature of women's varied and complex social reality.' b. hooks, 'Sisterhood, political solidarity between women', in S. Gunew (ed.), *Feminist Knowledge: Critique and Construct* (London, Routledge, 1990) 29.

[147] C. Johnson-Odim, above note 140 at 325.

[148] C. Mohanty, 'Cartographies of struggle', above note 142 at 13.

[149] M. Alexander and C. Mohanty, 'Genealogies, legacies, movements', in M. Alexander and C. Mohanty, above note 136 at xiii, xix.

[150] See chapter 7.

[151] See J. Gardam, 'An alien's encounter with the law of armed conflict', in N. Naffine and R. Owens (eds), *Sexing the Subject of the Law* (Sydney, Law Book Co. Ltd, 1996) 233.

non-stereotyped' images of women resulted in a paragraph referring to women's experiences as including 'balancing work and family responsibilities, as mothers, as professionals, as managers, as entrepreneurs'.[152] Dianne Otto has noted that this list of women's major life experiences 'neatly encapsulates the dominant possibilities for women which are approved by the Platform: the traditional role of mother remains central, but is now augmented by the addition of a role in the free market economy'.[153]

Feminist analyses rest on a commitment to challenge male dominance of women. What, then, are the most appropriate feminist tools and theories in examining international law? As we noted in chapter 1, feminist inquiry into international law can be compared to an archaeological dig. One obvious sign of power differentials between women and men is the absence of women in international legal institutions. Beneath this is the vocabulary of international law. It is striking that most international documents continue to use the generic male pronoun when referring to individuals generally, reinforcing the exclusion of women.[154] Digging further down, many apparently 'neutral' principles and rules of international law can be seen to operate differently with respect to women and men. Another, deeper, layer of the excavation reveals the gendered and sexed nature of the basic concepts of international law, for example, 'states', 'security', 'order' and 'conflict'. Permeating all stages of the dig is a silence from and exclusion of women. This phenomenon does not emerge as a simple gap or vacuum that weakens the edifice of international law and that might be remedied by some rapid construction work. It is rather an integral part of the structure of the international legal order, a critical element of its stability. The silences of the discipline are as important as its positive rules and rhetorical structures.

One technique for identifying and decoding the silences in international law is paying attention to the way that various dichotomies are used in its structure. International legal discourse rests on a series of distinctions: for example, objective/subjective, legal/political, logic/emotion, order/anarchy, mind/body, culture/nature, action/passivity, public/private, protector/protected, independence/dependence, binding/non-binding, international/domestic, intervention/non-intervention, sovereign/non-self-governing. Feminist scholars have drawn attention to the gendered coding of these systems of binary oppositions with the first term signifying 'male' characteristics and the second 'female'.[155]

---

[152] Beijing Platform for Action, para. 245(b).

[153] D. Otto, 'Holding up half the sky, but for whose benefit? A critical analysis of the Fourth World Conference on Women'; 6 *Australian Feminist Law Journal* (1996) 7 at 27.

[154] D. Spender, *Man Made Language* (London/Boston, Routledge & Kegan Paul, 1980) at 147–8.

[155] C. Cohn, 'War, wimps and women: talking gender and thinking war', in M. Cooke and A. Woollacott (eds), *Gendering War Talk* (Princeton, Princeton University Press, 1993) 227 at 231.

This is not to say that all, or even most, women or men actually possess these contrasting qualities. It is rather that using the vocabulary of objectivity, logic and order positions a person as being manly, which immediately gives their words a higher value; the use of subjective, emotional or 'disordered' discourse is coded as feminine and thus weakens a statement or argument.[156] Carol Cohn has written of her 'participant observation' study of North American defence and security affairs analysts that: 'Certain ideas, concerns, interests, information, feelings, and meanings [e.g. peace, emotion, concern for the environment] are marked in national security discourse as feminine, and are devalued.'[157] For this reason, they are both difficult to articulate and difficult to hear. They seem illegitimate, embarrassing and irrelevant.[158] In a similar way, international law typically values the 'manly' terms more greatly than their pairs. Thus the symbolic system and culture of international law are permeated by gendered values, which in turn reinforce more general stereotypes of women and men.

The silence of international law with respect to women needs to be challenged on every level and different techniques will be appropriate at different levels of the excavation. For this reason we adopt the method described by Margaret Radin as 'situated judgment' – using a variety of analytic strategies rather than a single feminist theory.[159] In some contexts, we rely on 'liberal' feminist techniques to point out that modern international law has failed to deliver on its promises of neutrality and equality and to challenge its illusory universality. Women have been almost completely excluded from international law-making arenas and it is important to document this and then to argue for the need for proper representation and participation of women. Simply 'adding women and mixing' is by itself inadequate because the international legal system is itself gendered. Its rules have developed as a response to the experiences of a male elite. Feminist analysis must thus explore the unspoken commitments of apparently neutral principles of international law and the ways that male perspectives are institutionalised in it. This involves some of the techniques and concepts suggested by 'cultural', 'radical', 'post-modern' and 'third world' feminisms. All these approaches are useful in examining the sex and gender of the building blocks of the international legal order, although such an eclectic method may also attract charges of theoretical incoherence.[160]

Feminist scholarship in the discipline of international relations deals with many issues central to the international legal system. For example, international relations scholars have examined the gendered nature of the state,

---

[156] *Ibid.* at 229–30.
[157] *Ibid.* at 231.
[158] *Ibid.*
[159] See above note 132 and accompanying text.
[160] E.g. F. Tesón, 'Feminism and international law', above note 19 at 648.

sovereignty and security in a range of contexts.[161] From different theoretical vantage points, they have made productive forays into the gendered way in which global politics is conducted and understood. We have been encouraged and stimulated by the work of these colleagues. We draw on it in this book and try to show its implications for international law. We hope that one result of this will be a closer dialogue between these artificially separated disciplines.[162]

A number of feminists have developed a useful overarching methodology for analysis of international law based upon dialogue. One formulation is 'world travelling' which depends upon what Maria Lugones has called a 'loving perception' of other women.[163] Isabelle Gunning has described three steps in the process of the multicultural dialogue involved in world travelling. First, we must be explicit about our own historical and cultural context. Second, we must try to understand how other women might see us. Third, we should recognise the complexities of the contexts of other women, in other words, to try to see them through their own eyes.[164] A similar method is that of 'rooting' and 'shifting' expounded by some European feminists. Each woman remains rooted in her own history and identity while shifting to understand the roots of other women in the dialogue. Nira Yuval-Davis has described two conditions of this process of 'transversalism': the process of shifting should not mean losing one's own roots and values nor should it homogenise 'other' women.[165] Again, Rosi Braidotti suggests the image of 'multiple literacies' to capture the global range of feminisms. This entails 'being able to engage in conversation in a variety of styles, from a variety of disciplinary angles, if possible in different languages'.[166] Unlike Gunning, however, who has contemplated the possibility of identifying shared values

[161] E.g. J. Tickner, *Gender in International Relations* (New York, Columbia University Press, 1992); J. Pettman, *Worlding Women: A Feminist International Politics* (Sydney, Allen & Unwin, 1996). On the tensions in the relationship between feminist and 'mainstream' international relations scholars see J. Tickner, 'You just don't understand: troubled engagements between feminists and IR theorists', 41 *International Studies Quarterly* (1997) 611.

[162] See A.-M. Slaughter, A. Tulumello and S. Wood, 'International law and international relations theory: a new generation of interdisciplinary scholarship', 92 *American Journal of International Law* (1998) 367.

[163] M. Lugones, 'Playfulness, "world-traveling", and loving perception', 2 *Hypatia* (1987) 3 at 18.

[164] I. Gunning, 'Arrogant perception, world-travelling and multicultural feminism: the case of female genital surgeries', 23 *Colombia Human Rights Law Review* (1991–92) 189 at 191.

[165] N. Yuval-Davis, 'Women, ethnicity and empowerment', in A. Oakley and J. Mitchell, above note 95 at 77, 95–7. Yuval-Davis has distinguished transversalism from 'universalism'. The latter, she has said, 'by assuming a homogenous point of departure ends up being exclusive instead of inclusive'. *Ibid.* at 96.

[166] R. Braidotti, 'The exile, the nomad, and the migrant: reflections on international feminism', 15 *Women's Studies International Forum* (1992) 7 at 10.

and common concerns among women from diverse backgrounds,[167] Braidotti has insisted that feminists 'relinquish the dream of a common language' and resign themselves to simply 'temporary political consensus on specific issues'.[168] In this book, we do not attempt to resolve the issue of whether 'world travelling' can deliver permanent or merely temporary agreement on particular issues. For our purposes, the value of the idea of world travelling in the context of international law is its emphasis on the multiplicity of women's stories and the range of their cultural, national, religious, economic and social concerns and interests.[169] Analysis of our discipline means confronting the inevitable tension between general theories and local experience, being receptive to a diversity of voices and perspectives. In other words, world travellers must use different modes of transport according to the terrain. As Elizabeth Grosz has observed, 'Feminists are not faced with pure and impure options. All options are in their various ways bound by the constraints of patriarchal power. The crucial political question is which commitments remain, in spite of their patriarchal alignments, of use to feminists in their political struggles? What kind of feminist strategy do they make possible or hinder?'[170]

Essentialism

Feminist analyses of international law raise the issue of essentialism in an acute form. Essentialism, or the notion that women have a fixed 'essence' or set of characteristics, has sparked a major debate within feminist theory. The problem of an essentialist approach is that it limits the possibilities of restructuring social and political life: '[Essentialist theories] rationalize and neutralize the prevailing sexual division of social roles by assuming that these are the only, or the best, possibilities, given the confines of the nature, essence, or biology of the two sexes.'[171] Thus essentialism confuses social relations with immutable attributes.

From an international perspective, essentialism does not account for the historical and social differences between women of different cultures.[172] It allows the use of monolithic categories such as 'third-world-women' which carry a baggage of poverty, oppressive traditions, illiteracy and overpopulation.[173]

---

[167] I. Gunning, 'Arrogant perception', above note 164 at 191.

[168] R. Braidotti, above note 166 at 10.

[169] G. Sen and C. Grown, *Development, Crises, and Alternative Visions: Third World Women's Perspectives* (New York, Monthly Review Press, 1987) at 18–19.

[170] E. Grosz, 'A note on essentialism and difference', in S. Gunew, above note 146 at 332, 342–3.

[171] *Ibid.* at 335.

[172] *Ibid.*

[173] C. Mohanty, 'Under western eyes: feminist scholarship and colonial discourses', 30 *Feminist Review* (1988) 61; M. Lugones and E. Spelman, 'Have we got a theory for you!', 6 *Hypatia* (1983) 578.

In reality, as Chandra Mohanty has pointed out, 'Women are constituted as women through the complex interaction between class, culture, religion and other ideological institutions and frameworks. They are not "women" – a coherent group – solely on the basis of a particular economic system or policy.'[174] For all these reasons, the term 'essentialism' (or its cognates, biologism, naturalism and universalism) have become, in Elizabeth Grosz's words, 'labels for danger zones or theoretical pitfalls' in feminist theory, both from an intellectual and a political perspective.[175]

Chandra Mohanty has proposed the idea of an 'imagined community' (borrowed from Benedict Anderson)[176] that is useful in feminist analysis of international law.[177] Mohanty has developed the notion in the context of problems of writing about third world feminisms in a general but worthwhile way, but it can be usefully extended to all women in an international context. For Mohanty, the epithet 'imagined' is used in contrast to existing boundaries – of nation, colour, sexuality and so on – to indicate the potential for collaborative endeavour across them; the term 'community' refers to the possibility of a 'horizontal comradeship' across existing hierarchies. An 'imagined community' of feminist interests does not imply a single set of feminist concerns, but rather a strategic, political alliance. Mohanty has written: 'it is not color or sex which constructs the ground for these struggles. Rather it is the *way* we think about race, class, and gender – the political links we choose to make among and between struggles.'[178] Another technique proposed to bridge identity and universality is that of 'reflective solidarity'. Reflective solidarity challenges the opposition between difference and universality by emphasising a 'universalism of difference'. In this sense identity is not opposed to universality, but is rather dependent on it.[179] Drawing on Habermas's notion of 'discursive universalism' in which debate and argument are vital as the foundation of any universal norm, Jodi Dean has argued for

> the importance of coming to an agreement about those aspects of our lives affecting us all, of working within our differences to find norms and practices worthy of the consent of each individual. The recognition of difference remains meaningless so long as it is not included as an element of our common life context and incorporated into the struggle to end exclusion and oppression.[180]

---

[174] *Ibid.* at 74.

[175] E. Grosz, above note 170 at 335.

[176] B. Anderson, *Imagined Communities: Reflections on the Origins and Spread of Nationalism* (London/New York, Verso, rev. edn 1991).

[177] C. Mohanty, 'Cartographies of struggle', above note 142 at 4.

[178] *Ibid.* (emphasis in original).

[179] J. Dean, *Solidarity of Strangers: Feminism after Identity Politics* (Berkeley, University of California Press, 1996) chapter 5.

[180] *Ibid.* at 174.

One strategy to overcome the hazards of essentialism in feminist work in international law is to focus on problems women appear to face whatever their background. In practice, women from very different backgrounds have worked successfully together at an international level to raise awareness of oppressive and discriminatory practices. For example, the four UN conferences on women (Mexico (1975), Copenhagen (1980), Nairobi (1985) and Beijing (1995)) and particularly their respective associated NGO fora indicate that women are able to use international arenas to negotiate a great range of differences to support both common projects and concerns of particular groups. The campaign for recognition of violence against women, prevalent in all countries and cultures, as a violation of women's human rights was especially effective as a unifying force throughout the global conferences on diverse subjects of the 1990s.

The tactic of identifying and addressing common global issues for women is complex. For example, there are disagreements about whether particular practices constitute violence against women, and deep divisions over the appropriate methods to deal with a problem.[181] Moreover, the search for 'universal' women's predicaments may homogenise women's experiences and obscure the position of women who suffer from multiple forms of discrimination, for example, because of their race, class, age and sexual orientation. Another strategy has been the use of networks across national boundaries in ways that bring together women with shared concerns, although they may have very different political aspirations.[182] The international legal system has been slow to recognise the diversity of women. The Beijing Conference in 1995 paid some attention to the intersection of a variety of obstacles to women's empowerment, for example race, age, language, ethnicity, culture, religion, disability, indigeneity, family and socio-economic status, or status as refugees or displaced persons, or as victims of environmental damage, disease or violence, although it ultimately failed to acknowledge sexual orientation as an aspect of women's identity.[183] But no further significance was drawn from this recognition of diversity between women in the Beijing Platform and, in any event, as noted above, the recognition of women's diversity was undermined by the limited vision of women's roles in the Beijing Platform.[184] Dianne Otto has commented: 'Women's "citizenship" within the global community is both limited to, and conditional upon, their position within the prescribed normative framework. This is contingent "citizenship" at the price of women's diversity and of fundamental global change.'[185]

---

[181] E.g. the debate over feminist responses to female genital mutilation, discussed in chapter 7.

[182] N. Yuval-Davis, above note 165 at 95–6.

[183] Beijing Platform for Action, para. 46.

[184] See notes 152–3 above and accompanying text.

[185] D. Otto, above note 153 at 27.

The term 'feminism' has little meaning if it does not extend beyond purely local concerns, but the use of feminist theories on a global level requires attention to the way that these theories can privilege some women's experiences over others. In some international contexts, 'women' may well be an appropriate category in the struggle against domination by men, while other situations call for a more particularised category. The language of international law is itself universalised, acknowledging cultural differences only in the most general and attenuated form. In the feminist excavation of the levels of the discipline, the gender of international law's 'universal' concepts and principles may be most effectively exposed when countered with contrary 'universal' models. In the early stages of feminist work in this area, fetishising the particular over the general may well blunt the bite of criticism. It may also, albeit unwittingly, support arguments of cultural relativism, legitimating a feminist form of the segregationist 'separate but equal' policy.[186] In this context Martha Nussbaum has pointed out that, in the name of anti-essentialism, some scholars, otherwise committed to the advancement of women, have espoused reactionary, oppressive and sexist positions.[187]

The category of 'women' has powerful theoretical and political potential in scrutinising international law. It has theoretical force in the sense that it is using a patriarchal tool against patriarchy, removing women from the category of the particular to which they are usually assigned. And it has political implications in its ability to mobilise.[188] Feminist analysis must negotiate a strategic path between theoretical purity and political principle.[189] Gayatri Spivak has explained the dilemma well:

> You pick up the universal that will give you the power to fight against the other side and what you are throwing away by doing that is your theoretical purity. Whereas the great custodians of the anti-universal are obliged therefore simply to act in the interest of a great narrative, the narrative of exploitation, while they keep themselves clean by not committing themselves to anything.[190]

The challenge is to develop 'situated perspectives', create 'imagined communities' or employ a 'discursive universalism' which encourage awareness

[186] J. Martin, 'Methodological essentialism, false difference, and other dangerous traps', 19 *Signs* (1994) 630 at 648.

[187] M. Nussbaum, 'Human functioning and social justice: in defence of Aristotelian essentialism', 20 *Political Theory* (1992) 202 at 212.

[188] E. Grosz, above note 170 at 343.

[189] *Ibid.* at 342. Annie Bunting has described a form of 'asymmetrical anti-essentialism', allowing oppressed groups to articulate 'essential' identities in political struggles, while challenging the right of dominant groups to employ general categories. A. Bunting, 'Theorizing women's cultural diversity in feminist international human rights strategies', in A. Bottomley and J. Conaghan (eds), *Feminist Theory and Legal Strategy* (Oxford, Blackwell Publishers, 1993) 6 at 12.

[190] G. Spivak, 'Criticism, feminism and the institution', *Thesis Eleven* 10/11 at 184, quoted in E. Grosz, above note 170 at 342.

of the differences between women as the bases of feminist international legal principles and strategies.

Exploring public/private distinctions in international law

We have argued that feminist analysis of international law requires use of a variety of theoretical perspectives and attention to both general and specific categories of women. In this section we use this multi-layered approach in investigating how distinctions between public and private spheres operate in international law. We have briefly described above some of the ways that public/private dichotomies structure the international legal system.[191] These distinctions operate on a number of levels and may evolve and mutate over time.

Beneath the various private/public dichotomies in international law lie divisions based on sex and gender. Historically, the formation of the European nation state depended on a sexual division of labour and the relegation of women to a private, domestic, devalued sphere.[192] Men dominated in the public sphere of citizenship and political and economic life. The state institutionalised the patriarchal family both as the qualification for citizenship and public life and as the basic socio-economic unit.[193] The functions of the state are still identified with men, while at the same time the state depends on the work of the 'private' sphere to sustain its operations. As Cynthia Enloe has pointed out:

> Governments need . . . wives who are willing to provide their diplomatic husbands with unpaid services so these men can develop trusting relationships with other diplomatic husbands. They need . . . a steady supply of women's sexual services to convince their soldiers that they are manly. To operate in the international arena, governments seek other government's recognition of their sovereignty; but they also depend on ideas about masculinized dignity and feminized sacrifice to sustain that sense of autonomous nationhood.[194]

International law operates in the public, male world. While it formally removes 'private' concerns from its sphere, the international legal system nevertheless strongly influences them. One form of influence is the fact that 'private' issues are left to national, rather than international, regulation.[195]

[191] See above text accompanying notes 46–50 and 120–4.

[192] R. Grant, 'The sources of gender bias in international relations theory', in R. Grant and K. Newland (eds), *Gender and International Relations* (Bloomington, Indiana University Press, 1991) 8 at 11–12.

[193] V. Peterson and A. Runyan, *Global Gender Issues* (Boulder, Westview Press, 1993) at 93.

[194] C. Enloe, *Bananas, Beaches, and Bases: Making Feminist Sense of International Politics* (London, Pandora Press, 1989) at 196–7.

[195] See K. Walker, 'An exploration of article 2(7) of the United Nations Charter as an embodiment of the public/private distinction in international law', 26 *New York University Journal of International Law and Politics* (1994) 173.

This means that laws concerning 'private' matters, such as the family, can quite properly (from an international perspective) take account of cultural and religious traditions that may allow the domination of women by men. Another aspect of the assignment of particular issues to the 'private', national, realm is that the state can devolve some of its powers to centres of authority in the private sphere that may have no concern with the unequal position of women or indeed may have an interest in maintaining it, such as the family, religious institutions, the education system, business, finance and the media.[196] Distinctions between public and private have both a descriptive and a normative aspect: public/private divisions such as international/national or state/civil society are seen to characterise the reality of the international community; at the same time, they are also connected with political choices about whether or not to intervene legally.[197]

Concern with public/private dichotomies in explaining the sexed and gendered nature of international law has been criticised by feminist scholars, for example, the American international lawyer, Karen Engle.[198] Engle has argued that the division obscures important aspects of women's lives by ignoring those parts that take place in public realms and by assuming that private spheres are inevitably bad for women. She has pointed to the 'liberating potential' of the private sphere for women in its capacity to accommodate rights such as the right to abortion, and to sexual and bodily freedom.[199] Being outside the scope of international legal regulation, she has contended, may well be the province of the powerful and she has pointed to the quest of multinational corporations to remain on the margins of international law.[200] Engle's reminder that the simple inclusion of women's lives in the public sphere of international legal regulation does not amount to inevitable progress is valuable. However, her faith in the potential of an international right to privacy to provide rights for women may be too optimistic given the very limited scope attached to it in international law. In any event, our argument is not that there is a monolithic public/private dichotomy that can be mapped on to international legal doctrine to explain the oppression of women. It is rather that a variety of distinctions, ostensibly between 'public' and 'private', shape international law and that many of them have gendered consequences that need to be evaluated.

A different type of critique of our concern with public/private distinctions in international law may be that they are a Western feminist obsession and

[196] S. Wright, 'Economic rights, social justice and the state: a feminist reappraisal', in D. Dallmeyer, above note 104 at 117, 121.
[197] N. Lacey, 'Theory into practice? Pornography and the public/private dichotomy', 20 *Journal of Law and Society* (1993) 93 at 94–5.
[198] K. Engle, 'After the collapse of the public/private distinction: strategizing women's rights', in D. Dallmeyer, above note 104 at 143.
[199] *Ibid.* at 148–9.
[200] K. Engle, 'Views from the margins: a response to David Kennedy', 1994 *Utah Law Review* 105.

inappropriate in global contexts. Feminist scholars have cautioned against general explanations of the worldwide domination of women by men. Particular cultural and social contexts, they have argued, must be taken into account and 'universal' analytic categories such as public/private distinctions run the risk of simply being shorthand for biological explanations of women's subordination.[201] The anthropologist Maila Stivens, for example, has pointed out that it is very difficult to specify what the private domain is in agrarian societies in South-East Asia.[202] She has noted the gendering of all levels of social life right across the traditional public/private division and argues that we should expand our notion of politics rather than analyse all societies within the confines of a particular Western construction of the public/private distinction.[203] A similar point has been made by Aida Hurtado in a comparison of the significance of a public/private distinction in the lives of white middle class women and black women in the United States:

> Women of Color have not had the benefit of the economic conditions that underlie the public/private distinction ... Welfare programs and policies have discouraged family life, sterilization programs have restricted reproduction rights, government has drafted and armed disproportionate numbers of people of Color to fight its wars overseas, and locally, police forces and the criminal justice system arrest and incarcerate disproportionate numbers of people of Color. There is no such thing as a private sphere for people of Color except that which they manage to create and protect in an otherwise hostile environment.[204]

The analysis of public/private distinctions in international law will not be useful if the content of each sphere is defined by Western experience and if women are regarded as always opposed to men in the same ways in all contexts and societies. For example in the West, women's social inferiority may be connected to their role in bearing and raising children,[205] but this is by no means a universal condition. In studying domestic violence in the South Asian immigrant community in the United States, Anannya Bhattacharjee has provided an excellent case study of the complex layering

---

[201] See H. Moore, *Feminism and Anthropology* (Cambridge, Polity Press, 1988) at 25–3; M. Rosaldo, 'The use and abuse of anthropology: reflections on feminism and cross-cultural understanding', 5 *Signs* (1980) 389.

[202] M. Stivens, 'Why gender matters in Southeast Asian politics', 1989 *Asian Studies Review* 4 at 7.

[203] A parallel observation is made about women lace-makers in India in M. Mies, *The Laceworkers of Naraspur: Indian Housewives Produce for the World Market* (London, Zed Books, 1982).

[204] A. Hurtado, 'Relating to privilege: seduction and rejection in the subordination of white women and women of color', 14 *Signs* (1989) 833 at 849.

[205] L. Imray and A. Middleton, 'Public and private: marking the boundaries', in E. Garmanikow *et al.*, above note 122 at 12, 13–14.

and mutability of notions of public and private.[206] In this context, the home, the workplace, the ethnic community, the nation of origin and United States citizenship and immigration laws all create 'private' spaces in which violence against women is accepted. On this analysis, recourse to the 'public' state to remedy 'private' violence is futile because the state is complicit in the violence. A similar situation prevails where the state uses law to articulate principles of religious fundamentalism.[207] What operates as 'public' in one context may well be 'private' in another, but women's activities are typically construed as private and marginalised.[208]

We use public/private distinctions at various points in this book to explain how an area of international law is gendered. This is not to say that distinctions between public and private are inherently problematic for women in an international context and that a feminist reconstruction of international law would require the collapse of all public/private distinctions in its definition. For example, the extension of international legal regulation to all 'private' activities is not a practical or useful strategy. A feminised international legal system would rather attempt to transcend *gendered* public/private dichotomies, incorporating and responding to women and their concerns. If the 'public' is understood, as Nicola Lacey has suggested, as involving susceptibility to political debate and dialogue, while the 'private' is the sphere from which people can withdraw from public scrutiny (not simply the area excluded by the public), women's experiences will not automatically be excluded or marginalised by the use of public/private dichotomies.[209]

Conclusion

Feminist excursions into international law have been reproved for criticising the male-centredness of international law while at the same time invoking the international legal order to improve the situation of women.[210] Are these contradictory moves? The implication of the charge is that feminists forfeit the right to invoke international law if they point out its biases. As we noted

---

[206] A. Bhattacharjee, 'The public/private mirage: mapping homes and undomesticating violence work in the South Asian immigrant community', in M. Alexander and C. Mohanty, above note 136 at 308.

[207] R. Coomaraswamy, 'To bellow like a cow: women, ethnicity and the discourse of rights', in R. Cook (ed.), *Human Rights of Women: National and International Perspectives* (Philadelphia, University of Pennsylvania Press, 1994) 39 at 50–1.

[208] H. Moore, above note 201 at 54–9.

[209] N. Lacey, 'Theory into practice', above note 197 at 110, drawing on I. Young, *Justice and the Politics of Difference* (Princeton, Princeton University Press, 1990) at 119–20.

[210] E.g. A. D'Amato, book review of R. Cook (ed.), *Human Rights of Women* (see above note 207), 89 *American Journal of International Law* (1995) 840.

above, feminist interventions in international law have to be conducted on a number of levels, inside the discipline, strengthening it to respond to the oppression of women, and outside looking in, drawing attention to the structural faults in the system. We do not want to assert that international legal doctrine is a monolithic force for the oppression of women and the advantage of men, but rather that it offers only a partial, and often contradictory and inconsistent, response to women's oppression. One of the major strategic advantages of international law is its universal vocabulary. Feminists may want to make use of this feature of international law, while at the same time arguing that its 'universality' must extend beyond a limited male view. Sandra Harding has made a similar point in her work on the Western scientific tradition:

> We do not imagine giving up speaking or writing just because our language is deeply androcentric; nor do we propose an end to theorizing about social life once we realize that thoroughly androcentric perspectives inform even our feminist revisions of the social theories we inherit . . . I am seeking an end to androcentrism, not to [the] systematic inquiry [of science]. But an end to androcentrism will require far-reaching transformations in the cultural meanings and practices of that inquiry.[211]

Feminist analysis of international law has two major roles. One is deconstruction of the explicit and implicit values of the international legal system, challenging their claim to objectivity and rationality because of the limited base on which they are built. All tools and categories of international legal analysis become problematic when the exclusion of women from their construction is understood. The 'international' the canon purports to represent is, in Elizabeth Grosz's words, in fact a 'veiled representation and projection of a masculine which takes itself as the unquestioned norm, the ideal representative without any idea of the violence that this representational positioning does to its others'.[212] Investigating the silences of international law is another way of discovering its gendered nature: why are some activities considered capable of international legal regulation while others are not? Deconstruction has transformative potential because it reduces the imaginative grip of the traditional theories. In this sense, all feminist theories are subversive strategies. They are 'forms of guerrilla warfare, striking out at points of patriarchy's greatest weakness, its blindspots'. They reveal the 'partial and partisan instead of the universal or representative position' of patriarchal discourse.[213]

---

[211] S. Harding, above note 85 at 1.

[212] E. Grosz, *Volatile Bodies: Towards a Corporeal Feminism* (Sydney, Allen & Unwin, 1994) at 103.

[213] E. Gross, 'What is feminist theory?', in C. Pateman and E. Gross (eds), *Feminist Challenges: Social and Political Theory* (Sydney, Allen & Unwin, 1986) 197.

The second role of feminist analysis of international law is that of reconstruction. This does not mean a strategy of simply increasing international legal regulation, making 'public' all that the legal system deems 'private'. It requires rebuilding the basic concepts of international law in a way that they do not support or reinforce the domination of women by men. The benefits of such a reconstruction would not be limited to women. Non-domination of women would allow the major aims of the UN Charter – the maintenance of international peace and security, the self-determination of peoples and the protection of fundamental human rights – to be defined in new, inclusive, ways. That task is considerable and this book is only a beginning.

3

Modes of international law-making

Introduction

This chapter and the next examine various modes of international law-making to investigate the interests and perspectives they support. Here, we describe the law with respect to customary international law, general principles of law and subsidiary sources of law. Chapter 4 looks more specifically at the law of treaties. We deal with the traditional sources of international law, as well as proposals to extend them, and we use the international legal response to violence against women as a case study of the problems and potential of the sources of international law. The tension between feminist theoretical and pragmatic goals described in chapter 2 is evident in this discussion. While we argue that the accepted sources of international law sustain a gendered regime, we also attempt to accommodate women-specific harms within the standard account of sources.

Sources of international law

Statute of the ICJ, article 38(1)

The sources of law define how new rules are made and existing rules are repealed or abrogated.[1] Analysis of them traditionally commences with article

---

[1] A. Cassese and J. Weiler (eds), *Change and Stability in International Law-Making* (Berlin/New York, De Gruyter, 1988). See the general discussion in the major text books, e.g. I. Brownlie, *Principles of Public International Law* (Oxford, Clarendon Press, 5th edn 1998) chapter 1; R. Jennings and A. Watts, *Oppenheim's International Law* (London, Longmans, 9th edn 1992) vol. 1 at 22–50; P. Malanczuk, *Akehurst's Modern Introduction to International Law* (London, Routledge, 7th edn 1997) chapter 3; M. Shaw, *International Law* (Cambridge, Grotius, 4th edn 1997) chapter 3. See also M. McDougal and M. Reisman, 'The prescribing function in the world constitutive process: how international law is made', 6 *Yale Studies in World Public*

38(1) of the Statute of the ICJ[2] which lists as sources: international conventions, whether general or particular; international custom; general principles of law; judicial decisions and the teachings of the most highly qualified publicists.[3] International conventions are binding upon parties to them.[4] Although the expression 'law-making treaties' is often used to describe multilateral agreements, a treaty creates rights and duties for third parties only in specified circumstances,[5] for example when it declares or generates customary international law.[6] Customary international law, binding upon all states, has two components: uniform and consistent state practice and *opinio juris sive necessitatis* (states' belief that the behaviour is required by law).[7] Both requirements operate at a high level of generality. Decision-makers identifying the operative rules of customary international law must choose from among the many daily activities and statements made in the name of states, those that they regard as evidence of state practice. Emphasis is given to the official acts of government: statements and claims made by political leaders in local, regional and global public fora; diplomatic communications; judicial and administrative decisions. The chain of claim and counter-claim that typically constitutes evidence of state practice may be affected by acquiescence or silence[8] or by 'persistent objection' to an activity.[9] *Opinio juris* is also derived from the behaviour of a state's ruling elite.

Order (1980) 249; D. Kennedy, 'The sources of international law', 2 *American University Journal of International Law and Policy* (1987) 1.

[2] Statute of the ICJ, 26 June 1945, 1 UNTS xvi.

[3] The Statute lists the sources of decision-making, not of international law. A distinction is sometimes drawn between 'formal' sources of law and 'material' sources. See G. Fitzmaurice, 'Some problems regarding the formal sources of international law', in *Symbolae Verzijl: Presentées au Professeur JHW Verzijl* (La Haye, Martinus Nijhoff, 1958) 153.

[4] Vienna Convention on the Law of Treaties, 23 March 1969, 1155 UNTS 331, article 34.

[5] *Ibid.*, articles 35–7.

[6] *Ibid.*, article 38. *North Sea Continental Shelf Cases* (Federal Republic of Germany v. Denmark; Federal Republic of Germany v. The Netherlands) 1969 ICJ Rep. 3 (Judgment of 20 February); *Fisheries Jurisdiction Case* (United Kingdom v. Iceland) Merits 1974 ICJ Rep. 3 (Judgment of 25 July); *Military and Paramilitary Activities in and against Nicaragua* (Nicaragua v. United States) Merits 1986 ICJ Rep. 14 (Judgment of 27 June) (*Nicaragua*, Merits).

[7] E.g. *Case Concerning the Continental Shelf* (Libyan Arab Jamahiriya v. Malta) 1985 ICJ Rep. 29 (Judgment of 3 June) at para. 27.

[8] I. McGibbon, 'The scope of acquiescence in international law', 31 *British Yearbook of International Law* (1954) 143.

[9] *Anglo-Norwegian Fisheries Case* (United Kingdom v. Norway) 1951 ICJ Rep. 116 (Judgment of 18 December). On the controversies surrounding the persistent objector rule see J. Charney, 'The persistent objector rule and the development of customary international law', 56 *British Yearbook of International Law* (1985) 1; T. Stein, 'The approach of the different drummer: the principle of the persistent objector in international law', 26 *Harvard International Law Journal* (1985) 457.

Despite their separate categorisation in article 38(1), treaties and customary international law do not operate in isolation from each other.[10] Customary international law is not codified in the same manner as a negotiated treaty text. However, the articulation of states' positions in negotiations can contribute to the generation of customary international law. Drafts, position papers and preliminary studies can clarify stances that may be incorporated within the text, or become part of future state practice. Customary international law that is created in this way shares some characteristics with treaty law. The absence of women from the formal treaty-making processes that is described in chapter 4 thus also affects the development of custom.

The content of the category of 'general principles of law recognised by all civilised nations' is controversial.[11] When drafted as part of the Statute of the PCIJ, article 38(1)(c) was a compromise between those who regarded general principles as derived from natural law and those who saw them as drawn from national law.[12] It is now widely accepted that article 38(1)(c) applies to principles of both international and domestic law.[13] The concept incorporates maxims normally found within state domestic law, including procedural principles, good faith[14] and *res judicata*. It does not, however, contemplate the incorporation of municipal law principles 'lock, stock and barrel' into international law.[15] The drafters of the Statute of the PCIJ suggested that general principles would form a safety net to avert the danger of a *non liquet* if neither custom nor treaty law provided an answer to the

[10] John Hazard has described custom and treaty law as 'intertwined' in A. Cassese and J. Weiler, above note 1 at 31.

[11] For the argument that the term 'civilised nations' is not exclusionary see T. Elias, *New Horizons in International Law* (Dordrecht, Sijthoff & Noordhoff, 1979) at 118. See further *ibid.* (2nd rev. edn 1992) at 295–6.

[12] On the intentions of the drafters of article 38(1)(c) see G. Van Hoof, *Rethinking the Sources of International Law* (Deventer, Kluwer, 1983) at 135–9; B. Cheng, *General Principles of Law as Applied by International Courts and Tribunals* (London, Stevens, 1953 reprinted 1987) at 6–22.

[13] D. O'Connell, *International Law* (London, Stevens, 2nd edn 1970) vol. 1 at 9.

[14] E.g. *Nuclear Tests Cases* (Australia v. France; New Zealand v. France) 1974 ICJ Rep. 253, 457 (Orders of 20 December) at para. 46.

[15] Judge McNair emphasised that 'the true view of the duty of international tribunals in this matter is to regard any features or terminology which are reminiscent of the rules and institutions of private law as an indication of policy and principles rather than as directly importing these rules and institutions.' *Status of South West Africa Case* 1950 ICJ Rep. 128 (Adv. Op. 11 July) at 148 (sep. op. Judge McNair). See M. Bassiouni, 'A functional approach to "general principles of international law"', 11 *Michigan Journal of International Law* (1990) 768 at 774; J. Lammers, 'General principles of law recognised by civilised nations', in F. Kalshoven (ed.), *Essays on the Development of the International Legal Order* (Alphen aan den Rijn, Sijthoff & Noordhoff, 1980) 53 at 62.

question before the Court.[16] General principles can also be used in interpreting treaties and articulating customary law.

Judicial decisions and the writings of well-known publicists are subsidiary sources of international law.[17] Although there is no formal doctrine of precedent in international law,[18] the articulation of principles by the ICJ, or other international adjudicators, can clarify customary international law and treaty provisions. Decisions of regional and domestic tribunals, notably state supreme courts, may also be used by decision-makers when determining the requirements of customary international law.[19]

Other sources

The traditional schema of sources in article 38(1) preserves state control over what is deemed law, but is an incomplete reflection of the realities of contemporary international law-making. Other important modalities of law-making have been identified, for example through the resolutions of international organisations, such as the General Assembly of the UN, the practice of international organisations and international codes of conduct.[20] An important feature of the international legal scene in the 1990s was global summits on broad, interlocking issues of international concern that have culminated in declarations and strategies for state and intergovernmental and non-governmental institutional action.[21] Despite the high level of preparations, the often intense negotiations and the large number of participating states, traditional international legal doctrine denies the status of formally binding law to the conclusions of these conferences.

[16] B. Cheng, above note 12 at 390; M. Bassiouni, above note 15 at 778. For the view that general principles 'trump' custom and conventions see A. Verdross, 'Les principes généraux du droit dans la jurisprudence internationale', 52 *Recueil des Cours* (1935) vol. II at 24–6, cited in B. Simma and P. Alston, 'The sources of human rights law: custom, *jus cogens* and general principles', 12 *Australian Yearbook of International Law* (1992) 82 at 88.

[17] Statute of the ICJ, article 38(1)(d).

[18] *Ibid.*, article 59.

[19] R. Lillich, 'The proper role of domestic courts in the international legal order', 11 *Virginia Journal of International Law* (1970) 9 at 11. See also R. Falk, *The Role of Domestic Courts in the International Legal Order* (Charlottesville, Virginia University Press, 1964).

[20] A. Pellet, 'The normative dilemma: will and consent in international law-making', 12 *Australian Yearbook of International Law* (1992) 22 at 27–40.

[21] These include the World Summit for Children, New York 1990; the World Conference on the Environment and Development, Rio de Janeiro 1992; the World Conference on Human Rights, Vienna 1993; the International Conference on Population and Development, Cairo 1994; the World Summit for Social Development, Copenhagen 1995; the Fourth World Conference on Women, Beijing 1995; and Habitat II, Istanbul 1996.

The concept of 'soft' law has been developed to cover non-legally binding instruments that nevertheless create expectations about future action.[22] States that reject the normative content of a particular instrument may simply emphasise its non-binding nature, while others assert the opposite view. The subject matter of many 'soft' law instruments is significant. States use 'soft' law structures for matters that are not regarded as essential to their interests ('soft' issues of international law) or where they are reluctant to incur binding obligations. Many of the issues that concern women thus suffer a double marginalisation in terms of traditional international law-making: they are seen as the 'soft' issues of human rights[23] and are developed through 'soft' modalities of law-making that allow states to appear to accept such principles while minimising their legal commitments.

On a traditional analysis, 'soft' law can develop into customary international law if supported by the appropriate state practice and *opinio juris*.[24] A non-binding instrument may also be the forerunner of a subsequent treaty on the same subject.[25] Indeed its programmatic and evolutionary function is widely accepted as one of the benefits of this form of recording consensus.[26] Georges Abi-Saab has identified three significant interdependent criteria for determining whether a soft law instrument has crystallised into customary international law: the circumstances of the adoption of the instrument, including voting patterns and expressed reservations; the concreteness of the document; and the existence of follow up procedures.[27] More broadly, Jonathan Charney has urged acceptance of 'universal' international law to supplement the traditional methods of international law-making.[28] He has derived 'universal' law from global multilateral fora and has used similar criteria to Abi-Saab to distinguish authoritative debates or resolutions within them. Charney has given weight to the extent participating states are made

[22] See further C. Chinkin, 'The challenge of soft law: development and change in international law', 38 *International and Comparative Law Quarterly* (1989) 850.

[23] See chapter 7.

[24] In the *Nicaragua* case, the ICJ gave weight to General Assembly resolutions prohibiting the use of force and illegal intervention as evidence of both state practice and *opinio juris*. *Nicaragua*, Merits, above note 6 at paras 183–6.

[25] E.g. the Declaration on the Elimination of Discrimination against Women, GA Res. 2263 (XXII), 7 November 1967, preceded the Convention on the Elimination of All Forms of Discrimination against Women, 18 December 1979, 1249 UNTS 13, reprinted in 19 *International Legal Materials* (1980) 33.

[26] R.-J. Dupuy, 'Declaratory law and programmatory law: from revolutionary custom to "soft law"', in N. Horn (ed.), *Studies in Transnational Economic Law*, vol. 1, *Legal Problems of Codes of Conduct for Multinational Enterprises* (Antwerp/Boston, Kluwer Deventer, 1980) 247.

[27] G. Abi-Saab, 'Cours général de droit international public', 207 *Recueil des Cours* (1987) 33 at 160–1. Compare *Texaco Overseas Petroleum Co and California Asiatic Oil Co* v. *Libya* 53 *International Law Reports* (1977) 389.

[28] J. Charney, 'Universal international law', 87 *American Journal of International Law* (1993) 529.

aware that the proposed rule is a refinement, codification, crystallisation or progressive development of existing principles of law, and the level of widespread support for the rule.[29] Reliance on states' votes emphasises that 'universal' law remains state law.[30]

Claims of the normative nature of soft law instruments have led on the one hand to strong reaffirmations of the exclusivity of the traditionally accepted sources and the place of states within them,[31] and, on the other, to assertions of the inadequacy of those sources in providing mechanisms for change and development in modern international law.[32] Harold Koh has described a 'brave new world of international law' where: 'transnational actors, sources of law, allocation of decision function and modes of regulation have all mutated into fascinating hybrid forms. International Law now comprises a complex blend of customary, positive, declarative and soft law.'[33]

Debates on the sources of international law

Although article 38(1) was drafted over seventy years ago to guide the PCIJ, it remains widely cited as the authoritative list of the sources of international law.[34] However, it has also generated considerable debate.[35] Certain questions have been consistently addressed. These include the requirements

---

[29] *Ibid.* at 544.

[30] Compare *Legality of the Threat or Use of Nuclear Weapons* 1996 ICJ Rep. 226 (Adv. Op. 8 July), reprinted in 35 *International Legal Materials* (1996) 809 at 879 where Judge Weeramantry (dissenting) referred to the millions of signatures on petitions against nuclear weapons that had been received by the Court.

[31] E.g. I. Brownlie, 'The rights of peoples in modern international law', in J. Crawford (ed.), *The Rights of Peoples* (Oxford, Clarendon Press, 1988) 1 at 15; P. Weil, 'Towards relative normativity in international law?', 77 *American Journal of International Law* (1983) 413; G. Danilenko, *Law-Making in the International Community* (Boston, Martinus Nijhoff, 1993); J. Klabbers, 'The redundancy of soft law', 65 *Nordic Journal of International Law* (1996) 167. See also the remarks of Vice-President Schwebel in his dissenting opinion in *Legality of the Threat or Use of Nuclear Weapons*, above note 30 at 839: 'The General Assembly has no authority to enact international law and cannot be lightly assumed to declare it . . . When faced with continuing and significant opposition, the repetition of General Assembly resolutions is a mark of ineffectuality in law formation as it is in practical effect.'

[32] E.g. B. Simma and P. Alston, above note 16 at 88.

[33] H. Koh, 'A world transformed', 20 *Yale Journal of International Law* (1995) ix. See also H. Koh, 'Why do nations obey international law?' 106 *Yale Law Journal* (1997) 2599.

[34] The importance of the sources listed in article 38(1) has been reaffirmed in *The Lotus Case* (France v. Turkey) 1927 PCIJ ser. A no. 10 (Judgment of 7 September); *North Sea Continental Shelf Cases*, above note 6; *Nicaragua*, Merits, above note 6; *Legality of the Threat or Use of Nuclear Weapons*, above note 30 at para. 64.

[35] See e.g. G. Van Hoof, above note 12; R. Higgins, *Problems and Process: International Law and How We Use It* (Oxford, Clarendon Press, 1994) chapter 2.

for establishing a rule of customary international law;[36] the weight to be accorded to what a state says rather than what it does;[37] the possibility of 'instant' custom;[38] the effect of treaties on third parties;[39] and the content of general principles of law.

Since the decolonisation era of the 1960s, other aspects of the sources of international law have become more controversial, for example the ways in which sources are manipulated to preserve the control over substantive principle by those states that had previously dominated the international legal system. Such issues include how and why a newly emergent state is bound by the customary international law in existence at the time of its acquiring statehood;[40] how 'law-breaking' by dissentient states transforms into new customary international law; how the requirement of uniformity applies in the generation of customary international law when the numerical majority of states dissents from the practice of the minority of economically and politically powerful states; the law-making effect of a multilateral treaty;[41] which treaties bind a successor state, and whether it is critical that the new state came into being through decolonisation rather than secession from, or union with, an existing state.[42] The hierarchy of sources of international law has also prompted debate, in particular the relationship between treaty and

[36] E.g. there is disagreement on the length of time needed to establish a consistent practice, on the degree of uniformity required and on the degree of consistency between state practice and *opinio juris*. See F. Kirgis, 'Custom on a sliding scale', 81 *American Journal of International Law* (1987) 147; K. Wolfke, 'Some persistent controversies regarding customary international law', 24 *Netherlands Yearbook of International Law* (1993) 1.

[37] E.g. the preference for state action in A. D'Amato, *The Concept of Custom in International Law* (Ithaca, Cornell University Press, 1971) and K. Wolfke, *Custom in Present International Law* (Dordrecht, Martinus Nijhoff, 2nd rev. edn 1993) as opposed to statements in M. Akehurst, 'Custom as a source of international law', 47 *British Yearbook of International Law* (1974–75) 1.

[38] B. Cheng, 'Custom: the future of general state practice in a divided world', in R. Macdonald and D. Johnston (eds), *The Structure and Process of International Law: Essays in Legal Philosophy, Doctrine and Theory* (Dordrecht, Martinus Nijhoff, 1983) 513.

[39] See C. Chinkin, *Third Parties in International Law* (Oxford, Clarendon Press, 1993) at 25–146.

[40] See A. D'Amato, above note 37; L. Henkin, *How Nations Behave: Law and Foreign Policy* (New York, Columbia University Press, 2nd edn 1979) at 112; J. Brierly, *The Law of Nations: An Introduction to the International Law of Peace* (Oxford, Clarendon Press, 6th edn 1963) at 52.

[41] See R. Baxter, 'Multilateral treaties as evidence of customary international law', 41 *British Yearbook of International Law* (1965–66) 275; A. Weisburd, 'Customary international law: the problem of treaties', 21 *Vanderbilt Journal of Transnational Law* (1988) 1; 'Interpreting state practice under treaties: a brief colloquy on the composition of customary international law', *ibid.* at 457.

[42] A. Cassese, *International Law in a Divided World* (Oxford, Clarendon Press, 1986) at 179–98; R. Jennings and A. Watts, above note 1 at 208–44.

customary international law.[43] Perhaps the most significant aspect of the debate on hierarchy is over the concept of *jus cogens*[44] which limits state sovereignty by asserting the fundamental values of the international legal system, including those based on the integrity of the human person.

Underlying this discussion are questions about the nature of international law and the impact of power relations on the making of international law.[45] Does individual state consent (voluntarism) remain the basis of legal obligation, as was forcefully asserted in *The Lotus Case*,[46] or has there been a shift towards a type of international 'democracy' in which a broader notion of the international community creates law? Could this type of system embrace the views of non-state actors? The notion of consent itself has been challenged as a basis for legal, as distinct from political, obligation. Thus Koskenniemi has argued that consent is either 'apologist', in that it cannot uphold an objective concept of law, or 'utopian' in that it derives from some non-consensual, non-statist base such as natural law.[47]

The deficiencies of international law-making have been particularly highlighted in fields of international law where exclusive state interests may conflict more directly with those of non-state actors.[48] Examples include human rights,[49] international economic law[50] and environmental law.[51] Traditional international law-making assumes a monolithic state voice that silences individuals and other non-elite groups in the international arena, except insofar as their interests are championed by states. International law nevertheless has an impact upon individuals. It may be directly applicable

[43] M. Akehurst, 'The hierarchy of the sources of international law', 47 *British Yearbook of International Law* (1974–75) 273; C. Parry, *The Sources and Evidences of International Law* (Manchester, Manchester University Press, 1968); R. Baxter, 'Treaties and custom', 129 *Recueil des Cours* (1970) 25; H. Chodosh, 'An interpretive theory of international law: the distinction between treaty and customary law', 28 *Vanderbilt Journal of Transnational Law* (1995) 973.

[44] Vienna Convention on the Law of Treaties, article 53 (peremptory norm of international law, *jus cogens*) and article 64 (an emergent norm of *jus cogens*). See further chapter 4.

[45] M. Byers, 'Custom, power and the power of rules: customary international law from an interdisciplinary perspective', 17 *Michigan Journal of International Law* (1995) 109.

[46] Above note 34 at 18.

[47] M. Koskenniemi, *From Apology to Utopia: The Structure of International Legal Argument* (Helsinki, Finnish Lawyers' Publishing Co., 1989) chapter 2.

[48] G. Van Hoof, above note 12 at 2.

[49] I. Gunning, 'Modernizing customary international law: the challenge of human rights', 31 *Virginia Journal of International Law* (1991) 211. See also the discussion in B. Simma and P. Alston, above note 16.

[50] I. Seidl-Hohenveldern, 'International economic soft law', 198 *Recueil des Cours* (1986) vol. III, 68; K. Hossain (ed.), *Legal Aspects of the New International Economic Order* (New York, Nichols Publishing Company, 1980).

[51] G. Palmer, 'New ways to make international environmental law', 86 *American Journal of International Law* (1992) 259.

within domestic legal systems, and domestic law in turn may influence the development of international law.

Debates about the sources of international law have not examined the way that international legal doctrine on sources is built on a gendered base. The vocabulary of international law-making relies on concepts that have a gendered dimension. For example, the sources of international law are based on a hierarchical and abstract model and they are presented as identifiable through rational means. As we discussed in chapter 2, this characterisation codes the sources as male and superior to sources of law that may be contextual and concrete. The distinction drawn between 'hard' and 'soft' law also rests on a dichotomy that has gendered significance, implying the superiority of the 'hard' (male) over the 'soft' (female). International legal scholarship does not discount the value of 'soft' law entirely,[52] but 'hard', binding law remains the preferred paradigm of international law, and all forms of international law-making are assessed in relation to this form. A striking description of the consensus system in international law as 'an enormously elaborate mating ritual that ends with the pretence of a consummation that has not taken place'[53] emphasises the view of consensus as a failed form of 'hard' decision-making.

Another gendered tendency in traditional law doctrines on sources is the emphasis on obligation formed through consent. The model of the individual, autonomous state freely choosing to accept or reject international law rules reinforces models of behaviour that are coded as male. As Nancy Hirschmann has pointed out: 'By declaring that all obligations, to be such, must be taken on voluntarily, consent theory ignores or denies what women's experience reveals . . . that obligations do in fact exist that are not chosen but stem from the character of human relationships.'[54]

Women's participation in international law-making

The gendered structure of international law-making will not be altered simply by ensuring that more women participate in its processes. It is important,

---

[52] See above notes 24–7 and accompanying text.

[53] R. Righter, *Utopia Lost: The United Nations and World Order* (New York, Twentieth Century Fund Press, 1995), quoted in R. Sabel, *Procedure at International Conferences: A Study of the Rules of Procedure of Conferences and Assemblies on International Inter-Governmental Organizations* (Cambridge, Cambridge University Press, 1997) at 307, quoted in a book review of Sabel by Philip Alston, 92 *American Journal of International Law* (1998) 353 at 354.

[54] N. Hirschmann, 'Freedom, recognition and obligation: a feminist approach to political theory', 83 *American Political Science Review* (1989) 1229, quoted in C. Ku, 'Treaties and gender bias: what frame(s) work(s)?', in *Contemporary International Law Issues: Opportunities at a Time of Momentous Change* (The Hague, Nederlandse Verenigning voor Internationaal Recht, 1993) 414.

however, to understand the obstacles to women's involvement in the development of international legal principles. In this section the campaign to have the issue of violence against women recognised as an international legal wrong incurring state responsibility will be used as a case study of these barriers. We describe the generation and articulation of such a norm by non-state actors and its emergence, primarily in 'soft' law form, within state-controlled arenas. We then consider whether such a norm has entered the corpus of international law through the generation of customary law, as a general principle of law, or in some other way.

Customary international law and 'soft' law

Diverse forms of violence against women are endemic in all states.[55] A number of doctrinal difficulties are encountered, however, in asserting that this violence breaches customary international law. First, state practice is not consistent with such a norm. Where the facts of state practice do not conform with assertions of legal norms, the reality may be disregarded in preference for the statements of governments that such actions are prohibited.[56] Jurists have proposed various devices to interpret state behaviour. For example, Frederick Kirgis has argued that state practice and *opinio juris* operate along a sliding scale requiring greater consistency in state practice where there is little evidence of *opinio juris*, but tolerating contradictory behaviour where there is greater consensus about its illegality. He has concluded that 'the more destabilizing or morally distasteful the activity . . . the more readily international decision-makers will substitute one element for the other'.[57] Similarly Oscar Schachter has argued that where the conduct is 'violative of the basic concept of human dignity' statements of condemnation are sufficient evidence of its illegitimacy under customary international law.[58] Christian Tomuschat has in turn propounded the deduction of custom from 'the core philosophy of humanity' that is sanctified in the unwritten constitution of the international community and the UN Charter.[59] This process is limited to fundamental human rights norms including those relating to the right to life, the prohibitions against torture and slavery and the equality of human beings. This deduction is envisaged as free-standing and as not entailing reference to state

[55] See chapter 1.
[56] E.g. the ICJ in the *Nicaragua* case found that, despite many instances of international armed conflict, there was sufficient evidence of contrary *opinio juris* expressed through the resolutions of the General Assembly to support principles of customary law prohibiting the use of force and wrongful intervention. *Nicaragua*, Merits, above note 6 at paras 186–90.
[57] F. Kirgis, above note 36 at 149.
[58] O. Schachter, 'International law in theory and practice: general course in public international law', 178 *Recueil des Cours* (1982) 21 at 334–8.
[59] C. Tomuschat, 'Obligations arising for states without or against their will', 241 *Recueil des Cours* (1993) vol. IV 195 at 303.

practice and *opinio juris*. Again, Michael Byers has analysed customary international law as a means of universalising public interest: the behaviour of states acts as an indicator of the degree to which they are interested in achieving a particular legal outcome.[60]

None of these approaches necessarily facilitates the assertion of a rule of customary international law condemning violence against women. First, unlike acknowledged human rights abuses, 'private' violence against women is not even formally condemned as illegal in many societies.[61] Second, the violence may be tolerated on social, traditional or religious grounds and as such is excluded from international concern.[62] Until 1993 there had been no generalised General Assembly statement condemning violence against women[63] and little indication that it was widely regarded as 'destabilizing or morally unacceptable' or contrary to the 'core philosophy of humanity'. There is no sign that the international community wishes to eliminate violence against women and impose state responsibility for failure to do so. Thus, there is no strong evidence of *opinio juris* to justify discounting the contrary state practice. Third, the connection between the dominance of women by men and systemic violence is also not well understood. Significantly, Schachter's list of human rights violations sufficiently condemned to be deemed contrary to customary international law despite widespread inconsistent practice includes slavery, genocide, torture, mass killings, prolonged arbitrary imprisonment, and systematic racial discrimination, or any consistent pattern of gross violations of human rights, but omits gender discrimination or gendered violence.[64] Fourth, the intensity of the condemnation of the behaviour and the identity of those denouncing it is significant in international law. In order to constitute *opinio juris*, condemnation must be through official government channels. The voices of women's groups rarely make such impact. Indeed, violence against women is often presented as a 'private' affair outside the control of the state.[65]

[60] M. Byers, above note 45.

[61] See further chapter 5.

[62] UN, *Women, Challenges to the Year 2000* (New York, UN, 1991) at 65–78.

[63] GA Res. 40/36, 29 November 1985, was limited to domestic violence. Its preamble identified the main harms of domestic violence as the undermining of the family structure, and contributing to psychological harms in, and delinquency of, children. See H. Charlesworth and C. Chinkin, 'Violence against women: a global issue', in J. Stubbs (ed.), *Women, Male Violence and the Law* (Sydney, Institute of Criminology Series no. 6, 1994) 135.

[64] O. Schachter, above note 58. This list follows that of the American Law Institute, *Restatement (Third) of the Foreign Relations Law of the United States* (St Paul, American Law Institute, 1987) at para. 702. Compare S. Wang, 'The maturation of gender equality into customary international law', 27 *New York University Journal of International Law and Politics* (1995) 899.

[65] C. Bunch, 'Women's rights as human rights: toward a re-vision of human rights', 12 *Human Rights Quarterly* (1990) 486. See chapter 2 for feminist analyses of

Another process that might generate customary principles would be through the elaboration of a treaty prohibition on violence against women. If such a treaty were concluded and widely ratified without broad reservations, it could be influential in creating a general norm.[66] To date the only such treaty is the Inter-American Convention on the Prevention, Punishment and Eradication of Violence against Women, adopted by the Organisation of American States (OAS) at Belem do Para and applicable only in its region.[67] The beginnings of a more broadly applicable treaty might be found in the Declaration on the Elimination of Violence against Women adopted by the General Assembly in 1993.[68] The Declaration was the result of a Canadian initiative in 1991 that progressed through a meeting of non-governmental experts in November 1991.[69] The expert working group's draft was submitted to an intersessional working group of the UN Commission on the Status of Women (CSW) in 1992, and then through the UN Economic and Social Council (ECOSOC) and the General Assembly.

The Declaration defines gender-based violence broadly and asserts that states should 'exercise due diligence to prevent, investigate and . . . punish acts of violence against women whether those acts are perpetrated by the State or private persons'.[70] The formulation of principles has been described as the first step in the law-making process by identifying the wrong and directing attention towards the substance of the potential rule.[71] Although it is formally a legally non-binding instrument, a declaration is considered to have greater weight than a resolution.[72] The Declaration on the Elimination of Violence thus has the potential to generate state practice and *opinio juris* to crystallise into customary international law. International doctrine pays attention to the method by which a declaration or resolution is adopted by an international organisation. If a vote is taken, it is considered important

---

public and private distinctions and chapter 7 for their impact on international human rights law.

[66] On the generation of custom through 'law-making' treaties see *North Sea Continental Shelf Cases*, above note 6 at 176–9.

[67] 9 June 1994, reprinted in 33 *International Legal Materials* (1994) 1534.

[68] UN Declaration on the Elimination of Violence Against Women, GA Res. 48/104, 20 December 1993. See further chapter 7.

[69] H. Charlesworth, 'Worlds apart: public/private distinctions in international law', in M. Thornton (ed.), *Public and Private Feminist Legal Debates* (Melbourne, Oxford University Press, 1995) 243 at 256–9.

[70] Declaration on the Elimination of Violence against Women, article 4(c).

[71] H. Meijers, 'How is international law made? The stages of growth of international law and the use of its customary rules', 9 *Netherlands Yearbook of International Law* (1978) 3.

[72] B. Sloan, 'General Assembly resolutions revisited', 58 *British Yearbook of International Law* (1987) 39 at 93. Sloan has argued that there is a presumption that a declaration constitutes law where an intent to declare law is evinced and it has been adopted unanimously, or at least nearly unanimously, or by genuine consensus.

for the establishment of *opinio juris* (or for 'universal' law in Charney's terms) that a resolution is adopted with as many affirmative votes as possible, especially from the most influential states.[73] One way to avoid negative votes is to have a resolution adopted by consensus, as occurred with the Declaration on the Elimination of Violence. Consensus removes the potential for confrontation at the time of vote-taking and presents the appearance of acceptance by all interest groups.[74] Its focus upon harmony and co-operation means that it may be perceived as consistent with feminist goals.[75] However, consensus may conceal the exploitation of power during negotiations to block provisions unwelcome to some actors; it may also be achieved only through elimination of controversial or far-reaching provisions. The position of the Declaration is equivocal in this regard. Although some of the text is ground-breaking,[76] some significant sections were removed in negotiations to facilitate the Declaration's adoption by the General Assembly. For example, at the intersessional meeting of the CSW in 1992, the United States and Sweden insisted on removing an explicit nexus between violence against women and human rights. A reference to 'degrading representation of women in the media' as a form of violence was also deleted from the experts' text.[77]

The ICJ has emphasised the importance of norm-generating, rather than aspirational, language in instruments that evidence custom.[78] The operative provisions of the Declaration by contrast contain mainly aspirational language, for example '[s]tates should condemn violence against women'[79] and '[t]he organs and specialized agencies of the United Nations system should ... contribute to the recognition and realization of the rights'.[80] Moreover, obligations to implement the purposes of the Declaration are not couched in mandatory terms.[81]

---

[73] *Legality of the Threat or Use of Nuclear Weapons*, above note 30 at para. 71. In this case the ICJ rejected the argument that General Assembly resolutions declaring the illegality of nuclear weapons constituted *opinio juris* since several had been adopted 'with substantial numbers of negative votes and abstentions'.

[74] Compare K. Zemanek, 'Majority rule and consensus technique in law-making diplomacy', in R. Macdonald and D. Johnston, above note 38 at 857; A. D'Amato, 'On consensus', 8 *Canadian Yearbook of International Law* (1970) 104; A. Cassese, 'Consensus and some of its pitfalls', 58 *Rivista di Diritto Internazionale* (1975) 754.

[75] E.g. the discussion of decision-making by consensus in R. Lederman, 'Looking back: the women's peace camps in perspective', in D. Russell (ed.), *Exposing Nuclear Phallacies* (New York/Oxford, Pergamon Press, 1989) 244. See also note 53.

[76] E.g. article 4 clarifies that custom, tradition or religion do not justify violence against women, and the specific inclusion of private actors.

[77] See H. Charlesworth and C. Chinkin, above note 63 at 25.

[78] *North Sea Continental Shelf Cases*, above note 6 at para. 72.

[79] Declaration on the Elimination of Violence against Women, article 4.

[80] *Ibid.*, article 5.

[81] *Ibid.*, article 4(a–q), article 5(a–h).

Although non-binding instruments cannot become binding merely through repetition, such restatement can provide evidence of a growing *opinio juris*.[82] What other instruments relate to violence against women? The General Assembly has built upon the 1993 Declaration by expressing concern for especially vulnerable groups of women, for example migrant workers.[83] The Convention on the Elimination of All Forms of Discrimination Against Women (the Women's Convention) does not explicitly condemn violence against women, but in General Recommendation no. 19, its monitoring body, the Committee on the Elimination of Discrimination Against Women (CEDAW) stipulated that 'gender based violence is a form of discrimination which ... impairs or nullifies the enjoyment by women of human rights and fundamental freedoms'.[84] The Vienna Conference on Human Rights in 1993 also stressed 'the importance of working towards the elimination of violence against women in public and private life' and urged states 'to combat violence against women'.[85] Similar provisions were included in the Cairo Programme of Action[86] and the Beijing Platform for Action.[87] The UN Crime Commission has also adopted resolutions condemning such violence.[88] The repetition of statements through a cross-section of international fora strengthens the argument for the requisite *opinio juris*.

Implementation and monitoring mechanisms are considered significant in enhancing the normative value of a 'soft' law instrument.[89] The Declaration on the Elimination of Violence against Women has no enforcement provisions, making it easier to dismiss as mere rhetoric. However, the appointment in 1994 by the UN Commission on Human Rights (CHR) of a Special Rapporteur to examine the causes and consequences of violence against women suggests an intention to monitor closely the Declaration's

[82] '... a series of resolutions may show the gradual evolution of the *opinio juris* required for the establishment of a new rule'. *Legality of the Threat or Use of Nuclear Weapons*, above note 30 at para. 70.

[83] Resolution on measures to prevent acts of violence against women migrant workers, GA Res. 49/165, 23 December 1994.

[84] General Recommendation no. 19 Violence Against Women, UN Doc. A/47/38, CEDAW/C/ 1992/L.1/Add. 15, 30 January 1992, paras 1 and 7.

[85] World Conference on Human Rights, Vienna Declaration and Programme of Action, 25 June 1993, UN Doc. A/CONF. 157/23, reprinted in 32 *International Legal Materials* (1993) 1661, II, para. 38.

[86] International Conference on Population and Development, Cairo, UN Doc. A/CONF. 171/13, 18 October 1994, para. 4.9.

[87] Fourth World Conference on Women, Declaration and Platform for Action, 15 September 1995, UN Doc. A/CONF. 177/20, reprinted in 35 *International Legal Materials* (1996) 401 (Beijing Platform for Action), Critical Area of Concern D, paras 112–30.

[88] UN Commission on Crime Prevention and Criminal Justice, Resolution on the Elimination of Violence against Women, 5th Session, Vienna, May 1996.

[89] G. Abi-Saab, above note 27 at 162.

implementation.[90] Similarly, CEDAW has been active in promoting its General Recommendation no. 19. By closely scrutinising states' reports and questioning their representatives on the incidence of gender-based violence and steps taken to reduce it, CEDAW has worked to create an understanding of the requirements of the Convention that is not directly attributable to its text.[91] These are of course 'soft' methods of enforcement,[92] but they nevertheless serve to enhance the continued visibility of the instrument. The binding nature of the Inter-American Convention on Violence against Women allows for 'harder' implementation mechanisms, which draw upon those of the Inter-American Convention on Human Rights, the American Commission and Court of Human Rights. Thus the Convention against Violence allows states parties and the Inter-American Commission on Women to request an advisory opinion on its interpretation[93] and provides an individual complaint mechanism.[94] Recourse to these procedures would provide an interpretative jurisprudence on the Convention that in turn might generate principles at least of regional customary international law,[95] and possibly custom of broader application.

This analysis has suggested how evidence of *opinio juris* can be assembled in order to argue that the Declaration on the Elimination of Violence against Women has contributed to customary international law. Consistent state practice is also needed to achieve this status. Actions of NGOs and individuals in urging governmental compliance with the Declaration are likely to be discounted in determining state practice. However, pressure can

---

[90] The appointment of the Special Rapporteur was approved in CHR Res. 1994/45, UN Doc. ESCOR, 1994, Supp. no. 4, 140, 11 March 1994. In 1997, the Special Rapporteur, Radhika Coomaraswamy's, mandate was extended for a further three years: CHR Res. 1997/44.

[91] General Recommendation no. 19, para. 2. See also General Recommendation no. 12, 3 March 1989. Declaration on the Elimination of Violence Against Women, article 4(m) states that information on violence against women and measures taken to combat it should be included in states' reports to all relevant human rights committees.

[92] P. Birnie, 'Legal techniques of settling disputes: the soft settlement approach', in W. Butler (ed.), *Perestroika and International Law* (Dordrecht, Martinus Nijhoff, 1990) 177.

[93] Article 11.

[94] Article 12. The Inter-American Commission on Human Rights held admissible on 9 October 1998 a case against Trinidad and Tobago which concerned the imposition of the death penalty on a woman for involvement in the murder of her common-law husband, who had allegedly long been violent towards her. The violence had not been raised during her trial. The applicant alleged violations of both the American Convention on Human Rights (articles 4, 5, 8 and 11) and the Inter-American Convention on Violence against Women, ratified by Trinidad and Tobago on 4 June 1996: *Trinidad and Tobago, Indravani Ramjattan* Inter-American Commission on Human Rights, Report no. 63/98 (Admissibility) Case no. 11837.

[95] On regional customary international law see the *Asylum Case* (Columbia v. Peru) 1950 ICJ Rep. 266 (Judgment of 20 November).

be brought to bear on states by groups monitoring implementation. A state might change its practice with respect to recognition and prosecution of crimes of violence against women to be consistent with international condemnation of such behaviour.[96] NGOs can assist in generating state practice by campaigning in domestic arenas for appropriate statements in parliaments and other official bodies. Bringing test cases in domestic, regional and international tribunals and intervening in appropriate cases can all encourage a change in state practice.

On the other hand, although an enormous amount of energy and commitment was required for women to bring 'soft law' instruments requiring the elimination of violence against women into the international arena, under traditional sources of international law their non-binding form reduces their normative effect. It is difficult to assert the existence of custom in the face of consistent opposition from powerful and influential states.[97] Even if an international prohibition of violence against women became widely accepted, it is possible that opposing states could claim to be 'persistent objectors' to the norm.[98] It may be argued that, if customary international law is diffuse, ambiguous and subject to rejection by persistent objectors, it is not a worthwhile status to seek for an issue such as the prohibition of violence against women. An alternative strategy might be to argue for the normative effect of General Assembly resolutions,[99] acknowledging the change in the sources of law that this entails.[100]

General principles of law

Can the Declaration on the Elimination of Violence against Women be asserted to rest on general principles of law and as such to be binding upon states? There has been a recent academic revival of interest in the potential

[96] E.g. *Criminal Injustice: Violence against Women in Brazil* (New York, Human Rights Watch, 1991); D. Thomas and M. Beasley, 'Domestic violence as a human rights issue', 12 *Human Rights Quarterly* (1993) 36; Report of the Special Rapporteur on Violence against Women, its Causes and Consequences, Ms Radhika Coomaraswamy, submitted in accordance with CHR resolution 1995/85, UN Doc. E/CN.4/1996/53, 5 February 1996.

[97] See above note 31.

[98] See above note 9.

[99] E.g. Reisman has argued that the three criteria for law-making can be present in soft law instruments: normative statements, expectations of authority and communication of the control intention. M. Reisman, 'The concept and functions of soft law in international politics', in E. Bello and B. Ajibola (eds), *Essays in Honour of Judge Taslim Olawale Elias* (Dordrecht, Martinus Nijhoff, 1992) 135.

[100] This has been said to amount to a 'revolutionary change in the structure of the system itself': O. Garibaldi, 'The legal status of General Assembly resolutions: some conceptual observations', *Proceedings of the 73rd Annual Meeting of the American Society of International Law* (Washington DC, American Society of International Law, 1979) 324 at 325.

of article 38(1)(c) which had largely become a 'historical remnant'.[101] For example, M. Cherif Bassiouni has argued that increasing global inter-dependence has exposed the inadequacies of customary international law and treaties in responding to major issues such as human rights, the environment, economic development and international criminality.[102] He has contended that general principles may be drawn upon to fill the gaps and that they may indeed become 'the most important and influential source of international law'.[103] This view has some support in the operation of the International Criminal Tribunals for the former Yugoslavia and Rwanda. While the Tribunals' jurisdiction is based upon customary international law and the authority of the Security Council,[104] their Rules of Procedure and Evidence have been created by moulding domestic criminal procedure and human rights standards to the needs of international criminal process.[105] However, it should be noted that in its Advisory Opinion on the *Legality of the Threat or Use of Nuclear Weapons*, the ICJ did not draw upon general principles, even of humanitarian law, as a basis for decision in the absence of conventional or customary law.[106]

Bruno Simma and Philip Alston have encouraged the use of general principles of law as a contemporary source of human rights law. They have argued that the concept of general principles derived from the international plane needs to be expanded: 'Principles brought to the fore in this 'direct' way ... would (and should) then percolate down into domestic fora, instead of being elevated from the domestic level to that of international law by way of analogy.'[107]

General principles drawn from international arenas may be found in statements of consensus, such as those expressed at global summits, and in the 'soft' law resolutions of the organs of the UN. An advantage identified by Simma and Alston in the revival of general principles for this purpose is that

[101] G. Van Hoof, above note 12 at 145.

[102] M. Bassiouni, above note 15 at 769. Schachter has also suggested that general principles of law are ripe for recruitment into international law in the areas of individual rights, contractual remedies, liability for extra-hazardous activities and restraints on the use of common property. O. Schachter, *International Law in Theory and Practice* (Dordrecht/Boston, Martinus Nijhoff, 1991) at 53.

[103] M. Bassiouni, above note 15 at 769.

[104] SC Res. 827, 25 May 1993; SC Res. 955, 8 November 1994. See further chapter 10.

[105] Rules of Procedure and Evidence, revised 30 January 1995, UN Doc. IT/32/Rev.3, as amended 17 December 1998, UN Doc. IT/32/Rev. 14. In *Prosecutor v. Dusko Tadic Jurisdiction of the Tribunal*, 10 August 1995, IT-94-I-T, the Trial Chamber discussed the sources of law used in preparing these Rules. Compare Rome Statute for the International Criminal Court, 17 July 1998, UN Doc. A/CONF. 183/9, reprinted in 37 *International Legal Materials* (1998) 999, article 21(1)(c).

[106] Above note 30. Compare the dissenting opinion of Judge Higgins, *ibid.* at 937–8, who considered this a failure of judicial process.

[107] B. Simma and P. Alston, above note 16 at 102.

it would retain the consensualist basis of international law while overcoming many of the conceptual and practical problems of customary international law, in particular the need to prove state practice and *opinio juris*. However, states might become more reluctant to express such general principles if they were to be incorporated into the body of international law in this way.

A serious concern with the use of general principles of domestic law in the international legal system is that they will simply transpose the problems of the former into the latter. National legal systems have been fashioned by men and reflect the interests of their designers.[108] Whether the national system is based upon a religious, capitalist or socialist ideology, the legal system reinforces the power structures of the male political elite. The subordination of women to men through both the structure and substance of law is one of the few truly universal features of national legal systems and there is little evidence of a general principle prohibiting gender-specific violence. Rather such violence has been tolerated or condoned.

Equity is a source of law sometimes considered to have the status of a general principle, which may be useful in this context.[109] Equity has been described as comprising 'general principles of justice as distinguished from any particular system of jurisprudence or the municipal law of any State'.[110] It can provide constraints upon state consent by bringing objective notions of fairness and distributive justice into international law.[111] Some treaties require recourse to equity,[112] and the ICJ has increasingly invoked the concept.[113] Equity can broaden the scope of legal argument in the sense that it allows a decision to be contextualised. It may be a suitable tool where there are competing interests and where the law is not highly developed as in the case of violence against women. The notion of equity can encompass fair economic and social arrangements,[114] and facilitate shifting of power imbalances. Vaughan Lowe has pointed out that:

[108] See generally R. Graycar and J. Morgan, *The Hidden Gender of Law* (Annandale, Federation Press, 1990).

[109] C. Rossi, *Equity and International Law: A Legal Realist Approach to International Decision-Making* (New York, Transnational Publishers, 1993).

[110] V. Lowe, 'The role of equity in international law', 12 *Australian Yearbook of International Law* (1992) 54.

[111] *Ibid.* at 78–80.

[112] E.g. UN Convention on the Law of the Sea, 10 December 1982, UN Doc. A/CONF. 62/122, reprinted in 21 *International Legal Materials* (1982) 1261, articles 59, 69, 70(4), 74, 83.

[113] The ICJ has drawn upon equity and equitable principles in a number of boundary delimitation cases, e.g. *Maritime Delimitation in the Area between Greenland and Jan Mayen* (Denmark v. Norway) 1993 ICJ Rep. 38 (Judgment of 14 June) at 211 (sep. op. Judge Weeramantry).

[114] In *Maritime Delimitation in the Area between Greenland and Jan Mayen*, Judge Weeramantry envisaged a new role for equity (which he viewed as being drawn from all global traditions and civilisations) in the development of environmental law and duties with respect to future generations. *Ibid.* at paras 235–42.

> Reliance on law tends to favour interests, institutions and actors which have been predominant in the past. By abandoning the language of law for the language of morality – autonomous equity – that inherent bias ... in the established legal system can be circumvented.[115]

Equity is, however, a variable concept and may be invoked to preserve the interests of the privileged. Indeed at the Fourth World Conference on Women in 1995 the notion of equity was used to resist claims to equality for women and girls. Some Islamic states argued against equal inheritance rights for females and males because different adult roles require an 'equitable' distribution of assets in correlation with responsibilities.[116] Although this argument was not ultimately endorsed, it demonstrates the potential appropriation of the language of equity.

In practice, resort to the concept of equity has been primarily restricted to boundary delimitation and individual instances of resource allocation between states. It has not operated more broadly to provide for structural justice between persons within a state, or even between states. In the first hearing before the Arbitral Tribunal established in Bosnia and Herzegovina as a consequence of the Dayton Peace Accords,[117] the Tribunal weighed the effect of its award on the populations in the respective areas and the international community's need for regional stability in the name of equity.[118] In such balancing exercises, the particular needs of women are unlikely to attract attention. Moreover it has been argued that the invocation of equity favours form over substance by allowing the appearance of legal regulation through objective standards, while in reality offering inadequate solutions to future conflict.[119]

Subsidiary sources of law

Article 38(1)(d) of the Statute of the ICJ lists judicial decisions as a subsidiary source of international law. In the 1990s there has been a proliferation of international tribunals that supplement the ICJ and the regional human rights courts.[120] Such judicial fora could be used for the identification and

---

[115] V. Lowe, above note 110 at 78.

[116] This argument was put forward in discussion of para. 274(d) of the Beijing Platform for Action. See D. Otto, 'Holding up half the sky: but for whose benefit?', 6 *Australian Feminist Law Journal* (1996) 7 at 14.

[117] General Framework Agreement for Peace in Bosnia and Herzegovina, initialled Dayton, Ohio, 21 November 1995, signed Paris, 14 December 1995, reprinted in 35 *International Legal Materials* (1996) 75.

[118] *Arbitral Tribunal for Dispute over Inter-Entity Boundary in Breko Area* (Republika Srpska v. Federation of Bosnia and Herzegovina), 14 February 1997, reprinted in 36 *International Legal Materials* (1997) 396.

[119] M. Koskennniemi, 'The politics of international law', 1 *European Journal of International Law* (1990) 4.

[120] E.g. the establishment of the *ad hoc* International Criminal Tribunals for the former Yugoslavia (1993) and Rwanda (1994) (see further chapter 10); the Tribunal

exploration of gender and sex issues, including those relating to violence against women. There are two potential limitations to this strategy: first, the lack of female participation in both domestic and international judicial tribunals; and second, the task of finding a tribunal with appropriate jurisdiction. In 1995 Judge Rosalyn Higgins became the first woman elected to the ICJ.[121] Women have been under-represented also on the regional human rights bodies.[122] The failure to elect women to the ICJ suggests a limited understanding of the stipulation in its Statute that 'in the [Court] as a whole the representation of the main forms of civilization and of the principal legal systems of the world should be assured'.[123] This requirement has been taken seriously with respect to representation of regional, economic and political diversity, but not with respect to women. Election of more women would have an educative and symbolic effect by underscoring the validity of the presence of women in the most prestigious and visible positions within international judicial fields.[124] There is much debate over whether women judges reason differently from men,[125] especially as they would almost certainly

---

on the Law of the Sea which was established after the UN Convention on the Law of the Sea entered into force in 1994; and the World Trade Organisation Appellate Body (1995).

[121] Madame Suzanne Bastid was judge *ad hoc* in Application for Revision and Interpretation of the Judgment of 24 February 1982 in the *Case Concerning the Continental Shelf* (Tunisia v. Libyan Arab Jamahiriya) 1985 ICJ Rep. 192 (Judgment of 10 December).

[122] In 1997 there was one woman judge on the European Court of Human Rights (ECHR) (Ms Elisabeth Palm, Sweden), three women on the European Commission of Human Rights and two on the Committee of Independent Experts under the European Social Charter, Council of Europe, Human Rights Information Bulletin No. 40 (Strasbourg, March–June 1997) 24–5. In 1998, after the establishment of the new permanent ECHR under the European Convention for the Protection of Human Rights and Fundamental Freedoms, 4 November 1950, 213 UNTS 221, Protocol No. 11 Restructuring the Control Machinery Established Thereby, 11 May 1994, reprinted in 33 *International Legal Materials* (1994) 960, eight out of 39 judges were women: Ms Elisabeth Palm (Sweden); Mme Francoise Tulkens (Belgium); Mme Viera Straznicka (Slovakia); Mme Nina Vajic (Croatia); Mme Wilhelmina Thomassen (Netherlands); Mme Margarita Tsatsa-Nikoloska (FRY of Macedonia); Mme Sophie Greve (Norway); Mme Snejana Botoucharova (Bulgaria). As of December 1998 there were no women among the seven judges of the Inter-American Court of Human Rights. Article 14(3) of the Protocol of June 1998, OAU AFCHPR PROT, to the African Charter on Human and Peoples' Rights, 26 June 1981, reprinted in 21 *International Legal Materials* (1982) 59, establishing an African Court of Human Rights requires the Assembly of the Organisation of African Unity to ensure adequate gender representation in the election of judges.

[123] Statute of the ICJ, article 9.

[124] E.g. S. Sherry, 'The gender of judges', 4 *Law and Inequality* (1986) 159; S. Sherry, 'Civic virtue and the feminine voice in constitutional adjudication', 72 *Virginia Law Review* (1986) 543.

[125] See further chapter 2 at notes 99–100 and accompanying text.

have received similar international legal training as their male colleagues. Studies of women trial judges in the United States have concluded that it is difficult to determine empirically whether women make different judicial decisions, particularly as there are very few cases decided by female judges.[126] The common practice of the ICJ of preparing a single majority judgment through a drafting committee ensures that only matters on which there is a high level of agreement will be included and reduces the scope for controversial approaches,[127] except in separate or dissenting opinions.[128] Moreover, the impact of any redress of sex imbalance in judiciaries alone may be difficult to gauge: personal attitudes, political outlooks, philosophical tendencies and ideological and cultural affinities all play an important role in decision-making.[129]

The jurisprudence of the European Court of Justice (ECJ) and the regional human rights courts suggests that male judges will identify and remedy instances of sex discrimination if the discrimination is direct and obvious. The ECJ has developed a progressive concept of sex equality in the context of work-related matters that is based upon European directives, applicable in member states.[130] The European Court of Human Rights (ECHR) has redressed instances of direct sex discrimination,[131] condemned violence against women in armed conflict[132] and upheld women's right to information about abortion services, even against strongly supported laws within the local community.[133] It has used reasoning that can be extended by analogy to enhance the rights of women. For example it has held that article 8 of the

---

[126] J. Gruhl, C. Spohn and S. Welch, 'Women as policymakers: the case of trial judges', 25 *American Journal of Political Science* (1981) 308.

[127] On the process of reaching judgment in the ICJ see R. Higgins, 'Remedies and the International Court of Justice: an introduction', in M. Evans (ed.), *Remedies in International Law: The Institutional Dilemma* (Oxford, Hart Publishing, 1998) 1 at 2–5.

[128] C. Weeramantry, 'The function of the International Court of Justice in the development of international law', 10 *Leiden Journal of International Law* (1997) 309 at 328–9.

[129] See especially K. Llewellyn, *Karl Llewellyn on Legal Realism* (Birmingham, Legal Classics Library, 1986); W. Twining, *Karl Llewellyn and the Realist Movement* (London, Weidenfeld & Nicolson, 1973, reprinted Norman, University of Oklahoma Press, 1985); M. McDougal, 'Fuller versus the American legal realists: an intervention', 50 *Yale Law Journal* (1941) 827.

[130] S. Prechal and N. Burrows, *Gender Discrimination Law of the European Community* (Aldershot, Dartmouth, 1990); T. Loenen, 'Changing the gender bias in the conceptualisation of equality by international judicial bodies', in *Contemporary International Law Issues: Opportunities at a Time of Momentous Change*, above note 54 at 424.

[131] E.g. *Abdulaziz, Cabales and Balkandali v. UK* 94 ECHR (ser. A) (1985) (discrimination in nationality laws).

[132] E.g. *Cyprus v. Turkey*, Application No. 6780/74; 6950/75, 10 July 1976; *Aydin v. Turkey* (1997) 3 *Butterworths Human Rights Cases* (1997) 300.

[133] *Open Door and Dublin Well Woman v. Ireland* 249 ECHR (ser. A) (1992) 25. See J. Crawford, 'Democracy and international law', 64 *British Yearbook of International Law* (1993) 115.

European Convention on Human Rights[134] imposes positive obligations upon states to adopt measures designed to secure respect for private life, even in the sphere of individual relations.[135] The Inter-American system has also promoted women's rights in particular contexts.[136] However, the regional systems have also been reluctant to extend human rights protection to issues of reproductive freedom and have not addressed systemic discrimination against women.[137] As discussed in chapter 10, the two *ad hoc* International Criminal Tribunals are developing a sizable jurisprudence and practice on the prosecution of crimes against women.

The subject matter jurisdiction of the regional and specialised tribunals makes the consideration of issues of gender and sex more possible, while their procedures are more amenable to submissions from non-state actors.[138] There is a danger, however, that the jurisprudence of these bodies will be viewed as specialist and marginal to the mainstream development of international law. Unlike these institutions, the structure of the jurisdiction of the ICJ poses obstacles for bringing cases that would directly raise issues of equality. First, the Court's jurisdiction in contentious cases is restricted to states[139] and it has been reluctant to extend the ambit of third party procedures.[140] A state wishing to commence proceedings against another state challenging the latter's treatment of women as contrary to international law would have to overcome a number of jurisdictional and admissibility hurdles. Article 29 of the Women's Convention establishes the jurisdiction of the ICJ

---

[134] Article 8(1) provides: 'Everyone has the right to respect for his private and family life, his home and his correspondence.'

[135] *Airey v. Ireland* 32 ECHR (ser. A) (1979). See also *X & Y v. the Netherlands* 91 ECHR (ser. A) (1985).

[136] E.g. *In the Matter of Viviana Gallardo et al*, Resolution of 4 September 1983, Int. Am. CHR (ser. A.) No. G101/81; *Mejia Egocheaga v. Peru* (1996) 1 *Butterworths Human Rights Cases* 229. See C. Medina, 'Toward a more effective guarantee of the enjoyment of human rights by women in the Inter-American system', in R. Cook (ed.), *Human Rights of Women: National and International Perspectives* (Philadelphia, University of Pennsylvania Press, 1994) 257; A. Ewing, 'Violence against women under the American Convention on Human Rights', 26 *Columbia Human Rights Law Review* (1995) 751. Compare C. Beyani, 'Toward a more effective guarantee of women's rights in the African human rights system', in R. Cook, *ibid.* at 285.

[137] E.g. in *Bruggemann and Scheuten v. Germany*, 21 *European Yearbook of Human Rights* (1978) 638, the European Commission held that the right to privacy does not guarantee a woman's right to choose to have an abortion.

[138] The ICJ is not alone in its restrictive approach towards submissions from individuals. In *US – Import Prohibition of Certain Shrimp and Shrimp Products*, a World Trade Organisation Panel held that it would not accept non-requested submissions from NGO sources: reprinted in 37 *International Legal Materials* (1998) 834 at 838–9. A distinction may be emerging between tribunals dealing with 'soft' issues of human rights which exercise greater flexibility in this regard and those dealing with 'hard' issues of interstate relations and trade.

[139] Statute of the ICJ, article 34(1).

[140] C. Chinkin, *Third Parties*, above note 39 at chapter 10.

over disputes concerning 'the interpretation or application' of the Convention. Many states have made reservations to this article.[141] If jurisdiction cannot be established under article 29, it might be based on the non-discrimination articles of the International Covenant on Civil and Political Rights.[142] This Covenant has its own enforcement mechanisms through the (as yet unused) provision for interstate complaint under article 41 and the right of individual petition under the Optional Protocol.[143] The Court has not had to decide whether the existence of an internal enforcement mechanism excludes its residual jurisdiction over disputes.[144] However the reluctance of states to use the interstate complaints procedures under those conventions where it is available[145] suggests that this route is unlikely.[146]

The question of admissibility is not necessarily resolved by a determination of jurisdiction.[147] Technical restrictions limit the potential of the ICJ to consider issues of women's equality. First, an applicant state has to show a legal interest in the subject matter of a dispute between itself and the respondent.[148] States that are not parties to the proceedings can rarely present arguments in their own interest, nor on behalf of an NGO, nor in the public interest.[149]

---

[141] See chapter 4.

[142] International Covenant on Civil and Political Rights, 16 December 1966, 999 UNTS 171, reprinted in 6 *International Legal Materials* (1967) 368, articles 2 and 26.

[143] 16 December 1966, 999 UNTS 3, reprinted in 6 *International Legal Materials* (1967) 383.

[144] Statute of the ICJ, article 36(1) accords the Court jurisdiction over 'all cases which the parties refer to it and all matters specially provided for in the Charter of the United Nations or in treaties or conventions in force'.

[145] States have also not used the interstate complaint mechanism under the International Convention on the Elimination of All Forms of Racial Discrimination, 21 December 1965, 660 UNTS 195, article 11; the Convention against Torture and Other Cruel, Inhuman or Degrading Treatment or Punishment, 10 December 1984, UN Doc. A/39/51, reprinted in 23 *International Legal Materials* (1984) 1027, substantive changes noted in 24 *International Legal Materials* (1985) 535, article 21. In Europe, the interstate procedure under the European Convention on Human Rights, article 24, has been infrequently used.

[146] However, the proceedings brought by Paraguay with respect to the imminent death sentence to be carried out on a Paraguayan national who had not been accorded access to his consul indicates that human rights issues can be raised before the ICJ: *Case Concerning the Vienna Convention on Consular Relations* (Paraguay v. United States of America) 1998 ICJ Rep. (Order of 9 April), reprinted in 37 *International Legal Materials* (1998) 810.

[147] *Case Concerning East Timor* (Portugal v. Australia) 1995 ICJ Rep. 90 (Judgment of 30 June).

[148] E.g. *Nuclear Tests Cases*, above note 14.

[149] *South West Africa Cases*, Second Phase (Ethiopia & Liberia v. South Africa), 1966 ICJ Rep. 4 (Judgment of 18 July). In *Nicaragua*, Judge Schwebel argued for public interest intervention: *Nicaragua*, Request for the Indication of Provisional Measures 1984 ICJ Rep. 169 (Order of 10 May) at 190, 196 (diss. op. Judge Schwebel); Declaration of Intervention of the Republic of El Salvador 1984 ICJ Rep. 215 (Order of 4 October) at 223 (diss. op. Judge Schwebel).

Since treatment of women in another state is unlikely of itself to be considered to create such a legal interest, the potential applicant would have to argue that co-membership of a treaty establishes mutual rights and obligations, breach of which can be legitimately challenged. Second, the third party right of intervention has been narrowly interpreted by the ICJ.[150] If a state were willing to request intervention under article 62 of the Court's Statute to present arguments about equality issues in a case arising between other parties, it would have to convince the Court that the proceedings affected some legal interest of its own. Intervention under article 63 requires construction of a Convention to which the intervening state is also a party.[151] The large numbers of states parties to the Women's Convention would make this a possibility if the construction of the Convention was in issue before the Court.

Third party argument can address issues not raised by the parties. The International Criminal Tribunal for the Former Yugoslavia has accepted (and sought) *amicus* briefs, for example on the prosecution of sexual assault cases.[152] The ICJ has not accepted any *amicus* brief in contentious cases, even from non-party states. A new approach might be considered by the ICJ, especially in its advisory jurisdiction where the Court can receive written or oral statements from states and international organisations.[153] Although its Statute does not appear to preclude information from NGOs,[154] the Court has denied similar access to them and to individuals.[155] The ICJ has even been reluctant to allow individuals access to its jurisdiction in the area of

[150] Statute of the ICJ, articles 62 and 63. C. Chinkin, *Third Parties*, above note 39 at chapter 7. *Case Concerning the Land, Island and Maritime Frontier* (El Salvador v. Honduras) (Nicaragua intervening) 1992 ICJ Rep. 351 (Judgment of 11 September) is the only case where a request to intervene under article 62 has been granted.

[151] See *Nicaragua*, Declaration of Intervention 1984 ICJ Rep. 215.

[152] In *Prosecutor v. Dusko Tadic, Decision on the Prosecutor's Motion Requesting Protective Measures for Victims and Witnesses*, Decision of 10 August 1995, IT-94-I-T, the Trial Chamber referred to two *amicus* briefs it had received. One was jointly presented by a group of American NGOs, the second by Christine Chinkin. The International Criminal Tribunal for Rwanda has also accepted *amicus* briefs. See further chapter 10.

[153] Statute of the ICJ, article 66(2) allows submission of oral or written statements by international organisations 'considered by the Court . . . as likely to be able to furnish information'.

[154] *Ibid.*, article 66(a).

[155] In *International Status of South West Africa* 1950 ICJ Rep. 128 (Adv. Op. 11 July) the International League for the Rights of Man was permitted to make statements under article 66(2). In the *Asylum Case*, ICJ Pleadings, vol. ii at 228 and *Namibia*, ICJ Pleadings vol. ii at 649, 652, 672, applications by non-state actors to make statements were rejected. In the *Nuclear Weapons* Advisory Opinion, 28 states made written submissions and 22 made oral statements. None were allowed from NGOs, although some associated with the World Court Project had requested permission to do so: *Legality of the Threat or Use of Nuclear Weapons*, above note 30 at paras 5–10.

staff employment within the UN system.[156] It has bypassed oral proceedings in such cases and avoided deciding whether individuals could appear before it.[157] These restrictions make it difficult for a woman to argue sex discrimination or harassment in her employment within the UN before the ICJ in the event of an adverse decision by the Administrative Tribunal. In these cases, the immunity of international organisations to the jurisdiction of municipal courts even makes successful recourse to national law unlikely.[158]

The ICJ's advisory jurisdiction may nevertheless be of value in achieving a judicial pronouncement on equality between women and men. The *Nuclear Weapons* advisory opinions were sought after an 'umbrella' NGO, the World Court Project, brought pressure on the World Health Organisation (WHO) through the World Heath Assembly to do so. In the WHO case, the Court advised that specialised agencies are only competent to request opinions within the 'scope of their activities' and declined to give an opinion.[159] The UN General Assembly's request for an advisory opinion was, however, accepted. For the Court to give an advisory opinion on some aspect of women's rights, a specialised agency would have to demonstrate that the issues fell directly within its authority, or the General Assembly would have to be persuaded to request the opinion. All these procedural restrictions restrict the opportunities for the development of jurisprudence on sex equality by the ICJ that could be utilised as a subsidiary source of international law.

The other subsidiary source of international law listed in article 38(1)(d) is the work of 'the most highly qualified publicists' of international law. The tradition of international law scholarship has been created almost completely by male scholars who have little interest in questions of sex and gender.[160] For example, Andrew Byrnes has pointed out that the leading work on international standards with respect to the treatment of prisoners

---

[156] The ICJ has advisory jurisdiction over decisions of the Administrative Tribunal, the Statute of which guarantees equality before the Court for the individual: Statute of the UN Administrative Tribunal, article 11 as amended in 1955 by GA Res. 957 (X), 8 November 1955.

[157] *Application for Review of Judgment No. 158 of the United Nations Administrative Tribunal* 1973 ICJ Rep. 166 (Adv. Op. 12 July); *Application for Review of Judgment No. 273 of the United Nations Administrative Tribunal* 1982 ICJ Rep. 325 (Adv. Op. 20 July); *Application for Review of Judgment No. 333 of the United Nations Administrative Tribunal* 1987 ICJ Rep. 18 (Adv. Op. 27 May).

[158] M. Singer, 'Jurisdictional immunity of international organizations: human rights and functional necessity concerns', 36 *Virginia Journal of International Law* (1995) 53. See further chapter 6.

[159] 1996 ICJ Rep. 233 at 235. On the background of the case see E. Krisjansdottír, 'The legality of the threat or use of nuclear weapons under international law: the arguments behind the World Court's Advisory Opinion', 30 *New York University Journal of International Law and Policy* (1998) 291.

[160] The paucity of leading international law texts written by women has been accentuated by the authority accorded to the writings of former justices of the ICJ

fails to address the way in which sexual violence is a major component of torture of women prisoners.[161] The Women's Convention may receive cursory attention in sections on human rights in international law texts or in collections of 'basic' texts, but other treaties relating to women are rarely mentioned. Feminist writings are sometimes adverted to briefly in more recent international law scholarship but this attention is usually limited to a brief extract of a single article.[162] Theoretical works consistently fail to consider the impact of feminist theories on international law. Gerry Simpson has noted that the response of the 'dominant liberal tradition' in international law has been one of 'blasé silence . . . feminism is tolerated providing it does not attack the sacred cows of liberalism, such as the autonomy of the self, the ideal of individual choice, or the imperatives of objectivity'.[163] The consequence is that the subsidiary sources of law replicate the silences and omissions of treaties and customary international law.

Contemporary international legal standards are determined by many other reference points. These include the views and conclusions of quasi-judicial bodies (for example, the UN human rights treaty bodies,[164] the regional human rights bodies, the UN Claims Commission,[165] the World Bank Inspection Panel,[166] the GATT (General Agreement on Tariffs and Trade)/ WTO (World Trade Organisation) Panels); statements of practice from international organisations (for example, statements of the Executive Committee of the UN High Commissioner for Refugees (UNHCR) or statements

---

and former holders of key government positions. Their works are widely cited, creating a self-reinforcing cycle of authoritative statements. E.g. A. McNair, *The Law of Treaties* (Oxford, Clarendon Press, 1961); G. Fitzmaurice, *Law and Procedure of the International Court of Justice* (Cambridge, Grotius, reprinted 1986); H. Mosler, 'The international society as a legal community', 140 *Recueil des Cours* (1974) 17; P. Jessup, *A Modern Law of Nations* (New York, Macmillan, 1948); H. Lauterpacht, *The Function of Law in the International Community* (Oxford, Clarendon Press, 1933); Jiminez de Arechaga, 'International law in the past third of a century', 159 *Recueil des Cours* (1978) 9; T. Elias, *The Modern Law of Treaties* (Dobbs Ferry, Oceana, 1974); T. Elias, *The International Court of Justice and some Contemporary Problems* (The Hague, Martinus Nijhoff, 1983). The work of Judge Rosalyn Higgins is a rare exception to this male domination, e.g. R. Higgins, above note 35.

[161] A. Byrnes, 'Women, feminism and international human rights law – methodological myopia, fundamental flaws or meaningful marginalisation?', 12 *Australian Yearbook of International Law* 205, discussing N. Rodley, *The Treatment of Prisoners under International Law* (Oxford, Clarendon Press, 1987).

[162] E.g. A. D'Amato (ed.), *International Law Anthology* (Cincinnati, Anderson Publishing Co., 1994) 389.

[163] G. Simpson, 'Is international law fair?', 17 *Michigan Journal of International Law* (1996) 61 at 62.

[164] See chapter 7.

[165] Established in accordance with SC Res. 687, 3 April 1991, SC Res. 692, 20 May 1991.

[166] I. Shihata, *The World Bank Inspection Panel* (Oxford, Clarendon Press, 1994).

of the UN High Commissioner for Human Rights); and the findings and reports of fact-finding missions, working parties, expert groups, thematic and country human rights rapporteurs and the UN Secretary-General. While these less formal sources generally follow the tradition of making women and their concerns invisible, in some cases their subject matter, the identity of the main contributors and the input from non-state actors have resulted in a greater awareness of the concerns of women.[167]

Broadening the sources of law

The chapter thus far has examined the orthodox and accepted sources of international law. More radical suggestions have been made for new methods of international law-making that focus less on the role of states and consider the actions of other actors within the international arena, notably those of NGOs and 'international civil society'.

NGOs

There has been a dramatic proliferation in the numbers and activities of NGOs in the past years.[168] This has been recognised by governments and NGO contributions are sought in various arenas. NGOs are increasingly achieving access to national policy-making bodies and offering advice to senior government officials.[169] In turn this has had an impact upon regional and international decision-making. For example, Karen Knop has pointed to the growing role of NGOs within the Organisation for Security and Co-operation in Europe (OSCE) process.[170] She has noted that NGOs are now 'sought-after participants in a political process' and that the 'growing receptiveness

[167] An example is the much greater attention paid by UNHCR to the specific needs of women refugees. See UNHCR Executive Committee Resolution No. 73 (XLIV) (1993), Refugee Protection and Sexual Violence; Guidelines on the Protection of Refugee Women (Geneva, UNHCR, 1991); Prevention and Response to Sexual Violence among Refugees (Geneva, UNHCR, 1993); UNHCR, Progress Report on Refugee Women, SC/1998/Inf.1, 25 May 1998 and Activities and Plans for Gender Mainstreaming, 25 May 1998. See further chapter 7.

[168] Secretary-General's Report, 15 June 1994, UN Doc. E/AC.70/1994/5, prepared in accordance with ECOSOC Res. 1993/214, para. 4. One hundred and fourteen international NGOs attended the First UN World Conference on Women in Mexico City in 1975 compared with some 2,900 at the Fourth in Beijing in 1995. Amnesty International, Report on the Fourth World Conference on Women, IOR 41/30/95, 22.

[169] Secretary-General's Report, above note 168 at para. 29.

[170] The OSCE is the successor to the Conference on Security and Co-operation (CSCE) in Europe. See V. Dronov, 'From CSCE to OSCE: historical retrospective', in M. Evans (ed.), *Aspects of Statehood and Institutionalism in Contemporary Europe* (Aldershot, Dartmouth, 1997) 105.

to NGO participation in the process has translated into [O]SCE provisions that allow NGOs to move from the corridors into the sessions'.[171] Similarly international NGOs have become increasingly visible and active in the negotiations before and during global summit meetings.

Despite their high profile, such NGO activities do not challenge the primacy of states in law-making. However influential their input, the final documents, whether in treaty or soft law form, are agreed on by states. More radical are proposals that have been made for the acceptance of the activities of NGOs as constitutive of practice for determining rules of customary international law.[172] This, it is argued, would reflect the contemporary dynamics of the formation of international law.[173] While this suggestion would import the different perspectives and priorities of NGOs into international law-making, it raises some significant questions. One issue would be deciding which of the thousands of NGOs in existence would have this status.[174] Another would be determining which of their activities could constitute 'practice'. A possible limitation on NGO participation in international law-making would be to focus on international NGOs that have observer status with the UN's ECOSOC.[175] This would ensure at least that the relevant NGOs had a formal commitment to the purposes and principles of the UN Charter. However, state hostility towards the mandates of particular NGOs can prevent ECOSOC recognition.[176] It is also important to note that the agendas of NGOs are not necessarily produced with greater democracy or transparency than the agendas of individuals or states.[177]

NGOs have been the catalyst for some significant advances in standard-setting in the traditional, state-based development of international law. Would increasing the law-making status of NGOs allow greater access to the international system for women? The answer is a qualified one. Although women's NGOs have been very active in the international arena, they are often

---

[171] K. Knop, 'Re/statements: feminism and state sovereignty in international law', 3 *Transnational and Contemporary Legal Problems* (1993) 293 at 310.

[172] The role of NGOs in treaty negotiation is discussed in chapter 4.

[173] See I. Gunning, above note 49 at 227–34. For a critique of Gunning's proposals see K. Knop, above note 171 at 311–15.

[174] NGOs in consultative status with ECOSOC increased from 41 to 987 between 1948 and 1993: Secretary-General's Report, above note 168 at para. 65.

[175] Charter of the UN, 26 June 1945, article 71.

[176] The dependence of NGOs on state approval was seen at the Fourth World Conference on Women where women's organisations from Tibet and Taiwan, anti-fundamentalist groups and pro-choice Catholic groups were denied accreditation. In 1994 the International Lesbian and Gay Association lost its ECOSOC consultative status after intense pressure from the United States. See D. Otto, 'NGOs in the UN system: the emerging role of international civil society', 18 *Human Rights Quarterly* (1996) 107 at 116–17.

[177] See the discussion of the great variety and varying 'legitimacy' of NGOs in the *Proceedings of the 92nd Annual Meeting of the American Society of International Law* (Washington DC, American Society of International Law, 1998) at 20–36.

poorly funded and resourced.[178] Moreover, international women's NGOs tend to be dominated by women from the North.[179] Within even 'progressive' NGOs, women and their concerns tend to be marginalised. For example, Joni Seager has described the widespread racism and sexism in many environmental organisations and the effect that this has on the agenda of the movement generally.[180] She has observed that the 'environmental establishment' tends to be male and white, while the grassroots organisations all over the world are primarily run by women.[181] Seager has argued that the increasing success of NGOs in political life has been associated with a rise in bureaucratisation and professional hierarchies. Success within the organisation depends on 'working in the way of men', adopting a particular form of aggressive politics within and outside the group. Power relations between women and men and between racial groups are regarded as irrelevant to the task of protecting the environment.[182] Until 'mainstream' NGOs themselves recognise these limitations of their work, women are not likely to benefit directly from assigning significant legal status to NGO activities.

International civil society

The role of 'international civil society' has been presented as a counterbalance to the domination of states although the phenomenon of transnational citizen movements pre-dates the emergence of the state system of international organisation.[183] The category of 'international civil society' is broader than that of NGOs and covers a range of both organised and unorganised, alternative and complementary groupings. In different contexts international civil society can embrace officials of international organisations, voluntary organisations, grassroots organisations and transnational social organisations.[184] The concept also can encompass religious movements, professional groups such as lawyers, physicians, scientists or media personnel, business, trade and commerce representatives, trade unions, and indeed any body of persons that seeks to influence governments, to develop new modes of governance, to change international imperatives and to occupy political space.[185]

The former UN Secretary-General, Boutros Boutros-Ghali, described civil society as a social movement depending upon citizen participation including:

[178] For a fuller discussion see chapter 4.

[179] See J. Elshtain, 'Exporting feminism', 48 *Journal of International Affairs* (1995) 541.

[180] J. Seager, *Earth Follies* (New York, Routledge, 1993) chapter 4.

[181] *Ibid.* at 176.

[182] *Ibid.* at 170–5.

[183] R. Coate, C. Alger and R. Lipschutz, 'The UN and civil society: creative partnerships for sustainable development', 21 *Alternatives* (1996) 93 at 99.

[184] *Ibid.*

[185] *Ibid.*

The ability to associate with fellow human beings, to undertake tasks in and on behalf of the community in which one lives, to express and represent the needs of a community, and to engage in a dialogue with the governance to which this community relates.[186]

Richard Falk has argued that the role of 'international civil society' challenges state-centred international law.[187] He has postulated that states are no longer the sole legitimate source of law-making and that ideas from other bodies should not be ignored when determining the international normative order. He has pointed to 'societal or populist' initiatives that respond to the failure of constitutional governments and international institutions to respond to particular events. International civil society thus acts without 'any authorization, directly or indirectly from government or the State'.[188] It is promoted as an expression of democracy where popular will is expressed by concerned citizens, and constituting a truly 'universal law.' Similarly, in response to what was considered to be the undemocratic character of the UN Security Council and the need for revitalisation of the General Assembly, in 1995 the Commission on Global Governance commended the 'transformation politics' of NGOs and international civil society and proposed an International Assembly of People and a Forum of Civil Society with direct access to the UN system.[189] UN Secretary-General Kofi Annan has accepted that an essential part of reforming the UN is revising and updating the ways the organisation interacts with civil society.[190]

Promoting the idea of civil society allows possibilities for a broader range of interests to be considered in the definition of social goals. However, the identity of the participants in this debate and the method of setting priorities and agendas and making decisions are all critical. The composition of 'international civil society' is at issue for women. Although it is viewed as heterogenous and 'representative', its components – public, political, religious, economic and legal spheres – are dominated by men.[191] A survey of

[186] Secretary-General's Report, above note 168.
[187] R. Falk, 'The rights of peoples (in particular of indigenous peoples)', in J. Crawford, above note 31 at 17.
[188] *Ibid.* at 27.
[189] *Our Global Neighbourhood: Report of the Commission on Global Governance* (New York, Oxford University Press, 1995) at 259.
[190] Report of the Secretary-General, *Reviving the United Nations: A Programme for Reform*, UN Doc. A/51/950, 14 July 1997, paras 201–16.
[191] Falk's examples of 'international civil society' include the MacBride Commission which investigated allegations of Israeli violations of international law during the invasion of Lebanon, 1982; the Permanent Peoples Tribunal which has examined human rights violations; the Nuremburg Tribunal organised by the German Green Party to investigate the nuclear arms race; and the Nuclear Warfare Tribunal, London, January 1985. R. Falk, above note 187 at 27–9.

NGOs carried out in 1995 found serious concerns about the domination of international fora by larger, white, organisations operating in the English language. It was noted that 'prejudices of racism, sexism and colonialism still endure'.[192] This notion of international civil society replicates the gendered division of national civil society into public and private spheres.[193] The 'invisible college' of international scholars – the network of leading international lawyers within universities, government departments and international organisations[194] – which articulates and evaluates developments in international law, is itself fettered by its limited composition and perspective.

Further, not all non-state actors have benign influence on international law. Some writers have emphasised the non-democratic nature of what has been termed 'globalisation from above' (the movements supporting economic capital flow and liberalisation of trade) which, it is urged, must be countered by the forces of 'globalisation from below', or civil society.[195] The UN Secretary-General has described an increase in groups that take advantage of the processes of globalisation, including access to vast audiences through the growth in electronic communications. He has pointed to the activities of terrorists, drug traffickers and those involved in organised crime, including prostitution and trafficking in women and children, and has called for multilateral action and the formation of partnerships to reverse the trend that strengthens these influences.[196]

Despite these problems, international civil society retains some potential for reshaping international law. International civil society can work both through constituted NGOs and through informal groupings of citizens to create

---

[192] R. Krut, *Globalization and Civil Society: NGO Influence in International Decision-Making* (New York, UN Research Institute for Social Development, 1997) at 13–16.

[193] See chapter 2. Compare A. Parashar, 'Reconceptualisations of civil society: third world and ethnic women', in M. Thornton (ed.), *Public and Private: Feminist Legal Debates* (Melbourne, Oxford University Press, 1995) 221. Most accounts of international civil society gloss over the role of women. For example, Richard Falk's catalogue, above note 191, of initiatives of international civil society omitted the 1976 International Tribunal of Crimes against Women, which sat in Brussels and heard evidence from women worldwide on oppression and crimes committed against them. See D. Russell (ed.), *Crimes Against Women: The Proceedings of the International Tribunal* (San Francisco, Frog in the Well, 1976, reprinted 1984). A similar tribunal was held at the 1993 World Conference on Human Rights in Vienna. More recently Richard Falk has cited the Gulf War Crimes Tribunal organised in 1992 under the leadership of Ramsey Clark as an aspect of international civil society. R. Falk, Foreword in B. Chimni, *International Law and World Order: A Critique of Contemporary Approaches* (New Delhi, Sage Publications, 1993) 9 at 12.

[194] See O. Schachter, 'The invisible college of international lawyers', 72 *Northwestern University Law Review* (1977) 217.

[195] R. Falk, 'The Nuclear Weapons advisory opinion and the new jurisprudence of global civil society', 7 *Transnational Law and Contemporary Problems* (1997) 333.

[196] Report of the Secretary-General, above note 190 at para. 209.

what have been termed 'transnational issue networks'.[197] Through mobilising information and sharing strategies, such networks seek to exercise leverage over national elites. These activities may empower those who have been silenced by formal state structures and bring together those with common interests at all levels. Three factors contributing to the current strength of issues networks have been identified: the growth of information and communication technologies; expansion of international conferencing; and the role of key individuals ('transnational moral entrepreneurs') in identifying new concerns and seizing opportunities to address them.[198] The positive results of women's global networking can be seen in the attention accorded to women's human rights at the World Conference on Human Rights in 1993, the acceptance of the Declaration on the Elimination of Violence against Women by the General Assembly and the inclusion of crimes against women in the jurisdiction of the international war crimes tribunals.[199]

Conclusion

The limitations of the sources of international law are complex for women. The process of international law-making has been described as confrontational rather than co-operative.[200] This is particularly true of customary international law where timely protest can exclude a state from the ambit of a particular principle. The commencement of proceedings before an international tribunal, which can result in the articulation of norms of customary international law, is deliberately adversarial. Treaty and 'soft' law negotiation may also be adversarial, especially where the allocation of scarce resources is at stake. International law-making, however, also contains non-adversarial elements of consensus decision-making and co-operation that suggest a move away from the supremacy of state sovereignty in law-making, although these law-making techniques can be manipulated by stronger powers or groupings of states.

Feminist analyses of the international legal order must grapple with the institutionalisation of state perspectives in law-making. Feminists have developed a complex view of the domestic state as a social process rather than as a legal category or set of institutions.[201] On this analysis, the state is not

---

[197] K. Sikkink, 'Human rights, principled issue-networks and sovereignty in Latin America', 47 *International Organization* (1993) 411. See also M. Keck and K. Sikkink, *Activists beyond Borders: Advocacy Networks in International Politics* (Ithaca, Cornell University Press, 1998).

[198] See K. Sikkink, above note 197.

[199] R. Coomaraswamy, 'Reinventing international law', in P. Van Ness (ed.), *Debating Human Rights* (London/New York, Routledge, 1999) 167 at 173–5 (describing the role of women's groups in international civil society).

[200] I. Gunning, above note 49.

[201] See further chapter 5.

an expression of a single set of interests, but has its own complex set of power relations and issues, which include those of sex and gender. Feminists thus can work to fracture a monolithic account of state interest and to ensure their concerns are heard at the national and international level.

However, this strategy leaves the current structures of international law-making untouched. One method for promoting change would be to challenge the positivist paradigm of international law through a 'communitarian' perspective that asserts the normativity of principles fundamental to the international community regardless of individual state consent.[202] Challenges have been made to the strictly consensual view of international law-making, especially through the doctrine of *jus cogens*,[203] and in the context of the creation and content of obligations owed *erga omnes*, that is to all members of the international community.[204] One expression of this trend is that of the ICJ in *Barcelona Traction*:

> an essential distinction should be drawn between the obligations of a state towards the international community as a whole, and those arising vis à vis another State in the field of diplomatic protection. By their very nature the former are the concern of all States. In view of the importance of the rights involved, all states can be held to have a legal interest in their protection; they are obligations *erga omnes*.[205]

Principles generated by such methods have been asserted to be inevitably unsatisfactory from a traditional perspective in that they create a hierarchy of normativity.[206] On the other hand, John Tasioulas has argued that the move to communitarianism is supported by the reasoning of the ICJ in the *Nicaragua* case, where it gave prominence to the values of co-existence and co-operation.[207]

> It affirms ... that it is only as members of the community of human kind as a whole – a community whose self-understanding is integrally oriented in part by the acknowledgement of shared values – that its components (be they states, peoples, organisations or individuals) can understand their own identities ... Membership of this community and subjection to at least its basic norms cannot be understood as an optional matter hinging on anterior expressions of state volition ... Thus customary obligations *omnium* and the peremptory norms of *jus cogens* encapsulate the fundamental aspects of the

[202] C. Chinkin, *Third Parties*, above note 39, chapter 16.
[203] See chapter 4.
[204] E.g. the *Case Concerning East Timor*, above note 147 at para. 29 (the right of peoples to self-determination as a right *erga omnes*).
[205] *Barcelona Traction Light and Power Company Case* (Belgium v. Spain) New Application 1970 ICJ Rep. 3 (Order of 5 February) at 32.
[206] P. Weil, above note 31.
[207] J. Tasioulas, 'In defence of relative normativity: communitarian values and the *Nicaragua* case', 16 *Oxford Journal of Legal Studies* (1996) 85.

antecedent commitment to world public order that undergirds the idea of an international community. Derogation from them ... involves an abnegation of a state's identity as a member of that community.[208]

While the ICJ sees the concept of obligations owed *erga omnes* in state terms,[209] Tasioulas has recognised the place of non-state actors in identifying such fundamental norms. The *omnes* need not be identified with states, but could be expressed through a wider range of voices. However, even if this view were adopted,[210] concerns about ensuring the inclusion of all women's voices in a broader, communitarian conception remain. How can the words of women be heard outside the privileged coterie of international lawyers?

Feminist questioning of the sources of international law raises an uneasy tension. On the one hand, we have argued that there are some possibilities for women's lives to be acknowledged in the orthodox account of sources. The formality of law and its claim of rational objective truth are exploited for the legitimacy they give women's claims. Indeed, the campaign with respect to violence against women has deliberately relied on these qualities. On the other hand, we have suggested that the design of the international legal system is gendered at a deep level and that its mantle of rationality and objectivity is a chimera. The strategic use of international law thus leads us to work with concepts that are problematic and inadequate.

[208] *Ibid.* at 117.
[209] E.g. *Case Concerning East Timor*, above note 147.
[210] The ICJ's Advisory Opinion in *The Legality of the Threat or Use of Nuclear Weapons*, above note 30, suggests this is far from the case.

4

The law of treaties

Introduction

Treaties have become increasingly important throughout the twentieth century as a means of securing states' commitment to legal obligations.[1] The major advantages of treaties as a source of international law are perceived to be the certainty of a written text and the comparative ease of determining the parties. The wide acceptance of the Vienna Convention on the Law of Treaties,[2] and the Vienna Convention on the Law of Treaties between States and International Organizations or between International Organizations[3] has clarified such matters as the validity, interpretation, acceptance, amendment, suspension and termination of treaties. Once perceived as essentially bilateral, setting out reciprocal rights and obligations, multilateral 'law-making' treaties now provide a regulatory framework across a broad range

[1] Vienna Convention on the Law of Treaties, 23 March 1969, 1155 UNTS 331, article 2(1)(a) defines a treaty as 'an international agreement concluded between States in a written form and governed by international law'. This is without prejudice to the legal force of international agreements not in written form, or between states and other subjects of international law; *ibid.* article 3. On the debates about what constitutes a treaty see J. Klabbers, *The Concept of Treaty in International Law* (The Hague, Kluwer International, 1996) at 15–36.

[2] Parts of the Vienna Convention have been accepted by the ICJ as constituting customary international law, e.g. *Legal Consequences for States of the Continued Presence of South Africa in Namibia (South West Africa) notwithstanding Security Council Resolution 276 (1970)* 1971 ICJ Rep. 16 (Adv. Op. 21 June); *Fisheries Jurisdiction Case* (United Kingdom v. Iceland) Merits 1974 ICJ Rep. 3 (Judgment of 25 July) at para. 36; *Gabcikovo-Nagymaros Project* (Hungary v. Slovakia) 1997 ICJ Rep. (Judgment of 25 September 1997), reprinted in 37 *International Legal Materials* (1998) 162, available at http://www.icj-cij.org.

[3] 20 March 1986, UN Doc. A/CONF.129/1, reprinted in 25 *International Legal Materials* (1986) 43. Vienna Convention on Succession of States in Respect of Treaties, 23 August 1978, UN Doc. A/CONF.80/31, reprinted in 72 *American Journal of International Law* (1978) 971.

of subject matters. These include areas of individual state commitment to international standards over matters once regarded as excluded from international scrutiny by the notion of domestic jurisdiction,[4] for example human rights and the environment. This chapter examines some of the gendered aspects of treaty law and the problems inherent in using this mechanism to improve the position of women. At the same time, it points out that the acceptance of international conventional standards can provide a useful yardstick for measuring the actions of national decision-makers.

The process of treaty-making

Treaty-making is sometimes seen as analogous to the process of contract-making in national law. Common to both these mechanisms is the idea of the autonomous person freely entering a binding agreement. The voluntarist understanding of international law underpins the law of treaties, emphasising the importance of consent as a basis for obligation. As we noted in chapter 3, this account of law is coded as 'male' in contrast to alternatives that give priority to communitarian values.

Treaty negotiation

Treaty-making is covered in the Vienna Convention on the Law of Treaties. Its provisions describe the doctrine of full powers whereby a state representative has authority to bind the state,[5] and the ways in which a state can give its consent to become bound through signature, exchange of instruments, ratification, acceptance, approval or accession.[6]

Throughout the process of treaty negotiation the interests of all participants are mediated in the search for a mutually acceptable text. The subject matter for international regulation derives from the interests of states as articulated within domestic or international fora. The low level of women's participation in national government policy formulation and decision-making bodies, especially those relating to foreign and economic policies and national security, ensures that matters considered of international concern are defined by men.[7] Women within negotiating teams may find it difficult to be taken seriously and to make their voices heard.[8] In 1927 an Australian woman delegate to the League of Nations was asked politely by the Chairman as she took her place among the forty-nine 'amazed and horrified' men

[4] Charter of the UN, 26 June 1945, article 2(7).
[5] Vienna Convention on the Law of Treaties, article 7.
[6] *Ibid.*, article 11.
[7] See chapter 6.
[8] Georgina Ashworth has said of her experiences at international conferences: 'The normal patterns of masculine exchanges were evidently confused by my

on the Fourth Committee (which dealt with finance, budgets and the codification of international law), 'Have you lost your way Madam?'[9] Today this question might still be asked as women participate in very low numbers in most treaty negotiation processes.

Not only are women under-represented in government bodies that play the leading roles in treaty-making, they also have little voice in the international law-making bodies. For example, there has never been a woman on the thirty-four-member International Law Commission (ILC) which has the responsibility for the codification and progressive development of international law under the UN Charter.[10] The ILC's work requires both detailed analysis of existing law and the recommendation of future trends within draft texts. Similar law-making work has been undertaken by other bodies both within[11] and outside the UN structure[12] that have few active women members in positions of influence. The 'invisible college' of scholars, described by Oscar Schachter as incorporating values and interests into the international legal process that do not necessarily reflect those of states,[13] has been traditionally dominated by men.[14] Similarly the writers of the most

---

presence . . . and minor penalties were extracted: catching the chairperson's eye was difficult, as though women were meant to offer only silent applause.' G. Ashworth, 'An elf among gnomes: a feminist in North-South relations', 17 *Millennium* (1988) 497 at 498.

[9] C. Ku, 'Treaties and gender bias: what frame(s) work(s)?', in *Contemporary International Law Issues: Opportunities at a Time of Momentous Change* (The Hague, Nederlandse Vereniging voor Internationaal Recht, 1993) 414, quoting C. Miller, 'Women in international relations: the debate in inter-war Britain', in R. Grant and K. Newland (eds), *Gender and International Relations* (Bloomington, Indiana University Press, 1991) 64.

[10] Charter of the UN, article 13. The ILC is a part-time body that since its inception has met annually in Geneva for ten to twelve weeks. In theory this has restricted membership to those who could meet this commitment, although there has been a high rate of absenteeism, for example by members who are government officials and whose other work takes priority. See generally I. Sinclair, *The International Law Commission* (Manchester, Manchester University Press, 1987); *Making Better International Law: The International Law Commission at 50* (New York, UN, 1998). Since 1998 the ILC has met experimentally in a 'split' session, in Geneva and New York. The assumption of such timetables, that members have the ability to work abroad for long periods, is unfounded for many, including those with primary responsibility for caring for family members.

[11] E.g. UN Commission on International Trade Law (UNCITRAL).

[12] E.g. the Harvard Research on International Law which prepared draft texts on such topics as the law of treaties and state responsibility, the Institut du Droit International, the International Law Association and the American Society of International Law.

[13] O. Schachter, 'The invisible college of international lawyers', 72 *Northwestern University Law Review* (1977) 217.

[14] This is exemplified by a panel at the American Society of International Law entitled 'Lawyers as statesmen: twentieth century United States attitudes toward

frequently cited texts have also been men.[15] There is an interactive process, as academics and non-governmental bodies draw upon the meticulous and detailed work of the ILC, and governments use these materials in preparing statements, briefs and policy positions, allowing what Oscar Schachter has called a *'pénétration pacifique* of ideas from government to non-government'.[16] The effect is an accumulation of material being consistently considered and evaluated from a single-gendered perspective.

NGOs and treaty-making

We considered the role of NGOs in international law-making generally in chapter 3. NGOs have to some limited extent lessened the state monopoly in the treaty-drafting process. NGO involvement at the international level is not a new phenomenon.[17] For example, women's NGOs have been strong in promoting humanitarian and social reform since before the time of the League of Nations.[18] The ground-breaking provision in the UN Charter that prohibited discrimination on the grounds of sex[19] was achieved largely through their efforts, as was the establishment of the Commission on the Status of Women (CSW).[20] The drafting of the UN Convention on the Rights of the Child (the Children's Convention)[21] is regarded as a high point of NGO involvement in international standard-setting. In 1983 during the early negotiation stage of the Convention, interested NGOs formed a committee which presented its ideas and views to government delegates in a unified and coherent way, and maintained a strong presence throughout the entire negotiation process.[22] NGO input into the early stages of norm articulation

---

international law', *Proceedings of the 90th Annual Meeting of the American Society of International Law* (Washington DC, American Society of International Law, 1996) 139.

[15] See chapter 3.

[16] O. Schachter, above note 13 at 217.

[17] See S. Charnovitz, 'Two centuries of participation: NGOs and international governance', 18 *Michigan Journal of International Law* (1997) 183. For an account of women's NGOs active before World War II see L. White, *International Non-Governmental Organizations* (New Brunswick, Rutgers University Press, 1951) at 179–84.

[18] C. Miller, above note 9.

[19] Charter of the UN, article 1(3).

[20] J. Connors, 'NGOs and the human rights of women at the United Nations', in P. Willetts (ed.), *'The Conscience of the World': The Influence of Non-Governmental Organisations in the UN System* (Washington DC, Brookings Institution, 1996) 147.

[21] 20 November 1989, GA Res. 44/25, reprinted in 28 *International Legal Materials* (1989) 1448.

[22] N. Cantwell, 'The origins, development and significance of the United Nations Convention on the Rights of the Child', in S. Detrick (ed.), *The United Nations Convention on the Rights of the Child: A Guide to the Travaux Préparatoires* (Dordrecht, Martinus Nijhoff, 1992) 19; C. Price Cohen, 'The role of nongovernmental organizations in the drafting of the Convention on the Rights of the Child', 12 *Human Rights Quarterly* (1990) 137.

is likely to be followed by an ongoing commitment to implementation and enforcement. NGOs pressure governments to ratify treaties and to fulfil their performance obligations once they have done so. The Children's Convention spells out this continued role by providing for communications between the Committee on the Rights of the Child and 'competent bodies'.[23]

The ongoing role of NGOs in standard setting is also recognised in non-binding instruments, such as the final documents of global conferences.[24] An example of such interaction between NGOs, a treaty body and government representatives, using non-binding instruments as an impetus to the negotiation of a binding one, was the campaign for a complaints mechanism in the form of an Optional Protocol to the Convention on the Elimination of All Forms of Discrimination Against Women (the Women's Convention).[25] The Vienna Declaration on Human Rights of 1993 stated that the CSW and Committee on the Elimination of Discrimination Against Women (CEDAW)[26] should examine the possibility of a complaints mechanism under the Convention.[27] The proposal was followed up by the Women in Law Project of the International Human Rights Law Group which worked with experts, including academics, current and former members of CEDAW and human rights specialists to produce a draft text.[28] In January 1995 CEDAW adopted Suggestion no. 7[29] essentially endorsing the draft text. In March 1995 the CSW adopted a draft resolution requesting the Secretary-General to invite governments, NGOs and international organisations to submit their views on an Optional Protocol to him. This initiative was supported in the Beijing Platform of Action.[30] After four years discussion

[23] Convention on the Rights of the Child, article 45(b).

[24] E.g. World Conference on Human Rights, Vienna Declaration and Programme of Action, 25 June 1993, UN Doc. A/CONF.157/23, reprinted in 32 *International Legal Materials* (1993) 1661, I, para. 38; International Conference on Population and Development, Cairo, UN Doc. A/CONF.171/13, 18 October 1994, chapter 15.

[25] 18 December 1979, 1249 UNTS 13, reprinted in 19 *International Legal Materials* (1980) 33.

[26] *Ibid.* article 18.

[27] Vienna Declaration and Programme of Action, II, para. 40.

[28] For an account of this process see A. Byrnes and J. Connors, 'Enforcing the human rights of women: a complaints procedure for the Convention on the Elimination of All Forms of Discrimination Against Women', 21 *Brooklyn Journal of International Law* (1996) 679. This article includes as an appendix the initial NGO draft of the Optional Protocol.

[29] CEDAW, Suggestion no. 7, Elements for an optional protocol to the Convention on the Elimination of All Forms of Discrimination Against Women, 14th session, UN Doc. A/50/38 1995.

[30] Fourth World Conference on Women, Declaration and Platform for Action, adopted 15 September 1995, UN Doc. A/Conf. 177/20, reprinted in 35 *International Legal Materials* (1996) 401(Beijing Platform for Action), para. 230(k).

in a CSW working group,[31] an Optional Protocol was finally adopted in 1999.[32]

NGO participation at the July 1998 Diplomatic Conference in Rome for the negotiation of a Statute for a Permanent International Criminal Court was also intense with NGOs involved throughout the various preparatory meetings and attending the Conference in great numbers. Indeed, they were described by a Canadian official as the 'new superpower'.[33] More generally, however, the effect of NGOs on both treaty-making and the agreement of non-binding instruments remains limited in important ways. Throughout treaty negotiations the interests of all participants are mediated in the search for a mutually acceptable text. This leads to compromises and trading of texts and states may seek to neutralise NGO influence in these processes. Thus some international bodies remain impervious to NGO activity[34] and access to international arenas remains susceptible to government exclusion.[35] NGO registration practices at the global conferences have not been consistent, nor can NGOs participate directly in formal drafting sessions unless governments concur. For example at Rome it was reported that at the request of a number of Arab states, NGOs were expelled from a meeting of the committee of the whole where gender-related matters were to be negotiated.[36]

NGO efforts may be channelled through one forum while the final decision-making occurs elsewhere. An example of this is the negotiating history of the draft Declaration on Indigenous Peoples, completed in 1994 by the Working Group on Indigenous Populations of the UN Subcommission on Prevention of Discrimination and Protection of Minorities.[37] The Working

---

[31] A. Byrnes, 'Slow and steady wins the race? The development of an optional protocol to the Women's Convention', *Proceedings of the 91st Annual Meeting of the American Society of International Law* (Washington DC, American Society of International Law, 1997) 383. The working group draft is contained in the Report on the Idea of an Optional Protocol, UN Doc. E/CN.6/1997/WG/L., March 1997.

[32] Optional Protocol to the Convention on the Elimination of All Forms of Discrimination Against Women, adopted by the CSW 12 March 1999, UN Doc. E/CN.6/1999/WG/L.2; adopted by the General Assembly, 15 October 1999 (GA Res. 54/4).

[33] *On the Record*, International Criminal Court Conference, Rome 1998, volume 1, issue 5 (19 June) 1.

[34] E.g. although the ILC has a broad authorisation to consult in its work there is apparently little formal contact with, or input from, NGOs: GA Res. 174 (II), 21 November 1947, Annex: Statute of the ILC, article 16(e), 26. There has also been little NGO involvement in GATT/WTO, although there are some signs of this changing: S. Charnovitz, above note 17 at 279.

[35] See chapter 3.

[36] *On the Record*, International Criminal Court Conference, Rome 1998, volume 1, issue 18 (11 July) 4.

[37] 26 August 1994, UN Doc. E/CN.4/1995/2, E/CN.4/Sub.2/1994/56, 28 October 1994, reprinted in 34 *International Legal Materials* (1995) 541.

Group encouraged participation by indigenous persons, dispensing with formal consultative status and according access to individuals as well as NGOs. It also offered training and workshop sessions to representatives and gave indigenous persons their first sustained point of entry into the UN system.[38] The draft Declaration, which was submitted to the Commission on Human Rights (CHR) in March 1995, took over a decade to prepare. The CHR then decided to establish its own governmental working group, restricting participation to NGOs with consultative status with the UN Economic and Social Council (ECOSOC), and instructing the working group to elaborate its own declaration, rather than to work from the draft Declaration prepared through the Subcommission.[39]

Women's NGOs have been successful at recent UN conferences in inserting some reference to women's interests into final conference texts.[40] However, men continue to dominate mainstream non-governmental bodies.[41] This has led to a failure to recognise the relevance of power imbalances between women and men to social and economic issues. In this sense, there must be caution about regarding the growing prominence of NGOs in international treaty-making as being inevitably of major benefit for women.

Reservations

The voluntarist account of international law underpins the right of a state to qualify its acceptance of treaty terms through reservations. The principles regulating the making of reservations to treaties, objections to reservations and the legal relations between reserving, objecting and acquiescing states are contained in the Vienna Convention on the Law of Treaties.[42] The Vienna Convention largely affirms the test formulated by the ICJ in the *Reservations* case which attempts to achieve balance between maintaining the

---

[38] M. Langton, 'The United Nations and indigenous minorities: a report on the United Nations Working Group on Indigenous Populations', in B. Hocking (ed.), *International Law and Aboriginal Human Rights* (Sydney, Law Book Co. Ltd, 1988) 83.

[39] As of December 1998, the CHR working group had not agreed on the text of a draft Declaration.

[40] See D. Sullivan, 'Women's human rights and the 1993 World Conference on Human Rights', 88 *American Journal of International Law* (1994) 152. Compare H. Charlesworth, 'Women as sherpas: are global summits useful for women?', 22 *Feminist Studies* (1996) 537 at 542. See chapter 10 for discussion of the Rome Statute for an International Criminal Court.

[41] G. Ashworth, above note 8. See also chapter 3.

[42] Articles 19 to 23. See D. Greig, 'Reservations: equity as a balancing factor', 16 *Australian Yearbook of International Law* (1995) 21; C. Redgewell, 'Universality or integrity? Some reflections on reservations to general multilateral treaties', 64 *British Yearbook of International Law* (1993) 245.

integrity of the text and securing widespread acceptance by allowing reservations unless they are incompatible with the object and purpose of the treaty.[43] Uncertainties and gaps within the Vienna Convention have led to academic critique and the inclusion of the subject on the agenda of the ILC.[44]

Standard-setting human rights treaties have proved to be especially vulnerable to reservations.[45] The bilateral model of reciprocity upon which the international law reservations regime is based is inadequate where the treaty objective is the attainment of common standards within all states parties, rather than the mutual acceptance of rights and obligations. Human rights institutions including the ECHR,[46] the Inter-American Court of Human Rights[47] and the Human Rights Committee[48] have adopted approaches to reservations consistent with the need to guarantee human rights, although these have been controversial.[49]

The Women's Convention has been particularly susceptible to reservations and 'interpretive declarations'.[50] As of December 1998 over fifty states

---

[43] *Reservations to the Convention on the Prevention and Punishment of the Crime of Genocide Case* 1951 ICJ Rep. 15 (Adv. Op. 28 May). The 'object and purpose' test is stipulated in the Vienna Convention on the Law of Treaties, article 19(c).

[44] See First Report on the Law and Practice Relating to Reservations to Treaties, Preliminary Report, 30 May 1995, UN Doc. A/CN.4/470; Second Report on the Law and Practice Relating to Reservations to Treaties, UN Doc. A/CN.4/447, and Add. 1, 21 May and 13 June 1996; Preliminary Conclusions of the ILC on Reservations to Normative Multilateral Treaties including Human Rights Treaties, Report of the ILC on the work of its forty-ninth session, UN Doc. A/52/10 (1997) 125 at para. 157.

[45] See M. Coccia, 'Reservations to multilateral treaties on human rights', 15 *California Western International Law Journal* (1985) 1; L. Lijnzaad, *Reservations to UN Human Rights Treaties: Ratify and Ruin?* (Dordrecht, Martinus Nijhoff, 1995).

[46] *Belilos v. Switzerland* 132 ECHR (ser. A) (1988) 1; *Loizidou v. Turkey*, Preliminary Objections (ser. A) 20 EHRR 99 (1995).

[47] *Effect of Reservations on Entry into force of the American Convention (articles 74 and 75)* 67 International Law Reports (1982) 558.

[48] Human Rights Committee, General Comment no. 24, on issues relating to reservations made upon ratification or accession to the Covenant (International Covenant on Civil and Political Rights) or the Optional Protocols thereto, or in relation to declarations under article 41 of the Covenant, 4 November 1994, UN Doc. HRI/Gen/1/Rev.2, para. 17.

[49] France, the United Kingdom and the United States reacted negatively to General Comment no. 24: Observations by Governments of the United States and United Kingdom on General Comment no. 24(52) relating to reservations, reprinted in 16 *Human Rights Law Journal* (1995) 433. See for comment R. Higgins, 'Introduction', in J.-P. Gardner (ed.), *Human Rights as General Norms and a State's Right to Opt Out* (London, British Institute of International and Comparative Law, 1997) xvii. See also B. Simma, 'Reservations to human rights treaties: some recent developments', in G. Hafner (ed.), *Liber Amicorum Professor Seidl-Hohenveldern* (The Hague, Kluwer Law International, 1998) 659. The General Comment is discussed further below.

[50] See *Belilos v. Switzerland*, above note 46.

had entered reservations to the Women's Convention.[51] A number of these are reservations to the Convention's dispute settlement procedures,[52] while others raise fundamental questions about the purpose of the Convention and the seriousness with which the international community regards its objective of achieving equality for women. Article 28(2) of the Women's Convention follows the Vienna Convention by prohibiting incompatible reservations. There is no, specific article to which reservations are prohibited, nor are there any non-derogable rights. The consequences of an incompatible reservation or of an objection to a reservation are not spelled out. One of the most sweeping reservations was the final paragraph of that from the Maldives: 'the Republic of Maldives does not see itself bound by any provisions of the Convention which obliges [sic] to change its Constitution and laws in any manner'.[53]Lesotho, Malaysia and Pakistan also subject the entire Women's Convention to their Constitutions.[54] Other states have made reservations to the effect that their domestic law prevails in specific instances,[55] although under the Vienna Convention on the Law of Treaties it is no defence to a breach of an international obligation that it conflicts with domestic law.[56] There is an expectation that states will ensure that their

[51] See http://www.un.org/Depts/Treaty, which is the source for the wording and information about reservations and objections thereto used in this section. See also B. Clark, 'The Vienna Convention reservations regime and the Convention on the Elimination of All Forms of Discrimination Against Women', 85 *American Journal of International Law* (1991) 281; R. Cook, 'Reservations to the Convention on the Elimination of All Forms of Discrimination Against Women', 30 *Virginia Journal of International Law* (1990) 643; C. Chinkin, 'Reservations and objections to the Convention on the Elimination of All Forms of Discrimination Against Women', in J.-P. Gardner, above note 49 at 64.
[52] Article 29(1). Article 29(2) allows reservations to this provision. In the *Reservations* case, above note 43, the ICJ upheld such reservations. Since 1990 a number of the former socialist states of Eastern Europe have withdrawn their reservations to article 29.
[53] Reservation made 1 June 1993, Note by the Secretary-General, Declarations, reservations, objections and notifications of withdrawal of reservations relating to the Convention on the Elimination of All Forms of Discrimination Against Women, UN modified effective from 23 June 1999. Doc. CEDAW/SP/1994/2.
[54] Lesotho reservation, 22 August 1995; Malaysian accession and reservation, 5 July 1995, modified effective from 6 February 1998, but not in this regard; Pakistan accession and reservation, 12 March 1996.
[55] E.g. Turkey has reserved 'with regard to the articles . . . dealing with family relations which are not completely compatible with the provisions of the Turkish Civil Code', 20 December 1985; Tunisia has reserved 'with regard to the provisions in article 9, paragraph 2 . . . which must not conflict with the provisions of chapter VI of the Tunisian Nationality Code', 20 September 1985. See further examples in articles cited above note 51.
[56] Vienna Convention on the Law of Treaties, article 27 states that: 'A party may not invoke the provisions of its internal law as justification for its failure to perform a treaty.'

domestic law conforms with their treaty obligations, and will alter their law where necessary.[57]

Reservations have been made to the first five articles of the Women's Convention which are critical to the fulfilment of its objectives.[58] A number of states parties have differently worded reservations to the common effect that the Convention is not binding insofar as its provisions conflict with Islamic *Shariah* law, or that the state is willing to comply with the Convention, provided that such compliance is not contrary to *Shariah* law. For example, the first paragraph of the Maldives' initial reservation was broad: 'The Government of the Maldives will comply with the provisions of the Convention, except those which the Government may consider contradictory to the principles of the Islamic Sharia upon which the laws and traditions of the Maldives is founded.' Similarly, on first acceding to the Convention, Libya stated: 'The accession is subject to the general reservation that such accession cannot conflict with the laws on personal status derived from the Islamic Shariah.'[59]

Libya has now withdrawn this reservation and replaced it by the following:

1. Article 2 of the Convention shall be implemented with due regard for the peremptory norms of the Islamic Shariah relating to determination of inheritance portions of the estate of a deceased person, whether female or male.
2. The implementation of paragraph 16(c) and (d) of the Convention shall be without prejudice to any of the rights guaranteed to women by the Islamic Shariah.[60]

This new reservation at least identifies the articles of the Convention to which it is applicable. However, reservations to article 2 are especially problematic.[61] For example, Egypt, which has made a number of other reservations, also has one specifically applicable to article 2. The Egyptian reservation states: 'The Arab Republic of Egypt is willing to comply with the content of this article [2], provided that such compliance does not run counter to the Islamic Shariah.'[62]

---

[57] Indeed, Giegerich has argued that reservations are solely to assist a state in adjusting its legal order to the required human rights standards and that it must do this and then withdraw all reservations within a reasonable period of time. T. Giegerich, 'Vorbehalte zu Menschenrechtsabkommen: zulassigkeit, gultigkeit und prufungskompetenzen von vertragsgremien', 55 *Zeitschrift fur Auslandisches Offentlicher Recht und Volkerrecht* (1995) 713 at 780 (English summary).

[58] See chapter 7.

[59] Reservation made 16 May 1989.

[60] Reservation made 5 July 1995.

[61] Article 2 requires governments to take specific legal action to implement the Convention and is therefore a central provision giving force to its objects and purposes.

[62] Reservation made 18 September 1981. Morocco made a similarly worded declaration to article 2, 21 June 1993.

These reservations are of questionable validity at international law. Their indeterminacy, imprecision and open-ended nature are contrary to the certainty required for the acceptance of a legal obligation. The intended legal or practical scope is often unexplained, even where the scope of the reservation has been reduced, as in the Libyan case. Disagreements among Islamic scholars as to the requirements of *Shariah* law adds to the uncertainty.[63] The extent of the reservations, and therefore of the obligations incurred, are subject to change in accordance with evolving interpretations and practice of the *Shariah* rather than in accordance with international legal standards.[64]

It is not only Islamic states that have made reservations to the opening articles. New Zealand has deferred to traditional customs within the Cook Islands by reserving articles 2(f) and 5(a) 'to the extent that the customs governing the inheritance of certain Cook Islands chief titles may be inconsistent with those provisions'.[65] Upon ratification of the Women's Convention in 1986, the United Kingdom made a reservation to article 2 which postponed review and amendment of admittedly discriminatory legislation until 'essential and overriding considerations of economic policy' allowed it.[66] States have also entered reservations to particular articles of the Convention. Kuwait indicated its antipathy to electoral reform after the 1990–91 Gulf War by reserving article 7(a) 'in as much as the provision in that paragraph conflicts with the Kuwaiti Electoral Act under which the right to be eligible for election and to vote is restricted to males'.[67] The most widely reserved articles

[63] See J. Connors, 'The Women's Convention in the Muslim World', in J.-P. Gardner, above note 49 at 85; U. Khaliq, 'Beyond the veil? An analysis of the provisions of the Women's Convention and the law as stipulated in Shar'iah', 2 *Buffalo Journal of International Law* (1995) 1. See also A. An-Na'im, 'Islam, Islamic law and the dilemma of cultural legitimacy for universal human rights', in C. Welch and V. Leary (eds), *Asian Perspectives on Human Rights* (Boulder, Westview Press, 1990) 31; D. Arzt, 'The application of international human rights law in Islamic states', 12 *Human Rights Quarterly* (1990) 202; R. Afshari, 'An essay on Islamic cultural relativism in the discourse of human rights', 16 *Human Rights Quarterly* (1994) 235; J. Leites, 'Modernist jurisprudence as a vehicle for gender role reform in the Islamic world', 22 *Columbia Human Rights Law Review* (1991) 251.

[64] For a fuller discussion of the compatibility of these reservations with the objects and purposes of the Convention see B. Clark and R. Cook, both above note 51.

[65] New Zealand reservation, 10 January 1985. Fiji has also reserved article 5(1): Fiji accession and reservation, 28 August 1995.

[66] Reservation made 7 April 1986. The United Kingdom also made reservations to articles 9, 10, 11, 13, 15 and 16. Similar reservations were made by the Government of the United Kingdom on behalf of the British Virgin Islands, the Falkland Islands (Malvinas), the Isle of Man, South Georgia and the South Sandwich Islands, and the Turks and Caicos Islands.

[67] Accession and reservation, 2 September 1994. Kuwait has made a similar reservation to the International Covenant on Civil and Political Rights, 16 December 1966, 999 UNTS 171, reprinted in 6 *International Legal Materials* (1967) 368, article 25(b). It also asserted that articles 2(I) and 3 (the non-discrimination provisions) must be exercised 'within the limits of Kuwaiti law': accession and reservation of 21 May 1996.

are those that require equality in private life, especially articles 9 and 16.[68] Reservations to these articles typically assert the primacy of personal status laws.[69]

With no institution competent to determine the compatibility of a reservation with the object and purpose of the treaty,[70] the Vienna Convention allows other states parties to enter objections to particular reservations. The legal significance of an objection is that there is no agreement between the reserving state and the objecting state as to the extent of the obligation incurred under the reserved clause, and that accordingly the clause is inapplicable.[71] An objecting state may also specify that it wishes to prevent the treaty as a whole being in force as between itself and the reserving state.[72] Fewer than 10 per cent of states have objected to the reservations made to the Women's Convention. Finland, Germany, Israel, Mexico, the Netherlands, Norway and Sweden have made objections to some of the broad reservations on the grounds of incompatibility with the object and purpose of the Convention.[73] More recent reservations have provoked a disapproving response. For example, the Maldavian reservation was objected to by Austria, Canada and Portugal, as well as by Finland, Germany, the Netherlands and Norway.[74] However, objections have generally been made without prejudice to the entry into force of the Convention between the reserving state and the objector.[75] With respect to reservations to article 2, it is unclear what area of common ground can remain between the reserving and objecting states.

The reservations and the failure of most states parties to the Women's Convention to object to sweeping reservations undermines their commitment to it. The impression is created that the Convention is not as binding

---

[68] E.g. Kuwait's reservation to article 9 which 'runs counter to the Kuwaiti Nationality Act which stipulates that the child's nationality shall be determined by that of his father.' See also reservations of Morocco, Cyprus, Egypt, Lebanon, Malaysia, Algeria, Bahamas, Fiji, France, Iraq, Jordan, Tunisia and Turkey.

[69] E.g. Singapore's accession and reservation 1995, 'reserves the right not to apply the provisions of articles 2 and 16 where compliance with these provisions would be contrary to their religious or personal laws.'

[70] The Secretary-General of the UN receives and circulates texts of reservations but enters no judgment as to their compatibility with the Convention: Convention on the Elimination of All Forms of Discrimination Against Women, article 28(1).

[71] Vienna Convention on the Law of Treaties, article 21.

[72] *Ibid.*, article 20(4)(b).

[73] http://www.un.org/Depts/Treaty.

[74] The reservations of Malaysia, Kuwait and Singapore have also been objected to by some of these same states, leading to some modifications.

[75] Exceptionally, Sweden stated in its objection to the reservation of the Maldives that it 'objects to these reservations and considers that they constitute an obstacle to the entry into force of the Convention between Sweden and the Republic of Maldives', 26 October 1994. A single instance of such an objection is unlikely to have little effect. If a sufficient number of other states were to follow suit there might be more pressure upon the reserving state to respond; alternatively this might persuade the state to withdraw from the Convention.

an international obligation as other treaties, and that these reservations need not be scrutinised against the yardstick of international standards of equality for women because of the religious and cultural sensitivity of the subject matter. In contrast there are few substantive reservations to the Convention on the Elimination of All Forms of Racial Discrimination (the Race Convention),[76] and none on the basis of religion or culture.[77] The historical association between the Women's Convention and the rise of Islamic fundamentalism in the 1980s[78] contrasts with that between the Race Convention and decolonisation and the right to self-determination of colonial peoples and those living under alien domination in the 1960s and 70s. The latter connection made for strong institutional and individual championship of the norm of non-discrimination on the basis of race, notably from the newly independent African and Asian states that were supported by the former Soviet Union. Their focal point within the General Assembly became condemnation of racial apartheid within South Africa. In contrast, reluctance to confront Islamic, oil-producing states has undermined parallel support for the elimination of gender apartheid, as demonstrated by the adverse response within the UN to proposals to tackle the reservations problem.

A 1986 initiative originated from the third meeting of states parties to the Women's Convention and resulted in an investigation by the Secretary-General into parties' views on reservations.[79] It was hoped that states would respond more frankly in this open forum than they do through the mechanism of unilateral objection. The initiative failed because of the linkage between the issue of broad reservations to the Women's Convention and Islamic states. Only seventeen states replied to the Secretary-General and most did not locate the issue within the framework of general international law. Over half the replies submitted did not address, or gave equivocal responses to, the crucial questions of compatibility and admissibility.[80]

CEDAW has long been concerned about the number and substance of reservations to the Women's Convention. In 1987 it proposed to ECOSOC that it 'promote or undertake studies on the status of women under Islamic laws' in order to be able to appraise more fully the effect of reservations. The Council declined to support this suggestion because of pressure from a number of Islamic states which saw the initiative as being hostile to Islamic

[76] International Convention on the Elimination of All Forms of Racial Discrimination, 21 December 1965, 660 UNTS 195, reprinted in 5 *International Legal Materials* (1966) 352.
[77] Most reservations to the Race Convention are to its dispute resolution provisions: B. Clark, above note 51 at 283.
[78] 1979, the year in which the Women's Convention was adopted by the General Assembly, was the year of the Iranian revolution.
[79] For a full analysis of this initiative and the Secretary-General's report see B. Clark, above note 51 at 283–4.
[80] *Ibid.*

values, a position supported by the UN General Assembly.[81] Lack of political backing, either from within the UN institutions or from sufficient states parties, means that CEDAW can do little more than continue to raise the question of reservations with individual states and to urge their removal, as it has done for example with the United Kingdom[82] and Australia.[83] Since even states with the broadest reservations remain parties to the Convention, they are obliged to submit to its reporting procedures.[84] CEDAW has consistently questioned states on the need for, and extent of, their reservations, in particular seeking information on the practical impact upon women's equality in the reserved areas.

CEDAW has adopted two General Recommendations on reservations. General Recommendation no. 4 expressed concern about the significant number of reservations that appeared to be incompatible with the object and purpose of the Convention and suggested that states parties reconsider such reservations with a view to withdrawing them.[85] Then, in General Recommendation no. 20 in 1992, CEDAW recommended that states should:

(a)   Raise the question of the validity and the legal effect of reservations to the Convention in the context of reservations to other human rights treaties;

(b)   Reconsider such reservations with a view to strengthening the implementation of all human rights treaties;

(c)   Consider introducing a procedure on reservations to the Convention compatible with that of other human rights treaties.[86]

In 1994 CEDAW reiterated the recommendations of the Vienna Conference on Human Rights that states be encouraged to limit the extent of any reservations they lodge to international human rights instruments, that they

---

[81] GA Res. 42/60, 30 November 1987, cited in A. Byrnes, *Report on the Seventh Session of the Committee on the Elimination of Discrimination Against Women and the Fourth Meeting of States parties to the Convention on the Elimination of All Forms of Discrimination Against Women* (Minnesota, International Women's Rights Action Watch, 1988).

[82] The United Kingdom's representative was subjected to close examination on the number and scope of British reservations when the second periodic report was examined in 1993: C. Chinkin and K. Werksman, *CEDAW No. 12, Report of the Twelfth Session of the Committee on the Elimination of All Forms of Discrimination Against Women* (Minnesota, International Women's Rights Action Watch, 1993).

[83] Report of the Committee on the Elimination of Discrimination against Women, UN Doc. A/52/38/Rev. 1 1997, 115 (considering Australia's third periodic report).

[84] Convention on the Elimination of All Forms of Discrimination Against Women, article 18.

[85] UN Doc. A/42/38, 10 April 1987.

[86] UN Doc. A/47/38, 30 January 1992, reprinted in A. Fraser and M. Kazantsis, *CEDAW No. 11, The Committee on the Elimination of Discrimination Against Women; the Convention on the Elimination of All Forms of Discrimination Against Women and Violence Against Women* (Minnesota, International Women's Rights Action Watch, 1992).

formulate their reservations as narrowly as possible, ensure none is incompatible with the object and purpose of the treaty and regularly review any reservations with a view to withdrawing them.[87] CEDAW also decided to amend its guidelines for the preparation of states' reports to contain a specific section on reservations. The guidelines require:

- State parties with substantive reservations to include information on them in their periodic reports.
- State parties to indicate why a reservation is considered necessary; whether reservations that may or may not have been made on the same rights in other conventions are consistent; the precise effect of a reservation in terms of national law and policy; plans to limit the effect of reservations and ultimately to withdraw them; and, where possible, a timetable for their withdrawal.
- States parties that have entered general reservations or reservations to Articles 2 and 3 to make a particular effort to report on their effect and interpretation.[88]

By requiring states to explain their reservations, CEDAW can investigate their scope, impact and the reasons for failure to comply with a timetable for their withdrawal, or for not submitting one. CEDAW has determined that its own concluding observations on states' reports should include a section on reservations and it has attempted to integrate its approach to reservations with that of other UN bodies. It has also requested the Secretary-General to write to states that had made substantive reservations in order to draw their attention to the Committee's concern.[89]

Despite its concerns, CEDAW has not adopted a recommendation similar to that of the Human Rights Committee with respect to reservations to the International Covenant on Civil and Political Rights (ICCPR).[90] The Human Rights Committee has challenged the exclusive competence of states parties to determine the compatibility of a reservation with the object and purposes of the treaty, considering that the special characteristics of human rights treaties and the inadequacies of the Vienna Convention regime on reservations and objections justify the Committee in assuming this task.[91] The Committee has concluded that an unacceptable reservation is severable from the ratification or accession to the Covenant, 'in the sense that the Covenant will be operative for the reserving party without benefit of the reservation'.[92] It has argued that in order to ensure they do not lead to a

---

[87] Vienna Declaration and Programme of Action, II, article 39.
[88] UN Doc. CEDAW/C/1994/WG. I/Rev.1, 31 January 1994.
[89] UN Doc. CEDAW/C/1994/WG.I/WP.1/Rev.1, 31 January 1994.
[90] General Comment No. 24, above note 48.
[91] 'In order to know the scope of its duty to examine a State's compliance . . . the Committee has necessarily to take a view on the compatibility of a reservation with the object and purpose of the Covenant and with general international law.' *Ibid.* at para. 18.
[92] *Ibid.*

'perpetual non-attainment of international human rights standards, reservations should not systematically reduce the obligations undertaken only to those presently existing in less demanding standards of domestic law'. The Human Rights Committee has also criticised imprecise, general reservations and emphasised that the effect of reservations on the treaty as a whole should be weighed.

Some states have challenged the Human Rights Committee's General Comment on the grounds that it usurps the position of states parties in determining the compatibility of reservations and that severing a reservation from an instrument of acceptance does not conform with the ratifying/ acceding party's intentions.[93] The ILC has also affirmed that the Vienna Convention regime is applicable to human rights treaties and that the object and purpose of the treaty are the most important criteria for determining the validity of the reservation.[94] While the ILC has regarded the human rights monitoring bodies as competent to comment upon, and make recommendations about, the admissibility of reservations,[95] it has argued that this does exclude the traditional role of contracting parties in responding to reservations[96] and that it is for the reserving state to respond to an inadmissible reservation either by withdrawing it, modifying it or withdrawing from the treaty.[97] More broadly there remains the question as to whether human rights treaties should be subject to a different regime on reservations than other treaties. The ECHR has regarded unacceptable reservations as severable,[98] whether they attempt to limit the reserving state's substantive obligations or the jurisdictional application of the European Convention on Human Rights.[99] As a judicial body, the ECHR has jurisdiction over 'all matters concerning the interpretation and application' of the Convention[100] and thus its claim to sever reservations is less controversial than that of the Human Rights Committee.

The Platform for Action of the Fourth World Conference on Women in

[93] Notably, the United States, France and the United Kingdom, above note 49.

[94] Second Report on the Law and Practice Relating to Reservations to Treaties, above note 44 at para. 1.

[95] *Ibid.*

[96] *Ibid.* at para. 6.

[97] *Ibid.* at para. 10. See B. Simma, 'The work of the International Law Commission at its forty-ninth session', 66 *Nordic Journal of International Law* (1997) 527.

[98] E.g. *Belilos v. Switzerland*, above note 46. See S. Marks, 'Three regional human rights treaties and their experience of reservations', in J.-P. Gardner, above note 49 at 35.

[99] E.g. *Loizidou v. Turkey*, above note 46.

[100] European Convention for the Protection of Human Rights and Fundamental Freedoms, 4 November 1950, 213 UNTS 221, as amended from 1 November 1998 by Protocol no. 11, article 32. Article 32(2) provides that in any dispute about the jurisdiction of the Court, the Court shall decide. The Court must assess reservations in the light of article 64.

1995 encouraged limiting reservations to the Women's Convention, their precise and narrow formulation to ensure their compatibility with the objects and purposes of the Convention and the withdrawal of incompatible reservations.[101] State practice indicates some positive response to this pressure to withdraw broad substantive reservations. As stated above, Libya, for example, withdrew its first extensive reservation. The more precise formulation of its replacement reservation is not as open-ended as the earlier reservation in its reference to article 2 and the particular issue of inheritance. Sub-section (2) is framed in terms of not withdrawing greater *Shariah* rights to women, but the reservation still fails to enumerate what those might be.[102] It is in any case arguably redundant in the light of article 23 of the Women's Convention.[103] At Beijing, the United Kingdom representative announced the government's commitment to withdrawing many of its reservations, a process that it had already commenced.[104]

Other proposals for dealing with the issue of reservations to the Women's Convention include that of diplomatic dialogue with the reserving state, which might involve requesting additional information about the reservation and formulating a preliminary objection to which the reserving state is invited to respond.[105] However, this positive state practice is offset by the

[101] Beijing Platform for Action, para. 230(b). See also GA Res. 51/68, 12 December 1996, in which the General Assembly urged states to limit reservations, to ensure that there was no incompatibility with the object and purposes of the Convention and to review reservations regularly with a view towards removing them.

[102] See above note 60. This new formulation did not satisfy the government of Finland which objected in the following terms: 'A reservation which consists of a general reference to religious law without specifying its contents does not clearly define to the other Parties of the Convention the extent to which the reserving State commits itself to the Convention and therefore may cast doubts about the commitment of the reserving state to fulfil its obligations under the Convention. Such a reservation is also . . . subject to the general principles of the observance of treaties according to which a party may not invoke the provisions of its internal law as justification for failure to perform a treaty.' Objection, 16 October 1996.

[103] Article 23 states that: 'Nothing in the present Convention shall affect any provisions that are more conducive to the achievement of equality between men and women which may be contained (a) In the legislation of a State Party; or (b) In any other convention, treaty or agreement in force for that State.'

[104] On 4 January 1995 the United Kingdom had removed its declaration to article 11 on the employment of women in underground work and its reservation to article 13. In March 1996 it withdrew its reservations to articles 1 and 2 and removed significant portions of its reservations to articles 9, 11, 15 and 16.

[105] Bulletin of Austrian Foreign Policy Activities, Document 90, Issues concerning reservations, Meeting in Vienna June 6 1995, Summary and Suggestions. In 1995 Austria followed this policy by indicating to Iran that it could not accept a reservation made by Iran to the Convention on the Rights of the Child that subjected its provisions to Islamic law 'unless Iran, by providing additional information or through subsequent practice ensures that the reservation is compatible with the provisions essential for the implementation of the object and purpose of the Convention'. Document 91, Osterreichische Erklarung zum Vorbehalt Irans Ubereinkommen uber die

continued inclusion of reservations even in the spate of new accessions that were made before and after the Beijing Conference. For example, Singapore's reservation referred to its diverse populations and declared that it would not 'apply the provisions of Articles 2 and 16 where compliance with these provisions would be contrary to their religious or personal laws'.[106] It also entered a 'protective' reservation allowing it to restrict, prohibit or impose conditions on employment where necessary or desirable to protect the heath of women or of the human foetus. Similarly Malaysia entered a reservation stating that it does not consider itself bound by many of the basic provisions of the Convention.[107]

The international law relating to reservations reflects the problems of constructing international communal norms in a system based on consent. In the particular context of the equality of women, some states have used the reservation mechanism effectively to hollow out the heart of their formal obligations.

Implementation of treaties into domestic law

The practical value of international standards depends largely on their implementation into domestic legal systems. In some states the formal position is that treaties automatically become the law of the land, while in others they must be transformed into national law through legislation.[108] It is thus quite possible for states to become parties to international agreements and yet to fail to incorporate the treaties into their domestic law, precluding reliance on the treaties. Even in the case of 'automatic' transformation into domestic law, judicial and executive devices allow for the evasion of international

---

Rechte des Kinds (BGBl. Nr 7/1993), New York, August 1995. This resulted in a reconsideration of the reservation by Iran.

[106] Acceded with reservations 5 October 1995.

[107] Acceded with reservations 5 July 1995, limited modification 6 February 1998.

[108] States that accept some form of automatic incorporation include the United States, France, the Netherlands, Germany and Italy. In such states the legislature plays a constitutional role in the ratification of treaties. See M. Leigh and M. Blakeslee, *National Treaty Law and Practice* (Washington DC, American Society of International Law, 1994); F. Jacobs and S. Roberts, *The Effect of Treaties in Domestic Law* (London, United Kingdom National Council of Civil Liberties, 1987); P. Alston and M. Chiam (eds), *Treaty-making and Australia: Globalisation versus Sovereignty* (Annandale, Federation Press, 1995); R. Higgins, 'The relationship between international and regional human rights norms and domestic law', 1992 *Commonwealth Law Bulletin* 1268. On incorporation of the European Convention on Human Rights see A. Drzemczewski, *The European Human Rights Convention in Domestic Law: A Comparative Study* (Oxford, Clarendon Press, 1983); J.-P. Gardner, *Aspects of Incorporation of the European Convention on Human Rights into Domestic Law* (London, British Institute of International and Comparative Law, 1993).

obligations.[109] The extent to which domestic courts require legislative incorporation of international obligations before they will rely on them has thus become a crucial factor in determining the domestic applicability of internationally accepted standards relating to the treatment of women. The practice of courts varies considerably from restrictive approaches[110] to more liberal ones.[111]

The *Unity Dow* case before the Botswanan Court of Appeal illustrates a broad approach. Unity Dow is a citizen of Botswana married to an American. Her children were born and raised in Botswana where she has spent her life apart from brief visits abroad. Two of her children were affected by a nationality law which provided that children whose fathers are Botswanan are also citizens wherever they may have been born but only children born outside marriage automatically acquire Botswanan citizenship through their mothers. The law also stipulated that foreign women who marry Botswanan citizens can apply for citizenship after two and a half years while foreign men married to Botswanan women must wait for ten years.[112] The law presented a number of practical problems to Botswanan women married to foreign men. The children had to have a Botswanan residence permit obtained by the non-citizen father. If the father lost his permission to reside in Botswana, their mother would either have to leave the country or risk losing custody of her children. In the event of separation or divorce, the children would have to reside with their father. The children had no citizenship rights, including no access to free tuition at the only university within Botswana. At age 18 they would become stateless unless they satisfied the residency requirements of Botswana (ten years) or the United States (five years).

The nationality law was challenged in the Botswanan courts as being discriminatory against women. Unity Dow argued that such discrimination was contrary to the Botswanan constitutional guarantees of liberty and of equality before the law. She also claimed that protection of the right to non-discrimination was required by Botswana's ratification of the African Charter

---

[109] E.g. the doctrine of 'self-executing' treaties allows the determination that some treaties do not have this quality: *Sei Fujii v. California* 242 P. 2d 617 (1952) (Sup. Ct California). In its ratification of the International Covenant on Civil and Political Rights, 8 June 1992, the United States made a declaration that articles 1 to 27 of the Covenant are not self-executing: http://www.un.org./Depts/Treaty.

[110] In the United Kingdom, for example, the need for incorporation of international law was explicitly reasserted by the House of Lords in the *International Tin Council Case (J. H. Rayner (Mincing Lane) Ltd v. Department of Trade and Industry)* [1990] 2 AC 418 at 476–7 (HL) (*per* Lord Templeman).

[111] E.g. *Minister for Immigration and Ethnic Affairs v. Ah Hin Teoh* (1995) 183 CLR 273 in which the Australian High Court held that treaties to which Australia is a party, but which are otherwise unincorporated into Australian law, should be taken into account in administrative decision-making.

[112] Citizenship Act Cap.01:01, sections 4 and 5.

of Human and People's Rights.[113] The Botswanan High Court accepted these arguments, influenced by Botswana's signing of the African Charter. While signing the treaty did not give it force of law in Botswana, Judge Horwitz considered that it supported a construction of the provision that was in harmony with international obligations.[114] He found it difficult 'if not impossible to accept that Botswana would deliberately discriminate against women in its legislation whilst at the same time internationally support non-discrimination against females or a section of them'.[115] The Court of Appeal upheld Dow's claim against a government appeal.[116] The Attorney-General's argument that the Constitution intended to preserve the fabric of Botswana customary law was rejected. The Court reaffirmed the significance of the African Charter, even though it had not been incorporated by legislation into domestic law, and of the General Assembly's Declaration on the Elimination of Discrimination Against Women, a non-binding instrument.[117] In the words of Judge Aguda:

> a court in this country, faced with the difficulty of interpretation as to whether or not some legislation breached any of the provisions entrenched in Chapter II of our Constitution which deal with Fundamental Rights and Freedoms of individuals, is entitled to look at the international agreements, treaties and obligations entered into before or after the legislation was enacted to ensure that such domestic legislation does not breach any of the ... obligations binding upon this country save upon clear and unambiguous language. In my view this must be so whether or not such international conventions, agreements, treaties, protocols or obligations have been specifically incorporated into our domestic law ... There is a clear obligation on this country like on all other African states signatories to the Charter to ensure the elimination [of] every discrimination against their women folk.[118]

The decision angered the government which apparently considered amending the Constitution. It took three years for the government to amend Botswanan law in accordance with the *Dow* ruling.[119] The arguments in the

---

[113] African Charter on Human Rights and Peoples' Rights, 26 June 1981, reprinted in 21 *International Legal Materials* (1982) 58. Article 18(3) provides: 'The state shall ensure the elimination of every discrimination against women and also ensure the protection of the rights of the woman and the child as stipulated in international declarations and conventions.' This provision has no counterpart in other human rights treaties.
[114] *Attorney-General of the Republic of Botswana v. Unity Dow* (High Court) [1991] LRC 574, reprinted in U. Dow (ed.), *Unity Dow, The Citizenship Case* (Gaborone, Lentswe La Lesedi Pty Ltd, 1995) 38 (*per* Judge Martin Horwitz).
[115] *Ibid.* at 40.
[116] The appeal was dismissed by a majority of 3 to 2. [1992] LRC 623.
[117] GA Res. 2263, 7 November 1967 (XXII).
[118] U. Dow, above note 114 at 168–70.
[119] Botswana enacted a new nationality law in August 1995.

Dow case have been used in similar claims in Sri Lanka, Pakistan, Bangladesh and Fiji.[120]

Judicial willingness to promote women's rights may provoke significant backlash. For example, a government may simply ignore a judicial holding,[121] or even take steps to reverse it.[122] An example of the latter is *Md Ahmed Khan v. Shah Bano Begum*, where an Indian Muslim woman was divorced by her husband who was unwilling to pay maintenance in accordance with the Indian Code of Criminal Procedure.[123] He claimed application of Muslim personal status law, which limits the period and basis of payment.[124] The Supreme Court of India upheld the wife's claim by according priority to the secular criminal law in preference to the religious-based personal law. This decision aroused considerable dissent from conservative Muslims, who regarded it as usurping the exclusive right of the *Ullamah* to interpret Muslim law and as denying their right to separate personal status laws. Muslim leaders activated widespread street demonstrations and lobbied the Indian government. After election setbacks and being fearful of community violence, the Indian government undid the *Shah Bano* decision by enacting legislation misleadingly titled the Muslim Women (Protection of Rights on Divorce) Act 1986.[125]

A series of statements from colloquia of Commonwealth judges has emphasised the significance of international standards in interpreting national

[120] Interights, UK supplied this information.

[121] E.g. in *Longwe v. Intercontinental Hotels* [1993] 4 Law Reports of the Commonwealth 221 (HC Zambia) it was held that denial of access to an unaccompanied woman to a hotel constituted discrimination on the grounds of gender and denial of fundamental rights. The Court allowed judicial notice to be taken of international human rights treaties. In the end, however, the hotel policy was not changed. S. Longwe, 'Foreword', in U. Dow, above note 114 at vii.

[122] E.g. the Australian government reacted to the *Teoh* decision, above note 111, by introducing legislation to override it. See H. Charlesworth, 'Dangerous liaisons: globalisation and Australian law', 20 *Adelaide Law Review* (1998) 57 at 67–8.

[123] *Md Ahmed Khan v. Shah Bano Begum* [1985] 3 S.C.R. 844. For commentary on the case see A. Rahman, 'Religious rights versus women's rights in India: a test case for international human rights law', 28 *Columbia Journal of Transnational Law* (1990) 473; R. Coomaraswamy, 'To bellow like a cow: women, ethnicity and the discourse of rights', in R. Cook (ed.), *Human Rights of Women: National and International Perspectives* (Philadelphia, University of Pennsylvania Press, 1994) 39; A. An-Na'im, above note 63 at 43–6.

[124] Indian Code of Criminal Procedure, section 125 provides maximum maintenance payments of 500 rupees a month to all destitute divorced women at the discretion of the magistrate. The husband claimed that his payment of 200 rupees per month for two years and a dower of three thousand rupees during *idaat* relieved him from further obligations.

[125] Despite its name, this legislation excludes all Muslims from section 125 of the Code of Criminal Procedure and codifies the law as it was before the case. Other provisions of the Act also have a negative impact upon women. See A. Rahman, above note 123 at 481.

law. For example, in 1988 the Bangalore Declaration asserted the 'vital duties of an independent judiciary in interpreting and applying national constitutions and law' in the light of universal human rights.[126] In 1994, senior judges from Commonwealth countries adopted the Victoria Falls Declaration of Principles for the Promotion of the Human Rights of Women,[127] which develops the Bangalore Principles in the context of women. The Victoria Falls Declaration states that:

> The judicial officers in Commonwealth jurisdictions should be guided by the Convention on the Elimination of All Forms of Discrimination Against Women when interpreting and applying the provisions of national constitutions and laws, including the common law and customary law, when making decisions.[128]

The Declaration also emphasises the importance of judicial and legal professional awareness and training in international human rights standards, of dissemination of these standards in local languages and of test case litigation.[129]

Regional systems provide examples of the direct influence of international standards on domestic law. The EC in particular has developed a significant body of law on sex equality through directives,[130] which in turn derive from the Treaty of Rome.[131] Under Community law these directives are directly applicable in the domestic law of member states without further incorporation. The Treaty on European Union (EU)[132] repeats the commitment to equal pay for equal work and builds upon the Treaty of Rome through the so-called Social Chapter, although the rejection of the social provisions by one member of the EU, the United Kingdom, required a scheme to allow it to opt out of progressive social obligations.[133]

---

[126] The Bangalore Principles are quoted in *Longwe v. Intercontinental Hotels*, above note 121 at 224.

[127] 19–20 August, 1994, Victoria Falls, Zimbabwe, reprinted in *Promotion of the Human Rights of Women and the Girl Child through the Judiciary: Commonwealth Declarations and Strategies for Action* (London, Commonwealth Secretariat, 1997).

[128] *Ibid.* at para. 11.

[129] See Beijing Platform for Action, para. 233. On the implementation of the Women's Convention through constitutional means, legislation, judicial decision-making and government policies in a number of states see I. Landsberg-Lewis (ed.), *Bringing Equality Home: Implementing the Convention on the Elimination of All Forms of Discrimination Against Women* (New York, Unifem, 1998).

[130] C. Barnard, *EC Employment Law* (Chichester, Chancery Law Publishing, 1995) chapter 4.

[131] Treaty Establishing the European Economic Community, 25 March 1957, 298 UNTS 11, article 119.

[132] Maastricht, 7 February 1992, Agreement on Social Policy concluded between the Member States of the EC with the exception of the United Kingdom of Great Britain and Northern Ireland, article 6.

[133] See further C. Chinkin, 'Comparative perspectives: the United Kingdom', in P. Alston and M. Chiam, above note 108 at 266.

Jus cogens

The modern treaty doctrine of *jus cogens* asserts the existence of fundamental legal norms from which no derogation is permitted. It imports notions
of universally applicable norms into the international legal process.[134] The
Vienna Convention on the Law of Treaties includes a formal, procedural
definition of the international law concept of *jus cogens*. Article 53 states
that:

> a peremptory norm of general international law is a norm accepted and recog-
> nised by the international community of States as a whole as a norm from
> which no derogation is permitted and which can be modified only by a subse-
> quent norm of general international law having the same character.

Article 64 of the Vienna Convention stipulates the procedural consequences
of concluding a treaty contrary to *jus cogens*: 'If a new peremptory norm of
general international law emerges, any existing treaty which is in conflict
with that norm becomes void and terminates.' The potential significance of
jus cogens is highlighted by the special procedures for a dispute concerning
the application or interpretation of articles 53 and 64. If no solution has
been reached within twelve months of an objection to a claim of *jus cogens*
being made, either party to the dispute may submit it in writing to the ICJ,
unless there has been an agreement to arbitrate.[135] This attempt to ensure
an authoritative determination of the issue counter-balances criticisms of
the imprecision of the doctrine and concerns about its destabilising impact
upon the principle of *pacta sunt servanda*.[136]

Provision for the jurisdiction of the ICJ may be undermined by reservations to the specific treaty. Consideration by the Court of a claim that a
provision of the Women's Convention, for example the definition of discrimination in article 1 or the obligations upon state parties in article 2,
constitutes *jus cogens* might be ousted by a reservation to article 29 of that
Convention, or to the substantive provision in question. Although article
66(a) of the Vienna Convention has never been put into operation, the
impact of reservations to the Women's Convention might be to pre-empt
any such procedural strategy.

---

[134] For a selection of different views on the topic of *jus cogens* see J. Sztucki,
Jus Cogens and the Vienna Convention on the Law of Treaties: A Critical Appraisal
(Vienna, Springer-Verlag, 1972); L. Hannikainen, *Peremptory Norms (Jus Cogens)
in International Law* (Helsinki, Finnish Lawyers' Publishing Co., 1988); N. Onuf
and R. Birney, 'Peremptory norms of international law: their source, function
and future', 4 *Denver Journal of International Law and Policy* (1974) 187; G.
Schwarzenberger, 'International *jus cogens*', 43 *Texas Law Review* (1965) 455.

[135] Vienna Convention on the Law of Treaties, article 66(a).

[136] *Ibid.*, article 26. For criticism of the doctrine of *jus cogens* see P. Weil,
'Towards relative normativity in international law?', 77 *American Journal of International Law* (1983) 413.

The consequences of a successful invocation of voidness through *jus cogens* are spelled out in the Vienna Convention. The parties shall:

(a)   eliminate as far as possible the consequences of any act performed in reliance on any provision which conflicts with the peremptory norm of general international law; and

(b)   bring their mutual relations into conformity with the peremptory norm of general international law.[137]

Where an existing treaty becomes void because of the emergence of a new norm of *jus cogens* that is in conflict with it, the parties are released from any further obligations under the treaty.[138] Prior rights or obligations are unaffected provided that 'their maintenance is not in itself in conflict with the new peremptory norm of general international law'.[139]

The freedom of states to enter into whatever treaty relations they wish is limited by fundamental values of the international community, as expressed through the doctrine of *jus cogens*. The doctrine has been rarely invoked in this context, although it may have had some restraining influence on the conclusion of treaties.[140] The importance of the doctrine of *jus cogens* lies therefore not in its practical application, but in its symbolic significance. It assumes that decisions with respect to normative priorities can be made and that certain norms can be designated as of fundamental significance. These are norms of 'relative indelibility' that cannot be overridden by treaty or acquiescence.[141] Discussions of the norms that may have attained this elevated status indicate that what is regarded as fundamental to international society are based upon men's experiences.[142] Contenders for *jus cogens* status include the prohibition of the use of force and aggression, the right to self-determination, the obligation to settle disputes peacefully and certain human rights norms.[143] The human rights norms that are typically asserted

[137] Vienna Convention on the Law of Treaties, article 71.

[138] *Ibid.*, article 71(2)(a).

[139] *Ibid.*

[140] See E. Schwelb, 'Some aspects of international *jus cogens* as formulated by the International Law Commission', 61 *American Journal of International Law* (1967) 946; G. Gaja, '*Jus cogens* beyond the Vienna Convention', 172 *Recueil des Cours* (1981) 271; G. Christenson, '*Jus cogens*: guarding interests fundamental to international society', 28 *Virginia Journal of International Law* (1988) 585.

[141] I. Brownlie, *Principles of Public International Law* (Oxford, Clarendon Press, 5th edn 1998) at 515.

[142] For a fuller discussion of the bias inherent in the doctrine of *jus cogens* see H. Charlesworth and C. Chinkin, 'The gender of *jus cogens*', 15 *Human Rights Quarterly* (1993) 63.

[143] E.g. the ILC Special Rapporteur, Sir Humphrey Waldock, proposed three categories of *jus cogens* norms: those prohibiting the use of force contrary to the UN Charter; international crimes so characterised by international law; and acts or omissions whose suppression is required by international law. Second Report on the Law

to constitute *jus cogens* are the prohibition of genocide, slavery, murder/ disappearances, the right to life, torture, prolonged arbitrary detention and systematic racial discrimination.[144] All these violations of human rights are of undoubted seriousness but the silences of the list indicate that women are peripheral to the understanding of fundamental community values. For example, prohibition of sex-based discrimination is not generally understood as a basic norm.[145]

Chapter 7 argues that definitions of human rights norms have a male bias, and that the substance of human rights law has been developed in accordance with male values. This claim can also be extended to the norms of *jus cogens*. That there can be gender-specific methods of genocide, such as systematic, mass rape to further ethnic cleansing or to produce children of their fathers' ethnicity, has only recently, and controversially, been argued.[146] Bruno Simma and Philip Alston have drawn attention to the priority given to civil and political rights over economic and social rights and have asked:

> whether any theory of human rights law which singles out race but not gender discrimination, which condemns arbitrary imprisonment but not death by starvation, and which finds no place for a right of access to primary health care is not flawed in terms both of the theory of human rights and of United Nations doctrine.[147]

A revised list of *jus cogens* norms might give prominence to a range of other rights: to sexual equality; to food;[148] to reproductive freedom; to freedom from fear of violence and oppression; and to peace.[149] This catalogue includes rights that have been challenged as insufficiently rigorously proved and as confusing policy goals with current international law.[150] However, the doctrine of *jus cogens* has an explicitly aspirational and promotional character. Its content would be much richer if women's lives contributed to

---

of Treaties, [1963] 2 *Yearbook International Law Commission* at 56–9, UN Doc. A/ CN.4/156 and Add. 1 to 3. See also [1966] 2 *Yearbook International Law Commission* at 247–8 where other examples were suggested by members of the ILC.

[144] American Law Institute, *Restatement (Third) of the Foreign Relations Law of the United States* (St Paul, American Law Institute, 1987) para. 702; M. Whiteman, 'Jus cogens in international law, with a projected list', 7 *Georgia Journal of International and Comparative Law* (1977) 609.

[145] However, Ian Brownlie has commented that the 'principle of religious non-discrimination must have the same status as the principle of non-discrimination as to sex.' I. Brownlie, above note 141 at 515, n. 29.

[146] *Kadic v. Karadzic* 70 F. 3rd 232 (2d Cir. 1995).

[147] B. Simma and P. Alston, 'The sources of human rights law: custom, jus cogens and general principles', 12 *Australian Yearbook of International Law* (1992) 82 at 94.

[148] See C. Chinkin and S. Wright, 'The hunger trap: women, food and self-determination', 14 *Michigan Journal of International Law* (1993) 262.

[149] See chapter 8.

[150] See I. Brownlie, 'The rights of peoples in modern international law', in J. Crawford (ed.), *The Rights of Peoples* (Oxford, Clarendon Press, 1988) 16.

the designation of international fundamental values allowing women to benefit from at least the same promise of the doctrine as men.

Treaty termination

Treaty obligations provide a yardstick against which state performance can be assessed. The description of the global position of women in chapter 1 reveals that many states violate their obligations under the Women's Convention and under the non-discrimination provisions of other human rights treaties. Further, as has been seen, even where domestic courts uphold women's claims based on international standards, they are not always implemented. The question then arises as to how states can be held to their obligations and what the sanctions are for non-compliance.

The Vienna Convention on the Law of Treaties seeks to uphold the continuity and stability of treaty regimes. A state may not therefore withdraw easily from a treaty, and the conditions for termination and suspension of treaty obligations are restrictive. A state may not withdraw or denounce a multilateral treaty unless the treaty explicitly or implicitly provides for this.[151] As there is no such provision in the Women's Convention, it can be assumed that withdrawal is not envisaged.[152] The Human Rights Committee has stated that once people are accorded human rights guarantees, such protection continues to belong to them despite any action by the state to divest them of those rights.[153] Indeed, withdrawal from treaty rights would not remove a state's obligations under customary international law.

Similarly, the drastic step of termination or suspension of a treaty in the case of material breach is counter-productive to continuation of human rights obligations.[154] Accordingly the Vienna Convention exempts 'provisions relating to the protection of the human person contained in treaties of

---

[151] Vienna Convention on the Law of Treaties, article 56. In *Gabcikovo-Nagymaros Project*, above note 2, the ICJ confirmed that in the absence of any provision concerning termination, the treaty could be terminated 'only on the limited grounds enumerated in the Convention'.

[152] This contrasts with the International Convention on the Elimination of All Forms of Racial Discrimination, article 21. In its General Comment no. 26 on issues relating to the continuity of obligations to the International Covenant on Civil and Political Rights, UN Doc. CCPR/C/21/Rev.1/Add.8/Rev.1, 8 December 1997, the Human Rights Committee concluded from the existence of this provision in the Race Convention that it was not mere oversight to omit reference to termination in other human rights treaties.

[153] *Ibid.* at para. 4.

[154] Vienna Convention on the Law of Treaties, article 60 defines material breach and its consequences. In addition, the breach of a treaty may give rise to legitimate counter-measures. See *Air Services Agreement* (France v. United States) 18 Reports of International Arbitral Awards (1978) 416.

a humanitarian character' from these consequences of breach.[155] Neverthe-less the issue remains of what responses may be made in the face of long-term breach of states' obligations with respect to women.[156] Human rights treaties contain monitoring provisions. The Women's Convention provides only for periodic state reporting to CEDAW of measures taken by states to implement the Convention.[157] Although states' reports might expose non-performance or breach, there is no tradition of censure by the treaty bodies but rather one of 'constructive dialogue', which is unlikely to lead to change in the face of intransigence. The 1999 Optional Protocol to the Women's Convention, which will allow individuals to bring complaints about viola-tions of the Convention to CEDAW, will allow a new type of pressure for change.[158]

The Women's Convention grants jurisdiction to the ICJ over disputes relating to the interpretation or application of the Convention, which might include allegations of material breach.[159] Despite this jurisdictional clause, the ruling in the *South West Africa* case[160] that an applicant state must have a legal interest in the dispute to bring a case would appear to reduce the prospects of such a case being brought before the Court. On the other hand it could be argued that such a restrictive interpretation would render article 29 meaningless. The many reservations made by states parties to article 29 militate, however, against this contention.

Conclusion

The law of treaties can be regarded with ambivalence by women. On the one hand, the global position of women has been recognised in a number of human rights treaties that have received many ratifications and accessions, providing greater certainty as to the extent of obligation than customary international law, and including monitoring and implementation provisions. Treaties also can be incorporated into national policies, guidelines and legislation. Women activists consequently tend to regard the attainment of treaty support for their goals as a benchmark of success. On the other hand,

---

[155] Vienna Convention on the Law of Treaties, article 60(5).

[156] In the *Legal Consequences for States of the Continued Presence of South Africa in Namibia (South West Africa) notwithstanding Security Council Resolution 276, 1970*, above note 2, the ICJ advised that South Africa's continued breach of man-date agreement meant that the General Assembly had validly terminated it.

[157] See chapter 7.

[158] See further chapter 7.

[159] Convention on the Elimination of All Forms of Discrimination Against Women, article 29(1).

[160] *South West Africa Cases*, Second Phase (Ethiopia & Liberia v. South Africa) 1966 ICJ Rep. 4 (Judgment of 18 July).

treaties as a source of law are limited by their voluntaristic nature, based on a model of individual state consent. The process of giving consent has largely excluded women and the subject matter and substantive content of most treaties reflect a limited perspective. In many instances, international standards are not implemented into domestic law or are simply not observed. The law of treaties reinforces voluntarism through doctrines such as that relating to reservations and limiting declarations. Further, the modest recognition of a communitarian system of values through the *jus cogens* doctrine is undermined in practice by the male-centred account of fundamental norms.

Two cases in 1999 illustrate the mixed value of treaties for women. *Apparel Export Promotion Council v. Chopra*[161] concerned an allegation of sexual harassment. The Supreme Court of India held that the message of international instruments such as the Women's Convention and the Beijing Declaration is 'loud and clear.' They 'cast an obligation on the Indian State to gender sensitise its laws' and on the courts to ensure that this message is not drowned.[162] It continued that courts and counsel must never forget the core principles embodied in international conventions and instruments and as far as possible to give effect to them. This is in strong contrast to the Supreme Court of Zimbabwe which, in *Venia Magaya v. Nakayi Shonhiwa Magaya,*[163] held that even if the Zimbabwe Constitution prohibited sex discrimination 'on account of Zimbabwe's adherence to gender equality enshrined in international human rights instruments', there are exceptions based, *inter alia* on customary law applied between Africans. In denying the claim to succession of the deceased's eldest child, who was female, in favour of a younger male child, the Court upheld African customary law noting that it would not be readily abandoned 'especialiy by those such as senior males who stand to lose positions of privilege.'[164] The Court stated that it was never contemplated that the Zimbabwean Legal Age of Majority Act 1982 would be interpreted to 'give women additional rights which interfered with and distorted some aspects of customary law.'[165]

[161] Civil Appeal Nos 226–227 of 1999, 20 January 1999.
[162] *Ibid.* at 25–6.
[163] Judgment No. SC 210/98, Civil Appeal No. 635/92, 2 November 1998 and 16 February 1999.
[164] *Ibid.* at 18.
[165] *Ibid.* at 16. Zimbabwe has made no reservations to the Women's Convention.

5

The idea of the state

Introduction

Statehood confers the capacity to claim rights and duties under international law.[1] Other entities, such as individuals and international intergovernmental and NGOs, can assert some degree of international personhood for particular purposes, but the state is considered the most complete expression of international legal personality.[2] The state is of course an artificial entity, a means of allocating political control over territory. Its decisions, policies and strategies are those of the individuals and groups comprising its decision-making elites. International law regards states as independent and autonomous members of the international community. It tends to obliterate the differences between states by considering all states as formally equal, whatever their size, population, geography or wealth.[3] In practice, however, disparities in size, population and wealth create great differences in power between states which are sometimes acknowledged in weighted voting systems in international organisations or differential treaty obligations.[4] The fiction of equality is preserved through such arrangements being presented as dependent on the consent of all states parties.[5]

The monolithic view of statehood upon which traditional international law doctrine depends significantly limits the scope of international law. One consequence is that it establishes a model for full international personality that

[1] On statehood generally see R. Jennings and A. Watts (eds), *Oppenheim's International Law* (London, Longmans, 9th edn 1992) chapters 2–4.

[2] D. O'Connell, *International Law* (London, Stevens, 2nd edn 1970) vol. 1 at 89–92.

[3] E.g. Charter of the UN, 26 June 1945, article 2(1): 'The [UN] is based on the principle of the sovereign equality of all its members.'

[4] E.g. UN Framework Convention on Climate Change, 9 May 1992, UN Doc A/AC.237/18, reprinted in 31 *International Legal Materials* (1992) 849.

[5] J. Crawford, 'The criteria for statehood in international law', 48 *British Yearbook of International Law* (1976–77) 93 at 108.

other claimants for international status cannot replicate. Moreover, the idea of statehood constructed by international law creates a barrier between the entity of the state and those within it. This is exemplified externally by the principles of non-intervention[6] and non-interference in the domestic affairs of states[7] and internally by doctrines of immunity and non-justiciability. International legal theory has little to say about national decision-making processes, providing limited constraints on national action mainly through human rights principles.[8] It is therefore not surprising that there has been little investigation by international lawyers of statehood's differential significance for women and men.

International legal doctrine on the state focuses on the criteria for, and the incidents of, statehood.[9] Martti Koskenniemi has pointed out that the international legal notion of statehood operates to privilege particular voices and to silence others,[10] but this insight has not yet been fully explored. This chapter examines the international legal notion of statehood, the doctrine of recognition, some of the major incidents of statehood – jurisdiction and state responsibility – and the concept of self-determination as a process for acquiring statehood. It discusses the invisibility of women in the construction and application of these legal principles and examines their impact upon women. International lawyers generally present the state as being without a sexed identity, a neuter,[11] and thus without consequences for sex or gender. By contrast, we argue that the paradigm state is constructed as a 'male' in international law, with 'female' features only in particular contexts. The 'sex' of the state makes it difficult to represent women's interests in international legal discourse. A related effect of the sex attributed to the state is to naturalise beliefs about sexual difference, which then help to sustain the oppression of women.

The concept of statehood in international law

The Montevideo Convention on Rights and Duties of States of 1933[12] sets out the traditional and accepted definition of a state in international law. Article 1 provides:

[6] Declaration on Principles of International Law Concerning Friendly Relations and Co-operation among States in Accordance with the Charter of the United Nations, GA Res. 2625 (XXV), 24 October 1970, principle III.

[7] Charter of the UN, article 2(7).

[8] See chapter 7.

[9] R. Jennings and A. Watts, above note 1 at 339.

[10] M. Koskenniemi, *From Apology to Utopia: The Structures of International Legal Argument* (Helsinki, Finnish Lawyers' Publishing Co., 1989) at 499.

[11] E.g. the Preface to the leading work by James Crawford, *The Creation of States in International Law* (Oxford, Clarendon Press, 1979) at ix, states: 'In this study . . . [t]he State is not . . . allocated a sex: where necessary the pronouns "it" and "its" are used.'

[12] 135 LNTS 19.

> The state as a person of international law should possess the following quali-
> fications: (a) a permanent population; (b) a defined territory; (c) government;
> and (d) capacity to enter into relations with other States.

These criteria are apparently neutral and value-free. Nevertheless, state practice since 1933 indicates that further considerations, such as the process of
formation of the state and even the observance of human rights, may be
relevant to statehood. New states are recognised by other states as members
of the international community if they are deemed to meet the international
criteria, and sometimes, when political expediency so demands, even if they
do not. We suggest here that the prerequisites for statehood in international
law endorse particular views of masculinity and femininity.

A permanent population

International legal doctrine does not require a minimum number of inhabitants for an entity to qualify as a state. Indeed, the Montevideo definition
gives no content to the notion of population, apart from the need for it to
be permanent. The constitution of a population appears in many respects as
a broad prerogative of statehood. The fact that the Vatican City is recognised as a state in international law[13] suggests that there is no problem if an
entity restricts its population almost entirely to adult men and that the
population is reproduced asexually, through recruitment.

The concept of permanent population as a criterion of statehood assumes
that populations are static. This is inaccurate in a number of ways. In the
1990s there were significant movements of peoples within and between states.
For example, the UNHCR estimated that in 1997 there were 50 million
forcibly displaced people around the world.[14] In some instances, long-term
political disputes mean that refugees become *de facto* part of the population
of the host state. States also deliberately manipulate populations through
settler policies in order to consolidate claims over territory.[15] Another form
of manipulation of demographic change is what has become termed 'ethnic
cleansing' – killing and forcing populations to flee a particular area. One
instance of this has been legitimated by the international community in the
1995 General Framework Agreement for Peace in Bosnia and Herzegovina
in the constitutional recognition of the Republika Srpska.[16] All these forms

[13] See below at note 61 and accompanying text.
[14] UNHCR, *The State of the World's Refugees 1997–98* (Oxford, Oxford University Press, 1997).
[15] See e.g. C. Drew, 'Self-determination, population transfer and the Middle East
peace accords', in S. Bowen (ed.), *Human Rights, Self-Determination and Political
Change in the Occupied Territories* (The Hague, Kluwer Law International, 1997) 119.
[16] Initialled Dayton, 21 November 1995, signed Paris, 14 December 1995, reprinted in 35 *International Legal Materials* (1996) 75 (Dayton Peace Accords), article
III, annexes 2 and 4.

of population stratagems have significance for women. Women and children
are disproportionately highly represented in many refugee flows; settler policies rely on high birth rates to entrench the settlers' security; and rape of
women has become central to policies of ethnic cleansing.[17] State policies on
population control, combined with cultural and economic preferences for
male children, have produced perhaps the most direct form of sexed population. The dramatic decline in the numbers of women described by Amartya
Sen[18] has created severe population imbalance between the sexes in some
states with enormous social implications. Despite their impact upon the
identity of the state, none of these deviations from the notion of a permanent population have been understood to affect the definition of a state in
international law.

Certain restraints on population have, however, been accepted as undermining a claim to statehood. For example, the 'homelands' or 'Bantustans'
created by South Africa were never accepted as states by the international
community. The UN General Assembly strongly condemned their establishment 'as designed to consolidate the inhuman policies of apartheid, to destroy
the territorial integrity of the country, to perpetuate white minority domination and to dispossess the African people of South Africa of their inalienable rights'.[19] In the same resolution, the General Assembly went on to
describe the declaration of independence of one Bantustan, the Transkei, as
invalid, and called upon UN members to refrain from having any dealings
with it. International practice, therefore, suggests that a certain form of
racial policy may be significant but that other forms of population change
such as those described above are insignificant in the assessment of whether
a particular group of people constitutes a permanent population. Sex is,
however, crucial in the construction of a population in the sense that heterosexual activity reproduces further generations of a population.

Another way that sex is relevant is through the notion of citizenship, the
legal recognition of being part of a particular population. The notion of
citizenship, developed in the Athenian *polis* that forms the basis of modern
Western understandings, was based on property and/or military service and so
effectively excluded women.[20] Women, slaves and children lived in the private
realm of production and reproduction that sustained and supported the public
world of politics and citizenship. One consequence was that female slaves
were sought and used for reproductive purposes to increase the economic
value of the slave holding. Another was that all women's sexuality was tightly

[17] See chapters 8 and 10.
[18] A. Sen, 'More than 100 million women are missing', *New York Review of Books*, 20 December 1990, 61. See further chapter 1.
[19] GA Res. 31/6 (1976).
[20] V. Peterson, 'Security and sovereign states: what is at stake in taking feminism seriously?', in V. Peterson (ed.), *Gendered States: Feminist (Re) Visions of International Relations Theory* (Boulder, Lynne Rienner Publishers, 1992) 31 at 34.

regulated so that it was at the service of men; still another was the relegation of all aspects of childbirth and child caring and rearing to the private, non-political sphere. In this way, a particular social and political mythology of sex differences was created: men's lives fit the requirements of citizenship more naturally than women's lives.[21] The notion of citizenship excludes other marginal groups as well, such as refugees and indigenous peoples. As Anne Orford has said, 'The rational, ruthlessly ordered world of sovereign states has no place for those portrayed as unruly, disordered, subversive, primitive or irrational.'[22] The modern post-colonial state also may draw boundaries around that part of its population entitled to full citizenship, for example by criminalising homosexuality and lesbianism.[23] Contemporary international law leaves questions of citizenship and nationality largely up to individual states[24] and allows people to be excluded from full citizenship on the grounds of sex or sexuality, for example by the denial of the right to vote, exclusion from military participation or denial of civil rights. Further, different criteria for the acquisition of citizenship on the basis of sex are not unusual.[25]

Defined territory

The territory of a state can vary greatly in size. The fact that the borders, or indeed existence, of a territorial entity are contested is considered no barrier to statehood.[26] What is considered critical is that there be 'a certain coherent territory effectively governed'.[27] A related international legal principle is the right of states to 'territorial integrity'. Article 2(4) of the UN Charter commits all member states to 'refrain in their international relations from the threat or use of force against the territorial integrity or political independence of any state'.[28]

This concern with the coherence and integrity of territory presents the state as a bounded, unified entity. The notions of boundaries, borders, circumferences and peripheries have considerable power in legal rhetoric. Thus

---

[21] *Ibid.* at 36–7.

[22] A. Orford, 'The uses of sovereignty in the new imperial order', 6 *Australian Feminist Law Journal* (1996) 63 at 72.

[23] M. Alexander, 'Not just (any) body can be a citizen: the politics of law, sexuality and postcoloniality in Trinidad and Tobago and the Bahamas', 48 *Feminist Review* (1994) 5.

[24] *Nottebohm Case* (Liechtenstein v. Guatemala) 1955 ICJ Rep. 4 (Judgment of 6 April).

[25] See International Law Association Committee on Feminism and International Law, *Preliminary Report on Women's Equality and Nationality in International Law* (London, International Law Association, 1998).

[26] J. Crawford, above note 11 at 37–8.

[27] *Ibid.* at 40.

[28] Declaration on Principles of International Law Concerning Friendly Relations and Co-operation among States in Accordance with the Charter of the United Nations, principle I. See chapter 8.

Jennifer Nedelsky has argued that the metaphor of boundary used in United States constitutional law to limit the power of a collective to deal with individuals is distorting and destructive because it rests on a flawed conception of the individual as detached from society. Just as a right to property is understood to define 'a sphere in which we can act largely unconstrained by collective demands and prohibitions',[29] the international legal notion of statehood is concerned to preserve a fixed territorial space of exclusive control and over which the international community has very limited standing.

The notion of a 'coherent' state territory in international law also has characteristics of the person found in the criminal law of common law systems. For example, Ngaire Naffine has described the subject of the law of assault as 'a discrete, distinct, volitional subject for whom the skin of his body is considered to represent a boundary from other distinct subjects. Consent is required if that boundary skin is to be transgressed . . . The mere touching of the skin represents an encroachment, a violation of the person's person if the touching is not wanted.'[30] Naffine has used a 'body bag' as the appropriate image for the heterosexual, male 'person' assumed in criminal law. She has argued that:

> The principal concern of law is (the policing of the boundaries of) the bounded heterosexual male body. Bodies [such as women's] which are not like this, or are not allowed to be like this, are somehow deviant and undeserving . . . They are 'unnatural', even 'loathsome', because they have apparently lost their clear definition.[31]

Naffine's account of criminal law illuminates international law, where concern with the preservation of the borders and security of states is dominant.[32] The state constituted by international law is a bounded, self-contained, closed, separate entity that is entitled to ward off any unwanted contact or interference. Most boundary delimitations are bilateral, of concern only to the parties involved, becoming of broader community concern only when violated. Like a heterosexual male body, the state has no 'natural' points of entry, and its boundedness makes forced entry the clearest possible breach of international law. The international reaction to Iraq's invasion of Kuwait in 1990 is a good example of this. Entities that cannot assert control over a coherent unified territory, or that straddle borders, such as many indigenous

[29] J. Nedelsky, 'Law, boundaries, and the bounded self', 30 *Representations* (1990) 162 at 165.

[30] N. Naffine, 'The body bag', in N. Naffine and R. Owens (eds), *Sexing the Subject of Law* (Sydney, Law Book Co. Ltd, 1997) 79 at 85.

[31] *Ibid.* at 84.

[32] E.g. the UN Secretary-General has described the dangers of a world of 'increasingly porous boundaries' with threats from drug trafficking, crime, terrorism and money laundering. Annual Report of the Secretary-General on the Work of the Organization, UN Doc. A/52/1, 3 September 1997 at para. 130.

minority peoples, do not qualify as full subjects of international law. This type of group is seen as having permeable, negotiable, penetrable, vulnerable boundaries in the same way that women's bodies have been constructed in criminal law. Images of orderly national domestic spaces separated by state boundaries from outside dangerous chaos and anarchy, to be found in the literature on international security,[33] similarly reflect the male sex of the state.

Boundaries feature prominently in the international legal imagery of colonial conquest. Exploration and discovery of 'virgin' territory were prerequisites of legal acquisition of territory through occupation.[34] Penetration of dark, unbounded territory (*terra nullius*) justified its ownership. Colonialism was represented in an erotic way, with the male coloniser taming, through intercourse, an unbounded, uncontrolled female people.[35] Colonised territories were presented as uncivilised, unable to protect their territory or to resist the well-organised incursions of a superior culture. Because many indigenous peoples have understood their relationship to land in a spiritual and inclusive way, rather than based on exclusive possession, their land was considered as belonging to no one. The doctrine of *terra nullius* indeed allowed the existence of people who did not assert territorial rights over a fixed area in a European manner to be legally obliterated.[36] Colonial ownership of a territory justified exploitation of all its resources.[37] The international legal account of colonialism validated the coloniser's perspective by factoring out anything inconsistent with his desires.

In the twentieth century territorial claims have expanded to include maritime areas and air space. Delimitation of such areas creates new problems to which traditional international law rules of acquisition of territory are inapplicable. New prescriptive regimes have been developed for these areas[38] which emphasise the durability of the concern with boundary drawing.[39]

---

[33] J. Tickner, 'Inadequate providers? A gendered analysis of states and security', in J. Camilleri, A. Jarvis and A. Paolini (eds), *The State in Transition* (Boulder, Lynne Rienner Publishers, 1995) 133; A. Orford, above note 22 at 67.

[34] See R. Jennings, *The Acquisition of Territory in International Law* (Manchester, Manchester University Press, 1962).

[35] J. Pettman, *Worlding Women: A Feminist International Politics* (Sydney, Allen and Unwin, 1996) at 27.

[36] E.g. *Milirrpum v. Nabalco Pty Ltd* (1997) 17 FLR 141 (Supreme Court of the Northern Territory); *Mabo v. Queensland No. 2* (1992) 175 CLR 1; H. Reynolds, *The Law of the Land* (Melbourne, Penguin Books, 1987) at 12–14.

[37] A. Anghie, 'Colonialism, environmental damage and the Nauru case', 34 *Harvard International Law Journal* (1993) 445.

[38] E.g. UN Convention on the Law of the Sea, 10 December 1982, UN Doc. A/CONF. 62/122, reprinted in 21 *International Legal Materials* (1982) 1261; Chicago Convention on International Civil Aviation, 7 December 1944, 15 UNTS 295.

[39] E.g. M. Evans, *Relevant Circumstances and Maritime Delimitations* (Oxford, Clarendon Press, 1989); J. Charney and L. Alexander (eds), *International Maritime Boundaries* (Dordrecht, Martinus Nijhoff, 1993).

Innovative schemes for equitable sharing of resources in the post-colonial era such as the concept of 'the common heritage of mankind'[40] have been controversial and resisted by a number of developed countries. In the context of the deep seabed and subsoil, the area beyond national jurisdiction and hence within the common heritage area, was greatly reduced by the extensive definition of the continental shelf.[41] The envisaged operation of mining that area for the common benefit has been subsequently modified because of pressure from developed states, notably the United States and some member states of the EU in ways that effectively undermine the spirit of common heritage in favour of 'market-oriented approaches'.[42]

Naffine has pointed out that the 'body bag' version of the person in the criminal law of common law systems has created a language and culture that construes the sexual act as one of domination and invasion – the penetration or piercing by a male of a passive (female) cavity. She has argued that this does not reflect the reality of many sexual encounters and prevents us from construing sexual relations in a more positive, mutually empowering, light; for example, as an act of interpersonal fusion or as the creation of something beyond the participants.[43] In a similar way, the rhetoric of territorial integrity in international law rests on a particular view of the male body and the nature of its sexual intercourse with the female body. An account of the state as a bounded entity assumes that states will be worse off if any aspect of their territorial sovereignty is sublimated.[44] Such rhetoric has undermined, for example, attempts in the UN to accommodate the claims to self-determination of indigenous peoples,[45] or to resolve territorial disputes. It is the basis of the nostalgia about an era of strong, impermeable boundaries (now seen to

[40] UN Convention on the Law of the Sea, Part XI; Treaty on the Principles Governing the Activities of States in the Exploration of Outer Space including the Moon and other Celestial Bodies, 27 January 1967, 610 UNTS 205, articles 1 and 2; Agreement Governing the Activities of States on the Moon and Other Celestial Bodies, 5 December 1979, reprinted in 18 *International Legal Materials* (1979) 1434, articles 1 and 2.

[41] UN Convention on the Law of the Sea, articles 76 to 85.

[42] Agreement Relating to the Implementation of Part XI of the UN Convention on the Law of the Sea of 10 December 1982, GA Res. 48/263, 28 July 1994, reprinted in 33 *International Legal Materials* (1994) 1309.

[43] N. Naffine, above note 30 at 92.

[44] E.g. the discussion of the importance of respect for territorial frontiers expressed in the principle *uti possidetis: Frontier Dispute Case* (Burkina Faso v. Mali) 1986 ICJ Rep. 554 (Judgment of 22 December) at paras 23–6.

[45] B. Kingsbury, 'Whose international law? Sovereignty and non-state groups', *Proceedings of the 88th Annual Meeting of the American Society of International Law* (Washington DC, American Society of International Law, 1994) 1; B. Kingsbury, '"Indigenous Peoples" in international law: a constructivist approach to the Asian controversy', 92 *American Journal of International Law* (1998) 414.

be undermined by increasing global interdependence) found in the modern literature of international relations and international law.[46]

Legal boundaries are alienating, a means of separating peoples,[47] but they also often represent areas where communities meet and interact.[48] Where legal boundaries are marked out there may be a need for practical steps for minimising disruption for the inhabitants on each side of the boundary and for enhancing transborder economic and social co-operation. Boundary commissions have long been used to facilitate the management of *sui generis* boundary regimes, and resource sharing arrangements have been devised. Such approaches to what have been termed integrative boundaries emphasise permeability and management rather than separation and isolation. The traditional international legal account of territorial integrity and legal sovereignty, to use Jennifer Nedelsky's terms, makes boundaries central and intercourse a violation.[49] This in turn reinforces the view of women within states as unbounded, submissive and unequal with men. Preoccupation with boundaries also undermines possibilities of understanding the autonomy of the individual state as dependent on, rather than likely to be antithetical to, the international community.

Government

International law requires that an entity have an organised and effective government before it can be considered a state.[50] Traditionally, there has been little concern with the *form* of the government, only its effectiveness. State practice indicates some outer limits on methods of achieving governmental stability, particularly at the time of the formation of a new entity. For example, the UN's refusal to recognise the declaration of independence of Ian Smith's government in Southern Rhodesia in 1965 was based on its purpose of enabling continued minority white rule, as well as its unilateral assertion.[51] The notion of governmental power assumed in the definition of statehood, however, does not question women's exclusion from systems of power worldwide; indeed it can be seen to depend for its smooth functioning

[46] A. Orford, 'The politics of collective security', 17 *Michigan Journal of International Law* (1996) 373.

[47] The language of separation is strong in R. Jennings and A. Watts, above note 1 at 661–70. See also the Dayton Peace Accords, article III and annex II, which establish the Inter-Entity boundary between the Republika Srpska and the Federation of Bosnia and Herzegovina.

[48] E.g. a river may naturally be the means for communication between peoples as well as a boundary. The mid-line and *thalweg* principles give no effect to this reality. See R. Jennings and A. Watts, above note 1 at 664.

[49] J. Nedelsky, above note 29 at 170.

[50] J. Crawford, above note 11 at 42.

[51] SC Res. 232, 1966; GA Res. 2379 (XXVI), 28 October 1968.

on particular versions of masculinity and femininity, which, like the Athenian *polis*, connect men with public political life and women with the private, domestic infrastructure that is necessary to sustain public life.

The criterion of an organised and effective government, like all the traditional international legal criteria of statehood, depends on a notion of state autonomy built on isolation and separation.[52] It enables the state to be seen as a complete, coherent, bounded entity that speaks with one voice, obliterating the diversity of voices within the state.[53] In this way, government can be seen as the head of the body of the state, which is made up of its population and territory. Just as a person's head (or mind) controls its bodily flesh, so a government controls its sometimes unruly body. The existence of a single head, voice and will in a state allows it to be seen as a rational (male) actor. The nineteenth-century political theorist, Bluntschli, declared that a secular state was masculine because it behaved like a man, 'consciously determining and governing itself.'[54] He contrasted the masculine character of the modern state with the feminine character of a religious community which 'does not consciously rule herself like a man, and act freely in her external life, but wishes only to serve God and perform her religious duties'.[55]

Capacity to enter into relations with other states

This criterion of statehood is generally understood to signify independence from the authority of other states, so that agreements with other states can be freely entered into. Independence, or its synonym in international law, sovereignty, is considered the principal criterion of statehood.[56] The Peace of Westphalia in 1648 was built on the notion of the sovereign state, one that could govern its people without external interference on any basis – religious, military, political or legal.[57] Sovereignty means both full competence to act in the international arena, for example by entering into treaties or by acting to preserve state security, and exclusive jurisdiction over internal matters, for example exercise of legislative, executive and judicial competence.[58] Thus sovereignty is a doubled-sided principle: externally, it signifies

---

[52] On the individualistic character of post-Westphalian international law see A. Cassese, *International Law in a Divided World* (Oxford, Clarendon Press, 1986) chapter 1.

[53] E.g. P. Guggenheim, 'Les principes de droit international public', 80 *Recueil des Cours* (1952) 1 at 83, 96.

[54] J. Bluntschli, *The Theory of the State* (Oxford, Clarendon Press, 1921 edn) at 207.

[55] *Ibid.* at 23.

[56] J. Crawford, above note 11 at 48.

[57] See chapter 2.

[58] J. Crawford, above note 5 at 108.

equality of power, and internally, it signifies pre-eminence of power. The standard view of international law as an essentially consensual regime is a concomitant of sovereignty – a fully sovereign entity can only voluntarily accept restraints on its activities. This capacity distinguishes states from other non-state entities such as indigenous peoples. Consent to the regime of international law thus becomes the vehicle by which the sovereign independence of states is reconciled with the practical imperatives of co-existence with other states.[59]

There are strong connections between the requirement of a defined territory, and the notions of independence and sovereignty. One aspect of the definition of territory and the creation of boundaries is precisely to foster independence and autonomy from other entities. International law doctrine endorses two main elements of statehood: 'the separate existence of an entity within reasonably coherent frontiers; and the fact that the entity is "not subject to the authority of any other State or group of States"'.[60] In this sense, independence involves many of the characteristics associated with the Western account of masculinity.

That capacity to enter into international relations depends upon the willingness of other states to allow particular interests an international voice is illustrated by the somewhat anomalous position of the Holy See. The territorial state of the Vatican City is governed by the Holy See, which is a non-member state maintaining a permanent observer mission to the UN.[61] The Holy See is regarded as the 'juridical personification' of the Roman Catholic Church.[62] It is a full member of some UN specialised agencies and some European intergovernmental organisations.[63] The Holy See receives and sends diplomatic representatives to other states. It can enter into treaties, address the UN General Assembly and participate as an associate member of the UN on the same basis as state delegations in UN conferences and meetings. It has exercised considerable influence within both the specialised agencies and at global conferences. For example, in 1996 it withdrew its contributions to UNICEF and waged a campaign to persuade other states to do likewise. It did so because UNICEF had signed on to a UN manual on women's needs in emergencies and refugee camps, which asserted the right to have access on the basis of free and voluntary choice to 'comprehensive information and services for reproductive health, including family planning and maternity'.[64] Similarly, the Holy See was the leader of a group of Catholic

[59] O. Schachter, 'Sovereignty – then and now', in R. Macdonald (ed.), *Essays in Honour of Wang Tieya* (Dordrecht, Martinus Nijhoff, 1994) 671 at 675.
[60] J. Crawford, above note 11 at 51–2.
[61] H. Cardinale, *The Holy See and the International Order* (Toronto, Macmillan, 1976) at 256–7; R. Jennings and A. Watts, above note 1 at 325–9.
[62] H. Cardinale, above note 61 at 115.
[63] *Ibid.* at 249–65.
[64] Y. Delph and K. Toner, 'First among equals', 18 *Conscience* (no. 3, 1997) 2.

states at the 1994 International Conference on Population and Development held in Cairo and at the 1995 Fourth World Conference on Women held in Beijing. The Holy See's influence was facilitated by the process of reaching consensus whereby one delegation is able to block, or threaten to block, a text with which it disagrees.[65] At both the Cairo and Beijing conferences, the Vatican combined forces with a number of Islamic states to resist recognition of women's sexual and reproductive rights and freedoms.[66] At the Diplomatic Conference in Rome in 1998 which adopted a statute for a permanent International Criminal Court, it was able to influence drafting on 'forced pregnancy' and the meaning of gender that signifed a step back from what was agreed at Beijing.[67] In the case of the Vatican, state acceptance thus gives a particular religious community privileged access to international fora.

Formal international status is not of course a prerequisite for international influence. Islam has no territorial or institutional centre comparable to the Holy See, but it nevertheless has significant leverage in the international community. Some Islamic leaders have asserted the irrelevance of state boundaries in upholding religious competence, for example the *fatwa* pronounced against Salman Rushdie for his portrait of Mohammed and Islam in *The Satanic Verses* and the use of *fatwas* against women authors, for example the Bangladeshi Taslima Nasreen.[68] The demands by Islamist groups for Nasreen's death for making allegations of the persecution of Bangladesh's Hindu minority caused her to flee her country in 1994. Such sentences of death are contrary to international law, particularly human rights norms relating to the right to a fair trial and to freedom of movement and expression.[69] As an assertion of extraterritorial criminal jurisdiction, the *fatwa* violates the sovereign rights of other states. At the same time, Islamic states invoke the argument of non-interference in domestic jurisdiction[70] to prevent international scrutiny of their compliance with international conventions, especially relating to the treatment of women.[71] Thus the Holy See uses the privileges of statehood to promote its agenda while the Islamic world can oscillate between claiming and ignoring the limitations of statehood to advance its interests.

---

[65] See chapter 3.

[66] H. Charlesworth, 'Women as sherpas: are global summits useful for women?', 22 *Feminist Studies* (1996) 537 at 542–3.

[67] Rome Statute for the International Criminal Court, 17 July 1998, UN Doc. A/CONF.183/9, reprinted in 37 *International Legal Materials* (1998) 999, articles 7(2)(f) and 7(3).

[68] See *Human Rights are Women's Right* (London, Amnesty International Publications, 1995) at 96.

[69] E.g. International Covenant on Civil and Political Rights, 16 December 1966, 993 UNTS 3, reprinted in 6 *International Legal Materials* (1967) 368, articles 12, 14 and 19.

[70] Charter of the UN, article 2(7).

[71] See discussion in chapter 4 on reservations.

Jus cogens

Modern international law has developed further criteria for statehood that move beyond the traditional requirements of factual effectiveness as a state. For example, James Crawford has argued that the doctrine of *jus cogens* in international law[72] affects statehood.[73] Thus, if a state-like entity comes into being in violation of a norm of *jus cogens*, it cannot claim statehood. One such norm that has been invoked in this context is the prohibition of race discrimination, and the examples of Southern Rhodesia and the Bantustans are referred to above. This raises the question of why race is considered an international legal concern in the context of statehood, but sex is not.

In chapter 1 we noted the limitations of the UN's approach to racism. Nevertheless, racial discrimination as state policy in South Africa has long been vociferously denounced within the UN, particularly in the General Assembly. After the onset of the process of decolonisation in the 1960s, which resulted in admission to UN membership of a great number of states whose populations were non-European, the entwined language of anti-colonialism and anti-racism became staple discourse in the General Assembly. One of the first specialised human rights treaties adopted by the UN was the International Convention on the Elimination of All Forms of Racial Discrimination[74] in 1965. The categories of economically developed and developing states almost completely mirrored the categories of United States/European and non-European populations and thus problems of inequality in wealth and resources became merged with concerns of racism. The linkage between colonialism and racism allowed states to take on the identity of their populations. Concerns of discrimination against groups or individuals because of their race were easily translated into concerns of discrimination against states themselves because of the race attributed to their populations, whatever the reality of racial mix. The charge of racism was applicable equally to economically advanced nations, which refused to make appropriate economic concessions to less developed nations, and to cases of discrimination against groups or individuals within states because of their race.

If the idea that states could be attributed with different races or religions has been accepted in some contexts, why has the sex of states not been recognised in international legal discourse? A partial answer is that discrimination on the basis of sex has never been understood by the international community of states to be as structured, serious or damaging as racism. It has never been proposed as a barrier to the creation of a state, even where there is an effective system of apartheid based on sex.[75] Discrimination against

[72] See further chapter 4.

[73] J. Crawford, above note 11 at 75–84.

[74] 21 December 1965, 660 UNTS 195, reprinted in 5 *International Legal Materials* (1966) 352.

[75] R. Cook, *The Elimination of Sexual Apartheid: Prospects for the Fourth World Conference on Women* (Washington DC, American Society of International Law, 1995).

women has been construed as natural and as a matter of individual concern, without any ramifications for the identity or nature of the state entity in which it occurs. The problem is sublimated because state entities are not understood to be discriminated against on the basis of their sex; indeed the concept of the sex of a state would not be understood, although the race of a state might be. Further, where there has been criticism of a state on the basis of its treatment of women, this has typically been construed as an attack on the particular religion and as interference with the right to express religious choice.[76]

The sex of the state

The sex of the state in international law is constructed through a process of opposition between female and male body types.[77] The notion of the independence and equality of states has been explicitly seen as analogous to manhood, in implicit contrast with the assumed dependence of womanhood.[78] Sometimes the state as the protector (man) guards its weaker people; at other times a vulnerable entity (woman) is protected by the men within it. One paradigm of the state is that it has clear boundaries, strong government and acts autonomously. It is contrasted with 'deviant' entities, such as groups without control over territory, colonised peoples or 'failed states', where although the government has lost authority, statehood is retained: no state has yet lost its membership of the UN through collapse into anarchy. Colonised peoples typically seek to achieve statehood, whereas failed states may be required to surrender their sovereignty while international powers determine their strategies for restoration of order and stability.[79] Thus when the Badinter Commission found that armed conflict between the elements of the Federation and lack of authority to observe cease-fire agreements meant that the former Yugoslavia was in 'the process of dissolution',[80] attention turned to the regulation of the formation of new states.

Another paradigm of the state is that of the nurturer of its people, who in turn will give their lives to defend it. The state is constructed as female when

---

[76] See chapter 4 on reservations and chapter 7 for a discussion of religious and cultural relativism.

[77] M. Davies, 'Taking the inside out: sex and gender in the legal subject', in N. Naffine and R. Owens, above note 30 at 25.

[78] '[J]ust as men may differ in strength, wealth and influence but are all equal and absolutely men, so sovereign states, big, little, and all, are equally and absolutely sovereign.' A. James, *Sovereign Statehood: The Basis of International Society* (London, Allen & Unwin, 1986) at 49.

[79] E.g. Dayton Peace Accords, annex 4: Constitution of Bosnia and Herzegovina, article 8.

[80] Badinter Arbitration Commission, European Community Conference on Yugoslavia, Opinion No. 1, 29 November 1991, reprinted in 92 *International Law Reports* 162.

it is attacked and in need of protection, and it depends on its (male) military to defend it.[81] The metaphor of rape is common when a state is invaded. Maternal imagery ('the mother country') can also be invoked to suggest the basic nurturing functions of a state. Saddam Hussein's famous threat of the 'mother of all battles' in the Gulf War in 1990 captures some of the paradoxical usages of femininity in protecting sovereignty. The state can likewise be constructed as male in the guise of the protector of its vulnerable population.[82] A variation on this story is that of the militarily strong male state coming to the rescue of the helpless female state.[83] The rhetoric of the Gulf War, for example, regularly depicted a vulnerable (female) Kuwait, ravished by the predatory (male) state of Iraq, being rescued by the virtuous masculine strength of the forces lead by the United States. At the same time, Iraq, in the person of its President, Saddam Hussein, was sometimes presented as having the 'female' traits of being capricious, irrational and temperamental in contrast to the sober, calculated behaviour of the allies.[84]

The male nature of the classic state is emphasised in studies of the notion of international security. For example, accepted security-seeking behaviour of states depends on notions of self-help, autonomy and power-seeking, attributes associated with manhood.[85] The ultimate basis of sovereignty is a state's ability to use force to defend its territory externally and its capacity to impose its rule by force internally.[86] This may require identifying certain of its inhabitants as imperilling the security of the state and therefore as being outside its legal protection.[87] The realist view of states has been described as one of 'primitive "individuals" separated from history and others by loner rights of sovereignty – backed up, for good measure, by military hardware – and involved in international conventions and institutions only on a voluntary basis'.[88] A similar, popular image is that of states as billiard

---

[81] J. Tickner, above note 33 at 129.

[82] *Ibid.*

[83] *Ibid.* at 133.

[84] On the rhetoric of the Gulf War see A. Farmanfarmaian, 'Did you measure up? The role of race and sexuality in the Gulf War', in C. Peters (ed.), *Collateral Damage: The 'New World Order' at Home and Abroad* (Boston, South End Press, 1992) 111; N. Chomsky, '"What we say goes": The Middle East in the New World Order', in *ibid.* at 49.

[85] J. Tickner, above note 33 at 125.

[86] A. James, above note 78 at 40–1.

[87] For an argument that the state is configured as heterosexual in that homosexuality is denoted by the state as a threat to its security and thus to its existence see M. Alexander, above note 23 at 6. See also V. Peterson and L. Parisi, 'Are women human? It's not an academic question', in T. Evans (ed.), *Human Rights Fifty Years On: A Reappraisal* (Manchester, Manchester University Press, 1998) 132 at 139–42 (describing how group reproduction and heterosexism are embedded in state-making).

[88] C. Sylvester, 'Feminists and realists view autonomy and obligation in international relations', in V. Peterson, *Gendered States*, above note 20 at 155, 157.

138

balls which knock haphazardly against each other and move on without leaving any imprint one on the other.

This version of statehood is in contrast to the view of the state created in the international economic system. The era of economic globalisation depends on the permeability of national boundaries and the subversion of distinctive national systems. The state may manipulate an image of sexualised and seductive femininity as an economic resource and thus promote state-sponsored sexism.[89] The shifting sexual identity of the state may result in contradictory images,[90] but its various identities accord with and reinforce complementary social 'realities' of womanhood and manhood. Differences between them are seen as 'natural'.

Recognition and statehood

Principles of recognition play an important, if contested, role in the international law of statehood.[91] We argue here that they also reinforce the 'male' character of the state. 'Recognition' of a state by other states or international institutions signifies its acceptance as a member of the international community. A distinction is drawn between recognition of states and recognition of governments, despite the close relationship between these concepts. International legal doctrine, however, formally maintains that the personality of the state is untouched by even radical changes in government.[92]

Recognition of statehood is generally regarded as a 'one-off' act. Once accorded, it continues even though the entity may later fail to meet even the minimal criteria set out in the Montevideo Convention.[93] The legal effect of an act of recognition is controversial. There is debate over whether recognition is constitutive or declaratory. The former implies that recognition by other states is an essential element of the claim to statehood; the latter that it is simply a political act that does not affect the true legal status of the

[89] G. Heng, '"A great way to fly": nationalism, the state, and varieties of third-world feminism', in M. Alexander and C. Mohanty (eds), *Feminist Genealogies, Colonial Legacies, Democratic Futures* (London, Routledge, 1997) 30.

[90] Indeed Edward Morgan has described the international law image of the state as a hermaphrodite: 'The hermaphroditic paradigm of international law: a comment on *Alvarez-Machain*', *Proceedings of the Canadian Council on International Law* (Ottawa, Canadian Council on International Law, 1992) 78.

[91] See generally H. Lauterpacht, *Recognition in International Law* (Cambridge, Cambridge University Press, 1948); J. Dugard, *Recognition and the United Nations* (Cambridge, Grotius Publications, 1987); I. Brownlie, *Principles of Public International Law* (Oxford, Clarendon Press, 5th edn 1998) at 85–104.

[92] J. Crawford, above note 11 at 28–9.

[93] Somalia from 1992 is an example of a state with no effective government, which is still assumed to maintain its statehood. See *Republic of Somalia v. Woodhouse Drake and Carey Suisse S.A.* [1993] Q.B. 54.

state in question. One asserted concomitant of the constitutive theory of recognition is that recognition becomes a legal duty if an entity fulfils the criteria for statehood.[94] By contrast, the declaratory theory of recognition contemplates considerable political discretion in state action with respect to recognition.[95]

State practice has generally favoured the declaratory view of recognition. However, the international community has occasionally responded collectively to claims of statehood when imposing a duty of non-recognition through Security Council resolutions, as for example in the cases of South West Africa/Namibia,[96] Southern Rhodesia,[97] the Turkish occupation of Northern Cyprus and subsequent assertion of the Turkish Republic of Northern Cyprus,[98] the Bantustans and the Iraqi invasion of Kuwait.[99] These cases all involved international illegality because of racism or the use of force. Although institutionalised governmental discrimination on the basis of race or ethnicity may prevent international recognition of new states, the case of South Africa shows that it will not result in the status of statehood being withdrawn.

Recognition practice in the case of the states formed from the former Yugoslavia and the Soviet Union indicates a curious fusion of both constitutive and declaratory approaches. In 1991, the EC had to determine its response to events in those states in the light of their continuing upheaval and disintegration, and its recognition of new entities was crucial in constituting them as states. The EC response to this issue of recognition was unusual in that it amounted to an institutional or communal formulation of uniform conditions before a series of unilateral acts of recognition.[100] It agreed on Guidelines on the Recognition of New States in Eastern Europe and in the Soviet Union that required, among other things:

> respect for the provisions of the Charter of the United Nations and the commitments subscribed to in the Final Act of Helsinki and in the Charter of Paris especially with regard to the rule of law, democracy and human rights
> . . .

---

[94] H. Lauterpacht, above note 91 at 6.

[95] *Tinoco Arbitration* (Great Britain v. Costa Rica) 1 Reports of the International Arbitral Awards (1923) 369.

[96] *Legal Consequences for States of the Continued Presence of South Africa in South West Africa (Namibia)* 1971 ICJ Rep. 16 (Adv. Op. 21 June) at 54, 56.

[97] In 1965 the Security Council demanded non-recognition of Southern Rhodesia as a state: SC Res. 216, 217, 20 UN SCOR Resolutions and Decisions S/INF/20/ Rev. 1 1965.

[98] SC Res. 541, 18 November 1983; SC Res. 550, 11 May 1984.

[99] The Security Council called upon states not to recognise the Iraqi annexation of Kuwait: SC Res. 662, 9 August 1990.

[100] See C. Warbrick, 'Recognition of states: recent European practice', in M. Evans (ed.), *Aspects of Statehood and Institutionalism in Contemporary Europe* (Aldershot, Dartmouth Publishing Co., 1997) 9.

and

guarantees for the rights of ethnic and national groups and minorities in accordance with the commitments subscribed to in the framework of the Conference on Security and Cooperation in Europe [now the Organisation for Security and Cooperation in Europe].[101]

The Guidelines made explicit higher standards for these new states than simply meeting the Montevideo criteria for statehood. Conformity with the Guidelines was determined by an Arbitration Commission established by the EC, the Badinter Commission, for those entities that applied for recognition as states. In fact, the commitment to performance in accordance with the Guidelines demanded by the EC was minimal and little attempt was made to ensure compliance.[102] Although individual states' acts of recognition were made on essentially political criteria and without strict regard for the opinions of the Badinter Commission, the acts of recognition of the former republics by member states of the EC were critical in constituting them as states.[103] Serbia and Montenegro, claiming to form the residual state of Yugoslavia, did not seek recognition and thus were not called upon to demonstrate even a formal commitment to the Guidelines. Serbia and Montenegro were, however, denied the right to succeed to the membership of the former Republic of Yugoslavia in the UN in a form of collective response to their role in the violence that surrounded the disintegration and dissolution of the former Yugoslavia.[104]

Recognition of governments, the acknowledgment by the executive that a particular regime can claim governmental authority in a state and will be so treated by the recognising state, is in issue in cases of an unconstitutional accession to power. In all other cases it is assumed that successive governments are legitimate. Many states have now abandoned the policy of recognition of governments, thereby avoiding complex political decisions about the level of formal approval to be offered a new regime.[105] A necessary condition for the recognition of a government is that it is in reasonably permanent 'effective control' of a state. Once this criterion is achieved to the satisfaction of the recognising state, state practice indicates considerable individual discretion in deciding whether or not to accord recognition to a

---

[101] 16 December 1991, reprinted in 62 *British Yearbook of International Law* (1991) 559. See generally R. Rich, 'Recognition of states: the collapse of Yugoslavia and the Soviet Union', 4 *European Journal of International Law* (1993) 36.

[102] R. Rich, above note 101 at 47–54.

[103] *Ibid.* at 55–6.

[104] *Ibid.* at 53–4. See *Case Concerning the Application of the Genocide Convention* (Bosnia and Herzegovina v. Yugoslavia) (Provisional Measures) 1993 ICJ Rep. 3 (Order of 8 April).

[105] See B. Weston, R. Falk and H. Charlesworth, *International Law and World Order* (St Paul, West Group, 3rd edn 1997) at 266–7.

regime.[106] State practice with respect to recognition of governments reveals that in some contexts institutionalised racial discrimination has been regarded as a barrier to recognition of a government.[107] However, concern with institutionalised discrimination against women has been much rarer. When the Taliban movement asserted power in much of Afghanistan in 1996–97, it forced women out of the paid workforce, imposed upon them strict dress codes and severely limited educational opportunities for girls and young women. The aim of these moves was said to be the creation of the world's purest Islamic state. While some countries recognised the Taliban government in 1997,[108] others did not. The United States, for example, stated that it would not recognise the Taliban because of 'their approach to human rights . . . their despicable treatment of women and children and their lack of respect for human dignity'.[109] It is unclear whether concern about the situation of women will be incorporated into any peace negotiations in Afghanistan. The UN Special Mission to Afghanistan has not indicated that the restrictions upon women's lives are relevant to the peace process itself, simply calling for an embargo on foreign arms supplies and for the establishment of a 'broad-based' government.[110]

Generally, notions of recognition in international law operate to ensure that members of the international community resemble each other, in a manner reminiscent of the practices of a men's club. Once an entity is accepted as a state, there is no further scrutiny of its status. Rules of recognition allow new claimants access to the exclusive privileges of statehood provided they do not overstep the accepted limits. The outer limits of variation appear to be the overtly racist origins of a state, the illegal use of force, the establishment of a 'puppet' regime[111] or some combination of these. Other factors, such as institutional discrimination against women, do

[106] M. Peterson, *Recognition of Governments: Legal Doctrine and State Practice* (New York, St Martin's Press, 1997) at 28.

[107] E.g. recognition of the Rabuka government in Fiji, which came to power in 1987 through a military coup, was affected by its alterations to the Fijian Constitution that gave privileges to the indigenous Fijian population at the expense of Fijians of Indian descent. See J. Bush, 'Defining group rights and delineating sovereignty: a case from the Republic of Fiji', 14 *American University International Law Review* (1999) 735.

[108] Pakistan, Saudi Arabia and the United Arab Emirates.

[109] S. Erlanger, 'In Pakistan, Albright denounces Afghan regime', *New York Times*, 19 November 1997.

[110] See the Report of the UN Secretary-General on Afghanistan, November 1997, available at http://www.unhchr.ch/html/menu4/garep/garep52.htm. Compare the views of the CHR's Special Rapporteur on Afghanistan, Dr Karmal Hossain in UN Doc. E/CN.4/1999/40, 24 March 1999.

[111] E.g. the non-recognition of the Heng Samrin government established in Kampuchea after the invasion by Vietnam in 1979. See C. Warbrick, 'The new British policy on recognition of governments', 30 *International and Comparative Law Quarterly* (1981) 568.

not impinge significantly on recognition practice and cause little disadvantage to the state in question. States built upon a system of sex discrimination have no particular identity in international law. Thus it is of little significance with respect to statehood that a particular nation state denies basic political rights to women, such as the right to vote or to participate in public life. It is correspondingly more difficult to describe and represent women's concerns in the vocabulary of statehood.

State jurisdiction

One of the incidents of statehood is the capacity to assert judicial, legislative and administrative jurisdiction over territory and nationals.[112] States have considerable discretion in the exercise of jurisdiction. While there has been extensive investigation of the way male perspectives have been built into the laws and practices of particular states,[113] traditional international law has little concern with this form of systemic injustice, except for the often modest restraints of human rights law.[114] Here we focus on aspects of jurisdiction that have an immediately international dimension.

One major issue in state jurisdiction is whether jurisdiction can be asserted beyond the accepted bases of territory and nationality.[115] Jurisdiction has been claimed by some states on the basis of the effects of extra-territorial behaviour. For example, the United States has legislated to make anti-competitive behaviour that affects United States' markets illegal, whether or not it is illegal in the state where it occurs.[116] Assertions of extra-territorial jurisdiction have typically been based upon concerns about local economic consequences of behaviour. The United States also uses extra-territorial jurisdiction to assert its political interests abroad.[117] However, there has not been a parallel concern with the social implications of overseas activities.

The growth of 'sex tourism' since the 1970s, particularly in South-East Asia, raises this issue. Mass tourism has encouraged the growth of an industry catering to the tourist demand for sexual services that are often illegal in tourist-producing countries. Local laws prohibiting sexual exploitation of

---

[112] I. Brownlie, above note 91 at 301.

[113] E.g. R. Graycar and J. Morgan, *The Hidden Gender of Law* (Annandale, Federation Press, 1990).

[114] See chapter 7.

[115] See Harvard Research Draft Convention on Jurisdiction with Respect to Crime,1935, 29 *American Journal of International Law* (1935) Supp.; V. Lowe (ed.), *Extraterritorial Jurisdiction: An Annotated Collection of Legal Materials* (Cambridge, Grotius Publications, 1983).

[116] See I. Brownlie, above note 91 at 310–12; M. Shaw, *International Law* (Cambridge, Cambridge University Press, 4th edn 1997) at 483–90.

[117] V. Lowe, 'U.S. extraterritorial jurisdiction: the *Helms-Burton* and *D'Amato* Acts', 46 *International and Comparative Law Quarterly* (1997) 378.

children are inadequately enforced and child prostitution has burgeoned in South-East Asia.[118] Some countries have responded to this phenomenon with a limited assertion of extra-territorial jurisdiction designed to criminalise sexual activity with minors that occurs overseas. For example, Australia has extended its criminal laws to sexual activity with minors overseas, although the law is restricted in scope because it applies only to Australian citizens or permanent residents.[119]

Another ground for the exercise of state jurisdiction extra-territorially is the principle of universal jurisdiction which contemplates the assertion of jurisdiction over non-nationals on the grounds that their acts were so heinous that international public policy requires that they be tried wherever they are found.[120] Hijacking and trafficking in narcotics are often included in this class.[121] One category of offences that undoubtedly attract universal jurisdiction is 'grave breaches' of international humanitarian law. 'Grave breaches' are defined in the four Geneva Conventions of 1949 and Protocol I of 1977 to cover what are considered to be the most serious violations of the treaties.[122] It is striking that the treaties do not include within the category of grave breaches violations of provisions explicitly protecting women.[123] By contrast, a draft Optional Protocol to the UN Convention on the Rights of the Child requires states to give effect to the principle of universal criminal jurisdiction with respect to sexual exploitation of children.[124] Developments in extending extra-territorial jurisdiction indicate how existing principles of criminal jurisdiction can be used to prosecute those who commit crimes against women.

The potential of civil jurisdiction to enforce the law of nations has been explored through a series of cases brought before United States courts.

---

[118] Report of the Working Group on Contemporary Forms of Slavery on its Fourteenth Session, UN Doc. E/CN 4/Sub 2/1089/39, 28 August 1989, para. 32.

[119] Crimes (Child Sex Tourism) Amendment Act 1994 (Cth). See also Penal Code chapter 2 para. 2 (Sweden); Child Sexual Abuse Prevention Act, 1994, 18 U.S.C. § 2423(b). See M. Healy, 'The extraterritorial prosecution of child sex tourists', 10 *Interights Bulletin* (1996) 161.

[120] I. Brownlie, above note 91 at 307–9; J. Murphy, 'International crimes', in O. Schachter and C. Joyner (eds), *United Nations Legal Order* (Cambridge, Cambridge University Press, 1995) vol. 2, 993.

[121] See I. Brownlie, above note 91 at 308.

[122] E.g. Geneva Convention Relative to the Protection of Civilian Persons in Time of War, 12 August 1949, 75 UNTS 287, article 147; Protocol Additional to the Geneva Conventions of 12 August 1949, and Relating to the Protection of Victims of International Armed Conflicts, 10 June 1977, 1125 UNTS 3, article 85.

[123] J. Gardam, 'Women and the law of armed conflict: why the silence?', 46 *International and Comparative Law Quarterly* (1997) 55. See further chapter 10.

[124] See Commission on Human Rights, Question of a draft optional protocol to the Convention on the Rights of the Child on the sale of children, child prostitution and child pornography, as well as the basic measures needed for their eradication, Report of the Working Group on its Fourth Session, UN Doc. E/CN.4/1998/103, 24 March 1998, article 2(a).

Claims have been made under the Alien Tort Claims Act of 1790[125] and the Torture Victim Protection Act of 1991[126] of violations of human rights committed abroad against non-United States nationals where service can be entered in the United States to commence proceedings.[127] In *Kadic v. Karadzic*[128] Croat and Muslim Bosnian women who claimed that they had been subject to systematic rape and forced impregnation and other atrocities by Bosnian Serb forces during the conflict in the Bosnia and Herzegovina in the early 1990s filed tort actions for 'genocide, rape, forced prostitution and impregnation, torture and other cruel, inhuman and degrading treatment, assault and battery, sex and ethnic inequality, summary execution and wrongful death' committed in Bosnia and Herzegovina, against Radovan Karadzic, leader of the self-styled Republika Srpska. Civil jurisdiction cannot result in any punishment, but the impact of a default judgment (typically for millions of dollars) against the defendant restricts access to the United States and validates the victims' accounts of crimes committed against them. Similar cases filed against corporate entities may be instrumental in ensuring corporate responsibility for actions committed abroad, including violations of the rights of women.[129]

Immunity from jurisdiction

A state's exercise of civil and criminal jurisdiction is limited by the principles of state and diplomatic immunity. Foreign state immunity is based on the notion of equality of states and requires that the courts of one state not adjudicate on the rights of another state.[130] The doctrine has been refined in many states to apply only to acts of government (*jure imperii*) and to exclude commercial activities (*jure gestionis*).[131] Its scope is nevertheless relatively

---

[125] Alien Tort Claims Act, 28 U.S.C. § 1350.
[126] Torture Victim Protection Act, 28 U.S.C. § 1350.
[127] The landmark case was *Filartiga v. Pena-Irala* 630 F. 2d 876 (2d Cir. 1980).
[128] 70 F. 3rd 232 (2d Cir. 1995).
[129] E.g. in *Doe v. Unocal Corp. et al.* 963 F. Supp. 880 (CD Cal. 1997) a civil action was brought against Unocal for violations of human rights, including rape, violence and enslavement of local farmers in furtherance of Unocal's joint venture with a state-owned company in Myanmar (Burma) for gas lines.
[130] *The Schooner Exchange v. McFadden* (1812) 7 Cranch 116.
[131] I. Brownlie, above note 91 at 329–32. In many states restrictive immunity has been adopted by legislation. See e.g. Foreign States Immunities Act 1976 (US), reprinted in 15 *International Legal Materials* (1976) 1388; State Immunity Act 1978 (UK); Foreign States Immunities Act 1985 (Cth) (Australia). There is no international treaty on the subject but see the European Convention on State Immunity, 1972, reprinted in 11 *International Legal Materials* (1972) 470; Inter-American Draft Convention on Jurisdictional Immunity of States, reprinted in 22 *International Legal Materials* (1983) 292.

wide because national courts have accepted an immunity argument when made by a head of state for a wide range of activities. This issue was also raised in the case of *Kadic v. Karadzic*. One of Karadzic's responses to the action was that he was entitled to immunity from suit on the basis that he was an invitee of the UN at the time that he was served with the papers. The United States Federal Court rejected Karadzic's assertion of immunity as an invitee. It accepted, however, that had Karadzic been head of a state recognised by the United States, he would have been able to assert immunity successfully. In *Al-Adsani v. Government of Kuwait* the United Kingdom Court of Appeal upheld a plea of immunity to jurisdiction in a claim alleging torture in a state security prison.[132] However, in November 1998 the House of Lords rejected a claim of state immunity to arrest and extradition proceedings to Spain on charges of torture, hostage taking and conspiracy made on behalf of the former Head of State of Chile, General Pinochet.[133] The majority of the House of Lords held that acts of torture and hostage taking could not be regarded as official functions of a head of state and therefore were not protected by immunity within the terms of the relevant legislation.[134]

The principle of diplomatic immunity is based on the same respect for the equality of states as foreign sovereign immunity but it can be claimed only by a specific category of persons – accredited diplomats[135] – the vast majority of whom are still men.[136] Diplomatic immunity is said to ensure the efficient functioning of the diplomatic process and the promotion of friendly relations between states.[137] Although they do not perform diplomatic functions, consuls are publicly recognised as agents of the sending states and are accordingly allowed some privileges and immunities in pursuit of their official business.[138] The vocabulary of diplomatic immunity depends on bounded imagery. Thus the notion of 'inviolability' – the protection of the diplomatic person from action or constraint – is central to the law of diplomatic immun-

---

[132] 12 March 1995, 107 International Law Reports 536 (1995).

[133] *R. v. Bow Street Metropolitan Stipendiary Magistrate*, ex parte *Pinochet Uguarte (no. 1)* [1998] 3 WLR 1456 (HL), reprinted in 37 *International Legal Materials* (1998) 1302; *R. v. Bow Street Stipendiary Magistrate*, ex parte *Pinochet Ugarte (no. 3)* [1999] 2 WLR 827 (HL), reprinted in 38 *International Legal Materials* (1999) 430.

[134] State Immunity Act 1978 section 20; Diplomatic Privileges Act 1964 section 39.2.

[135] Vienna Convention on Diplomatic Relations, 18 April 1961, 500 UNTS 95.

[136] C. Enloe, *Bananas, Beaches, and Bases: Making Feminist Sense of International Politics* (London, Pandora Press, 1989) at 93. On the history of the inclusion of women within the United Kingdom diplomatic service see *Women in Diplomacy The FCO 1782–1994* (London, Historical Branch LRD, 1994).

[137] J. Barker, *The Abuse of Diplomatic Privileges and Immunities: A Necessary Evil?* (Aldershot, Dartmouth Publishing Company, 1996) at 229.

[138] Vienna Convention on Consular Relations, 24 April 1963, 596 UNTS 261.

ity.[139] This point was made in a striking way by a diplomat, enraged at the determination of the New York police to enforce parking fines incurred by diplomats. He said: 'Diplomatic immunity is like virginity. Either you have it or you do not. I have never seen half a virgin.'[140]

Diplomatic immunity has been regularly invoked to avoid the application of the receiving state's criminal laws to diplomatic personnel in a number of cases involving sexual abuse of women, including offences committed by members of the family of the diplomatic agent.[141] One consequence of the protection of the diplomatic family from legal proceedings is that no action can be taken between family members to remedy, for example, violence within the home or to assert rights to custody of children.[142]

The utility of the immunity argument in preventing scrutiny of men's domination of women has been well described by Catharine MacKinnon. She has argued that the ideology of sovereignty supports patriarchal systems:

> Immunities govern and mark every level of this sovereignty scheme. Marital immunity has governed the family . . . Familiarity immunity still de facto governs acquaintance or intimate relations. Official immunity protects state actors within states. Sovereign immunity protects them in the law of nations.[143]

The unacknowledged dependence of governments in their international affairs on women's support, work and sexuality has been noted in chapter 2. The international law of immunity sustains the invisibility of women in this area and reinforces the notion of the impermeability of statehood and its recognised agents. The major inroads into the principle of the absolute immunity of the state and its agents has been in the name of commercial enterprise, leaving untouched the structures of domination and subordination within the state.

---

[139] J. Barker, above note 137 at 230–2.

[140] Quoted in 'Diplomats driven to distraction', *Guardian Weekly*, 13 April 1997, 16.

[141] Vienna Convention on Diplomatic Relations, article 37. See C. Ashman and P. Trescott, *Outrage: The Abuse of Diplomatic Immunity* (London, Star Books, 1986) at 58–87, 153–68.

[142] E.g. *Re P (Children Act: Diplomatic Immunity)* [1998] 1 Family Law Reports 624 (holding that diplomatic immunity prevented a mother bringing proceedings against her husband, an American diplomat, with respect to removal of the children from the jurisdiction); *Re P (Diplomatic Immunity: Jurisdiction)* [1998] 1 Family Law Reports 1026 (diplomatic immunity did not apply as the husband had ceased to be a diplomat and removal of the children was not part of his official functions but state immunity did apply as the removal was ordered by the government and accordingly an act of a governmental nature).

[143] C. MacKinnon, remarks in *Contemporary International Law Issues: New Forms, New Applications* (The Hague, Nederlandse Vereniging voor Internationaal Recht, 1997) 152.

State responsibility

Another incident of statehood is that of state responsibility.[144] The principles of state responsibility allocate liability for breach of an obligation imposed by international law. The centrality of the state to the international legal system is reflected in the law on responsibility: a breach of international law must be linked to a state in order for it to be justiciable in the international system.[145] The traditional rules of state responsibility have provided a number of obstacles to the recognition of women's concerns as issues of international law.

One major obstacle is the confinement of responsibility to particular activities of a state. The law of state responsibility distinguishes 'public' actions for which the state is accountable from those 'private' ones for which it does not have to answer internationally. Thus the conduct of persons not acting on the state's behalf, or which is not attributable to the state, generally is not considered an act of the state.[146] This distinction between public and private has significant repercussions for women. As discussed in chapters 3 and 7, the most widespread violence sustained by women around the world occurs in the 'private' sphere, particularly the home. This violence is typically not regarded as an international legal issue, even if the violence is tolerated by a legal and political system that provides inadequate remedies to the victims of violence.

A study of violence against women in Brazil showed how the doctrine of responsibility could be applied to incidents of domestic violence. It documented the ways in which both the substantive criminal law and the administration of the criminal justice system combined to provide effective impunity to men who murdered, assaulted or raped their partners.[147] Although over 70 per cent of reported cases of violence against women in Brazil took place in the home (compared to 10 per cent for men), domestic violence was treated either as a minor problem or simply as being outside the criminal justice system. In the case of wife murder, a defence of 'honour', dependent on an allegation that the wife had been unfaithful, operated in some

---

[144] See generally I. Brownlie, *State Responsibility* (Oxford, Clarendon Press, 1983); M. Spinedi and B. Simma (eds), *UN Codification of State Responsibility* (New York, Oceana Publications, 1987).

[145] ILC, Draft Articles on State Responsibility, provisionally adopted by the ILC on first reading, Report of the ILC on the Work of its Forty-eighth Session, UN Doc. A/CN.4/L.528/Add. 2, 16 July 1996, article 11. At its fiftieth session the ILC Drafting Committee indicated the proposed deletion of article 11: UN Doc. A/CN.4/L.569, 4 August 1998.

[146] ILC, Draft Articles on State Responsibility, articles 3 (imputability) and 14 (acts of insurrectional movements). At its fiftieth session the ILC Drafting Committee also indicated deletion of article 14.

[147] America's Watch, *Criminal Injustice: Violence against Women in Brazil* (New York, Human Rights Watch, 1991).

regions to exonerate a husband in 80 per cent of cases in which it was invoked.[148]

The study concluded that Brazil should be held internationally responsible for the situation because there was a discriminatory pattern of state responses to crimes of violence based on the sex of the victim. The international norm of non-discrimination had thus been violated.[149] The failure of the legislative, executive and judicial branches of the state to ensure the prevention, investigation and punishment of violence against women should incur international legal responsibility.[150] While reliance on the norm of discrimination may be useful in modifying the traditional law of state responsibility with respect to women, the principle of 'equal treatment' of women and men may be inadequate to deal with social structures that support violence against women. There is no reason why the maintenance of a legal and social system in which violence against women is endemic and accepted should not engage state responsibility directly, whether or not women are treated differently from men in this respect.

A number of techniques for broadening the basis for state responsibility are offered by decisions of regional human rights courts. In *Costello–Roberts v. U.K.*[151] the ECHR accepted that the state could be responsible for violations of human rights committed within private schools. In this sense a public/private distinction in education establishments did not relieve the state of its obligations under the European Convention on Human Rights.[152] The European Court found the Netherlands to be in breach of the Convention in *X & Y v. The Netherlands*[153] because its criminal law provided no remedy for a mentally disabled girl who had been sexually abused. The Court held that the protection of human rights imposed positive obligations on states and may require laws governing 'private' relations between individuals.[154] In *Velasquez Rodriguez v. Honduras*,[155] a case dealing with the 'disappearance' of a political activist, the Inter-American Court of Human Rights spoke of 'the duty of the States Parties [to the American Convention

---

[148] *Ibid.* at 4. Husband murder in parallel circumstances was treated as being considerably more serious. *Ibid.* at 35.

[149] *Ibid.* at 4.

[150] R. Cook, 'State accountability under the Women's Convention', in R. Cook (ed.), *Human Rights of Women: National and International Perspectives* (Philadelphia, University of Pennsylvania Press, 1994) 228 at 244–51.

[151] 19 EHRR 112 (1993).

[152] European Convention for the Protection of Human Rights and Fundamental Freedoms, 4 November 1950, 213 UNTS 221.

[153] 91 ECHR (ser. A) (1985).

[154] E.g. in *Airey v. Ireland* 32 ECHR (ser. A) (1979), the European Court required the state to take positive action to ensure enjoyment of human rights, in this case legal aid, to enable a woman to seek a judicial separation.

[155] Inter-American Court of Human Rights (ser. C) no. 4 (1988), reprinted in 28 *International Legal Materials* (1989) 294.

on Human Rights[156]] to organise the governmental apparatus and, in general, all the structures through which public power is exercised, so that they are capable of juridically ensuring the free and full enjoyment of human rights'. It went on to say:

> An illegal act which violates human rights and which is initially not directly attributable to a State (for example, because it is the act of a private person . . .) can lead to international responsibility of the State, not because of the act itself, but because of the lack of due diligence to prevent the violation or to respond to it . . . This duty to prevent includes all those means of a legal, political, administrative and cultural nature that promote the protection of human rights and ensure that any violations are considered and treated as illegal acts.[157]

In *Osman v. United Kingdom*[158] the ECHR also held that the right to life requires the state to take preventive, operational measures to protect an individual from the criminal acts of another person. The case concerned the stalking of a child and his family by an obsessed schoolteacher. Despite apparently strong indications of the degree of obsession, the Court found that the police did not at any decisive stage know, or have reason to know, that the lives of the child and his family were at risk. The Court held that in order to show violation of a positive obligation, the applicant must show that the authorities did not do all that could be reasonably expected of them in the particular circumstances to avoid the risk. In the context of violence against women, the concealed nature of many acts of domestic violence committed by men who otherwise do not appear to pose any threat may make it difficult to establish such failure.

These are significant statements of states' duties to extend human rights protection beyond the 'public' sphere. They indicate that inadequate laws regulating the 'private' sphere, a particular or systemic failure to enforce existing laws or a bias against women in the administration of justice, can entail state responsibility.[159] The Inter-American Convention on the Prevention, Punishment and Eradication of Violence Against Women contains explicit treaty provisions to this effect in the context of violence against women.[160] In cases where state responsibility for 'private' harm is not explicit, Rebecca Cook has proposed a number of ways in which the scope of

---

[156] 22 November 1969, 36 OASTS, 1114 UNTS 123.

[157] *Velasquez Rodriguez v. Honduras*, above note 155 at paras 172–5.

[158] ECHR (87/1997/871/1083), 28 October 1998.

[159] A. Ewing, 'Establishing state responsibility for private acts of violence against women under the American Convention on Human Rights', 26 *Columbia Human Rights Law Review* (1995) 751 at 787–91. See also X. Li, 'License to coerce: violence against women, state responsibility, and legal failures in China's family planning program', 8 *Yale Journal of Law and Feminism* (1996) 145.

[160] 9 June 1994, reprinted in 33 *International Legal Materials* (1994) 1535, article 7.

the traditional rules of state responsibility may be expanded.[161] Links must be established between the disadvantages women face and the exercise of power by states: 'States must be answerable for their acts and omissions, their initiatives, and their maintenance of the *status quo* despite evidence of pervasive inequality.'[162] Cook's methodology involves describing the situation of women in terms of international human rights standards, in particular evidence of systemic discrimination, and then identifying the state's duties of prevention and redress both in customary and conventional international law.[163]

The law of state responsibility can thus be interpreted in a progressive way to increase its relevance to women. Its focus on the liability of individual states is both an advantage and a disadvantage. The notion of individual state responsibility can be used to place pressure on a particular state to improve its response to assertions of women's rights. At the same time, the notion is inadequate in capturing the global nature of the domination of women, and the way that international society reinforces this.

Self-determination in international law

The principle of self-determination is an important aspect of the international law of statehood.[164] It has both 'internal' and 'external' dimensions: a sovereign state is in theory built on the self-determination of its population in the sense that the people should determine the way that government is organised; and the principle can also allow a particular group to reject claims of jurisdiction by other states and assert its own status as a state. In this sense, it provides a gloss on the notions of state sovereignty, the equality of states and non-intervention.[165]

The right to self-determination

The legal right to self-determination attaches to peoples or groups and allows them 'to choose for themselves a form of political organisation and their

[161] R. Cook, 'State responsibility for violations of women's human rights', 7 *Harvard Human Rights Journal* (1994) 125; R. Cook, 'Accountability in international law for violations of women's rights by non-state actors', in D. Dallmeyer (ed.), *Reconceiving Reality: Women and International Law* (Washington DC, American Society of International Law, 1993) 93.

[162] R. Cook, 'State responsibility for violations of women's human rights', above note 161 at 137.

[163] See also C. Romany, 'State responsibility goes private: a feminist critique of the public/private distinction in international human rights law', in R. Cook, *Human Rights of Women*, above note 150 at 85, 96–106.

[164] See R. Higgins, *Problems and Process: International Law and How We Use It* (Oxford, Clarendon Press, 1994) at 111; A. Cassese, *Self-Determination of Peoples* (Cambridge, Cambridge University Press, 1995).

[165] I. Brownlie, above note 91 at 602.

relation to other groups'.[166] It has been a focus of the General Assembly since 1960.[167] The right is given prominence in article 1 of both the UN Covenants on Human Rights.[168]

> All peoples have the right of self-determination. By virtue of that right they freely determine their political status and freely pursue their economic, social and cultural development.

The right also embraces disposition and control over natural resources, and the right not to be deprived of the means of sustenance. The linkage of the right to self-determination to the entire spectrum of political, civil, economic, social and cultural rights contained within the two Covenants emphasises its importance in international law.

Controversy surrounds self-determination as an international legal principle. It has been argued that it only properly applies to situations of colonial rule or foreign domination and is almost obsolete.[169] Particularly if manifested as a claim of secession, self-determination challenges the notion of territorial integrity and the international community has been slow to support claims made outside a European colonial context.[170] Thus although their claim to self-determination has been upheld by the ICJ,[171] the Saharawi people have not been able to free themselves from Moroccan control.[172] The practical application of the international law notion of self-determination has also been problematic in the context of claims by indigenous peoples.[173]

There are also a number of areas of contention in the doctrine of self-determination. One is the identification of the unit of self-determination – the definition of 'peoples' which may legitimately claim the right. Recognised criteria include ethnic and cultural particularity.[174] Subsequent difficulties

[166] *Ibid.* at 599.

[167] Declaration on the Granting of Independence to Colonial Territories and Peoples, GA Res. 1514 (XV), 14 December 1960. The Resolution builds upon the Charter of the UN, article 1(2).

[168] International Covenant on Civil and Political Rights, article 1; International Covenant on Economic, Social and Cultural Rights, 16 December 1966, 999 UNTS 3, reprinted in 6 *International Legal Materials* (1967) 360, article 1. See also African Charter on Human and Peoples' Rights, 26 June 1981, reprinted in 21 *International Legal Materials* (1982) 58, article 20.

[169] See D. Cass, 'Re-thinking self-determination: a critical analysis of current international law theories,' 18 *Syracuse Journal of International and Comparative Law* (1992) 21.

[170] This is emphasised by GA Res. 1514 which states in para. 6 that any attempt aimed at the partial or total disruption of territorial integrity of a state is incompatible with the UN Charter.

[171] *Western Sahara Case* 1975 ICJ Rep. 12 (Adv. Op. 16 October).

[172] See further chapter 8.

[173] See J. Crawford (ed.), *The Rights of Peoples* (Oxford, Clarendon Press, 1988); Draft Declaration on the Rights of Indigenous Peoples, 26 August 1994, UN Doc. E/CN.4/1995/2, E/CN.4/Sub.2/1994/2/56, 28 October 1994, reprinted in 34 *International Legal Materials* (1995) 541, article 3.

[174] GA Res. 1541 (XV).

may be caused by the need to identify who belongs within a group claiming the right to self-determination, who has the right to determine membership of the group and who speaks on behalf of the group. The basis of inclusion or exclusion may be challenged from within the group, by another group or by an individual wishing to assert or deny membership. Such challenges may reveal clashes of values or human rights violations in the denial of personal choice.[175] Tensions between the competing claims of individuals, representatives of the group and those of one or more established sovereign states may result.

Another contentious aspect in international law is the political arrangement that satisfies the right to self-determination. Self-determination is not synonymous with independence and may be achieved through other freely chosen political structures, for example through integration with an existing state or a form of free association.[176] Whatever form of arrangement is agreed, achievement of the right to self-determination has often been regarded as a single event. Once 'external' self-determination, that is freedom from foreign domination and control, has been gained, international protection of rights within the self-determined unit legally rests upon human rights guarantees and provisions for the protection of minorities.[177] A distinction has also been drawn between 'internal' and 'external' self-determination to indicate the right of a people to develop forms of governance within an existing state structure.[178]

It has been argued that there is an emerging international norm of a right to democratic governance.[179] Such a right is said to derive from a right to

---

[175] E.g. *Lovelace v. Canada* Communication no. 24/197 (1986), UN Doc. CCPR/C/OP/1 at 83. The case was brought under the first Optional Protocol to the International Covenant on Civil and Political Rights, 16 December 1966, 999 UNTS 171, reprinted in 6 *International Legal Materials* (1967) 383. The complainant was a member of the Maliseet Indian tribe who, under tribal law, had lost her right to live on the Tobique Indian reservation upon her marriage to a non-Indian. The Human Rights Committee held that this violated article 27 of the Covenant which guarantees persons belonging to minorities the right, in community with other members of their group, to enjoy their own culture. See further chapter 7.

[176] GA Res. 1541 (XV). The Resolution stresses that free association should be the 'result of a free and voluntary choice by the Peoples of the territory concerned expressed through informed and democratic processes'. Integration too must be freely chosen.

[177] E.g. International Covenant on Civil and Political Rights, article 27; Council of Europe Framework Convention for the Protection of National Minorities, 1 February 1995, reprinted in 34 *International Legal Materials* (1995) 351.

[178] On the concept of internal self-determination see A. Cassese, above note 164 at chapter 5; A. Rosas, 'Democracy and human rights', in A. Rosas and J. Helgesen (eds), *Human Rights in a Changing East-West Perspective* (London, Pinter Publications, 1990) 31.

[179] T. Franck, 'The emerging right to democratic governance', 86 *American Journal of International Law* (1992) 46.

internal self-determination and is consistent with article 25 of the ICCPR.[180] If this is accepted, it suggests an ongoing role for the right to self-determination in international law, beyond the single event of determination of the future political structure as described above.[181] While this linkage between internal self-determination and democratic government expands the understanding of self-determination in one respect, it is also limiting because of the location of the right within the public, political, arena of civil and political rights. The definition of self-determination in the UN Covenants is not limited to political representation and participation for it includes social and cultural development which extends the concept, at least in theory, into the private arena with group autonomy over societal organisation and mores. This incorporates family relations, cultural and religious traditions and sex and gender roles within society.

Throughout all the debates about the meaning of the right to self-determination, there has been little questioning of its equal application to, and meaning for, all those within the group. Self-determination assumes the right to autonomy, freedom from alien oppression and the right to choose an economic, political and social system 'free from outside intervention, subversion, coercion or constraint of any kind whatsoever'.[182] Once external self-determination has been achieved and internal self-determination is guaranteed, it is assumed that all members of the group will equally benefit, in other words that the terms 'self' and 'peoples' are homogenous. Individual and group aspirations and goals, both before and after the achievement of self-determination, are subsumed within those of the self-determining unit.

This assumption of group identity and commonality is of course open to challenge. The notion of a self-determining unit collapses many forms of diversity, but most particularly that of sex. The consequences of this limited definition are evident in the fact that apparently successful claims to self-determination typically fail to deliver the same level of personal freedom and autonomy for women as for men, despite there being in many cases a historical association between nationalist and feminist movements[183] and a high degree of women's participation in the decolonisation process.[184] Indeed,

---

[180] Article 25 provides that 'Every citizen shall have the right and the opportunity . . . (a) to take part in the conduct of public affairs, directly or through freely chosen representatives; (b) to vote and to be elected at genuine periodic elections . . . (c) to have access, on general terms of equality, to public service in his country.'

[181] J. Crawford, 'Democracy in international law', 64 *British Yearbook of International Law* (1993) 3.

[182] The wording is taken from a General Assembly Resolution on Afghanistan after the Soviet invasion in 1979. GA Res. ES-6/2, 14 January 1980.

[183] See generally K. Jayawardena, *Feminism and Nationalism in the Third World* (London, Zed Books, 1986).

[184] Karen Knop has made a detailed analysis of the participation of women in the plebiscites that preceded independence in many instances of decolonisation, even

in many cases it emerges that achievement of national self-determination has led to a regression in the position of women. Examples include Algeria's independence from French colonial rule, the overthrow of the Shah in Iran and the transition to democracy in Eastern Europe. A study of the situation of Palestinian women indicates the complexity of self-determination for women.[185]

Self-determination and Palestinian women

The vocabulary of self-determination has been contested by the international community in the context of the Palestinian people,[186] but the Palestinians themselves, and many states that recognise Palestinian statehood, accept this as the major aspiration.[187] How does the struggle for self-determination affect Palestinian women? Palestinian women of course are not an homogenous group, with, among other things, significant differences in religion, class and education, and many writers have cautioned against simplified depictions of 'third world women'.[188] But they have in common the history of the contested region, in particular the impact of the events leading to and following the creation of the state of Israel in 1948 and the Israeli occupation of the Sinai, Gaza and the West Bank in 1967.[189] During the occupation, women have been shaped by the different realities of life within Israel, within the occupied areas of the West Bank and the Gaza Strip, in Israeli prisons, in refugee camps, or in foreign states as immigrants or migrant

---

where women were unable to vote in national elections: K. Knop, *The Making of Difference in International Law: Interpretation, Identity and Participation in the Discourse of Self-Determination* (J.S.D. University of Toronto, 1998) chapter 6.

[185] Much of the information for this case study was gathered when we participated in a conference at the Gaza Centre for Human Rights, September 1994.

[186] Compare GA Res. ES-7/2, 1980 (referring to the Palestinian people's right to self-determination) with the Israel-Palestine Liberation Organization (PLO), Declaration of Principles on Interim Self-Government, Washington, 13 September 1993, reprinted in 32 *International Legal Materials* (1993) 1525 and the Agreement on the Gaza Strip and Jericho Area, Cairo, 4 May 1994, reprinted in 33 *International Legal Materials* (1994) 626 which do not mention self-determination. The Wye River Memorandum, Washington, 23 October 1998, also refers only to 'permanent status negotiations', not self-determination: text at http://www.arabic.news.com.

[187] Palestine National Council, Political Communiqué and Declaration of Independence, 15 November 1988, reprinted in 27 *International Legal Materials* (1988) 1660. Over 100 states have recognised the state of Palestine. See also GA Res. 43/177 which accords it observer status before the UN. For opposing views on the 1988 Declaration see F. Boyle, 'The creation of the state in Palestine', 1 *European Journal of International Law* (1990) 301 and J. Crawford, 'The creation of the state in Palestine', *ibid.*, at 307.

[188] L. Gandhi, *Postcolonial Theory* (Sydney, Allen & Unwin, 1998) at 81.

[189] The Sinai was returned to Egypt in 1979 under the Peace Treaty, Egypt/Israel, 26 March 1979, reprinted in 18 *International Legal Materials* (1979) 362.

workers.[190] Particular aspects of the military occupation have impinged specifically upon women, for example by undermining women's health. Control of water resources by the Israelis is a contributing factor to malnutrition, which falls disproportionately upon girls.[191] Health, especially reproductive health, has been adversely affected by Israeli use of pesticides and other chemicals in agriculture that has polluted water supplies, unsanitary conditions and the use of tear gas upon civilian populations. One observer has argued that: 'Inequities in distribution of health care by the Israeli administrative apparatus institutionalise sexist, racist and classist assumptions which equate "Palestinian" and "women" and reduce both to manifestations of 'nature' needing to be tamed and controlled.'[192] The Israeli punitive demolition of houses has disrupted family life, with the additional burden of finding shelter falling primarily upon women.[193] Daily confrontation with male enemy soldiers was threatening for women.[194] Palestinian women who have sought work abroad, usually in low-paying domestic service, have had to leave their families and have become vulnerable to other external forces such as the often brutal demands of employers,[195] and the disruption caused by the Iraqi invasion of Kuwait in 1990.[196]

Palestinian women have played various and prominent roles in the struggle for self-determination. They have long been deeply involved in opposition movements and in international campaigns against outside occupation.[197] In the late nineteenth century and early twentieth century, women's groups in Egypt and Palestine used both feminist and nationalist arguments against imperialism and neo-colonialism.[198] Women have continued to play a significant, if unsung, role in modern campaigns. After the 1967 war, Palestinian women in the West Bank and Gaza mobilised to resist Israeli occupation

---

[190] M. Rishmawi, 'The legal status of Palestinian women in the Occupied Territories', in N. Toubia (ed.), *Women of the Arab World* (London, Zed Books, 1988) 79.

[191] E. Young, 'A feminist politics of health care: the case of Palestinian women under Israeli occupation, 1979–82', in T. Mayer (ed.), *Women and the Israeli Occupation: The Politics of Change* (London, Routledge, 1994) 179 at 181.

[192] *Ibid.* at 182; R.-L. Punamaki, 'Relationships between political violence and psychological responses among Palestinian women', 27 *Journal of Peace Research* (1990) 75.

[193] U. Halabi, 'Demolition and sealing of houses in the Israeli Occupied Territories: a critical legal analysis', 5 *Temple International and Comparative Law Journal* (1991) 251.

[194] E. Young, above note 191 at 184.

[195] See Middle East Watch, *A Victory Turned Sour: Human Rights in Kuwait since Liberation* (New York, Human Rights Watch, 1991) for accounts of abuses suffered by Palestinian women in Kuwait.

[196] See chapter 8.

[197] L. Brand, *Palestinians in the Arab World: Institution Building and the Search for a State* (New York, Columbia University Press, 1988) at 196–203.

[198] S. Sharoni, 'Middle East politics through feminist lenses: toward theorizing international relations from women's struggles', 18 *Alternatives* (1993) 5.

and often were imprisoned.[199] The Women's Work Committee was established in 1978 and, with other similar organisations, provided a focus for women's political activity.[200] Palestinian women became active in resistance movements in refugee camps in Lebanon in the early 1980s, although their participation was, in the words of an observer, 'uneven in form, content and meaning'.[201] Generally, however, the feminist movement has been concentrated among urban, middle class intellectuals rather than among camp refugees and village women.[202]

The *intifada* gave considerable impetus to Palestinian women's political organisation, with women's activism moving beyond national aspirations to women's rights. As Zahira Kamal has noted, 'the intifada caused the Palestinian women to enter the long struggle to destroy (some) traditional social relationships down to their roots – especially their total dependence on men, traditional ways of thinking, and activities which are forced on [them]'.[203] Women became the backbone of the *intifada*, taking on the roles usually performed by men. At the same time, the imagery often used about women's role in nation-building depended on maternal stereotypes. Women were presented as heroic mothers of the nation – 'the middle-aged woman, usually in her national embroidered dress, who is often in demonstrations . . . [and who] has invented effective tactics for saving children in danger of being arrested or beaten by Israeli soldiers'.[204] On the other hand, the participation of Hanan Ashrawi and Zahira Kamal in the peace talks of 1991–92 brought women into the 'mainstream' of political activity in a way unique in world politics.

Retention of authority and control within the family has appeared important for the preservation of Palestinian men's self-respect and personal identity. Women are caught in a web of conflicting needs and interests and their own responses may also be contradictory. The primary concern of most Palestinian women is strengthening the Palestinian people. Notions of motherhood and sacrifice have become enshrined in the Palestinian struggle as a virtual national duty. Women who sought recognition in the public arena have been forced to combine this traditional view of their duties with their newly defined roles of providing economically for their families.[205]

---

[199] C. Cervenak, 'Promoting inequality: gender-based discrimination in UNWRA's approach to Palestinian refugee status', 16 *Human Rights Quarterly* (1994) 300 at 361.

[200] *Ibid.*

[201] J. Peteet, 'No going back: women and the Palestinian movement', 138 *Middle East Report* (Jan.–Feb. 1986) 20–4, quoted in S. Sharoni, above note 198 at 16.

[202] N. Abdo, 'Women of the intifada: gender, class and national liberation', 32 *Race and Class* (no 4. 1991) 19 at 32.

[203] Quoted in C. Cervenak, above note 199 at 362–3.

[204] N. Abdo, above note 202 at 25.

[205] S. Dajani, 'Between national and social liberation: the Palestinian women's movement in the Israeli occupied West Bank and Gaza Strip', in T. Mayer, above note 191 at 42.

Increased public visibility has not always meant greater equality at home where longstanding assumptions about women may continue unchallenged. Indeed Palestinian women have generally refrained from directly challenging patriarchal structures.[206]

Despite the long history of some Palestinian women's political involvement in the quest for self-determination, women's participation in the political process during transition and in self-government is by no means assured. The traditions of both customary and religious law are not sympathetic to women's rights or activities in the public, political sphere. These systems limit women's roles to that of 'nurturers and repositories of family honor'.[207] Eileen Kuttab has pointed out that the end of the *intifada* has, paradoxically, undermined Palestinian women's activism for equal rights. With independence seen as being within grasp, pressure is placed on women to give priority to the nationalist political struggle rather than to the need for social justice.[208] Women in Gaza have described a 'tokenist' pattern of allowing a single woman to hold various prominent positions. For example, in 1994 one woman judge (of a total of more than thirty judges) was appointed to the Gaza judiciary, and one woman minister (of a total of sixteen) was appointed to the Palestinian Authority with the portfolio of social affairs. Of ninety-three positions of Ambassador to other nations, only two were held by women. In the 1996 elections for the Palestinian Legislative Council, five women and eighty-three men were elected.[209]

The tension between Palestinian women's claims for rights and representation in the political process and the patriarchal Palestinian traditions seems to have been resolved in favour of the *status quo*. A good example of this is the PLO leadership's reaction to women's assertions of rights. In August 1994, the General Union of Palestinian Women adopted a set of 'Principles of Women's Rights' based on a number of international human rights treaties including the Convention on the Elimination of All Forms of Discrimination Against Women. The Union sought a commitment from Yasser Arafat that the principles would be incorporated into the Constitution and laws of a future Palestinian state. Arafat's response was that he supported the Principles, but only if they did not conflict with Islamic law.[210] Women have been excluded from the most important committees planning

---

[206] *Ibid.* at 44.

[207] A. Wing, 'Custom, religion, and rights: the future legal status of Palestinian women', 35 *Harvard International Law Journal* (1994) 149 at 152.

[208] E. Kuttab, paper given at conference organised by the Gaza Centre for Human Rights, September 1994.

[209] Three women were from the Gaza Strip (Intesar Alwasir, Jamilla Sidam and Rawyar Shawwa) and two were from the West Bank (Hanan Ashrawi and Dalal Salama). A total of twenty-four women stood for election to the Legislative Council and one for the Presidency (Ra'ees) (Samiha Khalil).

[210] E. Kuttab, above note 208.

self-government and the draft Constitution provides no clear guarantee of women's equality.[211]

Palestinian women have become increasingly vocal about their frustration over their lack of political participation in the creation of a Palestinian state. Dr Rita Giacaman, Director of Community Health at Bir Zeit University, has been quoted as saying, 'How come we did all that [during the *intifada*] and now we're not in decision-making positions? Most of the major decisions being made are by people outside who have no interest in women.'[212] The novelist Sahar Khalifa expressed the reservations of many Palestinian women in stating, 'I don't want to be a heroine for the sake of the nation; I don't want my body to be the bridge for the state; I want to undergo a transformation, to have the experience of changing, to reap the benefits of the struggle, not to serve as the fuel for the national flame.'[213]

Non-representation of women in political decision-making is one manifestation of the limited agenda of many liberation movements.[214] A further failure of nationalist movements is their lack of concern with inequalities based on wealth and class – 'women and the poor [in the Middle East] often bear the brunt of the sacrifice necessary for national liberation with little or no reward'.[215] As Nahla Abdo has pointed out, 'national liberation is not a movement for the liberation of gender and class oppression'.[216] The impoverished Palestinian women camp refugees are thus particularly disadvantaged. Palestinian women's lack of political representation is connected to their low levels of literacy and education and economic power. In 1994 32 per cent of Palestinian women were illiterate and 60 per cent left school at primary level. In the West Bank only 12 per cent of the workforce were women, while in the Gaza Strip the figure was 3.7 per cent.[217]

Another factor for Palestinian women generally is the influence Islamic fundamentalism may have on their lives. The Israeli occupation has encouraged the rise of the *Hamas* movement, compounding threats to women's human rights. In Nahla Abdo's words, *Hamas* has 'emerged [in the Occupied Territories] as a form of escapism from the total impasse the region has slipped into on almost all fronts: the economic, political, and cultural'. The

---

[211] Compare the Palestine National Council's Declaration of Independence of 15 November 1988, above note 187 at 1670, which guarantees non-discrimination on the basis of sex.

[212] A. Sipress, 'PLO's inner circle elbows women out', *The Australian*, 16 May 1994, 14.

[213] Quoted in S. Sharoni, above note 198 at 15.

[214] See chapter 8 for discussion of the inclusion of women's rights in the Saharawi Constitution.

[215] S. Sharoni, above note 198 at 15.

[216] N. Abdo, 'Middle East politics through feminist lenses: negotiating the terms of solidarity', 18 *Alternatives* (1993) 29 at 31.

[217] UNDP, *Report on Palestinian Women* (New York, UN, October 1994).

political activities of *Hamas* and similar movements have manipulated religious texts to legitimise their agendas at the expense of women.[218] Thus women's veiling, exclusion and oppression is connected with religious salvation. In this sense, women are as much outsiders for Muslim fundamentalists as are Westerners.[219]

An interesting feature of women's movements within the Palestinian liberation struggle is the solidarity they have forged with some Israeli women's groups. The *intifada* in particular encouraged Israeli women's political organisation against occupation of the Gaza Strip and West Bank, in making alliances with Palestinian women's groups, and in considering the links between militarism and sexism, connecting the oppression of Palestinians with the oppression of women in Israel.[220] Simona Sharoni has suggested that 'the institutionalization of "national security" as a top priority in Israel contributes to gender inequalities on the one hand, and legitimizes violence against Palestinians and against women on the other'.[221] She has noted 'in a context where every man is a soldier, every woman becomes an occupied territory'.[222]

Of particular concern in the Palestinian context is the treatment of women refugees by the UN Works and Relief Agency (UNWRA). UNWRA has always employed a patrilineal model for determining eligibility for registration as a UN 'Palestine refugee' that gives access to a range of benefits and services such as education, housing, food and health. Refugee status is passed through the father. Although Palestinian refugee women who marry non-refugees maintain their refugee status, they may not transmit this status to their children. Palestinian refugee men who marry non-refugee women may nevertheless pass on their status to their children.[223] Quite apart from the immediate tangible benefits of refugee status, the exclusion of a group of women has implications also for their status in the self-government negotiations. The UNWRA rules relating to refugee status appear to be based on both sexist and 'orientalist' stereotypes,[224] without any regard to particular situations or allowing women to have a voice in such decisions. The assumption was that Palestinian women would always follow their husbands for cultural and legal reasons.[225] Sex discrimination was justified in deference to what was perceived as Arab law and culture.[226]

---

[218] N. Abdo, 'Middle East politics', above note 216 at 36–7.

[219] *Ibid.*

[220] S. Sharoni, above note 198 at 19–20.

[221] *Ibid.* at 21.

[222] *Ibid.* at 22.

[223] C. Cervenak, above note 199 at 301–2.

[224] See generally E. Said, *Orientalism: Western Conceptions of the Orient* (Harmondsworth, Penguin, 1985).

[225] C. Cervenak, above note 199 at 347.

[226] *Ibid.* at 349.

This brief account of the role of Palestinian women in the struggle for self-determination indicates the complexity of their position. In this context, how useful is the international law of self-determination? Its major promise with respect to political self-determination is the achievement of group autonomy free from external control. If the ongoing premise of internal self-determination is accepted, it provides the formal guarantee of civil and political rights through the right to vote and to participate in public life. However, the introduction of 'democratic' forms of government does not prevent the continued exclusion of women from public policy and decision-making bodies. Carole Pateman has noted that the forms of liberal democracy were founded upon the deliberate exclusion of women from public life: 'By constructing women's nature as equipped only for domestic life and as incapable of developing a sense of justice, liberalism initially barred women from public life altogether.'[227] Although liberation struggles allowed women to enter public life, the post-liberation reality in numerous cases has been the political marginalisation of women and the loss of political and social gains that had been acquired. The effect of national self-determination for women has often been the replacement of public control by foreign males for that of males of their own community, while private control continues unabated.

Self-determination also includes social and cultural development. The decreasing public role allowed to women in the *intifada* as the religious bodies gained influence parallels experience elsewhere where the successful end to a national liberation struggle led to a reassertion of men's positions of power within both public and private arenas. The effectiveness of human rights instruments guaranteeing sex equality is further reduced where the legitimacy of the standards is challenged by conflict with social custom and religious belief.[228] Women are seen as the repositories of a society's culture, and powerful demands are made for the maintenance of their traditional roles. The assertion of women's right to equality with men is viewed as destabilising, undermining the position and strength of the family and traditional culture.

The third strand of self-determination is that of economic autonomy. Economic self-determination has particular significance for Palestinians who have been deprived of their land and its resources. Loss of ownership and control of their land has entailed a shift from an agricultural economy to a wage-based economy. Both women and men have been forced to work for the Israelis in poor working conditions in jobs of low economic value. This employment is vulnerable to periodic Israeli refusals to allow Palestinians from Gaza and the West Bank to enter Israel for security reasons, thereby denying them vital financial resources.

[227] C. Pateman, *The Disorder of Women: Democracy, Feminism and Political Theory* (Cambridge, Polity Press, 1989) at 21.
[228] See chapter 7.

161

Women's economic self-determination is impeded by other factors, in-cluding legal restrictions on land-holding and inheritance, lack of educa-tional opportunity, restrictions on employment prospects and male control of women's bodies. During the occupation lack of choice in the spacing and number of children was justified, and even sanctified, through the national imperative to have more (male) children. to ensure the continuity of the struggle.[229] The control and regulation of women's bodies serves to limit their socio-economic development through restricting access to the paid workforce. There are private restrictions upon women's participation in economic life in many Arab countries. A woman may be technically free to work in the paid, public workforce, but if a man is given the right to prevent his wife from participating in public, political or cultural activities outside the home this freedom is meaningless.[230] There is also symbolic significance in the relocation of women in the private sphere. Reassertion of control over women's bodies and returning women to the home signifies men's regaining control over what is 'theirs', a reappropriation of (male) collective identity and a symbol of having wrested control away from Israel.

Rethinking self-determination

The Palestinian example indicates some of the problems for women of the traditional understandings of the doctrine of self-determination. The right to self-determination attaches to 'peoples', groups that are defined by their history, ethnicity, culture or language. The fact that half of the group comprising the 'people' are accorded unequal status and are allowed little input into its decisions is not considered relevant at international law. The principle of self-determination is usually discussed as if there were a single relevant 'self', masking the fact that the most prominent identity is usually a construct of the most powerful players in the group.[231] The 'self' inter-national law allows to determine its political status and freely pursue eco-nomic, social and cultural development is male. Women *as women* are not

[229] R. Morgan, *The Demon Lover: On the Sexuality of Terrorism* (London, Man-darin, 1989) chapter 8.

[230] N. Al Sadawi, 'The political challenges facing Arab women at the end of the 20th century', in N. Toubia, above note 190 at 8.

[231] A further illustration of this point in the Canadian context is the concern expressed by women's groups about the intention of the province of Quebec to secede from Canada (as expressed by its male-dominated government). In a brief prepared by the 'Ad Hoc Committee of Canadian women on the Constitution' for the Canadian Supreme Court which was considering the matter, it was argued that women in Quebec would be disadvantaged by secession because the protection of the right to equality in the Canadian Constitution was superior to the Quebec form of protection. Factum of the Ad Hoc Committee of Canadian Women on the Con-stitution, 10 April 1997. For the decision in the case see *Reference re Secession of Quebec*, reprinted in 37 *International Legal Materials* (1998) 1342.

162

seen as able to constitute a group of their own because of the historical linkage of personhood with manhood.[232] Andrea Dworkin has turned traditional ideas of self-determination upside down by representing women as an occupied people – 'physically occupied inside, internally invaded . . . with a metaphysically compromised privacy'.[233] Dworkin has pointed out that while peoples under colonial occupation can legitimately pursue self-determination, women who reject male occupation are regarded as deviant.[234]

International law presents self-determination as the cornerstone of all human rights guarantees. It can therefore be viewed as broader than the narrow interpretations traditionally given to both 'external' and 'internal' self-determination. A broadly conceived concept of self-determination would embrace the idea of a secure and fulfilled existence within a freely chosen democratic political and economic framework.[235] The equal participation of women and men in the choices of political and economic forms would be crucial to its legitimacy. Self-determination would incorporate such rights as the right to life, to food, to education, to work, to shelter, to health, to be free from the fear or threat of violence and to reproductive freedom.[236]

Most of these rights have special significance in the context of Palestine: the right to food and health where there has been widespread malnutrition, where water supplies have been diverted and where contaminated water and unsanitary conditions have caused disease; the right to education where public educational establishments have been closed; the right to work where access to employment has been suspended; the right to shelter where housing has been deliberately destroyed as retribution; the right to be free from violence where there has been military occupation; and the right to reproductive freedom in the face of the exigencies of national survival. Satisfactory achievement of self-determination for all Palestinians must go beyond mere political autonomy to take account of these issues.

A right to self-determination that benefited women as much as men would require attention to a range of contexts.[237] First, such a right would address women's right to political expression, including the right to vote and to express dissent. Second, it would cover work and mobility rights, covering women's role in the labour force, their mobility and the provision of child

---

[232] V. Peterson and L. Parisi, above note 87 at 151.

[233] A. Dworkin, *Intercourse* (London, Secker & Warburg, 1987, Arrow edn 1988) at 146.

[234] *Ibid.*

[235] C. Chinkin and S. Wright, 'The hunger trap: women, food and self-determination', 14 *Michigan Journal of International Law* (1993) 262.

[236] Universal Declaration of Human Rights, GA. Res. 217, A (III), 10 December 1948, articles 23, 25, 26 and 29.

[237] The list is drawn from J. Giele, 'Introduction: comparative perspectives on women', in J. Giele and A. Smock (eds), *Women, Roles and Status in Eight Countries* (New York, Wiley, 1977), quoted in V. Moghadam, 'Women, work and ideology in the Islamic Republic', 20 *International Journal of Middle East Studies* (1988) 221.

care, and the provision of equal pay for equal work. Third, the right would grant women freedom in choice of partners and a comparable status to men if they are single, widowed or divorced. Fourth, the right would include real access to all levels of education. Fifth, it would cover women's access to health care and their right of control over their fertility. Sixth, the right would pay attention to cultural expression and the way that images of women are created. Another important aspect of self-determination for women is a commitment to the eradication of violence against them. Formal commitment to such objectives is not sufficient and mechanisms for their implementation and evaluation are also required.

Recasting the state

The state as depicted in international law is an inadequate representation of a complex phenomenon. However, its definition affects all aspects of the international legal system: the regulation of access to the system and the design of substantive principles. The sex of the state operates to legitimate understandings of sexual difference that rest on a model of (male) dominance and (female) subservience within states as natural and immutable.

Although international law texts generally treat the state as a 'natural' ordering of political space, there is increasing attention paid to recasting it. Some scholars have argued for new understandings of state sovereignty in the wake of its indiscriminate invocation to justify resistance to international accountability. Thus Oscar Schachter has suggested that claims of sovereignty should be tied in some way to the consent of those within a state.[238] He has also sketched a number of models of 'relative' sovereignty to replace the traditional notion of absolute sovereignty. The demands of individuals, community values and the environment all impose restraints on sovereignty. For example, sovereignty has been whittled away by human rights law, by sanctions imposed by international institutions and by international environmental law.[239] Globalisation and regionalism are often presented as other forces undermining traditional understandings of statehood. Thus Neil MacCormick has argued that the development of the EC has effectively subverted the notion of sovereign states and single centralised authorities in Europe.[240] He has described the new order as a diffusion of political and legal power centres: 'a world in which our normative existence and our practical life are anchored in, or related to, a variety of institutional systems, each of which has validity or operation in relation to some range of

[238] O. Schachter, above note 59 at 674.
[239] *Ibid.* at 677–9. See also L. Henkin, 'The mythology of sovereignty', in R. Macdonald, above note 59 at 351 (arguing for a new vocabulary of statehood that omits the term 'sovereignty').
[240] N. MacCormick, 'Beyond the sovereign state', 56 *Modern Law Review* (1993) 1.

concerns, none of which is absolute over all the others, and all of which, for most purposes, can operate without serious mutual conflict in areas of overlap'.[241] The concept of sovereign statehood as the central value of the international legal system has also been strongly defended. Martti Koskenniemi has argued that the formality of statehood is an important bulwark against authoritarianism.[242] He has emphasised the significance of formal procedures as the basis of legality rather than universal values based on 'unverifiable ... manipulable, notions of a contextless natural Good'.[243] Thus, 'In normal circumstances, states still provide the means to direct substantive disagreement into institutionalized debate.'[244]

Feminist scholars have long been interested in the nature of the state and its implications for the international and national social order. They have taken a variety of approaches to statehood.[245] Some feminist writings emphasise the potential of state intervention to redress sexual inequality. Although the state is regarded as currently captive to male interests, its restructuring is seen as a route to significant social change. This liberal feminist approach is the foundation of most of the existing initiatives to promote sexual equality in the international arena. The Women's Convention, for example, relies on considerable state intervention to remedy discriminatory treatment. This is also the approach of the Platform for Action adopted at the Fourth World Conference for Women in 1995. There are, however, problems for women in assuming state involvement is always beneficial. For example, in the context of the South, Radhika Coomaraswamy has pointed out: 'if the state is entrusted with the responsibility of ensuring women's rights, if it is always viewed as active and paternalistic in a benign manner ... this ... pose[s] serious questions. The nation-state in the third world does not carry this "Scandinavian aura"'.[246] Another aspect of the post-colonial state that is problematic for women is its manipulation of religion and religious codes to undermine international norms.[247] Moreover, states do not treat all women the same. Minority women are often in a particularly complex relationship with the state. They may experience neglect of their particular interests and also discriminatory intervention and scrutiny.[248]

[241] *Ibid.* at 17.
[242] M. Koskenniemi, 'The future of statehood', 32 *Harvard International Law Journal* (1991) 397.
[243] *Ibid.* at 402.
[244] *Ibid.* at 410.
[245] See S. Watson, 'The state of play: an introduction', in S Watson (ed.), *Playing the State* (Sydney, Allen & Unwin, 1990) 3 at 6–8.
[246] R. Coomaraswamy, 'To bellow like a cow: women, ethnicity, and the discourse of rights', in R. Cook, *Human Rights of Women*, above note 150 at 39, 44.
[247] *Ibid.* at 51.
[248] J. Pettman, 'A feminist perspective on peace and security', 4 *Interdisciplinary Peace Research* (1992) 58 at 66.

Another approach, drawing on Marxist-feminist analysis, regards the state as reinforcing male oppression within the family through maintaining the social conditions of reproduction. Thus state support for a specific form of household associated with capitalism – a family unit dependent on a woman's domestic labour and a man's wage – is seen as maintaining the subordination of women.[249] Other scholars have stressed the masculinity of central state institutions. For example, Catharine MacKinnon has presented the state as synonymous with the legal system which is seen as a direct expression of men's interests.[250]

The historical origins of the state in a sexual division of labour have been studied by feminist scholars.[251] They have noted the relegation of women to a private, domestic, devalued sphere and the domination of men in the public sphere of citizenship and political and economic life. The state institutionalised the patriarchal family as the qualification for citizenship and public life and also as the basic socio-economic unit.[252] The functions of the state were in effect identified with men. Grant has observed that 'women experienced the effects of wars and other manifestations of state conduct. But it was left to men – citizens of the state – to formulate policy for dealing with other states.'[253] One particular focus of feminist attention has been the relationship between militarism, the belief system that upholds the legitimacy of the military control exercised by the state, and the assumption that military values are conducive to creating an orderly and secure society,[254] and the nation state. Military expenditure diverts resources and expertise from development needs and from health and social welfare programmes.[255] This spending at the cost of social expenditures has a particularly negative impact on women, and contributes significantly to the feminisation of poverty.[256]

---

[249] M. McIntosh, 'The state and the oppression of women', in A. Kuhn and A. Wolpe (eds), *Feminism and Materialism: Women and Modes of Production* (London, Routledge and Paul, 1978) 254 at 255.

[250] C. MacKinnon, *Towards a Feminist Theory of the State* (Cambridge, Mass., Harvard University Press, 1989) at 162–3.

[251] R. Grant, 'The sources of gender bias in international relations theory', in R. Grant and K. Newland (eds), *Gender and International Relations* (Bloomington, Indiana University Press, 1991) 8 at 11–12.

[252] V. Peterson and A. Runyan, *Global Gender Issues* (Boulder, Westview Press, 1993) at 93.

[253] R. Grant, above note 251 at 14.

[254] B. Reardon, *Sexism and the War System* (New York, Teachers College Press, 1985) at 14.

[255] See R. Panjabi, 'From Stockholm to Rio: a comparison of the declaratory principles of international environmental law', 21 *Denver Journal of International Law and Policy* (1992) 215 at 260–1.

[256] B. Reardon, above note 254 at 14.

Feminist accounts of the state, then, range from one of a potential saviour to that of an unambiguously oppressive institution. The evidence that is available, however, suggests that these approaches are too abstract and universal to provide an accurate account of the relationship of states to women. Indeed Judith Allen has challenged the idea of the 'state' as a useful focus for feminist work. She has described the state as

> a category of abstraction that is too aggregative, too unitary and too unspecific to be of much use in addressing the disaggregated, diverse and specific (or local) sites that must be of most pressing concern to feminists. 'The state' is too blunt an instrument to be of much assistance (beyond generalizations) in explanations, analyses or the design of workable strategies.[257]

Wendy Brown has written in a similar vein that 'its multiple dimensions make state power difficult to circumscribe and difficult to injure. There is no single thread that, when snapped, unravels the whole of state or masculine dominance.'[258] Are local investigations more appropriate for feminist analysis than focusing upon categories such as the state?[259] If states are 'a complex set of interrelated but distinct institutions, relations, hierarchies, discourses, interests and players',[260] one method of accommodating insights into the intricate, shifting nature of states is to study particular mechanisms of power within them.[261] In this way, states can be seen as encompassing many different sites or arenas of power, some more susceptible than others to responding to the range of women's interests.[262] International lawyers must also be concerned with particular mechanisms of power between nation states and the way these mechanisms are accommodated. The methodology of challenging gendered dichotomies classifying the world according to male perspectives and priorities could be used to scrutinise established dichotomies of the international legal system: state/non-state; member/non-member; sovereignty/domestic jurisdiction; governmental/non-governmental; state action/non-state action. If we lift the veil of the state and see it as acting with a variety of motives and through a variety of actors, the rigidity of the dichotomies supporting the international legal system, and the place of the state within it, collapses.

The conceptual dominance of statehood in international legal theory shields the internal workings of the state from scrutiny. It makes concerns

---

[257] J. Allen, 'Does feminism need a theory of "The State"?', in S. Watson, above note 245 at 21, 22.
[258] W. Brown, *States of Injury* (Princeton, Princeton University Press, 1995) at 179.
[259] Allen has suggested that categories such as 'policing', 'law' and 'the body' are more significant for feminist scholarship. J. Allen, above note 257 at 22.
[260] S. Watson, above note 245 at 10.
[261] R. Pringle and S. Watson, 'Fathers, brothers, mates: the fraternal state in Australia', in S. Watson, *Playing the State*, above note 245 at 229.
[262] S. Watson, above note 245 at 7.

about the relationship between the state and civil society seem largely irrelevant.[263] This indifference must be challenged in any feminist rethinking of the state. Accepting statehood and sovereignty as givens in the international legal order narrows our imaginative universe and the possibilities of reconstruction. Indeed international law maintains the fiction of the sovereignty of the nation state which in reality is undermined by the policies of a range of actors including intergovernmental monetary institutions, multinational corporations and human rights bodies. Yet international legal doctrines such as those of state responsibility and immunity barely acknowledge this reality.

What direction does feminist analysis suggest for reconceiving the state? Runyan and Peterson have pointed out the unique character of feminist critiques of the state in that 'they have never been mounted in the name of women taking over state power'.[264] They deal instead with new conceptions of power. Some scholars have proposed that a feminist state could promote the ability of human beings to act in concert, creating networks and co-operation across state boundaries.[265] It might stress a primary affiliation to planet earth rather than the nation state, breaking from the contractual morality of orthodox theories.[266] But can we simply replace the autonomous individualised male model of the state with a female counterpart? A feminised state is predicted to have implications for international law-making, for example by making it more flexible. Thus Mona Harrington has proposed that a feminist international law should involve 'an ongoing formulation of rules responding to the particular shape of problems as they arise', devised democratically, rather than a more abstract, universal set of prescriptions created by sovereign states. Such strategies have major limitations, however.[267] First, they preserve the idea of the state as a unitary entity, thus undermining the potential status of non-states (individuals and groups) in international law. Second, they rest on contested images of women as 'naturally' caring and nurturing agents.

The EC Guidelines on Recognition, discussed above, might be seen to indicate an awareness of the importance of democracy and human rights. This

---

[263] K. Knop, 'Re/statements: feminism and state sovereignty in international law', 3 *Transnational Law and Contemporary Problems* (1993) 293 at 302; K. Knop, 'Why rethinking the sovereign state is important for women's human rights law', in R. Cook, *Human Rights of Women*, above note 150 at 153.

[264] A. Runyan and V. Peterson, 'The radical future of realism: feminist subversions of IR theory', 16 *Alternatives* (1991) 67 at 99.

[265] R. Keohane, 'International relations theory: contributions of a feminist standpoint', in R. Grant and K. Newland, above note 251 at 41, 44–5.

[266] *Ibid.* at 47–8.

[267] K. Knop, 'Borders of the imagination: the state in feminist international law', *Proceedings of the 88th Annual Meeting of the American Society of International Law* (Washington DC, American Society of International Law, 1994) 14 at 15–16.

is a first step in scrutinising a state's concern with domestic justice rather than the maintenance of power.[268] However, the 'one-off' nature of recognition prevents it being used as an effective method of ongoing scrutiny. Further, as noted above, compliance with the criteria in the Guidelines has not been closely monitored. Nevertheless, as Karen Knop has pointed out, 'The rhetorical scaffolding has been put in place and women can now use it to construct the argument that a state's international status should be conditional on other, gender-conscious ideas of representation and democracy.'[269]

Jennifer Nedelsky has proposed some directions for rethinking the notion of autonomy that could be useful in international law. She has rejected the traditional liberal dichotomy drawn between the autonomous individual and the collective, arguing that a more fruitful understanding of autonomy involves dependence on relationships with others.[270] On this analysis, interdependence and integration are vital elements of autonomy.[271] The approach suggests the value of de-emphasising the significance of boundaries and state sovereignty as essential components of states and giving prominence to the formation and preservation of relationships between states and other international actors. International autonomy should be understood as dependent on international society, rather than in conflict with it.

Another feminist strategy is to undermine the centrality of the state in international law. The emergence of an international civil society has been advocated as a counter-balance to the statism of international law.[272] Karen Knop has drawn attention to the value of international civil society – non-state groups and networks – as a site for the generation of international law: '[The] existence [of international civil society] at the edges of the system of states frees this mix of non-governmental organizations, unofficial groups of experts, and other initiatives from the calculus of self interest that often dictates the position of states, and enables it to be more responsive to women's aspirations and more creative in developing proposals for change.'[273] As Knop has acknowledged, however, civil society is not necessarily hospitable to women's interests. In many ways, international civil society tends to reflect the existing power imbalances in the nation state system. This emphasises the importance of women taking an active role in international civil society and also developing theoretical underpinnings for its role in the creation of international law.[274] This can encompass a range of activities,

[268] K. Knop, 'Re/statements', above note 263 at 290, 302.
[269] *Ibid.* at 302–3.
[270] J. Nedelsky, 'Reconceiving autonomy: sources, thoughts and possibilities', in A. Hutchinson and L. Green (eds), *Law and the Community: The End of Individualism?* (Toronto, Carswell, 1989) 219.
[271] *Ibid.* at 225, 234.
[272] See chapter 3.
[273] K. Knop, 'Re/statements', above note 263 at 316.
[274] *Ibid.* at 308.

from scholars at the margins challenging the basic assumptions of international law to the mainstream of traditional lobbying.

The dominance of the sovereign state in international law can also be challenged by women presenting their interests directly in the international arena. This could take the form of bringing cases concerning women's rights to relevant international bodies.[275] This tactic contests the role of states as the sole representatives of women at the international level by demonstrating that the state is not yet structurally capable of representing the diversity of women and their interests. At the same time, this strategy runs the risk of merely assimilating women to standards created for men. Further, not all international institutions are amenable to such interventions. For example the GATT system and the WTO[276] and the Security Council have remained largely impermeable to influence by NGOs.

In his critical defence of the international legal notion of the state, Martti Koskenniemi has argued that the 'formal-bureaucratic rationality' of the state safeguards against 'the totalitarianism inherent in a commitment to substantive values, which forces those values on people not sharing them'.[277] He has celebrated the 'wonderful artificiality' of statehood because the state allows a 'position of retreat in which we can reflect upon our sociological and ethical conceptions and their relations to the truth or acceptability of our preferred way of life'.[278] Our argument, however, is that statehood in international law is much more than a formal, abstract structure. It is committed to a particular version of sexual difference and is unable to represent the interests of women (or indeed of some men). Substantive values may be obscured in the structure of statehood, but they nevertheless affect a state's entire population. In this sense, statehood falls inevitably into the totalitarian trap Koskenniemi believes it avoids. By understanding that the state is both sexed and gendered, we can move from the fiction of abstract rationality to a debate about the substance of its values.

[275] This avenue is now made easier by the adoption of an Optional Protocol to the Convention on the Elimination of All Forms of Discrimination Against Women which allows for individual communications. See further chapter 7.

[276] The Singapore Statement on NGO-WTO relations urges WTO member states to undertake consultations with NGOs in the interests of transparency. Reprinted in 27 *Environmental Policy and Law* (1997) 159.

[277] M. Koskenniemi, above note 242 at 407.

[278] M. Koskenniemi, 'The wonderful artificiality of states', *Proceedings of the 88th Annual Meeting of the American Society of International Law* (Washington DC, American Society of International Law, 1994) 22.

6

International institutions

Introduction

One of the features of the transistion from the 'Westphalian' order, in which the interests of individual states were paramount, to the 'Charter' regime and the creation of an international community, is the increasing prominence of intergovernmental institutions.[1] These institutions are considered to have international legal personality and to contribute to the generation of international law through the practice of their judicial, 'legislative' and 'executive' branches.[2] They also are the subject of international legal regulation, undermining the traditional state-based focus of international law. This chapter investigates how international institutions contribute to the gendered character of international law. It documents the absence of women at senior levels in international institutions, using the UN as a case study, and evaluates the various measures taken to improve the situation. The chapter then considers whether imbalance in women and men's representation in an institution such as the UN is significant. It argues that the invisibility of women at decision-making levels has affected the treatment not only of 'women's' issues, but also the way all international concerns are understood.

International inter-governmental institutions

International institutions have many forms. The most significant from an international legal perspective is the UN organisation. In 1999 it had 188

---

[1] See generally D. Bowett, *The Law of International Institutions* (London, Stevens, 4th edn 1982); N. White, *The Law of International Organisations* (Manchester, Manchester University Press, 1996).

[2] On the international legal personality of the UN see *Reparation for Injuries Suffered in the Service of the UN* 1949 ICJ Rep. 174 (Adv. Op. 11 April).

member states and operated a complex system of organs, commissions, committees and specialised agencies. All member states are represented in the General Assembly which has the power to consider and adopt resolutions on 'any matter' within the Charter's scope.[3] The General Assembly is also responsible for approving the UN's budget, calling international conferences and overseeing the UN Secretariat and a multitude of subsidiary bodies. The General Assembly meets in annual three-month sessions at UN headquarters in New York, and occasionally in special sessions on specific issues. The fifteen-member Security Council, which meets in almost continuous session, has five permanent members,[4] each of which has the power to veto draft resolutions.[5] The ten non-permanent members are elected by the General Assembly for two-year terms. The main function of the Security Council is to assume 'primary responsibility for the maintenance of international peace and security'.[6] It considers situations that may involve international conflict or somehow implicate international peace and security. The Security Council has been granted the power to take action to maintain international peace and security, including ordering international sanctions[7] and authorising military action.[8] Unlike resolutions of the General Assembly, Security Council decisions are formally binding on UN members.[9] The other 'principal organs' established by the UN Charter are the ECOSOC (responsible for initiating and co-ordinating UN work with respect to economic, social, cultural, educational, health and related matters),[10] the Trusteeship Council (responsible for the now-completed task of supervising the transition of 'trust' territories to self-government),[11] the ICJ[12] and the Secretariat (headed by the Secretary-General).[13] Both the Security Council and the General Assembly have established subsidiary bodies.[14]

The UN system also includes various specialised agencies such as the financial bodies, the International Monetary Fund (IMF) and the International

[3] Charter of the UN, 26 June 1945, article 10.

[4] Republic of China (now Peoples' Republic of China), France, the USSR (now Russian Federation), the United Kingdom and the United States. Charter of the UN, article 23.

[5] *Ibid.*, article 27(3).

[6] *Ibid.*, article 24.

[7] *Ibid.*, article 41.

[8] *Ibid.*, article 42.

[9] *Ibid.*, article 25.

[10] *Ibid.*, chapter X.

[11] *Ibid.*, chapter XIII.

[12] *Ibid.*, chapter XIV.

[13] *Ibid.*, chapter XV.

[14] *Ibid.*, articles 7(2), 22 (General Assembly), 29 (Security Council). See *Prosecutor v. Dusko Tadic* (Jurisdiction) 105 International Law Reports 420 (Judgment of 10 August 1995, Trial Chamber; 2 October 1995, Appeal Chamber) on the competence of the Security Council to establish the International Criminal Tribunal for the Former Yugoslavia.

Bank for Reconstruction and Development (World Bank), trade institutions such as the GATT and the WTO and bodies with specialised mandates such as the ILO, the Food and Agriculture Organisation (FAO), the International Maritime Organisation (IMO), the International Civil Aviation Organisation (ICAO) and the WHO.

An important category of international intergovernmental institutions are political regional organisations such as the Association of South East Asian Nations (ASEAN), the Organization of African Unity (OAU), and the Organisation of American States (OAS). The last two have been instrumental in promoting human rights protections within their regions, as has the Council of Europe.[15] Other regional organisations are primarily for economic and trade purposes such as the EU and the North American Free Trade Association, although the EU has moved far beyond the original perception of common economic communities in terms of political and social integration. Some regional economic institutions have taken on security and peacekeeping functions, for example the Organisation of Eastern Caribbean States (OECS) and the Economic Community of West African States (ECOWAS),[16] while others were explicitly formed for these purposes, such as the North Atlantic Treaty Organisation (NATO) and the OSCE. Both of these latter organisations have had to adapt their membership and functions in the light of the political changes in Europe in the late 1980s and 1990s. The size, criteria for membership, functions and complexity of organisational structure of global and regional institutions differ greatly, making generalisations problematic.

The term 'international institutions' is usually regarded by international lawyers as covering inter-governmental institutions alone, although there are also a range of diverse international NGOs that have access to and influence the international legal system.[17] The primary focus of this chapter is the largest permanent international governmental institution, the UN, because of its size and claim to almost universal membership and also because of its significance in the international legal system. The problems we identify in the workings of the UN are, however, common to international institutions generally.[18]

[15] See chapter 7.
[16] E.g. the OECS action in Grenada in 1983, and ECOWAS action through the ECOWAS Monitoring Group (ECOMOG) in Liberia from 1990. See C. Gray, 'Regional arrangements and the United Nations collective security system', in H. Fox (ed.), *The Changing Constitution of the United Nations* (London, British Institute of International and Comparative Law, 1997) 91.
[17] See chapter 3.
[18] On the position of women in the League of Nations see M. Galey, 'Forerunners in women's quest for partnership', in A. Winslow (ed.), *Women, Politics, and the United Nations* (Westport/London, Greenwood Press, 1995) 1 at 4–6.

Women in the UN

Participation of women

Both the UN's membership and its bureaucracy are dominated by men. In 1998 nine of 185 member states had women as their head or acting head of mission to the UN[19] and only two of the fifty-three sessions of the General Assembly held since the founding of the UN in 1945 had been presided over by a woman president.[20] In 1996, women represented 22 per cent of the total diplomatic staff at national missions to the UN, a modest increase on the 1949 figure of 16 per cent.[21] Only the Third Committee of the General Assembly, dealing with social, cultural and humanitarian affairs, regularly has a significant number of women delegates and for this reason has been referred to within the UN as the 'Ladies' Committee'.[22] Very little attention has been paid to the balance of women and men on national delegations by the UN itself. Some of the strongest statements on this issue were made in the very first session of the General Assembly when France made a formal declaration asking that 'feminine participation should occupy a more important place in the various [national] delegations to the . . . United Nations'.[23]

Permanent representatives to the UN, of course, act on instructions from home governments and national governments the world over are dominated by men. Women's participation in government tends to vary inversely with the distribution of political power.[24] At the end of 1998, the governments of three states were led by a woman.[25] Women's participation in government is increasing at a very slow rate. In 1987 an average of 3.5 per cent of women were in cabinet ministries and 4.2 per cent of women were in national ministerial and other senior level decision-making posts.[26] These women tended to be relegated to fields which are considered the extension of 'female' concerns – health, welfare, education, culture, families and consumer

[19] Australia, the Dominican Republic, Finland, Guinea, Jamaica, Kazakhstan, Kyrgyzstan, Liechtenstein and Turkmenistan.

[20] Ambassador Vijaya Lakshmi Pandit of India in 1953 and Ambassador Angie E. Brooks of Liberia in 1969.

[21] Press Briefing on 16 March 1996 by UN Assistant Secretary-General, Rosario Green.

[22] M. Bruce, 'Women and policy-making in the United Nations', in N. Davidson and M. Croke (eds), *The United Nations and Decision Making: The Role of Women* (New York, UNITAR, 1978) 49 at 62.

[23] UN Doc. A/PV.29, 12 February 1946, reprinted in UN, *The United Nations and the Advancement of Women 1945–1996* (New York, UN, 1996) 97.

[24] See generally V. Randall, *Women and Politics: An International Perspective* (Chicago, Chicago University Press, 1987) chapter 3.

[25] Bangladesh (Prime Minister Sheikh Hasina Wajed), New Zealand (Prime Minister Jenny Shipley), Sri Lanka (President Chandrika Kumaratunga).

[26] UN, *Women in Politics and Decision-Making in the Late Twentieth Century: A United Nations Study* (Dordrecht, Martinus Nijhoff, 1992) at 63, 68.

affairs.[27] Women were completely absent from ministerial levels of government decision-making in the majority of the 155 countries surveyed. In
1987, the average global representation of women in national legislatures
was 9.7 per cent,[28] five years later, in 1993, it was 10.10 per cent,[29] and in
1997 the figure was 12.9 per cent[30] and in 1998, 12.6 per cent.[31] In 1996 the
percentage of women at ministerial level had increased to 6.8 per cent.[32]
While 48 of the 187 countries surveyed had no women at the ministerial
level, five countries had women holding 30 per cent of ministerial posts.[33]
Women ministers remained concentrated in social portfolios, rather than in
legal, economic, political or executive areas.[34]

The highest average participation of women (26.6 per cent) in national
legislatures in 1987 was in Eastern European countries, twice as high as the
average for Western industrialised nations.[35] The political and economic
restructuring associated with 'democratisation' in Eastern Europe since 1989
has, however, produced a striking decrease in women's participation in
national legislatures, with the 1991 average in Eastern Europe falling to
10.9 per cent.[36] In 1998, the figures remained low.[37] It appears that 'democratisation' allows legislatures to reflect more accurately the distribution of
power and wealth within a community and that the increasing importance
of parliaments results in a decrease in women's participation in national
legislatures.[38] UN data also indicate that there is no clear relationship
between a nation's 'development', measured in terms of national income, and
women's representation in legislatures.[39]

The bureaucracies that service national governments replicate the imbalance between the sexes in elected office. In 1987, there were no women in
any senior levels in fifty-one countries.[40] In 1996, women held 9.9 per cent
of senior official positions globally.[41] In most regions of the world, the

[27] V. Randall, above note 24 at 112.

[28] *Ibid.* at 9.

[29] Inter-Parliamentary Union, *Women in Parliament as at 30 June 1993* (Map)
(Geneva, Inter-Parliamentary Union, n.d.).

[30] UNDP, *Human Development Report* (New York, Oxford University Press, 1997)
at 154.

[31] See the data provided by the Inter-Parliamentary Union at http://www.ipu.org/
wmn-e/classif.htm.

[32] See the data provided by the UN Division for the Advancement of Women at
http://www.un.org/womenwatch/daw/public/womingov.htm.

[33] Barbados, Finland, Liechtenstein, Seychelles and Sweden. *Ibid.*

[34] *Ibid.*

[35] *Women in Politics*, above note 26 at 15.

[36] *Ibid.* at 16.

[37] See above note 31.

[38] *Women in Politics*, above note 26 at 16.

[39] *Ibid.* at 17. See also above note 32.

[40] *Women in Politics*, above note 26 at 62.

[41] See above note 32.

proportion of women increases as the decision-making level gets lower.[42] Moreover, women in senior positions are concentrated in social policy areas that are considered of low prestige and power compared with areas such as political affairs, economic management, and law and justice.[43] Within national workforces, women hold a global average of 10 per cent of management positions and less than 5 per cent of the highest positions.[44] The ILO has estimated that, at the present rate of change, it will take 475 years before women and men are represented in equal numbers in national positions of political and economic power.[45] Channels of political influence such as unions, interest organisations and the media exacerbate the problem by also marginalising women.[46]

Given the disproportionate representation of men in national decision-making structures, it is no surprise that states' nominees for 'expert' positions in the UN system are generally male. In almost eighty years, one woman has been elected to the World Court and no woman has ever sat on the ILC.[47] Few women have been elected to expert positions in the UN human rights system.[48] The staffing of the UN bureaucracy also mirrors national patterns. Article 8 of the UN Charter provides that: 'The United Nations shall place no restrictions on the eligibility of men and women to participate in any capacity and under conditions of equality in its principal and subsidiary organs.' This provision, lobbied for by the Committee of Women's Organizations at the San Francisco Conference, was phrased in negative terms rather than as a positive obligation to include women because a country's choice of delegates was considered to be an inviolable aspect of its sovereignty.[49] The relevance of article 8 to the Secretariat itself has rarely been considered. Its negative phrasing has long been interpreted as offering the minimal – and ineffective – promise of formal equality.

The UN Secretariat comprises two main categories of positions: General Service and Professional Posts. The latter consists of five rungs (P-1 to P-5), with two levels of 'Principal Officer' above it (D-1, D-2). Above this level are the highest levels of the bureaucracy: Assistant Secretary-General and Under-Secretary-General. Formal responsibility for the appointment of

---

[42] *Women in Politics*, above note 26 at 63.

[43] *Ibid.* at 61, 67. See also V. Randall, above note 24 at 116–17.

[44] 'Unequal race to the top', *World of Work* (no. 2, February 1993) 6.

[45] M. Ducel, 'Women in authority: the ideal and the reality', *World of Work* (no. 2, February 1993) 4.

[46] V. Randall, above note 24 at 112–15, 119–20.

[47] See chapter 4.

[48] See chapter 7.

[49] R. Russell, *A History of the United Nations Charter: The Role of the United States, 1940–1945* (Washington DC, Brookings Institution, 1958) at 793–4, n. 24. Article 8 is couched in less strong terms than the parallel provision in the Covenant of the League of Nations, 28 June 1919, 11 Martens (3rd) 323, 225 Parry's TS 195, article 7 (see chapter 1 at note 85 and accompanying text).

UN staff rests with the Secretary-General under regulations adopted by the General Assembly[50] and subject to the principles that govern the recruitment and employment of staff as set out in the UN Charter:

> The paramount consideration in the employment of the staff and in the determination of the conditions of service shall be the necessity of securing the highest standards of efficiency, competence, and integrity. Due regard shall be paid to the importance of recruiting the staff on as wide a geographical basis as possible.[51]

The final sentence of this paragraph has been fulfilled through the creation of a category of posts 'subject to geographical distribution'. Appropriate geographical representation is determined by a system of 'desirable ranges' for representation of nations of member states, based on the size of membership of the UN, assessed contributions of member states and population of member states. Such staff are appointed directly by the Secretary-General to posts in the professional category and above in the UN Secretariat for at least a year.[52] In practice many of the appointments to posts subject to geographical representation are made on the nomination of member states. Responsibility for the serious under-representation of women within the UN itself thus rests both with UN members which fail to nominate women for posts and with the UN leadership which has tolerated deeply misogynist attitudes in the Secretariat.

Almost half the UN staff are women, but three-quarters of the women are in the General Service category whose functions are chiefly to provide clerical and secretarial support.[53] *De facto* restrictions on women in decision-making roles in the UN have been in place since its foundation. No woman has ever held, or been formally nominated for, the post of Secretary-General. There has, however, been some progress at senior levels below that of Secretary-General. In 1990, Brian Urquhart and Erskine Childers noted that of the 136 UN

---

[50] Charter of the UN, article 101(1). Some UN subsidiary organs have a special status, conferred by the General Assembly, in staff appointments, e.g. the UNDP, the UNHCR and the UNICEF. See UN Common System: Composition of the Secretariat: Report of the Secretary-General, UN Doc. A/48/559, 5 November 1993, at 2.

[51] Article 101(3).

[52] In 1993, there were 2573 such staff. Staff excluded from the geographical distribution system include staff in UN subsidiary organs with special status in matters of appointment, staff in the UN Secretariat in posts with special language requirements and in General Service and related categories. See UN Doc. A/48/559 at 8.

[53] See UN Joint Inspection Unit, Advancement of the Status of Women in the United Nations Secretariat in an era of 'Human Resources Managment' and 'Accountability': A New Beginning? UN Doc. A/49/176, 17 June 1994, Table 4 (JIU Report). (The JIU is an independent body created by the General Assembly to audit UN practices.) This chapter deals with the representation of women within the UN in policy and decision-making roles and therefore focuses on the Professional category. Although women are well-represented within the General Service category, they suffer from a range of direct and indirect discriminations. See *ibid.* at paras 33–5.

agency heads appointed since 1946, one, Dr Nafis Sadik, Executive Director of the UNFPA, was a woman.[54] In 1998, there were ten women at the level of executive heads[55] and over thirty men in similar positions. The UN Secretary-General, Kofi Annan, created a new post of Deputy Secretary-General in 1998 and appointed a Canadian woman, Louise Fréchette, to the position.

Women have occasionally reached the highest career level of decision-making posts in the UN system – Under-Secretary-General – but they have never held more than a small fraction of these positions at any time and regularly there are no women at all at this level. The restructuring of the Secretariat undertaken in 1991 removed the two women then serving as Under-Secretaries-General from their posts and produced a 'streamlined' twenty-man cadre. In 1998, one woman and seventeen men held posts as Under-Secretary-General.[56] At the same time, there were three women and nine men in positions immediately below Under-Secretary-General, Assistant Secretary-General.[57] It is striking that the proportion of women in the highest echelons of the UN does not grow in a permanent way at all; indeed, it regularly goes backwards.[58] Even when rising to high ranks within the UN, women tend to be placed in positions that are the diplomatic equivalents of housekeeping – for example, conference organisation and translation – rather than being entrusted with more prestigious and powerful economic and political responsibilities. Moreover, women are distributed very unevenly throughout the Secretariat, with many UN units having no women at senior levels.[59] Another pattern seems to be the assignment of overwhelming or impossible tasks to women 'where the visibility is high and the chances of failure even greater'.[60]

---

[54] B. Urquhart and E. Childers, *A World in Need of Leadership: Tomorrow's United Nations* (Uppsala, Dag Hammarskjold Foundation, 1990) at 97.

[55] Sadako Ogata (UNHCR), Catherine Bertini (World Food Programme), Elizabeth Dowdeswell (UN Environment Program), Carol Bellamy (UNICEF), Martha Duemas-Loya (INSTRAW), Noleen Heyzer (UNIFEM), Nafis Sadik (UNFPA), Mary Robinson (UN High Commissioner for Human Rights) and Gro Harlem Brundtland (WHO).

[56] Improvement of the status of women in the Secretariat: Report of the Secretary-General, UN Doc. E/CN.6/1998/8, 12 February 1998, at 3.

[57] *Ibid.*

[58] E.g. in 1993 three women were Under-Secretary-Generals, with eighteen men at this level. A former UN staff member, Claire de Hedervary, has noted that the number of women in professional positions in the Secretariat in the 1950s was greater than the number in the 1960s. C. de Hedervary, 'The United Nations: "Good grief, there are women here"', in R. Morgan (ed.), *Sisterhood is Global: The International Women's Movement* (Garden City, Anchor Press/Doubleday, 1984) 695.

[59] JIU Report, above note 53 at para. 26. See also *Report of the Secretary-General*, above note 56 at 3, noting that in 1998 there were no senior women (D-1 and above) in the UN International Drug Control Programme nor in the Office of the Co-ordinator for Humanitarian Affairs.

[60] C. de Hedervary, above note 58 at 698.

At the bureaucratic levels below Assistant Secretary-General, the numbers of women have been rising. The rate of change has been very slow, however. In 1949, women formed 393 out of 1678 of professional staff.[61] In 1971 (the first year in which the Secretary-General reported to the General Assembly on the number of women by level in the Secretariat), 17 per cent of professional posts subject to geographical distribution were filled by women.[62] In 1972, the percentage of women was 18.5, in 1976, 20.9 and in 1981, just less than 22 per cent. Over ten years later, in 1992, the proportion was 30.2 per cent.[63] By 1998, women held 36.8 per cent of professional posts.[64] At the Director ('D-1 and above') level, women filled 2.6 per cent of posts in 1971,[65] a little over 10 per cent (37 of 356 posts) in 1992,[66] and 22.6 per cent in 1998.[67] Within the UN, women generally work in peripheral areas of concern. They also often are placed in extra-budgetary positions that have no security or career development.[68] The under-representation of women in all prestigious posts throughout the UN, whether or not they are subject to the distribution on the basis of geographical distribution (for example, language posts),[69] indicates that the problems go beyond the system of geographic distribution. Sex imbalance is even worse in most of the specialised agencies of the UN than in the Secretariat[70] and in staff categories such as project personnel.[71]

[61] Report of the Secretary-General to the Commission on the Status of Women on the participation of women in the work of the United Nations, UN Doc. E/CN.6/132, 16 March 1950, reprinted in *The United Nations and the Advancement of Women*, above note 23 at 126–31.

[62] JIU Report, above note 53 at para. 175.

[63] 'Women in the Secretariat: putting the principle into practice', *Instraw News* (no.18, Autumn 1992) 18 at 19.

[64] Report of the Secretary-General 1998, above note 56 at 3.

[65] JIU Report, above note 53 at para. 175.

[66] 'Women in the Secretariat', above note 63 at 18.

[67] Report of the Secretary-General 1998, above note 56 at 3.

[68] C. de Hedervary, above note 58 at 697.

[69] Women held 35 per cent of language posts at 31 December 1993. JIU Report, above note 53, table 4.

[70] E.g. on the position of women in the ILO see C. Lubin and A. Winslow, *Social Justice for Women: The International Labor Organization and Women* (Durham/London, Duke University Press, 1990) at 261–2. On the position of women in the Office of the UNHCR see the remarks of Roberta Cohen, *Proceedings of the 89th Annual Meeting of the American Society of International Law* (Washington DC, American Society of International Law, 1995) 196. The UNDP, UNFPA and UNICEF are exceptions. See K. Timothy, 'Women as outsiders: the glass ceiling at the United Nations', in F. D'Amico and P. Beckman (eds), *Women in World Politics: An Introduction* (Westport/London, Bergin & Garvey, 1995) 84 at 86–7; A. Winslow, 'Specialized agencies and the World Bank', in A. Winslow, above note 18 at 155, 168–72.

[71] Women held 12 per cent of these positions in 1991. JIU Report, above note 53 at para. 28. On the very low numbers of women involved in UN peacekeeping operations see J. Stiehm, 'Peacekeeping and peace research: men and women's work', 18 *Women & Politics* (1997) 27 at 33–9. See further chapter 9.

UN responses

The position of women in the UN has always been precarious. One former staff member described women in the Secretariat during the 1960s as 'an endangered species'.[72] However, little official attention seems to have been given to the issue of women within the UN Secretariat until the early 1970s. Statistics revealing the very low participation of women in professional posts in the UN were prepared for the CSW in 1950, but no action to remedy the situation was identified.[73] At almost every session of CSW between 1948 and 1963, a draft resolution on the participation of women in the UN system was adopted, urging the Secretary-General to appoint women to senior positions. These draft resolutions were presented for adoption to ECOSOC but it refused to accept them on the basis that the staffing of the Secretariat was up to the Secretary-General alone.[74] In 1970, the General Assembly adopted its first resolution on women's employment within the UN.[75] The resolution expressed the hope that the UN and its agencies would set an example with regard to the opportunities they afforded for the employment of women in the professional category. It urged the UN to take appropriate measures to ensure equal opportunity for the employment of qualified women in the UN and requested the Secretary-General to include data on women in his annual report to the General Assembly on the composition of the Secretariat. The Ad Hoc Group for Equal Rights for Women was formed within the Secretariat in 1971 by a group of women frustrated by overt discrimination against them.[76] In 1972, UNITAR held a seminar on 'The Situation of Women in the United Nations' and made recommendations on removing discrimination against women in the Secretariat.[77] Prompted by these developments, the General Assembly adopted further

[72] C. de Hedervary, above note 58 at 695.

[73] See for example Report of the Secretary-General to the Commission on the Status of Women on the participation of women in the work of the United Nations, UN Doc. E/CN.6/132, 16 March 1950, reprinted in *The United Nations and the Advancement of Women*, above note 23 at 126.

[74] L. Parker (ed.), *A Compilation of Documents on the Participation of Women in the Work of the United Nations System (1945–1988)* (a report of the Group on Equal Rights for Women at the Vienna International Centre, submitted as a background paper to the Commission on the Status of Women at its thirty-second session Vienna, 14–23 March 1988).

[75] GA Res. 2715 (XXV), 15 December 1970, reprinted in *The United Nations and the Advancement of Women*, above note 23 at 169.

[76] See C. de Hedervary, 'The Ad Hoc Group of Women: action on decision-making in the United Nations', in N. Davidson and M Croke, above note 22, vol. 2, 131.

[77] For a report of the seminar see A. Szalai, 'The situation of women in the UN': A Report based on the proceedings of the Colloquium of Senior UN Official held at 4–6 July 1972 at Schloss Hernstein, Austria (New York, UNITAR, 1973). A second seminar on the same topic was organized by UNITAR in 1977. Its proceedings are published in N. Davidson and M. Croke, above note 22.

resolutions.[78] In 1974, it set 1980 as a goal for the achievement of an 'equitable balance' of men and women staff members in the Secretariat.[79]

The issue was also on the agenda of the World Conference of the International Women's Year held in Mexico City in 1975. One of the goals in the World Plan of Action adopted by that conference was the improvement of women's representation within the Secretariat and in national delegations.[80] Ten years later, the *Forward-Looking Strategies for the Advancement of Women to the Year 2000*, adopted by the Nairobi Conference of the UN Decade for Women in 1985, included a recommendation that: 'The United Nations system should take all necessary measures to achieve an equitable balance between women and men staff members at managerial and professional levels in all substantive areas, as well as in field posts.'[81] The *Forward-Looking Strategies* called on all parts of the UN system to 'take all possible measures to achieve the participation of women on equal terms with men at all levels by the year 2000'.[82] The Nairobi Conference called for the taking of special measures – for example, 'the preparation of a comprehensive affirmative action plan including provisions for setting immediate targets and for establishing and supporting special mechanisms . . . to improve the status of women staff'[83] – and it endorsed regular reporting to UN bodies on this action. The Beijing Platform for Action in 1995 made no real advances on this issue, reiterating rather bland commitments for the UN to achieve overall gender equality by 2000.[84]

Successive Secretaries-General have made attempts to respond to the problems of women in the UN system. The Secretary-General, Dag Hammarskjold, assured the CSW in 1954 that he would not countenance discrimination against women in the Secretariat. He explained the small number of women in professional posts in the UN as a 'natural consequence of the fact that women had been so recently emancipated'. He was confident that 'as the proportion of trained women in national life increased, the change would be reflected in the staffs of the international organizations'.[85]

[78] E.g. GA Res. 39 (XXVII), 18 December 1972; GA Res. 3352 (XXIX), 18 December 1974.

[79] GA Res. 3352 (XXIX), 18 December 1974. See also GA Res. 3416 (XXX), 8 December 1975, GA Res. 31/26, 29 November 1976, GA Res. 32/17, 11 November 1977. At the same time, some of the specialised agencies of the UN adopted resolutions on the employment of women. See M. Bruce, above note 22 at 74–5.

[80] Resolution 8, World Conference of the International Women's Year, 1975.

[81] UN Doc. A/CONF.116/12 1985, para. 356. See also paras 79, 315 and 358.

[82] *Ibid.* at para. 358.

[83] *Ibid.*

[84] Fourth World Conference on Women, Declaration and Platform for Action, 15 September 1995, UN Doc. A/CONF.177/20 (1995), reprinted in 35 *International Legal Materials* (1996) 401 (Beijing Platform for Action), para. 193.

[85] Summary of statement made by the Secretary-General to the eighth session of the CSW, UN Doc. E/CN.6/SR. 149, 8 April 1954, reprinted in *The United Nations and the Advancement of Women*, above note 23 at 156.

In 1977 Secretary-General Kurt Waldheim published a statement on equality of men and women in the Secretariat.[86] The statement reaffirmed equality between the sexes as a guiding principle of the UN and announced a policy of equal opportunity in order to achieve the 'equitable balance' of men and women staff by 1980, as requested by the General Assembly. Guidelines for promoting Equal Treatment of Men and Women in the Secretariat were issued in 1982.[87] The Guidelines covered the use of sexist language, the assignment of work and sexual harassment. Revised guidelines have since been issued,[88] but there is still no comprehensive Secretariat policy on sexual harassment, despite the urging of the General Assembly. The position of co-ordinator of women's affairs, at Assistant Secretary-General level, was created in 1984, but eliminated in budget cuts two years later.[89] In 1985, at the request of the General Assembly, the Secretary-General made a comprehensive report on women in the Secretariat[90] and in 1986, he established a Steering Committee for the Improvement of the Status of Women in the Secretariat.[91] In its reports, the Committee has recommended a range of measures to increase the recruitment and promotion of women.[92] One proposal was that women's cumulative seniority be taken into account in promotion on the basis that women spend more time than men at every level of the career ladder.[93]

In 1985, the Secretary-General proposed an 'action programme' for women with the goal of 30 per cent of women in professional posts by 1990 and 35 per cent by 1995 and, 'all things being equal and to the extent possible', 25 per cent at D-1 level and above by 1995.[94] These targets were endorsed regularly by the General Assembly and the Secretary-General has been consistently encouraged to achieve them.[95] In 1992, the Secretary-General added a target for policy level positions (Under-Secretaries-General and Assistant Secretaries-General) of 'as close to 50/50 as possible' by 1995.[96] In his mess-

[86] UN Doc. ST/SGB/154, 8 March 1977. See also the FAO Director-General's Bulletin No 77/57 of 14 October 1977, reprinted in N. Davidson and M. Croke, above note 22, vol. 1, at 169–70.

[87] UN Doc. ST/IC/79/71/Rev.1, 8 March 1982.

[88] E.g. UN Docs. ST/AI/379 and ST/IC/1992/67, 29 October 1992.

[89] V. Peterson and A. Runyan, *Global Gender Issues* (Boulder, Westview Press, 1993) at 49. In 1997, the Secretary-General appointed Ms Angela King as his Special Adviser on Gender Issues and the Advancement of Women.

[90] Improvement of the Status of Women in the Secretariat: Report of the Secretary-General, UN Doc. A/C.5/40/30, 8 November 1985.

[91] UN Doc. ST/SGB/216, 7 March 1986.

[92] E.g. Sixth Report of the Steering Committee for the Improvement of the Status of Women in the Secretariat, UN Doc. ST/SGB/252, 20 October 1992.

[93] See K. Timothy, above note 70 at 91.

[94] Report of the Secretary-General 1985, above note 90.

[95] E.g. GA Res. 45/239 C, 21 December 1990; GA Res. 47/226 C, 8 April 1993.

[96] Secretary-General's statement to the Fifth Committee, UN Doc. ST/IC/1992/73, 12 November 1992, at 8.

age celebrating International Women's Day in 1993, the Secretary-General stated that he intended that 50 per cent of all the professional posts subject to geographical distribution would be held by women in 1995.[97] The same year, the Secretary-General issued an administrative instruction on 'Special Measures to Improve the Status of Women in the Secretariat'.[98] It relaxed various eligibility requirements to increase the pool of women for appointment or promotion to high-level posts and stated that 'the criteria for advancement should stress performance and potential and not simply nominal qualifications and seniority in grade'.[99] In 1994, a goal of 'complete parity' by 2000 was endorsed by the Secretary-General and a new five-year strategic plan of action announced.[100] This plan was somewhat more detailed than its predecessors, but contained few implementing teeth.

The issue of the position of women within the UN Secretariat has been raised so often formally and informally within the UN that a 1994 report by the JIU dealing with the problem opened with an extraordinary apology: 'The topic of women's advancement in the United Nations Secretariat has been around for so many years that any new study such as this one may be considered annoying . . . many decision-makers dislike being reminded again of this seemingly endless piece of unfinished business.'[101] Nevertheless, despite over twenty-five years of official recognition that the low representation of women in the UN Secretariat is a serious issue for the organisation, the advancement of women has been glacial.

The average rate of progress in professional posts is approximately 1 per cent growth a year overall, and half that rate in the senior positions at the D-1 and above level.[102] It is much slower again in language posts.[103] Targets are routinely not met, but no sanctions incurred. In 1995, the UN had not quite achieved the goal of 35 per cent of professional posts, with 34.1 per cent of women in posts subject to geographical distribution (and almost two

---

[97] UN Doc. E/CN.6/1993/15, para. 14. This commitment was reaffirmed on International Women's Day in 1994. See UN Doc. E/CN.6/1994/L.8.

[98] UN Doc. ST/AI/382, 3 March 1993, reprinted in *The United Nations and the Advancement of Women*, above note 23 at 456–7.

[99] *Ibid.* at para. 5.

[100] Report of the Secretary-General to the General Assembly on the Improvement of the Status of Women in the Secretariat, UN Doc. A/49/587, 1 November 1994, reprinted in *The United Nations and the Advancement of Women*, above note 23 at 503–11.

[101] JIU Report, above note 53 at iii.

[102] In June 1983, there were 22.3 per cent of women overall in posts subject to geographical distribution, 6 per cent of whom were in positions of D-1 and above. UN Doc. A/48/559 at 16, 21. It is important to note that the number of positions in the higher echelons has fallen overall: in 1983 there were 28 Under-Secretaries-General, compared with 21 in 1993, 25 Assistant Secretaries-General in 1983, 16 in 1993, 89 D-2 positions in 1983, 66 in 1993, 262 D-1 positions in 1983 and 243 in 1993.

[103] Between 1983 and 1993, the percentage of women in language posts rose from 33 per cent to 35 per cent. UN Doc. A/48/559 at 16.

decades short of the Secretary-General's more ambitious 1993 commitment to 50 per cent of women by 1995).[104] It was up to a decade behind in the goal of 25 per cent of D-1 and above positions by 1995.[105] Moreover, the women in the professional category are congregated at the lowest levels. In December 1993, while women held 14.3 per cent of Under-Secretary-General posts and 6.7 per cent of Assistant Secretary-General posts, they held 100 per cent of the positions at the lowest rung of the professional category (P-1)[106] and 49 per cent of P-2 posts.[107] In 1994, the JIU reported that 'If P-1s, P-2s and P-3s ran the organization, the "equitable balance" which the UN sought for 1980 would now be much closer to being achieved.'[108] By 1996, the Secretary-General argued that the goal of equal distribution of professional posts by 2000 was not realistic and urged the General Assembly to revise its targets – downwards.[109] In 1998, the Secretary-General referred again to the 'great challenge' of the 50 per cent by 2000 target.[110] The two specific initiatives he identified were the creation of action plans for each department with targets and the development of a reference manual of 'good practices' with respect to the recruitment of women.[111]

Why is the rhetoric of concern about the position of women in the UN so far from the reality? The 1990s budgetary crisis in the UN, which has led to a freeze on recruitment for professional posts, has made bold action difficult during this period.[112] The reduction of positions in the higher echelons over the last ten years also has had a retarding effect on attempts to change staff composition. But the causes of the imbalance between women and men go deeper. One factor concerns the way the system of geographical distribution of professional posts has operated. First, member states become involved in nominating candidates for high echelon positions and, almost invariably, tend to nominate men. In the UN, as elsewhere, women find

[104] Report of the Secretary-General on the Improvement of the Status of Women in the Secretariat, UN Doc. A/50/691, 27 October 1995, paras 6 to 10.

[105] This prediction is based on the June 1995 proportion of women in these posts (17.1 per cent) and a 1 to 2 per cent annual increase. In June 1995, the percentage of women in USG and ASG posts was 11.8 per cent, far short of the target announced these in 1992 of 'as close to 50/50' of USG and ASG positions (see above note 96).

[106] Women held all six of the P-1 posts.

[107] JIU Report, above note 53 at 4, Table 1.

[108] *Ibid.* at para. 15.

[109] Report of the Secretary-General on the Status of Women in the Secretariat, UN Doc. A/51/304, 1996.

[110] 1998 Report of the Secretary-General, above note 56 at 5–6.

[111] *Ibid.* at 6.

[112] It is noteworthy, however, that of staff members appointed during the freeze, in response to emergencies, only 37 per cent were women: UN Doc. A/48/513 at 8. The Secretary-General has commented that these figures 'reflect the fact that the many mechanisms in place to ensure the search for qualified women candidates have played no part during emergency recruitment conditions'. *Ibid.*

it difficult to be appointed to positions that depend on networking and support.[113] In 1993, there were no women UN staff members from forty-nine states who had nationals in posts subject to geographic distribution. Women from Africa, the Middle East and Eastern Europe are significantly less well-represented than women from other regions.[114] Second, equitable distribution of positions according to nationality continues to have a far greater priority than equitable distribution according to gender. This is perhaps unsurprising in an institution whose membership is defined by statehood. One problem is that the demands for more balanced gender representation are regarded as analogous to the claim of a particular member state whose nationals are under-represented on the UN staff. As Claire de Hedervary wrote in 1982: 'We have reached the stage at the United Nations where women are at least considered a part of the geographic distribution, a kind of . . . Member State. You recruit a Guatemalan, a Belgian, someone from Singapore – and then you recruit a woman.'[115] This elision of two distinct claims to equitable representation, sex and nationality, has obscured the urgency of the former. None of the power-brokers within the UN system have consistently insisted on the need for equal representation of women.[116] This also makes direct strategies such as a quota system or affirmative action plans impracticable. A further factor in the UN's poor record on women is the institutional view that women's family commitments prevents their complete dedication to the job, for example through their ability to travel,[117] as well as the design of job specifications to require regular changes in location.

The failure of the UN to improve significantly the position of women within it is also due to the fact that the implementation of General Assembly targets within the UN bureaucracy has historically attracted little active support from the UN administration.[118] In the 1994 JIU report, the UN's programmes to encourage the recruitment of women were described as 'apathetic and indecisive'.[119] They were seen as strong on targets, but weak on establishing responsibility and accountability for non-implementation. Responsibility for programmes promoting the recruitment of women in the UN is consistently shifted by managers onto others.[120] The annual report on the position of women in the Secretariat is regularly delivered late, which prevents proper scrutiny by states.[121] The content of the reports is almost

---

[113] 'Women in the Secretariat', above note 63 at 18, 19.
[114] UN Doc. A/48/513 at 5.
[115] C. de Hedervary, above note 58 at 696.
[116] See K. Timothy, above note 70 at 88–9.
[117] *Ibid.* at 89.
[118] C. de Hedervary, above note 58 at 697.
[119] JIU Report, above note 53 at para. 39.
[120] *Ibid.* at para. 42.
[121] *Ibid.* at para. 100.

entirely statistical with very little discussion of priorities or strategies,[122] although the 1995–2000 Strategic Plan of Action[123] is a modest improvement in this respect. Within the UN, plans of action are typically not implemented, guidelines on recruitment are routinely ignored, and sexism and discrimination against women still are not regarded as serious failings. Why is this so? The major reason underlines the circularity of the problem: there are not enough women at senior levels in the UN to insist on the urgency and importance of the task. Nor are there are systematic or transparent mechanisms by which senior managers are held accountable for the results they have achieved in recruiting and promoting women.[124] The performance of heads of departments and offices is poorly monitored in this respect[125] and programmes targeted at women are poorly resourced.[126] The lack of any coherent general Secretariat recruitment policy contributes to the imbalance in sex representation. The UN's JIU has referred to recruitment policy as a '*terra incognita* in which people are recruited into the organization in various vague ways'.[127] This allows outmoded organisational structures to continue and 'old boys' networks to flourish[128] – 'the present "non-system" works most to the advantage of the *status quo*, and to the detriment of those trying to catch up after years of neglect: women'.[129]

Although successive Secretaries-General have been careful publicly to support the importance of women's appointments in the Secretariat, whole-hearted commitment to women's equality is rare. In 1984, members of the Ad Hoc Group for Women told the then Secretary-General: 'Every year the women of the United Nations meet with you for what has become a ritual philosophical exchange. . . . We present the perennial problem and you reiterate your commitment to the principles of equality.'[130] Ten years later a similar frustration was expressed, albeit in the more indirect language of UN resolutions, by member states. In 1994, a General Assembly resolution emphasising that a 'visible commitment of the Secretary-General is essential to the achievement of the targets set by the General Assembly',[131] noted 'with concern' that the current rate of increase in women's employment in the UN was insufficient to achieve the objective of 35 per cent participation of women in posts subject to geographical distribution by 1995 and that the participation

[122] *Ibid.*
[123] See Report of the Secretary-General 1994, above note 100.
[124] *Ibid.* at para. 36.
[125] *Ibid.*
[126] *Ibid.* at para. 163.
[127] *Ibid.* at para. 50.
[128] *Ibid.* at para. 51.
[129] *Ibid.* at para. 68.
[130] Quoted in C. Enloe, *Bananas, Beaches, and Bases: Making Feminist Sense of International Politics* (London, Pandora Press, 1989) at 121–2.
[131] GA Res. 49/167, 23 December 1994, reprinted in *The United Nations and the Advancement of Women*, above note 23 at 652–3.

rate of women in posts at the D-1 level 'remains unreasonably low'.[132] The General Assembly also requested the Secretary-General to make full implementation of the 1995–2000 plan of action a specific performance indicator in the appraisal of all UN managers.[133]

The dissonance between Secretaries-General's words and action on women is illustrated by the dramatic, and quite unachievable, leap in targets for women in professional posts by 1995 from 35 per cent to 50 per cent announced by Boutros Boutros-Ghali in 1993. In such circumstances, targets come to appear as utopian goals without any dedication to their realisation. The UN Administrative Tribunal, for example, took a long time to accept any complaint from a woman that failure to appoint or promote was based on sex discrimination in violation of article 8 of the Charter.[134] The lack of commitment to women's equality has permeated the entire organisation. The JIU's 1994 report concluded that: 'Despite many United Nations declarations and conventions, two decades of detailed General Assembly resolutions, and strong policy statements and targets of past and current Secretaries-General, a decade's worth of "action programmes" to improve women's status in the Secretariat have been ineffective and have lost their momentum.'[135]

Responsibility for the lack of women's participation in the UN rests both with member states, which play a very significant role in the composition of the Secretariat, and with the Secretariat's own management. Few member states consistently display a strong concern with the levels of women's participation and they continue to nominate men disproportionately for all levels of UN appointment, particularly in the higher echelons.[136] Indeed, the more important the post, the more likely it is that a man will be nominated to fill it. Moreover, even when urging change upon the Secretariat, states have avoided the imposition of duties on themselves to send women as national delegates to UN fora.

Sexual harassment

The imbalance between women and men in the UN has fostered a culture of discrimination and sexism. The issue of sexual harassment of women in the UN Secretariat has become increasingly prominent. Sexual harassment is of

---

[132] UN Doc. E/CN.6/1994/L.8.

[133] GA Res. 49/222, 23 December 1994, reprinted in *The United Nations and the Advancement of Women*, above note 23 at 653–4.

[134] See Tribunal Administratif, Judgment no. 492, Affair no. 548: *Dauchy*, UN Doc. AT/DEC/492 1990.

[135] JIU Report, above note 53 at iii.

[136] This is despite resolutions such as GA Res. 45/239, 21 December 1990, which calls on states to nominate, encourage and identify more women candidates, especially for senior positions.

course manifest in many institutions and organisations,[137] and the UN is remarkable mainly for the inadequacy of the steps it has taken to eradicate it.[138] While guidelines for dealing with allegations of sexual harassment have been adopted in the Secretariat, no comprehensive policy on the issue has yet been devised[139] and final decision-making power in relation to them rests with the Secretary-General rather than with any independent tribunal. Furthermore, because UN staff members enjoy immunity from prosecution in national courts,[140] cases of sexual harassment cannot be dealt with by more effective national legal remedies.[141] A 1994 case (details of which were leaked despite the Secretary-General's ruling that it remain confidential) illustrates some of the problems with the UN's essentially *ad hoc* approach and with the reluctance of the UN's leadership to take the issue seriously.[142] An Under-Secretary-General was accused of sexual harassment by a more junior woman colleague, the victim arguing that her rejection of sexual advances had led to the harasser attempting to reclassify her position so that she would be no longer able to hold it. An Irish judge, Mella Carroll, was appointed to conduct an investigation into the matter and concluded that sexual harassment had occurred.[143] But her report was never made public and although the harasser ultimately resigned from his position,[144] he was reported to have received a very generous 'retirement' package and payment of his legal fees.[145] The Secretary-General announced that no compensation would be paid to the victim of the harassment.[146] When the victim of the harassment later brought

[137] See S. Halford, 'Feminist change in a patriarchal organisation: the experience of women's initiatives in local government and implications for feminist perspectives on state institutions', in M. Savage and A. Witz (eds), *Gender and Bureaucracy* (Oxford/Cambridge, Blackwell/Sociological Review, 1992) 157 at 179.

[138] On decisions of the UN Administrative Tribunal relating to sexual discrimination see C. Amerasinghe, *The Law of the International Civil Service* (Oxford, Clarendon Press, 1994) at 319.

[139] In March 1994, the CSW called on the Secretary-General to 'develop further comprehensive policy measures aimed at the prevention of sexual harassment in the Secretariat'. UN Doc. E/CN.6/1994/L.8, para. 8.

[140] Charter of the UN, article 105; Convention on the Privileges and Immunities of the United Nations, 13 February 1946, 1 UNTS 15.

[141] M. Singer, 'Jurisdictional immunity of international organizations: human rights and functional concerns', 36 *Virginia Journal of International Law* (1995) 53.

[142] The case is reported in some depth in P. Comeau, 'Guilty verdict handed down in "secret" UN sexual harassment hearing', 1 *Human Rights Tribune* (no. 3, March/April 1994) 19.

[143] Extracts from the report appear *ibid*.

[144] After resigning in February 1994, the official was apparently rehired by the Administrator of the UNDP to serve as a special advisor. After an outcry at this appointment, it was rescinded. *Ibid.* at 19–20. See also remarks of Ciciel Gross in *Proceedings of the 89th Annual Meeting of the American Society of International Law* (Washington DC, American Society of International Law, 1995) 191 at 194–5.

[145] P. Comeau, above note 142 at 20.

[146] *Ibid.*

a civil suit against the official in the New York Supreme Court, the UN argued that he was subject to immunity as an international civil servant.[147] Guidelines on sexual harassment released since this case stress the need to seek informal solutions to such problems, thus emphasising confidentiality and minimising adherence to publicly articulated standards.

Women's participation and representation in decision- and policy-making

The imbalance in the participation of women and men within the UN system is striking. What are its implications? First the imbalance raises issues of human rights. The UN has an institutional commitment to human rights and the equality of women and men through the UN Charter and a series of instruments negotiated and adopted in UN fora.[148] The definition of discrimination on the basis of sex in international law encompasses both direct and indirect discrimination against women.[149] In other words, whatever their motive, practices that result in unequal enjoyment of rights by women constitute discrimination. The Convention on the Elimination of All Forms of Discrimination Against Women (Women's Convention) makes specific reference to the need to take measures to eliminate discrimination against women in political and public life[150] and provides also that: 'States Parties shall take all appropriate measures to ensure to women, on equal terms with men and without any discrimination, the opportunity to represent their Governments at the international level and to participate in the work of international organizations'.[151] CEDAW has stressed the importance of these provisions and called on states parties to the Women's Convention to take temporary special measures to ensure that they are complied with.[152] The

---

[147] C. Gross, above note 144 at 194. See also *Mendaro v. The World Bank* 717 F. 2nd 610 (DC Cir. 1983) where the Bank's claim to immunity from suit under Title VII of the Civil Rights Act 1964 was upheld. The Court commented that requiring the Bank to comply with local employment practices would make it impossible for it to perform its functions. See also *Atkinson v. Inter-American Development Bank* 136 F. 3rd 1335 (DC Cir. 1998), reprinted in 38 *International Legal Materials* (1999) 91 (holding that a garnishee order for family support could not be enforced against an employee of the Bank).

[148] See chapter 7.

[149] Convention on the Elimination of All Forms of Discrimination Against Women, 18 December 1979, 1249 UNTS 13, reprinted in 19 *International Legal Materials* (1980) 33.

[150] *Ibid.*, article 7.

[151] *Ibid.*, article 8.

[152] CEDAW, General Recommendation no. 23, UN Doc. A/52/38/Rev.1, 13 January 1997. The Convention on the Elimination of All Forms of Discrimination Against Women, article 4, provides for transitional special measures.

UN's record on the employment of women and its resistance to improvement violate the standards of equality of the Women's Convention. The patterns of both member states' nominations and Secretariat practices impair women's rights to participation in global policy-making.

The claim that the unequal participation of women in the international system is an issue of human rights has been contested, particularly by Fernando Tesón.[153] Although he acknowledges that there is a 'statistical underrepresentation' of women, Tesón has argued that it is a 'category mistake' to criticise an undemocratic government for its failure to appoint women to posts of influence. The issue of lack of democracy for Tesón is in a much more serious category than sex discrimination, and in any event he would regard all appointments of an illegitimate government as morally invalid.[154] In the case of 'full members of the liberal alliance',[155] Tesón has acknowledged an injustice in the under-representation of women in public life only if this phenomenon is the result of states actively preventing women from exercising their right to vote or to stand for public office.[156]

Despite the terms of the Women's Convention, Tesón has dismissed the notion that the great imbalance in actual political participation between women and men is in itself a human rights issue.[157] In this sense, Tesón's criticism is based on his belief that equality on the basis of sex means formal equality: discrimination simply means formally equal treatment.[158] The problem with this model of equality, as many feminist scholars have pointed out,[159] is that it only offers equality when women and men are in identical positions, but fails to address the underlying causes and consequences of sex discrimination. Institutional practices may not directly discriminate against women, but they can effectively inhibit women's participation by relying on norms reflecting male life patterns as benchmarks of eligibility or success.[160] For example, in the international arena, requirements of extensive travelling depend on considerable domestic support, typically provided by wives.[161]

---

[153] F. Tesón, 'Feminism and international law: a reply', 33 *Virginia Journal of International Law* (1993) 647 at 651–4.

[154] *Ibid.* at 651–2.

[155] *Ibid.* at 652. This term is not further defined by Tesón.

[156] *Ibid.*

[157] *Ibid.* at 653–4.

[158] Tesón has conceded, however, that his 'Kantian' theory of international law would not preclude 'domestic electoral arrangements designed to heighten the probability of electing women in a given state'. He has explained that: 'Local conditions will vary, and in states where women have been previously excluded from politics it may be permissible and desirable to adopt preferential electoral arrangements.' *Ibid.* at 654.

[159] See chapter 2.

[160] K. Knop, 'Re/statements: feminism and state sovereignty in international law', 3 *Transnational Law and Contemporary Problems* (1993) 293 at 304.

[161] *Ibid.* at 304–5.

Apart from the human rights issues, does balanced participation of the sexes in international organisations really make a difference? The major concerns of the UN, it could be argued, do not have a gendered dimension. Security, peacekeeping and human rights are political and social concerns, that affect men and women equally. From this perspective, the slow rate of change in women's numbers in the UN is not a significant problem. Political scientists studying domestic political elections have pointed out that the characteristics of elected representatives may differ significantly from those of the electors and that this is not inevitably a matter of consequence.[162] As Anne Phillips has noted, 'Establishing an empirical under-representation of certain categories of people does not in itself add up to a normative case for their equal or proportionate presence. It may alert us to overt forms of discrimination that are keeping certain people out, but does not yet provide the basis for radical change.'[163]

Determining if and how balanced participation of women and men affects political agendas and cultures is complicated by a paucity of empirical data. No national government or international organisation yet has equal numbers of women and men. The imbalance appears normal and indeed inevitable, and maintains the necessity of 'natural' supportive female roles. Men can dominate government not least because women can be relied on to provide enough support, both at home and in low-level employment,[164] to sustain such activity. But research in a number of political contexts suggests a difference between women and men on political issues.[165] For example, it has been shown that women tend to support peace initiatives, protection of the environment, and the creation and maintenance of social services to a greater degree than men.[166] A study of Finnish women parliamentarians identified their major concerns as social legislation and cultural and educational policies, while their male colleagues gave prominence to transport, public utilities, and economic policy.[167] Women's increased participation in the European Parliament in 1979 coincided with an increased concern with issues of sex equality.[168] The style of decision-making also appears to change in institutions with a significant

[162] Anne Phillips, 'Democracy and representation: or, why should it matter who our representatives are?', in A. Phillips (ed.), *Feminism and Politics* (Oxford, Oxford University Press, 1998) 224 at 225.

[163] *Ibid.*

[164] M. Savage and A. Witz, above note 137 at 3, 11.

[165] C. Hamilton, 'Women in politics: methods of resistance and change', 12 *Women's Studies International Forum* (1989) 129; R. Kelly and J. Burgess, 'Gender and the meaning of power and politics', 9 *Women and Politics* (1989) 47.

[166] *Women in Politics*, above note 26 at 107.

[167] *Ibid.* at 108. See also V. Peterson and A. Runyan, above note 89 at 150 (citing United States studies indicating that women legislators were more interested in 'domestic' issues such as unemployment, housing, poverty, the homeless, health care and child care than men legislators).

[168] V. Randall, above note 24 at 155–6.

participation of women: debates are usually more focused and less polarised and tend to be couched in more accessible and more concrete language.[169]

However, evidence of the effects of women's participation in political decision-making is complex, and even more so in an international forum. In some cases it appears to have little beneficial impact for women generally. Thus the relatively high participation of women in Nordic politics has not delivered significant change in, for example, the position of women in labour markets.[170] Anne Phillips has noted that: 'Politics appears to be more of an independent variable than might have been expected and substantial political equalities look possible even in the absence of thoroughgoing social or economic reform.'[171] Women politicians are required to operate within male-defined political structures, and the question of whether or not they are appointed to positions on important policy committees may affect their ability to participate in politics.[172] Party politics, for example, can significantly constrain women's representation in political fora. In her study of women parliamentarians in India, Rai has described the 'gate-keeping' functions of political parties which control political agendas. She has concluded that 'institutional constraints, and systems of organisational incentives and disincentives are important explanations of the limited role that women can play in advancing the agenda of gender-justice through party-based political work'.[173] Women politicians are more likely to display allegiance to party platforms than to women's issues. While women vary in their acknowledgment that they have a 'women's' mandate to fulfil, even those who are committed in that way are likely to face a conflict between 'selling out' their ideals or becoming marginalised within the system.[174]

The terms 'participation' and 'representation' are not necessarily synonyms, although they are regularly used as such. Greater participation in political processes does not necessarily lead to greater representation because of the problem of ensuring the accountability of 'representatives'.[175]

---

[169] *Women in Politics*, above note 26 at 108. The Joint Inspector's report referred to some of this type of research, which, it said, 'suggests that women managers provide fresh perspectives, important managerial skills (such as building consensus and teamwork), and can encourage a much more open and creative work environment'. JIU Report, above note 53 at para. 157.

[170] A. Phillips, *Engendering Democracy* (Cambridge, Polity Press in association with Blackwell, 1991) at 19; H. Skjeie, 'The rhetoric of difference: on women's inclusion into political elites', 19 *Politics and Society* (1991) 233.

[171] A. Phillips, above note 170 at 19.

[172] N. Norton, 'Women, it is not enough to be elected: committee position makes a difference', in G. Duerst-Lahti and R. Kelly (eds), *Gender, Power, Leadership and Governance* (Ann Arbor, University of Michigan Press, 1995) 15.

[173] S. Rai, 'Gender and representation: women MPs in the Indian Parliament 1991–6', in A. Goetz (ed.), *Getting Institutions Right for Women in Development* (London/New York, Zed Books, 1997) 104 at 118.

[174] H. Skjeie, above note 170.

[175] A. Phillips, above note 170 at 19. See also S. Rai, above note 173 at 117–8.

Anne Phillips has noted that 'it is only when there are mechanisms through which women can formulate their own policies or interests that we can really talk of their "representation"'.[176] However, the increasing participation of women tends to increase the articulation of differences among women.[177] Of course the position of elected women in national politics is not directly comparable with that of women who are representatives of their state, for example at the General Assembly or ECOSOC, where they must follow state directions and may have little space to address women's concerns. For women in the Secretariat who are international civil servants, there is the added burden of operating within the complex, male-dominated bureaucracy.

The claim that women bring different attributes to public life to men also raises some thorny theoretical issues. Arguments for women's equal participation in decision-making based on the special qualities they might bring to the process often rely on the assumption that women have a 'different voice' to, and a different way of arriving at, moral judgments than, men. As we have seen in chapter 2, these are controversial assertions and may perpetuate myths about women's nature, rather than developing an understanding of the power relationships that attribute particular characteristics to women. This issue is an example of the tension in much feminist scholarship between regarding gender as an unfixed, socially constructed category on the one hand and privileging the special standpoint of women on the other.[178]

How women's equal participation in decision-making would affect the agenda and priorities of decision-making within the different UN fora is, then, not yet certain. But, whatever the evidence of a distinctive woman's influence in political decision-making, it is at least clear that the realities of women's lives under the present unbalanced system do not contribute in any significant way to the shaping of UN policy. The distinction between the two notions is often elided, as Ruth Roach Pierson has shown in the context of feminist attitudes to peace and war.[179] Pierson has pointed out that there is no necessary link between maternality and opposition to war.[180] From a historical perspective, she has disentangled the distinction between essentialist feminist positions on peace derived from women's role as nurturer and

---

[176] A. Phillips, above note 170 at 19. See also A. Phillips, *Democracy and Difference* (University Park, Pennsylvania State University, 1993) at 97–100.
[177] See R. Kelly, M. Saint-Germain and J. Horn, 'Female public officials: a different voice?', 515 *Annals of the American Academy of Political and Social Science* (1991) 77 at 87.
[178] C. Murphy, 'Seeing women, recognizing gender, recasting international relations', 50 *International Organization* (1996) 513 at 525–6.
[179] R. Pierson, '"Did your mother wear army boots?", Feminist theory and women's relations to war, peace and revolution', in S. Macdonald, P. Holden and S. Ardener (eds), *Images of Women in Peace and War: Cross-Cultural and Historical Perspectives* (Basingstoke, Macmillan, 1987) 205.
[180] *Ibid.* at 207.

mother on the one hand and, on the other, the historical exclusion of women from decisions relating to warfare.

So, too, in a broader international context, it is not necessary to identify particular attributes of women in order to observe their isolation from international decision-making. While women worldwide have tremendously different life experiences, they share at least a lack of access to power and a vulnerability to economic, social and sexual exploitation. Karen Knop has suggested that women's under-representation in decision-making could be characterised as impinging on their 'collective autonomy'.[181] She has written that 'women should be able to decide at least certain international issues not because they will decide them better than or even differently from men, but because they as a group ... should be able to make the decisions that affect their lives'.[182] Although the notion of women's 'collective autonomy' is a complex and contentious one on the international plane, given the great differences in women's positions and experiences, it provides a useful understanding of the significance of women's participation in international decision-making.

A separate element is the difficulty of men adequately representing women's interests, which are not a fixed or stable category, particularly in the international arena. Anne Phillips has argued, in the context of domestic political representation, that 'if women's interests were transparently obvious to any intelligent observer, there might be no particular case ... for insisting on representatives who also happen to be women'.[183] She has pointed out that if, on the contrary, women's interests are 'varied, unstable, perhaps still in the process of formation', the separation of the representative from what is to be represented is much more difficult. The imbalance in men's representation in national and international governmental structures allows male life experiences to be regarded as a general, rather than gendered, category.

Concern with participation and representation, and concomitant issues of legitimacy, are traditional and, indeed, natural in an international governmental organisation. In the UN system these concerns have been almost exclusively about issues of nationality and regionality.[184] All UN fora take participation of the various country groupings (based on geography, politics and economy) extremely seriously. The universality of the UN's mandate has been interpreted in ways that work against the recognition of particularities

---

[181] The notion derives from the work of Denise Réaume on institutional structures for ethnic and cultural groups. See K. Knop, above note 160 at 306.

[182] *Ibid.* at 306–7.

[183] A. Phillips, above note 170 at 15.

[184] For example, as noted in chapter 3, the Statute of the ICJ, 26 June 1945, 1 UNTS xvi provides that judges on the Court be drawn from a variety of legal systems (article 9). The Charter of the UN refers to the principle of 'equitable geographical distribution' in the election of non-permanent members of the Security Council (article 23) and 'the importance of recruiting [UN] staff on as wide a geographical basis as possible' (article 101).

of identity, other than nationality, except as marginal coda. Women typically find themselves recognised, if at all, in a category of 'women, indigenous persons and other minorities'. The implication is that women's issues are a special, minority concern. Gender is elided with minority racial membership, indigeneity, disability and other characteristics that deviate from the assumed international norm of personhood – a white man. Why is this grouping inappropriate? Most obviously, women are not a global minority. Numerically, they constitute a little over half of the global population. Second, the grouping inaccurately implies a commonality of perspective among women and attributes a single personality (and voice) to them. The UN's political and legal agenda is seriously skewed and lopsided by the institution's domination by men.

Women and their lives are invisible in all 'mainstream' areas of UN activity because women are not properly represented in its structures. In this sense, the UN's current agenda is a reflection of the silence of women. Cynthia Enloe has connected the male domination of the Security Council with its preoccupation with military issues and comparative lack of concern about development, health and environment programmes.[185] While this may be explained by the wording of chapter VII of the UN Charter, which gives the Security Council primary responsibility for international peace and security, it is perpetuated by the perception of security issues in the limited context of military activities.[186] Moreover, the disproportionate effect of Security Council actions on women and children goes unacknowledged and unchallenged.

Gender mainstreaming

The UN has responded to criticism of its marginalisation of women by instituting policies of 'gender mainstreaming'.[187] This process involves integrating concerns of gender into all the activities that are funded or undertaken by an organisation, and spreading responsibility for gender issues throughout the organisation, through appropriate guidelines and training, so that they become an aspect of the routine work of all staff.[188] The major practical

---

[185] C. Enloe, *The Morning After: Sexual Politics at the End of the Cold War* (Berkeley, University of California Press, 1993) at 259.

[186] See chapter 9.

[187] See Beijing Platform for Action, paras 79, 105, 123, 141, 164, 189, 202, 229, 238, 252 and 273. See the discussion of gender mainstreaming in the context of human rights in chapter 7.

[188] S. Razavi and C. Miller, *Gender Mainstreaming: A Study of Efforts by the UNDP, the World Bank and the ILO to Institutionalize Gender Issues* (Geneva, UN Research Institute for Social Development, 1995) at ii. See also Council of Europe Committee of Ministers, *Gender Mainstreaming: Conceptual Framework, Methodology and Presentation of Good Practices*, 26 March 1998, Doc. GR-EG (98) 1.

problem with the process of gender mainstreaming has been translating worthy commitments into action. Responsibility for gender issues has tended to remain with specialist staff and has encountered sustained resistance.[189] A review of the policy as implemented in the UNDP, World Bank and ILO found that there was inadequate budgeting for the gender components of projects, insufficient analytical skills and supervision of their implementation and a general lack of political commitment both within the organisation and at the country level.[190] The rhetoric of mainstreaming was adopted, with little monitoring or follow-up. At the World Bank, proponents of gender concerns were required to provide rigorous evidence of potential efficiency gains.[191] Although 'mainstreaming' has had very limited impact, the policy has allowed the reduction of resources for specialised women's units within UN agencies.

A conceptual limitation of the UN's gender mainstreaming policies is that 'gender' is assumed to be a synonym for women, leaving male gender identities unexamined. It requires women to change, but not men. In a case study of an FAO fish-farming project in sub-Saharan Africa, Elizabeth Harrison has described how 'gender issues', prominent in the project's rationale, ended up being marginalised.[192] This was not simply because of male resistance or organisational inadequacies. The interpretation of the gender mandate varied greatly among the stakeholders in the project, from those in the FAO in Rome, to field workers in Africa and local farmers. Gender is not an easily transmissible technical concept and can also be very threatening to those already holding power. In the FAO project, 'gender policy' became radically simplified. In the field, it ended up as little more than the collection of information on the numbers of women involved in fish farming and the goal of including more, without any impact on technical planning. Local project workers could not understand the pressure to include women in farming projects and resented it as irrelevant and inconvenient.[193]

Conclusion

Both the revivalist literature on the UN's renaissance prompted by the end of the cold war and the reformist writings generated by the UN's fiftieth anniversary almost entirely ignored one of the most significant problems facing this institution as it enters the twenty-first century – its exclusion and marginalisation

---

[189] See generally C. Cockburn, *In the Way of Women: Men's Resistance to Sex Equality in Organisations* (Basingstoke, Macmillan, 1991).

[190] S. Razavi and C. Miller, above note 188 at 65–6.

[191] *Ibid.* at 67.

[192] E. Harrison, 'Fish, feminists and the FAO: translating "gender" through different institutions in the development process', in A. Goetz, above note 173 at 61.

[193] *Ibid.* at 69–71.

of women.[194] The general silence about women in discussions of UN reform has made issues of sex and gender appear irrelevant to the process.[195]

The issue of the absence of women from UN decision-making processes, however, cuts across all the commonly identified concerns about the future of the UN: the UN's role in international security, peacekeeping and election monitoring, its bureaucratic inefficiency and financial accountability, the position of the Secretary-General, the protection of human rights and the environment, the promotion of economic development, and the membership of and relationship between the various UN bodies and institutions.[196] Examination of the way sex and gender have affected UN structures and work therefore allows new perspectives on the standard list of concerns. Spike Peterson and Anne Sisson Runyan have described the significance of a 'gender-sensitive lens' in world politics.[197] They have argued that it can transform the simple observation of the presence of men and the absence of women to an awareness that 'women are in fact an important part of the picture even though they are obscured when we focus on the men', and further to an understanding that 'constructions of masculinity are . . . dependent upon, opposing constructions of femininity'.[198] In this sense, the very categories into which the UN's work is compartmentalised and analysed – security, peacekeeping, human rights and economic development – are shaped by sex and gender. They are all constructs largely defined by male experiences. Indeed, the presence of men in the UN system can be seen as contingent on the absence of women.[199]

In the context of national political life, Carole Pateman has pointed out that for women to become citizens as *women* – 'as autonomous, equal, yet

---

[194] E.g. A. Roberts and B. Kingsbury (eds), *United Nations, Divided World: The United Nation's Role in International Relations* (Oxford, Clarendon Press, 2nd edn 1993) contains a few scattered references to women's rights, but does not mention the almost complete absence of women from senior levels of decision-making within the UN. Erskine Childers and Brian Urquhart's important guide to the improvement of the quality of leadership within the UN makes occasional critical reference to the paucity of women in high posts in the UN, describing the situation as 'appalling' and 'grotesque', but it, too, does not examine the issue further. Above note 54 at 30, 60.

[195] For example, in one of the rare analyses of this issue, Margaret Galey took an almost apologetic tone in writing: 'Raising the concept of sex-gender relations must surely seem unusual in a discussion of UN reform.' M. Galey, 'Gender roles and UN reform', 22 *Political Science and Politics* (1989) 813 at 815. For a useful early analysis of the position of women within the UN system see N. Davidson and M. Croke, above note 22.

[196] For a useful survey of reformist moves within the UN see M. Bertrand, 'The historical development of efforts to reform the UN', in A. Roberts and B. Kingsbury, above note 194 at 420. See also P. Wilenski, 'Reforming the United Nations for the post-cold war era', in M. Bustelo and P. Alston (eds), *Whose New World Order: What Role for the United Nations?* (Annandale, Federation Press, 1991) 122.

[197] V. Peterson and A. Runyan, above note 89 at 1–3.

[198] *Ibid.* at 7.

[199] *Ibid.* at 7–8.

sexually different beings from men' – the theory and practice of democracy will have to be radically transformed.[200] She has argued that the possibility for radical change is now more open than at other points in history, given the instability of patriarchal institutions and the force of feminist critiques.[201] These observations are equally applicable in the international context. While increasing the participation of women in the UN is only one aspect of the broader project of enhancing the UN's future, it is essential for increasing the UN's effectiveness and accountability and involves two distinct but related tasks.[202] First, women must participate equally in the UN and other global political structures. Second, the international power structures themselves must be challenged and reconstructed to accommodate the half of humanity currently on their margins.

What practical strategies can be implemented in order to achieve the goals of equal participation and of transformation? The first task requires that within the UN the present strategies to increase the proportion of women in policy positions must be much more closely monitored.[203] The practical commitment of the Secretary-General and all levels of UN management to this task is crucial. The Secretary-General should begin to appoint women as his special representatives and envoys to deal with particular issues.[204] The performance of managers should be measured by their success in recruiting women, especially at senior levels. A high-level permanent and properly resourced office for women staff issues within the UN should be created as well as a mentoring programme for newer women employees. Personnel policies should be reviewed to ensure that position specifications and entitlements do not directly or indirectly discriminate against women.[205] Women's participation will depend on the possibility of new working arrangements, such as flexible working hours, leave entitlements and career break schemes. A comprehensive sexual harassment policy must be adopted, accompanied by an adequate complaint resolution mechanism, and proper training in eradicating sexual harassment should be a requirement for all managers. Member states should consider withholding a portion of their dues if agreed targets for women in professional posts are not met. Membership of the UN should be contingent on a state's preparedness to introduce measures to secure equal representation of women in national political fora.[206] Member

---

[200] C. Pateman, *The Disorder of Women: Democracy, Feminism and Political Theory* (Cambridge, Polity, 1989) at 14.

[201] *Ibid.*

[202] V. Peterson and A. Runyan, above note 89 at 150.

[203] See GA Res. 53/119, 9 December 1998 (calling on the Secretary-General to implement fully and monitor the strategic plan of action for the improvement of the status of women).

[204] *Ibid.*

[205] K. Knop, above note 160 at 305.

[206] V. Peterson and A. Runyan, above note 89 at 154.

states also need to acknowledge their own responsibility to increase women's participation in the UN Secretariat and specialised agencies through their influence over the staff nomination process.

One response to the inadequate participation of women within UN structures has been the active participation of women's NGOs. In chapters 3 and 4 we described how women's NGOs have become increasingly sophisticated in participating in international law-making and in targeting global summit meetings and parallel NGO fora to ensure their concerns are included. Proposals to ensure the representation of international civil society at the General Assembly[207] are thus of potential significance for women, if their representation is taken seriously.

The achievement of the second task, the transformation of the structures of international power, builds on the participation of women, although it is clear that feminist changes in political agendas do not come easily. Peterson and Runyan have suggested that increasing women's participation in decision-making would allow, first, greater attention to be drawn to issues of women's reproductive roles and work; second, an increased demand for gender-differentiated research which would document how, for example, militarisation, poverty and environmental harm disadvantage women in particular; and third, a type of 'distributive gender justice' – change in policies that would transfer public resources from military and industrial practices to women to enable them to lead safer lives.[208]

As we noted in chapter 2, the transformation of international society also depends on the feminist strategy of reducing the imaginative grip of traditional concepts through challenging their 'objectivity' and 'impartiality' and analysing the gendered experiences on which they are based. For example, the narrow notion of 'security' presently animating the Security Council must be expanded to encompass consideration of the effect of threats to international peace and responses to them on the most vulnerable in society: women's systemic *insecurity* must be taken into account in any properly human meaning of security.[209]

At a basic level, challenging the sexed and gendered character of international institutions depends on a revision of the division of labour that confines women and men to different spheres of activity. As Peterson and Runyan have argued, 'For world politics to change, we must relate the gender politics of everyday life and personal experience to their consequences for systemic processes and global crises.'[210] If the nexus between sex and gender

---

[207] Report of the Secretary-General, Reviving the United Nations: A Programme for Reform, UN Doc. A/51/950, 14 July 1997.

[208] V. Peterson and A. Runyan, above note 89 at 150–1.

[209] See further chapter 9.

[210] V. Peterson and A. Runyan, above note 89 at 156–7. See also *Plan of Action to Correct Present Imbalances in the Participation of Men and Women in Political Life* (Geneva, Inter-Parliamentary Union, 1994) at 6–7.

and the division of labour into public and private spheres were broken, if women and men shared household and workplace responsibilities, the conditions for equal political participation in international organisations would be in place. At the same time, this could make the need for *representation* of women's interests less significant: the breakdown of the gendered public/private distinction would lead to 'a world in which gender should become less relevant and the abstractions of humanity more meaningful . . . [rather than] a world in which women have to speak continuously as women – or men are left to speak as men'.[211]

[211] A. Phillips, above note 170 at 7.

7

Human rights

Introduction

The notion of human rights describes what it is to be human and defines the 'rock bottom of human existence'.[1] Human rights law challenges the traditional state-centred scope of international law, giving individuals and groups, otherwise with very restricted access to the international legal system, the possibility of making international legal claims. In many ways, human rights law has been the most accessible and hospitable area of international law for women because it explicitly acknowledges women's lives, albeit in a limited fashion. The aim of this chapter is to investigate the ways in which human rights law recognises and promotes the concerns of women and to assess its potential for the advancement of women's interests. It begins with an account of the development of the human rights canon and feminist critiques of rights. The chapter then discusses women-specific human rights instruments and the reasons why they have not provided an adequate response to human rights abuses typically sustained by women. Finally, the chapter considers recent developments that suggest the potential of human rights law to protect the 'rock bottom' of women's lives.

The evolution of human rights law

Modern human rights law derives primarily from Western philosophical thought dealing with the relationship between those who govern and those who are governed, although it also has some resonance in other cultural traditions.[2] Of particular significance in its development have been the values of Judaeo-Christian morality, natural law principles and political theories

[1] J. Galtung, *Human Rights in Another Key* (Oxford, Polity Press, 1994) at 2.
[2] *Philosophical Foundations of Human Rights* (Paris, UNESCO, 1996).

associated with the rationalism of the French and American revolutions. These theories include Locke's social contract and natural rights theories, Montesquieu's theory of the separation of powers between the legislature, executive and judiciary, and Rousseau's theory of the sovereignty of the people.[3]

Human rights law is largely a product of the post-World War II international legal order.[4] It poses a profound challenge to the notion of state sovereignty because it asserts an international interest in the way states treat their populations. The UN Charter recognised in principle the importance of the protection of human rights by states,[5] and a series of both general and particular international instruments have since given definition and texture to this commitment.[6] The three major general instruments, the Universal Declaration of Human Rights (UDHR),[7] the International Covenant on Economic, Social and Cultural Rights (ICESCR) [8] and the International Covenant on Civil and Political Rights (ICCPR)[9] have become known as the 'international bill of rights'. Other instruments cover specific violations of rights (for example, genocide,[10] racial discrimination,[11] apartheid[12] and torture[13]) and specific protected groups (for example, women,[14] children[15] and

---

[3] A. Cassese, *International Law in a Divided World* (Oxford, Clarendon Press, 1986) at 288; L. Henkin, *The Age of Rights* (New York, Columbia University Press, 1990).

[4] For a survey of the antecedents of the UN human rights system see H. Steiner and P. Alston, *International Human Rights in Context* (Oxford, Clarendon Press, 1996) at 59–116.

[5] Charter of the UN, 28 June 1945, articles 1, 55 and 56.

[6] A useful guide to the development of international human rights law is T. Meron (ed.), *Human Rights in International Law* (New York, Oxford University Press, 1984). See also *The United Nations and Human Rights 1945–1995* (New York, UN, 1995).

[7] GA Res. 217A (III), 10 December 1948.

[8] 16 December 1966, 993 UNTS 3, reprinted in 6 *International Legal Materials* (1967) 360.

[9] 16 December 1966, 993 UNTS 171, reprinted in 6 *International Legal Materials* (1967) 368.

[10] Convention on the Prevention and Punishment of the Crime of Genocide, 9 December 1948, 78 UNTS 277.

[11] International Convention on the Elimination of All Forms of Racial Discrimination, 21 December 1965, 660 UNTS 195, reprinted in 5 *International Legal Materials* (1966) 352.

[12] International Convention on the Suppression and Punishment of the Crime of Apartheid, 30 November 1973, 1015 UNTS 243.

[13] Convention against Torture and Other Cruel, Inhuman or Degrading Treatment or Punishment, 10 December 1984, UN Doc. A/39/51, reprinted in 23 *International Legal Materials* (1984) 1027, substantive changes noted in 24 *International Legal Materials* (1985) 535.

[14] Convention on the Elimination of All Forms of Discrimination Against Women, 18 December 1979, 1249 UNTS 13, reprinted in 19 *International Legal Materials* (1980) 33.

[15] Convention on the Rights of the Child, 20 November 1989, GA Res. 44/25, reprinted in 28 *International Legal Materials* (1989) 1448.

migrant workers[16]). There is also a series of general regional human rights treaties that offer various forms of protection to human rights within the specified region,[17] and specialised regional treaties.[18] International human rights law is one of the most developed branches of international law. It has not only generated a considerable number of treaties and 'soft' law instruments, but has also developed relatively sophisticated monitoring regimes and institutions. The regional treaties can be invoked under specified circumstances by individuals claiming violations in special courts and commissions, and most of the UN treaties establish expert monitoring committees that oversee compliance in a number of ways. It is often argued that many international human rights standards meet the conditions for the creation of customary international law.[19]

The development of human rights law through the UN is often, if controversially, described in terms of 'generations'.[20] The first generation of rights consists of civil and political rights. First generation rights are typically characterised as rights that can be claimed by individuals against governments. Such rights protect against arbitrary interference by the state. Civil and political rights may be described as 'negative' in that they require abstention by the state from particular acts, such as torture, arbitrary deprivation of life, liberty and security. They focus on 'domesticating, restraining the state, making the state obey due process of law in principle created and upheld by the state'.[21] The core of first generation rights is the preservation of the autonomy of the individual. The major general document of the first generation of rights is the ICCPR.

The second generation of rights comprises economic, social and cultural rights. These are rights, such as those to health, housing and education, that

---

[16] International Convention on the Protection of the Rights of All Migrant Workers and Members of Their Families, 18 December 1990, GA Res. 45/158, reprinted in 30 *International Legal Materials* (1991) 1517.

[17] European Convention for the Protection of Human Rights and Fundamental Freedoms, 4 November 1950, 213 UNTS 221; American Convention on Human Rights, 22 November 1969, 1114 UNTS 123, reprinted in 9 *International Legal Materials* (1970) 673; African Charter on Human and Peoples' Rights, 26 June 1981, reprinted in 21 *International Legal Materials* (1982) 59.

[18] E.g. The European Convention for the Prevention of Torture and Inhuman or Degrading Treatment, 26 November 1987, reprinted in 27 *International Legal Materials* (1988) 1152; Inter-American Convention to Prevent and Punish Torture, 9 December 1985, reprinted in 25 *International Legal Materials* (1986) 519; Convention Governing the Specific Aspects of the Refugee Problems in Africa, 10 September 1969, 1001 UNTS 45.

[19] E.g. *The United Nations and Human Rights*, above note 6 at 7; *Filartiga v. Pena-Irala* 630 F. 2d 876 (1980).

[20] P. Alston, 'A third generation of solidarity rights: progressive development or obfuscation of international human rights law?', 29 *Netherlands International Law Review* (1982) 307.

[21] J. Galtung, above note 1 at 8.

require positive activity by the state to ensure their protection. They assume an active, interventionist role for governments and can be claimed by individuals and groups to secure their subsistence, with dignity, as human beings. The most detailed definition of second generation rights is in the ICESCR.[22] The comparative justiciability of the first and second generation rights is often raised in debates about the implementation of human rights.[23] Can governments be held accountable for violations of economic, social and cultural rights in the same way as they can for violations of civil and political rights? How can causal links be established between alleged violations of economic and social rights and state actions, or inaction? What standard of compliance is required – is it a general standard, or does it depend on the level of economic development of the state concerned?[24]

The third generation of rights encompasses peoples', or collective, rights, such as the rights to self-determination, development and peace, that can only be claimed by groups, rather than by individuals.[25] Claims of peoples' rights can be made against the international community, as well as particular nation states. The guarantee of collective rights assumes both that the benefits will flow to individuals within the group and that the interests of all members of the group will coincide. Many of the third generation rights are contained in 'soft' law instruments, such as UN General Assembly declarations and resolutions.[26] Their most complete translation into 'hard', treaty, norms is in the African Charter of Human and Peoples' Rights.[27]

Perhaps the most contentious of the third generation rights is the right to development.[28] The Declaration on the Right to Development was adopted by the UN General Assembly in 1986 (by vote, rather than consensus) after a decade of negotiation.[29] The Declaration is couched in general terms and its parameters are hard to determine. 'Development' is defined as 'a comprehensive economic, social, cultural and political process, which aims at the constant improvement of the well-being of the entire population and of all

[22] See also European Social Charter, 18 October 1961, 529 UNTS 89; Protocol Amending the Charter, 21 October 1991, reprinted in 31 *International Legal Materials* (1992) 155.

[23] See Committee on Economic, Social and Cultural Rights, General Comment no. 3, UN Doc.E/1991/23, 1990 Annex III.

[24] See generally F. Coomans and F. van Hoof (eds), *The Right to Complain about Economic, Social and Cultural Rights* (Utrecht, Netherlands Institute of Human Rights, 1995).

[25] *Lake Lubicon Band v. Canada* Communication no. 167/1984 (Human Rights Committee).

[26] E.g. Declaration on the Right of Peoples to Peace, GA Res. 39/11, 12 November 1984.

[27] African Charter of Human and Peoples' Rights, articles 19 to 24.

[28] For differing views on the right to development see F. Snyder and P. Slynn, *International Law of Development: Comparative Perspectives* (Abingdon, Professional Books Ltd, 1987).

[29] GA Res. 41/128, 4 December 1986.

individuals on the basis of their active, free and meaningful participation in development and in the fair distribution of benefits resulting therefrom'.[30] Thus the Declaration links human rights and economic relations by asserting that the aims of development are not simply economic growth but are primarily social and human, and it emphasises the interdependence of social justice at the national and international levels. The right to development is defined as an individual right 'by virtue of which every human person and all peoples are entitled to participate in, contribute to, and enjoy economic, social and cultural and political development, in which all human rights and fundamental freedoms can be fully realized'. It also 'implies the full realization of the right of peoples to self-determination, which includes, subject to the relevant provisions of both International Covenants on Human Rights, the exercise of their inalienable right to full sovereignty over all their natural wealth and resources'.[31] The problems of implementing the Declaration, and determining its status as a human right, are illustrated by the deliberations of two UN Working Groups on the Right to Development, one governmental group (1982–89) and another, expert group (1993–96), and the 1990 Global Consultation on the Realization of the Right to Development.[32] Yash Ghai has described the Declaration as 'a fuzzy document, trying to be all things to all persons'.[33]

Despite the absence of operational language in the Declaration, the idea of a right to development has taken on great symbolic significance in the UN system for both the South and the North. The South regards it as a recognition of fundamental economic inequality between South and North and the responsibility of the North to do something to redress it. In this sense, the right to development is the economic aspect of the political right to self-determination and was a central part of the South's advocacy of a 'New International Economic Order' in the 1970s.[34] Also, the connection made by the Declaration between human rights violations and the international political and economic system allows the shifting of responsibility for observance of human rights from individual states. This shift from the national arena to the international means, as Yash Ghai has pointed out, that specific rights are sacrificed to 'an ambiguous portmanteau right of development', whose definition and implementation is left up to the state.[35] The hostility of many Northern states to the Declaration stems from its linkage

[30] Declaration on the Right to Development, Preamble, para. 2.
[31] *Ibid.*, article 1.
[32] *The United Nations and Human Rights*, above note 6 at 74–80.
[33] Y. Ghai, 'Human rights and governance: the Asia debate', 15 *Australian Yearbook of International Law* (1994) 1 at 10.
[34] Declaration on the Establishment of a New International Economic Order, GA Res. 3201 (S-VI) 1 May 1974, reprinted in 13 *International Legal Materials* (1974) 715; Charter of Economic Rights and Duties of States, GA Res. 3281 (XXIX) 12 December 1974, reprinted in 14 *International Legal Materials* (1975) 251.
[35] Y. Ghai, above note 33 at 10.

of human rights language with international economic issues and the assertion of limits on international economic activity and trade policies, the need for restructuring of the global economy and the implication of a duty on developed states 'to promote more rapid development of developing countries'.[36] The 1993 Vienna Conference on Human Rights continued the tradition of ambiguity by specifically recognising the right to development as a universal and inalienable right and an integral part of the international human rights canon without further elaboration of its content.[37] In the 1990s the right to development has become linked to the environment through the concept of sustainable development. The UNDP is now seeking ways of integrating human rights throughout its policies on sustainable development.[38]

The generational metaphor in human rights law is controversial. First, very few rights fall neatly into a single category. For example, the right to freedom of thought, conscience and religion appears to be a quintessential individual civil right.[39] However, people form their thoughts and beliefs through shared ideas drawn from within their culture and express them, even internally, through their shared language. Culture and language are at the heart of peoples' rights, and peoples can only be sustained through adequate standards of living, education and health – economic and social rights.[40] Second, the metaphor implies a hierarchy in the development of human rights within the international community. It is largely the product of cold war politics and decolonisation.[41] Northern states have typically regarded civil and political rights as the most crucial for international protection and many commentators from the North still regard them as the paradigm against which all newer claims of rights must be measured. Indeed, some assert that civil and political rights are the only possible form of international human rights.[42] Civil and political rights fit easily into liberal accounts of rights because they attach to the individual and provide a buffer against governmental action. Nations of the South have usually given the strongest statements of support for economic, social and cultural rights and group or peoples' rights, particularly the right to development. The argument is sometimes made that economic under-development makes concern with civil and political rights irrelevant or, indeed, destructive in the context of fragile

[36] Declaration on the Right to Development, article 4.
[37] World Conference on Human Rights, Vienna Declaration and Programme of Action, 25 June 1993, UN Doc. A/CONF.157/23, reprinted in 32 *International Legal Materials* (1993) 1661, para. 10.
[38] UNDP, *Integrating Human Rights with Sustainable Human Development* (New York, UN, 1998).
[39] ICCPR, article 18.
[40] Professor Joan Fitzpatrick, lecture at the George Washington University Human Rights Course, Oxford, July 1998.
[41] See P. Alston, 'Revitalising the United Nations' work on human rights and development', 18 *Melbourne University Law Review* (1991) 216, 218–21.
[42] E.g. M. Cranston, 'Are there any human rights?', *Daedalus* (no. 4, 1983), 1.

states.[43] In turn, the status of third generation rights has been regularly challenged in the North. The apparent end of the cold war allowed the Vienna Conference to attempt to resolve this debate by the very general prescription that 'all human rights are universal, indivisible and interdependent and interrelated' and that they must accordingly be treated 'in a fair and equal manner, on the same footing, and with the same emphasis'.[44]

In any event, the notion of generations has not been rigidly translated in international legal instruments. Some span a number of generations: for example, the UDHR, adopted by the UN General Assembly in 1948, acknowledges both first and second generation rights, as do the Convention on the Elimination of All Forms of Discrimination (the Women's Convention) and the Convention on the Rights of the Child (the Children's Convention); both the ICCPR and the ICESCR protect the right to self-determination, an inherently group rather than individual right; and the African Charter on Human and Peoples' Rights includes rights from all three generations. Nevertheless, the stronger language of obligation[45] and the more effective enforcement measures[46] in the ICCPR compared to the ICESCR or instruments of the third generation rights have been used to support the assertion of the superiority of first generation rights. The collapse of many communist and socialist regimes since 1990 has also contributed to the sense that liberal values and rights have a permanence and solidity that other understandings of rights do not possess.[47]

Human rights law is under constant challenge. Most states formally accept the international regime,[48] but undermine their legal commitment by

[43] See Y. Ghai, above note 33 at 6.

[44] Vienna Declaration and Programme of Action, I, para. 5.

[45] Compare ICESCR, article 2.1 ('Each State Party to the present Covenant undertakes to take steps . . . to the maximum of its available resources, with a view to achieving progressively the full realization of the rights recognized in the present Covenant by all appropriate means, including particularly the adoption of legislative measures') with ICCPR, article 2.1 ('Each Party to the present Covenant undertakes to respect and to ensure to all individuals within its territory and subject to its jurisdiction the rights recognized in the present Covenant, without distinction of any kind').

[46] States parties to both the ICCPR and the ICESCR are obliged to make periodic reports on the implementation of their obligations. The former contains two additional mechanisms to monitor implementation: the possibility of complaints by states parties that other states parties are not fulfilling their treaty obligations (article 41); and the right of individual complaint against a state party: Optional Protocol to the ICCPR, 16 December 1966, 999 UNTS 302, reprinted in 6 *International Legal Materials* (1967) 383.

[47] See generally F. Fukuyama, *The End of History and the Last Man* (New York, Free Press, 1992).

[48] As of December 1999 the ICCPR had 144 parties; the ICESCR, 142; the International Convention on the Elimination of All Forms of Racial Discrimination, 155; the Convention on the Elimination of All Forms of Discrimination Against Women, 165; the Convention against Torture, 118; and the Convention on the Rights of the Child, 191.

use of extensive reservations,[49] claw-back and derogation provisions[50] that allow states to assert imperatives of national law, public safety and security[51] or inadequate national implementation.[52] Many states are responsible for widespread human rights violations. Another form of challenge focuses on the Western origins of human rights law allowing claims of cultural relativity. For example, at the Vienna Conference on Human Rights in 1993, a number of Asian states claimed that human rights as interpreted in the West were based on a commitment to individualism and were at odds with the Asian tradition of concern with the community.[53] The vulnerability of human rights law to non-observance is exacerbated when the law touches women's lives.

Feminist critiques of rights

An initial issue in any discussion of women and international human rights law is whether international formulations of rights are useful for women. Some feminist scholars have suggested, in the context of national laws, that campaigns for women's legal rights are at best a waste of energy and at worst positively detrimental to women. They have argued that, while the formulation of equality rights may be useful as a first step towards the improvement of the position of women, a continuing focus on the acquisition of rights may not be beneficial:[54] women's experiences and concerns are not easily translated into the narrow, individualistic, language of rights;[55] rights discourse overly simplifies complex power relations and their promise is constantly thwarted by structural inequalities of power;[56] the balancing of 'competing' rights by decision-making bodies often reduces women's power;[57]

[49] E.g. the United States ratification of the ICCPR in 1992. See H. Steiner and P. Alston, above note 4 at 766–71.

[50] R. Higgins, 'Derogations under human rights treaties', 48 *British Yearbook of International Law* (1976–7) 281.

[51] E.g. ICCPR, articles 18(3), 19(3), 21 and 22.

[52] E.g. H. Charlesworth, 'Australia's split personality: implementation of human rights treaty obligations in Australia', in P. Alston and M. Chiam (eds), *Treaty-Making and Australia* (Annandale, Federation Press, 1995) 129.

[53] Y. Ghai, above note 33 at 5–6. However this governmental view should be compared with the Bangkok NGO Declaration on Human Rights, 27 March 1993, *Report of the Regional Meeting for Asia on the World Conference on Human Rights*, UN Doc. A/CONF.157/ASRM/8- A/CONF.157/PC/59, 1993.

[54] E.g. E. Kingdom, *What's Wrong with Rights? Problems for Feminist Politics of Law* (Edinburgh, Edinburgh University Press, 1991).

[55] R. West, 'Feminism, critical social theory and law', 1989 *University of Chicago Legal Forum* 59.

[56] E. Gross, 'What is feminist theory?', in C. Pateman and E. Gross (eds), *Feminist Challenges: Social and Political Theory* (Sydney, Allen & Unwin, 1986) 190 at 192; C. Smart, *Feminism and the Power of Law* (London, Routledge, 1989) at 138–44.

[57] C. Smart, above note 56 at 138–44.

and particular rights, such as the right to freedom of religion or to the protection of the family, can in fact justify the oppression of women.[58] Feminists have examined the interpretation by national tribunals of rights apparently designed to benefit women and pointed to their often androcentric construction.[59] Other critiques of rights include the claim that statements of rights are indeterminate and thus highly manipulable both in a technical and a more basic sense. Recourse to the language of rights may give a rhetorical flourish to an argument, but provides only an ephemeral polemical advantage, often obscuring the need for political and social change.[60] To assert a legal right, it is sometimes argued, is to mischaracterise our social experience and to assume the inevitability of social antagonism by affirming that social power rests in the state and not in the people who compose it.[61] The individualism promoted by traditional understandings of rights limits their possibilities by ignoring 'the relational nature of social life'.[62] This aspect of the critique of rights echoes reservations about rights held in the South: the notion of adversarial rights held against the state can be interpreted, not as a symbol of civilisation and progress, but as a sign of a malfunctioning community.[63] Talk of rights is said to make contingent social structures seem permanent and to undermine the possibility of their radical transformation. Indeed it has been claimed that the only consistent function of rights has been to protect the most privileged groups in society.[64]

[58] H. Charlesworth, C. Chinkin and S. Wright, 'Feminist approaches to international law', 85 *American Journal of International Law* (1991) 613 at 635–8; D. Arzt, 'The application of international human rights law in Islamic states', 12 *Human Rights Quarterly* (1990) 202 at 203; H. Holmes, 'A feminist analysis of the Universal Declaration of Human Rights', in C. Gould (ed.), *Beyond Domination: New Perspectives on Women and Philosophy* (Totowa, Rowman & Allanheld, 1983) 250 at 252–5.

[59] Canadian feminists have made a distinctive contribution to this critique in their analysis of judicial interpretation of the Canadian Charter of Rights and Freedoms of 1982. E.g. E. Sheehy, 'Feminist argumentation before the Supreme Court of Canada in *R. v. Seaboyer; R. v. Gayme*: the sound of one hand clapping', 18 *Melbourne University Law Review* (1991) 450; J. Fudge, 'The effect of entrenching a Bill of Rights upon political discourse: feminist demands and sexual violence in Canada', 17 *International Journal of the Sociology of Law* (1989) 445. See also, in the United States context, F. Olsen, 'Statutory rape: a feminist critique of rights analysis', 63 *Texas Law Review* (1984) 387.

[60] M. Tushnet, 'An essay on rights', 62 *Texas Law Review* (1984) 1363 at 1371–2.

[61] See P. Gabel and P. Harris, 'Building power and breaking images: critical legal theory and the practice of law', 11 *New York Review of Law and Social Change* (1982–83) 369 at 375–6.

[62] M. Tushnet, 'Rights: an essay in informal political theory', 17 *Politics and Society* (1989) 403 at 410.

[63] R. Coomaraswamy, 'To bellow like a cow: women, ethnicity and the discourse of rights', in R. Cook (ed.), *Human Rights of Women: National and International Perspectives* (Philadelphia, University of Pennsylvania Press, 1994) 43.

[64] D. Kairys, 'Freedom of speech', in D. Kairys (ed.), *The Politics of Law* (New York, Pantheon Books, 1982) 140 at 141.

Feminist critiques of rights have been remarkably rare in the literature on *international* women's rights.[65] Perhaps the comparatively radical, and vulnerable, nature of human rights law within the international legal order has protected it from internal critique. Those concerned with the protection of human rights in general may well be reluctant to challenge the form of human rights law at a fundamental level, fearing that such a critique may be used to reduce the hard-fought-for advances in the area. Many commentators and activists assume that the quest for rights for women is an important and useful strategy internationally.[66] Nevertheless we must ask whether this task is worth the energy that must be expended on it. Can the human rights canon usefully respond to women's concerns across the globe? Are we simply creating new sites for the subtle oppression of women? Our response here is that campaigns for women's rights to be recognised as human rights can play a useful, strategic role in advancing women's equality, particularly when used in conjunction with other political and social strategies, but that the limited nature of rights must be acknowledged.

While the acquisition and assertion of rights is by no means the only solution for the domination of women by men, it is an important tactic in the international arena. Human rights offer a framework for debate over basic values and conceptions of a good society. One report has outlined six reasons for the importance of the human rights discourse. First, it provides a normative legal basis even if it is not perfectly drafted; second it is obligatory, not optional for states; third, the use of a human rights entry point brings the entire human rights structure to bear; fourth, international human rights should be matched by a corresponding legal basis within states; fifth, human rights require active and effective remedies; and finally, human rights require accountability in national and domestic arenas.[67] Because women in most societies operate from such a disadvantaged position, rights discourse offers a recognised vocabulary to frame political and social wrongs. Martha Minow has described the problems in denying rights discourse to traditionally dominated groups: 'I worry about criticizing rights and legal language just when they have become available to people who had previously lacked access to them. I worry about those who have telling those who do not, "you do not need it, you should not want it." '[68] In a similar vein, Patricia Williams has pointed out that for African-Americans, talk of rights has been a constant source of hope:

[65] See K. Engle, 'International human rights and feminism: when discourses meet', 13 *Michigan Journal of International Law* (1992) 317.

[66] E.g. D. Sullivan, 'Women's human rights and the 1993 World Conference on Human Rights', 88 *American Journal of International Law* (1994) 152.

[67] Commission on Human Rights, Right to Food, High Commissioner for Human Rights, UN Doc. E/CN.4/1998/21, 15 January 1998.

[68] M. Minow, 'Interpreting rights: an essay for Robert Cover', 96 *Yale Law Journal* (1987) 1860 at 1910.

'Rights' feels so new in the mouths of most black people. It is still so deliciously empowering to say. It is a sign for and a gift of selfhood that is very hard to contemplate restructuring . . . at this point in history. It is the magic wand of visibility and invisibility, of inclusion and exclusion, of power and no power . . .[69]

The empowering function of rights discourse for women, particularly in the international sphere where women are still almost completely invisible, is a crucial aspect of its value. As has been observed in the context of South Africa, rights talk can often seem naive and unpragmatic, but its power relies on a deep faith in justice and rightness.[70]

Rights discourse also offers a focus for international feminism that can translate into action if responses to women's claims are inadequate. It affirms 'a community dedicated to invigorating words with a power to restrain, so that even the powerless can appeal to those words'.[71] At the same time, the language of rights offers the traditional powerholders some comfort. This point has been made about black South Africans' claims of rights:

At this stage of nation-building, when we are sitting down with our oppressors, the rights rhetoric is very helpful. It helps to allay their fears: we will not lock them up or kick them out or boot them into the country; we want to escape this cycle of domination, subordination, resistance and revolution, which never ends. As an internationally accepted aspiration, it appeals to the best in all of us. They have their right to their freedoms, we have the right to forgive.[72]

In discussing the experience of African-Americans with the United States constitutional guarantees of rights, Patricia Williams has noted that 'the problem with rights discourse is not that the discourse is itself constricting but that it exists in a constricted referential universe'.[73] This observation is particularly apt with respect to women's international human rights law which operates within the narrow referential universe of the international legal order. The need to develop a feminist rights discourse so that it acknowledges gendered disparities of power, rather than assuming all people are equal in relation to all rights, is crucial. The challenge is then to invest a rights vocabulary with meanings that undermine the current skewed distribution of economic, social and political power.[74] In societies of the South, this task may be particularly complex. In South Asia, for example, Radhika Coomaraswamy has pointed out that 'rights discourse is a weak discourse',

---

[69] P. Williams, 'Alchemical notes: reconstructing ideals from deconstructed rights', 22 *Harvard Civil Rights-Civil Liberties Law Review* (1987) 401 at 431.

[70] Albie Sachs, quoted in *Economic and Social Rights and the Right to Health* (Cambridge, Harvard Law School Human Rights Program, 1995) at 42.

[71] M. Minow, above note 68 at 1881.

[72] A. Sachs, above note 70 at 13.

[73] P. Williams, *The Alchemy of Race and Rights* (Cambridge, Harvard University Press, 1991) at 159.

[74] M. Minow, above note 68 at 1910.

especially in the context of women and family relations.[75] She has argued that the very notion of rights has little resonance in many cultures, for example the countries of South Asia,[76] and that the discourse of women's rights assumes a free, independent, individual woman, an image that may be less powerful in protecting women's rights than other ideologies, such as 'women as mothers'.[77]

Adetoun Ilumoka has made a similar observation with respect to Africa, pointing out that the enforcement of rights is rarely an arena of struggle, and that the language of freedom, justice and fair play is considerably more powerful.[78] In the African context, Ilumoka has argued, 'addressing the problem of poverty is a priority human rights issue . . . [and] international economic policies . . . are a main source of violation of [women's] human rights'.[79] She has suggested that the language of rights may have a particular force in this context, because the generators of the international economic policies, UN agencies and the developed North, also see themselves as guardians of human rights. The language of rights is thus a complex instrument at an international level and ways of adapting it to respond to local and regional circumstances need to be devised.

The significance of rights discourse outweighs its disadvantages. Human rights provides an alternative and additional language and framework to the welfare and protection approach to the global situation of women, which presents women as victims or dependents.[80] It allows women to claim specific entitlements from a specified obligation-holder. Because human rights discourse is the dominant progressive moral philosophy and a potent social movement operating at the global level,[81] it is important for women to engage with, and contest, its parameters.

Women's rights in international law

At first sight, the international law of human rights offers considerable protection to women. The concerted activity of women's groups at the inter-

[75] R. Coomaraswamy, above note 63 at 55.

[76] *Ibid.*

[77] Compare S. Hossain, 'Equality in the home: women's rights and personal laws in South Asia', in R. Cook, above note 63 at 456 (arguing for the relevance of international human rights in Bangladesh).

[78] A. Ilumoka, 'African women's economic, social, and cultural rights – towards a relevant theory and practice', in R. Cook, above note 63 at 307, 319.

[79] *Ibid.* at 321.

[80] C. Brautigam, 'Mainstreaming a gender perspective in the work of the United Nations human rights treaty bodies', *Proceedings of the 91st Annual Meeting of the American Society of International Law* (Washington DC, American Society of International Law, 1997) 389 at 390.

[81] V. Peterson, 'Whose rights? A critique of the "givens" in human rights discourse', 15 *Alternatives* 303 at 303–4. For an investigation of the way moral philosophies have been generated in the international sphere see A. Orford, 'Locating the international: military and monetary interventions after the Cold War', 38 *Harvard International Law Journal* (1997) 443.

national level from early in the twentieth century is reflected in the range of instruments dealing with women.[82] Provisions in treaties dealing with women have been categorised as falling into three categories: protective, corrective and non-discriminatory.[83] Some treaties contain elements of all three categories. 'Protective' treaties assume that women should be treated differently to men in particular circumstances because they are physically different to and more vulnerable than men. Examples include the ILO's Convention Concerning Night Work of Women Employed in Industry,[84] which limits the amount of night work women can undertake, and provisions of the Third Geneva Convention that require particular treatment for women prisoners of war.[85] While special provisions for women acknowledge the differences in women and men's lives, 'protective' laws also tend to stereotype women as weak and helpless. Women's interests are not necessarily paramount in such 'protective' regimes. In the labour sphere they also protected 'men's work' and exceptions were made for other imperatives, such as when the national interest so required in the 'serious emergency' of the 1930s. 'Corrective' treaties attempt to improve women's treatment without making overt comparisons to the situation of men. Conventions dealing with trafficking in women[86] or with the requirement for women to marry only with their full and free consent[87] are examples of 'corrective' treaties.

The major focus of the protection of women's rights has been the right to equal treatment and non-discrimination on the basis of sex.[88] The UN Charter was the first international agreement to establish non-discrimination on the basis of sex as a basic right. It refers in its Preamble to 'the equal rights of men and women' and includes as a purpose of the UN the promotion and encouragement of respect for human rights and fundamental freedoms for all without distinction based on sex.[89] The references to discrimination on the basis of sex were inserted in the Charter as the result of concerted

---

[82] See further J. Connors, 'NGOs and the human rights of women at the United Nations', in P. Willetts (ed.), *'The Conscience of the World': The Influence of Non-Governmental Organisations in the UN System* (Washington DC, Brookings Institution, 1996) 147.

[83] N. Hevener, 'An analysis of gender based treaty law: contemporary developments in historical perspective', 8 *Human Rights Quarterly* (1986) 70 at 71.

[84] Revised 9 July 1948, 81 UNTS 285.

[85] Geneva Convention Relative to the Treatment of Prisoners of War, 12 August 1949, 75 UNTS 135, articles 14, 16 and 49.

[86] E.g. Convention for the Suppression of the Traffic in Women and Children, 24 April 1950, 53 UNTS 39.

[87] E.g. Convention on the Nationality of Married Women, 29 January 1957, 309 UNTS 65.

[88] A useful guide to the literature on women's rights is R. Cook and V. Oosterveld, 'A select bibliography of women's human rights', 44 *American University Law Review* (1995) 1429.

[89] Charter of the UN, 26 June 1945, article 1(3). Other references in the Charter to non-discrimination on the basis of sex are in articles 13, 55(c) and 76(c).

lobbying by women delegates and NGOs accredited to the San Francisco conference.[90] The UN and some of its agencies, as well as regional organisations, have since adopted a range of treaties and declarations that elaborate the principle of non-discrimination in certain contexts. The international legal system has dealt with non-discrimination on the basis of sex in both generally applicable and women-specific instruments.

General instruments

The right of women to equal treatment and non-discrimination on the basis of sex is part of the traditional canon of human rights. General human rights treaties at both the global and regional levels contain rights of non-discrimination on a number of bases that include sex and prohibit distinctions based on sex with respect to the enjoyment of rights.[91] For example, article 3 of the ICCPR provides that 'States Parties . . . undertake to ensure the equal right of men and women to the enjoyment of all civil and political rights set forth in the present Covenant'. More generally, article 26 provides:

> All persons are equal before the law and are entitled without any discrimination to the equal protection of the law. In this respect, the law shall prohibit any discrimination and guarantee to all persons equal and effective protection against discrimination on any ground such as race, colour, sex, language, religion, political or other opinion, national or social origin, property, birth or other status.

The Human Rights Committee has adopted a General Comment on article 26,[92] which gives it a broad meaning. It has made clear that article 26 is an autonomous right to equality and is not limited to those rights already provided for in the ICCPR. In other words, the right to equality applies across the spectrum of civil, political, economic, social and cultural rights. A second important aspect of the General Comment is its definition of the term 'discrimination', unelaborated in the text of article 26 itself. The comment refers to the definition of discrimination in both the Convention on the Elimination of All Forms of Racial Discrimination (the Race Convention)[93] and the Women's Convention[94] and adapts this to the context of the ICCPR:

> the Committee believes that the term 'discrimination' as used in the Covenant should be understood to imply any distinction, exclusion, restriction or preference which is based on any ground such as race, colour, sex, language, religion,

[90] *The United Nations and the Advancement of Women 1945–1996* (New York, UN, 1996) at 10.
[91] E.g. ICCPR, articles 2, 3 and 26; ICESCR, articles 3 and 7; American Convention on Human Rights, article 1; African Charter of Human and Peoples' Rights, articles 2 and 18(3); European Convention on Human Rights, article 14.
[92] General Comment no. 8, UN Doc. CCPR/C/21/Rev.1/Add.1, 21 November 1989.
[93] Convention on the Elimination of All Forms of Racial Discrimination, article 1.
[94] Convention on the Elimination of All Forms of Discrimination Against Women, article 1.

political or other opinion, national or social origin, property, birth or other status, and which has the purpose or effect of nullifying or impairing the recognition, enjoyment or exercise by all persons, on an equal footing, of all rights and freedoms.

This definition makes clear that a discriminatory intention is not necessary to establish discrimination and that article 26 extends to both direct and indirect discrimination.

Third, the Committee was explicit that equality does not always mean identical treatment. It acknowledged the possibility of different treatment in particular circumstances (for example the prohibition in article 6 of the ICCPR on the imposition of the death sentence on those under 18 or on pregnant women). It also pointed out that 'the principle of equality sometimes requires States parties to take affirmative action in order to diminish or eliminate conditions which cause or help to perpetuate discrimination prohibited by the Covenant'.[95] A fourth significant aspect of the General Comment is its observation that 'not every differentiation of treatment will constitute discrimination, if the criteria for such differentiation are reasonable and objective and if the aim is to achieve a purpose which is legitimate under the Covenant.' This passage is a tacit adoption of criteria developed by the ECHR to measure ostensibly discriminatory national laws.[96] Such a justification for differential treatment has been interpreted to involve showing that it has been adopted in pursuit of a legitimate aim (such as the efficient teaching of children in schools in cases of language discrimination[97]) and that there is a reasonable relationship of proportionality between the means employed and the aims sought to be realised – the so-called 'margin of appreciation' doctrine.[98]

The interpretation of article 26 in the context of individual cases brought before the Human Rights Committee under the first Optional Protocol to the ICCPR has been relatively narrow. The Committee has been more concerned to respond to cases of direct ('disparate treatment') than indirect ('disparate impact') discrimination. The Human Rights Committee has declared national laws that discriminate on their face between men and women to be in violation of article 26. For example, Mauritian immigration legislation that required foreign husbands to apply for residence permits, but did not make the same requirement of foreign wives, was found to violate several provisions of the ICCPR, including article 26.[99] So too a Peruvian law that prevented a married

---

[95] Compare Convention on the Elimination of All Forms of Discrimination Against Women, article 4.

[96] *Belgian Linguistics Case* 1 EHRR 252 (1968).

[97] Compare *Minority Schools in Albania* PCIJ ser. A/B, no. 64 (1935).

[98] H. Steiner and P. Alston, above note 4 at 600–39.

[99] *Aumeeruddy-Cziffra v. Mauritius* Communication no. 9/35. See International Law Association Committee on Feminism and International Law, *Women's Equality and Nationality in International Law* (London, International Law Association, 1998).

woman from taking legal action with respect to matrimonial property was held to discriminate against women.[100] Two Dutch women's challenge to national social security laws, which required married women, but not men, to prove that they were breadwinners before obtaining unemployment benefits, was also upheld by the Committee.[101]

Other cases of alleged discrimination have not, however, been closely scrutinised by the Human Rights Committee, which has in the past allowed a considerable margin of appreciation to states. For example *Vos v. The Netherlands*[102] involved discrimination with respect to access to a disability allowance on the death of a spouse. Dutch law allowed disabled men to retain the right to a disability allowance when their wives died, but on the death of their husbands, disabled women were only eligible for a widow's pension which in Ms Vos' case was less than the disability pension. Ms Vos had been divorced for 22 years at the time of her former husband's death and had been supporting herself when she became disabled. The Human Rights Committee found no violation of article 26 in this case. It accepted the Dutch government's justification of the distinction as reasonable and objective on a number of grounds: first that at the time of the legislation's enactment 'it was customary for husbands to act as bread-winners for their families'; second, that the law was 'necessary . . . to avoid the necessity of entering the person concerned in the records of two different bodies'; and third that generally the widow's pension was more than the disability allowance because most married women worked part-time and therefore qualified for only partial disability benefits.

Women-specific instruments

A number of international instruments focus entirely or in part on discrimination against women.[103] These include the Convention on the Political Rights of Women,[104] the Convention on the Nationality of Married Women, and the Convention on Consent to Marriage, Minimum Age for Marriage and Registration of Marriages.[105] The most wide-ranging of the international human rights treaties devoted to women is the Women's Convention, adopted

[100] *Avellanal v. Peru* Communication no. 22/1986.
[101] *Zwaan de Vries v. The Netherlands* Communication no. 182/1984; *Broeks v. The Netherlands* Communication no. 172/1984.
[102] Communication no. 218/1986.
[103] For a useful overview of these instruments see R. Cook, 'Women', in O. Schachter and C. Joyner (eds), *The United Nations Legal Order* (Cambridge, Cambridge University Press, 1995) 433. See also M. Halberstam and E. De Feis, *Women's Legal Rights: International Covenants as an Alternative to ERA?* (Dobbs Ferry, Transnational Publishers, 1987) at 18–33.
[104] 20 December 1952, 193 UNTS 135.
[105] 7 November 1962, 521 UNTS 231.

by the UN General Assembly in 1979.[106] The Convention contains a broader definition of discrimination than that contained in the earlier treaties, covering both equality of opportunity (formal equality) and equality of outcome (*de facto* equality). It states that discrimination against women means: any distinction, exclusion or restriction made on the basis of sex which has the effect or purpose of impairing or nullifying the recognition, enjoyment or exercise by women, irrespective of their marital status, on a basis of equality of men and women, of human rights and fundamental freedoms in the political, economic, social, cultural, civil or any other field.[107] The Women's Convention also covers discrimination in the civil, political, social, economic and cultural fields.[108] Article 2 requires states to take legal and other measures to ensure the practical realisation of the principle of sex equality. The Convention refers to a range of arenas where states parties must work to eliminate discrimination: political and public life,[109] international organisations,[110] education,[111] employment,[112] healthcare,[113] financial credit,[114] cultural life,[115] the rural sector[116] and the law.[117] It contemplates the use of 'temporary special measures' to accelerate *de facto* equality between women and men.[118]

The Women's Convention has been ratified widely by states from all regions of the world[119] and makes advances for women's rights in a number of ways. Its transcendence of the divide between first and second generation rights acknowledges that, for women, protection of civil and political rights is meaningless without attention to the economic, social and cultural context in which they operate. It identifies areas where discrimination against women is most marked and where women most need guarantees of rights. The Women's Convention also attempts to overcome the public/private dichotomy observed in international law. For example, it asserts women's equal rights to participate in public decision-making bodies at all levels and

[106] See generally L. Rehof, *Guide to the Travaux Préparatoires of the United Nations Convention on the Elimination of All Forms of Discrimination against Women* (Dordrecht, Martinus Nijhoff, 1993).
[107] Convention on the Elimination of All Forms of Discrimination Against Women, article 1.
[108] *Ibid.*, article 3.
[109] *Ibid.*, article 7.
[110] *Ibid.*, article 8.
[111] *Ibid.*, article 10.
[112] *Ibid.*, article 11.
[113] *Ibid.*, article 12.
[114] *Ibid.*, article 13(b).
[115] *Ibid.*, article 13(c).
[116] *Ibid.*, article 14.
[117] *Ibid.*, article 15.
[118] *Ibid.*, article 4.
[119] States that have not ratified or acceded to the Convention include Afghanistan, the Holy See, a number of the Pacific Island states, Saudi Arabia, Iran and the United States.

also explicitly affirms women's right to equality in a limited way within the 'private' arena of the family,[120] unlike other human rights instruments which designate the family as a unit to be protected.[121]

Inadequacies of human rights law for women

By its nature, human rights law is vulnerable to non-observance. As we noted above, the basis of human rights principles is that a government's power over its people is limited in a variety of ways. This claim poses a direct challenge to the idea of state sovereignty and states have identified many avenues of resistance to it. Despite problems of implementation and enforcement, human rights law has an important role in the international community as a statement, in Johan Galtung's phrase, of the 'elements of humanity':[122] it sets out a particular understanding of the basic conditions necessary for a good life. Our argument is that, in this important symbolic function, human rights law privileges one category of persons, men, over another, women. Although women have achieved some recognition in the international system for the protection of human rights, it has not been an adequate response to the situation of women described in chapter 1. This section explains this claim in greater detail.

Marginalisation of women's rights

In many ways, the creation of a specialised 'women's' branch of human rights law, of which the Women's Convention is the flagship, has allowed its marginalisation. 'Mainstream' human rights institutions have tended to ignore the application of human rights norms to women. The Human Rights Committee, for example, has outlined the scope of the right to life without reference to the issue of female infanticide,[123] athough more recently its comments on states' reports indicate a broader approach. Similarly, a 1993 study of the work of the then UN Commission on Human Rights' Special Rapporteur on Torture, Professor Kooijmans, found that he rarely considered the application of norms of international human rights law or international humanitarian law to women.[124] Well-documented cases of torture and

---

[120] Convention on the Elimination of All Forms of Discrimination Against Women, article 16.

[121] E.g. Universal Declaration of Human Rights, article 16; ICCPR, article 23.

[122] J. Galtung, above note 1 at 2.

[123] A. Byrnes, 'Women, feminism and international human rights law: methodological myopia, fundamental flaws or meaningful marginalisation?', 12 *Australian Yearbook of International Law* (1992) 205 at 216–23.

[124] *Token Gestures: Women's Human Rights and UN Reporting 1. The UN Special Rapporteur on Torture* (Washington DC, International Human Rights Law Group, 1993) at 5–6.

ill-treatment of women went uninvestigated or were treated in a desultory fashion.[125] Although the Special Rapporteur identified rape as torture in some contexts, he did so inconsistently. He did not discuss the frequency with which rape and sexual assault were used as forms of torture, nor the situations in which they were likely to occur. The connection between rape and gender was not adverted to in the reports of the Special Rapporteur.[126] His condemnation of rapes in Bosnia-Herzegovina focused on the harm resulting to ethnic communities and failed to acknowledge the harm inflicted on women as individuals because of their sex and gender.[127]

The Special Rapporteur's work underlines the traditional male-centred nature of the UN 'mainstream' and suggests that the UN's separation of 'general' and 'women's' matters disadvantages women. There is a strategic dilemma with respect to international legal structures and women. On the one hand, the attempt to improve the position of women through more generally applicable measures has allowed women's concerns to be submerged by what are regarded as more 'global' issues.[128] On the other hand, the price of the creation of separate institutional mechanisms and special measures dealing with women within the UN system has typically been the creation of a 'women's ghetto', given less power, fewer resources and a lower priority than 'mainstream' human rights bodies. Moreover, Anne Gallagher has noted that the methods of investigating and documenting human rights abuses can often obscure, or even conceal, abuses against women. Thus the UN's 'fact finding' in Rwanda in 1994 did not detect systematic sexual violence against women until nine months after the genocide, when women began to give birth in unprecedented numbers.[129]

In 1994, the UN Commission on Human Rights appointed the Sri Lankan jurist, Radhika Coomaraswamy, as Special Rapporteur on Violence against Women.[130] This was the first gender-specific mandate of a Special Rapporteur. In her reports, Ms Coomaraswamy has drawn attention to the phenomenon of violence against women in a systematic manner and made valuable proposals for change. But the very nature of the mandate may be viewed as an ambivalent advance for women in the international legal order because it can be read as implying that violence against women does not constitute torture, nor is it within the mandates of 'general' Special

---

[125] *Ibid.* at 10–11, 14–15.
[126] *Ibid.* at 7.
[127] *Ibid.* at 7–8.
[128] L. Reanda, 'The Commission on the Status of Women', in P. Alston (ed.), *The United Nations and Human Rights: A Critical Appraisal* (Oxford, Clarendon Press, 1992) 267.
[129] A. Gallagher, 'Ending the marginalisation: strategies for incorporating women into the United Nations human rights system', 19 *Human Rights Quarterly* (1997) 283 at 292.
[130] CHR Res. 1994/45, UN Doc. ESCOR, 1994, Supp. no. 4., 11 March 1994. The mandate was renewed in 1997, CHR Res. 1997/44.

Rapporteurs, such as those on the right to life, disappearances and religious intolerance.[131]

The segmentation of women's human rights issues is replicated in the work of NGOs. In the 1990s, a number of 'mainstream' NGOs, such as Amnesty International, have begun to document abuse of women that falls within the traditional scope of human rights law.[132] Less attention has been given to the way that the very structure of this law has been built on the silence of women.

Inadequate enforcement and implementation

Ineffective implementation of existing provisions relating to women's right to equality have reduced the force of international legal regulation. Implementation of the Women's Convention is affected by its relatively weak language, the reservations states parties have made to its terms and by the limited monitoring methods provided for in the Convention itself. The operative language of the Convention is much weaker, compared, for example, with the Race Convention. Most of the obligations imposed on states parties to the Women's Convention involve taking 'all appropriate measures', a term that leaves considerable discretion to individual states. The Race Convention contains more immediately binding obligations. The qualified language of the Women's Convention is further undermined by the large number of far-reaching reservations and declarations that have been made by states parties.[133]

The only method provided for monitoring the Women's Convention is that of states parties making periodic reports to the CEDAW, established by article 18 of the Convention. The reporting system under human rights treaties generally has been strongly criticised as being inefficient and inefficacious.[134] Its shortcomings are particularly clear in the context of the Women's Convention. For example, if a state is not due to report under the Convention, there is no available mechanism for challenging a state's actions. This inadequacy was highlighted at the 1993 CEDAW meeting where no effective response could be made to the well-documented atrocities committed

[131] The Special Rapporteur on Religious Intolerance has noted that the Commission on Human Rights has emphasised the need for a gender perspective and has stated that he intends to pay particular attention in future to the status of women. UN Doc. A/52/477, 16 October 1997.

[132] E.g. *Women in the Front Line: Human Rights Violations Against Women* (New York, Amnesty International, 1991); *Human Rights are Women's Right* (London, Amnesty International, 1995). See further E. Watson, 'Amnesty International and women's human rights: an organisational dilemma', 4 *Australian Journal of Human Rights* (1997) 126.

[133] See chapter 4.

[134] A. Bayefsky, 'Making the human rights treaties work', in L. Henkin and J. Hargrove (eds), *Human Rights: An Agenda for the Next Century* (Washington DC, American Society of International Law, 1994) 229 at 233–6.

against women in the former Yugoslavia. CEDAW wrote a letter to the UN Commission on Human Rights expressing concern and requesting reports from the states of the former Yugoslavia.[135]

By contrast, 'mainstream' human rights instruments offer a range of monitoring techniques. The ICCPR, the Race Convention and the Convention against Torture all contain two other monitoring mechanisms: the right of complaint by one state against another for violation of the treaty[136] and the right of individual communication to the treaty-monitoring body.[137] These procedures are accepted at the option of the state party. The reason for the distinction in monitoring procedures between the Race and the Women's Conventions is not clear. It may have been based on what Laura Reanda has described as 'a deeply held view that the condition of women, embedded as it is in cultural and social traditions, does not lend itself to fact-finding mechanisms and complaints procedures such as those developed in the human rights sphere'.[138] She has noted that the ultimately unsuccessful proposals to allow the CSW to review complaints and to receive information from NGOs were strongly opposed by socialist and developing nations on the grounds that 'violations of women's rights [could not] be placed on the same footing as those occurring under repressive and racist regimes'.[139] Although CEDAW has been particularly active in monitoring reports and in issuing lucid General Recommendations on the interpretation of the Convention, it has been hampered by resources even more limited than those of other treaty-monitoring bodies.[140] From its inception CEDAW sat for only two weeks annually, less than any other human rights treaty body,[141] although in 1993 and 1994 the General Assembly granted it

---

[135] C. Chinkin and K. Werksman, *Report of the Twelfth Session of the Committee on the Elimination of All Forms of Discrimination Against Women* (Minneapolis, International Women's Rights Action Watch, 1993).

[136] ICCPR, article 41; International Convention on the Elimination of All Forms of Racial Discrimination, article 11; Convention against Torture, article 21.

[137] Optional Protocol to the ICCPR, article 1; International Convention on the Elimination of All Forms of Racial Discrimination, article 14; Convention against Torture, article 22.

[138] L. Reanda, above note 128 at 274. On the development of a complaints procedure for the Women's Convention see below notes 277 to 283 and accompanying text.

[139] L. Reanda, above note 128 at 288.

[140] See N. Burrows, 'International law and human rights: the case of women's rights', in T. Campbell *et al.* (eds), *Human Rights: From Rhetoric to Reality* (New York, Basil Blackwell, 1986) 8 at 93–5; A. Byrnes, 'The "other" human rights treaty body: the work of the Committee on the Elimination of Discrimination Against Women', 14 *Yale Journal of International Law* (1989) 1; T. Meron, 'Enhancing the effectiveness of the prohibition of discrimination against women', 84 *American Journal of International Law* (1990) 213 at 214.

[141] Convention on the Elimination of All Forms of Discrimination Against Women, article 20.

an extra week. Following the Fourth World Conference on Women at Beijing the General Assembly adopted an amendment to article 20 allowing CEDAW to meet in two sessions each year.[142]

The influence of cultural relativism

One strong response to the creation of a universal system of human rights protection has been assertions of the philosophy of cultural relativism. Indeed it has been argued that 'cultural relativism dominates social, political and academic thought today'.[143] The claim is that if international human rights norms conflict with particular cultural standards, the particularity of culture must take precedence over universalising trends.[144] Critics of universal human rights standards point to the Western ethical basis of human rights law and reject this as a basis for commitments in other traditions. At the same time, Western states have developed their own form of cultural relativism in the human rights area in arguing for very broad 'margins of appreciation' in implementing their human rights obligations, based on the particularity of their national circumstances.[145] While concerns of cultural relativism arise with respect to human rights generally, it is striking that 'culture' is much more frequently invoked in the context of women's rights than in any other area. Indeed, Radhika Coomaraswamy has predicted that in Asia especially, the first decade of the twenty-first century will be marked by the collision of national cultural movements and women's rights.[146]

Appeals to cultural relativism have grown in intensity and frequency as the scope of the international human rights regime grows wider. The phenomena of non-acceptance of human rights treaties, substantive reservations to their terms, 'claw-back' provisions that reassert the primacy of domestic law and widespread rejection of compulsory international adjudication on human rights issues indicate that there is continuing disparity between international standards and many cultural traditions.[147] Claims of cultural relativism are rejected by many proponents of human rights because

[142] GA Res. 50/202, 23 February 1996.

[143] K. Barry, *Female Sexual Slavery* (New York, New York University Press, 1984) at 163.

[144] See generally A. Renteln, 'The unanswered challenge of relativism and the consequences for human rights', 7 *Human Rights Quarterly* (1985) 514; A. An-Na'im, 'Religious minorities under Islamic law and the limits of cultural relativism', 9 *Human Rights Quarterly* (1987) 1.

[145] C. Flinterman, 'The universality of human rights and cultural diversity', in *Contemporary International Law Issues: Conflicts and Convergence* (The Hague, Nederlandse Verenignng voor Internationaal Recht, 1995) 330.

[146] R. Coomaraswamy, 'Reinventing international law', in P. Van Ness (ed.), *Debating Human Rights* (London/New York, Routledge, 1999) 167 at 180–1.

[147] See the discussion of reservations to the Convention on the Elimination of All Forms of Discrimination Against Women in chapter 4.

they challenge the validity and retard the development of universal stand-ards.[148] Such proponents have pointed out that subordinating human rights to cultural traditions provides no objective yardstick against which state behaviour may be assessed; that it allows human rights to be traded as negotiable commodities; that it reconstructs the 'domestic jurisdiction' screen behind which authoritarian governments can shelter; and that it is based on the assumption that human rights standards are good for people in some parts of the world, but irrelevant elsewhere.

National and international bodies have had to grapple with claims that set individual rights and cultural practices or standards against each other, particularly in the context of women's rights. One example of this is *Lovelace v. Canada*.[149] Sandra Lovelace was born and registered as a female member of the Maliseet Indian tribe. Under Canadian law, after her marriage to a non-Indian she had lost her rights and privileges as a member of the tribe, including the right to live on the Tobique Indian reservation.[150] Lovelace made a communication under the first Optional Protocol asserting that this law violated articles 26 and 27[151] of the ICCPR. In determining that the legislation breached article 27, the Human Rights Committee held that 'persons who are brought up on a reserve, who have kept ties with their community and wish to maintain these ties must normally be considered as belonging to that minority'. *Lovelace* illustrates the identity conflict between Sandra Lovelace, who identified herself as an Indian, and wished to return home after the breakdown of her marriage, and the group who considered that women (but not men) who married outside the group ceased to have group identity. The group were supported in this view by the Canadian legal system, reflecting a shared cultural acceptance that the identity of married women is determined by reference to their husbands. Native Indian women had differing responses to the decision. The primary goal for some was to redress the discriminatory provisions of the Indian Act; for others the goal was the replacement of the Act by a form of indigenous self-government. Still others saw the case as imposing Western assumptions of sex equality, although the Human Rights Committee did not in fact address the claim under article 26. Mary Ellen Turpel (Aki-Kwe) asked: 'Before imposing upon us the logic of gender equality (with White men), what

[148] E.g. F. Tesón, 'International human rights and cultural relativism', 25 *Virginia Journal of International Law* (1985) 869; N. Kim, 'Towards a feminist theory of human rights: straddling the fence between western imperialism and uncritical absolutism', 25 *Columbia Human Rights Law Journal* (1993) 47.
[149] Communication no. 24/197 (1986), UN Doc. CCPR/C/OP/1 at 83.
[150] Indian Act, section 12(1)(b).
[151] Article 27 provides: 'In those States in which ethnic, religious or linguistic minorities exist, persons belonging to such minorities shall not be denied the right, in community with the other members of their group, to enjoy their own culture, to profess and practise their own religion, or to use their own language.'

about ensuring for our cultures and political systems equal legitimacy with the Anglo-Canadian cultural perspective which dominates the Canadian State?'[152]

Another example of the conflict between women's rights and customary norms is that of *Otieno*.[153] Wamboi Otieno claimed in the Kenyan courts the right to bury her husband outside his Luo tribal lands.[154] The marriage had taken place under the African Christian Marriage Act, based upon English law, rather than under Luo tribal law and the couple had lived in Nairobi. Otieno's claim was successfully challenged by her husband's brother who demanded that the body be buried on tribal land, in accordance with customary law, to protect the family from the harm that would ensue from violation of customary law. The Kenyan Court of Appeal asserted that 'a Luo man can never opt out of custom, and that a woman married to a Luo man becomes part of his household and subject to his law regardless of the specific legal form of their marriage'. Thus the wife's claim to status under civil law was disregarded in the face of conflicting custom.

A third example is *Md Ahmed Khan v. Shah Bano Begum*,[155] discussed in chapter 4. An Indian Muslim woman who was being divorced after forty years of marriage claimed the maintenance payments under the Indian Code of Criminal Procedure rather than those lower payments available under Muslim personal status law. After the Supreme Court of India upheld her claim, opposition and protests from within the conservative Muslim community ultimately persuaded the government to reverse the decision through the inaccurately-named Muslim Women (Protection of Rights on Divorce) Act 1986. Shah Bano Begum was thus disadvantaged by three layers of adverse identity: as a woman; as a Muslim woman within the predominantly Hindu society; and as a Muslim woman who wished to assert rights not supported by her community.[156]

A major conceptual difficulty with cultural relativism is that the notion of culture is itself endlessly mutable. All social values and hierarchies in their own time frames can be described as forms of culture. In this sense, 'to argue from culture is to prove too much'.[157] If all cultures are seen as special, resting on values that cannot be investigated in a general way, it is difficult to make any assessment from an international perspective of the significance of particular concepts and practices for women. Feminists have

[152] M. E. Turpel (Aki-Kwe), 'Patriarchy and paternalism: the legacy of the Canadian State for First Nations Women', 6 *Canadian Journal of Women and Law* (1993) 174 at 183.
[153] *Virginia Otieno v. Joash Ougo* (1982–88) 1 KAR 1049.
[154] A. Goldfarb, 'A Kenyan wife's right to bury her husband: applying CEDAW', 14 *ILSA Journal of International Law* (1990) 1.
[155] [1985] 3 S.C.R. 844.
[156] R. Coomaraswamy, 'To bellow like a cow', above note 63 at 53–4.
[157] G. Binion, 'Human rights: a feminist perspective', 17 *Human Rights Quarterly* (1995) 509 at 522.

pointed out that we need to investigate the gender of the 'cultures' that relativism privileges. Relativism is typically concerned with dominant cultures in particular regions and these are, among other things, usually constructed from male histories, traditions and experiences. Arati Rao has argued that the notion of culture favoured by international actors must be unmasked for what it is: a falsely rigid, ahistorical, selectively chosen set of self-justificatory texts and practices whose partiality raises the question of exactly whose interests are being served and who comes out on top.[158] Rao has proposed a series of questions to assess claims of culture, particularly those used to counter women's claims of rights: whose culture is being invoked? what is the status of the interpreter? in whose name is the argument being advanced? and who are the primary beneficiaries of the claim?[159]

In many ways, feminist and 'cultural' writings provide parallel critiques of international human rights law. Annie Bunting has pointed out that both see the dominant discourse as being based on individualistic and particular moral philosophies which serve to exclude the perspectives of 'others' and both challenge it as being founded on liberal notions of the self and on liberal prioritisation of civil and political rights. The two critiques are looking at the centre from different places on the margin.[160] A major difference in the structure of the critiques, however, is that the cultural critique is typically directed at the area of women's human rights, whereas the feminist critique is a broader challenge to the whole canon of human rights law. Cultural relativism is concerned with narrowing the scope of international law in that it places culture in a 'private' sphere outside international regulation and challenge, while feminists usually argue for a broadening of international legal regulation through redefining public and private spheres.

Lovelace, Otieno and *Shah Bano* indicate how cultural relativism and the critique of essentialism[161] are distinct, but related, challenges to the international recognition of women's rights. It has been pointed out that the Western enthusiasm for the articulation of women's rights not only ignores local feminisms and the historical realities of colonialism and the roles imposed upon, or accepted by, women in colonial encounters but also makes untenable, essentialist, assumptions about the sameness of the position of women worldwide.[162] One widely debated issue that raises concerns of both cultural

---

[158] A. Rao, 'The politics of gender and culture in international human rights discourse', in J. Peters and A. Wolper (eds), *Women's Rights, Human Rights: International Feminist Perspectives* (New York, Routledge, 1995) 167 at 174.

[159] *Ibid.*

[160] A. Bunting, 'Theorizing women's cultural diversity in feminist international human rights strategies', in A. Bottomley and J. Conaghan (eds), *Feminist Theory and Legal Strategy* (Oxford, Blackwell Publishers, 1993) 6 at 10.

[161] See chapter 2.

[162] V. Nesiah, 'Toward a feminist internationality: a critique of U.S. feminist legal scholarship', in R. Kapur (ed.), *Feminist Terrains in Legal Domains* (New Delhi, Kali, 1996) 11.

relativism and Western essentialism is that of what is termed female circumcision, genital surgery or genital mutilation.[163] Female genital mutilation involves the removal of parts of female genitalia, often without anaesthetic, most commonly when girls are very young. The operation is traditionally performed by an older woman. Various forms of genital mutilation are practised in countries throughout Asia, Africa and the Middle East, ranging from excision of the clitoris and inner and outer labia (infibulation) to removal of the tip of the clitoris (clitoridectomy). Many health consequences arise, such as the possibility of infection, or even tetanus from the unsterile instruments used in the procedure, as well as haemorraging, dysuria and dysmenorrhea. Genital surgeries also can cause complications in childbirth.[164] The justifications for this practice are primarily social and cultural. The significance of female genital surgeries is varied in different societies. It can be regarded as a form of initiation of girls into womanhood and a prerequisite for marriage; a way of enhancing fertility; a means of preserving virginity and discouraging prostitution; a method of maintaining female hygiene; and an important aspect of political and social cohesion.

The issue of female genital surgeries has been raised in international fora under the umbrella term 'traditional practices'. The CSW began to investigate traditional practices in the early 1950s and ECOSOC and the General Assembly adopted resolutions encouraging states to abolish practices such as these that violated human rights.[165] There was little controversy in the UN about the need to eradicate practices that harmed women and girls, but there were disagreements about the methods that should be used, whether it was an issue of human rights and, indeed, whether international concern about the issue constituted a violation of the domestic jurisdiction of UN member states.[166] When the WHO was asked, in 1951 and again in 1961, to undertake a study of the health effects of traditional practices on young girls, it refused to do so on the basis that the practices were ritual and cultural and beyond its sphere of competence.[167] The issue did not come on

---

[163] The issue of appropriate terminology is much debated. UN documents refer to the practice as female genital mutilation, but some scholars attempt to avoid the judgment of that term by using the terms of 'surgery' or 'circumcision'. See I. Gunning, 'Arrogant perception, world travelling and multicultural feminism: the case of female genital surgeries', 23 *Columbia Human Rights Law Review* (1992) 189; S. Wynter, '"Genital mutilation" or "symbolic birth"? Female circumcision, lost origins, and the aculturalism of feminist/western thought', 47 *Case Western Reserve Law Review* (1997) 501.

[164] For a discussion of the health aspects of genital surgeries see R. Cerny Smith, 'Female circumcision: bringing women's perspectives into the international debate', 65 *Southern California Law Review* (1992) 2449 at 2451; I. Gunning, above note 163 at 196–7.

[165] GA Res. 445 C (XIV), 28 May 1952; GA Res. 843 (IX), 17 December 1954.

[166] See *The United Nations and the Advancement of Women*, above note 90 at 22–4.

[167] *Ibid.* at 23.

to the international human rights agenda again until it was taken up by the Subcommission on Prevention of Discrimination and Protection of Minorities in 1983.[168] Generally, the issue of female genital mutilation has been discussed as implicating women's and girls' right to health.[169] This has proved to be the most acceptable context for international focus on the issue because it does not directly challenge its cultural or gender dimensions.[170] However, such an analysis may lead to the problematic conclusion that the surgeries are appropriate if medically supervised.[171] In 1993, the UN General Assembly's Declaration on the Elimination of Violence Against Women defined violence as including female genital mutilation 'and other traditional practices harmful to women'.[172]

States in which female genital surgeries are widely practised have reacted in a variety of ways. Some states have adopted national legislation outlawing the practice and have enforced the law to varying degrees.[173] Many states have been resistant to critical international attention being focused on the procedure. They have argued that cultural practices are properly part of their domestic jurisdiction and of no justified international concern, or that the goal of eradication can only be achieved in a gradual manner. While women within these states may often support the goal of eradication, the preoccupation that some Western feminists have displayed with respect to the phenomenon of female genital mutilation has raised considerable ire.[174] Women in countries where genital surgeries are practised have queried the

---

[168] On the Subcommission's handling of the issue see K. Brennan, 'The influence of cultural relativism on international human rights law: female circumcision as a case study', 7 *Law and Inequality* (1989) 367.

[169] E.g. Fourth World Conference on Women, Declaration and Platform for Action, UN Doc A/CONF.177/20, 15 September 1995, reprinted in 35 *International Legal Materials* (1996) 401 (Beijing Platform for Action), para. 281 (I). The Convention on the Rights of the Child, article 24(3) requires states parties to take all effective and appropriate measures with a view to abolishing traditional practices prejudicial to the health of children.

[170] For an argument in favour of what she terms 'clinicalization' see L. Obiora, 'Bridges and barricades: rethinking polemics and intransigence in the campaign against female circumcision', 47 *Case Western Reserve Law Review* (1997) 275 and the rejection of this view by Dawit in a letter to the symposium on the topic: *ibid.* at 268.

[171] I. Gunning, above note 163 at 237.

[172] GA Res. 48/104, 20 December 1993. See also Beijing Platform for Action, para. 113.

[173] E.g. in December 1997 the Egyptian Supreme Administrative Court upheld a ban on female genital mutilation, rejecting a claim of Islamic justification: 11 *The Women's Watch* (Minneapolis, International Women's Rights Action Watch, December 1997) 1.

[174] The labelling of the practice by some states as persecution within the terms of the Convention Relating to the Status of Refugees, 28 July 1951, 189 UNTS 150, article 1 emphasises the polarity of views. See e.g. in the United States *In re Kasinga* Interim Decision 3278 (Board of Immigration Appeals, 1996); S. Dawit and S. Mekuna, 'The west just doesn't get it', *New York Times*, 7 December 1993, 27.

usefulness of legal strategies and have urged the adoption of other stances such as economic empowerment and education.[175] It has also been pointed out that other general issues, such as poverty and social justice and gendered issues such as trafficking, child marriages and female infanticide, have a more deleterious effect on the position of women than the surgeries and yet have not attracted the same attention. There are sometimes elements of both prurience and racial superiority in the writings of Western feminists on the topic. Scholars have pointed out that some accepted practices in the West, such as cosmetic surgery, are of equal potential danger to women's health and replicate the emphasis on women as sexual beings but have never been regarded as issues of international concern.[176] The participation of women as the chief actors in the practice makes an analysis based on the male oppression of women more complex.[177]

Isabelle Gunning has argued that 'culturally challenging' practices such as female genital surgeries require responses other than punishment and force – for example, education and dialogue. She has suggested that the structures of international human rights law are capable of responding flexibly to such practices precisely because they are non-coercive and emphasise education. Gunning's technique of 'world-travelling' offers a balance between emphasising the interconnectedness of all women and respecting the independent position of women in particular situations.[178] It allows rejection of the harmful constructs of culture and tradition while respecting the genuine differences among people.[179] In turn, the methodology encourages reflection and scrutiny of the dominant norms of international human rights law.

The Vienna Declaration of 1993 expressed 'respect' for cultural and religious diversity, but reaffirmed the universality of human rights. It considered cultural and religious practices in the context of violence against women, but did not offer any resolution of the tension between rights to culture and religion and women's rights. It called only for the eradication of conflict between women's rights and 'the harmful effects of certain traditional or religious practices, cultural prejudices and religious extremism', without stipulating that such eradication should promote women's rights.[180] Extensive debate over the relative priorities of women's rights and religious

---

[175] E.g. L. Obiora, above note 170.

[176] I. Gunning, above note 163 at 213–14. For criticism of Gunning's views on this point see E. Gifford, '"The courage to blaspheme": confronting barriers to resisting female genital mutilation', 4 *UCLA Women's Law Journal* (1994) 329.

[177] K. Engle, 'Female subjects of public international law: human rights and the exotic other female', 26 *New England Law Review* (1992) 1509.

[178] I. Gunning, above note 163. See also S. Hom, 'Female infanticide in China: the human rights specter and thoughts towards (an)other vision', 23 *Columbia Human Rights Law Journal* (1991–92) 249.

[179] M. Minow, quoted in *Economic and Social Rights and the Right to Health*, above note 70 at 3.

[180] Vienna Declaration and Programme of Action, II, para. 38.

and cultural beliefs was also a feature of the Beijing Conference. During the negotiations over the text of the Platform for Action, it was proposed that a footnote be inserted to ensure that all the actions in relation to health should not be considered to be universally applicable, but should be seen as being subject to national laws and priorities, 'consistent with the various religious and ethical values and cultural backgrounds of its people'.[181] The footnote was eventually deleted, in a trade-off for the deletion of all references to 'sexual orientation' in the Platform.[182] The final text of the Platform repeats the unsatisfactory and ambiguous language of the Vienna Declaration.[183]

The limited understanding of 'equality' in international law

A major reason for the circumscribed protection of women in international human rights law is that the existing law identifies sexual equality with equal treatment. This 'liberal' feminist approach explains the centrality of the norm of non-discrimination, rather than a fuller set of rights, in the international law on women's rights.[184] For example, the rationale of the Convention on the Political Rights of Women, the Convention on the Nationality of Married Women and the norm of non-discrimination contained in both the ICCPR[185] and ICESCR[186] is to place women in the same position as men in the public sphere. This is also the strategy of the Women's Convention, although it extends to a limited extent into the private sphere. The activities of the CSW have similarly been informed by such an approach.[187] The shortcomings of understanding the global situation of women as a product of unequal treatment compared to men have been canvassed in chapter 2. The fundamental problem for women is not simply discriminatory treatment compared with men, although this is a manifestation of the larger problem. Women are in an inferior position because they lack real economic, social or political power in both the public and private worlds. As Noreen Burrows has written:

[181] See D. Otto, 'Holding up half the sky, but for whose benefit? A critical analysis of the Fourth World Conference on Women', 6 *Australian Feminist Law Journal* (1996) 7 at 19.

[182] *Ibid.*

[183] 'While the significance of national and regional peculiarities and various historical, cultural and religious backgrounds must be borne in mind, it is the duty of States, regardless of their political, economic and cultural systems, to promote and protect all human rights and fundamental freedoms ... full respect for various religious and ethical values, cultural backgrounds and philosophical convictions of individuals and their communities should contribute to the full enjoyment by women of their human rights.' Beijing Platform for Action, para. 9.

[184] Compare the Convention on the Rights of the Child which contains a catalogue of children's rights.

[185] Articles 2 and 26.

[186] Articles 2 and 3.

[187] L. Reanda, above note 128; N. Burrows, above note 140 at 87–8.

> For most women, what it is to be human is to work long hours in agriculture
> or the home, to receive little or no remuneration, and to be faced with political
> and legal processes which ignore their contribution to society and accord no
> recognition of their particular needs.[188]

For these reasons, even the comparatively broad definition of discrimination contained in the Women's Convention may not have much cutting edge against the problems women face worldwide. The non-discrimination approach of the Women's Convention was translated directly from the 1965 Race Convention.[189] Although this can be understood as a strategy to ensure the international acceptability of the Women's Convention, the appropriateness of the model can be questioned. Indeed, one of the obstacles faced by women in the area of international law is the general consensus at the state level that oppression on the basis of race is considerably more serious than oppression on the basis of gender.[190] The discrimination prohibited by the Women's Convention is, with the exception of the obligation in article 6 to suppress all forms of traffic in women and exploitation of prostitution of women, confined to accepted human rights and fundamental freedoms. If these rights and freedoms are defined in a gendered way, access to them will be unlikely to promote any real form of equality. The Convention's endorsement of affirmative action programmes in article 4 similarly assumes that these measures will be temporary techniques to allow women eventually to perform exactly like men.

The Human Rights Committee's consideration of individual communications under article 26 of the ICCPR in cases such as *Vos*, discussed above, illustrates the problems of an 'equality as sameness' approach. It privileges outmoded historical assumptions about working habits of women and administrative convenience over the right to equality.[191] As Anne Bayefsky has written of *Vos*: 'the decision fails entirely to recognize that th[e Dutch] legislative distinction [between disabled widows and disabled widowers] bore the hallmarks of classic stereotyping of women with its accompanying consequences of degradation and second class'.[192] Moreover, the views adopted by the Human Rights Committee seem to assume that for the legislation to

---

[188] N. Burrows, above note 140 at 82.

[189] L. Reanda, above note 128 at 286; N. Burrows, above note 140 at 86–8.

[190] This approach is well illustrated by the comment of an Indian delegate at the 1985 Copenhagen UN Mid-Decade for Women Conference that, since he had experienced colonialism, he knew that it could not be equated with sexism. Quoted in C. Bunch, *Passionate Politics Essays 1968–1986: Feminist Theory in Action* (New York, St. Martin's Press, 1987) at 297.

[191] *Vos*, above note 102 and accompanying text. A dissenting opinion signed by two of the Human Rights Committee members argued that the differential treatment was unjustifiable. The Committee plans to adopt a General Comment on article 3 in 2000, setting out the right of men and women to equal enjoyment of the rights contained in the Covenant.

[192] A. Bayefsky, 'The principle of equality or non-discrimination in international law', 11 *Human Rights Law Journal* (1990) 1 at 15.

violate article 26 there must be some sort of discriminatory intent rather than examining the actual effect of the legislation.

The male-centred view of equality offered in international law is tacitly reinforced by the focus in the Women's Convention on public life, the economy, the legal system and education, and its only limited recognition that oppression within the private sphere, that of the domestic and family worlds, contributes to women's inequality.[193] It does not, for example, explicitly prohibit violence against women perhaps because of the conceptual difficulty of compressing a harm characterised as private into the public frame of the Convention, or perhaps because this does not fit directly into the equality model. In its General Recommendation no.19, CEDAW described gender-based violence as a form of discrimination against women,[194] thereby underlining the significance of the private sphere as a site for the oppression of women.

In 1995, the Beijing Declaration and Platform for Action elaborated in detail the international understanding of women's equality. Equality is generally presented as women being treated in the same way as men, or at least having the same opportunity to be so treated, with little consideration of whether the existing male standards are appropriate. The Platform calls for women's equal participation in a wide range of areas – from the economy[195] and politics[196] to environmental management.[197] The assumption appears to be that women's inequality is removed once women participate equally in decision-making fora.[198] This account of equality ignores the underlying structures and power relations that contribute to the oppression of women. While increasing the presence of women is certainly important, it does not of itself transform these structures. We also need to understand and address the gendered aspects of fundamental concepts such as 'the economy', 'work', 'democracy', 'politics' and 'sustainable development'.[199]

'Human' rights as men's rights

The international law of human rights is inadequate as a response to the global position of women because it has been developed in a gendered way. Here we attempt to justify this claim, using examples from each 'generation' of rights. Despite their apparently different philosophical bases, the three generations are remarkably similar in their exclusion of women's perspectives.

[193] Convention on the Elimination of All Forms of Discrimination Against Women, Preamble, article 5.
[194] UN Doc. A/47/38, CEDAW/C/1992/L.1/Add.15. See chapter 3.
[195] E.g. Beijing Platform for Action, paras 58 to 66.
[196] *Ibid.*, paras 190 to 195.
[197] *Ibid.*, paras 253 to 255.
[198] D. Otto, above note 181 at 13. See also Y. Lee, 'Violence against women: reflections on the past and strategies for the future – an NGO perspective', 19 *Adelaide Law Review* (1997) 45.
[199] D. Otto, above note 181 at 14, 20–2.

With the exception of the Children's Convention and the International Convention on the Protection of the Rights of All Migrant Workers and Members of Their Families, all the 'general' human rights instruments use only the masculine pronoun. The importance of language in constructing and reinforcing the subordination of women has been much analysed by feminist scholars,[200] and the consistently masculine vocabulary of human rights law operates both directly and more subtly to exclude women. Such word use is significant in reinforcing hierarchies based on sex and gender, even if it is intended to be generic. The origins of the use of the masculine as generic were explicitly to give prominence and deference to men.[201] Moreover, it is often unclear whether the intention in using masculine terms is to signify a generic category. As Helen Bequaert Holmes has written, 'A man is sure that he is included; a woman is uncertain.'[202]

Another feature of the human rights treaties is the attention they pay to the idea of the family. The family is presented as 'the natural and fundamental group unit of society' and is thus 'entitled to protection by society and the State'.[203] Human rights instruments assume a certain model of the family, that is, a heterosexual married couple and their offspring. Spike Peterson and Laura Parisi have argued that this identification of the family as a heterosexual union serves to further the gendered division of identity, authority and power within society.[204] Indeed, it is assumed that the purpose of marriage is to have children. Within the marriage the woman will be economically dependent on her husband, so that if she is widowed, she will have a special claim on social security.[205] Emphasis on the family as the natural foundation of society assumes its permanence and suggests that human rights are not applicable within the family circle. The sacrosanct image of the family in human rights law discourages intervention and proper scrutiny of whether the rights to life, liberty, freedom from slavery and security of the person are realised in particular family contexts.[206] International human rights law rests on and reinforces a distinction between public and private worlds, and this distinction operates to muffle, and often completely silence, the voices of women.[207] In the sphere of human rights, a number of actors have an interest in preserving the dichotomy between public (regulated) action and private (unregulated) action. Powerful entities

[200] See e.g. D. Spender, *Man Made Language* (London/Boston, Routledge & Kegan Paul, 1980).
[201] *Ibid.* at 147–8.
[202] H. Holmes,. above note 58 at 259.
[203] E.g. Universal Declaration of Human Rights (UDHR), article 16(3).
[204] V. Peterson and L. Parisi, 'Are women human? It's not an academic question', in T. Evans (ed.), *Human Rights Fifty Years On: A Reappraisal* (Manchester, Manchester University Press, 1998) 132 at 145.
[205] E.g. UDHR, article 23.
[206] H. Holmes, above note 58 at 253.
[207] See chapter 2.

in the private arena, such as religious and commercial institutions, benefit from a lack of international human rights scrutiny.[208]

First generation rights

The epithet 'civil and political' to describe those rights that make up the traditional first generation of international human rights law suggests the defining nature of a public/private dichotomy in their content. These are rights that the individual can assert against the state: the public world of the state must allow the private individual protection and freedom from intervention in particular areas. The primacy traditionally given to civil and political rights by Western international lawyers and philosophers is directed towards protection for men within public life and their relationship with government. Although the civil and political rights (in the traditional sense) of women should be fully protected, violations of these rights are not the harms from which women most need protection.[209]

The operation of a public/private distinction at a gendered level is most clear in the definition of civil and political rights, particularly those concerned with protection of the individual from violence. The construction of these norms obscures the most pervasive harms done to women. One example of this is often considered the most important of all human rights,[210] the right to life contained in article 6 of the ICCPR[211] and in regional human rights treaties.[212] The right is primarily concerned with the arbitrary deprivation of life through public action.[213] Protection from arbitrary deprivation

[208] G. Binion, above note 157 at 517–18.

[209] See C. Chinkin, 'Strategies to combat discrimination against women', in M. O'Flaherty and G. Gisvold (eds), *Post-War Protection of Human Rights in Bosnia and Herzegovina* (The Hague, Kluwer Law International, 1998) 173.

[210] Y. Dinstein, 'The right to life, physical integrity and liberty', in L. Henkin (ed.), *The International Bill of Rights: The Covenant on Civil and Political Rights* (New York, Columbia University Press, 1981) 114.

[211] See also UDHR, article 3.

[212] European Convention for the Protection of Human Rights and Fundamental Freedoms, article 2; African Charter on Human and Peoples' Rights, article 4; American Convention on Human Rights, article 4.

[213] There is debate among various commentators as to how narrowly the right should be construed. Fawcett has suggested that the right to life entails protection only from the acts of government agents: J. Fawcett, 'The application of the European Convention on Human Rights', in W. Friedmann, L. Henkin and O. Lissitzyn (eds), *Transnational Law in a Changing Society; Essays in Honour of Philip C. Jessup* (New York, Columbia University Press, 1972) 228 at 238–9. Dinstein noted that it may be argued under article 6 that 'the state must at least exercise due diligence to prevent the intentional deprivation of the life of one individual by another'. He seemed, however, to confine the obligation to take active precautions against loss of life only in cases of riots, mob action or incitement against minority groups: Y. Dinstein, above note 210 at 119. Ramcharan has argued for a still wider interpretation of the right to life, 'plac[ing] a duty on the part of each government to pursue policies which are designed to ensure access to the means of survival for every

of life or liberty through public actions, important as it is, does not, however, address the ways in which being a women is in itself life-threatening and the special ways in which women need legal protection to be able to enjoy their right to life. As chapter 1 explained, from conception to old age, womanhood is full of risks: of abortion and infanticide because of the social and economic pressure to have sons in some cultures; of malnutrition because of social practices of giving men and boys priority with respect to food; of less access to health care than men; and of endemic violence against women in all states. Although the empirical evidence of violence against women is overwhelming and undisputed, it has not been adequately reflected in the development of human rights law. The significant documented violence against women around the world remains unaddressed by the international legal notion of the right to life because that legal system is focused on 'public' actions by the state.[214]

The international prohibition on torture is similarly limited.[215] A central feature of the international legal definition of torture is that it takes place in the public realm: it must be 'inflicted by or at the instigation of or with the consent or acquiescence of a public official or other person acting in an official capacity'.[216] Although many women are victims of torture in this 'public' sense,[217] by far the greatest violence against women occurs in the 'private' non-governmental sphere. Thus in 1996 in her second report, the UN Special Rapporteur on Violence against Women made the case for defining severe forms of domestic violence as torture.[218] She showed the similarities between torture and domestic violence: both the torture victim and the abused women are isolated and live in a state of terror; they suffer physically and psychologically; they develop coping mechanisms that come to dominate their existence; both forms of violence are committed intentionally in

---

individual within its country'. B. Ramcharan, 'The concept and dimensions of the right to life', in B. Ramcharan (ed.), *The Right to Life in International Law* (Dordrecht/Boston, Martinus Nijhoff, 1985) 1 at 6. The examples of major modern threats to the right to life offered by Ramcharan, however, do not encompass violence outside the 'public' sphere. *Ibid.* at 7–8.

[214] The Human Rights Committee in its General Comments no. 6, 27 July 1982 and no. 14, 9 November 1984 has, however, urged a non-restrictive interpretation of the right to life and has acknowledged infant mortality, malnutrition and epidemics as threats to the right.

[215] A more detailed analysis of the international law prohibition on torture from a feminist perspective is contained in H. Charlesworth, C. Chinkin and S. Wright, above note 58 at 628–9. See also C. Chinkin, 'Torture of the girl child', in G. Van Bueren (ed.), *Childhood Abused: Protecting Children against Torture, Cruel, Inhuman and Degrading Treatment and Punishment* (Aldershot, Dartmouth Publishing Co./Ashgate Publishing Co., 1998) 81.

[216] UN Convention against Torture, article 1(1).

[217] See e.g. *Women in the Front Line*, above note 132.

[218] See Report of the Special Rapporteur on Violence against Women, its Causes and Consequences, 5 February 1996, UN Doc. E/CN.4/1996/53.

order to terrorise, intimidate, punish or to extort confessions of often non-existent deviant behaviour. She concluded that:

> Battered women, like official torture victims, may be explicitly punished for infraction of constantly changing and impossible to meet rules. Both may be intimidated and broken by the continual threat of physical violence and verbal abuse; and both may be most effectively manipulated by intermittent kindness.[219]

If violence against women is understood not just as aberrant behaviour but as part of the structure of the universal subordination of women, it cannot be considered a purely 'private' issue. Charlotte Bunch has pointed out that such violence is caused by 'the structural relationships of power, domination and privilege between men and women in society. Violence against women is central to maintaining those political relations at home, at work and in all public spheres.'[220] These structures are supported by the male-dominated hierarchy of the nation state. The maintenance of a legal and social system in which violence or discrimination against women are endemic and where such actions are trivialised or discounted should engage state responsibility to exercise due diligence to ensure the protection of women.[221] Thus if, for example, state laws require female obedience to male relatives, provide for a defence of 'honour'[222] or deny an offence of marital rape,[223] or if law enforcement agencies routinely ignore complaints by women of domestic violence, the state is acquiescing in that violence and fails to satisfy the standard of due diligence.

In 1993, the UN General Assembly adopted the Declaration on the Elimination of Violence Against Women which supports this approach.[224] The Declaration is a valuable development in women's international human rights law because it affirms that violence against women is an international issue and because it defines gender-based violence in a broad manner. Violence against women is analysed as 'a manifestation of historically unequal power relationships between men and women'. The Declaration, however, also illustrates the problem of accommodating harms against women within a human rights framework. Apart from a reference to human rights in the Preamble, the Declaration does not clearly present violence against women as a general human rights concern. It appears as a discrete and special issue rather than an abuse of, for example, the rights to life or equality. The failure

---

[219] *Ibid.* at para. 47.

[220] C. Bunch, above note 190 at 491.

[221] R. Cook, 'State responsibility for violations of women's human rights', 7 *Harvard Human Rights Journal* (1994) 126.

[222] For an influential case study of such a system see *Criminal Injustice: Violence against Women in Brazil* (New York, Human Rights Watch, 1991).

[223] In *SW v. UK; CR v. UK*, 21 EHRR 363 (1995) the ECHR found that a conviction for marital rape did not offend against the principle of non-retroactivity even though there had not previously been such an offence in the United Kingdom.

[224] See chapter 3 for a discussion of its normative status in international law.

to explicitly link violence against women with abuse of human rights was due to some states' opposition to the nexus on the basis that this would devalue the traditional notion of human rights.[225] If the relevance of the Declaration to the interpretation of 'general' human rights had been made more explicit, it could more strongly influence the mainstream human rights bodies and encourage them to view violence against women as being within their mandates rather than just the province of the specialised women's institutions.

Apart from the rights to life and freedom from torture, other rights in the traditional civil and political catalogue have been interpreted in ways that offer very little freedom or protection to women. The right to liberty and security of the person set out in article 9 of the ICCPR, for example, has been considered to operate only in the context of direct action by the state. It has only recently been understood to address the fear of sexual violence, which is a significant aspect of many women's lives.[226] The right to free movement within a territory and to have the free choice of residence have not been interpreted to cover situations where women are forbidden by husbands or other male relatives to leave their homes.[227] The right to freedom of expression has been defined in some national contexts as including the right to make, distribute and use pornography, which contributes directly to the level of violence against women.[228] And although the right to privacy has been valuable for women in some national contexts,[229] it can also be interpreted as protecting from scrutiny the major sites for the oppression of women – home, family, religion and culture.

There has, however, been some recognition of the gendered dimensions of certain civil and political rights. For example, in *Longwe v. Intercontinental Hotels*, the High Court of Zambia held that a hotel policy of prohibiting entry to unaccompanied women violated rights of freedom of movement, assembly and association, as well as being discriminatory.[230] Gendered aspects of slavery and the slave trade have been increasingly acknowledged and human rights bodies have been urged to examine such practices as servile marriages, trafficking in women, enforced prostitution and pimping as forms of female sexual slavery.[231] The Women's Convention does not

[225] H. Charlesworth and C. Chinkin, 'Violence against women: a global issue', in J. Stubbs (ed.), *Women, Male Violence and the Law* (Sydney, Institute of Criminology Series no. 6, 1994) 13 at 25.

[226] R. West, above note 55 at 67.

[227] N. Toubia (ed.), *Women of the Arab World* (New York, St Martin's Press, 1988), Introduction.

[228] See C. MacKinnon, *Feminism Unmodified: Discourses on Life and Law* (Cambridge, Harvard University Press, 1987) at 163–97.

[229] K. Engle, 'After the collapse of the public/private distinction: strategizing women's rights', in D. Dallmeyer (ed.), *Reconceiving Reality: Women and International Law* (Washington DC, American Society of International Law, 1993) 143 at 148.

[230] [1993] 4 Law Reports of the Commonwealth 221.

[231] K. Barry, above note 143.

identify these as violations of women's human rights, much less as slavery, but only requires states to 'take all appropriate measures, including legislation, to suppress all forms of traffic in women and exploitation of prostitution of women'.[232] In 1983 the Special Rapporteur on the Suppression of Traffic in Persons and the Exploitation of Prostitution analysed prostitution as a form of slavery.[233] The Subcommission on Prevention of Discrimination and Protection of Minorities created a Working Group in 1975 to review developments in the law against slavery. The Group, which has been known since 1988 as the Working Group on Contemporary Forms of Slavery, has recognised the gendered manifestations of such practices.[234] Alongside economic, sexual and other forms of exploitation, the Working Group identified corruption that has spread to the highest social spheres as an 'inescapable element' in contemporary slavery. The 1998 report of the Special Rapporteur on Slavery, Ms Gay McDougall, on providing a legal framework for prosecuting sexual slavery and slavery-like practices during armed conflict stated that: 'Sexual slavery . . . encompasses situations where women and girls are forced into "marriage", domestic servitude or other forced labour that ultimately involves forced sexual activity' as well as forced prostitution.[235] In 1998 the International Criminal Tribunal for Rwanda found that rape and sexual violence against women constitute genocide in the same way as any other acts that are carried out with the intention to destroy a national, ethnical, racial or religious group.[236]

Second generation rights
Second generation rights – economic, social and cultural rights – might be thought to apply in both public and private spheres and thus offer more to women's lives.[237] Certainly, the fact that these rights do not neatly fit the 'individual v. state' paradigm has contributed to their more controversial status, the weaker language of obligation and weaker methods of implementation at international law. The definition of these rights as set out in the ICESCR, however, indicates the tenacity of a gendered public/private distinction in human rights law. The ICESCR creates a public sphere by assuming that all effective power rests with the state. But, as Shelley Wright

[232] Convention on the Elimination of All Forms of Discrimination Against Women, article 6.
[233] UN Doc. E/1983/7, 17 March 1983.
[234] UN Doc. E/CN.4/Sub.2/AC.2/1998/CRP.1.
[235] Special Rapporteur on Contemporary Forms of Slavery, Systematic Rape, Sexual Slavery and Slavery-like Practices, 22 June 1998, UN Doc. E/CN.4/Sub2/1998/13.
[236] *Prosecutor v. Jean-Paul Akayesu*, Judgment of 2 September 1998, ICTR-96-4-T. See further chapter 10.
[237] Compare B. Stark, 'The "other" half of the International Bill of Rights as a postmodern feminist text', in D. Dallmayer, above note 229 at 19.

has pointed out, 'For most women, most of the time, indirect subjection to the State will always be mediated through direct subjection to individual men or groups of men.'[238] The ICESCR, then, does not touch on the economic, social and cultural context in which most women live. For example, the definition of the right to just and favourable conditions of work in article 7 is confined to work in the public sphere. Marilyn Waring has documented the tremendous amount of economic activity by women all over the world that is rendered invisible precisely because it is performed by women without pay and considered as being within the private, domestic sphere.[239] Article 7's guarantee to women of 'conditions of work not inferior to those enjoyed by men, with equal pay for equal work' is thus rather hollow in the light of the low valuation of the extent and economic value of women's domestic work. Further, even within the paid, public sector, the sexual division of labour that clusters women in typically low-paying jobs that are deemed 'suitable' for women, means that there is often no male comparator, again exposing the deficiencies of the equality paradigm. It is notable that the ILO did not conclude a Convention on homeworkers, the majority of whom are women, until 1996.[240] Mohanty has shown how homeworking is perceived as a leisure activity pursued by housewives, while the marketing and distribution of the finished products, which is mainly performed by men, is categorised as economically productive.[241] Another example is the right to food, set out in article 11 of the ICESCR. This is even more clearly relevant to the private, domestic sphere and yet its elaboration has not taken account of the many transactions involving providing, preparing and serving food that are integral to the lives of women.[242] There are opposing tensions for women with respect to economic and social rights: on the one hand, according them full effect would enhance women's lives but much of the social burden of performance of such 'caring' rights is likely to fall upon women.[243]

[238] S. Wright, 'Economic rights and social justice: a feminist analysis of some international human rights conventions', 12 *Australian Yearbook of International Law* (1992) 241 at 249.

[239] M. Waring, *Counting for Nothing: What Men Value and What Women are Worth* (Wellington, Allen & Unwin, 1988); M. Waring, *Three Masquerades: Essays on Equality, Work and Human Rights* (Auckland, Auckland University Press, 1996) chapter 2.

[240] Convention no. 177 Concerning Home Work, 20 June 1996, reprinted in 12 *International Journal of Comparative Labour Law and Industrial Relations* (1996) 252.

[241] C. Mohanty, 'Women workers and capitalist scripts: ideologies of domination, common interests, and the politics of solidarity', in M. Alexander and C. Mohanty (eds), *Feminist Genealogies, Colonial Legacies, Democratic Futures* (New York/London, Routledge, 1997) 3 at 12.

[242] See C. Chinkin and S. Wright, 'The hunger trap: women, food and development', 14 *Michigan Journal of International Law* (1993) 262.

[243] B. Stark, 'Nurturing rights: an essay on women, peace and international human rights', 13 *Michigan Journal of International Law* (1991) 144.

As noted above, the definition of cultural and religious rights can often reinforce a distinction between public and private worlds that operates to the disadvantage of women. In secular states, culture and religion are typically seen as 'private' spheres protected from legal regulation, particularly with respect to discrimination against women. By contrast, in religious states, religion is an aspect of the public domain and its tenets are enforced through state support. While the right to gender equality on the one hand, and religious and cultural rights on the other, can be reconciled by limiting the latter,[244] in political practice cultural and religious freedom are accorded much higher priority nationally and internationally.

Interpretations of economic, social and cultural rights tend to ignore their ramifications for women. For example, in his final report in 1992, the Subcommission on Prevention of Discrimination and Protection of Minorities' Special Rapporteur on The Realization of Economic, Social and Cultural Rights, Danilo Turk, discussed barriers to the observance of these rights.[245] He identified problems ranging from structural adjustment policies, to income distribution and deficient political will but did not deal at all with the more basic issue of the relevance of these rights to women. The Committee on Economic, Social and Cultural Rights, which monitors the ICESCR has, however, shown more signs of taking women seriously than other expert committees in the UN human rights system. In its concluding remarks to states' reports it has drawn attention to sex discrimination in the enjoyment of rights under the ICESCR.[246] For example, the Committee's General Comment on the right to adequate housing in article 11(1) of the ICESCR specifically refers to the relevance of the right to female-headed households.[247]

One of the most consistent themes at the 1995 Beijing Conference was the impact on women's economic, social and cultural rights of the structural adjustment programmes imposed by the international monetary institutions.[248] Indeed, it has been argued that the severity of the socio-economic conditions caused by structural adjustment programmes in Africa undermines the relevance and utility of rights discourse for African women.[249] For example,

[244] See D. Sullivan, 'Gender equality and religious freedom: toward a framework for conflict resolution', 24 *New York University Journal of International Law and Politics* (1992) 795.

[245] UN Doc. E/CN.4/Sub.2/1992/16.

[246] E.g. it has queried discriminatory work practices, the position of women migrant workers, the position of women heads of household in the context of agrarian reforms and the application of housing programmes. See Consideration of Reports Submitted by States under Articles 16 and 17 of the Covenant, UN Doc. E/C.12/1/ Add.7/Rev.1, 2 December 1996.

[247] General Comment no. 4, UN Doc. E/1992/23, 13 December 1991.

[248] K. Guest, 'Post-modernism/pre-modernism: alive and well in Beijing', in S. Mitchell and R. Das Pradhan (eds), *Back to Basics from Beijing* (Canberra, Australian Council for Overseas Aid, 1997) 110.

[249] A. Kuenyehia, 'The impact of structural adjustment programs on women's international human rights: the example of Ghana', in R. Cook, above note 63 at 422.

such programmes in Ghana were designed to stimulate economic growth, enhance production, strengthen the balance of payments and increase domestic saving and investment.[250] Currency devaluation increased the cost of imported goods, and higher taxes meant increased petroleum and utility tariffs. Basic food prices increased, employment levels were reduced and government spending was cut back.[251] Emphasis on export of agricultural commodities reduced the land available to women for subsistence farming while increasing the total burden of their work.[252] Akua Kuenyehia has written:

> For women in Ghana and other African countries facing structural adjustment, the problems seem endless. They continue to have the responsibility for child care, producing food, gathering fuelwood and water, and taking care of sick members of the family. These functions are economically invisible and yield little or no cash. Additionally, they have to engage in economic ventures to earn income in a climate that has been rendered increasingly hostile by a process of adjustment that has completely marginalized their productive activities.[253]

This situation works against all aspects of women's rights: reduction in access to health, sanitation and education has first impact on women. Compliance with structural adjustment programmes gives governments an excuse not to implement obligations under the Women's Convention.[254] Moreover, Anne Orford has argued that interventionist monetary policies mandated by the IMF can disrupt stability, threaten internal peace and undermine civil society, all of which in turn contribute to increased violence against women.[255]

Third generation rights

Third generation rights that have been championed within the UN by developing nations in particular have been only cautiously accepted by the 'mainstream' international human rights community because of their challenge to the Western, liberal model of individual rights invocable against the sovereign. The philosophical basis of group rights rests on a primary commitment to the welfare of the community over and above the interests of particular individuals. As we have noted above, theories of collective rights assume that the interests of all members of a particular group will coincide. The articulation of collective rights generates a number of questions: how is the group to be defined and by whom? how is membership retained? what is

[250] *Ibid.* at 423.
[251] *Ibid.* at 424.
[252] *Ibid.* at 425.
[253] *Ibid.* at 431.
[254] *Ibid.* at 433.
[255] A. Orford, above note 81 at 455–6 (using economic rescheduling in Yugoslavia in the late 1980s as illustrative).

the relationship between rights of the group and the rights of individuals within the group? how is conflict between them to be resolved?[256]

On one analysis, it might seem that such rights would be of particular promise to women, whose lives typically have the quality of connectedness with others, centring more around the family, the group and the community than the individual. The theoretical and practical development of third generation rights has, however, delivered very little to women. For example, as chapter 5 explains, the right to self-determination, allowing 'all peoples' to 'freely determine their political status and freely pursue their economic, social and cultural development' has been invoked, and supported, recently in a number of contexts that allow the oppression of women.

The international legal definition of the right to development provides another example of the privileging of a male perspective and a failure to accommodate the realities of women's lives. The problematic nature of current development practice for women in the South goes of course much deeper than the international legal formulation of the right to development, but the rhetoric of international law reflects and reinforces a system sustaining the domination of women. The 1986 Declaration on the Right to Development describes the content of the right as the entitlement 'to participate in, contribute to and enjoy economic, social, cultural and political development, in which all human rights and fundamental freedoms can be fully realised'.[257] The right is apparently designed to apply to all individuals within a state and is assumed to benefit men and women equally.[258] Article 8 of the Declaration states that 'effective measures should be undertaken to ensure that women have an active role in the development process'.

Despite this specific reference to women, the Declaration fails to take into account the realities of women's lives. First, the Declaration does not specify discrimination against women as a major obstacle to development, nor to the fair distribution of its benefits. For example, one aspect of the right to development is the obligation on states to take 'resolute steps' to eliminate 'massive and flagrant violations of the human rights of peoples and human beings'. The examples given of such violations include apartheid and race discrimination but do not include sex discrimination.[259] Although subsequent UN deliberations have referred to the gender implications of the right to development, these concerns are generally presented as discrete, soluble by the application of special protective measures, rather than as central to development.[260]

---

[256] See W. Kymlicka, *Multicultural Citizenship* (Oxford, Clarendon Press, 1995) chapter 3.

[257] Declaration on the Right to Development, article 1.1.

[258] *Ibid.*, Preamble.

[259] *Ibid.*, article 5.

[260] E.g. Report prepared by the Secretary-General on the Global Consultation on the Realization of the Right to Development as a Human Right, UN Doc. E/CN.4/

A second problem with the Declaration is the model of development upon which it is built. Although the formulation of the right to development includes a synthesis of all recognised human rights, its core is redress of economic inequality. Development means in effect industrialisation and a market economy. The domination of women by men within the family and in society does not enter the traditional development calculus. The limitations of the idea of development enshrined in international law are highlighted by research that has documented the critical role women play in the economies of the South, particularly in agriculture, and at the same time the widespread inequality of women within their families and communities.[261] 'Development' has delivered little to women because economic visibility depends on working in the public sphere. Unpaid work in the home or the subsistence economy is categorised as 'unproductive, unoccupied, and economically inactive'.[262]

The failure to value 'private' women's work is one basis for the observation that overall, the process of development exacerbates the problems of women in the South.[263] The differential valuation of the work of women to that of men often means that, within the family, women will not have an equal claim to food and other necessities. Drèze and Sen have pointed to the significance of perceptions of relative economic contributions in the familial division of food, resources and health care in the developing world.[264] They have noted that paid employment is regarded as more significant than unpaid work. The narrow notion of development also operates to exclude women from some aid programmes because they are not considered workers, or because they are regarded as less productive than men.[265] When aid is provided to women, it is often in their guise as mothers. Another consequence of the economic paradigm of development is that women may be regarded as providing a lesser return on training and education.[266]

1990/9 at paras 15, 42, 51, 52, 59. However, the UNDP's policy on integrating human rights into sustainable human development emphasises that sustainable human development must work to eliminate discrimination against women, to redress past discrimination and to educate and empower women.

[261] E.g. J. Drèze and A. Sen, *Hunger and Public Action* (Oxford, Oxford University Press, 1989), chapter 4.

[262] *Ibid.* at 57.

[263] J. Momsen and J. Townsend, *Geography of Gender in the Third World* (Albany, State University of New York Press, 1987). See further H. Pietila and J. Vickers, *Making Women Matter: The Role of the United Nations* (London, Zed Books, 1994) chapter 2.

[264] J. Drèze and A. Sen, above note 261 at 52.

[265] R. Pfanner, 'Australian foreign aid and women in the third world', in N. Grieve and A. Burns (eds), *Australian Women: New Feminist Perspectives* (Melbourne, Oxford University Press, 1986) 305 at 307.

[266] M. Waring, *Counting for Nothing*, above note 239 at 10.

The international formulation of the right to development, then, reinforces gendered public/private distinctions. It does not regard systemic discrimination on the basis of sex as a barrier to development, despite the global evidence of the disparity between the economic position of women and men. Moreover, in using the 'neutral' language of development and economics, international law reinforces the pervasive, and detrimental, assumption that women's work is of a different value to men's.

Trade liberalisation promoted by free trade arrangements such as the Uruguay round of GATT and the North American Free Trade Agreement[267] has undermined the effectiveness of human rights discourse for women.[268] Vandana Shiva has made the point strongly, asserting that economic globalisation 'is deeper and wider than Structural Adjustment Policies or GATT – it is the ruling ideology that centres on the replacement of governmental and state planning by corporate strategic planning and the establishment of global corporate rule'.[269] She has argued that although the process is made to appear 'natural, spontaneous and inevitable', in reality it is deeply political and shaped primarily by the interests of transnational corporations.

The forces of economic globalisation are both non-transparent and non-accountable under the traditional state-centred structures of international law.[270] From the perspective of women, this process turns on its head the public/private distinction of traditional human rights law, for it redefines understandings of the role of the public sector, facilitates privatisation and requires governments to act primarily in accordance with commercial dictates rather than those of social justice and human rights.[271] However, women may benefit, at least in the short term, because increased investment and export processing can increase women's access to paid employment and offer alternatives to unemployment.[272] At the same time, the commodification

---

[267] 17 December 1992, reprinted in 32 *International Legal Materials* (1993) 296, 605.

[268] K. Guest, 'Exploitation under erasure: economic, social and cultural rights engage economic globalisation', 19 *Adelaide Law Review* (1997) 73. Guest has pointed out that the GATT and the WTO are not referred to in the Beijing Platform for Action, despite the impact of their policies upon women's lives.

[269] V. Shiva, *Women, Ecology and Economic Globalisation: Searching for an Alternative Vision* (New Delhi, Indian Association of Women's Studies, 1995) at 4–5.

[270] E.g. R. Krut, *Globalization and Civil Society: NGO Influence in International Decision-Making* (New York, UN Research Institute for Social Development, 1997) at 1.

[271] A. Orford, above note 81 at 471. The position is, however, complex: see for example V. Nesiah, above note 162, on the position of Sri Lankan women working for multinational corporations.

[272] C. Barbieri, 'Women workers in transition: the potential impact of the NAFTA labor side agreements on women workers in Argentina and Chile', 17 *Comparative Labor Law Journal* (1996) 526; S. Wright, 'Women in the global economic order: a feminist perspective', 10 *American University Journal of International Law and Policy* (1995) 861.

of the basics of everyday life – food, land, seeds, plants and animals – has meant that resources and knowledge that were formerly under local, often women's, control to generate sustenance and survival are now in the hands of the corporate sector, with their use motivated primarily by profit.

Women and human rights law

Despite the significant problems in making human rights law relevant to women's lives, human rights has been an area of intense activity for women. Various developments in the 1990s indicate the potential of this area of law.

Invocation of international rights in national fora

While the international law of human rights provides a very limited response to the injustices and inequality many women face, it has allowed at least some individual victories in national courts. As we have seen, the international understanding of the right to equality is a restricted one, but even this circumscribed notion may be useful in particular national contexts.[273] One example is the case of Unity Dow in Botswana, discussed in chapter 4, where Dow argued successfully that the Botswanan Constitution should be read in the light of the international law principle of sex equality.[274] On the other hand, progressive judicial decisions based on human rights principles have sometimes remained unenforced,[275] or have been overturned by legislatures.[276]

A complaints mechanism for the Women's Convention

We noted above that the Women's Convention, unlike other human rights instruments, had no procedure by which complaints of non-implementation could be made. NGOs lobbying for a complaints mechanism achieved some recognition in the Vienna Declaration in 1993.[277] A draft 'Optional Protocol' to the Women's Convention was prepared by independent experts at a meet-

---

[273] See A. Byrnes, 'Human rights instruments relating specifically to women, with particular emphasis on the Convention on the Elimination of All Forms of Discrimination Against Women', in A. Byrnes, J. Connors and L. Bik (eds), *Advancing the Human Rights of Women: Using International Human Rights Standards in Domestic Litigation* (London, Commonwealth Secretariat, 1997) 39 at 50–5. For an excellent practical guide to advocacy strategy in national and international arenas see *Women's Human Rights Step by Step* (Washington DC, Women, Law and Development, 1997).

[274] *Attorney-General of Botswana v. Unity Dow* [1992] LRC (Const) 623.

[275] E.g. *Longwe v. Intercontinental Hotels*, above note 230.

[276] E.g. *Shah Bano*, above note 155.

[277] Vienna Declaration and Programme of Action, II, para. 40.

ing in Maastricht in 1994.[278] The principles of the draft were then adopted by the CEDAW and then were circulated to states for comment in 1995 by the CSW. After four years of debate in an 'open-ended' working group of CSW, an Optional Protocol was adopted by the General Assembly in October 1999.[279]

The original Maastricht draft was modelled on existing treaty complaints mechanisms, but in many respects it offered a broader procedure. For example, the draft extended the category of those who could bring complaints to individuals, groups or organisations claiming to be affected by a violation and individuals, groups or organisations 'with a sufficient interest'. This would have allowed complaints of systemic discrimination rather than simply individual complaints. The broader standing provisions were strongly resisted by states and were deleted at the 1998 CSW meeting.[280] Another innovation of the Maastricht draft was a provision that would have placed an obligation on states to remedy violations identified through the complaints mechanism. Views adopted by treaty-monitoring committees under existing complaints mechanisms are not expressly stated to bind the state concerned and states regularly attempt to resist the force of the committees' views by arguing that they are recommendations only. The Maastricht provision was dropped in 1998 because of resistance (particularly from the United Kingdom and the United States), with the only requirement on states being to give 'due consideration' to CEDAW's views and to respond to them.[281] A third significant innovation in the Maastricht draft was giving the CEDAW the power to inquire into allegations of systemic violations of the Women's Convention without a specific complaint. This provision survived,[282] but was made subject to an 'opt-out' provision.[283]

Although the Optional Protocol to the Women's Convention is not significantly stronger than the existing treaty complaints mechanisms, the availability of the procedure will strengthen the force of the Convention. It will allow women in states that accept the Optional Protocol to invoke international standards and scrutiny when national laws are inadequate. It will also generate a body of jurisprudence interpreting the Women's Convention. The linking of the complaints mechanism of the Inter-American Convention on Violence against Women with that of the Inter-American Convention on Human Rights[284] offers a similar prospect.

[278] A. Byrnes and J. Connors, 'Enforcing the human rights of women: a complaints procedure for the Women's Convention', 21 *Brooklyn Journal of International Law* (1996) 679.

[279] GA Res. 54/4, 15 October 1999.

[280] See *ibid.*, article 2.

[281] *Ibid.*, article 7.4.

[282] *Ibid.*, articles 8 and 9.

[283] *Ibid.*, article 10.

[284] Inter-American Convention on the Prevention, Punishment and Eradication of Violence against Women, 9 June 1994, reprinted in 33 *International Legal Materials* (1994) 1534, articles 11 and 12.

Gender 'mainstreaming' in human rights treaty bodies

One response to the problems women face in the international human rights system has been the policy of 'gender mainstreaming'. At the Vienna Conference on Human Rights in 1993, it was accepted that the human rights of women should form 'an integral part of the United Nations human rights activities'.[285] The Office of the High Commissioner for Human Rights has made efforts to integrate gender into all human rights activities and is co-operating with the Division for the Advancement of Women.[286] The Office is developing a policy on gender and on strategies for its effective implementation. ECOSOC and the CHR have requested and encouraged the country specific and thematic special rapporteurs, experts and working groups to include sex-disaggregated data in their reports, to address women-specific violations of human rights and to co-operate and exchange information with the Special Rapporteur on Violence against Women.[287]

Guidelines designed to 'mainstream' gender perspectives in the international human rights system were formulated in 1995 by the annual meeting of the Chairpersons of the human rights treaty bodies. The reaction of the treaty-monitoring bodies to calls for 'gender mainstreaming' has been varied, however.[288] The reactions appear to depend on the presence of at least one or two committee members who have a real commitment to the issue. At one end of the spectrum, there have been significant advances. For example, the Committee on Economic, Social and Cultural Rights has generally taken the task of gender mainsteaming seriously, referring to the position of women regularly in its concluding observations on states parties, reports and in General Comments. Its reporting guidelines are, however, uneven with respect to gender issues. For example, gender is not referred to with respect to some important articles such as the right to free primary education.[289] By contrast, the Committee on the Elimination of Racial Discrimination (CERD) showed reluctance to advert to gender considerations in its concluding observations or general comments, although the intersection of race and sex discrimination is an important and controversial area. Indeed, the Chairman of CERD stated in 1996 that directives to integrate gender into states parties' reports were 'fundamentally misconceived'.[290] So too the Committee against Torture has not displayed any concern with the gendered aspects of torture.

[285] Vienna Declaration and Programme of Action, I, para. 18; II, para. 37.

[286] The question of integrating the human rights of women throughout the UN system, Report of the Secretary-General, UN Doc. E/CN.4/1998/49, 25 March 1998.

[287] For details of progress in this regard see *ibid.* at paras 43 to 53.

[288] For details of the response of all the human rights treaty bodies see *ibid.* at paras 23 to 41; *Women 2000*, December 1998.

[289] See A. Gallagher, above note 129 at 301–2. But see Plans of Action for Primary Education (article 14), General Comment II: UN Doc. E/C.12/1999/4, 10 May 1999.

[290] Quoted in A. Gallagher, above note 129 at 304. However in 1998 CERD

The Human Rights Committee, which monitors the ICCPR, is regarded as one of the most progressive of the treaty-monitoring bodies with respect to women. It has adopted a number of useful General Comments on articles of the ICCPR that show a sensitivity to gender issues; and in 1995 the Committee amended its reporting guidelines to request states parties to provide information on the position of women. As Jane Connors has pointed out, however, the Committee is not consistent in its concern with gender.[291] Most of the Committee's General Comments do not address the position of women. A 1996 General Comment on torture did not examine the gendered dimensions of the right to be free from torture, although it did refer to the need for states parties to address the infliction of torture or cruel, inhuman or degrading treatment by private actors.[292] On the other hand, the Committee has used its concluding observations in a number of cases in a progressive way. For example, in 1996, the concluding comments on Peru's periodic report under the ICCPR expressed concern about criminalisation of abortion even in cases of rape, which resulted in 'backyard' abortions being the major cause of maternal mortality. The Committee stated that 'these provisions not only mean that women are subject to inhumane treatment but are possibly incompatible with articles 3 [the right of men and women to equal enjoyment of the rights set out in the ICCPR], 6 [the right to life] and 7 [the right to be free from torture and cruel, degrading and inhuman treatment] of the Covenant'.[293]

Thus, overall, gender mainsteaming has had a mixed fate. It has been relatively easy to obtain revision of reporting guidelines and much more difficult to obtain practical follow-through, for example through the systematic questioning of states.[294]

Conclusion

The international community appears to have made considerable progress with respect to women and human rights. For example, at the Vienna World Conference on Human Rights in 1993, the international community formally recognised that the human rights system did not adequately respond to women's lives and committed itself to the view that the human rights of women were 'an inalienable, integral and indivisible part of human rights'.

---

agreed to draft a General Recommendation on Gender Dimensions of Racial Discrimination: UN Doc. CERD/C/SR. 1283, 12 August 1998.

[291] J. Connors, 'General human rights instruments and their relevance to women', in A. Byrnes *et al.*, above note 273 at 33.

[292] General Comment no. 20 (44), UN Doc. HRI/GEN/1/Rev.2 at 30 10 April 1996. The proposed General Comment on article 3, above note 191, is expected to provide a gender analysis of all the Covenant rights.

[293] Quoted in C. Brautigam, above note 80 at 393.

[294] *Ibid.*

It also accepted that gender-specific violations of human rights were part of the human rights agenda.[295] The Beijing Declaration and Platform for Action acknowledged that women's rights were human rights and described the human rights of women and the girl child as an inalienable, integral and indivisible part of all human rights and fundamental freedoms.[296] It should be noted, however, that the assertion that 'women's rights are human rights' is not contained in the Platform, apparently because of an anxiety of states about recognising 'new' human rights.[297] Thus the Platform distinguishes between human rights of women (which are universal) and women's rights (which are not).

Although the Beijing Platform for Action gives a nod in the direction of the diversity of women's experiences,[298] it nevertheless presents women in a very limited, encumbered, way. The major role for women remains that of the UDHR – wife and mother.[299] Attempts to raise the diversity of women's identities, most particularly with respect to sexual orientation, were unsuccessful.[300]

The new discourse of 'women's rights as human rights' is limited also in the way it understands the notion of equality. Although there have been significant moves in the recognition of some women-specific harms, particularly violence against women, the major remedy proposed for the global subordination of women is an increased role in decision-making. This allows women only access to a world already constituted by men, not to a world transformed by the interests of women. Dianne Otto has argued:

> In the absence of a recognition that the decision-making structures must themselves change, it is not clear what difference women's equal participation would make. Ultimately, it may merely equally implicate women in the perpetuation of the masculinist liberal forms of minimalist representative democracy and capitalist economics.[301]

[295] Vienna Declaration and Programme of Action, I, para. 18.

[296] Beijing Platform for Action, para. 213.

[297] D. Otto, 'A post-Beijing reflection on the limitations and potential of human rights discourse for women', in K. Askin and D. Koenig (eds), *Women and International Human Rights Law* (New York, Transnational Publishers, 1999) 115.

[298] Beijing Platform for Action, para. 46, recognises that:

> women face barriers to full equality and advancement because of such factors as their race, age, language, ethnicity, culture, religion or disability, because they are indigenous women or because of other status. Many women encounter specific obstacles related to their family status, particularly as single parents; and to their socio-economic status, including their living conditions in rural, isolated or impoverished areas. Additional barriers also exist for refugee women, other displaced women, including internally displaced women as well as for immigrant women and migrant women, including migrant women workers. Many women are also particularly affected by environmental disasters, serious and infectious diseases and various forms of violence against women.

[299] See chapter 2.

[300] D. Otto, above note 181 at 25–7.

[301] D. Otto, above note 297 at 127.

The new discourse also gives prominence to civil and political rights of women at the expense of economic and social rights. In particular, health and reproductive rights were controversial at Beijing. The feminisation of poverty, although clearly acknowledged in the Beijing Platform, was not placed in a rights context. It has been noted that the Platform 'assumes . . . that capitalism has the ability to deliver economic equality to the poor women of the world and . . . that the obligation of states to guarantee certain economic and social rights is made redundant by the more "efficient" processes of free market forces'.[302] Focusing on economic and social rights would draw attention to 'the operation of systems of privilege among women' and the inequitable structures of global capital.[303]

Women's international human rights must be developed on a number of fronts. First, it is important to document the relevance of the traditional canon of human rights to women. Second, the instruments and institutions of international law with respect to women must be supported and strengthened. Third, the boundaries of the traditional human rights canon must be redefined to accommodate women's lives. At the same time, rights that focus on harms sustained by women in particular need to be identified and developed, challenging the public/private distinction by bringing rights discourse into the private sphere. This has been described by Radhika Coomaraswamy as a fourth generation of women's rights.[304] The definition of specifically women's rights is one way of moving beyond the limitations of the non-discrimination focus of women's international human rights law. These rights may include those associated with reproductive choice and childbirth.[305] Other potential women's rights include the right to a minimum wage for work within the home or in subsistence farming, and the right to literacy.

Human rights are, in essence, what we want to take out of the agenda of short-term politics.[306] They create 'a protective sphere for vital interests, which people need to persuade them that they may accept vulnerability, run risks, undertake adventures in the world, and operate as citizens and as people'.[307] The two major challenges to all human rights, and especially to those of women, in the twenty-first century will be the forces of religious extremism and of economic globalisation.

---

[302] *Ibid.*

[303] *Ibid.* See also Y. Lee, above note 198.

[304] R. Coomaraswamy, 'Reinventing international law', above note 146 at 181–2.

[305] N. Burrows, above note 140 at 85; Programme of Action of the International Conference on Population and Development, UN Doc. A/Conf. 171/13, 18 October 1994, chapter VII.

[306] R. Unger, quoted in *Economic and Social Rights and the Right to Health*, above note 70 at 13.

[307] *Ibid.*

8

The use of force
in international law

Introduction

The control and regulation of state violence is one of the cornerstones of post-UN Charter international law. The primary purpose of the UN is '[t]o maintain international peace and security ... to take effective collective measures for the prevention and removal of threats to the peace, and for the suppression of acts of aggression or other breaches of the peace'.[1] The Charter's principles include the prohibition of the unilateral use of force in international relations[2] and the obligation upon states to settle their international disputes peacefully.[3] As a corollary to the prohibition of unilateral use of force, the Charter provides for a collective security regime.[4]

In this chapter we examine the prohibition of the use of force in international law. We first describe the impact of armed conflict upon women to indicate some of the ways in which women are particularly affected by it. We then discuss the way that international law deals with armed conflict[5] and argue that its gendered character produces an inadequate response to the realities of the lives of women caught up in conflict. Chapter 9 in turn considers the related international legal notions of peaceful resolution of disputes and collective security.

The impact of armed conflict on women

The consequences of armed conflict are horrific for all caught up in it. Since World War II deaths and injuries of civilian women, men and children have

---

[1] Charter of the UN, 26 June 1945, article 1.
[2] *Ibid.*, article 2(4).
[3] *Ibid.*, articles 2(3) and 33.
[4] *Ibid.*, articles 1(5), (6) and chapter VII.
[5] Chapter 10 considers international humanitarian law.

far exceeded those suffered by the military[6] and in the 1990s over 90 per cent of conflict-related casualties have been civilians.[7] Large numbers of women and children have been maimed by the small arms circulating within civilian society.[8] Both women and men non-combatants suffer many forms of harm during and after armed conflict and they are both targeted for different kinds of injury. The elderly, the sick, the poor and the young are particularly vulnerable in conflict.[9] Our concern in this chapter is, however, particularly with the reaction of the international legal system to the effect of armed conflict on women.[10] In many areas of armed conflict men sustain specific harms at a disproportionate rate to women. For example, men are the targets of 'disappearances' in times of conflict and political oppression at significantly higher levels.[11] But, as we argued in chapter 7, international law has responded more readily to the harms typically sustained by men than to those directed against women.[12] Further, the consequences for women family members of disappeared men are not always acknowledged.[13]

The construction of social sex and gender roles, combined with the generally subordinate social and economic position of women, mean that women suffer in particular ways during[14] and after conflict.[15] Women's experiences of

[6] A. Fetherston and C. Nordstrom, *Overcoming Conceptual Habitus in Conflict Management: UN Peacekeeping and Warzone Ethnography* (Canberra, Peace Research Centre, Australian National University, 1994, Working Paper no. 147).

[7] J. Pettman, *Worlding Women: A Feminist International Politics* (Sydney, Allen & Unwin, 1996) at 89.

[8] The UN Secretary-General has noted that 90 per cent of those killed or wounded by small arms are civilians and of those 80 per cent are women and children: Annual Report of the Secretary-General on the Work of the Organization, UN Doc. A/53/1, 27 August 1998 at para. 50.

[9] See G. Machel, The Impact of Armed Conflict on Children, UN Doc. A/51/306, 26 August 1996.

[10] See J. Vickers, *Women and War* (London, Zed Books, 1993) chapter 2.

[11] A. Jones, 'Does "gender" make the world go round? Feminist critiques of international relations', 22 *Review of International Studies* (1996) 405.

[12] E.g. the Working Group on Disappearances was formed in 1980 by the UN Commission on Human Rights, CHR Res. 20 (XXXVI), 1980, while the mandate of the Special Rapporteur on Violence against Women was not established until 1994.

[13] See *Women in Afghanistan: A Human Rights Catastrophe* (London, Amnesty International, 1995) at 15.

[14] The Fourth World Conference on Women in 1995 noted that: 'While entire communities suffer the consequences of armed conflict and terrorism, women and girls are particularly affected because of their status in society and sex.' Fourth World Conference on Women, Declaration and Platform for Action, 15 September 1995, UN Doc. A/CONF. 177/20, reprinted in 35 *International Legal Materials* (1996) 401 (Beijing Platform for Action), para. 135. See also J. Gardam, 'Women and the law of armed conflict: why the silence?', 46 *International and Comparative Law Quarterly* (1997) 55.

[15] E.g. the continuing impact of armed conflict on women in Bosnia-Herzegovina three years after the General Framework Agreement for Peace in Bosnia and Herzegovina, initialled Dayton, 21 November 1995, signed Paris, 14 December 1995,

conflict have varied greatly depending upon such factors as national identity, race, class, economic circumstances, urban or rural location, family situation, age, employment and health. Other variables are whether they were actively involved in combat, were imprisoned or detained, or attempted to maintain civilian life within or outside the war zone. In chapter 5, for example, we described the different effects of the Israeli/Palestinian conflict on groups of Palestinian women. In her analysis of women in South Africa's 'twilight war' in the 1980s, Cock has shown how women of different class and race were affected in quite separate ways.[16] She has described women as becoming 'protectors', 'protected', 'resisters', 'militarists' and 'victims'; in each case women's sex and gender was a defining factor in their experience of the conflict. Cock has argued that: 'War is a gendering activity . . . thus changing gender relations is one of the essential tasks for reducing the risks of war in the future.'[17]

Rape and sexual violence

Rape and sexual violence in times of armed conflict are well-documented. Women become victims of violence from both enemy and 'friendly' forces.[18] Indeed, licence to rape has been included as a term of employment for mercenary soldiers.[19] In the context of the armed conflicts accompanying the disintegration of the Former Yugoslavia in the 1990s, rape was described by the UN Security Council as 'massive, organised and systematic'.[20] It was used to 'humiliate, shame, degrade and terrify [an] entire ethnic group'.[21] As well as the immediate degradation, pain and terror, rape survivors frequently experience long-term physical injury and psychological trauma. Fear and shock are also experienced by women who were not themselves subjected to attack.[22]

---

reprinted in 35 *International Legal Materials* (1996) 75. See 'Women: war in peace', *Guardian*, 14 December 1998, G2, 6.

[16] See generally J. Cock, *Women and War in South Africa* (London, Open Letters, 1992).

[17] *Ibid.* at x.

[18] See chapter 9.

[19] E.g. the case of the Moroccan soldiers fighting with Free French forces in Italy in 1943: M. Walzer, *Just and Unjust Wars: A Moral Argument with Historical Illustrations* (New York, Basic Books, 2nd edn 1992) chapter 8.

[20] SC Res. 820, 17 April 1993.

[21] Tadeusz Mazowiecki, Special Rapporteur of the Commission on Human Rights, Report Pursuant to Commission Resolution 1992/S-1/1 of 14 August 1992, UN Doc. E/CN.4/1993/50, 10 February 1993. See also EC Investigative Mission into the Treatment of Muslim Women in the Former Yugoslavia, Warburton Report, Annex I to letter from the Permanent Representative of Denmark to the UN Secretary-General, 2 February 1993, UN Doc. S/25240 (1993).

[22] G. Ashworth, *Of Violence and Violation: Women and Human Rights* (London, Change, 1985). See also A. Wing and S. Merchan, 'Rape, ethnicity, and culture: spirit injury from Bosnia to Black America', 25 *Columbia Human Rights Law Review* (1993) 1.

Rape carries the risk of sexually transmitted disease and pregnancy. Women have to face the prospect of childbirth, or of seeking an abortion, at a time of great dislocation with reduced health care and intense social and cultural pressures, sometimes against abortion and sometimes against keeping a child conceived by rape.

Women's sexuality is also used as a reward and prop for male military action. For example, thousands of women were forced into government-sanctioned military brothels to act as 'comfort women' for Japanese troops during World War II.[23] The 'comfort women' were not considered prisoners of war and they were not referred to in the Peace Treaties with Japan.[24] Demands for official compensation, apologies and punishment of those responsible have been rejected by the Japanese government.[25] Sexual demands are not limited to territory in which conflict is current: prostitution associated with military bases and establishments for rest and recreation is accepted as inevitable.[26] The economic realities that make military prostitution inescapable for many women, and their procurement through force and fraud, constitute a form of sexual slavery.[27]

Millions of women and children have fled from armed conflict, remaining for years in refugee camps, in foreign countries or as displaced persons within their own countries.[28] Violent attacks often occur during flight, in camps and in host states. Sexual demands may be made in return for necessities such as food and shelter, the approval of personal documentation and even the grant of refugee status.[29] Although the domestic law of some states has changed in the 1990s,[30] in many legal systems fear of continued sexual

[23] The number of such women has been estimated to be between 100,000 and 200,000. See U. Dolgopol and S. Paranjape, *Comfort Women: The Unfinished Ordeal* (Geneva, International Commission of Jurists, 1994); U. Dolgopol, 'Women's voices, women's pain', 17 *Human Rights Quarterly* (1995) 127; G. Hicks, *The Comfort Women* (Sydney, Allen & Unwin, 1995).

[24] The Treaty of Peace with Japan, 8 September 1951, 183 UNTS 46, article 16 provides for indemnification of those prisoners of war 'who suffered undue hardship'.

[25] The Japanese government has refused to make payment on the basis that the peace treaties at the end of World War II settled all outstanding issues. Filipina and South Korean women have commenced class civil actions in Japanese courts. *Reuters News*, 16 May 1997.

[26] C. Enloe, *Does Khaki become You? The Militarisation of Women's Lives* (London, Pluto Press, 1983 reprinted 1988) chapter 2; C. Enloe, *Bananas, Beaches, and Bases: Making Feminist Sense of International Politics* (London, Pandora Press, 1989) chapter 4.

[27] K. Barry, *Female Sexual Slavery* (New York, New York University Press, 1984) at 70–6.

[28] S. Forbes Martin, *Refugee Women* (London/New Jersey, Zed Books, 1992). UNHCR, Guidelines on the Protection of Refugee Women (Geneva 1991).

[29] UNHCR, Executive Committee Resolution No. 73 (XLIV) 1993, Refugee Protection and Sexual Violence.

[30] E.g. Canada: Immigration and Refugee Board Guidelines on Gender-Related Persecution, 9 March 1993; Australia: Department of Immigration and Multicultural

abuse is not accepted as constituting a 'well-founded fear of persecution' for the purposes of refugee classification.[31]

Sexually manifested violence in armed conflict is an aspect of the subordinate position of women globally, described in chapter 1. It is connected to ideas of male soldiers' privileges, to the power of the military's lines of command as well as by class and ethnic differences among women.[32] It is also linked to the idea of women as property, thus 'to rape a woman is to humiliate her community'.[33] Men are exhorted to fight to protect their possessions: their land, their ports, their resources, their women. Imagery of women can be manipulated to make conflict seem inevitable, for example the idea of the vulnerable woman who must be protected.[34] As Ann Tickner has pointed out, 'certain people (usually gendered feminine) are being protected by certain others (always gendered masculine)... This protector/ protected relationship is one of inequality: those who are protected lack agency or ability to provide for their own protection.'[35] Thus the need for an international response to the Iraqi invasion of Kuwait in 1990 was linked to claims of infanticide, rape and torture.[36] These images were compounded by explicit sexual and racial elements that projected the construct of the virile white male defender of women and children, upholding Western values against a racial inferior.[37] The vulnerability of women to sexual attack is

---

Affairs, Refugee and Humanitarian Visa Application Guidelines on Gender Issues for Decision Makers, July 1996. The Refugee Women's Legal Group prepared Gender Guidelines for the Determination of Asylum Claims in the United Kingdom in July 1998 but these have not yet been adopted by the government.

[31] Convention Relating to the Status of Refugees, 28 July 1951, 189 UNTS 150, article 1; Protocol Relating to the Status of Refugees, 31 January 1967, 606 UNTS 267.

[32] B. Reardon, *Sexism and the War System* (New York, Teachers College Press, 1985) at 39. See also C. Enloe, 'The gendered gulf', in C. Peters (ed.), *The 'New World Order' at Home and Abroad: Collateral Damage* (Boston, South End Press, 1992) 93 at 97.

[33] R. Seifert, 'War and rape: a preliminary analysis', in A. Stiglmayer (ed.), *Mass Rape: The War against Women in Bosnia-Herzegovina* (Lincoln, University of Nebraska Press, 1994) 82.

[34] On the power of imagery see S. Macdonald, 'Drawing the lines – gender, peace and war: an introduction', in S. Macdonald, P. Holden and S. Ardner (eds), *Images of War in Peace and War: Cross-Cultural and Historical Perspectives* (Basingstoke, Macmillan, 1987) 1.

[35] J. Tickner, 'Feminist approaches to issues of war and peace', in D. Dallmeyer (ed.), *Reconceiving Reality: Women and International Law* (Washington DC, American Society of International Law, 1993) 267 at 271–2.

[36] A. Farmanfarmaian, 'Did you measure up? The role of race and sexuality in the Gulf War', in C. Peters, above note 32 at 111, 113.

[37] Similar images were essential to the whole colonial enterprise. See M. Alexander and C. Mohanty, 'Introduction: genealogies, legacies, movements', in M. Alexander and C. Mohanty (eds), *Feminist Genealogies, Colonial Legacies, Democratic Futures* (London, Routledge, 1997) xiii at xxi.

appropriated by government, military and the media for these purposes.[38] Whether the alleged atrocities actually occurred becomes irrelevant.

Daily survival

Armed conflict is a struggle to survive for those who remain at home,[39] as well as those who are interned.[40] Economic and social hardships are increased by the physical danger of attacks involved in leaving the home for routine activities such as shopping.[41] The imposition of economic sanctions and the creation of black markets exacerbate shortages and cause prices to hike.[42] Continuation of professional life, and thus of regular income, may become impossible. Caring for physically and psychologically injured fighters, the elderly and traumatised children falls most heavily upon women.[43] Women whose male relatives are killed may be left financially unassisted.[44] In an attempt to prevent this, governments may resort to previously discouraged, or forbidden, practices such as polygamy.[45] In other situations women who have remarried after believing their husbands to have been killed are subsequently punished.[46] Collapse of governmental agencies, including those for maintaining law and order, and the physical concentration of fighters within an area all undermine community restraints on human rights abuses.[47] Women also suffer from a higher incidence of violence at home during armed conflict, whether or not they are living within the combat

[38] S. Gibson, 'The discourse of sex/war: thoughts on Catharine MacKinnon's 1993 Oxford Amnesty Lecture', 1 *Feminist Legal Studies* (1993) 179. The lecture referred to is C. MacKinnon, 'Crimes of war, crimes of peace', in S. Shute and S. Hurley (eds), *On Human Rights: The Oxford Amnesty Lectures 1993* (New York, Basic Books, 1993) 83.

[39] N. Mousavizadeh (ed.), *The Black Book of Bosnia: The Consequences of Appeasement* (New York, Basic Books, 1996) has described civilian struggles for survival in all parts of the former Yugoslavia.

[40] E.g. M. Brooks, 'Passive in war? Women internees in the Far East 1942-5', in S. Macdonald *et al.*, above note 34 at 166.

[41] For graphic descriptions of life during the siege of Sarajevo see J. di Giovanni, *The Quick and the Dead: Under Siege in Sarajevo* (London, Phoenix, 1994).

[42] B. Bhatia, M. Kawar and M. Shahin, *Unheard Voices: Iraqi Women on War and Sanctions* (London, Change, 1991); R. Clark, *The Fire This Time: US War Crimes in the Gulf* (New York, Thunder's Mouth Press, 1992).

[43] G. Goodwin-Gill and I. Cohn, *Child Soldiers: The Role of Children in Armed Conflict* (Oxford, Clarendon Press, 1994); J. Kuper, *International Law Concerning Child Civilians in Armed Conflict* (Oxford, Clarendon Press, 1997).

[44] *Women and War* (Geneva, International Committee of the Red Cross, 1995) at 18.

[45] E.g. in Iraq during the Iran–Iraq war: S. Ladin, *IWRAW to CEDAW: Country Reports* (Minneapolis, International Women's Rights Action Watch, 1992) at 9.

[46] *Women in Afghanistan*, above note 13.

[47] See *Mejia Egocheaga and another v. Peru* (Case 10.970; Report 5/96) (1996) 1 Butterworths Human Rights Cases 229 (see further chapter 10).

zone.[48] Long-term conflict or territorial occupation has particular consequences for women, caused by both the occupiers[49] and by other members of their own society,[50] for example by prioritising women's role as childbearers[51] or as preservers of the national cultural heritage.[52]

Changing roles of women in armed conflict

The position of women during armed conflict is not always entirely negative. In Pat Barker's account of life in Britain during World War I in *Regeneration*, a character reflects that '[Women] seemed to have changed so much during the war, to have expanded in all kinds of ways, whereas men over the same period had shrunk into a smaller and smaller space.'[53] War has presented some women with the opportunity to gain freedoms and to enjoy new status.[54] Women's active participation in nationalist and revolutionary struggles has sometimes facilitated their subsequent assertion of political and social rights.[55] For example, the Iraqi Women's Federation played an important role during the Iran–Iraq war in helping Iraqi women to exercise their roles in all walks of life and thus helping to eliminate 'backward beliefs assigning a lowly role to women'.[56] However, it has been very difficult for

[48] E.g. during the Gulf War 1990–91, the number of rapes in Israel increased. In Croatia during the conflicts surrounding the dissolution of former Yugoslavia, violence against women within the family rose by almost 30 per cent. R. Seifert, above note 33 at 66.

[49] See chapter 5 for a discussion of the effects of occupation upon Palestinian women. Women in Israel are also affected by the occupation in different ways. See N. Yuval-Davis, 'The Israel example', in W. Chapkis (ed.), *Loaded Questions: Women in the Military* (Amsterdam, Transnational Institute, 1981) 73.

[50] On the outside/inside commission of violence against women under structural systems of oppression such as foreign occupation and apartheid see A. Wing, 'A critical race feminist conceptualization of violence: South African and Palestinian women', 60 *Albany Law Review* (1997) 943.

[51] E.g. during the war between Iran and Iraq, President Saddam Hussein of Iraq said in a radio broadcast: 'Our motto must be that each family produce at least five children ... and that the family which does not produce at least four children deserves to be harshly reprimanded.' Quoted in S. Ladin, above note 45 at 9.

[52] In the context of Palestine see K. Warnock, *Land Before Honour* (London, Macmillan, 1990) at 52.

[53] P. Barker, *Regeneration* (London, Penguin Books, 1991) at 90.

[54] E.g. Cynthia Enloe has described how the *intifada* denied Palestinian men opportunities to prove their manhood but presented women's household and other chores as 'national imperatives' essential to the continuing struggle: *Bananas, Beaches and Bases*, above note 26 at 58.

[55] L. Kornblum, 'Women warriors in a men's world: the combat exclusion', 2 *Law and Inequality* (1984) 351 at 380.

[56] Iraq's initial report on the application of the Convention on the Elimination of All Forms of Discrimination Against Women, 18 December 1979, 1249 UNTS 13, reprinted in 19 *International Legal Materials* (1980) 33, UN Doc. CEDAW/C/5/Add.66/Rev.1, 16 August 1990.

women to retain social and political advancement after the conflict is over,[57] with women required to give up power and responsibility by government policies designed to return men to employment and to restore traditional sex and gender roles.[58] The adoption of new economic systems post-conflict can also have adverse consequences for women. For example, after the collapse of communist regimes in Eastern Europe, the new capitalist systems have undermined the economic and social position of women.[59] In some instances women have responded to conflict by creating networks that transcend the opposing parties or have organised in response to the harms they have suffered.[60] Images of women are used for diverse, and often contradictory, purposes in times of conflict. Women can be depicted as maternal comforters, victims, manipulators of men, and sterling citizens, taking over men's work.[61] Sometimes women may be able to take short-term advantage of opportunities that are opened up by the dislocation of normal life, but they may quickly lose the gains they have made.

Women and the use of force

Women are rarely involved in decisions about the use of armed conflict and in its processes. Nationally, government bodies dealing with defence and international relations have few women representatives,[62] and this exclusion is replicated internationally.[63] Women seldom sit as members of delegations on the Security Council and are inadequately represented in security and

---

[57] See the case studies in C. Berkin and C. Lovett (eds), *Women, War and Revolution* (New York, Holmes & Meier, 1980).

[58] C. Enloe, *Does Khaki Become You?*, above note 26 at 188. For discussion of this in the context of the Gulf War see C. Enloe, *The Morning After: Sexual Politics at the End of the Cold War* (Berkeley, University of California Press, 1993).

[59] *Hidden Victims Women in Post-Communist Poland* (New York, Human Rights Watch, 1992); J. Jaquette and S. Wolchick (eds), *Women and Democracy* (Baltimore, Johns Hopkins University Press, 1998) 125–2.

[60] E.g. women's committees were formed in response to disappearances in South America: M. Acosta, 'Women's human rights groups in Latin America', in D. Forsythe (ed.), *Human Rights and Development* (London, Macmillan 1989) 3. See also M. Zalewski, 'Well, what is the feminist perspective on Bosnia?', 71 *International Affairs* (1995) 339 at 355 (discussing the formation of a Women's Party in Serbia crossing ethnic lines, and cross-community work in Northern Ireland).

[61] See N. Huston, 'Tales of war and tears of women', 3 *Women's Studies International Forum* (1982) 275 at 279.

[62] *Women – Challenges to the Year 2000* (New York, UN, 1991) at 75; *Women in Decision-Making: Facts and Figures on Women in Political and Public Decision Making in Europe* (Network of Experts Publication, 2nd edn 1994).

[63] Report of the Secretary-General, Peace: Women in International Decision-Making, UN Doc. E/CN.6/1995/12, 21 February 1995.

conflict resolution committees.[64] Why does this matter? We have examined in chapter 6 the significance of women's participation in international decision-making. It is clear that there is no inevitable or natural connection between womanhood and disdain for the use of force,[65] or between masculinity and support for the use of force. Whether greater participation of women in international decision-making would result in different types of decisions being made is difficult to establish, but it would at least would allow for a greater diversity of considerations to be taken into account.

Women are also peripheral participants in armed conflict. Women formed 7 per cent of forces in Operation Desert Storm in Kuwait in 1990–91, although not in combat positions.[66] Only a few states allow women to hold military posts that might directly involve combat.[67] The presence of women in the military is often accompanied by allegations of sexism, sexual harassment and abuse.[68] The basis for official exclusion of women from combat positions seems to be that women are intrinsically unsuited for such activity. A number of states have, for example, made reservations to the Convention on the Elimination of All Forms of Discrimination Against Women which stipulates equality in public life, on the basis that the principle of equality cannot be extended to combat and combat-related duties.[69]

The question of whether the right to equal exposure to combat is valuable for women has been hotly debated. On the one hand exclusion of women

[64] Commission on the Status of Women, Review and Appraisal of the Implementation of the Nairobi Forward-Looking Strategies for the Advancement of Women, 22 November 1989, UN Doc. E/CN.6/1990/5, 65.

[65] J. Tickner, above note 35 at 273; J. Elshtain, *Women and War* (New York, Basic Books, 1987 reprinted 1995). See further C. Chinkin, 'Women and peace: militarism and oppression', in K. Mahoney and P. Mahoney (eds), *Human Rights in the Twenty-First Century: A Global Challenge* (Dordrecht, Martinus Nijhoff, 1993) 405.

[66] Report of the Secretary-General, Peace: Women in International Decision-Making, above note 63 at para. 31. At the time of the Gulf War the United States Congress upheld a law banning women from combat assignments. In 1992 a Presidential Commission recommended that women be allowed on combat ships but remain excluded from ground or air combat: *Reuters News*, 3 November 1992.

[67] These include Belgium, Canada, Luxembourg, the Netherlands, Norway, Venezuela and Zambia: Report of the Secretary-General, Peace: Women in International Decision-Making, above note 63 at para. 23.

[68] E.g. at the 1991 Convention of the Tailhook Association (a private group of US Navy and Marine aviators) 83 defence forces women were sexually harassed and assaulted. Investigation revealed the pervasiveness of sexual abuse within United States forces: C. Enloe, *The Morning After*, above note 58 at 212–14.

[69] 18 December 1979, 1249 UNTS 13, reprinted in 19 *International Legal Materials*, article 7. Note by the Secretary-General, Declarations, reservations, objections and notifications of withdrawal of reservations relating to the Convention on the Elimination of All Forms of Discrimination Against Women, UN Doc. CEDAW/SP/1994/2. States with such reservations include Australia, Austria, Germany, New Zealand and Thailand.

from combat duties denies them equality with men. Some feminists have argued that this effectively relegates women to the status of second class citizens, protected or not according to the whim of the protectors.[70] Ann Scales has described how the exclusion of women from the draft disenfranchised them from legal protest against the Vietnam war. Women were denied standing to make their voices heard and were thus removed from the public arenas of both the courts and the combat zone.[71] Feminists have also pointed out that the reasons for keeping women out of combat positions are less about the requirements of national security and more about the assertion of a particular understanding of masculinity. If the military are presented as the protectors of the state and of women, emphasising sex differences camouflages and reinforces the naturalness of men's domination of women.[72] Catharine MacKinnon has said:

> Somehow it takes the glory out of the foxhole, the buddiness out of the trenches, to imagine us out there. You get the feeling they might rather end the draft, they might even rather not fight wars at all than have to do it with us.[73]

The threat to military cohesion, responsibility and loyalty posed by women is also implicit in debates about the admission of homosexuals to the military.[74] The inclusion of 'the other' is seen to undermine the integrity, autonomy and masculinity of the nation's fighters and to present a threat to 'national security'.

An alternative feminist position sees the demand for equal participation in the military as problematic. The claim is seen as implying that citizenship involves the ability to have recourse to arms and that militaristic values are important to society. It is said to justify the use of armed force by men and women rather than exploring ways for its reduction.[75] It also does not encompass any blueprint for change that might be effective in promoting domestic peace, and therefore international peace and security.

---

[70] Judith Hicks Stiehm has argued that women should engage in combat precisely to transform themselves from being 'protected' to becoming 'protectors': J. Stiehm, 'The protected, the protector, the defender', 5 *Women's Studies International Forum* (1982) 367.

[71] As Ann Scales has explained: 'I wanted to be part of it. I wanted to be a history-maker on the terms I understood history-making to involve. I wanted at least to have standing to resist.' A. Scales, 'Militarism, male dominance and law: feminist jurisprudence as oxymoron?', 12 *Harvard Women's Law Journal* (1989) 25.

[72] M. Burguières, 'Feminist approaches to peace: another step for peace studies', 19 *Millennium* (1990) 1 at 5.

[73] C. MacKinnon, *Feminism Unmodified: Discourses on Life and Law* (Cambridge, Harvard University Press, 1987) at 38.

[74] W. Chapkis, 'Sexuality and militarism', in E. Isaksson (ed.), *Women and the Military System* (Hemel Hempstead, Harvester Wheatsheaf, 1988) 106.

[75] See further C. Chinkin, above note 65.

The use of force under international law

The principles of international law relating to armed conflict can be seen as resting on a series of dichotomies: international/internal; independence/dependence; intervention/non-intervention; order/anarchy; integrity/disintegration; self-defence/illegal use of force. These binary oppositions are coded in a gendered way, with the first term connected with 'male' characteristics and the second, 'female'.[76] The international legal regime upholds the first set of concepts: for example article 2(4) of the UN Charter prohibits the unilateral use of force in international relations against the territorial integrity or political independence of any state.

Self-defence

The only UN Charter exception to this prohibition is article 51 which reiterates the 'inherent' right of states to individual and collective self-defence.[77] The enormous literature on the legal doctrine of self-defence[78] assumes that the use of force by states is inevitable and that legal doctrines need to be interpreted accordingly.[79] The concept of self-defence is not defined in article 51 and customary international law criteria remain applicable. These require the use of force to be necessary, proportionate and reasonable, that there be no alternative course of action, nor time for deliberation.[80] The ICJ clarified some aspects of self-defence under customary international law in the *Nicaragua* case, setting out two preconditions to the legitimate use of force in collective self-defence.[81] First, the target state must have declared

[76] C. Cohn, 'War, wimps and women: talking gender and thinking war', in M. Cooke and A. Woollacott (eds), *Gendering War Talk* (Princeton, Princeton University Press, 1993) 227 at 231. See further chapter 2.

[77] Article 51 states: 'Nothing in the present Charter shall impair the inherent right of individual or collective self-defence if an armed attack occurs against a Member of the United Nations, until the Security Council has taken measures to maintain international peace and security.'

[78] E.g. D. Bowett, *Self-Defence in International Law* (Manchester, Manchester University Press, 1958); I. Brownlie, *International Law and the Use of Force* (Oxford, Clarendon Press, 1963); M. McDougal and F. Feliciano, *Law and Minimum World Public Order: The Legal Regulation of International Coercion* (New Haven, Yale University Press, 1961); O. Schachter, 'Self-defense and the rule of law', 83 *American Journal of International Law* (1989) 259; S. Alexandrov, *Self-Defense against the Use of Force in International Law* (The Hague, Kluwer, 1996).

[79] See A. Cassese, *Violence and Law in the Modern Age* (Cambridge, Polity Press, 1986) especially chapter 2.

[80] *The Caroline Case* 29 BFSP 1137–38; 30 BFSP 195–6 (1841); *Legality of the Threat or Use of Nuclear Weapons* 1996 ICJ Rep. 226 (Adv. Op. 8 July), reprinted in 35 *International Legal Materials* (1996) 809 at para. 41.

[81] *Case Concerning Military and Paramilitary Activities in and against Nicaragua* (Nicaragua v. United States of America) Merits 1986 ICJ Rep. 14 (Judgment of 27 June) (*Nicaragua*, Merits) at para. 176.

that it had been subject to an armed attack and second, it must have requested assistance from the state purporting to act in collective self-defence. The ICJ also considered the related customary international norm of non-intervention, holding that illegal intervention not amounting to an armed attack does not legitimate the use of armed force either in self-defence or as a form of counter-intervention.[82]

As we discussed in chapter 5, the notion of the state and its attributes that is assumed in international law is a limited one. The emphasis on the integrity of territory in the law on the use of force mimics the idea of the individual, detached and separate from society, entitled to resist any unsolicited contact. The image of the autonomous (male) individual, on which the idea of statehood and the concern with sovereignty within territorial boundaries rests, makes the interests of the international community and of individuals appear of secondary importance to those of a single, threatened state. It also reinforces images of women as unbounded and unequal to men within the state.

The inadequacy of the international legal regime on the use of force is illustrated by the reaction to the invasion of Kuwait by Iraq in 1990. The invasion was quickly condemned by the international community. Kuwait's right to individual and collective self-defence in response to an armed attack was asserted and economic sanctions imposed to facilitate the removal of Iraqi forces from Kuwait.[83] Without any assessment of the effectiveness of economic sanctions, the use of 'all necessary means' was shortly afterwards mandated by the Security Council to achieve this objective.[84] Allied forces under American command subsequently defeated the Iraqi forces. The surrender of Iraqi President Saddam Hussein in accordance with the stringent terms of Security Council Resolution 687[85] signified the triumphant

[82] *Ibid.* at para. 195. See also Declaration on the Inadmissibility of Intervention in the Domestic Affairs of States and the Protection of their Independence and Sovereignty, GA Res. 2131 (XX), 21 December 1965; Declaration on Principles of International Law Concerning Friendly Relations and Co-operation among States in Accordance with the Charter of the UN, GA Res. 2625 (XXV), 24 October 1970.

[83] SC Res. 660, 2 August 1990; SC Res. 661, 6 August 1990; SC Res. 665, 25 August 1990.

[84] SC Res. 678, 29 November 1990. It has been debated whether this was collective action under UN Charter, chapter VII or collective self-defence under article 51: e.g. B. Weston, 'Security Council Resolution 678 and Persian Gulf decision making: precarious legitimacy', 85 *American Journal of International Law* (1991) 516; C. Greenwood, 'New world order or old? The invasion of Kuwait and the rule of law', 55 *Modern Law Review* (1992) 153; E. Rostow, 'Until what? Enforcement action or collective self-defence?', 85 *American Journal of International Law* (1991) 506; D. Greig, 'Self-defence and the Security Council: what does Article 51 require?', 40 *International and Comparative Law Quarterly* (1991) 366.

[85] 3 April 1991. The Resolution provided *inter alia* for a ceasefire; destruction of Iraqi chemical and biological weapons; on-site inspections of weapon-making facilities; return of Kuwaiti property; and the establishment of a Compensation

completion of this operation. The expulsion of Iraq from Kuwait in 1991 is regularly presented as a paradigm of the successful military operation of international law.[86]

Much attention was given to the actions of Saddam Hussein after the military surrender in 1991, but little was given to those of the returned Kuwaiti government.[87] The 'liberation' of Kuwait was accompanied by significant violations of women's rights. First, no Kuwaiti woman could be said to be 'liberated' in the narrow sense of formal participation in democratic rights as Kuwait continued to deny suffrage to women.[88] Second, women were not freed from the fear and actuality of violence that accompanied the occupation.[89] A rape epidemic was reported in Kuwait after 'liberation' at levels worse than during the Iraqi occupation. Particular victims were women migrant workers from Sri Lanka, the Philippines, Palestine and India raped by armed men in Kuwaiti army or police uniform. The attitude of these men was reportedly that the women 'deserved' their treatment for 'supporting' the Iraqis, or that the attackers could be excused some excesses because of their recent difficult time.[90] Although there was no evidence of deliberate government policy, Kuwaiti government responsibility could be based upon its failure to protect civilians by investigating allegations and prosecuting accused persons, especially where rapes were committed by men in uniform.[91] Instead a climate of impunity prevailed. Third, a large number of women domestic workers were unable to leave Kuwait and sought refuge in various embassies in Kuwait City in early 1992. In many cases their employers had taken their passports and refused to pay their fares home, effectively trapping them in a modern form of slavery. Although these women were effectively hostages, international law offered them no protection.[92]

Commission and Compensation Fund financed from the future sales of Iraqi oil. The measures that undermine Iraqi sovereignty aim both to punish Iraq and to render it impotent against any future hostile activities, thus highlighting the 'virility' of the allies referred to above.

[86] E.g. G. Evans, *Cooperating for Peace: The Global Agenda for the 1990s and Beyond* (Sydney, Allen & Unwin, 1993).

[87] See J. Vickers, above note 10 at 62–7.

[88] See chapter 4 for reservations on this point by Kuwait to human rights treaties.

[89] *A Victory Turned Sour: Human Rights in Kuwait Since Liberation* (New York, Human Rights Watch, 1991); *Punishing the Victim: Rape and Mistreatment of Asian Maids in Kuwait* (New York, Human Rights Watch, 1992).

[90] *A Victory Turned Sour*, above note 89 at 23.

[91] *Ibid.* at 21–4.

[92] The International Convention Against the Taking of Hostages, 17 December 1979, reprinted in 18 *International Legal Materials* 1456, article 1, does not cover this situation, as the aim was not to compel a third party to do or abstain from doing any act as a condition of release of the hostages.

The use of force in international law

Self-determination

The unilateral use of force has been contemplated and justified beyond the context of self-defence where it is argued that it is necessary to uphold other values enshrined within the UN Charter, for example the protection of human rights. Use of force in support of peoples fighting for their legitimate right of self-determination has accordingly been justified,[93] an argument bolstered by the Declaration on the Principles of Friendly Relations.[94] Some writers have argued that this should be understood more broadly to justify the use of force in support of internal self-determination, or to uphold an entitlement to democracy.[95] How has the use of force in the context of self-determination affected women?

One example is the dispute over the Western Sahara. The General Assembly has asserted since 1966 that the future of the phosphate-rich territory should be determined in accordance with the principle of self-determination,[96] a view reaffirmed by the ICJ in 1975.[97] After the Court's advisory opinion, and without a referendum, Morocco invaded the territory claiming that historic ties pre-dating Spanish colonisation justified its reclamation.[98] A tripartite agreement in 1976 between Spain, Morocco and Mauritania divided the territory between Morocco and Mauritania, with Spain retaining a financial interest in the phosphates. The Saharawi resistance movement, the Polisario, continued its armed guerilla struggle for self-determination against Morocco and Mauritania until 1978 when the latter withdrew.

[93] E.g. M. Reisman, 'Coercion and self-determination: construing Charter article 2(4)', 78 *American Journal of International Law* (1984) 642; M. Reisman, 'Sovereignty and human rights in contemporary international law', 84 *American Journal of International Law* (1990) 866; L. Fielding, 'Taking the next step in the development of new human rights: the emerging right of humanitarian assistance to restore democracy', 5 *Duke Journal of Comparative and International Law* (1994) 329.

[94] GA Res. 2625: 'Every State has the duty to refrain from any forcible action which deprives peoples . . . of their right to self-determination and freedom and independence. In their actions against and resistance to such forcible action in pursuit of the exercise of the right to self-determination such peoples are entitled to seek and to receive support.'

[95] M. Reisman, 'Sovereignty and human rights', above note 93 at 871–2; L. Fielding, above note 93 at 355. On the entitlement to democracy see T. Franck, 'The emerging right to democratic governance', 86 *American Journal of International Law* (1992) 46; J. Crawford, 'Democracy and international law', 64 *British Yearbook of International Law* (1993) 113. See also Document of the Copenhagen Meeting of the Conference on the Human Dimension of the CSCE, reprinted in 32 *International Legal Materials* (1993) 163.

[96] E.g. GA Res. 2229 (XXI), 20 December 1966; GA Res. 40/50, 2 December 1985.

[97] *Western Sahara Case* 1975 ICJ Rep. 12 (Adv. Op. 16 October).

[98] T. Franck, 'The stealing of the Sahara', 70 *American Journal of International Law* (1976) 694.

Although the Polisario has not been able to defeat the Moroccan occupation of the territory, the Polisario Saharan Arab Democratic Republic has
been recognised by a number of states. However, the Polisario have received
little support from Western states.[99] On 6 September 1991 a ceasefire, maintained and monitored by the UN peacekeeping force, MINURSO, took
effect as part of an agreement to hold a referendum. Over 60,000 applicants
for voting in the referendum have been identified. Despite a long impasse,[100]
a new settlement plan was agreed to in September 1997.[101]

Moroccan occupation of the Western Sahara has forced many Saharawi
people into refugee camps in Algeria. The refugees are predominantly
female.[102] Through their role in the liberation struggle as played out in the
camps, Saharawi women have made considerable political, social and educational progress.[103] The National Union of Saharawi women was created in
1979 on the initiative of the Polisario with the objectives of mobilising women
to play their role in the liberation struggle and to orientate women in social
and political life, education and professional training. Practical organisation
was through a National Committee, subdivided to cover such matters as
external affairs, information and culture. Socially, women have worked
through these committees to promote pre-school education, health, justice and
production in the camps. They have trained as doctors, nurses, nutrition
experts, technicians, agriculturists, administrators and teachers. Politically, the
Polisario leadership has promised an expanded role for women in a liberated
Saharawi Arab Democratic Republic. Article 30 of the Saharawi Constitution
accepted by the Eighth National Popular Congress in June 1991 states:

> The State works for the protection of all political, economic, social and cultural
> rights of the Saharawi woman and is attentive to guarantee her participation
> in the building of society and the development of the country.

In many ways, denial of the right of self-determination to the Saharawi
people has provided women with the space to assert their own interests
within the group. Saharawi women recognise that if self-determination is
achieved they will have to confront the problem of maintaining the legal

---

[99] Algeria has backed the Polisario. Factors other than self-determination have
influenced some states. For example, desire for access to the fishing resources off the
coast of the Western Sahara led the EC to conclude an agreement with Morocco:
EC, *Official Journal* L99, 16 April 1988, 49.
[100] Report of the Secretary-General on the situation concerning Western Sahara,
UN Doc. S/1996/343, 8 May 1996.
[101] Report of the Secretary-General on the situation concerning Western Sahara,
UN Doc. S/1997/742, 24 September 1997. The referendum had not taken place by
the end of 1999.
[102] The majority of the men do not live in the camps as they are in the army:
Western Sahara home page http://www.arso-org/05.3htm.
[103] *Ibid.*

and social status they have acquired through exile[104] and have attempted to address the issue in advance, for example by forming links with women elsewhere.[105] The experience of women in other states, for example Algeria, suggests that a successful outcome to the group claim to self-determination can have an adverse impact upon women within the group.[106] However, official reports on the Western Sahara focus on the referendum without any reference to the gendered dimensions of self-determination.[107]

Another example of the assertion of the right to use force in the context of self-determination is the ongoing conflict in Afghanistan, which had its first contemporary manifestations in the extension of Soviet power in the cold war order. In 1979 Soviet forces entered Afghanistan and established a government headed by Babrak Karmal. The military invasion was condemned by the General Assembly of the UN, although the Soviet veto prevented Security Council action.[108] The violation of the territorial integrity and political independence of Afghanistan were offered by the United States as reasons to support the local Afghan resistance movement, the *mujahideen*, alongside such states as Saudi Arabia and Pakistan.[109] The 1988 Geneva Peace Agreements provided for the subsequent withdrawal of Soviet forces and repatriation of refugees.[110] Civil war between different factions has continued in Afghanistan with a high level of civilian casualties. In September 1996 the Taliban, a fundamentalist Islamist group, claimed victory after occupying Kabul, although, as of December 1998, fighting still continued.

The United States' initial support for the self-determination of the Afghan

[104] *Today's Refugees, Tomorrow's Leaders*, Report of the Saharawi Women's Conference, Houses of Parliament, UK, 28 October 1993.

[105] E.g. the International Forum for Solidarity with Saharawi Women, 6–8 February 1996, Final Resolution and International Platform for Support of Saharawi Women: Western Sahara home page, above note 102.

[106] See further chapter 5.

[107] E.g. Report of the Secretary-General on the Situation concerning Western Sahara, UN Doc. S/1998/316.

[108] GA Res. ES–6/2, 14 January 1980. The Soviet Union argued that it had been invited into Afghanistan under the terms of the bilateral 1978 Treaty of Friendship. Interventions justified in terms of requests for assistance were a feature of cold war use of force: D. Harris, *Cases and Materials on International Law* (London, Sweet & Maxwell, 5th edn 1998) at 890–4.

[109] See M. Reisman, 'The resistance in Afghanistan is engaged in a war of national liberation', 81 *American Journal of International Law* (1987) 906; M. Reisman and J. Silk, 'Which law applies to the Afghan conflict?', 82 *American Journal of International Law* (1988) 459.

[110] Bilateral Agreements between the Republic of Afghanistan and the Islamic Republic of Pakistan on the Principles of Mutual Relations, in particular on Non-Interference and Non-Intervention; on the Voluntary Return of Refugees; on the Interrelationships for the Settlement of the Situation relating to Afghanistan; and Declaration on International Guarantees, 14 April 1988, reprinted in 27 *International Legal Materials* (1988) 581.

resistance movement ignored the implications for Afghan women, particularly the *mujahideen*'s commitment to an oppressive, rural, patriarchal society. Unlike the Saharawi refugee camps where women have been able to determine the parameters of daily life, the *mujahideen* imposed a strict fundamentalist regime upon Afghani refugees in Pakistan and Iran, confining women to their own quarters, isolating them and depriving them of their traditional tasks within a rural community. Women with no male family escorts have been especially vulnerable, being unable to collect rations and to dispose of human waste, a situation which has contributed to malnutrition, ill health and further social isolation.[111] While the Soviet-backed regime had encouraged educating girls (indeed one source of hostility towards the Karmal government by the *mujahideen* was their expansion of economic and educational opportunities for women and girls),[112] in the refugee camps preference was accorded to boys within UNHCR education facilities.[113] Similarly, during the 1980s a growing number of women were able to work outside the home in non-traditional roles;[114] since 1996, the Taliban has denied women a role in civil society. It has imposed strict criminal and dress codes and has banned women from public places, including education and the workplace.[115] Since many women have lost male relatives in the prolonged conflict, this restriction affects their own survival. Other prohibitions on women's activities include prohibitions on using the public baths in Kabul and attending landmine awareness classes.[116]

[111] S. Forbes Martin, above note 28 at 9–10. See also *Women in Afghanistan*, above note 13 at 11–12. On the devastating effect of *purdah* on Afghan refugee women see C. Chinkin and S. Wright, 'The hunger trap: women, food and self-determination', 14 *Michigan Journal of International Law* (1993) 262 at 281 n. 49.

[112] C. Enloe, *Bananas, Beaches, and Bases*, above note 26 at 57.

[113] Total enrolment in UN schools in 1988 was 104,000 boys and 7800 girls: *New York Times*, 27 March 1988, 16, quoted in C. Enloe, *ibid.*

[114] United States Department of State, Afghanistan Report on Human Rights Practices 1997, issued by the Bureau of Democracy, Human Rights and Labor, 30 January 1998.

[115] See Press Release issued by the Special Rapporteur on Violence against Women, expressing her concern about violations for women and girls of the rights to liberty, security of the person, freedom from discrimination, equal access to education and to work. UN Doc. HR/96/65, 7 November 1996.

[116] B. Rubin, 'Women and pipelines: Afghanistan's proxy wars', 73 *International Affairs* (1997) 283 at 294–5. Beijing Platform for Action, para. 143(e) recognises that women and children are particularly affected by the indiscriminate use of anti-personnel landmines. It has been noted that in areas under Taliban control there has been a reduction in (reported) rapes and violent acts against women: United States Department of State, above note 114, but a study on the health of women in Kabul under the Taliban concluded that the effects of war and denial of human rights have had a profound adverse impact on women's health: Z. Rasekh, H. Bauer, M. Manos and V. Lacopino, 'Women's health and human rights in Afghanistan', 280 *Journal of the American Medical Association* (1998) 449.

The cases of the assertion of the right to self-determination in the Western Sahara and Afghanistan illustrate the various ways that women are factored out of the scope of international law decisions relating to the use of force. In the case of the Western Sahara, women appear to have taken on significant social positions in the refugee camps, but there is no attention paid to preservation of these advances in the international monitoring of the process of self-determination. The support offered by the United States for the right to use force to achieve self-determination in Afghanistan took no account of its implications for women[117] and no guarantees of women's rights were included in the 1988 Geneva Peace Agreements. The blanket discrimination of the Taliban has, however, prompted international responses. The General Assembly and Security Council have denounced discrimination against women and girls in Afghanistan.[118] The latter has recorded its concern about possible repercussions on international relief and reconstruction[119] and has urged the Afghan factions to put an end to discrimination against girls and women.[120] Some Western aid agencies have discontinued operations in Afghanistan.[121] With different political agendas, some states have also spoken out against the Taliban's policies with respect to women, including India,[122] Iran[123] and the institutions of the EU.[124] Despite this criticism, sanctions have not been imposed by the Security Council.[125] It also remains uncertain

[117] Compare United States opposition to the 1979 Revolution in Iran in which the oppression of women was used as a justification for this stance: C. Enloe, *Bananas, Beaches, and Bases*, above note 26 at 57.

[118] E.g. GA Res. 52/145, 12 December 1997; SC Res. 1193, 28 August 1998; SC Res. 1214, 8 December 1998; GA Res. 53/65, 25 February 1998.

[119] E.g. SC Res. 1076, 22 October 1996.

[120] E.g. SC Res. 1193, 28 August 1998; SC Res. 1214, 8 December 1998. While the Security Council has denounced the violations of human rights and humanitarian law with respect to women, it did not use the stronger description of 'flagrant violation of international law' as it did with respect to the Taliban's murder of Iranian diplomats.

[121] Aid agencies have been divided on their approach to the Taliban. E.g. Save the Children and Oxfam suspended operations while others sought accommodation with the authorities: *The Times*, 31 October 1996. See M. Keating, 'Women's rights and wrongs', *The World Today*, January 1997, 11; D. Cammack, 'Gender relief and politics during the Afghan war', in D. Indra (ed.), *Engendering Forced Migration: Theory and Practice* (New York, Berghahn Books, 1999) at 94.

[122] India is apprehensive of the impact of a Pakistani-supported fundamentalist regime in Afghanistan on separatism in Kashmir.

[123] Iran views the Taliban as excluding Shiite Muslims from power and support as a United States strategy to encircle Iran: B. Rubin, above note 116.

[124] E.g. European Commission, 9 October 1996; European Parliament, Resolutions of 23 October 1997 (26) and 19 February 1998; European Council, 26 June 1998.

[125] The Security Council has called upon states to 'end the supply of arms and ammunition to all parties' but has not imposed an arms embargo or other sanctions: SC Res. 1214, 8 December 1998. Aid and co-operation have been suspended by the EU, with the exception of humanitarian aid. Now see SC Res. 1267, 15 October 1999.

whether such criticism would influence decisions about recognition of,[126] or dealings with, the Taliban if it restored peace and stability in the country.[127] It has been noted that, since 1979, the major role of women in Afghan politics has been as 'symbols of legitimization for political groups led by men'.[128]

Humanitarian intervention

Another controversial justification for the use of force is as a response to gross violations of human rights within another state, often referred to as the doctrine of 'humanitarian intervention'.[129] While unilateral intervention into the affairs of another state is *prima facie* contrary to the Declaration on the Principles of Friendly Relations, it has been claimed that where the coercive action is followed by free elections its legitimacy can be more readily accepted,[130] or that the use of force for humanitarian motives is morally, if not legally, justified in extreme cases.[131]

[126] As of December 1998 only three states had recognised the Taliban: Pakistan, Saudi Arabia and the United Arab Emirates.

[127] In May 1998, a Memorandum of Understanding on humanitarian assistance in Afghanistan was agreed between the UN and the Taliban: Secretary-General's report to the Security Council on the human rights situation in Afghanistan, UN Doc. S 11998/532, para. 40. Although the Secretary-General stated that the agreement with the Taliban deals with gender 'in a preliminary way', it urges only gradual adherence to the principle of non-discrimination.

[128] B. Rubin, above note 116 at 291.

[129] For a range of opposing views on international law in this area see R. Lillich (ed.), *Humanitarian Intervention and the United Nations* (Charlottesville, University of Virginia Press, 1973). See also F. Tesón, *Humanitarian Intervention: An Inquiry into Law and Morality* (Irvington-on-Hudson, Transnational Publishers, 2nd edn 1997); M. Walzer, above note 19; M. Bazlyer, 'Re-examining the doctrine of humanitarian intervention in light of the atrocities in Kampuchea and Ethiopia', 23 *Stanford Journal of International Law* (1987) 547; S. Simon, 'Contemporary legality of unilateral humanitarian intervention', 24 *California Western International Law Journal* (1993) 117; S. Murphy, *Humanitarian Intervention: The United Nations in an Evolving World Order* (Philadelphia, University of Pennsylvania Press, 1996). Humanitarian intervention in turn is closely connected with, but distinct from, the use of force to rescue a state's own nationals from some imminent danger within another state, a claim sometimes seen as an offshoot of the right to self-defence. E.g. J. Paust, 'The seizure and recovery of the Mayaguez', 85 *Yale Law Journal* (1975–6) 774; the Israeli raid on Entebbe, 1976, 15 *International Legal Materials* (1976) 1224; the United States attempt to rescue the hostages in Tehran, above note 92. See N. Ronzitti, *Rescuing Nationals Abroad through Military Coercion and Intervention on Grounds of Humanity* (Dordrecht, Martinus Nijhoff, 1985).

[130] M. Reisman, 'Sovereignty and human rights', above note 93 at 871; M. Reisman, 'Haiti and the validity of international action', 89 *American Journal of International Law* (1995) 82 (justifying collective action in Haiti after the military overthrow of the elected government of President Aristide).

[131] F. Tesón, above note 129 at 15–17. Richard Falk has labelled this approach 'advocating civil disobedience on an international level': M. Bazlyer, above note 129 at 577, n. 130. NATO use of force against Yugoslavia in March–June 1999 was justified on these grounds.

Collective and unilateral intervention in the internal affairs of a state has inspired much theoretical debate, as well as controversy over its practical applicability. In a strongly argued defence of humanitarian intervention, Fernando Tesón has argued that the ultimate justification for the continuation of the state is the protection of the natural rights of its citizens.[132] A government violating those rights therefore forfeits domestic and international legitimacy, and foreign intervention to suppress government abuse is justified. Tesón would support lawful intervention only in cases of gross violations of civil and political rights, although he has made an exception for the systematic denial of food.[133] He has argued that foreign intervention to protect socio-economic rights in states where civil and political rights are observed is an unjustifiable intrusion into their territorial and political sovereignty because such decisions are matters of government policy, not of human rights.[134] This limited approach is especially problematic for women. First, as has been seen, even considerable denial of women's civil and political rights has not led to forceful intervention, for example in Kuwait, Saudi Arabia or Afghanistan.[135] Second, as we have discussed in chapter 7, in many instances violations of women's economic and social rights may be as life-threatening as denial of civil and political rights. An analogy can be drawn between the principle of non-intervention in the domestic affairs of a state and the protection traditionally accorded in national legal systems to the family unit against state intrusion. In both cases, 'non-intervention' may in fact turn out to have active consequences by preserving existing power structures and shielding abusers of human rights from any accountability. Those who flee as refugees are often perceived as the problem, rather than those who caused the flight. The traditional analysis of intervention on humanitarian grounds does not take women into account in consideration of either its justifications or its consequences.

The forms of intervention contemplated by international law themselves create problems. While legal justifications for the ending of human rights abuses are valuable, intervention by force may lead to intensified coercive action in which women may suffer further gender-specific harms. Moreover, any widespread violation of human rights will be the result of a complex

---

[132] F. Tesón, above note 129 at 82.

[133] Other writers have argued for the extension of the doctrine to violations of subsistence rights – air, water, adequate food, clothing and shelter: D. Luban, 'Just war and human rights', 9 *Philosophy and Public Affairs* (1979–80) 160.

[134] Intervention may be authorised by the Security Council under UN Charter, chapter VII on humanitarian grounds for denial of economic and social rights. For example in Somalia, SC Res. 794, 3 December 1992 authorised 'all necessary means to establish as soon as possible a secure environment for humanitarian relief operations in Somalia'.

[135] On 20 August 1998, the United States took unilateral action in the form of missile strikes against Afghanistan in response to attacks on its embassy in Kenya and for its alleged shielding of the suspected terrorist, Osama bin Laden.

interaction of social, historic, political, cultural, economic and, possibly, religious factors. International intervention in the form of a military episode cannot respond to the intricate and structural roots of human rights abuses, and may indeed exacerbate them. Such intervention must be accompanied by a long-term commitment to protection and restructuring. International institutions themselves may help to create crises that then become candidates for international intervention. For example, Anne Orford has pointed to the destabilising role played by international monetary institutions in the period before the conflicts in the former Yugoslavia.[136]

Conclusion

Although the Charter makes the maintenance of international peace and security the primary purpose of the UN, the nation state system focuses upon legal justifications for the use of force, most notably national self-defence. This focus is perhaps at its most striking in the statement of the ICJ in its *Nuclear Weapons* Advisory Opinion that it could not conclude 'definitively whether the threat or use of nuclear weapons would be lawful or unlawful in an extreme circumstance of self-defence in which the very survival of a State would be at stake'.[137] How can the notion of peace be revived and developed in international law so that it can be sustained in a more positive way?

International law texts before 1945 distinguished between the laws of war and the laws of peace.[138] While war was regarded as an appropriate instrument of international relations, the laws of war were concerned with the rights and obligations of belligerents and third parties during the conduct of hostilities.[139] The laws of peace were applicable to legal relations between states during a time of non-war. This distinction required a definition of the condition of war and a identification of the participants in it, which were achieved by a formal declaration of war.[140] By contrast, the UN Charter's

[136] A. Orford, 'Locating the international: military and monetary interventions after the cold war', 38 *Harvard International Law Journal* (1997) 443.

[137] *Legality of the Threat or Use of Nuclear Weapons*, above note 80 at para. 105. This conclusion was reached by seven votes to seven, with the casting vote of the President of the Court.

[138] E.g. L. Oppenheim, *International Law: A Treatise* (London/New York, Longmans, Green & Co., 2nd edn, 1906) comprised vol. I, *Peace* and vol. II, *War and Neutrality*.

[139] A distinction was drawn between the legitimacy of war in international relations, the *jus ad bello* and the conduct of war, the *jus in bellum*. See R. Mushkat, 'When war may justifiably be waged: an analysis of historical and contemporary legal perspectives', 15 *Brooklyn Journal of International Law* (1989) 223; M. Walzer, above note 19 at 34–47, 51–63.

[140] A formal declaration of war indicates both the conditions for settlement and the public nature of war, and informs third powers of the condition of warfare: R. Mushkat, above note 139 at 232–3.

prohibition of the use of force and the obligation upon states to settle disputes peacefully might be thought to constitute a right to peace. Indeed a right to peace has been described as the *raison d'être* of modern international law.[141] The right has been located in the UN Charter, as amplified by resolutions of the General Assembly,[142] and other institutions,[143] although it is articulated only in one human rights treaty, the African Charter on Human and Peoples' Rights.[144]

One problem with defining peace is that in reality there is no clear dichotomy between war and peace. States interact along a spectrum of relations ranging from genuine peace to open conflict, with many levels of coercive and non-coercive behaviour in between.[145] For example, a state may engage in, authorise or assist terrorist activities against another state;[146] it may engage in covert assistance to rebels against the government of another state;[147] it may threaten the integrity of another state;[148] it may make coercive trade or other economic demands against another state, or impose economic sanctions;[149] and a state's repressive internal policies may cause people to flee engendering economic and political destabilisation in neighbouring

[141] P. Alston, 'Peace as a human right', 11 *Bulletin of Peace Proposals* (1980) 319.

[142] Declaration on the Preparation of Societies for Life in Peace, GA Res. 33/73, 15 December 1978; Declaration of the Right of Peoples to Peace, GA Res. 39/11, 12 November 1984. Both declarations were adopted during the cold war and reflect the political rhetoric of the time.

[143] E.g. UN Commission on Human Rights, Res. 5 (xxxii) 1976 states: 'Everyone has the right to live in conditions of international peace and security and fully to enjoy economic, social and cultural rights, and civil and political rights.'

[144] African Charter on Human and Peoples' Rights, 26 June 1981, reprinted in 21 *International Legal Materials* (1982) 59, article 23(1).

[145] M. McDougal, 'Peace and war: factual continuum with multiple legal consequences', 49 *American Journal of International Law* (1955) 63.

[146] E.g. the sinking by agents of the French Directorate General of External Security of the *Rainbow Warrior* in Auckland harbour in 1985. See *R v. Marfart & Prieur* 74 International Law Reports (1987) 241; UN Secretary-General, Ruling, 6 July 1986, *ibid.* at 256. Another example is the alleged involvement of Libya in the Lockerbie affair: *Case Concerning Questions of Interpretation and Application of the 1971 Montreal Convention arising from the Aerial Incident at Lockerbie* (Libyan Arab Jamahiriya v. United Kingdom; Libyan Arab Jamahiriya v. United States) Preliminary Objections 1998 ICJ Rep. (Judgment of 27 February). France was not at war with New Zealand and Libya was not at war with the United States, the United Kingdom or France.

[147] E.g. United States assistance to the *Contras* against the Sandinista government in *Nicaragua*, Merits, above note 81 at 20.

[148] See R. Sadurska, 'Threats of force', 82 *American Journal of International Law* (1988) 239.

[149] E.g. economic sanctions were imposed by the United States and other Western states against Iran after the seizure of the hostages in Tehran in 1979; against the Soviet Union and Afghanistan after the Soviet invasion in 1979–80; against Poland after the imposition of martial law in 1980. See E. Zoller, *Peacetime Unilateral*

territories.[150] International law has no unifying category for these situations, other than the contested notion of aggression.[151]

The complexities of defining peace are illustrated in the activities of the women's peace movements in the United Kingdom and United States in the 1980s which challenged the traditional notions of national peace and security as military preparedness.[152] Ironically, these activities led to a number of women being charged with the offence of 'breach of the peace' in national law. The legal outcomes of these trials generally ignored a broader concept of peace and focused on domestic legal notions of order and trespass. Even acts of civil disobedience by the women did not fit into the paradigm of acceptable citizen protest.[153] Nevertheless such actions may mobilise support and highlight the inconsistencies in international concepts of peace and security. In August 1996 four women peace campaigners were acquitted in the United Kingdom of charges of an estimated £1.5 criminal damage to a military aircraft that was due for export to Indonesia. The women admitted damaging the aircraft, but argued that their actions were justified because they 'were using reasonable force to prevent a crime' – the genocide of the East Timorese people by Indonesia.[154]

Another approach to defining peace is to identify its elements. If peace is understood as more than the absence of war or aggression, encompassing social justice, it requires positive steps for its fulfilment. The General Assembly Declaration on the Preparation of Societies for Life in Peace, adopted in a cold war environment, takes this approach.[155] It combines positive obligations to promote human rights at the local, regional and international levels with the negative obligation not to impede progress towards peace.

Remedies: An Analysis of Countermeasures (Dobbs Ferry, Transnational Books, 1984); O. Elageb, *The Legality of Non-Forcible Counter-Measures in International Law* (Oxford, Clarendon Press, 1988). Since 1990 economic sanctions have been used more regularly (see chapter 9).

[150] E.g. the Kurdish refugee flow from Iraq creating a threat to peace in the region, SC Res. 688, 5 April 1991.

[151] GA Res. 3314, 14 December 1974. The definition was a cold war compromise that was reached by the Special Committee on the Question of Defining Aggression twenty years after it was established.

[152] See generally R. Lederman, 'Looking back: the women's peace camps in perspective', in D. Russell (ed.), *Exposing Nuclear Phallacies* (Oxford, Pergamon Press, 1989) 244.

[153] A. Scales, above note 71 at 53. Harris and King have suggested that: '[C]ivil disobedience, the practice of militant non-violence by women in peace actions, can be seen as a form of *écriture féminine*, or a new "feminine text".' A. Harris and Y. King (eds), *Rocking the Ship of State: Toward a Feminist Peace Politics* (Boulder and London, Westview Press, 1989) at 2.

[154] 'Plane wreckers claim moral as well as legal victory', *Guardian*, 1 August 1996; 'Ploughing a deep furrow', *Guardian*, 7 August 1996, 5.

[155] GA Res. 33/73, 15 December 1978. Compare GA Declaration on the Right of Peoples to Peace, GA Res. 39/11, 12 November 1984.

Thus states are required to refrain from some actions (planning, preparing, initiating a war of aggression, propaganda for a war of aggression) to discourage others (colonialism, racism, racial discrimination, apartheid, advocacy of hatred and prejudice) and to promote equitable political, economic, social and cultural co-operation, to take up actions conducive to the furtherance of the ideals of peace, humanism and freedom, and to respect the right to self-determination of peoples.[156] The Declaration's explicit references suggest some of its limitations: racism and apartheid are specified as impediments to peace, but sexism and misogyny are not. By contrast, the Beijing Conference in 1995 recognised that women's empowerment and full participation on the basis of equality in all spheres of life are essential components of peace.[157]

Focusing upon the right to peace as a group right may obscure the particular needs of women and the reality that the greatest threat of violation of a woman's peace comes from the male members of the same group. For women the primary constituent of a right to peace might be freedom from the fear or reality of poverty or personal violence. On this analysis, peace is not achieved until states take seriously their internal obligations to ensure freedom from fear of violence at home, within the community or committed by state agents.

The right to peace should be seen as an individual and collective right imposing duties both upon states and individuals. The ILC Draft Articles on State Responsibility adopted on First Reading in 1996 designated 'a serious breach of an international obligation of essential importance for maintenance of international peace and security' as an international crime of state.[158] The significance of this designation is that all states are deemed injured by the commission of an international crime which gives rise to obligations *erga omnes*.[159] Article 19 has been much criticised[160] and may well not remain in the final text, although the concept of obligations owed *erga omnes* is now established international law.[161] Even in the 1996 draft, article 19(3)(a) applied only to the maintenance of peace in the limited

---

[156] In *Legality of the Threat or Use of Nuclear Weapons*, above note 80 at para. 99, the ICJ emphasised the importance of negotiations for disarmament.

[157] Beijing Declaration, paras 13, 18: 'peace is inextricably linked with the advancement of women'. See also Convention on the Elimination of All Forms of Discrimination Against Women, Preamble: 'the cause of peace require[s] the maximum participation of women on equal terms with men in all fields'.

[158] ILC, Draft Articles on State Responsibility, adopted on First Reading, UN Doc. A/CN.4/L.528/Add. 2, 16 July 1996, article 19(3)(a).

[159] *Ibid.*, article 40(3).

[160] See J. Weiler, A. Cassese and M. Spinedi, *International Crimes of State: A Critical Analysis of the ILC's Draft Article 19 on State Responsibility* (Berlin/New York, De Gruyter, 1989).

[161] See e.g. *Case Concerning East Timor* (Portugal v. Australia) 1995 ICJ Rep. 90 (Judgment of 30 June) at para. 29.

external sense – prohibition of aggression. Internal behaviour was the subject of article 19(3)(c), which designated 'a serious breach on a widespread scale of an international obligation of essential importance for safeguarding the human being' as an international crime. The examples given of such violations included apartheid, but not laws that discriminated on the basis of sex. The challenge is to define a right to peace that recognises the right to equality on the basis of sex as an essential aspect of human existence and to refocus international law away from force and towards peace.

9

Peaceful settlement of disputes

Introduction

The corollary of the prohibition of the use of force in international relations, discussed in chapter 8, is the obligation to settle disputes peacefully.[1]
This chapter examines some of the concepts and processes of international
dispute resolution through the lens of sex and gender. It argues that the
international legal understanding of peaceful dispute resolution and the
related concept of collective security are built on very limited bases that
sustain impoverished ideas of peace and security.

Identification of an international dispute

The ICJ has defined a dispute as 'a disagreement on a point of law or fact,
a conflict of legal views or interests between parties'.[2] Articulation of the
disagreement through the formulation and rejection of specific claims is
necessary for a dispute to be identified. International disputes are frequently
rooted in historical events and reflect geographical, political, religious, ideological or economic differences.[3] Many international disputes are longstanding
with the participants existing in an uneasy state of tension until escalation is
sparked by a specific event that may result in armed conflict. Curtailing
hostilities does not necessarily resolve the underlying dispute, but may provide some respite from ongoing conflict.

It is unusual for women, or women-specific issues, to be perceived as

[1] Charter of the UN, 26 June 1945, articles 2(3) & 33.
[2] *Case Concerning East Timor* (Portugal v. Australia) 1995 ICJ Rep. 90 (Judgment of 30 June) at para. 22. In earlier jurisprudence, the Court had stipulated 'two'
parties were necessary to a dispute: *Mavrommatis Palestine Concession* PCIJ ser. A,
no. 2, 11 (Judgment of 13 August).
[3] See C. Chinkin and R. Sadurska, 'The anatomy of international disputes', 7
Ohio State Journal on Dispute Resolution (1991) 39.

integral to an international dispute. The invisibility of women in international affairs, the widespread acceptance of religious and cultural justifications for the unequal treatment of women and the lack of international significance attached to women's lives explain this omission. Even where women are major actors in an international incident, this reality is rarely identified in dispute settlement. For example, transborder refugee flows frequently both provoke, and are the consequence of, international disputes, but although women constitute large numbers of refugees,[4] they do not figure separately in negotiations about resettlement. Other forms of discrimination, by contrast, have been at the core of significant international disputes. Racial discrimination was at issue in the respective disputes between the UN and South Africa[5] and the UN and Southern Rhodesia.[6] Acknowledgement of the potential for discrimination against minorities to escalate into international disputes motivated the inclusion of special provisions and procedures for their protection in the post-World War I peace treaties.[7] Events in the 1990s, such as those surrounding the disintegration of the former Yugoslavia, genocide in Rwanda and the treatment of the Kurdish and Shi'ite minorities in Iraq, indicate that these forms of discrimination are significant in contributing to international disputes. The multiple discriminations of race, ethnicity and sex suffered by women are not, however, seen as part of these disputes, nor as relevant to their resolution.

The position of women migrant workers illustrates states' failure to articulate claims with respect to the treatment of women. For example, the fate of the foreign women workers trapped in Kuwait after the Gulf War in 1992, referred to in chapter 8, was not considered a significant international legal issue. However, the large numbers of women seeking work outside their country of origin is not a private matter of personal choice. Those states that send labour benefit from the repatriation of foreign earnings[8] while recipient states enjoy the cheap labour. Migrant workers have no citizenship

[4] Fourth World Conference on Women, Declaration and Platform for Action, 15 September 1995, UN Doc. A/CONF. 177/20, reprinted in 35 *International Legal Materials* (1996) 401 (Beijing Platform for Action), para. 136.

[5] The dispute was over the apartheid regime of the South African government and its failure to comply with the international mandate over South West Africa (Namibia). In *Legal Consequences for States of the Continued Presence of South Africa in Namibia (South West Africa) Notwithstanding Security Council 276 (1970)* 1971 ICJ Rep. 16 (Adv. Op. 21 June) the ICJ avoided determining that the UN was in dispute with South Africa by noting its listing as a 'situation'.

[6] The Security Council imposed economic sanctions against Southern Rhodesia: SC Res. 217, 20 November 1965.

[7] W. McKean, *Equality and Discrimination under International Law* (Oxford, Clarendon Press, 1983) at 27–51.

[8] E.g. there were 4.2 million migrant Philippine workers employed in over forty states and remittances amounted to some $5.98 billion from 1986–1991; in 1988 remittances were equivalent to 58 per cent of exports for Bangladesh, over 20 per cent for Pakistan, Sri Lanka and India and 14 per cent for the Philippines: J. Pettman,

rights where they work and the private locations of domestic workers hide the abuses suffered by many and their isolation and powerlessness. Despite the social and economic significance of these migration patterns, the working conditions are subject to limited international regulation.[9] This contrasts with the significant body of conventional and customary law for the protection of other people working abroad for the benefit of their own state, for example diplomatic and consular staff,[10] and members of armed forces.[11]

Promotion of the export of labour by states has sometimes led to indifference to illegal trafficking of workers. Trafficking has increased as a consequence of reduced government commitment to social expenditure, for example as part of the transition to a free market economy in Eastern Europe, and of structural adjustment programmes. Economic hardship, organised criminal rings, fraud and violence have fostered the international trafficking of women and children.[12] These issues, however, are not considered the stuff of international disputes, nor sufficient for the exercise of extra-territorial jurisdiction. By contrast, claims of General Noriega's involvement in international drug trafficking supported the United States' use of force against Panama in 1989 that resulted in his arrest and conviction within the United States.[13] Similarly the United States has justified its violation of the territorial sovereignty of Mexico as being necessary to arrest another alleged drug trafficker.[14] Extra-territorial jurisdiction has also been asserted to protect the commercial interests of American nationals against the expropriation of their property by the Castro regime in Cuba.[15] The potential for these actions to

---

Worlding Women: A Feminist International Politics (Sydney, Allen & Unwin, 1996) at 71.

[9] See ILO Convention no. 97 concerning Migration for Employment (Revised) 1 July 1949; ILO Convention no. 143 concerning Migrations in Abusive Conditions and the Promotion of Equality of Opportunity and Treatment of Migrant Workers, 9 December 1978, 1120 UNTS 323; International Convention on the Protection of the Rights of All Migrant Workers and Members of their Families, GA Res. 45/158, 18 December 1990, reprinted in 30 *International Legal Materials* (1991) 1517.

[10] See Vienna Convention on Diplomatic Relations, 18 April 1961, 500 UNTS 95; Vienna Convention on Consular Relations, 24 April 1963, 596 UNTS 261.

[11] Armed forces serving abroad are protected by Status of Forces agreements: A. Watts and R. Jennings, *Oppenheim's International Law* (London, Longmans, 9th edn 1992) at 1154–65. Several conventions have been adopted to protect other people on official business: *ibid.* at 1174–8.

[12] Beijing Platform for Action, paras 122 and 130; Report on the mission of the Special Rapporteur on Violence Against Women to Poland on the issue of trafficking and forced prostitution of women (24 May to 1 June 1996), UN Doc. E/CN.4/1997/47/Add. 1, 10 December 1996.

[13] See e.g. A. D'Amato, 'The invasion of Panama was a lawful response to tyranny', 84 *American Journal of International Law* (1990) 516.

[14] *United States v. Alvarez-Machain* 504 U.S. 655 (1992).

[15] Cuban Liberty and Democratic Solidarity (Libertad) Act 1996, 22 USCA § 6021–6091, commonly known as the Helms-Burton Act.

provoke significant international disputes between itself and its trading allies has not deterred the United States from taking strong steps against trafficking in drugs and in property once owned by Americans in Cuba.[16]

The general myopia with respect to the human rights of women and labour conditions of female migrant workers makes unusual the 1995 dispute that arose between the Philippines and Singapore over the latter's execution of the domestic worker, Flor Contemplacion, following her conviction for the murder of another maid and a child in her care. The incident caused the most serious rift between member states of the ASEAN since the alliance was formed in 1967.[17] The Philippines foreign minister resigned, Filipino workers were banned from going to Singapore, hundreds returned to the Philippines, diplomatic relations were severed and an independent commission of investigation was established.[18] A Philippine Presidential panel was established to examine the position of Filipino overseas workers.[19] Another international dispute arose following the death sentence passed upon a 16-year-old Filipina woman worker in the United Arab Emirates for killing her employer.[20] Sara Balabagan's plea of self-defence to rape was accepted at her first trial where she was convicted of manslaughter but was rejected at a retrial by an Islamic court that sentenced her to death. After international protest the sentence was commuted to one year's imprisonment and one hundred lashes. This case was internationalised by the concern expressed by the Special Rapporteur on Extra-judicial, Summary and Arbitrary Executions and by the submission of two communications to the government of the United Arab Emirates by the Special Rapporteur on Violence against Women.[21] In these instances the Philippines exceptionally invoked the doctrine of diplomatic protection of aliens in support of its female migrant workforce. However, the complaints focused upon the official action of the

[16] The EU submitted its dispute with the United States over the Helms-Burton Act to the WTO dispute settlement procedures. In April 1997 negotiations between the United States and the EU resulted in a provisional resolution of the dispute: EU–United States, Memorandum of Understanding, Concerning the United States Helms Burton and the United States Iran and Libya Sanctions Act, 11 April 1997, reprinted in 36 *International Legal Materials* (1997) 529.

[17] *Reuters News*, 17 April 1995.

[18] Singapore and the Philippines agreed that a neutral panel of United States pathologists would conduct an autopsy on the murder victims. Relations between the two states were normalised after the panel reported its factual findings supporting Singaporean experts: *Reuters News*, 17 July 1995. President Ramos also called for an international mechanism to protect the human rights of migrant workers in Asia: *Associated Press*, 18 April 1995.

[19] The panel produced a 200-page report that documented the inability of Philippine embassies abroad to protect Filipino workers from abuse: *Reuters News*, 6 July 1995.

[20] Report of the Special Rapporteur on Violence against Women, its Causes and Consequences, 5 February 1996, UN Doc. E/CN.4/1996/53 at para. 8.

[21] *Ibid.*

recipient state (legal imposition of harsh penal sanctions) and only indirectly addressed the private abuses underlying the public events.

Dispute resolution under the UN Charter

The obligation upon states to seek peaceful settlement of disputes is stipulated in article 2(3) of the UN Charter and is reiterated in numerous General Assembly resolutions.[22] Chapter VI of the Charter provides the framework for the peaceful settlement of disputes while chapter VII provides for 'Action with respect to threats to the peace, breaches of the peace, and acts of aggression'. UN organs are competent to assist states in the resolution of their disputes under chapter VI.[23] Peace-making options available to the Security Council under chapter VI merge with its powers under chapter VII. Attempts by the international community to minimise the destructive consequences of a dispute that has escalated to present a threat to international peace and security are likely to include ongoing efforts at resolution under chapter VI, as well as more coercive collective action under chapter VII.[24]

In his blueprint, *An Agenda for Peace* and its 1995 *Supplement*,[25] the then Secretary-General of the UN, Boutros Boutros-Ghali, sought to improve the effectiveness of co-operative action within the framework of the Charter for dispute and conflict prevention, containment and resolution. He built upon the provisions of chapters VI and VII and the practice of peacekeeping evolved by UN organs during the cold war[26] to articulate the associated concepts of preventive diplomacy, peace-making, peacekeeping and peace-building.[27] Boutros-Ghali defined these terms functionally.[28] The objectives

[22] E.g. Declaration on Principles of International Law Concerning Friendly Relations and Co-operation among States in Accordance with the Charter of the United Nations, GA Res. 2625 (XXV), 24 October 1970; Manila Declaration on the Peaceful Settlement of International Disputes, GA Res. 37/10, 15 November 1982; Declaration on the Prevention and Removal of Disputes and Situations which may Threaten International Peace and Security and on the Role of the United Nations in this Field, GA Res. 43/51, 5 December 1988.
[23] S. Ratner, 'Image and reality in the UN's peaceful settlement of disputes', 6 *European Journal of International Law* (1995) 426.
[24] Charter of the UN, articles 41 and 42.
[25] *An Agenda for Peace, Preventive Diplomacy, Peacemaking and Peace-keeping*, Report of the Secretary-General pursuant to the Statement adopted by the Summit Meeting of the Security Council on 31 January 1992, 17 June 1992, UN Doc. A/47/277; *Supplement to An Agenda for Peace*, 1 January 1995, UN Doc. A/50/60-S/1995/1. See also An Agenda for Peace, GA Res. 47/120 B, 20 September 1993.
[26] See *Certain Expenses of the United Nations Case* 1962 ICJ Rep. 151 (Adv. Op. 20 July).
[27] *An Agenda for Peace*, above note 25 at para. 15.
[28] *Ibid.* at paras 20 to 22; *Supplement to An Agenda for Peace*, above note 25 at paras 23 to 56.

of preventive diplomacy, averting the eruption of disputes and the spread of conflict, demand pre-emptive action. Peace-making attempts to bring disputing parties to agreement, essentially through chapter VI processes. Peacekeeping involves the deployment of military, police and civilian personnel, under the auspices of the UN or a regional organisation,[29] in the troubled area, traditionally with the consent of all parties. Post-conflict peace-building attempts to prevent repetition by establishing structures to 'strengthen and solidify peace'.[30]

These distinct, but overlapping, tasks indicate that dispute resolution occurs across a continuum. It does not start when a dispute (or overt conflict) erupts, but much earlier through identification of potential disagreement and the seeking of measures to prevent escalation (preventive diplomacy). It may continue through the management of an overt dispute, involving attempts at resolution and containment (peace-making) through to short-term peacekeeping measures and efforts to find long-term solutions (peace-building). Boutros-Ghali sought to amplify and adapt chapters VI and VII to meet the needs of the international community in the post-cold war era. The next sections consider the basis and content of these concepts more fully and their relevance to women.

The concept of collective security

The notion of collective security underpins the UN Charter's regime for dispute resolution. In essence collective security signifies that an armed attack upon one member of a community would be taken to constitute an attack upon all, and justify action by the others in collective self-defence.[31] Chapter VII of the UN Charter sets out a collective security regime vesting considerable powers in the Security Council to respond to threats to international peace and security.[32] The use, or threat of use, of the veto by all

[29] E.g. peacekeeping forces from the ECOWAS were deployed in Liberia alongside UN forces: Annual Report of the Secretary-General on the Work of the Organization, 1997, UN Doc. A/52/1 at para. 114. In the Annual Report of the Secretary-General on the Work of the Organization, 1998, UN Doc. A/53/1 at para. 41, the Secretary-General emphasised the importance of regional organisations, especially since the causes of conflict are often regional or local.

[30] *An Agenda for Peace*, above note 25 at para. 21.

[31] Regional and bilateral examples of collective security treaties include Inter-American Treaty of Reciprocal Assistance, 2 September 1947, 21 UNTS 77; NATO, 4 April 1949, 34 UNTS 243; Pacific Security Treaty (ANZUS) 1 September 1951, 131 UNTS 273.

[32] Charter of the UN, article 39: 'The Security Council shall determine the existence of any threat to the peace, breach of the peace or act of aggression, and shall make recommendations, or decide what measures shall be taken in accordance with Articles 41 and 42, to maintain or restore international peace and security.'

permanent members of the Security Council[33] during the cold war ensured that chapter VII was little used, and that the regional defence treaties assumed significant political importance. The apparent end of the cold war has allowed the Security Council to activate these powers in a number of circumstances, such as enforcement action in response to allegations of international terrorism;[34] support for the provision of humanitarian relief;[35] the maintenance of no-fly zones;[36] the establishment of two international criminal tribunals;[37] and the restoration of democracy.[38] While the Charter's objective of the maintenance of international peace and security supports collective action authorised by the Security Council, there is concern that the Security Council has relied upon broad assertions of power without clarifying its limits.[39]

The concept of collective security requires a threshold understanding of what 'a threat to international peace' entails. *An Agenda for Peace* recognised that international peace comprises more than state security from military attack and protection by national military establishments: 'Peace-making and peace-keeping operations, to be truly successful, must come to include comprehensive efforts to identify and support structures which will tend to consolidate peace and advance a sense of confidence and well-being among people'.[40]

International peace, on this analysis, requires scrutiny of domestic policies as well as of external relations. Its maintenance involves establishing

---

[33] *Ibid.*, article 27. 3.

[34] E.g. SC Res. 731, 21 January 1992; SC Res. 748, 31 March 1992 imposing sanctions against Libya for failure to renounce terrorism and to respond to requests for the extradition of those allegedly responsible for the bombing of PanAm Flight 103 over Lockerbie, 21 December 1988; SC Res. 1267, 15 October 1999 (Afghanistan).

[35] E.g. SC Res. 688, 5 April 1991 (humanitarian relief to the Iraqi civilian population); SC Res. 775, 28 August 1992; SC Res. 794, 3 December 1992 (humanitarian assistance in Somalia).

[36] E.g. SC Res. 781, 9 October 1992 (no-fly zone over Bosnia and Herzegovina).

[37] E.g. SC Res. 808, 22 February 1993; SC Res. 827, 25 May 1993 (Former Yugoslavia); SC Res. 955, 8 November 1994 (Rwanda).

[38] E.g. SC Res. 940, 31 July 1994 (in Haiti).

[39] *Case Concerning Questions of Interpretation and Application of the 1971 Montreal Convention arising from the Aerial Incident at Lockerbie* (Libyan Arab Jamahiriya v. United Kingdom) Request for Indication of Provisional Measures 1992 ICJ Rep. 3. See J. Gardam, 'Legal restraints on Security Council military enforcement action', 17 *Michigan Journal of International Law* (1996) 285. Compare ICTY, *Prosecutor v. Dusko Tadic, Jurisdiction of the Tribunal*, 10 August 1995, IT-94-I-T; Decision on the Defence Motion for Interlocutory Appeal on Jurisdiction, 2 October 1995, IT-94-I-AR72; J. Alvarez, 'Nuremburg revisited: the Tadic case', 7 *European Journal of International Law* (1996) 24.

[40] *An Agenda for Peace*, above note 25 at para. 55.

conditions that inhibit violent conflict between or within states. In this wider sense peace relates to social and economic justice.[41] It has been argued that gross structural inequities in the global arena impede genuine peace and allow only an uneasy absence of overt conflict until a crisis erupts.[42] Peace is therefore intimately connected with respect for, and observance of, human rights and economic justice in what has been called the 'peace, human rights, and development' dialectic.[43] While *An Agenda for Peace* can be seen to offer a broad account of the idea of peace by connecting it to a respect for human rights,[44] it has been limited by the UN's narrow understanding of human rights. Thus, when cold war politics allowed, the Security Council used systemic human rights violations to justify imposing collective measures under article 41, for example the denial of human rights and self-determination in Southern Rhodesia.[45] Apartheid in South Africa was similarly deemed to constitute a serious threat to international peace and security.[46] The General Assembly also recognised the relationship between systemic oppression, deprivation, terrorism and breach of the peace.[47] Systemic oppression of women has not, however, been regarded as a comparable threat to international peace.

What is the content of the idea of 'collective security' in international law? The term 'collective security' is not actually used in the Charter although the idea of collective measures is given some substance in chapter VII. First, the concept of the collective is very circumscribed. The collective is defined as simply the Security Council, rather than any broader community of states or other interests. Second, the security offered is understood narrowly. Security orthodoxy has seen security as protecting the political and physical integrity of sovereign states and it has promoted the idea of peace through national strength. State security requires internationally recognised boundaries upheld through military action and the inherent right

---

[41] The Secretary-General has described a concept of 'preventive peace-building' which attempts to reduce poverty and promote development and democratisation: Annual Report of the Secretary-General 1998, above note 29 at para. 28.

[42] P. Alston, 'Peace as a human right', 11 *Bulletin of Peace Proposals* (1980) 319.

[43] S. Marks, 'The peace-human rights-development dialectic', 11 *Bulletin of Peace Proposals* (1980) 339. See also A. Eide, 'The right to peace', 10 *Bulletin of Peace Proposals* (1979) 157.

[44] *An Agenda for Peace*, above note 25 at para. 11.

[45] SC Res. 217, 20 November 1965.

[46] International Convention on the Suppression and Punishment of the Crime of Apartheid, 30 November 1973, 1015 UNTS 243 article 1(1).

[47] E.g. The GA Declaration on the Granting of Independence to Colonial Territories and Peoples states: 'The subjection of peoples to alien subjugation, domination and exploitation constitutes a denial of fundamental human rights, is contrary to the Charter of the United Nations and is an impediment to the promotion of world peace and co-operation.' GA Res. 1514 (XV) 1960.

of self-defence.[48] During the cold war, collective insecurity was perceived as threats to the balance of hegemony between the two superpowers through overt or covert military intervention in other states. Since the end of the cold war, threats to international peace and security have been identified by the Security Council in a range of situations, including matters that, although initially internal to the states involved, developed into threats to international security.[49] Indeed, UN Secretary-General, Boutros Boutros-Ghali, argued that peace and development were interrelated and acknowledged the connection between socio-political conditions and threats to the peace.[50] In a similar vein, the Australian Foreign Affairs Minister Gareth Evans promoted an idea of 'cooperative security' as a substitute for collective security.[51] Notions of 'cooperative' or 'common' security[52] are broader than the idea of military security, including threats to a state's economic well-being, political stability and social harmony, to its citizens' health, and to its environment.[53] On these accounts, threats to security may also include large-scale humanitarian crises.[54]

Even these relatively progressive understandings of what 'security' entails, however, remain centred on the preservation of the sovereign state from external threats and the activities of other states. They do not investigate the way that power relations work within states and how these power relations affect a state's 'external' activities. For example, Gareth Evans described the Gulf War as offering a chance to use the Charter's collective security provisions 'exactly as intended'.[55] But it is important to note the extensive threats to security involved in this incident. We know now that the Gulf War action was accompanied by significant sexual assault and abuse of women both in Iraq and Kuwait and within the US military forces.[56] The economic sanctions placed on Iraq at the end of the war have had particularly

---

[48] V. Peterson, 'Security and sovereign states: what is at stake in taking feminism seriously?', in V. Peterson (ed.), *Gendered States: Feminist (Re)Visions of International Relations Theory* (Boulder, Lynne Rienner Publishers, 1992) 31.

[49] E.g. the claims of the Kurds in Southern Iraq, SC Res. 731, 21 January 1992; support of terrorist acts by Libya, SC Res. 748, 31 March 1992.

[50] B. Boutros-Ghali, *An Agenda for Development* (New York, UN, 1995). See also *An Agenda for Peace*, above note 25 at para. 5.

[51] G. Evans, *Co-operating for Peace: The Global Agenda for the 1990s and Beyond* (Sydney, Allen & Unwin, 1993).

[52] *Our Global Neighbourhood: Report of the Commission on Global Governance* (New York, Oxford University Press, 1995) at 78–84.

[53] G. Evans, above note 51 at 5–6.

[54] *Ibid.* at 153–8.

[55] *Ibid.* at 147. Evans did note the failure with respect to preventive diplomacy: *ibid.* at 68–9.

[56] A. Orford, 'The politics of collective security', 17 *Michigan Journal of International Law* (1996) 373 at 377–9; *Punishing the Victim: Rape and Mistreatment of Asian Maids in Kuwait* (New York, Human Rights Watch, 1992).

bad effects on Iraqi women.[57] In other contexts, economic globalisation and the restructuring policies of the international monetary institutions may be implicated in the creation of security crises.[58] The premise of both security traditionalists and progressives, that responsibility for maintaining security rests essentially with states, also means that little attention is paid to the role of non-state actors, such as multinational corporations, in generating insecurity. The UN system of collective security assumes that there will be an active, finite, episode of 'collective' intervention (by sanctions or by military force) in response to a security crisis. This model both obscures and legitimates the much more pervasive forms of intervention inherent in the international economic system.[59] At the operational level, the complexities of military intervention to carry out humanitarian objectives and to relieve civilian populations of hardship, such as lack of food supplies, in the face of warring communities were starkly exposed in Somalia and Bosnia-Herzegovina in the early 1990s. The experiences in Somalia, especially the deaths of a number of Pakistani and American forces at the hands of such factions, have reduced the willingness to embark upon similar actions.[60]

The connection of security and miltary activity reinforces the values of militarism – the belief system that upholds the legitimacy of the military control that the state exercises, and the assumption that military values are conducive to creating an orderly and secure society.[61] Militarism imposes a particular construction of masculinity that affects the way women are treated within the state.[62] For example, the aftermath of the Gulf War gave new life to militarism in the United States which has a direct and deleterious impact on women's lives.[63] Moreover, national military expenditure, including research and development programmes, diverts money from social development needs.[64] Thus at the end of the cold war the United States spent fewer

[57] A. Orford, above note 56 at 379–81.

[58] A. Orford, 'Locating the international: military and monetary interventions after the cold war', 38 *Harvard International Law Journal* (1997) 443 at 451–9.

[59] *Ibid.* Frances Olsen has made a similar point with respect to intervention in families in domestic law. F. Olsen, 'The family and the market: a study of ideology and legal reform', 96 *Harvard Law Review* (1983) 1497 at 1517–20.

[60] For an account of such problems see *Peace Keeping and Human Rights* (New York, Amnesty International, 1994) at 19–21.

[61] B. Reardon, *Sexism and the War System* (New York, Teachers College Press, 1985) at 14.

[62] C. Enloe, *The Morning After: Sexual Politics at the End of the Cold War* (Berkeley, University of California Press, 1993) at 16.

[63] *Ibid.* at 381–2. See also L. Boose, 'Techno-muscularity and the "boy eternal": from the quagmire to the Gulf', in M. Cooke and A. Woollacott (eds), *Gendering War Talk* (Princeton, Princeton University Press, 1993) 67.

[64] 'The impact of militarisation on development and human rights', Statement by the Study Group on Militarisation of the International Peace Research Association, reprinted in 9 *Bulletin of Peace Proposals* 170 (1980). Post-cold war see Beijing Platform for Action, paras 138, 143; Z. Cervenka, 'The effect of militarization on

public funds on education than on the military.[65] The costs of the military to national society would be even greater if the unrecognised, unpaid, financial and social contributions of women were included.[66]

Despite the Boutros-Ghali's recognition of the importance of disarmament, arms control and non-proliferation of weapons of mass destruction,[67] the theme of militarism is pervasive in his blueprint for security. Thus, he regarded the availability of troops and equipment for international peace-keeping, including the proposal for a rapid reaction force, as crucial.[68] State and collective security appears to require (male) protectors of the state, and of those within it. Boutros-Ghali did not explore the impact of military deployment, including the social costs of the stationing of military forces upon civilian populations, nor the personal security of women from those 'protectors'. For example, there is growing evidence of the insecurity created for women through the presence of UN peacekeepers. Thus, prostitution in Cambodia increased dramatically during UN operations.[69] There have been allegations of harassment, rape and sexual assault committed against men, women and children by UN troops in Cambodia and Somalia.[70] It has been claimed that not only did the UN Protection Force (UNPROFOR) in Bosnia and Herzegovina fail to assist Bosnian Muslim women forcibly detained in rape camps, but that commanders refused to investigate allegations that UNPROFOR soldiers had themselves had sex with detained women.[71]

Implicit in even the progressive accounts of international security is the assumption that women and men experience issues of international security in the same ways. *An Agenda for Peace* identified racial discrimination and

---

human rights in Africa', in G. Shepherd and M. Anikpo (eds), *Emerging Human Rights: The African Political Economy Context* (New York, Greenwood Press, 1990) 129.

[65] C. Johnson *et al.*, *Child Poverty in America* (Washington DC, Children's Defense Fund, 1991) at 16, cited in H. Sklar, 'Brave new world order', in C. Peters (ed.), *The 'New World Order' at Home and Abroad: Collateral Damage* (Boston, South End Press, 1992) 3 at 32.

[66] C. Enloe, *Does Khaki Become You? The Militarisation of Women's Lives* (London, Pluto Press, 1983, reprinted 1988).

[67] *Supplement to an Agenda for Peace*, above note 25 at paras 57 to 59.

[68] *Ibid.* at para. 44.

[69] Numbers of prostitutes increased from 6000 in 1991 to 20,000 in 1992 after the arrival of the UN Transitional Authority in Cambodia (UNTAC): A. Orford, 'The politics of collective security', above note 56 at 379. This is not a new phenomenon. See E. Van den Haag, *The War in Katanga, Report of a Mission* (American Committee for Aid to Katanga Freedom Fighters, 1962) at 10.

[70] *Somalia: Human Rights Abuses by the United Nations Forces* (New York, Human Rights Watch, July 1993). On the abuse of Cambodian women and children during UNTAC's tenure see J. Stiehm, 'Peacekeeping and peace research: men's and women's work', 18 *Women & Politics* (1997) 27 at 44–5.

[71] D. Rieff, *Slaughterhouse: Bosnia and the Failure of the West* (London, Vintage, 1995) at 121.

ethnic hatred as constituting threats to the peace but failed to draw any connection between the oppression of women and the systemic violence that is a historical manifestation of that subordination. Nor did it acknowledge gender as a locus of structural inequality. The characterisation of women in *An Agenda for Peace* is also very limited: women are essentially in need of protection. Thus Boutros Boutros-Ghali understood democracy to require respect for minority *rights*, but only for the 'needs' of the 'more vulnerable groups of society, especially women and children'.[72] Insecurity in both its narrow and broader conceptions is closely bound up with unequal relations between women and men. The alleviation of military, economic and environmental insecurities involves the resolution of unjust social relations based on domination and subordination within states.[73]

The components of collective security, then, have been understood in a very constrained light. The symbolic system and culture of collective security is permeated by gendered values, which in turn reinforce more general stereotypes of women and men. One way of seeing this is to look at the language used in accounts of collective security. Collective security discourse rests on a series of dichotomies: logic/emotion, order/anarchy, mind/body, culture/nature, aggression/passivity, external/internal, public/private, protector/protected, independence/dependence. Many scholars have shown that the binary opposition is coded in a gendered way with the first term signifying male characteristics and the second female. Security talk typically values the first terms more greatly than their pairs.[74] For example, the collective security literature makes death and destruction abstract and sanitised.[75] This codes it as male. Nowhere is there acknowledgement of 'the emotional, the concrete, the particular, the human bodies and their vulnerability, human lives and their subjectivity'.[76] Moreover, the idea of security is tied to the idea of warding off, of rejection, an ideal of an independent, autonomous entity. As Anne Orford has written:

> Those international lawyers who represent the current period in world history as one of order threatened by chaos . . . represent only one perspective: that of those who had a stake in the old order. Th[is] story . . . does not describe the experience of many groups. All those who have been excluded from full citizenship in Western democracies . . . such as women, indigenous peoples, the mentally ill, or refugees, are not in the process of moving beyond the sovereign state, but were *already* beyond it, both materially and symbolically.[77]

[72] *An Agenda for Peace*, above note 25 at para. 81.
[73] J. Tickner, *Gender in International Relations* (New York, Columbia University Press, 1992) at 128. See also C. Enloe, *The Morning After*, above note 62 at 38–9.
[74] C. Cohn, 'War, wimps and women: talking gender and thinking war', in M. Cooke and A. Woollacott, above note 63 at 227, 231.
[75] *Ibid.* at 232.
[76] *Ibid.*
[77] A. Orford, 'The politics of collective security', above note 56 at 400.

How can we think about the causes of insecurity more broadly? Johan Galtung has developed the notion of structural violence which highlights causes other than warfare, for example poverty, as the major cause of death and suffering.[78] Scholars from the South identify the interconnections of poverty, environmental degradation, discrimination, exploitation, militarisation and violence as the causes of insecurity.[79] Jan Pettman has suggested that we think about what or who most threatens particular groups of people.[80] For women, this draws attention to the threats posed, not by foreign states, but by more local actors, including the men in their families. Eradication of the global gendered power imbalance that sustains violence against women is integral to the maintenance of international peace and security. Military intervention is an inappropriate and destructive mechanism if the causes of insecurity are poverty or discrimination.

Peace-making

Peace-making is understood in international law as the resolution, or at least the management and containment, of a dispute.[81]

Peaceful dispute resolution

Article 33 of the UN Charter lists negotiation, enquiry, good offices, conciliation, mediation, arbitration, adjudication and resort to regional arrangements as the first steps in dispute resolution. These methods are not otherwise defined and are stated to be without prejudice to any other process states may agree upon for themselves. The system is consensual in that no state may pursue any process without the consent of the other parties to the dispute.[82] The UN may be actively involved in such processes through the designation of 'distinguished statesmen' to serve in this capacity.[83] The Secretary-General too may offer her or his good offices to parties in dispute or conflict.[84]

Methods such as negotiation, mediation and conciliation may be confrontational, with all sides striving for the best individual result at the expense

---

[78] J. Galtung, *Peace: Research, Education, Action* (Copenhagen, Ejlers, 1975).
[79] E.g. G. Sen and C. Grown, *Development, Crises, and Alternative Visions: Third World Women's Perspectives* (New York, Monthly Review Press, 1987).
[80] J. Pettman, above note 8 at 105.
[81] See generally J. Merrills, *International Dispute Settlement* (Cambridge, Cambridge University Press, 3rd edn 1998).
[82] Statute of the ICJ, 26 June 1945, 1 UNTS xvi, article 36.
[83] *An Agenda for Peace*, above note 25 at para. 37.
[84] T. Franck, 'The Secretary-General's role in conflict resolution: past, present and pure conjecture', 6 *European Journal of International Law* (1995) 360.

of the other parties.[85] In a global environment dominated by nation states with land and maritime boundaries and ever-decreasing resources, competitive negotiations are likely to benefit the most powerful actors. However, increasing prominence has been given to problem-solving or co-operative approaches that favour reformulating a dispute as a shared problem to which a mutually acceptable solution must be sought.[86] Continuing environmental degradation, diminishing resources, shared access to resources, the interdependence of trade and economic interests, trans-boundary health risks and the potential consequences of conflict all indicate the need for a problem-solving approach to international disputes.

Arbitration and adjudication are distinguished from the negotiatory processes by their adversarial nature and legally binding outcomes. Although settlement of most international disputes is attempted through negotiatory processes, adjudication before the ICJ is consistently given greater attention by international law scholars. This emphasis reflects the primacy accorded to the rule of law upheld through adjudicative processes in Western legal thought, but distorts the reality of international dispute settlement. However, the practical reasons for this attention are evident. Unlike the private nature of other processes, ICJ pleadings and judgments are public documents allowing interested persons access to the parties' claims, arguments and judicial reasoning.

'Alternative' dispute resolution and women

Negotiatory processes are often termed 'alternative' forms of domestic dispute resolution (ADR) in the sense that they are alternatives to litigation.[87] There has been an upsurge of enthusiasm for ADR, especially mediation, within Western jurisdictions in the 1980s and 90s that has resulted in numerous programmes within courts, government departments, social agencies, universities and private business organisations. The virtues of ADR are seen as its comparative cheapness, speediness and flexibility, the parties' involvement in fashioning the outcomes in accordance with their underlying interests and the 'win-win' potential of non-judicial remedies.[88]

It has been suggested in the domestic context that disputants using ADR are addressing conflict in a more 'feminine' way than the confrontation

[85] Such negotiation is termed 'competitive', 'zero-sum' or 'adversarial'. See generally R. Fisher and W. Ury, *Getting to Yes: Negotiating Agreement Without Giving In* (Boston, Houghton Mifflin, 1981; 2nd edn New York, Penguin Books, 1991).

[86] *Ibid.*; C. Menkel-Meadow, 'Towards another view of legal negotiation: the structure of problem-solving', 31 *University of California, Los Angeles Law Review* (1984) 754.

[87] H. Astor and C. Chinkin, *Dispute Resolution in Australia* (Sydney, Butterworths, 1992) chapter 2.

[88] *Ibid.* at 41–53.

involved in litigation and that use of ADR might therefore be particularly beneficial for women.[89] Some feminist scholars have argued that the non-confrontational nature of problem-solving techniques are especially advantageous for women in that they provide the space for women's voices to be heard and their interests to be identified.[90] The focus upon dialogue and seeking solutions that foster long-term relationships has been seen as 'the product of a feminist conception of dispute resolution and transaction planning'.[91] It has been argued that emphasis on rights in the formal justice system offers a 'male' way of approaching problems, while the focus on relationships in ADR is better suited to women's experiences.[92] Such arguments are grounded in the assumption that women may reason in a 'different voice' to men, discussed in chapter 2. Pursuing options for settlement may be empowering for women who are often perceived as disempowered by adjudication. Further, ADR processes allow for different, fluctuating perceptions of reality to be considered rather than the two-sided presentation in adjudication in which one side's view is 'right', the other 'wrong.' The notion of a single, readily determined reality prevents the understanding of different, alternative worldviews, each with its own reality and rationality.[93]

The claim that ADR is a more women-oriented process than adjudication has been challenged.[94] Women may be more interested in preserving relationships than in clarifying their own interests and thus give insufficient weight to the latter. Most significantly, the party with the least access to power in litigation will be in the same position in ADR and a weaker party who fears that her or his vital interests may be discounted may prove unwilling to make concessions. A third party facilitator may then apply pressure to reach a compromise. From a more practical perspective it is feared that disputes in which women directly participate, such as family disputes, will be diverted to ADR and so deprive them of some legal protections.[95] Thus, general assertions cannot be made that either ADR or adjudication is more advantageous for women, or for any disempowered disputant. Structural power imbalances are not altered by process. In some circumstances, the judicial articulation of rights can provide greater protection for the powerless than negotiatory processes, that are conducted within the 'shadow

[89] See e.g. J. Rifkin, 'Mediation from a feminist perspective: promise and problems', 2 *Law and Equality* (1984) 21.

[90] H. Astor and C. Chinkin, above note 87 at 109.

[91] *Ibid.* at 92.

[92] *Ibid.*

[93] T. Northrup, 'Getting to maybe: the uneasy partnership between conflict theory and feminist theory', paper presented at the Annual Meeting International Studies Association, Washington DC, March 1994.

[94] H. Astor and C. Chinkin, above note 87 at 92–5, 105–12.

[95] *Ibid.* at 258. Grillo has argued the need for procedural protections for women in mediation: T. Grillo, 'The mediation alternative: process dangers for women', 100 *Yale Law Journal* (1990–1) 1545.

of the law'.[96] In other circumstances, less formal processes may be more responsive to the 'weaker' party.

Women and international dispute resolution

How does this debate transpose to the international arena? At the Fourth World Conference on Women at Beijing in 1995 it was accepted that: 'An environment that promotes ... the peaceful settlement of disputes, in accordance with the principles of non-threat or use of force ... is an important factor for the advancement of women.'[97] It is important to note that international 'alternative' processes were originally formulated as alternatives to war rather than to adjudication,[98] which was not institutionalised until the Statute of the PCIJ in 1919. Dispute settlement forms part of the conduct of international affairs from which women are generally excluded. Women rarely act as international arbitrators, mediators, judges, conciliators or members of official fact-finding bodies.[99] Moreover, the equal participation of women in peace settlement, especially in decision-making processes,[100] would not of itself ensure attention to women's concerns. The statist orientation of international law means that individuals are not present in their own capacity in international dispute resolution processes and their interests are represented (if at all) by state negotiators. Thus even where women's interests have been identified in a dispute, their voices will not customarily be heard except as mediated through those representatives.

There are other concerns about whether problem-solving forms of dispute resolution in the international arena can benefit women. Formal dispute resolution processes and peace negotiations are normally held at the international level between those far removed from the arenas of dispute or violence. Participants are political leaders and international representatives who often ignore the efforts at reconciliation of people who have lived through and survived the violence. Fetherston and Nordstrom have noted that 'while the power elites work to effect military conquests or cease-fires, the locals at the ground institute strategies to mitigate the destructive impact of war and violence'.[101] The dissonance between the process of dispute resolution and the effects of conflict on women are illustrated by the draft-

[96] R. Mnookin and L. Kornhauser, 'Bargaining in the shadow of the law: the case of divorce', 88 *Yale Law Journal* (1979) 950.

[97] Beijing Platform for Action, para. 131. See also para. 145(b).

[98] Convention for the Pacific Settlement of Disputes, The Hague, 29 July 1899, TS No. 392; Convention for the Pacific Settlement of Disputes, The Hague, 18 October 1907, TS No. 536.

[99] See chapter 10.

[100] Beijing Platform for Action, para. 142(a).

[101] A. Fetherston and C. Nordstrom, *Overcoming Conceptual Habitus in Conflict Management: UN Peacekeeping and Warzone Ethnography* (Canberra, Peace

ing of the General Framework Agreement for Peace in Bosnia and Herzegovina in November 1995 (the Dayton Accords).[102] Despite the evidence of the use of rape and sexual abuse as significant instruments of war, Bosnian women did not participate within the negotiations. The Dayton Accords do not require the authorities in either of the entities in Bosnia and Herzegovina to address women's specific needs or to provide compensation for the harms they suffered.[103] They allow women no explicit role in reconstruction and change within the state, while responding to the violations has been reserved to the international community. Such silence does not facilitate reintegration and leaves civilians vulnerable to further abuse.[104] Similarly the Security Council meetings that adopted the ceasefire resolution against Iraq in 1991 did not advert to the position of Iraqi women.[105] By contrast the decisions of the Governing Council of the United Nations Compensation Commission (UNCC) to consider individual claims arising from the Iraqi invasion of Kuwait, have taken women into account.[106] The UNCC has determined that 'serious personal injury, includes *inter alia* physical or mental injury arising from sexual assault and that compensation will be payable for non-pecuniary injuries arising from mental pain and anguish caused by sexual assault or witnessing such assault on his or her spouse, child or parent'.[107]

In both the Bosnian and Iraqi peace settlements, the priorities were determined by international policy-makers who did not regard the position of women during and after the respective conflicts as being relevant. At Dayton the emphasis on reconciliation between the opposing sides excluded the allocation of blame and the naming of specific violations that had occurred during the conflict.[108] By contrast, in the case of Iraq, recognition of offences

---

Research Centre, Australian National University, 1994, Working Paper no. 147) at 12. See also C. Nordstrom, *Warzones: Cultures of Violence, Militarisation and Peace* (Canberra, Peace Research Centre, Australian National University, 1994, Working Paper no. 145).

[102] Initialled Dayton, Ohio, 21 November 1995, signed Paris, 14 December 1995, reprinted in 35 *International Legal Materials* (1996) 75.

[103] U. Dolgopol, 'A feminist appraisal of the Dayton Peace Accords', 19 *Adelaide Law Review* (1997) 59.

[104] *Ibid.* at 60–1.

[105] SC Res. 687, 3 April 1991.

[106] *Ibid.* para. 16. The UNCC was established by SC Res. 692, 20 May 1991. See R. Bettauer, 'The UN Compensation Commission: developments since October 1992', 89 *American Journal of International Law* (1995) 416.

[107] Decision taken by the Governing Council of the UNCC, during its second session: UN Doc. S/AC.26/1991/3, 23 October 1991.

[108] Rules of Procedure and Evidence of the International Criminal Tribunal for the Former Yugoslavia, as amended 17 December 1998, IT/32/Rev. 14, rule 106 allows for a claim for compensation by victims through national courts pursuant to a judgment of the Tribunal.

against women coincided with the allies' broader demands for punishment of Iraq and reparations adjudicated by the UNCC and were therefore accommodated.

Despite the political imperatives that determine whether or not women's interests are included, reconciliation after conflict should always require recognition of the particular harms inflicted upon women and the need for redress. Silence about rape and other abuses of women in conflict will undermine long-lasting reconstruction. A Bosnian woman attending the Beijing Conference in 1995, whose daughter had been raped in the Bosnian conflict, asked one of us: 'How can I tell my daughter we have negotiated with the men who did this to her? How can I explain that her body was worth nothing?' Should negotiations even be commenced with political leaders who have sanctioned, or at least not repudiated, such abuses?[109] The continuation of international or national criminal proceedings alongside the political process (as in the context of the former Yugoslavia) to some extent allays these concerns but moral and legal dilemmas remain in the context of decisions to use 'truth commissions' or to grant amnesty to those who admit their guilt.[110] The particular experiences and concerns of women survivors have not been routinely documented or addressed in 'objective' fact-finding missions.

An innovative proposal to redress the marginalisation of women in peace-making is that for the African Women Committee on Peace. The Committee would be involved at all levels in the new institutions and mechanisms being created by the Organisation of African Unity for conflict prevention, management and resolution.[111] The proposal envisages an autonomous committee comprising sixteen women (six government representatives, five NGO representatives and five individuals selected in their personal capacity) to liaise with peace movements at national, regional and local levels and ensure women's participation in all African peace initiatives, including those involving fact-finding, negotiation and mediation processes. The committee will also promote the participation of women at high levels of decision-making, including national cabinets, the armed forces, diplomatic services and international organisations. If this proposal is made fully operational, it will not only provide information on the impact of women's involvement in peace discussions but will also encourage the engagement of experienced women in other foreign policy settings.

[109] See A. D'Amato, 'Peace vs. accountability in Bosnia', 88 *American Journal of International Law* (1994) 500.
[110] See further *Truth Commissions: A Comparative Assessment* (Cambridge, Harvard Law School Human Rights Program, 1997).
[111] Report of the Secretary-General on the Implementation of the African Platform for Action: Women, Peace and Development, OAU Doc. CM/2016 (LXVI), May 1997, Annex I. The proposal was endorsed by the UN Economic Commission for Africa, Res. 829 (XXXII), 8 May 1997.

Peacekeeping

Peacekeeping is not explicitly referred to in the UN Charter. It evolved during the cold war as a means to mitigate the non-operation of the chapter VII collective security system through the use of the veto[112] and has been increasingly used in the 1980s and 1990s.[113]

The scope of peacekeeping

In 1992 the then Secretary-General described the conditions of success for peacekeeping as: a clear and practicable mandate, party co-operation in implementing that mandate, the continuing support of the Security Council and member states' readiness to contribute human and other resources.[114] Peacekeeping as originally conceived rested upon the consent of the territorial state, impartiality in the conflict and non-use of force except in defence of the peacekeepers.[115] Since 1990 peacekeeping has been embarked upon in situations that have been rooted in internal instability[116] and consent has not always been possible.[117] International peacekeeping then requires much more than the separation of opposing forces, the creation of buffer zones or the observance of armistice or ceasefire lines, objectives that typified such operations during the cold war. Peacekeeping has become multi-functional. It may be directed at providing humanitarian assistance during a conflict and the conditions of impartiality and non-use of force may become intolerably strained by the requirement to protect the civilian population.[118] Agreement between the opposing sides as to the peacekeepers' mandate may be impossible to achieve,[119] forcing military commanders to make inappropriate concessions with fighting forces. Peacekeeping may commence after negotiations have succeeded and be directed at helping the parties to implement a settlement and thus merge into peace-building.[120] Unclear mandates, or divergence between the political mandate expressed by the Security Council

[112] *Certain Expenses of the United Nations* 1962 ICJ Rep. 151 (Adv. Op. 20 July).
[113] See G. Evans, above note 51 at 99–106.
[114] *An Agenda for Peace*, above note 25 at para. 50.
[115] On 'quantitative and qualitative changes' in peacekeeping since the end of the cold war see *Supplement to An Agenda for Peace*, above note 25 at paras 8 to 22.
[116] Thirteen out of twenty-one peacekeeping operations established since 1988 and nine out of eleven operations established since January 1992 have related to intra-state conflict: *ibid.* at para. 11.
[117] E.g. in Somalia in 1992, no consent was given to peacekeeping: *ibid.* at paras 34 to 35.
[118] E.g. the safe areas or safe havens that were established in Bosnia and Herzegovina: *ibid.* at paras 18 to 19.
[119] *Ibid.* at para. 19.
[120] *Ibid.* at para. 20, citing Namibia, Angola, El Salvador, Cambodia and Mozambique.

and the realities of the conflict, have further undermined the effectiveness of peacekeeping,[121] as has the inability of the Security Council to restore systems of internal justice.[122]

Peacekeeping: the absence of women

The overwhelming maleness of national military forces is replicated at the international level. Between 1957 and 1989 there were only twenty women (mainly nurses) in the approximately 20,000 military personnel who served in UN missions. This figure has increased but only to little more than 4 per cent of military personnel.[123] The change may be explained both by the gradual increase of women in national armed forces and by the changed functions of peacekeeping forces, but it is still lower than in some national militaries.

An Agenda for Peace does not examine the participation of women within UN peace-making or peacekeeping, nor the implications of their omission. Boutros-Ghali subsequently recommended to the General Assembly a target of 50 per cent women in UN field missions,[124] but achievement of this goal is dependent upon the inclusion of women by member states contributing troops. Similarly, member states appear reluctant to give women decision-making responsibilities within UN peacekeeping. From 1957 to 1993 no females were appointed to such positions. Since 1994 there have been a few female appointments to professional posts in the peacekeeping area of the UN Secretariat.[125] Greater attention has been paid to the inclusion of women in some instances. For example in Namibia, which is generally regarded as one of the most successful peacekeeping operations, 40 per cent of the professional staff were women and women held three of the senior field posts.[126]

---

[121] R. Thakur, 'From collective to cooperative security? The Gareth Evans vision of the United Nations', in S. Lawson (ed.), *The New Agenda for Global Security: Cooperating for Peace and Beyond* (Sydney, Allen & Unwin, 1995) 19 at 23, 29.

[122] M. Koskenniemi, 'The police in the temple, order, justice and the United Nations: a dialectical view', 6 *European Journal of International Law* (1995) 325.

[123] *Women 2000* (New York, UN, December 1995) breaks down the positions held by women in UN forces. It points out that greater use of civilian police officers in UN forces is likely to increase female participation as the number of women in national civilian police forces is increasing faster than within the military. See also J. Stiehm, above note 70.

[124] UN Doc. 27 October 1995 A/50/691, para. 59.

[125] In 1994 the first female staff member was posted from the Royal Netherlands Army to the Field Administration and Logistics Division in the Department of Peace-Keeping Operations, above note 123: *Women 2000*.

[126] *The World's Women: 1995 – Trends and Statistics* (New York, UN, 1995) at 156.

Peaceful settlement of disputes

It is not certain that greater female participation would change the character of peacekeeping missions. It has been suggested that including more women in military, police and civilian forces would bring some positive differences in values and perspectives to peacekeeping,[127] especially modern multi-functional peacekeeping operations.[128] For example, it might reduce incidents of sexual harassment and deter abuse of the local population. Evidence also suggests that good relations and trust between peacekeepers and the local community can be more easily developed by women UN personnel[129] and that women victims of abuse are more likely to give evidence to women interviewers.[130] Nevertheless, there needs to be considerably greater commitment to the inclusion of women for such potential advantages to be realised and for other consequences to be assessed.[131]

Legal protection and regulation of peacekeepers

Another issue that has assumed importance is that of the legal regime applicable to the actions of UN authorised peacekeepers. As a result of the growing number of severe attacks on peacekeepers, a New Zealand initiative for a convention for the protection of UN forces was adopted in 1994.[132] The treaty offers less protection to civilians engaged in UN operations than to military members. This imbalance is a particular problem for women who are more likely to be employed in the former category.[133]

Less attention has been given to clarifying the legal relationship between vulnerable civilians and their international protectors. The UN is not considered able to be a party to an armed conflict nor an occupying power, so the Geneva Conventions and Protocols are not directly applicable to UN peacekeepers.[134] Although agreements concluded between troop-supplying states and the UN incorporate the Geneva Conventions, their applicability

[127] *Women 2000*, above note 123 at 9.
[128] Adoption of the Report of the Commission [on the Status of Women] on its Forty-Second Session, UN Doc. E/CN.6/1998/L.2/Add. 1, 10 March 1998, 11.
[129] Report of the Secretary-General, Peace: Women in International Decision-Making, UN Doc. E/CN.6/1995/12, 21 February 1995, at para. 38.
[130] *Shattered Lives: Sexual Violence during the Rwandan Genocide and its Aftermath* (New York, Human Rights Watch, 1996) at 24–6.
[131] The Secretary-General has outlined a number of ways in which the participation of women served as a catalyst for changed attitudes and initiatives in Report of the Secretary-General 1995, above note 129 at para. 38.
[132] Convention on the Safety of United Nation and Associated Personnel, GA Res. 49/59, 9 December 1994. See also *An Agenda for Peace*, above note 25 at para. 66.
[133] W. Sharp, 'Protecting the avatars of international peace and security', 7 *Duke Journal of Comparative and International Law* (1996) 93.
[134] The Geneva Conventions, 12 August 1949, 75 UNTS 31ff, common article 2. See C. Greenwood, 'Protection of peacekeepers: the legal regime', 7 *Duke Journal of Comparative and International Law* (1996) 185.

is limited.[135] Peacekeepers are bound by their national military codes and should comply with international human rights standards and the Code of Conduct for Law Enforcement Officials.[136] However, the Security Council remains politically and legally unaccountable for harms caused by personnel acting under its authority. Concern has been expressed about the different levels and lines of authority and command that exist in any deployment of military forces by the UN.[137] Secretary-General Boutros-Ghali emphasised the importance of unity of command to the functioning of an operation as an integrated whole and warned that intrusion of national imperatives could jeopardise overall coherence. Troops assembled from different backgrounds and cultures bring with them diverse attitudes, including those with respect to service and local women. Boutros Boutros-Ghali did not address the importance of unified authority to the maintenance of order, legitimacy and authority of the operation *vis à vis* the civilian population. Agreements for the supply and deployment of troops need to include explicit terms with respect to the civilian, especially female, population.

The code of conduct for peacekeepers which addresses appropriate behaviour towards women must be disseminated to all involved[138] with pre-operation training on its requirements and on gender sensitivity and awareness.[139] It should be kept under constant review and monitoring mechanisms put into place.[140] A readily accessible complaints procedure for violation of those guidelines is needed and troop-donating countries should allow disciplinary action to be taken against their forces for behaviour falling below the required standards.[141] The World Bank Inspection Panel, which allows for inspection of allegations that the Bank has failed to comply

---

[135] See Model Agreement between the UN and Member States contributing personnel and equipment to UN peacekeeping operations, Report of the Secretary General, UN Doc. A/46/185, 23 May 1991. See also Model Status-of-Forces Agreement for peacekeeping operations, Report of the Secretary-General, UN Doc. A/45/594,1990; C. Gray, 'Host-state consent and United Nations peacekeeping in Yugoslavia', 7 *Duke Journal of Comparative and International Law* (1996) 241.

[136] GA Res. 34/169, 1979. See also Basic Principles on the Use of Force and Firearms by Law Enforcement Officials, adopted by the Eighth UN Congress on the Prevention of Crime and the Treatment of Offenders, Havana, Cuba, September 1990.

[137] *Supplement to An Agenda for Peace*, above note 25 at paras 37 to 42.

[138] Thematic issues before the CSW, Report of the Secretary-General, UN Doc. E/CN.6/1998/5, 23 January 1998, para. 79; Secretary-General's Bulletin on the Observance by United Nations Forces of International Law, UN Doc. ST/SGB/1999/13, 9 August 1999.

[139] See the proposal for intergovernmental colleges for peace-making: M. Reisman, 'Preparing to wage peace: toward the creation of an international peace-making command and staff college', 88 *American Journal of International Law* (1994) 76.

[140] Thematic issues before the CSW, above note 138 at para. 79. The Report also suggests that in such training the expertise of the Division for the Advancement of Women, UNIFEM and UNICEF should be utilised.

[141] *Ibid.* at para. 80.

with its own practices and policies, has been suggested as a model.[142] In the absence of international machinery, domestic disciplinary action against alleged wrongdoers is required. This has been undertaken by some states,[143] but with mixed results. In Belgium paratroopers were acquitted of alleged offences in Somalia;[144] two Italian generals resigned after photographs were published of rape of a Somali woman by an Italian soldier;[145] and a Royal Commission investigated crimes committed by Canadian troops in Somalia and Bosnia.[146] The Report, *Dishonoured Legacy*, published in July 1997, found poor leadership and discipline in a badly planned mission, but the Canadian Defence Minister did not accept its findings.[147]

Preventive diplomacy and peace-building

Peace-building occurs at both ends of the spectrum of collective measures for dispute containment and resolution. The first aim of an international society committed to the maintenance of peace and security must be early identification of potential flashpoints and the pursuit of diplomatic measures to prevent violence.[148] Preventive diplomacy accordingly envisages measures to curtail disputes, and for their geographic, physical and personal containment.[149] Parties may initiate such steps, for example through the inclusion of treaty provisions for regular consultation, and the establishment of mechanisms to facilitate such discussions. The UN and regional organisations can also assist preventive diplomacy through information

---

[142] A. Orford, 'A radical agenda for collective security reform', *Proceedings of the Second Annual Meeting of the Australian and New Zealand Society of International Law* (Canberra, Centre for International and Public Law, 1994) 71 at 81. See D. Bradlow, 'International organizations and private complaints: the case of the World Bank Inspection Panel', 34 *Virginia Journal of International Law* (1994) 553; I. Shihata, *The World Bank Inspection Panel* (Oxford, Oxford University Press, 1994). Nevertheless the Inspection Panel model is open to criticism, notably on the grounds that it is for the Bank's Board to determine its response to the Panel's findings.

[143] E.g. Italy and Belgium, *Observer*, 22 June 1997. Bangladesh is reported to discipline any infractions and to send offenders home: *Reuters News*, 20 June 1997.

[144] The most notorious was the acquittal of two paratroopers accused of roasting a child over a fire. The court martial accepted the soldiers' evidence of the incident as a joke and concluded that 'there was no evidence that the attack was meant to hurt the child'. *Tribune Media Services* (TMS), 6 July 1997.

[145] *Associated Press*, 23 June 1997.

[146] In Bosnia allegations were of sexual abuse, torture of civilians and other misconduct against the inmates and staff of the Bakovici mental hospital that Canadian troops had been assigned to protect: *Guardian Weekly*, 26 January 1997, 5.

[147] *TMS*, 4 July 1997.

[148] *An Agenda for Peace*, above note 25 at para. 15.

[149] *Ibid.* at para. 20.

gathering and analysis, fact-finding and monitoring mechanisms, and, with consent, the use of troops for preventive deployment. However, resistance to international interference in states' 'domestic jurisdiction'[150] remains pervasive. Despite the evident benefits of preventing conflict through early warning and 'quiet diplomacy', Boutros Boutros-Ghali identified the reluctance of states to accept UN help in both interstate and internal conflicts as the biggest obstacle to preventive action.[151]

Peace-building after cessation of conflict postulates measures for internal reconstruction and for external co-operation between states. The former may include the convening of elections, allowing for wider participation in government and decision-making, human rights implementation mechanisms,[152] economic measures, landmine clearance, reclamation of land for agriculture and farming, and verification processes. The latter may require refugee repatriation, economic and trade agreements, and co-operative projects on resources, transport and development. The same measures are often appropriate for preventive diplomacy and may follow peacekeeping.

Peace-building can occur as part of a comprehensive settlement that attempts to address the long-term root causes of conflict, as well as to secure cessation of hostilities. In some long-lasting conflicts, women have planned for the anticipated repatriation and societal reconstruction. For example refugee women from the Western Sahara who have acquired relevant skills, in such areas as administration, management, health care, work relations and education, have deliberated upon ways of optimising their contribution within a new political structure and have built international networks, primarily with other women, to enhance international awareness of their position.[153]

Peace-building envisages a new political and social domestic order. Boutros Boutros-Ghali emphasised the importance of democratic participation in this process, including the empowerment and active involvement of women.[154] This is rarely the case in practice.[155] For example, in Somalia, women were

---

[150] Charter of the UN, article 2(7).

[151] *Supplement to An Agenda for Peace*, above note 25 at paras 26 and 27. The UN Protection Force in the former Yugoslav Republic of Macedonia is the only example of a purely preventive UN force: Annual Report of the Secretary-General, 1998, above note 29 at para. 44.

[152] E.g. the establishment of the Human Rights Commission in Bosnia and Herzegovina and the UN Human Rights Field Operation in Rwanda: *Shattered Lives*, above note 130 at 97–8.

[153] See chapter 8.

[154] 'Existing evidence indicates that in the areas of peace, security, conflict resolution and international peace negotiations, the participation of women in general and in decision-making in particular is lower than in any other area.' Report of the Secretary-General, Peace: Women in International Decision-Making, above note 129.

[155] A. Orford, 'The politics of collective security', above note 56 at 389–90.

excluded from decision-making once some internal order had been re-stored.[156] Women in Eastern Europe have found themselves largely at the margins of decision-making in the political and economic transition of the former socialist states.[157] Deep-rooted assumptions about the sexual division of labour and the location of women in the private arena may prevent international agencies from focusing upon this aspect of reconstruction and it may be viewed as an area in which deference should be paid to local sensibilities.

Some examples of nation-building can be contrasted. In the UN Transition Assistance Group in Namibia from 1989 to 1990 there was a deliberate policy of recruiting trained women to military and civilian posts at all levels, including senior decision-making.[158] Their tasks included disarmament, monitoring the repatriation of refugees and the release of political prisoners, and supervising voter education programmes and the elections. Part of the credit for ensuring women's participation has been attributed to the personal commitment of the Special Representative to Namibia, Matti Aahtisaari. This experience was not repeated in the UN Mission in Cambodia from 1991 to 1993. There were some women among the international civilian staff but this was essentially a male operation with no women in senior decision-making roles. A Community Relations Office was established in Cambodia to help address the ill-feelings of the local population towards UNTAC, but it has been argued that: 'A visible presence of female officers would have enabled the Cambodian population, especially women and children, to regard the civilian police as an ally in their daily struggle for survival' and would have gone some way towards dispelling the impression of 'an army of occupation.'[159]

The legal regime for reconstruction provides a framework for peace-building. In South Africa and Bosnia the destructive impact of past discrimination has been constitutionally addressed and priority directed towards reconciliation between peoples bitterly divided by racial or ethnic difference. In South Africa the Constitution was negotiated nationally and includes the broadest anti-discrimination clause of any national constitution.[160] Women

[156] See H. Osman, 'Somalia: will reconstruction threaten women's progress?', 8 *Ms Magazine* (no. 5, March/April 1995) 12.

[157] N. Funk and M. Mueller, *Gender Politics and Post-Communism* (New York/London, Routledge, 1993); S. Ramet, *Gender Politics in the Western Balkans* (University Park, Pennsylvania State University Press, 1997).

[158] See above note 126.

[159] *Women 2000*, above note 123 at 8.

[160] Constitution of the Republic of South Africa, Act 108 1996, 10 December 1996, chapter 2, Bill of Rights, article 9(3) prohibits discrimination on 'one or more grounds' including gender, sex, pregnancy, marital status and sexuality. See C. Romany, 'Black women and gender equality in a new South Africa: human rights and the intersection of race and gender', 21 *Brooklyn Journal of International Law* (1996) 857.

were involved in the negotiation process through church and political groups and the publication of a Women's Rights Charter.[161] In Bosnia the Constitution was concluded through an external international peace process, culminating in the Dayton Peace Accords, negotiated between neighbouring states and international powers. The Constitution, which is part of the Dayton Accords, requires Bosnia and Herzegovina to become (or to remain) a party to international human rights treaties, including the Convention on the Elimination of All Forms of Discrimination Against Women.[162] The European Convention for the Protection of Human Rights and Fundamental Freedoms and its Protocols have been incorporated as direct law in Bosnia with priority over all other law.[163] Internal human rights monitoring bodies have been established.[164] Other than the requirement that Bosnia adhere to the Women's Convention, no mention is made of the particular needs, or potential contribution, of women in the reconstruction of society. It is not yet clear whether either the South African or Bosnian system represent practical progress in the advancement of women.[165]

Another model for peace-building is the Agreement on a Firm and Lasting Peace in Guatemala,[166] regarded as the most important UN peace-building operation.[167] In the context of resolving a long and destructive civil war in Guatemala, weight has been attached in the Agreement to strengthening human rights guarantees, especially with respect to the resettlement of uprooted populations. Attention has been given to the protection of female-headed families, widows and orphans, seriously affected by the war. The government (whose negotiation team included one woman) has committed itself to promote legislation against sexual harassment, to form an Office for the Defence of Indigenous Women's Rights and to implement women's human rights. The government has formally recognised the importance of women's active participation in the economic and social development of the state and has agreed to address the specific situation of women and to introduce policies to increase their opportunities.[168] In contrast, the fact that

---

[161] *Ibid.*

[162] Dayton Accords, article VII and annex 6.

[163] 4 November 1950, 213 UNTS 221 and eleven Protocols. Dayton Peace Accords, annex 4, the Constitution of Bosnia and Herzegovina, article 2.

[164] *Ibid.* annex 6, Agreement on Human Rights, article II.

[165] See further C. Chinkin, 'Strategies to combat discrimination against women', in M. O'Flaherty and G. Gisvold (eds), *Post-War Protection of Human Rights in Bosnia-Herzegovina* (The Hague, Martinus Nijhoff, 1998) 173.

[166] Agreement on a Firm and Lasting Peace in Guatemala, Government of Guatemala Unidad Revolucionaria Nacional Guatemalteca, 29 December 1996, reprinted in 36 *International Legal Materials* (1997) 258.

[167] Annual Report of the Secretary-General 1998, above note 29 at para. 66.

[168] The Security Council expressed its full support for the process and authorised the use of military observers and medical personnel for the verification of the cease-fire agreement: SC Res. 1094, 20 January 1997.

the genocide in Rwanda was seen as 'internal' meant that there was no international peace settlement. The burden of reconstruction is falling heavily upon women who constitute 70 per cent of the population.[169] In addition to the overwhelming psychological, physical and social problems they face, these women continue to be treated as second class citizens under Rwandan law. In numerous instances, survivors suffer from the perpetrators' apparent lack of accountability for the traumas they have suffered. In 1996 the justice, law enforcement, health and rehabilitation ministries had not co-ordinated ways of addressing women's needs.[170] Little international aid has been targeted for reconstruction or for gender-related issues,[171] although the political and social conditions to rebuild the country are dependent on the empowerment of Rwandan women.[172]

Economic sanctions

International law contemplates the use of economic sanctions to respond to threats to international peace and security,[173] as well as to supplement peace-making and peacekeeping measures. There is a broad range of such measures available to the Security Council, including withholding recognition, restrictions upon air and maritime traffic, economic and trading measures including limitations on exports and imports, freezing of foreign assets and arms embargoes.[174] Sanctions can be temporary and targeted at a specific state, or permanent and broadly applicable. While sanctions are generally punitive, there are also 'positive' sanctions that are directed at changing state behaviour through persuasion.[175]

Before the Iraqi invasion of Kuwait in 1990, the Security Council had only twice used its powers to authorise economic sanctions under the UN Charter:[176] against Southern Rhodesia after its unilateral declaration of

[169] Fifty per cent of households are headed by women: *Shattered Lives*, above note 130 at 2.

[170] *Ibid.* at 5.

[171] By 1996 the international community had spent US $2.5 billion on refugee camps compared with US $ 572 million in Rwanda itself: *ibid.* at 98–9.

[172] *Ibid.* at 5.

[173] Charter of the UN, article 41. The article also authorises the Security Council 'to call upon member states to apply such measures.'

[174] Unilateral sanctions can include other measures such as withdrawal of diplomatic or consular staff and closure of missions, withdrawal of, or requirements for, visas, and the cessation of sporting and cultural exchanges. See G. Simons, *Economic Sanctions* (London, Pluto Press, 1999).

[175] Kuyper has analysed the South African case as the first example of positive sanctions – 'the financing of specific projects through the intermediary of anti-apartheid organizations.' P. Kuyper, 'Trade sanctions, security, and human rights and commercial policy', in M. Maresceau (ed.), *The European Community's Commercial Policy after 1992: The Legal Dimension* (Dordrecht, Martinus Nijhoff, 1993) 401.

[176] Charter of the UN, article 41.

independence;[177] and against South Africa.[178] Both situations concerned systemic racial discrimination. Since 1990 different collective measures have been directed *inter alia* against Iraq and Iraqi-occupied Kuwait,[179] Liberia,[180] Somalia,[181] Libya,[182] Haiti,[183] the former Yugoslavia,[184] Sudan,[185] Angola[186] and Rwanda.[187] It is questionable whether the UN Charter prerequisite, that the situation constitutes a threat to international peace and security,[188] has been fulfilled in all cases. This is especially significant as the perceived ineffectiveness of economic measures may subsequently be used to justify more coercive action, without any full assessment of whether an article 39 situation exists. Further, failure to spell out the objectives of sanctions makes it difficult to determine when they have been achieved.[189]

Monitoring the application and impact of sanctions is difficult, not least because of the unwillingness of target states to provide reliable economic and social data. Sanctions also have undesirable collateral effects, for example on the work of humanitarian agencies and on third states.[190] The UN Charter allows states with special economic problems caused by sanctions to consult with the Security Council.[191] The Sanctions Committee hears these claims and may make recommendations to the President of the Security Council.[192] Less attention has been paid to the adverse effects upon the civilian population, which in practice is more likely to bear the brunt of punitive measures than the government whose policies have led to their imposition. Although exceptions are regularly made in sanctions provisions

---

[177] SC Res. 216, 13 November 1965; SC Res. 217, 20 November 1965.

[178] SC Res. 181, 7 August 1963 (voluntary arms embargo); SC Res. 418, 4 November 1977 (mandatory arms embargo).

[179] SC Res. 661, 6 August 1990. In this and all the following examples, the Security Council passed a succession of resolutions. Those listed are illustrative only and are not intended to provide a comprehensive list of Security Council action.

[180] E.g. SC Res. 788, 19 November 1992; SC Res. 985, 13 April 1995.

[181] E.g. SC Res. 733, 23 January 1992.

[182] E.g. SC Res. 731, 21 January 1992; SC Res. 748, 31 March 1992.

[183] E.g. SC Res. 841, 6 June 1993.

[184] E.g. SC Res. 713, 25 September 1991; SC Res. 757, 30 May 1992; SC Res. 760, 18 June 1992; SC Res. 787, 16 November 1992; SC Res. 820, 17 April 1993.

[185] E.g. SC Res. 1070, 6 August 1996.

[186] E.g. SC Res. 1127, 28 August 1997 (sanctions against UNITA).

[187] E.g. SC Res. 918, 17 May 1994.

[188] Charter of the UN, article 39.

[189] *Supplement to An Agenda for Peace*, above note 25 at para. 68.

[190] *Ibid.* at para. 70.

[191] Charter of the UN, article 50.

[192] Eg. SC Res. 669, 24 September 1990 mandated the Sanctions Committee established under SC Res. 661 to consider claims under Charter of the UN, article 50 caused by economic sanctions against Iraq.

for medical and other humanitarian needs,[193] the level of deprivation experienced, for example, by the Iraqi civilian population through the continuation of sanctions, suggests that there has been insufficient concern to ensure that collective sanctions do not themselves violate human rights standards.[194] Research on the effect of sanctions in Iraq suggests that their effect falls heavily upon women. In a 1991 study, 80 per cent of women interviewed reported that their domestic responsibilities had become more onerous with the onset of sanctions. Sanctions lead to rationing of basic commodities, including food and water. Black markets had raised prices and 50 per cent of women interviewed had exhausted their savings attempting to acquire these necessities.[195] Although extreme hardships have been documented by UN specialised agencies,[196] and the Committee on Economic and Social Rights has noted that sanctions almost always have a 'dramatic impact' on the rights contained in the ICESCR,[197] the Security Council is not formally accountable for the consequences of its peace-making or peacekeeping activities under article 41.[198] The Committee on Economic and Social Rights argues that both the affected state and the parties imposing sanctions have obligations flowing from the ICESCR that are neither nullified nor diminished by a decision with respect to the maintenance of international peace and security. This includes the obligation to 'take steps individually and through international assistance and cooperation . . . to respond to any disproportionate suffering experienced by vulnerable groups within the targeted country'.[199] The Secretary-General in turn has welcomed 'smart sanctions'

[193] *Supplement to An Agenda for Peace*, above note 25 at paras 72 and 74 asserts that such provision should always be made and that a mechanism within the Security Council should ensure its application.

[194] ILC, Draft Articles on State Responsibility, adopted on First Reading, UN Doc. A/CN.4/L.528/Add. 2, 16 July 1996, article 50 prohibits counter-measures that: are contrary to Charter of the UN, article 2(4); constitute extreme economic or political coercion; contravene the inviolability of diplomatic persons or premises; derogate from basic human rights; or contravene a rule of *jus cogens*.

[195] A. Orford, 'The politics of collective security', above note 56 at 380. See also B. Bhatia, M. Kawar and M. Shahin, *Unheard Voices: Iraqi Women on War and Sanctions* (London, Change, 1991).

[196] UNICEF estimated in late 1991 that 87,000 Iraqi children had died as a result of sanctions: *Associated Press*, 29 December 1991.

[197] 16 December 1966, 999 UNTS 3, 16 December 1966, reprinted in 6 *International Legal Materials* (1967) 360. See The relationship between economic sanctions and respect for economic, social and cultural rights, General Comment no. 8, UN Doc. E/C.12/1997/8, 5 December 1997. The Committee noted, at paras 4 and 5, that the humanitarian exemptions from sanctions are limited in scope and do not ensure respect for economic, social and cultural rights within the targeted country.

[198] Beijing Platform for Action, para. 14(i) requires governments, international and regional organisations to take measures 'with a view to alleviating the negative impact of economic sanctions on women and children.'

[199] *Ibid.* at para. 14.

that seek to pressure deviant regimes rather than civilian populations[200] and has reiterated that the harms of sanctions must be borne in mind when they are imposed and evaluated.[201] Neither the Committee nor the Secretary-General have referred to the particular burden of sanctions upon women, although the consequences for children are noted.

Conclusion

International interest in dispute resolution processes has had a number of practical manifestations including compulsory dispute resolution clauses in treaties, greater recourse to the ICJ than at any previous time in its history and greater use of arbitration, especially for international commercial disputes.[202] There has been renewed interest in peace-making, peacekeeping and peace-building. Collective international or regional action has assisted negotiated settlements to long-continuing disputes in Namibia, Cambodia, South Africa, Central America, the Middle East, Northern Ireland, Bosnia and Herzegovina, and elsewhere. However a peaceful settlement does not necessarily entail substantive agreement or durability,[203] nor guard against subsequent continuation of the dispute. Indeed, agreements on processes and institutions for reconstruction can mask continuing conflict.[204]

Despite statements on the importance of including women in international conflict resolution,[205] there has been little increase in women's actual participation or in analysis of its significance. Moreover, it cannot be assumed that merely including women within peace negotiations would ensure adequate inclusion of their interests, or changes in the political agendas addressed. Nevertheless there are lessons that can be drawn for effective dispute resolution from feminist scholarship. First, feminist analysis has drawn attention to the importance of considering power imbalance in dispute resolution. In the international context, power disparities are a frequent feature of disputes. Formal legal argument can emphasise the need for fair procedural treatment and the public articulation of legal rights and duties can protect less powerful litigants from excessive or abusive exercise

---

[200] E.g. SC Res. 1173, 12 June 1998 targeting UNITA forces within Angola.

[201] Annual Report of the Secretary-General, 1998, above note 29 at paras 62 to 64.

[202] C. Chinkin, 'The peaceful settlement of disputes: new grounds for optimism?', in R. Macdonald (ed.), *Essays in Honour of Wang Tieya* (Dordrecht, Martinus Nijhoff, 1994) 165.

[203] E.g., the peace agreement signed at Arusha, 4 August 1993 between the governments of Rwanda, Tanzania, Uganda, Burundi and Zaire which envisaged power-sharing even as extremists prepared for genocide: G. Prunier, *The Rwanda Crisis: History of a Genocide* (New York, Columbia University Press, 1995) at 159–206.

[204] M. Koskenniemi, above note 122 at 403.

[205] Notably in Beijing Platform for Action, Critical Area E.

of power by their opponents.[206] These safeguards may be less rigorously observed in private negotiatory procedures. For this reason devices that exclude non-state interests from international adjudication such as the restriction of the ICJ's contentious jurisdiction to states,[207] its unwillingness to accept an *actio popularis* or submissions of *amici curiae*,[208] or to accommodate third party interests, contribute to the marginalisation of the powerless.[209] On the other hand, appeals to legal resolution may be ineffective for the less powerful where the substantive legal principles support the interests of those that control the attributes of power. Thus broader participation in international law-making is important to develop a more equitable body of law, and greater access to the formal and informal processes that rest upon that law. While the focus of our concern is greater participation by women in both law-making and law-applying institutions, this point is equally applicable to other groups disadvantaged under international law, such as indigenous peoples.[210]

The second lesson that international lawyers can draw from feminist analysis relates to the concepts of co-operation and good neighbourliness prescribed within the UN Charter. The growing number of international problems that require co-operative attempts at resolution means that states have a broader common interest in enhancing good neighbourliness.[211] The notion of international community is given a different resonance through examples of women's networking and co-operation across boundaries, especially between women of hostile communities. An example is the effort of Palestinian and Israeli women to promote tolerance and to work together.[212] Palestinian women have also developed links with women further afield, from the Maghreb, the Mashreq and Europe. In 1994 the Marrakesh Declaration negotiated by women from these regions affirmed the need to continue the peace process, and undertook to promote educational and peace

[206] E.g. *Military and Paramilitary Activities in and against Nicaragua* (Nicaragua v. United States) Merits 1986 ICJ Rep. 14 (Judgment of 27 June) and *Case Concerning Certain Phosphate Lands in Nauru* (Nauru v. Australia) Preliminary Objections 1992 ICJ Rep. 240 (Judgment of 26 June).

[207] Statute of the ICJ, article 34.

[208] See chapter 3.

[209] This point is well illustrated by the *Case Concerning East Timor* (Portugal v. Australia) 1995 ICJ Rep. 90 (Judgment of 30 June), where the East Timorese, who were most affected by Indonesian actions, had no standing before the ICJ. Their interests were not considered by the Court because of the absence of Indonesia, a third party to the dispute.

[210] M. Reisman, 'Protecting indigenous rights in international adjudication', 89 *American Journal of International Law* (1995) 350.

[211] D. Hutchinson, 'The material scope of the obligation under the United Nations Charter to take action to settle international disputes', 14 *Australian Yearbook of International Law* (1992) 1 at 36.

[212] J. Vickers, *Women and War* (London, Zed Books, 1993) at 136–8, 146–8.

programmes and networks that would explore and emphasise common interests and values while respecting different contexts.[213]

Third, feminist writings shed light on the nature of discourse between
participants from diverse social and cultural backgrounds and the barriers
to understanding and co-operation. Interstate relations are shaped and
reshaped through a continuous process of communication, consultation
and negotiation. These communications are coloured by various factors, for
example wide disparities in available resources and economic development
between states. Conflict theorists argue that in prolonged conflict social
identity becomes dependent upon the perception of the self as 'good' and
the other as 'the enemy'. This danger is especially applicable to longstanding
international disputes where participants may rely upon assumptions about
the attitudes of their adversaries that may no longer be grounded in reality.
Feminist writers have described the fluidity of the concept of self and the
problems of an essentialist identity of self and the other for constructive
dialogue. For example, feminists of colour have pointed out that white,
Western feminists are frequently insensitive to their concerns, standing points
and history.[214] The common interest in seeking ways to end the subordinate
place of women in all societies can be concealed through failure to understand the importance of differences between women. Assumptions are made
as to common interests without identifying where there is such commonality
and where there is divergence. There is a risk of assuming that only the
'other' has cultural biases and that the 'self' is culturally neutral. Failure to
explore difference can be an impediment to identifying common ground and
therefore to dispute resolution. A genuine dialogue requires identification of
the cultural starting point of all involved and of the erroneous assumptions
that might be made.[215] Attempts must be made to understand the feelings
and perspectives of the other person and of their social and cultural background;[216] the 'exotic other' must be engaged.[217] The 'world traveller' model
discussed in chapter 2 is especially important for international mediators
who might assume themselves (and be assumed by others) to be culturally
and politically neutral in a dispute between identified parties. The issue is
not simply one of difference, but of power.[218]

---

[213] European Parliament, *Women of Europe Newsletter* (no. 45, June 1994).

[214] See chapter 2.

[215] An Expert Group meeting on women's contribution to a culture of peace
emphasised the importance of cross-cultural exchanges, dialogues respectful of
pluralities and difference and exploring alternative conflict resolution procedures
and models of governance: Report of the Secretary-General, Monitoring the Implementation of the Nairobi Forward Looking Strategies for the Advancement of
Women, Priority Theme Peace, UN Doc. E/CN.6/1996/6, 30 January 1996, Annex.

[216] See M. Clech Lam, 'Feeling foreign in feminism', 19 *Signs* (1994) 865.

[217] K. Engle, 'Female subjects of public international law: human rights and the
exotic other female', 26 *New England Law Review* (1992) 1509.

[218] T. Northrup, above note 93.

Fourth, there is a danger that attention to process can become a substitute for dealing with the underlying issues. Dispute resolution processes do not rectify the structural reasons for disagreement within the international arena and at best they facilitate accommodation between disputing parties. If the concept of peace is understood as more than the absence of conflict, the underlying causes of conflict, including the gendered distribution of wealth and power, economic disparities, inadequate resources, violation of human rights and environmental destruction, become relevant. The peaceful settlement of international disputes requires more than the presence of women in its processes. It requires the willingness to develop and revalue ways of thinking that are silenced and obscured in the current international legal system.[219]

There have been some indications of changed perspectives in response to the political crises at the end of the 1990s, although their potential is uncertain. The concept of security remains primarily rooted in the protection of state interests in territory, resources and promoting investment, thereby prioritising the interests of foreign investors above those of people to personal security. However individual states and the Security Council have ventured upon some innovative enterprises that perhaps challenge this assessment. After the human disasters of Somalia, Rwanda and Bosnia in the 1990s, where the international response was too late, too little or without the political will to establish and perform an effective mandate, the 1999 NATO bombing of Yugoslavia was carried out ostensibly for the protection of human rights.[220] Formal long term commitment to reconstruction has been made in Bosnia,[221] Kosovo,[222] Haiti[223] and East Timor.[224] These all remain contested arenas with controversy in particular about the appropriate balance between international intervention and local autonomy. Unlike the other cases, the importance of some of the issues discussed in this chapter has been explicitly recognised in East Timor. Thus the Security Council underlined the importance of personnel in the United Nations Transitional Administration in East Timor (UNTAET) having training in humanitarian law, human rights and refugee law 'including child and gender-related provisions, negotiation and communication skills, cultural awareness and civilian-military co-ordination.' If these requirements are broadly interpreted, and applied to all tasks of state-building, they could provide a model for the rethinking discussed above.

---

[219] C. Cohn, above note 74 at 239.
[220] See differing opinions about this campaign in 'Editorial Comments: NATO's Kosovo Intervention', 93 *American Journal of Internationa Law* (1999) 831–69.
[221] Dayton Accords, above note 102.
[222] SC Res. 1244, 10 June 1999.
[223] SC Res. 1212, 25 November 1998.
[224] SC Res. 1275, 25 October 1999.

10

Redrawing the boundaries of international law

Introduction

This book has argued that sex and gender shape international law. It has questioned the universality and objectivity of international law because of the exclusion of women from its substance, methodologies and processes. It has examined the assumptions of the international legal order that inculcate particular conceptions of gender and reinforce in turn ideas about 'femininity' and 'masculinity'. Women are only visible in very limited contexts in international law. Outside the human rights context of the prohibition on sex discrimination,[1] women's presence on the international stage is generally focused on their reproductive and mothering roles that are accorded 'special' protection.[2] The woman of international law is painted in heterosexual terms within a traditional family structure that is defined as the 'natural and fundamental group unit of society'.[3] She is constructed as 'the other', the shadow complement to the man of decision and action.

Harold Koh has described an 'epochal transformation of international law' in the 1990s.[4] The characteristics of this 'new' international law include a marked decline in national sovereignty, a proliferation of international regimes, institutions and non-state actors, the rapid development of customary and treaty-based rules, the erosion of the significance of 'domestic

[1] Convention on the Elimination of All Forms of Discrimination Against Women, 18 December 1979, 1249 UNTS 13, reprinted in 19 *International Legal Materials* (1980) 33.
[2] E.g. J. Gardam, 'An alien's encounter with the law of armed conflict', in N. Naffine and R. Owens (eds), *Sexing the Subject of Law* (Sydney, Law Book Co. Ltd, 1996) 233 at 241.
[3] International Covenant on Civil and Political Rights, 16 December 1966, 999 UNTS 171, reprinted in 6 *International Legal Materials* (1967) 368, article 23.
[4] H. Koh, 'Why do nations obey international law?', 106 *Yale Law Journal* (1997) 2599 at 2604.

jurisdiction' preserved by article 2(7) of the UN Charter, and the increasing integration of domestic and international systems. How has this apparent transformation responded to the realities of women's lives? This chapter examines an area where women's lives appear to have affected the evolution of the international legal order. It describes the development of institutions, principles and processes of international humanitarian and criminal law that has taken place in the 1990s,[5] in which the situation of women has to some extent been addressed. We argue that, despite this acknowledgement of women's experiences, the 'new' international criminal law does not represent a significant shift in the boundaries of international law.

Women in international criminal law

From late 1991 and throughout 1992 extensive media coverage created widespread pressure for an international legal response to the atrocities committed against women and men in the conflicts accompanying the disintegration of the former Yugoslavia. In particular, sufficient outrage was expressed about the extensive rapes and other violent assaults against women to ensure that they could not be ignored, or discounted as a normal phenomenon of armed conflict.[6]

The Security Council's response to the demands for action was incremental. To collect information on the allegations of war crimes,[7] it established a Commission of Experts to undertake an independent investigation.[8] Following the report of the Commission, the Security Council requested the UN Secretary-General to submit proposals for the establishment of an *ad hoc* tribunal for the prosecution of war crimes in the former Yugoslavia.[9] The Secretary-General's Report was adopted in May 1993, and the International Criminal Tribunal for Former Yugoslavia (ICTY) established.[10] In 1994 events in Rwanda led the Security Council to take similar steps[11] to establish a second *ad hoc* tribunal 'to prosecute persons for genocide and

[5] See T. Meron, 'War crimes law comes of age', 92 *American Journal of International Law* (1998) 462.

[6] E.g. D. Rieff, *Slaughterhouse: Bosnia and the Failure of the West* (London, Vintage, 1995) at 42–52.

[7] SC Res. 798, 18 December 1992; SC Res. 820, 17 April 1993. See also GA Res. 47/121, 17 December 1992.

[8] SC Res. 780, 6 October 1992.

[9] SC Res. 808, 22 February 1993. The Security Council was acting under chapter VII of the UN Charter.

[10] SC Res. 827, 25 May 1993. Statute of the ICTY, reprinted in 31 *International Legal Materials* (1993) 1203, available at http://www.un.org/icty.

[11] A Commission of Experts to investigate crimes against humanity in Rwanda was established by SC Res. 935, 1 July 1994. Its Final Report was submitted to the Security Council on 9 December 1994, UN Doc. S/1994/1405.

other serious violations of international humanitarian law' in that country, the International Criminal Tribunal for Rwanda (ICTR).[12] In July 1998 a further step was taken by the adoption of a Statute (Treaty) for a permanent International Criminal Court (ICC) by a Diplomatic Conference in Rome.[13] The Statute was the culmination of five years' work after the completion of a draft text by the ILC in 1994.[14]

Throughout the processes of creation and operation of the two *ad hoc* tribunals and the drafting of the ICC Statute, the interests of women have been accorded comparatively serious attention. The following sections outline the ways this has been manifested.

Women's participation in the Tribunals

In reacting to the allegations of sexual violence against women and appointing staff to the international criminal Tribunals, a greater degree of understanding of the need for women's participation has been shown than has been the case in other international institutions.[15] Nevertheless the number of women in key positions remains low. Initially, there were no women members of the Commission of Experts created by the Security Council to investigate allegations of atrocities in the former Yugoslavia. When the resignation of one member and the death of another created vacancies, the Secretary-General selected two women, Professor Christine Cleiren from the Netherlands and Judge Hanne Sophie Greve from Norway.[16] Professor Cleiren was allocated responsibility for preparing a special report on the legal aspects of rape and sexual assault. The Commission of Experts carried out an investigation of rape in Croatia, the first of its kind carried out during a war. An all-woman investigation team included prosecution experts and female mental health experts.[17] Their findings were included in the Final Report of the Commission before it was dissolved and its investigative functions continued by Tribunal staff.[18]

---

[12] SC Res. 955, 8 November 1994. Statute of the ICTR, reprinted in 33 *International Legal Materials* (1995) 1598, available at http://www.ictr.org.

[13] Rome Statute for the ICC, 17 July 1998, UN Doc. A/CONF.183/9, reprinted in 37 *International Legal Materials* (1998) 999.

[14] J. Crawford, 'The ILC adopts a Statute for an International Criminal Court', 89 *American Journal of International Law* (1995) 404. The question of a permanent international criminal court had been originally referred to the ILC by the General Assembly in 1948: GA Res. 260 (III), 9 December 1948.

[15] See chapter 6.

[16] Both were appointed on 19 October 1993.

[17] M. Bassiouni, 'The United Nations Commission of Experts established pursuant to Security Council Resolution 780 (1992)', 88 *American Journal of International Law* (1994) 784.

[18] Final Report of the Commission of Experts Established Pursuant to Security Council Resolution 780 (1992), UN Doc. S/1994/674, 27 May 1994, paras 232–53.

The Secretary-General recommended in his Report that, 'Given the nature of the crimes committed and the sensitivities of victims of rape and sexual assault, due consideration should be given in the appointment of staff to the employment of qualified women.'[19] Although this suggestion did not find its way into the text of the Statutes for either the ICTY or the ICTR, it was included in Rule 34(B) of the Rules of Procedure and Evidence of both Tribunals with respect to appointments to the Victim and Witnesses Unit by the Registry. Despite limited resources, the Units have provided some counselling and support services, especially in cases of rape and sexual assault, as well as physical security and financial compensation for witnesses while they are participating in proceedings.[20] The Secretary-General has appointed a number of women to the office of the prosecution. The second Chief Prosecutor for the ICTY and ICTR was Louise Arbour, a former judge from Canada, and the third Chief Prosecutor was Carla del Ponte from Switzerland. A Legal Adviser for gender-related crimes, Patricia Viseur-Sellers, has been appointed within the prosecution department. Other initiatives have been the formation of sexual assault investigative teams, in-house workshops on issues of sexual violence.

Tribunal judges are elected by the General Assembly from a list submitted by the Security Council. The criteria make no reference to sex or gender.[21] Geographical distribution is important and no two judges may be from the same state.[22] The first bench of the ICTY included two women out of eleven judges, Judge Elisabeth Odio-Benito from Costa Rica and Judge Gabrielle Kirk McDonald from the United States. The elections in 1997 produced a similarly constituted Tribunal. Judge Kirk McDonald retained her position (and until November 1999 held the Presidency) while Judge Odio-Benito did not, but Judge Florence Ndepele Mwachande Mumba from Zambia was elected. Elections in October 1998 for three additional judges to create a third Trial Chamber were all won by men. The ICTR has a single woman, Judge Navanethem Pillay from South Africa. The inclusion of women judges from the outset is an improvement on, for example, the composition of the ICJ, but it is still far from adequate representation. One

---

[19] Report of the Secretary-General Pursuant to Paragraph 2 of the Security Council Resolution 808 (1993), UN Doc. S/25704, 3 May 1993, at para. 88.

[20] The Victims and Witnesses Unit applies the Declaration of Basic Principles of Justice for Victims of Crime and Abuse of Power, GA Res. 40/34, 29 November 1985. Witnesses' expenses have been reimbursed, including expenses incurred for child care while in The Hague.

[21] Statute of the ICTY, article 13(1) provides that judges shall be of high moral character, impartiality and integrity with appropriate qualifications for judicial office in their own states. Due account shall also be taken of expertise in criminal law, international law and international humanitarian law. The Statute of the ICTR, article 12 is almost identical.

[22] Statute of the ICTY, article 13(2)(c) and (d).

possible means of increasing the number of women judges would have been to provide that if a male and female nominee received equal votes the female should be considered elected.[23] The ICC Statute requires states in selecting judges to 'take into account the need ... for ... [a] fair representation of female and male judges'.[24] This condition is placed third, after requirements of representation of legal systems and equitable geographical representation, and there is no indication as to how this is to be achieved in a secret ballot. States parties are also required to take into account the need for specific legal expertise 'including, but not limited to, violence against women and children'.[25]

The presence of women in international tribunals can make a difference. Women investigators and prosecutors facilitate the collection of evidence from women survivors who might be reluctant to talk to men about offences committed against them. The Legal Adviser on gender within the prosecution department of the ICTY and the ICTR has been instrumental in indicting accused persons for crimes against women, and women judges have been sensitive to the need to hear evidence of gender-based crimes. In the *Akayesu* case before the ICTR, evidence of rape and sexual assault did not emerge until the sole women member of the Tribunal, Judge Pillay, persisted in questioning witnesses about it.[26] The appointment of women to professional posts has symbolic, as well as practical, significance. Women appear in criminal proceedings most often as victims, especially in the war crimes tribunals, although the 1997 indictment of Pauline Nyiramasuhuko, former Minister of the Family and the Promotion of Women in Rwanda, for her active participation in the genocide shows that no assumptions can be made about the role of women in the commission of international crimes.[27] There remains the danger, however, that the inclusion of women will be perceived as appropriate for a tribunal dealing with, *inter alia*, offences against women, as is suggested by the Secretary-General's linkage between the nature of the crimes to be investigated and the employment of qualified women, quoted above. That the same importance is not attached to the inclusion of women in other authoritative institutions is illustrated by the failure of states to

---

[23] A precedent is found in the ILC Statute. In ILC elections, if two candidates from the same state receive the same number of votes, the elder is elected: Statute of the ILC, GA Res. 174 (II), 21 November 1947 (as amended), article 9(2).

[24] Rome Statute for the ICC, article 36(8)(a)(iii).

[25] *Ibid.*, article 36(8)(b).

[26] *Prosecutor v. Jean-Paul Akayesu*, Judgment of 2 September 1998, ICTR-96-4-T. See below at text accompanying note 101.

[27] *Butare* Indictment, 26 May 1997, ICTR-97-21-1. See *Rwanda Not So Innocent When Women Become Killers* (London, Africa Watch, 1995).

ensure that any women were elected to newly constituted tribunals such as the Tribunal on the Law of the Sea[28] and the seven member appellate panel for the WTO.[29]

Jurisdiction of the Tribunals

The jurisdiction of the *ad hoc* Tribunals includes violations of international humanitarian law,[30] genocide[31] and crimes against humanity.[32]

International humanitarian law
The 1993 Report of the Secretary-General recommending the establishment of the ICTY emphasised that the Tribunal should apply those rules of international humanitarian law 'which are beyond doubt part of customary law so that the problem of adherence of some but not all States to specific conventions does not arise'.[33] He concluded that the Geneva Conventions of 1949,[34] the Hague Convention (IV),[35] the Genocide Convention[36] and the Nuremberg Charter[37] were 'without doubt' customary international law.[38] Events in Rwanda were not considered to be part of an 'international' armed conflict and thus the jurisdiction of the ICTR for violations of the

---

[28] Established under the UN Convention on the Law of the Sea, 10 December 1982, UN Doc. A/CONF.62/122, reprinted in 21 *International Legal Materials* (1982) 1261, part XV. Only one state, the Philippines, nominated a woman candidate, Ms Haydee Yorac.
[29] See further chapter 3.
[30] Statute of the ICTY, articles 2 and 3; Statute of the ICTR, article 4.
[31] Statute of the ICTY, article 4; Statute of the ICTR, article 2.
[32] Statute of the ICTY, article 5; Statute of the ICTR, article 3.
[33] Report of the Secretary-General, above note 19 at para. 34.
[34] Convention for the Amelioration of the Condition of the Wounded and Sick in Armed Forces in the Field, 75 UNTS 31; Convention for the Amelioration of the Condition of the Wounded, Sick and Shipwrecked Members of Armed Forces at Sea, 75 UNTS 85; Convention Relative to the Treatment of Prisoners of War, 75 UNTS 135; Convention Relative to the Protection of Civilian Persons in Time of War, 75 UNTS 287, 12 August 1949.
[35] Hague Convention on the Regulation of the Laws and Customs of War on Land, 18 October 1907, 36 Stat. 2277, 1 Bevans 631.
[36] Convention on the Prevention and Punishment of the Crime of Genocide, 9 December 1948, 78 UNTS 277.
[37] Charter Annexed to the Agreement for the Establishment of an International Military Tribunal, 8 August 1945, 5 UNTS 251.
[38] Report of the Secretary-General, above note 19 at para. 35. See A. Cassese, 'The status of rebels under the 1977 Geneva protocols on non-international armed conflict', 30 *International and Comparative Law Quarterly* (1981) 416.

laws of war is limited to common article 3 of the four Geneva Conventions, which provides a minimum code of conduct in non-international armed conflict, and the 1977 Additional Protocol II to the Geneva Conventions which applies in such circumstances.[39]

To what extent does international humanitarian law cover rape and other violent acts against women? Despite the long history of rape and sexual assault against women during armed conflicts, and evidence offered to tribunals of such offences, they had not figured prominently in either the legal restraints on warfare nor directly in judgments of war crimes trials. There has long been an understanding of the illegality of violent attacks on non-combatant women,[40] indeed rape was included in the first recorded war crimes trial in 1474.[41] Nevertheless the first Geneva Conventions in 1864 were for the benefit of those who became *hors de combat* through injury or capture, that is members of the fighting forces, who were invariably men.[42] It was not until 1949 that explicit reference was made to rape and sexual assault in the Fourth Geneva Convention – the first Convention directed at the protection of civilians. However, the obligations are limited: states parties are under an obligation to protect women in international armed conflict 'against any attack on their honour, in particular against rape, enforced prostitution, or any form of indecent assault'.[43] This provision does not explicitly prohibit the listed offences but instead presents women as needing protection. It creates a dichotomy between the warrior as protector and the woman as the protected, making the use of force seem justified. By designating rape as a crime against 'honour' rather than one of violence, the provision presents women as male and family property. In 1977 two Protocols

[39] Statute of the ICTR, article 4; Protocol additional to the Geneva Conventions of 12 August 1949, and relating to the Protection of Victims of Non-International Armed Conflicts, 8 June 1977, 1125 UNTS 609, reprinted in 16 *International Legal Materials* (1977) 1391 (Protocol II).

[40] T. Meron, 'Shakespeare's Henry the Fifth and the law of war', 86 *American Journal of International Law* (1992) 1.

[41] K. Askin, *War Crimes against Women: Prosecution in International War Crimes Tribunals* (The Hague, Martinus Nijhoff, 1997) at 202–3.

[42] For a feminist account of humanitarian law see J. Gardam, 'A feminist analysis of certain aspects of international humanitarian law', 12 *Australian Yearbook of International Law* (1992) 265; J. Gardam, 'The law of armed conflict: a gendered perspective', in D. Dallmeyer (ed.), *Reconceiving Reality: Women and International Law* (Washington DC, American Society of International Law, 1993) 171; J. Gardam, 'Gender and non-combatant immunity', 3 *Transnational Law and Contemporary Problems* (1993) 345.

[43] Fourth Geneva Convention, article 27. For a discussion of these and other articles relevant to the protection of women see Y. Khushalani, *Dignity and Honour of Women as Basic and Fundamental Human Rights* (The Hague, Martinus Nijhoff, 1982) chapter 5; F. Krill, 'The protection of women in international humanitarian law', 249 *International Review of the Red Cross* (November–December 1985) 337.

were adopted to update the Geneva Conventions.[44] Protocol I does not refer to the notion of women's honour, but women continue to be portrayed as the objects of special respect and protection.[45] Protocol II, applicable in non-international armed conflicts, omits the language of protection and simply prohibits 'outrages upon personal dignity, in particular humiliating and degrading treatment, rape, enforced prostitution and any form of indecent assault'.[46] This formula identifies rape as a crime against dignity, not as a violent attack upon personal integrity.

Other references to women in the Geneva Conventions emphasise their reproductive, mothering and caring roles. For example Protocol I states:

> Pregnant women and mothers having dependant infants who are arrested, detained or interned for reasons related to the armed conflict, shall have their cases considered with the utmost priority.[47]

Analysis of the thirty-four provisions within the Geneva Conventions that apparently provide safeguards for women in armed conflict indicates that the primary target for protection is children.[48] This reduces the status of women without children and obscures the fact that girls are especially vulnerable to forms of sexual attack. For these reasons Judith Gardam has concluded that international humanitarian law has constructed a gender hierarchy parallel to that found in human rights law that has discounted the interests of women in favour of those of combatants and in the name of the notion of 'military necessity'.[49]

'Grave breaches' of the Geneva Conventions are made subject to universal jurisdiction exercisable in national courts[50] and thus are regarded as the most significant violations of international humanitarian law. Rape, enforced prostitution and sexual assault are not explicitly designated grave breaches. Since the category of grave breaches is defined to include acts 'wilfully causing great suffering or serious injury to body or health',[51] it has been

---

[44] Protocol additional to the Geneva Conventions of 12 August 1949, and relating to the Protection of Victims of International Armed Conflicts, 8 June 1977, 1125 UNTS 3, reprinted in 16 *International Legal Materials* (1977) 1391 (Protocol I); Protocol II, above note 39.

[45] Protocol I, article 76 states that: 'Women shall be the object of special respect and shall be protected in particular against rape, forced prostitution, and any other form of indecent assault.'

[46] Protocol II, article 4(2)(e).

[47] Protocol I, article 76(2).

[48] J. Gardam, 'Women and the law of armed conflict: why the silence?', 46 *International and Comparative Law Quarterly* (1997) 55 at 57. See also J. Kuper, *International Law Concerning Child Civilians in Armed Conflict* (Oxford, Clarendon Press, 1997).

[49] J. Gardam, above note 48.

[50] E.g. Fourth Geneva Convention, article 146.

[51] *Ibid.*, article 147; Statute of the ICTY, article 2(c).

argued that sexual violence falls within the definition.[52] Of course specific inclusion would have foreclosed contrary argument. Protocol I includes among its list of grave breaches 'degrading practices involving outrages on personal dignity based on racial discrimination'[53] but makes no reference to sex discrimination. Although non-grave breaches may nevertheless constitute war crimes, the legal distinction between 'grave' and 'other' breaches may lead to the latter being perceived as less significant and as not meriting enforcement.

The ICC Statute provides that the category of war crimes means grave breaches of the Geneva Conventions and 'other serious violations of the laws and customs applicable in international armed conflict'.[54] The definition of 'other serious violations' includes the commission of rape, sexual slavery, enforced prostitution, forced pregnancy and enforced sterilisation and adds 'any other form of sexual violence also constituting a grave breach of the Geneva Conventions'.[55] This supports an interpretation of specified grave breaches such as torture or inhuman treatment, wilfully causing great suffering, serious injury and unlawful confinement, as including sexual violence.

Common article 3 to the four Geneva Conventions provides a minimum standard of behaviour that applies to both government and non-government forces in some non-international (internal) conflicts.[56] Prohibited actions include violence to life and the person, cruel treatment and torture, and humiliating and degrading treatment. Again, it is not made explicit that forms of sexual violence can fall within these terms. The ICTR Statute, however, does so expressly through the familiar formula of prohibiting 'outrages upon personal dignity, in particular humiliating and degrading treatment, rape, enforced prostitution, and any form of indecent assault'.[57]

The inclusion of crimes committed during non-international armed conflict within the ICC Statute was controversial. In the end, however, common article 3 of the Geneva Conventions was reiterated and supplemented by reference to the 'laws and customs applicable in armed conflict not of an international character'. The enumeration of such offences includes the same

---

[52] The International Committee of the Red Cross took this position as early as 1958. Letter from the Secretary-General addressed to the President of the Security Council, UN Doc. S/1994/1405. See also C. Chinkin, 'Rape and sexual abuse of women in international law', 5 *European Journal of International Law* (1994) 326; T. Meron, 'Rape as a crime under international humanitarian law', 87 *American Journal of International Law* (1993) 424 at 426–7.

[53] Protocol I, article 85(3).

[54] Rome Statute for the ICC, article 8(2)(a) and (b).

[55] *Ibid.*, article 8(2)(b) and (s).

[56] Common article 3 applies to 'armed conflict not of an international character occurring in the territory of one of the High Contracting Parties'. Protocol II extends the protections in non-international armed conflict.

[57] Statute of the ICTR, article 4(e).

list as for international conflict: rape, sexual slavery, enforced prostitution, forced pregnancy, enforced sterilisation and 'any other form of sexual violence also constituting a serious violation of [common] article 3'.[58]

The distinction between international and non-international conflict in humanitarian law has a gendered dimension because it underpins a much more detailed legal regime protecting combatants (men) engaged in international conflicts and considerably weaker legal protection for the civilian population (in which almost all women are located) in times of both international and non-international conflict. The distinction has no basis in the reality of the lives of those caught up in conflict.

Moreover, the technicality of the law requires careful application of laws to the facts. Under the Fourth Geneva Convention, the only persons against whom a grave breach can be committed are those who are 'in the hands of a Party to the conflict or Occupying Power of which they are not nationals'.[59] In the first trial before the ICTY, the *Tadic* case,[60] the limitations of this defining category were made apparent. In the conflict in Bosnia and Herzegovina, there was no 'Party to the conflict or Occupying Power' of a different nationality to the Bosnian Muslim victims, unless the Bosnian Serbs could be considered as agents of the government of the Federal Republic of Yugoslavia (FRY). The Trial Chamber concluded that there was no evidence to support this contention.[61] After the withdrawal of the troops of the FRY from Bosnia and Herzegovina in May 1992, the forces of Republika Srpska were held to be allies of the FRY in attempting to carve out a Greater Serbia from the remnants of Yugoslavia.[62] The acts of the Bosnian Serbs were not considered imputable to the FRY and the victims were not therefore protected persons in the terms of the Geneva Convention. Tadic was accordingly acquitted of grave breaches of the Geneva Conventions.[63] The Appeals Chamber reversed this ruling in July 1999.

Genocide

A second jurisdictional possibility is that rape be considered a form of genocide. The international legal definition of genocide requires:

> an intention to destroy, in whole or in part, a national, ethnical, racial or religious group through the commission of such acts as killing or causing serious bodily or mental harm to members of the group; deliberately inflicting

---

[58] Rome Statute for the ICC, article 8(2)(e)(vi).

[59] Fourth Geneva Convention, article 4.

[60] *Prosecutor v. Dusko Tadic* a/k/a/ Dule, 7 May 1997, IT-94-IT, reprinted in 36 *International Legal Materials* (1997) 908.

[61] T. Meron, 'Classification of armed conflict in the Former Yugoslavia: Nicaragua's fallout', 92 *American Journal of International Law* (1998) 236.

[62] *Prosecutor v. Dusko Tadic*, above note 60 at para. 606.

[63] *Ibid.* at para. 608. Judge McDonald dissented on this point. For the appeal decision see http//www.un.org/icty.

on the group conditions of life calculated to bring about its physical destruction in whole or in part; imposing measures to prevent births within the group; forcibly transferring children of the group to another group.[64]

Although this definition covers sterilisation and forced termination of pregnancy, sexual violence does not appear to fall within the legal notion of genocide.[65] Nevertheless it has been argued that where rape has been carried out on a massive and systematic basis with the intent of destroying the victims' family and community life, of 'cleansing' an area of all other ethnicities by causing mass flight and the birth of children with the rapists' blood, it becomes genocidal.[66] In reviewing the indictments against the Bosnian Serbs, Radovan Karadzic and Ratko Mladic, a Trial Chamber of the ICTY invited the prosecution to broaden the scope of its characterisation of genocide, suggesting that: 'The systematic rape of women . . . is in some cases intended to transmit a new ethnic identity to the child. In other cases humiliation and terror serve to dismember the group.'[67] This characterisation is further supported by the phenomenon of forced detention of women, first for impregnation and subsequently to prevent abortion.[68]

So, too, in Rwanda, it has been contended that rape and sexual brutality in Rwanda was not incidental to the genocide but was an integral part of the aim to eradicate the Tutsi.[69] The NGO, Human Rights Watch, reported that: 'Taken as a whole, the evidence indicates that many rapists expected, consequent to their attacks, that the psychological and physical assault on each Tutsi woman would advance the cause of the eradication of the Tutsi people.'[70] In the *Akayesu* decision in 1998, the ICTR accepted such reasoning. Finding the former Bourgmestre of Taba guilty of genocide, the Tribunal held that sexual violence had been integral to the intended destruction of the Tutsi and that Tutsi women had been systematically raped.[71] It was

[64] Genocide Convention, article II. The Statute of the ICTY, article 4, the Statute of the ICTR, article 2 and the Rome Statute for the ICC, article 6 all repeat this definition.

[65] In its commentary to the Draft Code of Crimes against the Peace and Security of Mankind, adopted by the ILC at its forty-eighth session, UN Doc. A/51/10 (1996), the ILC omits any mention of rape as genocidal in its commentary to article 17 on genocide.

[66] See Preliminary Statement, *Kadic v. Karadzic*, Civil Action No. 43, CN 1163, United States District Court, Southern District of New York; *Kadic v. Karadzic* 70 F. 2d 232 (1995).

[67] Trial Chamber I, *Review of Indictment pursuant to Rule 61, Karadzic and Mladic cases*, 11 July 1996, IT-95-5-R61, IT-95-18-R61, paras 94 and 95.

[68] 'It would seem that the aim of many rapes was enforced impregnation: several witnesses also said that the perpetrators of sexual assault – often soldiers – had been given orders to do so': *ibid.* at para. 64.

[69] *Shattered Lives: Sexual Violence during the Rwandan Genocide and its Aftermath* (New York, Human Rights Watch, 1996) at 34–6.

[70] *Ibid.* at 35.

[71] *Prosecutor v. Jean-Paul Akayesu*, above note 26 at para. 7.8.

sufficient that Akayesu had encouraged the rapes of Tutsi women through his attitude and public utterances, with the required element of intent to destroy in whole or in part the Tutsi people. The Tribunal also held that measures to prevent births within a group can include mental as well as physical pressure where, for example, a person who has been raped subsequently refuses to bear children.[72] In the case brought by Bosnia and Herzegovina against Yugoslavia, the ICJ will have to determine state responsibility (as opposed to individual criminal responsibility) for acts of genocide.[73] Any statement by this Court on the gendered dimensions of genocide would add considerably to the jurisprudence of the *ad hoc* Tribunals and bring these issues within mainstream international law.

Crimes against humanity

A third possible head of jurisdiction applicable to sexual violence in armed conflict is that of crimes against humanity. Crimes against humanity were defined in the Nuremberg Charter as:

> murder, extermination, enslavement, deportation, and other inhumane acts committed against any civilian population before or during the war, or persecutions on political, racial, or religious grounds in execution of or in connection with any crime within the jurisdiction of the Tribunal whether or not in violation of the domestic law of the country where perpetrated.[74]

The four occupying powers in Germany included rape as a crime against humanity in Control Council Law No. 10,[75] and this was followed in the Statute of the ICTY.[76] The 1996 ILC Draft Code of Crimes against the Peace and Security of Mankind also includes 'rape, enforced prostitution and other forms of sexual abuse' as constituting crimes against humanity.[77] In its consideration of persecution as a crime against humanity, the ILC noted that gender-based persecution could be so designated under article 18(e),[78] but decided instead 'to limit the possible grounds for persecution to those contained in existing legal instruments'. Similarly while sex and gender-based discrimination might also fall within article 18(f),[79] the ILC

---

[72] *Ibid.* at para. 6.3.1.

[73] *Application of the Convention on the Prevention and Punishment of the Crime of Genocide* (Bosnia and Herzegovina v. Yugoslavia) Preliminary Objections 1996 ICJ Rep. (Judgment of 11 July).

[74] Charter Annexed to the Agreement for the Establishment of an International Military Tribunal, article 6(c).

[75] Control Council for Germany, Official Gazette, 31 January 1946 at 50, cited in T. Meron, above note 52.

[76] Statute of the ICTY, article 5(g).

[77] Article 18(j).

[78] Article 18(e): persecution on political, racial, religious or ethnic grounds.

[79] Article 18(f): institutionalised discrimination on racial, ethnic or religious grounds involving the violation of fundamental human rights and freedoms and resulting in seriously disadvantaging a part of the population.

noted that it might not necessarily amount to a 'crime against the peace and security of mankind'[80] and again declined to extend the prohibited grounds of institutionalised discrimination to include sex or gender. The ICC Statute does, however, include as a distinct crime against humanity persecution against 'any identifiable group or collectivity' on a number of specified grounds including gender.[81] This definition of persecution could be used in other contexts, for example to facilitate claims of refugee status for women persecuted for failure to conform with societal expectations of appropriate behaviour for women, or violence against women.[82]

The historic association between crimes against humanity and armed conflict was continued in the ICTY Statute.[83] The Appeals Chamber of the ICTY has, however, affirmed that no nexus between crimes against humanity and armed conflict is required by customary international law.[84] In *Tadic* the Trial Chamber clarified the concept of crimes against humanity in a number of other ways significant for trials of sexual attacks. It held that: 'a single act by a perpetrator taken within the context of a widespread or systematic attack against a civilian population entails individual responsibility and an individual perpetrator need not commit numerous offences to be held liable'.[85] Thus each perpetrator of rape in the context of a mass attack can be held guilty of a crime against humanity. Further, the requirement that the offences be committed in a 'systematic or organised' fashion can be inferred from the nature of the crimes and can be satisfied by either a state policy or that of non-state forces, including terrorist groups or organisations.[86] The ICTR Statute extends the concept of crimes against humanity to: 'Crimes . . . committed as part of a widespread or systematic attack against any civilian population on national, political, ethnic, racial or religious grounds.'[87] The ICC Statute uses similar language to the ICTR Statute on this issue and does not require the existence of armed conflict as a threshold requirement for crimes against humanity. It also defines the term 'attack

---

[80] On the complexities of defining 'crimes against the peace and security of mankind' separately from the jurisdiction of an international criminal court see J. Allain and J. Jones, 'A patchwork of norms: a commentary on the 1996 Draft Code of Crimes against the Peace and Security of Mankind', 8 *European Journal of International Law* (1997) 100.

[81] Rome Statute for the ICC, article 7(1)(h).

[82] Convention Relating to the Status of Refugees 28 July 1951, 189 UNTS 150. See *R. V. Immigration Appeal Tribunal*, ex parte *Shah* [1999] 2 All ER 545.

[83] Statute of the ICTY, article 5.

[84] *Decision on Defence Motion for Interlocutory Appeal on Jurisdiction, Tadic Case*, 2 October 1995, IT-94-1-T. The ILC Draft Code of Crimes against the Peace and Security of Mankind, article 18, also affirms that there is no requirement that the acts be committed in time of war.

[85] *Prosecutor v. Dusko Tadic*, above note 60 at para. 649.

[86] *Ibid.*

[87] Statute of the ICTR, article 3.

against any civilian population' as the commission of acts 'pursuant to or in furtherance of a State or organizational policy'.[88]

Although the 'new' international criminal law developed in the 1990s has paid increased attention to the situation of women in times of conflict, the three heads of jurisdiction of the two *ad hoc* Tribunals, international humanitarian law, genocide and crimes against humanity, have obscured rape and other violent crimes against women. The earlier omission of rape from the formal definition of 'grave breaches' of international humanitarian law allowed the perception that it is only where rape reaches the systematic or widespread level required for crimes against humanity that it becomes punishable as an international crime. The emphasis in genocide is on the group defined in ethnic, racial or religious terms and in crimes against humanity on the civilian population rather than on crimes against women. The *ad hoc* Tribunals have shown considerable sensitivity to the situation of women, but they have been constrained by the language of their statutes. The ICC Statute makes some advances in this respect. For example, it includes rape, sexual slavery and other forms of sexual violence in the enumeration of serious violations of the laws and customs of war and separates them from outrages on personal dignity, humiliating and degrading treatment.[89] The ICC Statute also specifically includes the same offences as crimes against humanity as well as defining forms of sexual violence as war crimes in armed conflict not of an international character.[90] At the same time, the Statute does not expressly state that rape and sexual violence can also constitute other crimes within the Court's jurisdiction, such as torture.

Prosecution policies and judicial interpretation

The continuing lack of clarity in the Tribunals' statutes made the form of indictments critical for the evolution of normative principles on rape and sexual violence. Investigations of crimes against women in the former Yugoslavia and in Rwanda have raised numerous practical and legal problems. The former include the dispersal of victims and witnesses across the globe; the unwillingness of women to speak of crimes committed against them through humiliation, shame, fear of public or family ostracism or fear of reprisal; the constant demand for accounts of their experiences from media, NGOs, medical and support agencies, and, eventually, official investigators; the passage of time and the desire not to relive such atrocities; and the feeling of some victims that rape and sexual assault were not as devastating as the loss of community, home and possessions, and the violent deaths or disappearances of family members. Legal problems include the articulation

[88] Rome Statute for the ICC, article 7(2)(a).
[89] *Ibid.*, article 8(2)(b)(xxi) and (xii).
[90] *Ibid.*, article 8(2)(c)(e)(vi).

of offences under the appropriate heads of jurisdiction and assembling sufficient admissible evidence for conviction.

Despite the reference in the Fourth Geneva Convention, there was no international law definition of rape.[91] In first charging rape, the prosecution for the ICTY could have relied upon the Yugoslav criminal law that was applicable to all those involved. It would, however, have been undesirable that an international tribunal should rely on specific local laws in the development of its jurisprudence on an international criminal law and the prosecution has emphasised elements of the prohibited conduct rather than simply asserting rape.[92] Thus it has indicted the crime of 'forcible sexual penetration of a person' by an accused, or by a third person under the control of the accused.[93] This formulation allows consideration of the elements of the offence without importing understandings of rape from any particular municipal legal system. It also emphasises the elements of violence and force. The terminology is broad enough to cover any form of penetration (for example by weapons) and to include male victims of sexual abuse. Such 'deconstruction' of the elements of the crime focuses on the conduct of the accused and more readily enables it to be understood as encompassing aspects of other crimes.[94] The ICTY prosecution has accordingly included counts of sexual assault in some innovative indictments, notably those issued in June 1996.[95] In its review of the indictment in the *Nikolic* case, the Trial Chamber considered that sexual assaults of women forcibly detained at Susica camp could come within the definition of torture,[96] which was subsequently confirmed by the judgments in the *Celebici* camp cases[97] and *Furundzija*,[98] the first war crimes prosecution in which rape and sexual assault was the single charge.

[91] 'No definition of rape can be found in international law.' *Prosecutor v. Anto Furundzija*, Judgment of 10 December 1998, IT-95-17/1-T, at para. 175.

[92] P. Viseur-Sellers, 'The *ad hoc* tribunals' response to gender based crimes', paper prepared for UN Expert Group meeting on Gender-based Persecution, Toronto, Canada, November 1997.

[93] *Gagovic & Others ('Foca')* Indictment, confirmed 26 June 1996, IT-96-23-I.

[94] Viseur-Sellers has argued that this form of 'deconstruction' removes fixation on rape by replacing it with a recognition of sexually violent conduct as evidence of a range of violations of international humanitarian law. P. Viseur-Sellers, above note 92.

[95] The *Foca* Indictment, above note 93, includes charges of crimes against women as crimes against humanity, enslavement under article 5(c), torture under article 5(f), rape under article 5(g) and grave breaches of the Geneva Conventions and violations of the laws and customs of war.

[96] Trial Chamber I, *Review of Indictment pursuant to Rule 61, Nikolic case*, IT-95-2-R61.

[97] Trial Chamber II ruled that 'whenever rape and other forms of sexual violence meet the aforementioned criteria, then they shall constitute torture, in the same manner as any other acts that meet this criteria'. *Prosecutor v. Delalic and Others*, Judgment of 16 November 1998, IT-96-21-T, at para. 496.

[98] *Prosecutor v. Anto Furundzija*, above note 91 at para. 171.

The ICTR was slower to indict mass rapes, the organised sexual mutilation of Tutsi women and their deliberate impregnation by Hutus.[99] NGOs became concerned that crimes against women were deemed insignificant when viewed against the overall Rwanda genocide rather than understood as gender-specific manifestations of that crime.[100] Indeed in *Akayesu* the first evidence of mass rape was introduced spontaneously by a witness, although the charge had not been included in the indictments. It was pursued by the only woman judge on the ICTR, Judge Pillay, who was a member of the Trial Chamber. The indictments were then amended[101] and evidence heard of mutilations, rapes and sexual violence that led to death.[102] In *Akayesu* the Trial Chamber asserted that rape is a form of aggression the central components of which cannot be captured by a 'mechanical description' of objects and body parts.[103] It commented upon the lack of international legal definition of rape and offered its own: rape is 'a physical invasion of a sexual nature, committed on a person under circumstances which are coercive'. The Chamber continued: 'Sexual violence, including rape, is not limited to physical invasion of the human body and may include acts which do not involve penetration or even physical contact', such as intimidation and duress. The ICTY Trial Chamber in *Furundzija* derived the objective elements of rape from general principles of law of the major legal systems of the globe. It emphasised that the 'prohibition embraces all serious abuses of a sexual nature inflicted upon the physical and moral integrity of a person by means of coercion, threat of force or intimidation in a way that is degrading and humiliating for the victim's dignity'.[104] The Tribunal affirmed that rape can also be a crime distinct from torture in that it may 'amount to a grave breach of the Geneva Conventions, a violation of the laws or customs of

---

[99] The Report on the Situation of Human Rights in Rwanda submitted by Mr Rene Degni-Segui, Special Rapporteur of the Commission on Human Rights, UN Doc. E/CN.4/1996/68, 29 January 1996, concluded that 'rape was the rule and its absence the exception'.

[100] *Amicus* brief regarding rape in Rwanda, respecting amendment of the indictment and supplementation of the evidence to ensure the prosecution of rape and other sexual violence within the competence of the Tribunal, submitted by J. Birenbaum and L. Wyndels, Working Group on Engendering the Rwandan Criminal Tribunal, R. Copelon, International Women's Human Rights Law Clinic and J. Green, Center for Constitutional Rights, 1997.

[101] In June 1997 the prosecutor made a motion to amend the indictment in the case of Jean-Paul Akayesu to include charges of rape as genocide.

[102] Similarly in *Kayeshima*, evidence of rape and sexual mutilation during the genocide was presented: *Prosecutor v. Kayeshima* ICTR 95-1-T-8. See P. Viseur-Sellers, 'Gender-based crimes in humanitarian law', in *Contemporary International Law Issues: New Forms, New Applications* (The Hague, Nederlandse Vereniging voor Internationaal Recht, 1997) 137 at 150.

[103] *Prosecutor v. Jean-Paul Akayesu*, above note 26 at paras 6.4 and 7.7.

[104] *Prosecutor v. Anto Furundzija*, above note 91 at paras 174 to 186.

war'[105] and is contrary to customary international law.[106] Thus through an evolutionary process involving NGO pressure and prosecutorial and judicial interpretation, an international legal understanding of the meaning and jurisdictional basis of rape and sexual assault is emerging.

Rules of procedure and evidence

The procedural rules used in criminal trials can be as significant as the substantive laws applied. The UN Secretary-General acknowledged this explicitly in the context of women by proposing that 'protective' measures be included in the Rules of Procedure and Evidence of the ICTY,[107] 'especially in cases of rape or sexual assault'.[108] A number of Rules accordingly provide for the protection of victims and witnesses in proceedings before Trial Chambers.[109] Rule 96 addresses the situation faced by victims of rape and sexual assault in the following terms:[110] In cases of sexual assault:

(i)   . . . no corroboration of the victim's testimony shall be required;
(ii)   consent shall not be allowed as a defence if the victim (a) has been subjected to or threatened with or has had reason to fear violence, duress, detention or psychological oppression, or (b) reasonably believed that if the victim did not submit, another might be so subjected . . .
(iii)   before evidence of the victim's consent is admitted, the accused shall satisfy the Trial Chamber *in camera* that the evidence is relevant and credible;
(iv)   prior sexual conduct of the victim shall not be admitted in evidence.

Rule 96 is significant in its response to many criticisms of treatment of rape victims in national legal systems. First, its elimination of the need for corroboration of a victim's testimony indicates an understanding of both the facts of rape and its psychological impact. There are many reasons why survivors may be unable to produce corroborating evidence, including silence because of fear of retribution or rejection by their families and reluctance

---

[105] *Ibid.* at para. 172.

[106] *Ibid.* at para. 168.

[107] The Rules of Procedure and Evidence were drawn up by the Judges of the ICTY. In accordance with the Statute of the ICTR, article 14, the Judges of the ICTR adopted similar Rules on 29 June 1995. The Rules relied on in this section are Rules of Procedure and Evidence, ICTY, IT/32/Rev.14, 17 December 1998; Rules of Procedure and Evidence, ICTR, 8 June 1998.

[108] Report of the Secretary-General, above note 19 at para. 108.

[109] Rules of Procedure and Evidence, rule 75. See also rules 69, 79 and 89.

[110] For an analysis of the drafting history of rule 96 see K. Fitzgerald, 'Problems of prosecution and adjudication of rape and other sexual assaults under international law', 8 *European Journal of International Law* (1997) 638.

to seek medical assistance, even if available.[111] Second, it restricts the availability of consent as a defence to rape. Many domestic rape trials turn on whether there was consent to intercourse, especially where the alleged attacker was known to the victim. Rule 96 recognises that the notion of consent is of less importance in times of armed conflict and approaches the question of consent from the standpoint of the victim. It is her reasonable belief of the consequences if she does not submit that is determinative, not that of the accused as to her consent. An earlier version of rule 96 had excluded the defence of consent altogether,[112] acknowledging the sexually coercive circumstances of armed conflict. It is not clear that the rule in its present form will entirely prevent the trauma experienced by women alleging rape through humiliating and aggressive questioning on their prior sexual conduct by defence counsel determined to present them as 'immoral' women and as therefore unreliable witnesses.[113]

The apparent sensitivity of the Rules of Procedure to the situation of victims of rape was thrown into doubt by the interruption to the trial in the *Furundzija* case before the ICTY in 1998.[114] The credibility of evidence of rape by a single witness, the victim 'A', was challenged by the defence after the trial had ended. The defence alleged that the prosecutor had failed to reveal evidence that the victim had received counselling and treatment for the psychological trauma she had suffered and that this condition and treatment could affect A's reliability with respect to the crimes she alleged had been committed against her.[115] The prosecution argued that the documents relating to the treatment A had undergone were irrelevant to witness A's ability to testify accurately, that this case was no different from other cases of rape, and that the defence was overstating the importance of this 'new' material.[116] The Trial Chamber's initial response was to categorise as 'serious misconduct' the prosecution's failure to disclose the counselling treatment and to reopen the case to give the defence the opportunity to recall and cross-examine witnesses on the medical, psychological or psychiatric treatment received by the victim. The Trial Chamber also ordered the prosecution to disclose any documents relating to such treatment

---

[111] See Preliminary Report submitted by the Special Rapporteur on Violence against Women, its Causes and Consequences, Ms Radhika Coomaraswamy, in accordance with Commission on Human Rights Resolution 1994/45, 22 November 1994, UN Doc. E/CN.4/1995/42, para. 281.

[112] K. Fitzgerald, above note 110 at 640–1.

[113] E.g. J. Scutt, *Women and the Law* (Sydney, Law Book Co. Ltd, 1990) at 475–7.

[114] *Prosecutor v. Anto Furundzija*, above note 91.

[115] *Prosecutor v. Anto Furundzija, Defendant's Motion to Strike the Testimony of Witness A Due to Prosecutorial Misconduct, or in the Event of a Conviction a New Trial*, 9 July 1998. ICTY-95-17/1-T10.

[116] *Prosecutor v. Anto Furundzija, Prosecutor's response to Defence Motion to Strike Testimony of Witness A or Order a New Trial*, 13 July 1998. ICTY-95-17/1-T10.

after May 1993.[117] In its conviction of the accused on 10 December 1998, the Trial Chamber upheld the witness's recollection of events and affirmed that 'there is no reason why a person with PTSD [post-traumatic stress syndrome] cannot be a perfectly reliable witness'.[118] Nevertheless the re-opening of the case indicates the vulnerable position of women who give evidence of sexual violence and the possibility of impugning their credibility at trial.[119]

Other issues of protection of victims and witnesses, especially in cases of sexual assault, have emerged in the work of the *ad hoc* tribunals. For example, in trial motions in the *Tadic* case before the ICTY,[120] the prosecution sought confidentiality for certain witnesses from press and media, protection from the potential trauma of having to confront the accused in open court, and anonymity, including from the accused, for as long as possible, for particular witnesses. In its majority decision, the Trial Chamber held that certain factors can weigh against public hearings and even against the accused knowing the identity of all witnesses. The decision emphasised the overriding preference for a public trial, especially in the light of the Tribunal's educative function. The crucial question was ensuring a fair trial in accordance with the Statute of the Tribunal and relevant human rights guarantees.[121]

The Statute provides that:

> the accused shall be entitled to the following minimum guarantees, in full equality:
> (e) To examine or have examined, the witnesses against him and to obtain the attendance and examination of witnesses . . . under the same conditions as witnesses against him.[122]

The Trial Chamber held that this guarantee must be balanced against other interests including those of the victim (for example victims' rights to security and privacy) and of the international community in the fair administration

---

[117] *Prosecutor v. Anto Furundzija, Decision on Defendant's Motion to Strike the Testimony of Witness A Due to Prosecutorial Misconduct, or in the Event of a Conviction a New Trial*, 16 July 1998.

[118] *Prosecutor v. Anto Furundzija*, above note 91 at para. 109.

[119] On 3 February 1999 the defence filed a motion to quash the decision and to request a retrial on the basis that Judge Mumba, the presiding judge, had been active in promoting the acceptance of rape as a violation of the laws of war and of women's human rights in general.

[120] See *Prosecutor v. Dusko Tadic, Decision on the Prosecutor's Motion Requesting Protective Measures for Victims and Witnesses*, 10 August 1995, IT-94-I-T, para. 46 on the need to minimise the trauma of trial for victims of sexual assault.

[121] The rights of the accused to a fair trial listed in the Statute of the ICTY, article 21, closely follow the European Convention for the Protection of Human Rights and Fundamental Freedoms, Rome, 4 November 1950, 213 UNTS 221, article 6 and ICCPR, article 14.

[122] Statute of the ICTY, article 21(e).

of criminal justice.[123] The Chamber also referred to the Tribunal's unique legal framework, especially its explicit mandate to protect witnesses and victims in the context of a continuing conflict that had caused 'terror and anguish' to the civilian population.[124] This mandate was seen to distinguish the Statute from human rights treaties that contain no such affirmative obligation and focus solely upon the rights of the accused. The Chamber drew upon national jurisprudence and that of the institutions of the European Convention on Human Rights to formulate guidelines on witness anonymity.[125] It held that for anonymity to be accorded there must be a real fear for the safety of victims and witnesses; the witness's evidence must constitute an important part of the case; there must be no evidence of unreliability; the Tribunal must be unable to supply adequate witness protection; and the measures must be strictly necessary to justify the unavoidable prejudice to the accused. Judge Stephen, dissenting, considered that an accused (who has no choice but to appear before the Tribunal) must receive absolute guarantees of fairness, including the right to confront witnesses whose participation is voluntary.[126] A Trial Chamber in the subsequent *Blaskic* case approved Judge Stephen's position,[127] but did not entirely rule out the possibility of anonymity where the prosecutor had provided proof of the kind of factors enumerated in the *Tadic* case.

The *Tadic* guidelines do not envisage anonymity for all, or even most, witnesses and it is clear that it will only be exceptionally accorded. They provide for the weighing of relevant factors in each individual application. The importance of the issue of identity will also vary. For example in a 'chain of command' case where the defendant was not present during the commission of offences, the identity of those testifying is less important than where the accused is the alleged perpetrator. In 'bystander' cases the identity of witnesses is happenstance. In many situations of rape, the identity of the victims is quite irrelevant. Women have told of being taken in turn, or arbitrarily 'selected' for sexual abuse. In these circumstances it is hard to understand why knowledge of the identity of a victim is essential to

---

[123] *Prosecutor v. Dusko Tadic, Decision on the Prosecutor's Motion Requesting Protective Measures for Victims and Witnesses*, above note 120 at para. 53. 'A fair trial means not only fair treatment to the defendant but also to the prosecution and witnesses . . . it is in the public interest for the International Tribunal to discharge its obligation to protect victims and witnesses . . .': *ibid.* at para. 56.

[124] Statute of the ICTY, article 22; rule 69 in Part Five, Pre-trial Proceedings and rule 75, in Part Six, Proceedings before Trial Chambers.

[125] *Prosecutor v. Dusko Tadic, Decision on the Prosecutor's Motion Requesting Protective Measures for Victims and Witnesses*, above note 120 at para. 77.

[126] N. Stephen, 'Toward transnational norms of criminal procedure: emerging issues of defendants' rights', in *Contemporary International Law Issues: New Forms, New Applications*, above note 102 at 1, 10.

[127] *Prosecutor v. Blaskic, Decision on the Application of the Prosecutor Requesting Protective Measures for Victims and Witnesses*, 5 November 1996, IT-95-I4-T.

the prosecution case. The Trial Chamber in *Tadic* also prescribed procedural safeguards for accused persons confronted by anonymous witnesses.[128] The judges must know each witness's identity and must be able to observe the demeanour of the witnesses to assess the reliability of testimony. The defence must be given ample opportunity to question the witness on issues unrelated to identity and current whereabouts and anonymity is not permanent, but lasts only as long as there is reason to fear for the witness's security.[129]

The majority ruling of the Trial Chamber in the *Tadic* case on anonymity provoked a very critical response from some international lawyers on the grounds that it would deny accused persons a fair trial and may lead to the conviction of accused persons on the basis of tainted evidence.[130] It has been argued that the long-fought-for rights of the accused must not be compromised in favour of the recently conceived notion of victims' rights that has not been carefully articulated.[131] The formulation of victims' rights through case law rather than by constitutional or statutory means has also been challenged.[132] The right to a fair trial is typically interpreted as a right of an accused to procedural safeguards to prevent an unjust conviction. It must be balanced against the right of victims of crime to be able to recount their experiences without intimidation. Giving priority to the right to a fair trial over other rights in the context of sexual violence illustrates the claim that human rights law has been predicated upon the concerns of men and that it fails to take account of the life experiences of women.[133]

[128] The ECHR considered similar issues in *Kostovski v. The Netherlands* 166 ECHR (ser. A) 3 (1989). In *Doorson v. The Netherlands*, Judgment of 26 March 1996 (i.e. after the *Tadic Protective Measures* decision) 22 EHRR 330 (1996), the ECHR held that the conviction of a drug dealer secured largely on the basis of anonymous evidence did not breach the European Convention on Human Rights, article 6. The difficulty of reconciling the conflicting interests is illustrated by the fact that the issue came again before the European Court in *Van Mechelen and Others v. The Netherlands* (Case No. 55/1996/674/861–4), Judgment of 23 April 1997, 25 EHRR 647 (1998).

[129] *Prosecutor v. Dusko Tadic, Decision on the Prosecutor's Motion Requesting Protective Measures for Victims and Witnesses*, above note 120 at para. 71. In *Decision on the Prosecutor's Motion to Withdraw Protective Measures for Witness K*, 12 November 1996, the Chamber withdrew anonymity after witness K indicated her willingness to testify in open court. In *Decision on the Prosecutor's Motion to Withdraw Protective Measures for Witness L*, 5 December 1996, protective measures were withdrawn from witness L.

[130] M. Leigh, 'The Yugoslav Tribunal: use of unnamed witnesses against accused', 90 *American Journal of International Law* (1996) 235; M. Leigh, 'Witness anonymity is inconsistent with due process', 91 *American Journal of International Law* (1997) 80. Compare C. Chinkin, 'Due process and witness anonymity', 91 *American Journal of International Law* (1997) 75; O. Swaak-Goldman, 'The ICTY and the right to a fair trial: a critique of the critics', 10 *Leiden Journal of International Law* (1997) 215.

[131] M. Leigh, 'Witness anonymity is inconsistent with due process', above note 130 at 83.

[132] *Ibid.*

[133] See chapter 7.

Concerns about persuading witnesses to testify are not restricted to sexual assault trials, nor to international tribunals. The Special Rapporteur on Violence against Women has found that women are unwilling to testify in cases of trafficking and prostitution for fear of reprisals against them and their families.[134] She has shown how such trafficking has acquired the character of organised crime that makes women very reluctant to testify.[135] Protective measures, together with safeguards for the accused, are indispensable for the curtailment of crimes that prevent witnesses from enjoying their rights to liberty, movement and physical integrity.

The ICC Statute sets out the entitlement of the accused to a fair trial.[136] It also states that the Court 'shall take appropriate measures to protect the safety, physical and psychological well-being, dignity and privacy of victims and witnesses'.[137] The same provision specifies that the Court shall have regard to all relevant factors, including gender and the nature of the crime, specifically 'sexual or gender violence'. Although this article is more detailed than the parallel provision of the Statute of the ICTY,[138] it does not refer directly to the possibility of anonymity of witnesses. The ICC Statute allows the Prosecutor to withhold evidence 'for the purposes of any proceedings conducted prior to the commencement of the trial' where disclosure may gravely endanger witnesses or their families.[139] This provision, however, is limited to pre-trial procedures and measures taken under it must not be 'prejudicial to or inconsistent with the rights of the accused', a formulation that does not require the accused's rights to be balanced against protective measures for witnesses. It remains to be seen whether the Rules of Procedure and Evidence clarify the position,[140] and continue the approach of the *ad hoc* Tribunals to provide some procedural protections to witnesses. According anonymity to witnesses has been strongly opposed in the context of the ICC, including by major human rights NGOs.[141] However, it is clear that alternatives to witness anonymity, such as witness protection programmes, are not adequate to protect a woman who has been raped from rejection by her own family.

---

[134] Report on the mission of the Special Rapporteur to Poland on the issue of trafficking and forced prostitution of women (24 May to 1 June 1996), UN Doc. E/CN.4/1997/47/Add. 1, 10 December 1996, paras 86 to 88.

[135] *Ibid.* at 59.

[136] Rome Statute for the ICC, article 67.

[137] *Ibid.*, article 68.

[138] Statute of the ICTY, article 22.

[139] Rome Statute for the ICC, article 68(5).

[140] The Rules of Procedure and Evidence will be drafted by states, not the judges as was the case with the ICTY. They will enter into force upon adoption by a two thirds majority of the members of the Assembly of States Parties, Rome Statute for the ICC, article 51.

[141] See Amnesty International, 'The International Criminal Court: Ensuring an effective role for victims', Memorandum for the Paris Seminar, April 1999, AI Index IOR 40/06/99 (London, 1999) at 19–25.

Has international criminal law been transformed?

The jurisdiction and emerging jurisprudence of the *ad hoc* Tribunals suggest that the silence about the suffering of women in all forms of armed conflict has been broken. Other developments in international criminal law reinforce this perception. For example, the extent of sexual slavery practised by the Japanese military during World War II has been exposed, and to some limited extent, addressed.[142] Rape in armed conflict was declared a violation of human rights law by both the World Conference on Human Rights[143] and the Fourth World Conference on Women.[144] The exercise of civil jurisdiction by United States courts over violations of the law of nations, regardless of the location of the commission of the offences or the nationality of the victim or the accused,[145] has been extended to acts of sexual violence in armed conflict against women.[146] In practical terms the default judgment entered against Radovan Karadzic inhibits his ability to enter the United States and provides some compensation for the inability of the ICTY to exercise jurisdiction over him.[147]

At the regional level, the decision of the Inter-American Commission of Human Rights in *Mejia Egocheaga v. Peru* is significant.[148] Raquel Mejia was raped by soldiers in Peru after they had abducted her husband, a known political activist. When she learned of her husband's death, Mejia filed criminal charges in Peru but, fearing reprisal, did not mention the rape. Some years later, after receiving political asylum in Sweden, Mejia lodged a petition with the Inter-American Commission on Human Rights alleging violations of her rights, including that of freedom from torture, to private life and the duty of the state to guarantee the exercise of the Inter-American Convention on Human Rights.[149] The Commission made a number of important statements with respect to the allegations of rape. First, the facts as alleged by Mejia were presumed to be true, although she had not reported

---

[142] U. Dolgopol, 'Women's voices, women's pain', 17 *Human Rights Quarterly* (1995) 127; G. Hicks, *The Comfort Women* (St Leonards, Allen & Unwin, 1995).

[143] World Conference on Human Rights, Vienna Declaration and Programme of Action, 25 June 1993, UN Doc. A/CONF. 157/23, reprinted in 32 *International Legal Materials* (1993) 1661, II, 38.

[144] Fourth World Conference on Women, Declaration and Platform for Action, 15 September 1995, UN Doc. A/CONF. 177/20, reprinted in 35 *International Legal Materials* (1996) 401 (Beijing Platform for Action), para. 145(d) and (e).

[145] Such jurisdiction was first established in *Filartiga v. Pena-Irala* 630 F. 2d 876 (1980).

[146] *Kadic v. Karadzic* 70 F. 2d 232 (2d Cir. 1995).

[147] Karadzic, along with Ratko Mladic, has been indicted by the ICTY under rule 61 but as of December 1999 has not been arrested: *Karadzic and Mladic* IT-95-5-R 61; IT-95-18-R 61.

[148] *Mejia Egocheaga v. Peru* (1996) 1 Butterworths Human Rights Cases 229.

[149] American Convention on Human Rights, 22 November 1969, reprinted in 9 *International Legal Materials* (1970) 673, articles 1(1), 5,8, 11 and 25.

rape immediately after its occurrence and there was no corroborating evidence. The Commission accepted that there was strong circumstantial evidence of the responsibility of Peruvian army troops. The rapist was wearing Peruvian army fatigues and was in the company of soldiers. The petitioner was living in an area under emergency rule where the military commonly perpetrated numerous human rights violations.[150] Her allegations were supported by the abundant information contained in reports of inter-governmental organisations and NGOs of rapes by security forces in Peru as part of their campaign to intimidate, humiliate and punish civilians suspected of collaborating with insurgents. Such rapes were committed with impunity and the Commission noted that there were no effective domestic remedies within Peru for the impartial investigation and prosecution of allegations of sexual abuse by members of the security forces. Accordingly Mejia's omission to report the offences did not amount to a failure to seek domestic remedies. Second, the Commission affirmed that:

> Current international law establishes that sexual assault committed by members of security forces, whether as a result of a deliberate practice promoted by the state or as a result of failure by the state to prevent the occurrence of this crime, constitutes a violation of the victim's human rights, especially the right to physical and mental integrity.[151]

The Commission also applied article 27 of the Fourth Geneva Convention and article 76 of Protocol I to support its pronouncement that 'any act of rape committed individually constitutes a war crime'. It referred to the declaration of the International Committee of the Red Cross that the 'serious offence' of deliberately causing great suffering includes sexual abuse. In the context of non-international armed conflict, common article 3 of the Geneva Conventions and article 49(2) of Protocol II include the prohibition of rape and other sexual abuse 'insofar as they are the outcome of harm deliberately influenced (sic) on a person'.[152] The Commission found that rape can constitute torture under the Geneva Conventions as well as coming within article 5 of the Inter-American Convention. It emphasised that 'rape is a physical and mental abuse that is perpetrated as a result of an act of violence'.[153] It is also a method of psychological torture through the humiliation, victimisation and fear of public ostracism that are inflicted. The purposive element of torture is satisfied by the use of rape for personal punishment and intimidation. The facts did not involve the 'traditional' elements of torture, detention or interrogation, but the situation where women

---

[150] *Mejia Egocheaga*, above note 148 at 245.

[151] *Ibid.* at 251.

[152] *Ibid.* at 252, citing Y. Sandoz, C. Swinarski and B. Zimmerman (eds), *ICRC Commentary on the Additional Protocols of 8 June 1977 to the Geneva Conventions of 12 August 1949* (Geneva, Martinus Nijhoff Publishers, 1987) 1375.

[153] *Mejia Egocheaga*, above note 148 at 253.

who themselves have played no political role are singled out because of their association with a known (or suspected) activist. A Human Rights Watch report with respect to Peru found that women may become subject to abuse from both government and anti-government forces.[154] In the *Egocheaga* case, the Commission accepted that the deliberate outrage to dignity that is caused by rape makes it a violation of the concept of private life within article 11 of the Inter-American Convention. Finally, it addressed remedies. It recommended to the government that it conduct a full investigation into the sexual abuse of Raquel Mejia in order to identify and punish the perpetrators in accordance with national law, and to pay her fair compensation.

The assertion that rape committed by unidentified members of the security forces constitutes torture attributable to the state is comparable with the indictments issued by the ICTY in the '*Foca*' case.[155] A Trial Chamber of the ICTY has also accepted that 'rape and other forms of sexual assault inflicted on women . . . may fall within the definition of torture'.[156] Taken together, these statements provide evidence of an understanding of violations of international humanitarian law and human rights that incorporate the experiences of women. The collapsing of the conceptual boundaries between the two categories of law also takes account of experiences that do not differentiate between international armed conflict, internal conflict and 'normal' conditions.

The ECHR has also contributed to the developing jurisprudence. In *Aydin v. Turkey*[157] the Court held that rape in detention by a state official is an especially grave and abhorrent form of ill-treatment that causes deep psychological scars. The accumulation of physical and mental violence suffered by the petitioner in the case and 'the especially cruel act of rape to which she was subjected' constituted torture contrary to the European Convention on Human Rights.[158] The Court also considered the responsibility of the state with respect to investigation. In this case the allegations had not been treated seriously. There had been no attempt to locate witnesses, nor to seek corroboration. The medical examination was inconsistent with the 'requirements of a fair and effective' investigation of rape in custody and had been directed more at ascertaining whether the complainant was a virgin than determining whether she had been raped. The Court required that a person alleging rape be examined 'with all appropriate sensitivity by medical professionals with particular experience in the area and whose independence is not circumscribed by instructions given to the prosecuting authority as to

---

[154] *Untold Terror: Violence against Women in Peru's Armed Conflict* (New York, Human Rights, 1992).

[155] Above note 93.

[156] Trial Chamber I, *Review of Indictment pursuant to Rule 61, Nikolic case*, 20 October 1995, IT-95-2-R61, para. 33.

[157] *Aydin v. Turkey* (1997) 3 Butterworths Human Rights Cases 300.

[158] *Ibid.* at paras 83 to 87.

the scope of the examination.'[159] These defects in the investigation were held to violate the European Convention.[160]

All these developments suggest that the international legal system has responded well in taking women's lives into account in the context of international criminal law. In some ways, however, the response has been very limited. Although the agreement for a permanent ICC is a response to the criticism of selectivity with respect to the *ad hoc* Tribunals, there are still shortcomings. For example, in the context of the ICC, jurisdiction over war crimes is intended particularly for crimes committed as 'part of a plan or policy or as part of a large-scale commission' of offences.[161] Although rapes and sexual violence in the former Yugoslavia have been perceived in such terms, this may not always be the case. There is a tendency to regard the sexual abuse in the former Yugoslavia as exceptional and not as a regularly occurring aspect of conflict. The ICC Statute defines enslavement as a crime against humanity to include the exercise of powers of ownership 'in the course of trafficking in persons, in particular women and children'. This appears to be a useful provision with which to combat the global dimensions of organised trafficking in women,[162] but it is again limited by the requirement that it be part of a 'widespread or systematic attack directed against any civilian population'. There is no general understanding of trafficking of persons as a crime against humanity.

Pressure from the Vatican and some Arab states during the drafting of the ICC Statute limited the recognition of women's experiences. For example, the final text places 'forced pregnancy' as a crime against humanity in the context of ethnic cleansing by defining it as the 'unlawful confinement of a woman made forcibly pregnant, with the intent of affecting the ethnic composition of the population or carrying out other grave violations of international law'.[163] National laws relating to pregnancy are expressly unaffected by this provision. The definition would not cover, for example, women who are forcibly 'married' and impregnated, or who are pregnant after rape and denied abortions under national laws.

Another limitation of the international legal system is the adequacy of international legal remedies for crimes involving sexual violence. Establishment of war crimes tribunals are a first step that need to be accompanied by long-term, financial and practical assistance such as medical care, shelter, support, counselling, resettlement and retraining. The focus of the *ad hoc*

---

[159] *Ibid.* at paras 103 to 109.
[160] Article 13.
[161] Rome Statute for the ICC, article 8(1).
[162] The Special Rapporteur on Violence against Women has described the epidemic proportions of trafficking in women and children in Central and Eastern Europe in the 1990s: Report on the mission of the Special Rapporteur to Poland, above note 134 at para. 44.
[163] Rome Statute for the ICC, article 7(2)(f).

war crimes Tribunals has been on punishing the wrongdoers, not on providing compensation and support to those who have suffered. The Rules of both Tribunals provide for claims of compensation through national courts,[164] but as at the end of 1998 there have been no such claims. The ICC Statute provides that the Court shall establish principles for reparations for victims, 'including restitution, compensation and rehabilitation'.[165] An order may be made to this effect against a convicted person and an order for reparations against the Trust Fund established by the Statute.[166]

Violence against women in armed conflict and in peacetime conditions are not distinct phenomena but form part of the same spectrum of behaviour. They are both the product of systemic relations of male power and domination. The focus on the systematic offences in the former Yugoslavia and Rwanda, and the failure to make explicit that any rape committed in armed conflict is a war crime, entails the risk of creating the assumption that 'lesser' rapes may still be committed with impunity. The ideal of justice animating the 'new' international criminal law rests on an understanding of peace and order obtained through force.[167] War crimes trials allow a return to the 'order' of the *status quo*, but this public order is dependent both on the acceptability of violence and on the private order of the domination of women.

Another aspect of the 'new' international criminal law from the perspective of women is that its emphasis remains on women's sexual and reproductive identities, and on harms committed by opposing forces. The numerous other forms of harm to women in armed conflict that were outlined in chapter 8 are still not addressed. For example, the Special Rapporteur on the Former Yugoslavia has emphasised the urgency of rehabilitation measures for children traumatised and physically injured by the war and who require expert psychological, educational and medical care.[168] That much of this social burden is likely to fall heavily upon women is not acknowledged; nor are there recommendations that women should be targeted for appropriate resources. Neither the law nor practice relating to armed conflict include women as agents of change or as survivors, but instead continue to view them as passive victims of international affairs. In this sense the law itself has not been transformed but has taken only limited steps to acknowledge what men have been forced to accept as the consequences of armed conflict upon women. This is a haphazard process that depends upon the

[164] Rules of Procedure and Evidence of the ICTY, rule 106.
[165] Rome Statute for the ICC, article 75.
[166] *Ibid.*, article 75.
[167] See S. Chesterman, 'Never again . . . and again: law, order, and the gender of war crimes in Bosnia and beyond', 22 *Yale Journal of International Law* (1997) 299 at 319.
[168] Situation of Human Rights Abuses in the Territory of the Former Yugoslavia, UN Doc. E/CN.4/1996/63, at paras 4, 208.

vigilance of civil society and the willingness and expertise of those in author-itative positions. It is also subject to backlash and revisionism.

Conclusion

The development of international criminal law in the 1990s has shown that concerted campaigning can produce some changes in the substance and procedures of international law. This is especially likely in subject matters that are themselves undergoing rapid transformation and where the position of women has been brought to the forefront through the efforts of women's NGOs. However, the approaches described are limited in that they are aimed only at tinkering with the international legal regime for the treatment of women in armed conflict and the definitions of genocide and crimes against humanity to include violence against women. They do not move beyond the 'add women and stir' approach described in chapter 2 and would not lead to a restructuring of the international legal system that would address the continued subordination of women. Although the vocabulary of 'gender' has been adopted in international criminal law, there are few signs that its significance is appreciated. Thus in the ICC Statute, 'gender' is defined as simply 'the two sexes, male and female, within the context of society'.[169] This definition, the result of lobbying by the Holy See and the Catholic and Islamic states to ensure that the term 'gender' could not be construed as including homosexuality,[170] presents gender as primarily an issue of biology rather than one of social construction and thus has limited transformative edge.

The institutional and substantive compartmentalisation of international law reinforces the resistance of international law to structural change. Indeed, those areas that have been most receptive to the needs of women such as human rights and international criminal law, are themselves marginalised areas of international law which are generally given scant coverage in general international law courses and texts. They are perceived as less central to the discipline than, for example, issues of statehood, identification of the sources of law, the use of force and allocation of territory and resources. Within the UN, issues of social justice and economic development fall within the mandate of the General Assembly and the ECOSOC rather than that of the Security Council, which has primary responsibility over the maintenance of international peace and security. The specialised working parties, commit-tees and commissions developed by the former have little contact with the latter. The structures of international trade and finance remain outside the framework of the UN and co-ordination between these various institutions

---

[169] Rome Statute for the ICC, article 7(3).

[170] See C. Steains, 'Gender issues in the Statute of the International Criminal Court', in R. Lee (ed.), *The International Criminal Court* (The Hague, Kluwer Law International, 1999) 357.

remains *ad hoc* and sporadic. The lack of a centralised law-making authority, coupled with systemic fragmentation, prevents the development of a coherent international legal policy. The same issues have to be fought in each separate arena where different agendas, priorities and personalities contribute to diverse outcomes. Progress achieved in one context will not necessarily be replicated elsewhere in the international system and may indeed be thwarted by contrary practices or policies.

In any event, from a feminist perspective, a more basic question is whether the pursuit of legal change is a worthwhile strategy. Feminists have mixed views on the utility of law reform in domestic legal systems and many have warned against attributing power to law to alter basic political and economic inequalities based upon sex and gender, or indeed giving legitimacy to an oppressive system.[171] These reservations may even be stronger in an international legal system where enforcement and efficacy are more controversial and uncertain. Would redrawing the boundaries of international law have any capacity to achieve changes beneficial to women in a world where forms of power would continue to be held by men? Carol Smart has warned against assuming that apparent reforms will be interpreted and applied by influential decision-makers in the way that is intended. She has argued that: 'The main dilemma for any feminist engagement with law is the certain knowledge that, once enacted, legislation [or, in the case of international law, treaties and soft law instruments] is in the hands of individuals and agencies far removed from the values and politics of the women's movement.'[172]

In our view, feminists should tackle international law on a number of levels at the same time. We should use existing mechanisms and principles wherever possible to improve women's lives. We should also work to reform the letter of the law so that it more adequately responds to concerns of women. We must insist that the equal participation of women in the international legal system and its institutions is a condition of their legitimacy. Beyond this we can contribute to the Grotian project of redrawing the boundaries of international law by challenging and questioning the 'objectivity' of the international legal system and its hierarchy based on gender. We must critically interrogate the categories we use as if they were somehow natural or inevitable. Standard dichotomies such as war/peace, order/disorder or security/insecurity have operated in international law to filter out the experiences of women. As Carol Cohn has pointed out, a radical shift in perspective and boundary-drawing will only occur through a 'commitment and ability to develop, explore, rethink and revalue those ways of thinking that get silenced and devalued'.[173] We must ask the questions that will force

---

[171] C. Smart, *Feminism and the Power of Law* (London, Routledge, 1989) at 144.
[172] *Ibid.* at 164.
[173] C. Cohn, 'War, wimps and women: talking gender and thinking war', in M. Cooke and A. Woollacott (eds), *Gendering War Talk* (Princeton, Princeton University Press, 1993) 227 at 239.

us to rethink the boundaries: how are apparently natural dichotomies gendered?; why is the category 'woman' so limited in international law?; why is it so difficult to perceive women as a group for the purposes of self-determination, refugee status or national identity?; why can we conceive of a state in terms of religion or in terms of race, while a 'feminist' state seems bizarre?; in what ways do the traditional rules of international law fail to respond to the new realities of the global order?; what would be the elements of an international theory of personal, political, social and economic equality?

Critics may take umbrage at this proposed range of tasks, arguing that feminist challenges to the objectivity of international law preclude any reliance on international legal principles in specific contexts.[174] On this account, feminists should not be both activist and subversive at the same time. But this approach does not recognise that international law has both regulative and symbolic functions. We should use its regulative aspects where we can to respond to particular harms done to women, and harness its symbolic force to reshape the way women's lives are understood in an international context, thus altering the boundaries of international law.

[174] See e.g. A. D'Amato, book review of R. Cook (ed.), *Human Rights of Women: National and International Perspectives* (Philadelphia, University of Pennsylvania Press, 1994), 89 *American Journal of International Law* (1995) 840.

Bibliography

Abdo N., 'Women of the intifada: gender, class and national liberation', 32 *Race and Class* (no.4, 1991) 19

Abdo N., 'Middle East politics through feminist lenses: negotiating the terms of solidarity', 18 *Alternatives* (1993) 29

Abi-Saab G., 'Cours général de droit international public', 207 *Recueil des Cours* (1987) 33

Abi-Saab G., 'Whither the international community?', 9 *European Journal of International Law* (1998) 248

Acosta M., 'Women's human rights groups in Latin America', in Forsythe D. (ed.), *Human Rights and Development* (London, Macmillan, 1989) 3

Africa Watch, *Rwanda Not So Innocent When Women Become Killers* (London, Africa Watch, 1995)

Afshari R., 'An essay on Islamic cultural relativism in the discourse of human rights', 16 *Human Rights Quarterly* (1994) 235

Akehurst M., 'Custom as a source of international law', 47 *British Yearbook of International Law* (1974–5) 1

Akehurst M., 'The hierarchy of the sources of international law', 47 *British Yearbook of International Law* (1974–5) 273

Alexander M., 'Not just (any) body can be a citizen: the politics of law, sexuality and postcoloniality in Trinidad and Tobago and the Bahamas', 48 *Feminist Review* (1994) 5

Alexander M. and Mohanty C. (eds), *Feminist Genealogies, Colonial Legacies, Democratic Futures* (New York, Routledge, 1997)

Alexander M. and Mohanty C., 'Genealogies, legacies, movements', in Alexander M. and Mohanty C. (eds), *Feminist Genealogies, Colonial Legacies, Democratic Futures* (New York, Routledge, 1997) xiii

Alexandrov S., *Self-Defense against the Use of Force in International Law* (The Hague, Kluwer, 1996)

Allain J. and Jones J., 'A patchwork of norms: a commentary on the 1996 Draft Code of Crimes against the Peace and Security of Mankind', 8 *European Journal of International Law* (1997) 100

Allen J., 'Does feminism need a theory of "The State"?', in Watson S. (ed.), *Playing the State* (Sydney, Allen & Unwin, 1990) 10

338

Al Sadawi N., 'The political challenges facing Arab women at the end of the 20th century', in Toubia N. (ed.), *Women of the Arab World* (London, Zed Books, 1998) 79

Alston P., 'Peace as a human right', 11 *Bulletin of Peace Proposals* (1980) 319

Alston P., 'A third generation of solidarity rights: progressive development or obfuscation of international human rights law?', 20 *Netherlands International Law Review* (1982) 307

Alston P., 'Revitalising the United Nations' work on human rights and development', 18 *Melbourne University Law Review* (1991) 216

Alston P. (ed.), *The United Nations and Human Rights: A Critical Appraisal* (Oxford, Clarendon Press, 1992)

Alston P. and Chiam M. (eds), *Treaty-making and Australia: Globalisation versus Sovereignty* (Annandale, Federation Press, 1995)

Alvarez J., 'Nuremburg revisited: the *Tadic* case', 7 *European Journal of International Law* (1996) 24

Amerasinghe C., *The Law of the International Civil Service* (Oxford, Clarendon Press, 1994)

American Law Institute, *Restatement (Third) of the Foreign Relations Law of the United States* (St Paul, American Law Institute, 1987)

Americas' Watch, *Criminal Injustice: Violence against Women in Brazil* (New York, Human Rights Watch, 1991)

Amnesty International, *Women in the Front Line: Human Rights Violations against Women* (New York, Amnesty International, 1991)

Amnesty International, *Peace Keeping and Human Rights* (New York, Amnesty International, 1994)

Amnesty International, *Human Rights are Women's Right* (London, Amnesty International, 1995)

Amnesty International, *Women in Afghanistan: A Human Rights Catastrophe* (London, Amnesty International, 1995)

Anderson B., *Imagined Communities: Reflections on the Origins and Spread of Nationalism* (London/New York, Verso, revised ed. 1991)

Anghie A., 'Colonialism, environmental damage and the Nauru case', 34 *Harvard International Law Journal* (1993) 445

Anghie A., 'Francisco de Vitoria and the colonial origins of international law', 5 *Social and Legal Studies* (1996) 32

Anghie A., 'Finding the peripheries: sovereignty and colonialism in nineteenth-century international law', 40 *Harvard International Law Journal* (1999) 1

Anker, R. 'Theories of occupational segregation by sex: an overview', 136 *International Labour Review* (1997) 315

An-Na'im A., 'Religious minorities under Islamic law and the limits of cultural relativism', 9 *Human Rights Quarterly* (1987) 1

An-Na'im A., 'Islam, Islamic law and the dilemma of cultural legitimacy for universal human rights', in Welch C. and Leary V. (eds), *Asian Perspectives on Human Rights* (Boulder, Westview Press, 1990) 31

Arzt D., 'The application of international human rights law in Islamic states', 12 *Human Rights Quarterly* (1990) 202

Ashman C. and Trescott, P., *Outrage: The Abuse of Diplomatic Immunity* (London, Star Books, 1986)

Ashworth G., *Of Violence and Violation: Women and Human Rights* (London, Change, 1985)

Ashworth G., 'An elf among gnomes: a feminist in North-South relations', 17 *Millennium* (1988) 497

Askin K., *War Crimes against Women: Prosecution in International War Crimes Tribunals* (The Hague, Martinus Nijhoff, 1997)

Askin K. and Koenig D. (eds), *Women and International Human Rights Law* (Ardsley, Transnational Publishers Inc., 1999)

Astor H. and Chinkin C., *Dispute Resolution in Australia* (Sydney, Butterworths, 1993)

Australian Law Reform Commission, *Equality before the Law* (parts I and II) (Sydney, Law Reform Commission, 1994)

Barbieri C., 'Women workers in transition: the potential impact of the NAFTA labor side agreements on women workers in Argentina and Chile', 17 *Comparative Labor Law Journal* (1996) 526

Barker J., *The Abuse of Diplomatic Privileges and Immunities: A Necessary Evil?* (Aldershot, Dartmouth Publishing Co., 1994)

Barker P., *Regeneration* (London, Penguin Books, 1991)

Barnard C., *EC Employment Law* (Chichester, Chancery Law Publishing, 1996)

Barry K., *Female Sexual Slavery* (New York, New York University Press, 1984)

Bartlett K., 'Feminist legal methods', 103 *Harvard Law Review* (1990) 829

Bassiouni M., 'A functional approach to "general principles of international law"', 11 *Michigan Journal of International Law* (1990) 768

Bassiouni M., 'The United Nations Commission of Experts established pursuant to Security Council resolution 780 (1992)', 88 *American Journal of International Law* (1994) 784

Baxter R., 'Multilateral treaties as evidence of customary international law', 41 *British Yearbook of International Law* (1965–6) 275

Baxter R., 'Treaties and custom', 129 *Recueil des Cours* (1970) 25

Bayefsky A., 'The principle of equality or non-discrimination in international law', 11 *Human Rights Law Journal* (1990) 1

Bayefsky A., 'Making the human rights treaties work', in Henkin L. and Hargrove J. (eds), *Human Rights: An Agenda for the Next Century* (Washington DC, American Society of International Law, 1994) 229

Bazilli S. (ed.), *Putting Women on the Agenda* (Johannesburg, Ravan Press, 1991)

Bazlyer M., 'Re-examining the doctrine of humanitarian intervention in light of the atrocities in Kampuchea and Ethiopia', 23 *Stanford Journal of International Law* (1987) 547

Bedjaoui M., *Towards a New International Economic Order* (New York, Holmes & Meier, 1979)

Bello E. and Ajibola B. (eds), *Essays in Honour of Judge Taslim Olawale Elias* (Dordrecht, Martinus Nijhoff, 1992)

Benn S. and Gaus G. (eds), *Public and Private in Social Life* (London, Croom Helm, 1983)

Berkin C. and Lovett C. (eds), *Women, War and Revolution* (New York, Holmes & Meier, 1980)

Bertrand M., 'The historical development of efforts to reform the UN', in Roberts A. and Kingsbury B. (eds), *United Nations, Divided World: The United Nations' Role in International Relations* (Oxford, Clarendon Press, 2nd ed. 1993) 194

Bettauer R., 'The UN Compensation Commission: developments since October 1992', 89 *American Journal of International Law* (1995) 416

Beyani C., 'Toward a more effective guarantee of women's rights in the African human rights system', in Cook R. (ed.), *Human Rights of Women: National and International Perspectives* (Philadelphia, University of Pennsylvania Press, 1994) 285

Bhatia B., Kawar M. and Shahin M., *Unheard Voices: Iraqi Women on War and Sanctions* (London, Change, 1991)

Bhattacharjee A., 'The public/private mirage: mapping homes and undomesticating violence work in the South Asian immigrant community', in Alexander M. and Mohanty C. (eds), *Feminist Genealogies, Colonial Legacies, Democratic Futures* (New York, Routledge, 1997) 308

Binion G., 'Human rights: a feminist perspective', 17 *Human Rights Quarterly* (1995) 509

Birnie P., 'Legal techniques of settling disputes: the soft settlement approach', in Butler W. (ed.), *Perestroika and International Law* (Dordrecht, Martinus Nijhoff, 1990) 177

Bluntschli J., *The Theory of the State* (Oxford, Clarendon Press, 1921 ed.)

Boose L., 'Techno-muscularity and the "boy eternal": from the quagmire to the Gulf', in Cooke M. and Woollacott A. (eds), *Gendering War Talk* (Princeton, Princeton Unversity Press, 1993) 67

Bottomley A. and Conaghan J. (eds), *Feminist Theory and Legal Strategy* (Oxford, Blackwell Publishers, 1993)

Boutros-Ghali B., *An Agenda for Development* (New York, United Nations, 1995)

Boutros-Ghali B., 'A Grotian moment', 18 *Fordham International Law Journal* (1995) 1609

Bowen S. (ed.), *Human Rights, Self-Determination and Political Change in the Occupied Palestinian Territories* (The Hague, Kluwer, 1997)

Bowett D., *Self-Defence in International Law* (Manchester, Manchester University Press, 1958)

Bowett D., *The Law of International Institutions* (London, Stevens, 4th ed. 1982)

Boyle F., 'The creation of the state in Palestine', 1 *European Journal of International Law* (1990) 301

Bradlow D., 'International organizations and private complaints: the case of the World Bank Inspection Panel', 34 *Virginia Journal of International Law* (1994) 553

Braidotti R., 'The exile, the nomad, and the migrant: reflections on international feminism', 15 *Women's Studies International Forum* (1992) 7

Brand L., *Palestinians in the Arab World: Institution Building and the Search for a State* (New York, Columbia University Press, 1988)

Brautigam C., 'Mainstreaming a gender perspective in the work of the United Nations human rights treaty bodies', *Proceedings of the 91st Annual Meeting of the American Society of International Law* (Washington DC, American Society of International Law, 1997) 389

Brennan K., 'The influence of cultural relativism on international human rights law: female circumcision as a case study', 7 *Law and Inequality* (1989) 367

Brierly J., *The Basis of Obligation in International Law* (Oxford, Clarendon Press, 1958)

Brierly J., *The Law of Nations: An Introduction to the International Law of Peace* (Oxford, Clarendon Press, 6th ed. 1963)

Brooks M., 'Passive in war? Women internees in the Far East 1942–5', in Macdonald S., Holden P. and Ardner S. (eds), *Images of War in Peace and War: Cross Cultural and Historical Perspectives* (Basingstoke, Macmillan, 1987)

Brownlie I., *International Law and the Use of Force* (Oxford, Clarendon Press, 1963)

Brownlie I., *State Responsibility* (Oxford, Clarendon Press, 1983)

Brownlie I., 'The rights of peoples in modern international law', in Crawford J. (ed.), *The Rights of Peoples* (Oxford, Clarendon Press, 1988) 1

Brownlie I., *Principles of Public International Law* (Oxford, Clarendon Press, 4th ed. 1990; 5th ed. 1998)

Bruce M., 'Women and policy-making in the United Nations', in Davidson N. and Croke M. (eds), *The United Nations and Decision Making: The Role of Women* (New York, UNITAR, 1978) 49

Bull H., Kingsbury B. and Roberts A. (eds), *Hugo Grotius and International Relations* (Oxford, Oxford University Press, 1990)

Bunch C., *Passionate Politics: Essays 1968–1986: Feminist Theory in Action* (New York, St. Martin's Press, 1987)

Bunch C., 'Women's rights as human rights: toward a re-vision of human rights', 12 *Human Rights Quarterly* (1990) 486

Bunting A., 'Theorizing women's cultural diversity in feminist international human rights strategies', in Bottomley A. and Conaghan J. (eds), *Feminist Theory and Legal Strategy* (Oxford, Blackwell Publishers, 1993) 6

Burguières M., 'Feminist approaches to peace: another step for peace studies', 19 *Millennium* (1990) 1

Burrows N., 'International law and human rights: the case of women's rights', in Campbell T. *et al.* (eds), *Human Rights: From Rhetoric to Reality* (New York, Basil Blackwell, 1986) 8

Bush J., 'Defining group rights and delineating sovereignty: a case from the Republic of Fiji', 14 *American University International Law Review* (1999) 735

Bustelo M. and Alston P. (eds), *Whose New World Order: What Role for the United Nations?* (Annandale, Federation Press, 1991)

Butler W. (ed.), *Perestroika and International Law* (Dordrecht, Martinus Nijhoff, 1990)

Byers M., 'Custom, power and the power of rules: customary international law from an interdisciplinary perspective', 17 *Michigan Journal of International Law* (1995) 109

Byrnes A., *Report on the Seventh Session of the Committee on the Elimination of Discrimination Against Women and the Fourth Meeting of States Parties to the Convention on the Elimination of All Forms of Discrimination Against Women* (Minneapolis, International Women's Rights Action Watch, 1988)

Byrnes A., 'The "other" human rights treaty body: the work of the Committee on the Elimination of Discrimination Against Women', 14 *Yale Journal of International Law* (1989) 1

Byrnes A., 'Women, feminism and international human rights law – methodological myopia, fundamental flaws or meaningful marginalisation?', 12 *Australian Yearbook of International Law* (1992) 205

Byrnes A., 'Slow and steady wins the race? The development of an optional protocol to the Women's Convention', *Proceedings of the 91st Annual Meeting of the*

American Society of International Law (Washington DC, American Society of International Law, 1997) 383

Byrnes A., 'Human rights instruments relating specifically to women, with particular emphasis on the Convention on the Elimination of All Forms of Discrimination Against Women', in Byrnes A., Connors J. and Bik L. (eds), *Advancing the Human Rights of Women: Using International Human Rights Standards in Domestic Litigation* (London, Commonwealth Secretariat, 1997) 39

Byrnes A. and Connors J., 'Enforcing the human rights of women: a complaints procedure for the Convention on the Elimination of All Forms of Discrimination Against Women', 21 *Brooklyn Journal of International Law* (1996) 679

Byrnes A., Connors J. and Bik L. (eds), *Advancing the Human Rights of Women: Using International Human Rights Standards in Domestic Litigation* (London, Commonwealth Secretariat, 1997)

Cammack D., 'Gender relief – politics during the Afghan war', in Indra D. (ed.), *Engendering Forced Migration* (1994) 94

Camilleri J., Jarvis A. and Paolini A. (eds), *The State in Transition* (Boulder, Lynne Rienner Publishers, 1995)

Campbell T., D. Goldberg, S. McLean and T. Mullen (eds), *Human Rights: From Rhetoric to Reality* (New York, Basil Blackwell, 1986)

Cantwell N., 'The origins, development and significance of the United Nations Convention on the Rights of the Child', in Detrick S. (ed.), *The United Nations Convention on the Rights of the Child: A Guide to the Travaux Préparatoires* (Dordrecht, Martinus Nijhoff, 1992) 19

Cardinale H., *The Holy See and the International Order* (Toronto, Macmillan, 1976)

Carty A., 'Critical international law: recent trends in the theory of international law', 2 *European Journal of International Law* (1991) 66

Cass D., 'Re-thinking self-determination: a critical analysis of current international law theories', 18 *Syracuse Journal of International and Comparative Law* (1992) 21

Cass D., 'Navigating the newstream: recent critical scholarship in international law', 65 *Nordic Journal of International Law* (1996) 341

Cassese A., 'Consensus and some of its pitfalls', 58 *Rivista di Diritto Internazionale* (1975) 754

Cassese A., 'The status of rebels under the 1977 Geneva protocols on non-international armed conflict', 30 *International and Comparative Law Quarterly* (1981) 416

Cassese A., *International Law in a Divided World* (Oxford, Clarendon Press, 1986)

Cassese A., *Violence and Law in the Modern Age* (Cambridge, Polity Press, 1986)

Cassese A., *Self-Determination of Peoples* (Cambridge, Cambridge University Press, 1995)

Cassese A. and Weiler J. (eds), *Change and Stability in International Law-Making* (Berlin/New York, De Gruyter, 1988)

Cerny Smith R., 'Female circumcision: bringing women's perspectives into the international debate', 65 *Southern California Law Review* (1992) 2449

Cervenak C., 'Promoting inequality: gender-based discrimination in UNWRA's approach to Palestinian refugee status', 16 *Human Rights Quarterly* (1994) 300

Cervenka Z., 'The effect of militarization on human rights in Africa', in Shepherd G. and Anikpo M. (eds), *Emerging Human Rights: The African Political Economy Context* (New York, Greenwood Press, 1990) 129

Chapkis W. (ed.), *Loaded Questions: Women in the Military* (Amsterdam, Transnational Institute, 1981)

Chapkis W., 'Sexuality and militarism', in Isaksson E. (ed.), *Women and the Military System* (Hemel Hempstead, Harvester Wheatsheaf, 1988) 106

Charlesworth H., 'The public-private distinction and the right to development in international law', 12 *Australian Yearbook of International Law* (1992) 190

Charlesworth H., 'Alienating Oscar? Feminist analysis of international law', in Dallmeyer D. (ed.), *Reconceiving Reality: Women and International Law* (Washington DC, American Society of International Law, 1993) 1

Charlesworth H., 'General principles as sources of international law', in *Contemporary International Law Issues: Opportunities at a Time of Momentous Change* (The Hague, Nederlandse Verenigning voor Internationaal Recht, 1993) 421

Charlesworth H., 'What are women's human rights?', in Cook R. (ed.), *Human Rights of Women: National and International Perspectives* (Philadelphia, University of Pennsylvania Press, 1994) 58

Charlesworth H., 'Transforming the United Men's club: feminist futures for the United Nations', 4 *Transnational Law and Contemporary Problems* (1994) 421

Charlesworth H., 'Worlds apart: public/private distinctions in international law', in Thornton M. (ed.), *Public and Private Feminist Legal Debates* (Melbourne, Oxford University Press, 1995) 243

Charlesworth H., 'The silences of Gareth Evans' "Blue Book"', in Lawson S. (ed.), *The New Agenda for Global Security: Cooperating for Peace and Beyond* (Sydney, Allen & Unwin, 1995) 133

Charlesworth H., 'Australia's split personality: implementation of human rights treaty obligations in Australia', in Alston P. and Chiam M. (eds), *Treaty-Making and Australia* (Annandale, Federation Press, 1995) 129

Charlesworth H., 'Women as sherpas: are global summits useful for women?' 22 *Feminist Studies* (1996) 537

Charlesworth H., 'Feminist critiques of international law and their critics', [1994–5] *Third World Legal Studies* (1996) 1

Charlesworth H., 'Cries and whispers: responses to feminist analyses of international law', 65 *Nordic Journal of International Law* (1996) 557

Charlesworth H., 'Sexing the state', in Naffine N. and Owens R. (eds), *Sexing the Subject of Law* (Sydney, Law Book Co. Ltd., 1997) 251

Charlesworth H., International human rights law: prospects and problems for Palestinian women" in Bowen S. (ed.), *Human Rights, Self-Determination and Political Change in the Occupied Palestinian Territories* (The Hague, Kluwer, 1997) 79

Charlesworth H., 'Dangerous liaisons: globalisation and Australian law', 20 *Adelaide Law Review* (1998) 57

Charlesworth H., 'Feminist methods in international law', 93 *American Journal of International Law* (1999) 379

Charlesworth H., 'The challenges of human rights law for religious traditions', in Janis M. and Evans C. (eds), *Religion in International Law* (The Hague, Martinus Nijhoff, 1999) 401

Charlesworth H. and Chinkin C., 'The gender of jus cogens', 15 *Human Rights Quarterly* (1993) 63

Charlesworth H. and Chinkin C., 'Violence against women: a global issue', in Stubbs J. (ed.), *Women, Male Violence and the Law* (Sydney, Institute of Criminology Series no. 6, 1994) 135

Charlesworth H., Chinkin C. and Wright S., 'Feminist approaches to international law', 85 *American Journal of International Law* (1991) 613

Charlesworth S., *Stretching Flexibility: Enterprise Bargaining, Women Workers and Changes to Working Hours* (Sydney, Human Rights and Equal Opportunity Commission, 1996)

Charney J., 'The persistent objector rule and the development of customary international law', 56 *British Yearbook of International Law* (1985) 1

Charney J., 'Universal international law', 87 *American Journal of International Law* (1993) 529

Charney J. and Alexander L. (eds), *International Maritime Boundaries* (Dordrecht, Martinus Nijhoff, 1993)

Charnovitz S., 'Two centuries of participation: NGOs and international governance', 18 *Michigan Journal of International Law* (1997) 183

Chatterjee S., 'The Charter of Economic Rights and Duties of States: an evaluation after fifteen years', 40 *International and Comparative Law Quarterly* (1990) 669

Chayes A. and Chayes A., *The New Sovereignty: Compliance with International Regulatory Agreements* (Cambridge, Harvard University Press, 1995)

Cheng B., 'Custom: the future of general state practice in a divided world', in Macdonald R. and Johnston D. (eds), *The Structure and Process of International Law: Essays in Legal Philosophy, Doctrine and Theory* (Dordrecht, Martinus Nijhoff, 1983) 513

Cheng B., *General Principles of Law as Applied by International Courts and Tribunals* (London, Stevens, 1953 reprinted 1987)

Chesterman S., 'Never again . . . and again: law, order, and the gender of war crimes in Bosnia and beyond', 22 *Yale Journal of International Law* (1997) 299

Chimni B., *International Law and World Order: A Critique of Contemporary Approaches* (New Delhi, Sage Publications, 1993)

Chinkin C., 'The challenge of soft law: development and change in international law', 38 *International and Comparative Law Quarterly* (1989) 850

Chinkin C., *Third Parties in International Law* (Oxford, Clarendon Press, 1993)

Chinkin C., 'Women and peace: militarism and oppression', in Mahoney K. and Mahoney P. (eds), *Human Rights in the 21st Century: A Global Challenge* (Dordrecht, Martinus Nijhoff, 1993) 405

Chinkin C., 'Rape and sexual abuse of women in international law', 5 *European Journal of International Law* (1994) 326

Chinkin C., 'The peaceful settlement of disputes: new grounds for optimism?', in Macdonald R. (ed.), *Essays in Honour of Wang Tieya* (Dordrecht, Martinus Nijhoff, 1994) 165

Chinkin C., 'Comparative perspectives: the United Kingdom', in Alston P. and Chiam M. (eds), *Treaty-making and Australia: Globalisation versus Sovereignty* (Annandale, Federation Press, 1995) 266

Chinkin C., 'Reservations and objections to the Convention on the Elimination of All Forms of Discrimination Against Women', in Gardner J-P. (ed.), *Human Rights as General Norms and a State's Right to Opt Out* (London, British Institute of International and Comparative Law, 1997) 64

Bibliography

Chinkin C., 'Due process and witness anonymity', 91 *American Journal of International Law* (1997) 75

Chinkin C., 'Women's human rights: guaranteed by universal standards or discounted by cultural bias?', 5(2) *Collected Courses of the Academy of European Law* (1997) 11

Chinkin C., 'Strategies to combat discrimination against women', in O'Flaherty M. and Gisvold G. (eds), *Post-War Protection of Human Rights in Bosnia and Herzegovina* (The Hague, Kluwer Law International, 1998) 173

Chinkin C., 'Torture of the girl child', in Van Bueren G. (ed.), *Childhood Abused: Protecting Children against Torture, Cruel, Inhuman and Degrading Treatment and Punishment* (Aldershot, Dartmouth Publishing Co./Ashgate Publishing Co., 1998) 81

Chinkin C. and Sadurska R., 'The anatomy of international disputes', 7 *Ohio State Journal on Dispute Resolution* (1991) 39

Chinkin C. and Werksman K., *CEDAW No. 12, Report of the Twelfth Session of the Committee on the Elimination of All Forms of Discrimination Against Women* (Minneapolis, International Women's Rights Action Watch, 1993)

Chinkin C. and Wright S., 'The hunger trap: women, food and self-determination', 14 *Michigan Journal of International Law* (1993) 262

Chodosh H., 'An interpretive theory of international law: the distinction between treaty and customary law', 28 *Vanderbilt Journal of Transnational Law* (1995) 973

Chomsky N., '"What we say goes": The Middle East in the New World Order', in Peters C. (ed.), *Collateral Damage: The 'New World Order' at Home and Abroad* (Boston, South End Press, 1992) 49

Chow R., 'Violence in the other country: China as crisis, spectacle, and woman', in Mohanty C., Russo A. and Torres L. (eds), *Third World Women and the Politics of Feminism* (Bloomington, Indiana University Press, 1991) 81

Christenson G., '*Jus cogens*: guarding interests fundamental to international society', 28 *Virginia Journal of International Law* (1988) 585

Clark B., 'The Vienna Convention reservations regime and the Convention on the Elimination of All Forms of Discrimination Against Women', 85 *American Journal of International Law* (1991) 281

Clark R., *The Fire This Time: The US War Crimes in the Gulf* (New York, Thunder's Mouth Press, 1992)

Clech Lam M., 'Feeling foreign in feminism', 19 *Signs* (1994) 865

Coate R., Alger C. and Lipschutz R., 'The UN and civil society: creative partnerships for sustainable development', 21 *Alternatives* (1996) 93

Coccia M., 'Reservations to multilateral treaties on human rights', 15 *California Western International Law Journal* (1985) 1

Cock J., *Women and War in South Africa* (London, Open Letters, 1992)

Cockburn C., *In the Way of Women: Men's Resistance to Sex Equality in Organisations* (Basingstoke, Macmillan, 1991)

Cohn C., 'War, wimps and women: talking gender and thinking war', in Cooke M. and Woollacott A. (eds), *Gendering War Talk* (Princeton, Princeton University Press, 1993) 227

Comeau P., 'Guilty verdict handed down in "secret" UN sexual harassment hearing', 1 *Human Rights Tribune* (no. 3, March/April 1994) 19

Commission on Global Governance, *Our Global Neighbourhood* (New York, Oxford University Press, 1995)

Commonwealth Secretariat, *Promotion of the Human Rights of Women and the Girl Child through the Judiciary: Commonwealth Declarations and Strategies for Action* (London, Commonwealth Secretariat, 1997)

Connors J., 'NGOs and the human rights of women at the United Nations', in Willetts P. (ed.), *The Conscience of the World: The Influence of Non-governmental Organizations in the United Nations System* (Washington DC, Brookings Institution, 1996) 147

Connors J., 'The Women's Convention in the Muslim World', in Gardner J-P. (ed.), *Human Rights as General Norms and a State's Right to Opt Out* (London, British Institute of International and Comparative Law, 1997) 85

Connors J., 'General human rights instruments and their relevance to women', in Byrnes A., Connors J. and Bik L. (eds), *Advancing the Human Rights of Women: Using International Human Rights Standards in Domestic Litigation* (London, Commonwealth Secretariat, 1997) 33

Cook R., 'Reservations to the Convention on the Elimination of All Forms of Discrimination Against Women', 30 *Virginia Journal of International Law* (1990) 643

Cook R., 'Accountability in international law for violations of women's rights by non-state actors', in Dallmeyer D. (ed.), *Reconceiving Reality: Women and International Law* (Washington DC, American Society of International Law, 1993) 93

Cook R. (ed.), *Human Rights of Women: National and International Perspectives* (Philadelphia, University of Pennsylvania Press, 1994)

Cook R, 'State accountability under the Women's Convention', in Cook R. (ed.), *Human Rights of Women: National and International Perspectives* (Philadelphia, University of Pennsylvania Press, 1994) 228

Cook R., 'State responsibility for violations of women's human rights', 7 *Harvard Human Rights Journal* (1994) 125

Cook R., *The Elimination of Sexual Apartheid: Prospects for the Fourth World Conference on Women* (Washington DC, American Society of International Law, 1995)

Cook R., 'Women', in Schachter O. and Joyner C. (eds), *United Nations Legal Order* (Cambridge, Cambridge University Press, 1995) 433

Cook R. and Oosterveld V., 'A select bibliography of women's human rights', 44 *American University Law Review* (1995) 1429

Cooke M. and Woollacott A. (eds), *Gendering War Talk* (Princeton, Princeton Unversity Press, 1993)

Coomans F. and van Hoof F. (eds), *The Right to Complain about Economic, Social and Cultural Rights* (Utrecht, Netherlands Institute of Human Rights, 1995)

Coomaraswamy R., 'Of Kali born: women, violence and the law in Sri Lanka', in Schuler M. (ed.), *Freedom from Violence: Women's Strategies from Around the World* (New York, UNIFEM, 1992) 49

Coomaraswamy R., 'To bellow like a cow: women, ethnicity and the discourse of rights', in R. Cook (ed.), *Human Rights of Women: National and International Perspectives* (Philadelphia, University of Pennsylvania Press, 1994) 39

Coomaraswamy R., 'Reinventing international law', in Van Ness P. (ed.), *Debating Human Rights* (London/New York, Routledge, 1999) 167

Cranston M., 'Are there any human rights?', *Daedalus* (no. 4, 1983) 1

Crawford J., 'The criteria for statehood in international law', 48 *British Yearbook of International Law* (1976–7) 93

Crawford J., *The Creation of States in International Law* (Oxford, Clarendon Press, 1979)

Crawford J. (ed.), *The Rights of Peoples* (Oxford, Clarendon Press, 1988)

Crawford J., 'The creation of the state in Palestine', 1 *European Journal of International Law* (1990) 307

Crawford J. 'Democracy and international law', 64 *British Yearbook of International Law* (1993) 113

Crawford J., 'The ILC adopts a Statute for an International Criminal Court', 89 *American Journal of International Law* (1995) 404

Dajani S., 'Between national and social liberation: the Palestinian women's movement in the Israeli occupied West Bank and Gaza Strip', in Mayer T. (ed.), *Women and the Israeli Occupation: The Politics of Change* (London, Routledge, 1994)

Dallmeyer D. (ed.), *Reconceiving Reality: Women and International Law* (Washington DC, American Society of International Law, 1993)

Dalton C., 'Where we stand: observations on the situation of feminist legal thought', 3 *Berkeley Women's Law Journal* (1987–88) 1

D'Amato A., 'On consensus', 8 *Canadian Yearbook of International Law* (1970) 104

D'Amato A., *The Concept of Custom in International Law* (Ithaca, Cornell University Press, 1971)

D'Amato A., 'The invasion of Panama was a lawful response to tyranny', 84 *American Journal of International Law* (1990) 516

D'Amato A. (ed.), *International Law Anthology* (Cincinnati, Anderson Publishing Co., 1994)

D'Amato A., 'Peace vs. accountability in Bosnia', 88 *American Journal of International Law* (1994) 500

D'Amato A., book review of Cook R. (ed.), *Human Rights of Women: National and International Perspectives* (Philadelphia, University of Pennsylvania Press, 1994), 89 *American Journal of International Law* (1995) 840

D'Amico F. and Beckman P. (eds), *Women in World Politics: An Introduction* (Westport/London, Bergin and Garvey, 1995)

Danilenko G., *Law-Making in the International Community* (Boston, Martinus Nijhoff, 1993)

Davidson N. and Croke M. (eds), *The United Nations and Decision Making: The Role of Women* (New York, UNITAR, 1978)

Davies M., 'Taking the inside out: sex and gender in the legal subject', in Naffine N. and Owens R. (eds), *Sexing the Subject of Law* (Sydney, Law Book Co. Ltd., 1997) 25

Dawit S. and Mekuna S., 'The west just doesn't get it', *New York Times*, 7 December 1993, 27

Dean J., *Solidarity of Strangers: Feminism after Identity Politics* (Berkeley, University of California Press, 1996)

de Hedervary C., 'The Ad Hoc Group of Women: action on decision-making in the United Nations', in Davidson N. and Croke M. (eds), *The United Nations and Decision Making: The Role of Women* (New York, UNITAR, 1978) vol. 2, 131

de Hedervary C., 'The United Nations: "Good grief, there are women here"', in Morgan R. (ed.), *Sisterhood is Global: The International Women's Movement* (Garden City, Anchor Press/Doubleday, 1984) 695

Delph Y. and Toner K., 'First among equals', 18 *Conscience* (no. 3, 1997) 2

Detrick S. (ed.), *The United Nations Convention on the Rights of the Child: A Guide to the Travaux Préparatoires* (Dordrecht, Martinus Nijhoff, 1992)

di Giovanni J., *The Quick and the Dead: Under Siege in Sarajevo* (London, Phoenix, 1994)

Dinstein Y., 'The right to life, physical integrity and liberty', in Henkin L. (ed.), *The International Bill of Rights: The Covenant on Civil and Political Rights* (New York, Columbia University Press, 1981) 114

Dolgopol U., 'Women's voices, women's pain', 17 *Human Rights Quarterly* (1995) 127

Dolgopol U., 'A feminist appraisal of the Dayton Peace Accords', 19 *Adelaide Law Review* (1997) 59

Dolgopol U. and Paranjape S., *Comfort Women: The Unfinished Ordeal* (Geneva, International Commission of Jurists, 1994)

Dorsey G., 'The McDougal-Lasswell proposal to build a world public order', 82 *American Journal of International Law* (1988) 41

Dow U. (ed.), *Unity Dow, The Citizenship Case* (Gaborone, Lentswe La Lesedi Pty Ltd, 1995)

Drew C., 'Self-determination, population transfer and the Middle East peace accords', in Bowen S. (ed.), *Human Rights, Self-Determination and Political Change in the Occupied Territories* (The Hague, Kluwer Law International, 1997)

Drèze J. and Sen A., *Hunger and Public Action* (Oxford, Oxford University Press, 1989)

Dronov V., 'From CSCE to OSCE: historical retrospective', in Evans M. (ed.), *Aspects of Statehood and Institutionalism in Contemporary Europe* (Aldershot, Dartmouth, 1997) 105

Drzemczewski A., *The European Human Rights Convention in Domestic Law: A Comparative Study* (Oxford, Clarendon Press, 1983)

Ducel M., 'Women in authority: the ideal and the reality', *World of Work* (no. 2, February 1993) 4

Duerst-Lahti G. and Kelly R. (eds), *Gender, Power, Leadership and Governance* (Ann Arbor, University of Michigan Press, 1995)

Dugard J., *Recognition and the United Nations* (Cambridge, Grotius Publications, 1987)

Dunne T. and Wheeler N. (eds), *Human Rights in Global Politics* (Cambridge, Cambridge University Press, 1999)

Dupuy R-J., 'Declaratory law and programmatory law: from revolutionary custom to "soft law"', in Horn N. (ed.), *Studies in Transnational Economic Law*, vol. 1, *Legal Problems of Codes of Conduct for Multinational Enterprises* (Antwerp/ Boston, Kluwer Deventer, 1980) 247

Dworkin A., *Intercourse* (London, Secker and Warburg, 1987, Arrow ed. 1988)

Eide A., 'The right to peace', 10 *Bulletin of Peace Proposals* (1979) 157

Elageb O., *The Legality of Non-Forcible Counter-Measures in International Law* (Oxford, Clarendon Press, 1988)

Elias T., *The Modern Law of Treaties* (Dobbs Ferry, Oceana, 1974)

Elias T., *The International Court of Justice and some Contemporary Problems* (The Hague, Martinus Nijhoff, 1983)

Elias T., *New Horizons in International Law* (Dordrecht, Sijthoff and Noordhoff, 1979; 2nd revised ed. 1992)

Elshtain J., *Women and War* (New York, Basic Books, 1987, reprinted 1995)

Elshtain J., 'Exporting feminism', 48 *Journal of International Affairs* (1995) 541

Engle K., 'International human rights and feminism: when discourses meet', 13 *Michigan Journal of International Law* (1992) 317

Engle K., 'Female subjects of public international law: human rights and the exotic other female', 26 *New England Law Review* (1992) 1509

Engle K., 'After the collapse of the public/private distinction: strategizing women's rights', in Dallmeyer D. (ed.), *Reconceiving Reality: Women and International Law* (Washington DC, American Society of International Law, 1993) 143

Engle K., 'Views from the margins: a response to David Kennedy', 1994 *Utah Law Review* 105

Enloe C., *Does Khaki Become You? The Militarization of Women's Lives* (London, Pluto Press, 1983, reprinted 1988)

Enloe C., *Bananas, Beaches, and Bases: Making Feminist Sense of International Politics* (London, Pandora Press, 1989)

Enloe C., 'The gendered gulf', in Peters C. (ed.), *The 'New World Order' at Home and Abroad: Collateral Damage* (Boston, South End Press, 1992) 93

Enloe C., *The Morning After: Sexual Politics at the End of the Cold War* (Berkeley, University of California Press, 1993)

Evans G., *Cooperating for Peace: The Global Agenda for the 1990s and Beyond* (Sydney, Allen & Unwin, 1993)

Evans M., *Relevant Circumstances and Maritime Delimitations* (Oxford, Clarendon Press, 1989)

Evans M. (ed.), *Aspects of Statehood and Institutionalism in Contemporary Europe* (Aldershot, Dartmouth Publishing Co., 1997)

Evans M. (ed.), *Remedies in International Law: The Institutional Dilemma* (Oxford, Hart Publishing, 1998) 1

Evans T. (ed.), *Human Rights Fifty Years On: A Reappraisal* (Manchester, Manchester University Press, 1998)

Ewing A., 'Establishing state responsibility for private acts of violence against women under the American Convention on Human Rights', 26 *Columbia Human Rights Law Review* (1995) 751

Falk R., 'The inadequacy of contemporary theories of international law – gaps in legal thinking', 50 *Virginia Law Review* (1964) 231

Falk R., *The Role of Domestic Courts in the International Legal Order* (Charlottesville, Virginia University Press, 1964)

Falk R., *The End of World Order: Essays on Normative International Relations* (New York, Holmes & Meier, 1983)

Falk R., 'The rights of peoples (in particular of indigenous peoples)', in Crawford J. (ed.), *The Rights of Peoples* (Oxford, Clarendon Press, 1988) 17

Falk R., 'Foreword', in Chimni B., *International Law and World Order: A Critique of Contemporary Approaches* (New Delhi, Sage Publications, 1993) 9

Falk R., 'Casting the spell: the New Haven school of international law', 104 *Yale Law Journal* (1995) 1991

Falk R., 'The Nuclear Weapons advisory opinion and the new jurisprudence of global civil society', 7 *Transnational Law and Contemporary Problems* (1997) 333

Farmanfarmaian A., 'Did you measure up? The role of race and sexuality in the Gulf War', in Peters C. (ed.), *Collateral Damage: The 'New World Order' at Home and Abroad* (Boston, South End Press, 1992) 111

Fawcett J., 'The application of the European Convention on Human Rights', in Friedmann W., Henkin L. and Lissitzyn O. (eds), *Transnational Law in a Changing Society: Essays in Honour of Philip C. Jessup* (New York, Columbia University Press, 1972) 228

Fetherston A. and Nordstrom C., *Overcoming Conceptual Habitus in Conflict Management: UN Peacekeeping and Warzone Ethnography* (Canberra, Peace Research Centre Working Paper no.147, Australian National University, 1994)

Fielding L., 'Taking the next step in the development of new human rights: the emerging right of humanitarian assistance to restore democracy', 5 *Duke Journal of Comparative and International Law* (1994) 329

Finley L., 'Transcending equality theory: a way out of the maternity and workplace debate', 86 *Columbia Law Review* (1986) 1118

Fisher R. and Ury W., *Getting to Yes: Negotiating Agreement Without Giving In* (Boston, Houghton Mifflin, 1981; 2nd ed. New York, Penguin Books, 1991)

Fitzgerald K., 'Problems of prosecution and adjudication of rape and other sexual assaults under international law', 8 *European Journal of International Law* (1997) 638

Fitzmaurice G., 'Some problems regarding the formal sources of international law', in *Symbolae Verzijl: Presentées au Professeur JHW Verzijl* (La Haye, Martinus Nijhoff, 1958) 153

Fitzmaurice G., *Law and Procedure of the International Court of Justice* (Grotius, Cambridge, reprinted 1986)

Flax J., 'Postmodernism and gender relations in feminist theory', 12 *Signs* (1987) 621

Flinterman C., 'The universality of human rights and cultural diversity', in *Contemporary International Law Issues: Conflicts and Convergence* (The Hague, Nederlandse Vereniging voor Internationaal Recht, 1995) 330

Forbes Martin S., *Refugee Women* (London/New Jersey, Zed Books, 1992)

Forsythe D. (ed.), *Human Rights and Development* (London, Macmillan, 1989)

Fox H. (ed.), *The Changing Constitution of the United Nations* (London, British Institute of International and Comparative Law, 1997)

Franck T., 'The stealing of the Sahara', 70 *American Journal of International Law* (1976) 694

Franck T., *The Power of Legitimacy Among Nations* (New York, Oxford University Press, 1990)

Franck T., 'The emerging right to democratic governance', 86 *American Journal of International Law* (1992) 46

Franck T., *Fairness in International Law and Institutions* (New York, Oxford University Press, 1995)

Franck T., 'The Secretary-General's role in conflict resolution: past, present and pure conjecture', 6 *European Journal of International Law* (1995) 360

Fraser A. and Kazantsis M., *CEDAW No. 11, The Committee on the Elimination of Discrimination Against Women; the Convention on the Elimination of All Forms of*

Discrimination Against Women and Violence Against Women (Minneapolis, International Women's Rights Action Watch, 1992)

Friedmann W., Henkin L. and Lissitzyn O. (eds), *Transnational Law in a Changing Society: Essays in Honour of Philip C. Jessup* (New York, Columbia University Press, 1972)

Frug M.J., 'A postmodern feminist legal manifesto (an unfinished draft)', 105 *Harvard Law Review* (1992) 1045

Fudge J., 'The effect of entrenching a Bill of Rights upon political discourse: feminist demands and sexual violence in Canada', 17 *International Journal of the Sociology of Law* (1989) 445

Fukuyama F., *The End of History and the Last Man* (New York, Free Press, 1992)

Funk N. and Mueller M. (eds), *Gender Politics and Post-Communism* (New York/ London, Routledge, 1993)

Gabel P. and Harris P., 'Building power and breaking images: critical legal theory and the practice of law', 11 *New York Review of Law and Social Change* (1982–83) 369

Gaja G., '*Jus cogens* beyond the Vienna Convention', 172 *Recueil des Cours* (1981) 271

Galey M., 'Gender roles and UN reform', 22 *Political Science and Politics* (1989) 813

Galey M., 'Forerunners in women's quest for partnership', in Winslow A. (ed.), *Women, Politics, and the United Nations* (Westport/London, Greenwood Press, 1995) 1

Gallagher A., 'Ending the marginalisation: strategies for incorporating women into the United Nations human rights system', 19 *Human Rights Quarterly* (1997) 283

Galtung J., *Peace: Research, Education, Action* (Copenhagen, Ejlers, 1975)

Galtung J., *Human Rights in Another Key* (Oxford, Polity Press, 1994)

Gandhi L., *Postcolonial Theory: A Critical Introduction* (Sydney, Allen & Unwin, 1998)

Gardam J., 'A feminist analysis of certain aspects of international humanitarian law', 12 *Australian Yearbook of International Law* (1992) 265

Gardam J., 'The law of armed conflict: a gendered perspective', in Dallmeyer D. (ed.), *Reconceiving Reality: Women and International Law* (Washington DC, American Society of International Law, 1993) 171

Gardam J., 'Gender and non-combatant immunity', 3 *Transnational Law and Contemporary Problems* (1993) 345

Gardam J., 'An alien's encounter with the law of armed conflict', in Naffine N. and Owens R. (eds), *Sexing the Subject of Law* (Sydney, Law Book Co. Ltd, 1996) 233

Gardam J., 'Legal restraints on Security Council military enforcement action', 17 *Michigan Journal of International Law* (1996) 285

Gardam J., 'Women and the law of armed conflict: why the silence?' 46 *International and Comparative Law Quarterly* (1997) 55

Gardner J-P., *Aspects of Incorporation of the European Convention on Human Rights into Domestic Law* (London, British Institute of International and Comparative Law, 1993)

Gardner J-P. (ed.), *Human Rights as General Norms and a State's Right to Opt Out* (London, British Institute of International and Comparative Law, 1997)

Garibaldi O., 'The legal status of General Assembly resolutions: some conceptual observations', *Proceedings of the 73ʳᵈ Annual Meeting of the American Society of*

International Law (Washington DC, American Society of International Law, 1979) 324

Garmanikow E., Morgan D., Purvis J. and Taylorson D. (eds), *The Public and the Private* (Aldershot, Gower, 1983)

Garmanikow E. and Purvis J., 'Introduction', in Garmanikow E., Morgan D., Purvis J. and Taylorson D. (eds), *The Public and the Private* (Aldershot, Gower, 1983) 1

Ghai Y., 'Human rights and governance: the Asia debate', 15 *Australian Yearbook of International Law* (1994)

Gibson S., 'The discourse of sex/war: thoughts on Catharine MacKinnon's 1993 Oxford Amnesty Lecture', 1 *Feminist Legal Studies* (1993) 179

Giegerich T., 'Vorbehalte zu Menschenrechtsabkommen: zulassigkeit, gultigkeit und prufungskompetenzen von vertragsgremien', 55 *Zeitschrift für Auslandisches Offentlicher Recht und Volkerrecht* (1995) 713

Giele J., 'Introduction: comparative perspectives on women', in Giele J. and Smock A. (eds), *Women, Roles and Status in Eight Countries* (New York, Wiley, 1977)

Giele J. and Smock A. (eds), *Women, Roles and Status in Eight Countries* (New York, Wiley, 1977)

Gifford E., '"The courage to blaspheme": confronting barriers to resisting female genital mutilation', 4 *UCLA Women's Law Journal* (1994) 329

Gilligan C., *In a Different Voice: Psychological Theory and Women's Development* (Cambridge, Harvard University Press, 1982)

Gilligan C., 'Getting civilized', in Oakley A. and Mitchell J. (eds), *Who's Afraid of Feminism? Seeing through the Backlash* (New York, The New Press, 1997) 13

Ginwala F., 'Women and the elephant: the need to redress gender inequality', in Bazilli S. (ed.), *Putting Women on the Agenda* (Johannesburg, Ravan Press, 1991) 62

Goetz A. (ed.), *Getting Institutions Right for Women in Development* (London/New York, Zed Books, 1997)

Goldfarb A., 'A Kenyan wife's right to bury her husband: applying CEDAW', 14 *International Law Students' Association Journal of International Law* (1990) 1

Goodwin-Gill G. and Cohn I., *Child Soldiers: The Role of Children in Armed Conflict* (Oxford, Clarendon Press, 1994)

Gould C. (ed.), *Beyond Domination: New Perspectives on Women and Philosophy* (Totowa, Rowman & Allanheld, 1983) 250

Grant R., 'The sources of gender bias in international relations theory', in Grant R. and Newland K. (eds), *Gender and International Relations* (Bloomington, Indiana University Press, 1991) 8

Grant R. and Newland K. (eds), *Gender and International Relations* (Bloomington, Indiana University Press, 1991)

Gray C., 'Host-state consent and the United Nations peacekeeping in Yugoslavia', 7 *Duke Journal of Comparative and International Law* (1996) 241

Gray C., 'Regional arrangements and the United Nations collective security system', in Fox H. (ed.), *The Changing Constitution of the United Nations* (London, British Institute of International and Comparative Law, 1997) 91

Graycar R. and Morgan J., *The Hidden Gender of Law* (Annandale, Federation Press, 1990)

Greenwood C., 'New world order or old? The invasion of Kuwait and the rule of law', 55 *Modern Law Review* (1992) 153

Greenwood C., 'Protection of peace-keepers: the legal regime', 7 *Duke Journal of Comparative and International Law* (1996) 185

Greig D., 'Self-defence and the Security Council: what does Article 51 require?' 40 *International and Comparative Law Quarterly* (1991) 366

Greig D., 'Reservations: equity as a balancing factor', 16 *Australian Yearbook of International Law* (1995) 21

Grieve N. and Burns A. (eds), *Australian Women: New Feminist Perspectives* (Melbourne, Oxford University Press, 1986)

Grillo T., 'The mediation alternative: process dangers for women', 100 *Yale Law Journal* (1990–1) 1545

Gross C., Remarks in *Proceedings of the 89th Annual Meeting of the American Society of International Law* (Washington DC, American Society of International Law, 1995) 191

Gross E., 'What is feminist theory?', in Pateman C. and Gross E. (eds), *Feminist Challenges: Social and Political Theory* (Sydney, Allen & Unwin, 1986) 197

Grosz E., 'A note on essentialism and difference', in Gunew S. (ed.), *Feminist Knowledge: Critique and Construct* (London/New York, Routledge, 1990) 332

Grosz E., *Volatile Bodies: Towards a Corporeal Feminism* (Sydney, Allen & Unwin, 1994)

Gruhl J., Spohn C. and Welch S., 'Women as policymakers: the case of trial judges', 25 *American Journal of Political Science* (1981) 308

Guest K., 'Post-modernism/pre-modernism: alive and well in Beijing', in Mitchell S. and Das Pradhan R. (eds), *Back to Basics from Beijing* (Canberra, Australian Council for Overseas Aid, 1997) 110

Guest K., 'Exploitation under erasure: economic, social and cultural rights engage economic globalisation', 19 *Adelaide Law Review* (1997) 73

Guggenheim P., 'Les principes de droit international public', 80 *Recueil des Cours* (1952) 1

Gunew S. (ed.), *Feminist Knowledge: Critique and Construct* (London/New York, Routledge, 1990)

Gunning I., 'Modernizing customary international law: the challenge of human rights', 31 *Virginia Journal of International Law* (1991) 211

Gunning I., 'Arrogant perception, world-travelling and multicultural feminism: the case of female genital surgeries', 23 *Colombia Human Rights Law Review* (1991–2) 189

Hafner G. (ed.), *Liber Amicorum Professor Seidl-Hohenveldern* (The Hague, Kluwer Law International, 1998)

Halabi U., 'Demolition and sealing of houses in the Israeli Occupied Territories: a critical legal analysis', 5 *Temple International and Comparative Law Journal* (1991) 251

Halberstam M. and De Feis E., *Women's Legal Rights: International Covenants as an Alternative to ERA?* (Dobbs Ferry, Transnational Publishers, 1987)

Halford S., 'Feminist change in a patriarchal organisation: the experience of women's initiatives in local government and implications for feminist perspectives on state institutions', in Savage M. and Witz A. (eds), *Gender and Bureaucracy* (Oxford/Cambridge, Blackwell/Sociological Review, 1992) 157

Hamilton C., 'Women in politics: methods of resistance and change', 12 *Women's Studies International Forum* (1989) 129

Imray L. and Middleton A., 'Public and private: marking the boundaries', in Garmanikow E. *et al.* (eds), *The Public and the Private* (Aldershot, Gower, 1983) 12

Indra D. (ed.), *Engendering Forced Migration* (1994)

International Committee of the Red Cross, *Women and War* (Geneva, International Committee of the Red Cross, 1995)

International Human Rights Law Group, *Token Gestures: Women's Human Rights and UN Reporting 1. The UN Special Rapporteur on Torture* (Washington DC, International Human Rights Law Group, 1993)

Isaksson E. (ed.), *Women and the Military System* (Hemel Hempstead, Harvester Wheatsheaf, 1988)

Jacobs F. and Roberts S., *The Effect of Treaties in Domestic Law* (London, United Kingdom National Council of Civil Liberties, 1987)

Jaquette J. and Wolchik S. (eds), *Women and Democracy* (Baltimore/London, Johns Hopkins University Press, 1998)

James A., *Sovereign Statehood: The Basis of International Society* (London, Allen & Unwin, 1986)

Jang D., Lee D. and Morello-Frosch R., 'Domestic violence in immigrant and refugee communities: responding to the needs of immigrant women', 13 *Response* (no. 4, 1990)

Janis M. and Evans C. (eds), *Religion in International Law* (The Hague, Martinus Nijhoff, 1999)

Jayawardena K., *Feminism and Nationalism in the Third World* (London, Zed Books, 1986)

Jejeebhoy S. and Cook R., 'State accountability for wife beating: the Indian challenge', 349 *The Lancet* (Supplement on Women's Health) (1997) 10

Jennings R., *The Acquisition of Territory in International Law* (Manchester, Manchester University Press, 1962)

Jennings R. and Watts A., *Oppenheim's International Law* (London, Longmans, 9th ed. 1992)

Jessup P., *A Modern Law of Nations*, (New York, Macmillan, 1948)

Jiminez de Arechaga, 'International law in the past third of a century', 159 *Recueil des Cours* (1978) 9

Johnson C. *et al.*, *Child Poverty in America* (Washington DC, Children's Defense Fund, 1991)

Johnson-Odim C., 'Common themes, different contexts', in Mohanty C., Russo A. and Torres L. (eds), *Third World Women and the Politics of Feminism* (Bloomington, Indiana University Press, 1991) 314

Jones A., 'Does "gender" make the world go round? Feminist critiques of international relations', 22 *Review of International Studies* (1996) 405

Kairys D. (ed.), *The Politics of Law* (New York, Pantheon Books, 1981)

Kairys D., 'Freedom of speech', in Kairys D. (ed.), *The Politics of Law* (New York, Pantheon Books, 1981) 140

Kaldor M., 'Transnational civil society', in Dunne T. and Wheeler N. (eds), *Human Rights in Global Politics* (Cambridge, Cambridge University Press, 1999) 195

Kalshoven F. (ed.), *Essays on the Development of the International Legal Order* (Alphen aan den Rijn, Sijthoff and Noordhoff, 1980)

Kapur R. (ed.), *Feminist Terrains in Legal Domains* (New Delhi, Kali, 1996)

Keating M., 'Women's rights and wrongs', *The World Today*, January 1997, 11

Keck M. and Sikkink K., *Activists beyond Borders: Advocacy Networks in International Politics* (Ithaca, Cornell University Press, 1998)

Kelly R. and Burgess J., 'Gender and the meaning of power and politics', 9 *Women and Politics* (1989) 47

Kelly R., Saint-Germain M. and Horn J., 'Female public officials: a different voice?', 515 *Annals of the American Academy of Political and Social Science* (1991) 77

Kennedy D., 'The sources of international law', 2 *American University Journal of International Law and Policy* (1987) 1

Kennedy D., 'A new stream of international law scholarship', 7 *Wisconsin International Law Journal* (1988) 1

Keohane R., 'International relations theory: contributions of a feminist standpoint', in Grant R. and Newland K. (eds), *Gender and International Relations* (Bloomington, Indiana University Press, 1991) 41

Khaliq U., 'Beyond the veil? An analysis of the provisions of the Women's Convention and the law as stipulated in Shar'iah', 2 *Buffalo Journal of International Law* (1995) 1

Khushalani Y., *Dignity and Honour of Women as Basic and Fundamental Human Rights* (The Hague, Martinus Nijhoff, 1982)

Kim N., 'Towards a feminist theory of human rights: straddling the fence between western imperialism and uncritical absolutism', 25 *Columbia Human Rights Law Journal* (1993) 47

Kingdom E., *What's Wrong with Rights? Problems for Feminist Politics of Law* (Edinburgh, Edinburgh University Press, 1991)

Kingsbury B., 'Whose international law? Sovereignty and non-state groups', *Proceedings of the 88th Annual Meeting of the American Society of International Law* (Washington DC, American Society of International Law, 1994) 1

Kingsbury B., '"Indigenous Peoples" in international law: a constructivist approach to the Asian controversy', 92 *American Journal of International Law* (1998) 414

Kirgis F., 'Custom on a sliding scale', 81 *American Journal of International Law* (1987) 147

Klabbers J., *The Concept of Treaty in International Law* (The Hague, Kluwer International, 1996)

Klabbers J., 'The redundancy of soft law', 65 *Nordic Journal of International Law* (1996) 167

Knop K., 'Re/statements: feminism and state sovereignty in international law', 3 *Transnational and Contemporary Legal Problems* (1993) 293

Knop K., 'Borders of the imagination: the state in feminist international law', *Proceedings of the 88th Annual Meeting of the American Society of International Law* (Washington DC, American Society of International Law, 1994) 14

Knop K., 'Why rethinking the sovereign state is important for women's human rights law', in Cook R. (ed.), *Human Rights of Women: National and International Perspectives* (Philadelphia, University of Pennsylvania Press, 1994) 153

Knop K., *The Making of Difference in International Law: Interpretation, Identity and Participation in the Discourse of Self-Determination* (JSD thesis, University of Toronto, 1998)

Koh H., 'A world transformed', 20 *Yale Journal of International Law* (1995) ix

Koh H., 'Review essay: why do nations obey international law?', 106 *Yale Law Journal* (1997) 2599

Kornblum L., 'Women warriors in a men's world: the combat exclusion', 2 *Law and Inequality* (1984) 351

Koskenniemi M., *From Apology to Utopia: The Structure of International Legal Argument* (Helsinki, Finnish Lawyers' Publishing Co., 1989)

Koskenniemi M., 'The politics of international law', 1 *European Journal of International Law* (1990) 4

Koskenniemi M., 'The future of statehood', 32 *Harvard International Law Journal* (1991) 397

Koskenniemi M., 'The wonderful artificiality of states', *Proceedings of the 88ᵗʰ Annual Meeting of the American Society of International Law* (Washington DC, American Society of International Law, 1994) 22

Koskenniemi M., 'The police in the temple, order, justice and the United Nations: a dialectical view', 6 *European Journal of International Law* (1995) 325

Koskenniemi M., book review of Dallmeyer D., (ed.), *Reconceiving Reality: Women and International Law* (Washington DC, American Society of International Law, 1993), 89 *American Journal of International Law* (1995) 227

Krill F., 'The protection of women in international humanitarian law', 249 *International Review of the Red Cross* (November-December 1985) 337

Kristansdottír E., 'The legality of the threat or use of nuclear weapons under international law: the arguments behind the World Court's Advisory Opinion', 30 *New York University Journal of International Law and Policy* (1998) 291

Krut R., *Globalization and Civil Society: NGO Influence in International Decision-Making* (New York, UN Research Institute for Social Development, 1997)

Ku C., 'Treaties and gender bias: what frame(s) work(s)?', in *Contemporary International Law Issues: Opportunities at a Time of Momentous Change* (The Hague, Nederlandse Vereeniging voor Internationaal Recht, 1993) 414

Kuenyehia A., 'The impact of structural adjustment programs on women's international human rights: the example of Ghana', in Cook R. (ed.), *Human Rights of Women: National and International Perspectives* (Philadelphia, University of Pennsylvania Press, 1994)

Kuhn A. and Wolpe A. (eds), *Feminism and Materialism: Women and Modes of Production* (London, Routledge & Paul, 1978)

Kuper J., *International Law Concerning Child Civilians in Armed Conflict* (Oxford, Clarendon Press, 1997)

Kuyper P., 'Trade sanctions, security, and human rights and commercial policy', in Maresceau M. (ed.), *The European Community's Commercial Policy after 1992: The Legal Dimension* (Dordrecht, Martinus Nijhoff, 1993) 401

Kymlicka W., *Multicultural Citizenship* (Oxford, Clarendon Press, 1995)

Lacey N., 'Legislation against sex discrimination: questions from a feminist perspective', 14 *Journal of Law and Society* (1987) 411

Lacey N., 'Theory into practice? Pornography and the public/private dichotomy', 20 *Journal of Law and Society* (1993) 93

Ladin S., *IWRAW to CEDAW: Country Reports* (Minneapolis, International Women's Rights Action Watch, 1992)

Lammers J., 'General principles of law recognised by civilised nations', in Kalshoven F. (ed.), *Essays on the Development of the International Legal Order* (Alphen aan den Rijn, Sijthoff and Noordhoff, 1980) 53

Landsberg-Lewis I., *Bringing Equality Home. Implementing the Convention on the Elimination of All Forms of Discrimination against Women* (New York, UNIFEM, 1998)

Langton M., 'The United Nations and indigenous minorities: a report on the United Nations Working Group on Indigenous Populations', in Hocking B. (ed.), *International Law and Aboriginal Human Rights* (Sydney, Law Book Co. Ltd, 1988) 83

Lasswell H. and McDougal M., *Jurisprudence for a Free Society: Studies in Law, Science, and Policy* (New Haven, New Haven Press, 1992)

Lauterpacht H., *The Function of Law in the International Community* (Oxford, Clarendon Press, 1933)

Lauterpacht H., 'The Grotian tradition in international law', 23 *British Yearbook of International Law* (1946) 1

Lauterpacht H., *Recognition in International Law* (Cambridge, Cambridge University Press, 1948)

Lawson S. (ed.), *The New Agenda for Global Security: Cooperating for Peace and Beyond* (Sydney, Allen & Unwin, 1995)

Lederman R., 'Looking back: the women's peace camps in perspective', in Russell D. (ed.), *Exposing Nuclear Phallacies* (New York/Oxford, Pergamon Press, 1989) 244

Lee R. (ed.), *The International Criminal Court* (The Hague, Kluwer Law International, 1999)

Lee Y., 'Violence against women: reflections on the past and strategies for the future – an NGO perspective', 19 *Adelaide Law Review* (1997) 45

Leigh M., 'The Yugoslav Tribunal: use of unnamed witnesses against accused', 90 *American Journal of International Law* (1996) 235

Leigh M., 'Witness anonymity is inconsistent with due process', 91 *American Journal of International Law* (1997) 80

Leigh M. and Blakeslee M., *National Treaty Law and Practice* (Washington DC, American Society of International Law, 1994)

Leites J., 'Modernist jurisprudence as a vehicle for gender role reform in the Islamic world', 22 *Columbia Human Rights Law Review* (1991) 251

Li X., 'License to coerce: violence against women, state responsibility, and legal failures in China's family planning program', 8 *Yale Journal of Law and Feminism* (1996) 145

Lijnzaad L., *Reservations to UN Human Rights Treaties: Ratify and Ruin?* (Dordrecht, Martinus Nijhoff, 1995).

Lillich R., 'The proper role of domestic courts in the international legal order', 11 *Virginia Journal of International Law* (1970) 9

Lillich R. (ed.), *Humanitarian Intervention and the United Nations* (Charlottesville, University of Virginia Press, 1973)

Llewellyn K., *Karl Llewellyn on Legal Realism* (Birmingham, Legal Classics Library, 1986)

Locke J., *Two Treatises of Government* (J. Harrison and P. Laslett (eds), Oxford, Oxford University Press, 1965)

Loenen T., 'Changing the gender bias in the conceptualisation of equality by international judicial bodies', in *Contemporary International Law Issues: Opportunities at a Time of Momentous Change*, (The Hague, Nederlandse Verenigning voor Internationaal Recht, 1993) 424

Lowe V. (ed.), *Extraterritorial Jurisdiction: An Annotated Collection of Legal Materials* (Cambridge, Grotius Publications, 1983)

Lowe V., 'The role of equity in international law', 12 *Australian Yearbook of International Law* (1992) 54

Lowe V., 'US extraterritorial jurisdiction: the *Helms-Burton* and *D'Amato* Acts', 46 *International and Comparative Law Quarterly* (1997) 378

Luban D., 'Just war and human rights', 9 *Philosophy and Public Affairs* (1979–80) 160

Lubin C. and Winslow A., *Social Justice for Women: The International Labor Organization and Women* (Durham, Duke University Press, 1990)

Lugones M., 'Playfulness, "world-traveling", and loving perception', 2 *Hypatia* (1987) 3

Lugones M. and Spelman E., 'Have we got a theory for you!', 6 *Hypatia* (1983) 578

Mabandla B., 'Promoting gender equality in South Africa', in Bazilli S. (ed.), *Putting Women on the Agenda* (Johannesburg, Ravan Press, 1991) 75

MacCormick N., 'Beyond the sovereign state', 56 *Modern Law Review* (1993) 1

Macdonald R. (ed.), *Essays in Honour of Wang Tieya* (Dordrecht, Martinus Nijhoff, 1994)

Macdonald R. and Johnston D. (eds), *The Structure and Process of International Law: Essays in Legal Philosophy, Doctrine and Theory* (Dordrecht, Martinus Nijhoff, 1983)

Macdonald S., 'Drawing the lines – gender, peace and war: an introduction', in Macdonald S., Holden P. and Ardner S. (eds), *Images of War in Peace and War: Cross Cultural and Historical Perspectives* (Basingstoke, Macmillan, 1987) 1

Macdonald S., Holden P. and Ardner S. (eds), *Images of War in Peace and War: Cross-Cultural and Historical Perspectives* (Basingstoke, Macmillan, 1987)

MacKinnon C., *Sexual Harassment of Working Women* (New Haven, Yale University Press, 1979)

MacKinnon C., *Feminism Unmodified: Discourses on Life and Law* (Cambridge, Harvard University Press, 1987)

MacKinnon C., *Towards a Feminist Theory of the State* (Cambridge, Harvard University Press, 1989)

MacKinnon C. 'From practice to theory, or what is a white woman anyway?', 4 *Yale Journal of Law and Feminism* (1991) 13

MacKinnon C, 'Crimes of war, crimes of peace', in Shute S. and Hurley S. (eds), *On Human Rights: The Oxford Amnesty Lectures 1993* (New York, Basic Books, 1993) 83

MacKinnon C., *Only Words* (London, Harper Collins, 1995)

Mahoney K.and Mahoney P. (eds), *Human Rights in the 21st Century: A Global Challenge* (Dordrecht, Martinus Nijhoff, 1993) 405

Maine H., *Ancient Law* (London, J. Murray, 1863)

Malanczuk P., *Akehurst's Modern Introduction to International Law* (London, Routledge, 7th ed. 1997)

Maresceau M. (ed.), *The European Community's Commercial Policy after 1992: The Legal Dimension* (Dordrecht, Martinus Nijhoff, 1993)

Margolis E., 'The hydrogen bomb experiments and international law', 64 *Yale Law Journal* (1955) 629

Marks S., 'The peace-human rights-development dialectic', 11 *Bulletin of Peace Proposals* (1980) 339

Marks S., 'Three regional human rights treaties and their experience of reservations', in Gardner J-P. (ed.), *Human Rights as General Norms and a State's Right to Opt Out* (London, British Institute of International and Comparative Law, 1997) 35

Martin J., 'Methodological essentialism, false difference, and other dangerous traps', 19 *Signs* (1994) 630

Mayer T. (ed.), *Women and the Israeli Occupation: The Politics of Change* (London, Routledge, 1994)

McClintock A., *Imperial Leather: Race, Gender and Sexuality in the Colonial Context* (New York, Routledge, 1995)

McDougal M., 'Fuller versus the American legal realists: an intervention', 50 *Yale Law Journal* (1941) 827

McDougal M., 'Peace and war: factual continuum with multiple legal consequences', 49 *American Journal of International Law* (1955) 63

McDougal M. and Chen L., 'Human rights of women and world public order: the outlawing of sex-based discrimination', 69 *American Journal of International Law* (1975) 497

McDougal M. and Feliciano F., *Law and Minimum World Public Order: The Legal Regulation of International Coercion* (New Haven, Yale University Press, 1961)

McDougal M. and Reisman M., 'The prescribing function in the world constitutive process: how international law is made', 6 *Yale Studies in World Public Order* (1980) 249

McDougal M. and Schlei N., 'The hydrogen bomb tests in perspective: lawful measures for security', 64 *Yale Law Journal* (1955) 648

McGibbon I., 'The scope of acquiescence in international law', 31 *British Yearbook of International Law* (1954) 143

McIntosh M., 'The state and the oppression of women', in Kuhn A. and Wolpe A. (eds), *Feminism and Materialism: Women and Modes of Production* (London, Routledge & Paul, 1978) 254

McKean W., *Equality and Discrimination under International Law* (Oxford, Clarendon Press, 1983)

McNair A., *The Law of Treaties* (Oxford, Clarendon Press, 1961)

Medina C., 'Toward a more effective guarantee of the enjoyment of human rights by women in the Inter-American system', in Cook R. (ed.), *Human Rights of Women: National and International Perspectives* (Philadelphia, University of Pennsylvania Press, 1994) 257

Meijers H., 'How is international law made? The stages of growth of international law and the use of its customary rules', 9 *Netherlands Yearbook of International Law* (1978) 3

Menkel-Meadow C., 'Towards another view of legal negotiation: the structure of problem-solving', 31 *University of California, Los Angeles Law Review* (1984) 754

Menkel-Meadow C., 'Portia in a different voice: speculations on a women's lawyering process', 1 *Berkeley Women's Law Journal* (1985) 39

Menkel-Meadow C., 'The trouble with the adversary system in a postmodern, multicultural world', 38 *William and Mary Law Review* (1996) 5

Meron T. (ed.), *Human Rights in International Law* (New York, Oxford University Press, 1984)

Meron T., 'Enhancing the effectiveness of the prohibition of discrimination against women', 84 *American Journal of International Law* (1990) 213

Meron T., 'Shakespeare's Henry the Fifth and the law of war', 86 *American Journal of International Law* (1992) 1

Meron T., 'Rape as a crime under international humanitarian law', 87 *American Journal of International Law* (1993) 424

Meron T., 'Classification of armed conflict in the Former Yugoslavia: Nicaragua's fallout', 92 *American Journal of International Law* (1998) 236

Meron T., 'War crimes law comes of age', 92 *American Journal of International Law* (1998) 462

Merrills J., *International Dispute Settlement* (Cambridge, Cambridge University Press, 3rd ed. 1998)

Middle East Watch, *A Victory Turned Sour: Human Rights in Kuwait since Liberation* (New York, Human Rights Watch, 1991)

Mies M., *The Laceworkers of Naraspur: Indian Housewives Produce for the World Market* (London, Zed Books, 1982)

Miller C., 'Women in international relations: the debate in inter-war Britain', in Grant R. and Newland K. (eds), *Gender and International Relations* (Bloomington, Indiana University Press, 1991)

Minda G., *Postmodern Legal Movements: Law and Jurisprudence at the Century's End* (New York, New York University Press, 1995)

Minow M., 'Interpreting rights: an essay for Robert Cover', 96 *Yale Law Journal* (1987) 1860

Mitchell S. and Das Pradhan R. (eds), *Back to Basics from Beijing* (Canberra, Australian Council for Overseas Aid, 1997)

Mnookin R. and Kornhauser L., 'Bargaining in the shadow of the law: the case of divorce', 88 *Yale Law Journal* (1979) 950

Moghadam V., 'Women, work and ideology in the Islamic Republic', 20 *International Journal of Middle East Studies* (1988) 221

Mohanty C., 'Under western eyes: feminist scholarship and colonial discourses', 30 *Feminist Review* (1988) 61

Mohanty C., Russo A. and Torres L. (eds), *Third World Women and the Politics of Feminism* (Bloomington, Indiana University Press, 1991)

Mohanty C., 'Cartographies of struggle: third world women and the politics of feminism', in Mohanty C., Russo A. and Torres L. (eds), *Third World Women and the Politics of Feminism* (Bloomington, Indiana University Press, 1991) 81

Mohanty C., 'Women workers and capitalist scripts: ideologies of domination, common interests, and the politics of solidarity', in Alexander M. and Mohanty C. (eds), *Feminist Genealogies, Colonial Legacies, Democratic Futures* (New York/London, Routledge, 1997) 3

Momsen J. and Townsend J., *Geography of Gender in the Third World* (Albany, State University of New York Press, 1987)

Moore H., *Feminism and Anthropology* (Cambridge, Polity Press, 1988)

Morgan E., 'The hermaphroditic paradigm of international law: a comment on *Alvarez-Machain*', *Proceedings of the Canadian Council on International Law* (Ottawa, Canadian Council on International Law, 1992) 78

Morgan R. (ed.), *Sisterhood is Global: The International Women's Movement* (Garden City, Anchor Press/Doubleday, 1984)

Morgan R., *The Demon Lover: On the Sexuality of Terrorism* (London, Mandarin, 1989)

Morgenthau H., *Politics Among Nations: The Struggle for Power and Peace* (New York, Alfred A. Knopf, 5th ed. 1973)

Morrison T. (ed.), *Race-ing Justice, En-gendering Power* (New York, Pantheon Books, 1992)

Mosler H., 'The international society as a legal community', 140 *Recueil des Cours* (1974) 17

Mousavizadeh N. (ed.), *The Black Book of Bosnia: The Consequences of Appeasement* (New York, Basic Books, 1996)

Mullerson R., 'Sources of international law: new tendencies in Soviet thinking', 83 *American Journal of International Law* (1989) 498

Murphy C., 'Seeing women, recognizing gender, recasting international relations', 50 *International Organization* (1996) 513

Murphy J., 'International crimes', in Schachter O. and Joyner C. (eds), *United Nations Legal Order* (Cambridge, Cambridge University Press, 1995) vol. 2, 993.

Murphy S., *Humanitarian Intervention: The United Nations in an Evolving World Order* (Philadelphia, University of Pennsylvania Press, 1996)

Mushkat R., 'When war may justifiably be waged: an analysis of historical and contemporary legal perspectives', 15 *Brooklyn Journal of International Law* (1989) 223

Naffine N., *Law and the Sexes: Explorations in Feminist Jurisprudence* (Sydney, Allen & Unwin, 1990)

Naffine N., 'The body bag', in Naffine N. and Owens R. (eds), *Sexing the Subject of Law* (Sydney, Law Book Co. Ltd., 1997) 79

Naffine N. and Owens R. (eds), *Sexing the Subject of Law* (Sydney, Law Book Co. Ltd., 1997)

Nedelsky J., 'Reconceiving autonomy: sources, thoughts and possibilities', in Hutchinson A. and Green L. (eds), *Law and the Community: The End of Individualism?* (Toronto, Carswell, 1989) 219

Nedelsky J., 'Law, boundaries, and the bounded self', 38 *Representations* (1990) 162

Nesiah V., 'Towards a feminist internationality: a critique of US feminist legal scholarship', in Kapur R. (ed.), *Feminist Terrains in Legal Domains* (New Delhi, Kali, 1996) 11

Nordstrom C., *Warzones: Cultures of Violence, Militarisation and Peace* (Canberra, Peace Research Centre Working Paper no. 145, Australian National University, 1994)

Northrup T., 'Getting to maybe: the uneasy partnership between conflict theory and feminist theory', paper presented at the Annual Meeting International Studies Association, Washington DC, March 1994

Norton N., 'Women, it is not enough to be elected: committee position makes a difference', in Duerst-Lahti G. and Kelly R. (eds), *Gender, Power, Leadership and Governance* (Ann Arbor, University of Michigan Press, 1995) 15

Nussbaum A., *A Concise History of the Law of Nations* (New York, Macmillan, 2ⁿᵈ ed. 1962)

Nussbaum M., 'Human functioning and social justice: in defence of Aristotelian essentialism', 20 *Political Theory* (1992) 202

Oakley A. and Mitchell J. (eds), *Who's Afraid of Feminism? Seeing Through the Backlash* (New York, The New Press, 1997)

Oakley A., 'A brief history of gender', in Oakley A. and Mitchell J. (eds), *Who's Afraid of Feminism? Seeing Through the Backlash* (New York, The New Press, 1997) 29

Obiora L., 'Bridges and barricades: rethinking polemics and intransigence in the campaign against female circumcision', 47 *Case Western Reserve Law Review* (1997) 275

O'Connell D., *International Law* (London, Stevens, 2nd edn 1970)

O'Donovan K., *Sexual Divisions in Law* (London, Weidenfeld & Nicholson, 1985)

O'Flaherty M. and Gisvold G. (eds), *Post-War Protection of Human Rights in Bosnia and Herzegovina* (The Hague, Kluwer Law International, 1998)

Olsen F., 'The family and the market: a study of ideology and legal reform', 96 *Harvard Law Review* (1983) 1497

Olsen F., 'Statutory rape: a feminist critique of rights analysis', 63 *Texas Law Review* (1984) 387

Olsen F., 'The myth of state intervention in the family', 18 *University of Michigan Journal of Law Reform* (1985) 835

Olsen F., 'Feminism and critical legal theory: an American perspective', 18 *International Journal of the Sociology of Law* (1990) 199

Olsen F., 'Children's rights: some feminist approaches to the United Nations Convention on the Rights of the Child', 6 *International Journal of Law and the Family* (1992) 192

Onuf N. and Birney R., 'Peremptory norms of international law: their source, function and future', 4 *Denver Journal of International Law and Policy* (1974) 187

Oppenheim L., *International Law: A Treatise* (London/New York, Longmans, Green and Co., 1ˢᵗ edn 1905, 1906)

Orford A., 'A radical agenda for collective security reform', *Proceedings of the Second Annual Meeting of the Australian and New Zealand Society of International Law* (Canberra, Centre for International and Public Law, 1994) 71

Orford A., 'The uses of sovereignty in the new imperial order', 6 *Australian Feminist Law Journal* (1996) 63

Orford A., 'The politics of collective security', 17 *Michigan Journal of International Law* (1996) 363

Orford A., 'Locating the international: military and monetary interventions after the cold war', 38 *Harvard International Law Journal* (1997) 443

Osman, H., 'Somalia: will reconstruction threaten women's progress?', 8 *Ms Magazine* (no. 5, March/April 1995) 12

Otto D., 'NGOs in the UN system: the emerging role of international civil society', 18 *Human Rights Quarterly* (1996) 107

Otto D., 'Subalternity and international law: the problems of global community and the incommensurability of difference', 5 *Social and Legal Studies* (1996) 337

Otto D., 'Holding up half the sky, but for whose benefit? A critical analysis of the Fourth World Conference on Women', 6 *Australian Feminist Law Journal* (1996) 7

Otto D., 'A post-Beijing reflection on the limitations and potential of human rights discourse for women', in Askin K. and Koenig D. (eds), *Women and International Human Rights Law* (Ardsley, Transnational Publishers Inc., 1999) vol. 1, 115

Palmer G., 'New ways to make international environmental law', 86 *American Journal of International Law* (1992) 259

Panjabi R., 'From Stockholm to Rio: a comparison of the declaratory principles of international environmental law', 21 *Denver Journal of International Law and Policy* (1992) 215

Parashar A., 'Reconceptualisations of civil society: third world and ethnic women', in Thornton M. (ed.), *Public and Private: Feminist Legal Debates* (Melbourne, Oxford University Press, 1995) 221

Parker L. (ed.), *A Compilation of Documents on the Participation of Women in the Work of the United Nations System (1945–1988)* (a report of the Group on Equal Rights for Women at the Vienna International Centre, submitted as a background paper to the Commission on the Status of Women at its 32nd session, Vienna, 14–23 March 1988)

Parry C., *The Sources and Evidences of International Law* (Manchester, Manchester University Press, 1968)

Pateman C., 'Feminist critiques of the public/private dichotomy', in Benn S. and Gaus G. (eds), *Public and Private in Social Life* (London, Croom Helm, 1983) 281

Pateman C., *The Disorders of Women: Democracy, Feminism and Political Theory* (Cambridge, Polity Press, 1989)

Pateman C. and Gross E. (eds), *Feminist Challenges: Social and Political Theory* (Sydney, Allen & Unwin, 1986)

Paust J., 'The seizure and recovery of the Mayaguez', 85 *Yale Law Journal* (1975–6) 774

Pellet A., 'The normative dilemma: will and consent in international law-making', 12 *Australian Yearbook of International Law* (1992) 22

Peteet J., 'No going back: women and the Palestinian movement', 138 *Middle East Report* (Jan.-Feb. 1986) 20

Peters C. (ed.), *Collateral Damage: The 'New World Order' at Home and Abroad* (Boston, South End Press, 1992)

Peters J. and Wolper A. (eds), *Women's Rights Human Rights* (New York, Routledge, 1995)

Peterson M., *Recognition of Governments: Legal Doctrine and State Practice* (New York, St. Martin's Press, 1997)

Peterson V., 'Whose rights? A critique of the "givens" in human rights discourse', 15 *Alternatives* (1989) 303

Peterson V. (ed.), *Gendered States: Feminist (Re)Visions of International Relations Theory* (Boulder, Lynne Rienner Publishers, 1992)

Peterson V., 'Security and sovereign states: what is at stake in taking feminism seriously?', in Peterson V. (ed.), *Gendered States: Feminist (Re)Visions of International Relations Theory* (Boulder, Lynne Rienner Publishers, 1992) 31

Peterson V. and Parisi L., 'Are women human? It's not an academic question', in Evans T. (ed.), *Human Rights Fifty Years On: A Reappraisal* (Manchester, Manchester University Press, 1998) 132

Peterson V. and Runyan A., *Global Gender Issues* (Boulder, Westview Press, 1993) 93

Bibliography

Pettman J., 'A feminist perspective on peace and security', 4 *Interdisciplinary Peace Research* (1992) 58

Pettman J., *Worlding Women: A Feminist International Politics* (Sydney, Allen & Unwin, 1996)

Pfanner R., 'Australian foreign aid and women in the third world', in Grieve N. and Burns A. (eds), *Australian Women: New Feminist Perspectives* (Melbourne, Oxford University Press, 1986) 305

Phillips A., *Engendering Democracy* (Cambridge, Polity Press in association with Blackwell, 1991)

Phillips A., *Democracy and Difference* (University Park, Pennsylvania State University, 1993)

Phillips A. (ed.), *Feminism and Politics* (Oxford, Oxford University Press, 1998)

Phillips A., 'Democracy and representation: or, why should it matter who our representatives are?', in Phillips A. (ed.), *Feminism and Politics* (Oxford, Oxford University Press, 1998) 224

Pierson R., '"Did your mother wear army boots?" Feminist theory and women's relations to war, peace and revolution', in Macdonald S., Holden P. and Ardener S. (eds), *Images of Women in Peace and War: Cross-Cultural and Historical Perspectives* (Basingstoke, Macmillan, 1987) 205

Pietila H. and Vickers J., *Making Women Matter: The Role of the United Nations* (London, Zed Books, 1994)

Polan D., 'Toward a theory of law and patriarchy', in Kairys D. (ed.), *The Politics of Law* (New York, Pantheon, 1982) 294

Prechal S. and Burrows N., *Gender Discrimination Law of the European Community* (Aldershot, Dartmouth, 1990)

Price Cohen C., 'The role of nongovernmental organizations in the drafting of the Convention on the Rights of the Child', 12 *Human Rights Quarterly* (1990) 137

Pringle R. and Watson S., 'Fathers, brothers, mates: the fraternal state in Australia', in Watson S. (ed.), *Playing the State* (Sydney, Allen & Unwin, 1990) 7

Prunier G., *The Rwanda Crisis: History of a Genocide* (New York, Columbia University Press, 1995)

Punamaki R-L., 'Relationships between political violence and psychological responses among Palestinian women', 27 *Journal of Peace and Research* (1990) 75

Purvis N., 'Critical legal studies in public international law', 32 *Harvard International Law Journal* (1991) 81

Radin M., 'The pragmatist and the feminist', 63 *Southern California Law Review* (1990) 1699

Rahman A., 'Religious rights versus women's rights in India: a test case for international human rights law', 28 *Columbia Journal of Transnational Law* (1990) 473

Rai S., 'Gender and representation: women MPs in the Indian Parliament 1991-6', in Goetz A. (ed.), *Getting Institutions Right for Women in Development* (London/New York, Zed Books, 1997) 104

Ramcharan B. (ed.), *The Right to Life in International Law* (Dordrecht/Boston, Martinus Nijhoff, 1985)

Ramcharan B., 'The concept and dimensions of the right to life', in Ramcharan B. (ed.), *The Right to Life in International Law* (Dordrecht/Boston, Martinus Nijhoff, 1985) 1

Randall V., *Women and Politics: An International Perspective* (Chicago, University of Chicago Press, 1987)

Rao A, 'The politics of gender and culture in international human rights discourse', in Peters J. and Wolper A. (eds), *Women's Rights Human Rights* (New York, Routledge, 1995) 167

Rasekh Z., Bauer H., Manos M. and Lacopino V., 'Women's health and human rights in Afghanistan', 280 *Journal of the American Medical Association* (1998) 449

Ratner S., 'Image and reality in the UN's peaceful settlement of disputes', 6 *European Journal of International Law* (1995) 426

Rawls J., 'The law of peoples', in Shute S. and Hurley S. (eds), *On Human Rights: The Oxford Amnesty Lectures* (New York, Basic Books, 1993) 41

Razavi S. and Miller C., *Gender Mainstreaming: A Study of efforts by the UNDP, the World Bank and the ILO to institutionalize gender issues* (Geneva, UN Research Institute for Social Development, 1995)

Reanda L., 'The Commission on the Status of Women', in Alston P. (ed.), *The United Nations and Human Rights: A Critical Appraisal* (Oxford, Clarendon Press, 1992) 267

Reardon B., *Sexism and the War System* (New York, Teachers College Press, 1985)

Redgewell C., 'Universality or integrity? Some reflections on reservations to general multilateral treaties', 64 *British Yearbook of International Law* (1993) 245

Rehof L., *Guide to the Travaux Préparatoires of the United Nations Convention on the Elimination of All Forms of Discrimination against Women* (Dordrecht, Martinus Nijhoff, 1993)

Reisman M., 'Coercion and self-determination: construing Charter article 2(4)', 78 *American Journal of International Law* (1984) 642

Reisman M., 'The resistance in Afghanistan is engaged in a war of national liberation', 81 *American Journal of International Law* (1987) 906

Reisman M., 'Sovereignty and human rights in contemporary international law', 84 *American Journal of International Law* (1990) 866

Reisman M., 'The concept and functions of soft law in international politics', in Bello E. and Ajibola B. (eds), *Essays in Honour of Judge Taslim Olawale Elias* (Dordrecht, Martinus Nijhoff, 1992) 135

Reisman M., 'The view from the New Haven school of international law', *Proceedings of the 86th Annual Meeting of the American Society of International Law* (Washington DC, American Society of International Law, 1992) 118

Reisman M., 'Preparing to wage peace: toward the creation of an international peacemaking command and staff college', 88 *American Journal of International Law* (1994) 76

Reisman M., 'Haiti and the validity of international action', 89 *American Journal of International Law* (1995) 82

Reisman M., 'Protecting indigenous rights in international adjudication', 89 *American Journal of International Law* (1995) 350

Reisman M. and Silk J., 'Which law applies to the Afghan conflict?', 82 *American Journal of International Law* (1988) 459

Renteln A., 'The unanswered challenge of relativism and the consequences for human rights', 7 *Human Rights Quarterly* (1985) 514

Reynolds H., *The Law of the Land* (Melbourne, Penguin Books, 1987)

Rich R., 'Recognition of states: the collapse of Yugoslavia and the Soviet Union', 4 *European Journal of International Law* (1993) 36

Rieff D., *Slaughterhouse: Bosnia and the Failure of the West* (London, Vintage, 1995)

Rifkin J., 'Mediation from a feminist perspective: promise and problems', 2 *Law and Equality* (1984) 21

Righter R., *Utopia Lost: The United Nations and World Order* (New York, Twentieth Century Fund Press, 1995)

Rishmawi M., 'The legal status of Palestinian women in the Occupied Territories', in Toubia N. (ed.), *Women of the Arab World* (London, Zed Books, 1988) 79

Roberts A. and Kingsbury B. (eds), *United Nations, Divided World: The United Nations' Role in International Relations* (Oxford, Clarendon Press, 2nd ed. 1993)

Rodley N., *The Treatment of Prisoners under International Law* (Oxford, Clarendon Press, 1987)

Romany C., 'State responsibility goes private: a feminist critique of the public/private distinction in international human rights law', in Cook R., *Human Rights of Women: National and International Perspectives* (Philadelphia, University of Pennyslvania Press, 1994) 137

Romany C., 'Black women and gender equality in a new South Africa: human rights and the intersection of race and gender', 21 *Brooklyn Journal of International Law* (1996) 857

Ronzitti N., *Rescuing Nationals Abroad through Military Coercion and Intervention on Grounds of Humanity* (Dordrecht, Martinus Nijhoff, 1985)

Rosaldo M., 'The use and abuse of anthropology: reflections on feminism and cross-cultural understanding', 5 *Signs* (1980) 389

Rosas A., 'Democracy and human rights', in Rosas A. and Helgesen J. (eds), *Human Rights in a Changing East-West Perspective* (London, Pinter Publications, 1990) 31

Rossi C., *Equity and International Law: A Legal Realist Approach to International Decision-Making* (New York, Transnational Publishers, 1993)

Rostow E., 'Until what? Enforcement action or collective self-defence?' 85 *American Journal of International Law* (1991) 506

Rubin B., 'Women and pipelines: Afghanistan's proxy wars', 73 *International Affairs* (1997) 283

Runyan A. and Peterson V., 'The radical future of realism: feminist subversions of IR theory', 16 *Alternatives* (1991) 67

Russell D. (ed.), *Crimes Against Women: The Proceedings of the International Tribunal* (San Francisco, Frog in the Well, 1976, reprinted 1984)

Russell D. (ed.), *Exposing Nuclear Phallacies* (New York/Oxford, Pergamon Press, 1989)

Russell R., *A History of the United Nations Charter: The Role of the United States, 1940–1945* (Washington DC, Brookings Institution, 1958)

Sabel R., *Procedure at International Conferences: A Study of the Rules of Procedure of Conferences and Assemblies on International Inter-Governmental Organizations* (Cambridge, Cambridge University Press, 1997)

Sadurska R., 'Threats of force', 82 *American Journal of International Law* (1988) 239

Said E., *Orientalism: Western Conceptions of the Orient* (Harmondsworth, Penguin, 1985)

Sandoz Y., Swinarski C. and Zimmerman B. (eds), *ICRC Commentary on the Additional Protocols of 8 June 1977 to the Geneva Conventions of 12 August 1949* (Geneva, Martinus Nijhoff Publishers, 1987)

Santow G., 'Social roles and physical health: the case of female disadvantage in poor countries', 40 *Social Sciences and Medicine* (1995) 141

Savage M. and Witz A. (eds), *Gender and Bureaucracy* (Oxford/Cambridge, Blackwell/ Sociological Review, 1992)

Scales A., 'The emergence of feminist jurisprudence: an essay', 95 *Yale Law Journal* (1986) 1373

Scales A., 'Militarism, male dominance and law: feminist jurisprudence as oxymoron?', 12 *Harvard Women's Law Journal* (1989) 25

Schachter O., 'The invisible college of international lawyers', 72 *Northwestern University Law Review* (1977) 217

Schachter O., 'International law in theory and practice: general course in public international law', 178 *Recueil des Cours* (1982) 21

Schachter O., 'Self-defense and the rule of law', 83 *American Journal of International Law* (1989) 259

Schachter O., *International Law in Theory and Practice* (Dordrecht/Boston, Martinus Nijhoff, 1991)

Schachter O., 'Sovereignty – then and now', in Macdonald R. (ed.), *Essays in Honour of Wang Tieya* (Dordrecht, Martinus Nijhoff, 1994) 671

Schachter O. and Joyner C. (eds), *United Nations Legal Order* (Cambridge, Cambridge University Press, 1995)

Schuler M. (ed.), *Freedom from Violence: Women's Strategies from Around the World* (New York, UNIFEM, 1992) 49

Schwarzenberger G., 'International *jus cogens*', 43 *Texas Law Review* (1965) 455

Schwelb E., 'Some aspects of international *jus cogens* as formulated by the International Law Commission', 61 *American Journal of International Law* (1967) 946

Scott J., 'Gender: a useful category of analysis', 91 *American Historical Review* (1986) 1053

Scutt J., *Women and the Law* (Sydney, Law Book Co., 1990)

Seager J., *Earth Follies* (New York, Routledge, 1993)

Seidl-Hohenveldern I., 'International economic soft law', 198 *Recueil des Cours* (1986) vol. III, 68

Seifert R., 'War and rape: a preliminary analysis', in Stiglmayer A. (ed.), *Mass Rape: The War against Women in Bosnia-Herzegovina* (Lincoln, University of Nebraska Press, 1994) 82

Sen A., 'More than 100 million women are missing', *New York Review of Books*, 20 December 1990, 61

Sen A., *Development as Freedom* (New York, Alfred A. Knopf, Inc., 1999)

Sen G. and Grown C., *Development, Crises, and Alternative Visions: Third World Women's Perspectives* (New York, Monthly Review Press, 1987)

Shahabuddeen M., 'Developing countries and the idea of international law', in Macdonald R. (ed.), *Essays in Honour of Wang Tieya* (Dordrecht, Martinus Nijhoff, 1994) 721

Sharoni S., 'Middle East politics through feminist lenses: toward theorizing international relations from women's struggles', 18 *Alternatives* (1993) 5

Sharp W., 'Protecting the avatars of international peace and security', 7 *Duke Journal of Comparative and International Law* (1996) 93

Shaw M., *International Law* (Cambridge, Grotius, 4th ed. 1997)

Sheehy E., 'Feminist argumentation before the Supreme Court of Canada in *R. v. Seaboyer; R. v. Gayme*: the sound of one hand clapping', 18 *Melbourne University Law Review* (1991) 450

Shepherd G. and Anikpo M. (eds), *Emerging Human Rights: The African Political Economy Context* (New York, Greenwood Press, 1990)

Sherry S, 'Civic virtue and the feminine voice in constitutional adjudication', 72 *Virginia Law Review* (1986) 543

Sherry S., 'The gender of judges', 4 *Law and Inequality* (1986) 159

Shihata I., *The World Bank Inspection Panel* (Oxford, Clarendon Press, 1994)

Shiva V., *Women, Ecology and Economic Globalisation: Searching for an Alternative Vision* (New Delhi, Indian Association of Women's Studies, 1995)

Shute S. and Hurley S. (eds), *On Human Rights: The Oxford Amnesty Lectures* (New York, Basic Books, 1993)

Sikkink K., 'Human rights, principled issue-networks and sovereignty in Latin America', 47 *International Organization* (1993) 411

Simma B., 'The work of the International Law Commission at its forty-ninth session', 66 *Nordic Journal of International Law* (1997) 527

Simma B., 'Reservations to human rights treaties: some recent developments', in Hafner G. (ed.), *Liber Amicorum Professor Seidl-Hohenveldern* (The Hague, Kluwer Law International, 1998) 659

Simma B. and Alston P., 'The sources of human rights law: custom, *jus cogens* and general principles', 12 *Australian Yearbook of International Law* (1992) 82

Simma B. and Paulus A., 'The "international community": facing the challenge of globalization', 9 *European Journal of International Law* (1998) 266

Simon S., 'Contemporary legality of unilateral humanitarian intervention', 24 *California Western International Law Journal* (1993) 117

Simons G., *Imposing Economic Sanctions* (London, Pluto Press, 1999)

Simpson G., 'Imagined consent: democratic liberalism in international legal theory', 15 *Australian Yearbook of International Law* (1994) 103

Simpson G., 'Is international law fair?', 17 *Michigan Journal of International Law* (1996) 61

Simpson G. and Charlesworth H., 'Objecting to objectivity: the radical challenge to legal liberalism', in Hunter R., Ingleby R. and Johnstone R. (eds), *Thinking About Law* (Sydney, Allen & Unwin, 1995) 85

Sinclair I., *The International Law Commission* (Manchester, Manchester University Press, 1987)

Singer M., 'Jurisdictional immunity of international organizations: human rights and functional necessity concerns', 36 *Virginia Journal of International Law* (1995) 53

Sipila H., 'Introduction', in Whittick A., *Women into Citizens* (London, The Athenaeum Publishing Co. Ltd, 1979) 1

Sjolander C., 'The rhetoric of globalization: what's in a wor(l)d?', 51 *International Journal* (1996) 603

Skjeie, H., 'The rhetoric of difference: on women's inclusion into political elites', 19 *Politics and Society* (1991) 233

371

Sklar H., 'Brave new world order', in Peters C. (ed.), *The 'New World Order' at Home and Abroad: Collateral Damage* (Boston, South End Press, 1991) 3

Slaughter A.-M., 'International law in a world of liberal states', 6 *European Journal of International Law* (1995) 503

Slaughter A.-M., Tulumello A. and Wood S., 'International law and international relations theory: a new generation of interdisciplinary scholarship', 92 *American Journal of International Law* (1998) 367

Sloan B., 'General Assembly resolutions revisited', 58 *British Yearbook of International Law* (1987) 39

Smart C., 'Feminist jurisprudence', (talk at La Trobe University, Melbourne, 2 December 1987)

Smart C., *Feminism and the Power of Law* (London, Routledge, 1989)

Snyder F. and Sathirathai S., *Third World Attitudes Towards International Law: An Introduction* (Dordrecht, Martinus Nijhoff, 1987)

Snyder F. and Slynn P., *International Law of Development: Comparative Perspectives* (Abingdon, Professional Books Ltd., 1987)

Spender D., *Man Made Language* (London/Boston, Routledge & Kegan Paul, 1980)

Spinedi M. and Simma B (eds), *UN Codification of State Responsibility* (New York, Oceana Publications, 1987)

Spivak G., 'Criticism, feminism and the institution', *Thesis Eleven* 10/11 184

Stark B., 'Nurturing rights: an essay on women, peace and international human rights', 13 *Michigan Journal of International Law* (1991) 144

Stark B., 'The "other" half of the international bill of rights as a postmodern feminist text', in D. Dallmeyer (ed.), *Reconceiving Reality: Women and International Law* (Washington DC, American Society of International Law, 1993) 19

Steains C., 'Gender issues in the Statute of the International Criminal Court', in Lee R. (ed.), *The International Criminal Court* (The Hague, Kluwer Law International, 1999) 357

Stein T., 'The approach of the different drummer: the principle of the persistent objector in international law', 26 *Harvard International Law Journal* (1985) 457

Steiner H. and Alston P., *International Human Rights in Context* (Oxford, Clarendon Press, 1996)

Stephen N., 'Toward transnational norms of criminal procedure: emerging issues of defendants' rights', in *Contemporary International Law Issues: New Forms New Applications* (The Hague, Nederlandse Vereniging voor Internationaal Recht, 1997) 137

Stiehm J., 'The protected, the protector, the defender', 5 *Women's Studies International Forum* (1982) 367

Stiehm J., 'Peacekeeping and peace research: men and women's work', 18 *Women and Politics* (1997) 27

Stienstra D., *Women's Movements and International Organizations* (London, Macmillan, 1994)

Stiglmayer A. (ed.), *Mass Rape: The War against Women in Bosnia-Herzegovina* (Lincoln, University of Nebraska Press, 1994)

Stivens M., 'Why gender matters in Southeast Asian politics', [1989] *Asian Studies Review* 4

Stone J., *Legal Controls of International Conflict* (Sydney, Maitland Publications, 1954)

Stubbs J. (ed.), *Women, Male Violence and the Law* (Sydney, Institute of Criminology Series no. 6, 1994)

Sullivan D., 'Gender equality and religious freedom: toward a framework for conflict resolution', 24 *New York University Journal of International Law and Politics* (1992) 795

Sullivan D., 'Women's human rights and the 1993 World Conference on Human Rights', 88 *American Journal of International Law* (1994) 152

Swaak-Goldman O., 'The ICTY and the right to a fair trial: a critique of the critics', 10 *Leiden Journal of International Law* (1997) 215

Sylvester C., 'Feminists and realists view autonomy and obligation in international relations', in Peterson V. (ed.), *Gendered States: Feminist (Re) Visions of International Relations Theory* (Boulder, Lynne Rienner Publishers, 1992) 155

Sylvester C., *Feminist Theory and International Relations in a Postmodern Era* (Cambridge, Cambridge University Press, 1994)

Szalai A., 'The situation of women in the UN': a report based on the proceedings of the Colloquium of Senior UN Officials held at 4–6 July 1972 at Schloss Hernstein, Austria (New York, UNITAR, 1973)

Sztucki J., *Jus Cogens and the Vienna Convention on the Law of Treaties: A Critical Appraisal* (Vienna, Springer-Verlag, 1972)

Tasioulas J., 'In defence of relative normativity: communitarian values and the *Nicaragua* case', 16 *Oxford Journal of Legal Studies* (1996) 85

Tesón F., 'International human rights and cultural relativism', 25 *Virginia Journal of International Law* (1985) 869

Tesón F., 'Realism and Kantianism in international law', *Proceedings of the 86th Annual Meeting of the American Society of International Law* (Washington DC, American Society of International Law, 1992) 113

Tesón F., 'The Kantian theory of international law', 92 *Columbia Law Review* (1992) 53

Tesón F., 'Feminism and international law: a reply', 33 *Virginia Journal of International Law* (1994) 647

Tesón F., *Humanitarian Intervention: An Inquiry into Law and Morality* (Irvington-on-Hudson, Transnational Publishers, 2nd ed. 1997)

Tesón F., *A Philosophy of International Law* (Boulder, Westview, 1998)

Thakur R., 'From collective to cooperative security? The Gareth Evans vision of the United Nations', in Lawson S. (ed.), *The New Agenda for Global Security: Cooperating for Peace and Beyond* (Sydney, Allen & Unwin, 1995) 19

Thomas D. and Beasley M., 'Domestic violence as a human rights issue', 12 *Human Rights Quarterly* (1993) 36

Thomas J., 'History and international law in Asia: a time for review?', in Macdonald R. (ed.), *Essays in Honour of Wang Tieya* (Dordrecht, Martinus Nijhoff, 1994) 813

Thornton M. (ed.), *Public and Private: Feminist Legal Debates* (Melbourne, Oxford University Press, 1995)

Thornton M., 'The cartography of public and private', in Thornton M. (ed.), *Public and Private: Feminist Legal Debates* (Melbourne, Oxford University Press, 1995) 2

Tickner J., *Gender in International Relations* (New York, Columbia University Press, 1992)

Tickner J., 'Feminist approaches to issues of war and peace', in Dallmeyer D. (ed.), *Reconceiving Reality: Women and International Law* (Washington DC, American Society of International Law, 1993) 267

Tickner J., 'Inadequate providers? A gendered analysis of states and security', in Camilleri J., Jarvis A. and Paolini A. (eds), *The State in Transition* (Boulder, Lynne Rienner Publishers, 1995) 133

Tickner J., 'You just don't understand: troubled engagements between feminists and IR theorists', 41 *International Studies Quarterly* (1997) 611

Timothy K., 'Women as outsiders: the glass ceiling at the United Nations', in D'Amico F. and Beckman P. (eds), *Women in World Politics: An Introduction* (Westport/London, Bergin and Garvey, 1995) 84

Today's Refugees, Tomorrow's Leaders, Report of the Saharawi Women's Conference, Houses of Parliament, UK, 28 October 1993

Tomuschat C., 'Obligations arising for states without or against their will', 241 *Recueil des Cours* (1993) vol. IV 195

Toubia N. (ed.), *Women of the Arab World* (New York, St. Martin's Press, 1988)

Tunkin V., 'Co-existence and international law', 95 *Recueil des Cours* (1958) 1

Turpel M. (Aki-Kwe), 'Patriarchy and Paternalism: the legacy of the Canadian State for First Nations women', 6 *Canadian Journal of Women and Law* (1993) 174

Tushnet M., 'An essay on rights', 62 *Texas Law Review* (1984) 1363

Tushnet M., 'Rights: an essay in informal political theory', 17 *Politics and Society* (1989) 403

Twining W., *Karl Llewellyn and the Realist Movement* (London, Weidenfeld & Nicolson, 1973, reprinted Norman, University of Oklahoma Press, 1985)

UN, *The World's Women 1970–90: Trends and Statistics* (New York, United Nations, 1991)

UN, *Women, Challenges to the Year 2000* (New York, United Nations, 1991)

UN, *Women In Politics and Decision-Making in the Late Twentieth Century: A United Nations Study* (Dordrecht, Martinus Nijhoff, 1992)

UN, *The World's Women 1995: Trends and Statistics* (New York, United Nations, 1995)

UN, *The United Nations and Human Rights 1945–1995* (New York, United Nations, 1995)

UN, *Women in a Changing Global Economy: 1994 World Survey on the Role of Women in Development* (New York, United Nations, 1995)

UN, *The United Nations and the Advancement of Women 1945–1996* (New York, United Nations, 1996)

UN, *Making Better International Law: The International Law Commission at 50* (New York, United Nations, 1998)

UNDP, *Report on Palestinian Women* (New York, United Nations, October 1994)

UNDP, *Human Development Report* (New York, Oxford University Press, 1995)

UNDP, *Human Development Report* (New York, Oxford University Press, 1997)

UNDP, *Human Development Report* (New York, Oxford University Press, 1998)

UNDP, *Integrating Human Rights with Sustainable Human Development* (New York, United Nations, 1998)

UNICEF, *The State of the World's Children* (Oxford, Oxford University Press, 1995)

United States Department of State, Afghanistan Report on Human Rights Practices 1997, issued by the Bureau of Democracy, Human Rights and Labor, 30 January 1998

Urquhart B. and Childers E., *A World in Need of Leadership: Tomorrow's United Nations* (Uppsala, Dag Hammarskjold Foundation, 1990)

Van Bueren G., *The International Law on the Rights of the Child* (Dordrecht, Martinus Nijhoff, 1995)

Van Bueren G. (ed.), *Childhood Abused: Protecting Children against Torture, Cruel, Inhuman and Degrading Treatment and Punishment* (Aldershot, Dartmouth Publishing Co./Ashgate Publishing Co., 1998)

Van den Haag E., *The War in Katanga, Report of a Mission* (American Committee for Aid to Katanga Freedom Fighters, 1962)

Van Hoof G., *Rethinking the Sources of International Law* (Deventer, Kluwer, 1983)

Van Ness P. (ed.), *Debating Human Rights* (London/New York, Routledge, 1999)

Verdross A., 'Les principes généraux du droit dans la jurisprudence internationale', 52 *Receuil des Cours* (1935) vol. II, 24

Vickers J., *Women and War* (London, Zed Books, 1993)

Viseur-Sellers P., 'The ad hoc tribunals' response to gender based crimes', paper prepared for UN Expert Group meeting on Gender-based Persecution, Toronto, Canada, November 1997

Viseur-Sellers P., 'Gender-based crimes in humanitarian law, in *Contemporary International Law Issues: New Forms, New Applications* (The Hague, Nederlandse Vereniging voor Internationaal Recht, 1997) 137

Walker K., 'An exploration of article 2(7) of the United Nations Charter as an embodiment of the public/private distinction in international law', 26 *New York University Journal of International Law and Politics* (1994) 173

Walter N., *The New Feminism* (London, Virago, 2nd edn 1999)

Walters M., 'American gothic: feminism, melodrama and the backlash', in Oakley A. and Mitchell J. (eds), *Who's Afraid of Feminism? Seeing through the Backlash* (New York, The New Press, 1997) 56

Walzer M., *Just and Unjust Wars: A Moral Argument with Historical Illustrations* (New York, Basic Books, 2nd ed. 1992)

Wang S., 'The maturation of gender equality into customary international law', 27 *New York University Journal of International Law and Politics* (1995) 899

Warbrick C., 'The new British policy on recognition of governments', 30 *International and Comparative Law Quarterly* (1981) 568

Warbrick C., 'Recognition of states: recent European practice', in Evans M. (ed.), *Aspects of Statehood and Institutionalism in Contemporary Europe* (Aldershot, Dartmouth Publishing Co., 1997) 9

Waring M., *Counting for Nothing: What Men Value and What Women are Worth* (Wellington, Allen & Unwin, 1988)

Waring M., *Three Masquerades: Essays on Equality, Work and Human Rights* (Sydney, Allen & Unwin, 1996)

Warnock K., *Land Before Honour* (London, Macmillan, 1990)

Watson E., 'Amnesty International and women's human rights: an organisational dilemma', 4 *Australian Journal of Human Rights* (1997) 126

Watson J., 'A realistic jurisprudence of international law', [1980] *The Year Book of World Affairs* 265

Watson J., 'State consent and the sources of international law', *Proceedings of the 86th Annual Meeting of the American Society of International Law* (Washington DC, American Society of International Law, 1992) 108.

Watson P., '(Anti) feminism after Communism', in Oakley A. and Mitchell J. (eds), *Who's Afraid of Feminism? Seeing through the Backlash* (New York, The New Press, 1997) 144

Watson S. (ed.), *Playing the State* (Sydney, Allen & Unwin, 1990)

Watson S., 'The state of play: an introduction', in Watson S. (ed.), *Playing the State* (Sydney, Allen & Unwin, 1990) 3

Weeramantry C., 'The function of the International Court of Justice in the development of international law', 10 *Leiden Journal of International Law* (1997) 309

Weil P., 'Towards relative normativity in international law?', 77 *American Journal of International Law* (1983) 413

Weiler J., Cassese A. and Spinedi M., *International Crimes of State: A Critical Analysis of the ILC's Draft Article 19 on State Responsibility* (Berlin/New York, De Gruyter, 1989)

Weisburd A., 'Customary international law: the problem of treaties', 21 *Vanderbilt Journal of Transnational Law* (1988) 1

Weisburd A., 'Interpreting state practice under treaties: a brief colloquy on the composition of customary international law', 21 *Vanderbilt Journal of Transnational Law* (1988) 457

Welch C. and Leary V. (eds), *Asian Perspectives on Human Rights* (Boulder, Westview Press, 1990)

West R., 'Feminism, critical social theory and law', [1989] *University of Chicago Legal Forum* 59

Weston B., 'Security Council Resolution 678 and Persian Gulf decision making: precarious legitimacy', 85 *American Journal of International Law* (1991) 516

Weston B., Falk R. and Charlesworth H., *International Law and World Order* (St Paul, West Group, 3rd edn 1997)

White L., *International Non-Governmental Organizations* (New Brunswick, Rutgers University Press, 1951)

White N., *The Law of International Organisations* (Manchester, Manchester University Press, 1996)

Whiteman M., '*Jus cogens* in international law, with a projected list', 7 *Georgia Journal of International and Comparative Law* (1977) 609

Whittick A., *Women into Citizens* (London, The Athenaeum Publishing Co. Ltd, 1979)

Whitworth S., *Feminism and International Relations* (London, Macmillan, 1994)

Wilenski P., 'Reforming the United Nations for the post-cold war era', in Bustelo M. and Alston P. (eds), *Whose New World Order: What Role for the United Nations?* (Annandale, Federation Press, 1991) 122

Willetts P. (ed.), *The Conscience of the World: The Influence of Non-governmental Organizations in the United Nations System* (Washington DC, Brookings Institution, 1996)

Williams P., 'Alchemical notes: reconstructing ideals from deconstructed rights', 22 *Harvard Civil Rights-Civil Liberties Law Review* (1987) 401

Williams P., *The Alchemy of Race and Rights* (Cambridge, Harvard University Press, 1991)

Williams W., 'Equality's riddle: pregnancy and the equal treatment/special treatment debate', 13 *New York University Review of Law and Social Change* (1985) 325

Wilson B., 'Will women judges really make a difference?', 28 *Osgoode Hall Law Journal* (1990) 507

Wing A., 'Custom, religion, and rights: the future legal status of Palestinian women', 35 *Harvard International Law Journal* (1994) 149

Wing A., 'A critical race feminist conceptualization of violence: South African and Palestinian women', 60 *Albany Law Review* (1997) 943

Wing A. and Merchan S., 'Rape, ethnicity, and culture: spirit injury from Bosnia to Black America', 25 *Columbia Human Rights Law Review* (1993) 1

Winslow A. (ed.), *Women, Politics, and the United Nations* (Westport/London, Greenwood Press, 1995)

Winslow A., 'Specialized agencies and the World Bank', in Winslow A. (ed.), *Women, Politics, and the United Nations* (Westport/London, Greenwood Press, 1995) 155

Wolfke K., 'Some persistent controversies regarding customary international law', 24 *Netherlands Yearbook of International Law* (1993) 1

Wolfke K., *Custom in Present International Law* (Dordrecht, Martinus Nijhoff, 2nd revised ed. 1993)

Women in Decision-Making: Facts and Figures on Women in Political and Public Decision Making in Europe (Network of Experts Publication, 2nd ed. 1994)

Women in Diplomacy. The FCO 1782-1994 (London, Historical Branch LRD, 1994)

Women's Human Rights Step by Step (Washington DC, Women, Law and Development, 1997)

Wright S., 'Economic rights and social justice: a feminist analysis of some international human rights conventions', 12 *Australian Yearbook of International Law* (1992) 241

Wright S., 'Economic rights, social justice and the state: a feminist reappraisal', in Dallmeyer D. (ed.), *Reconceiving Reality: Women and International Law* (Washington DC, American Society of International Law, 1993)

Wright S., 'Women in the global economic order: a feminist perspective', 10 *American University Journal of International Law and Policy* (1995) 861

Wynter S., '"Genital mutilation" or "symbolic birth"? Female circumcision, lost origins, and the aculturism of feminist western thought', 47 *Case Western Reserve Law Review* (1997) 501

Young E., 'A feminist politics of health care: the case of Palestinian women under Israeli occupation, 1979-82', in Mayer T. (ed.), *Women and the Israeli Occupation: The Politics of Change* (London, Routledge, 1994) 179

Young I., *Justice and the Politics of Difference* (Princeton, Princeton University Press, 1990)

Young O., 'International law and social science: the contributions of Myres S. McDougal', 66 *American Journal of International Law* (1972) 60

Yuval-Davis N., 'The Israel example', in Chapkis W. (ed.), *Loaded Questions: Women in the Military* (Amsterdam, Transnational Institute, 1981) 73

Yuval-Davis N., 'Women, ethnicity and empowerment', in Oakley A. and Mitchell J. (eds), *Who's Afraid of Feminism? Seeing through the Backlash* (New York, The New Press, 1997) 77

Zalewski M., 'Well, what is the feminist perspective on Bosnia?', 71 *International Affairs* (1995) 339

Zemanek K., 'Majority rule and consensus technique in law-making diplomacy', in Macdonald R. and Johnston D. (eds), *The Structure and Process of International Law: Essays in Legal Philosophy, Doctrine and Theory* (Dordrecht, Martinus Nijhoff, 1983) 857

Zoller E., *Peacetime Unilateral Remedies: An Analysis of Countermeasures* (Dobbs Ferry, Transnational Books, 1984)

Table of cases

Table of cases

Table of cases

Table of cases

Table of cases

Table of cases

Table of Treaties
(in chronological order)

385

Other International Instruments

Abbreviations

CHR United Nations Commission on Human Rights
ECOSOC United Nations Economic and Social Council
GA United Nations General Assembly
Res. Resolution
SC United Nations Security Council
UNHCR United Nations High Commissioner for Refugees
WHA World Health Assembly
WHO World Health Organisation

Index

Please note that page references with an 'n' included denote references to footnotes

401

Muslim, *Shariah* law 105, 106, 116, 158
See also Palestine, *Hamas* movement in; treaties, reservations to
International Research and Training Institute for the Advancement of Women, *see* United Nations, International Research and Training Institute for the Advancement of Women

Jejeebhoy, S. 13
Johnson-Odim, C. 47
jurisdiction in international law
  domestic *see* domestic jurisdiction
  extra-territorial 19, 135, 143, 277–8
  immunity from *see* immunity
  statehood 143–5
  universal 144, 315
jus cogens 16, 27–8, 69, 94, 118–21, 123, 136–7

Kamal, Z. 157
Karadzic, R. 145, 146, 330
Kenya, application of customary law in 224–5
Khalifa, S. 159
Kirgis, F. 71
Kirk McDonald, G. 311
Knop, K. 169, 194
Koh, H. 67, 308
Koskenniemi, M. 21–2, 29–30, 34–5, 69, 125, 165, 170
Kuenyehia, A. 240
Kuttab, E. 158
Kuwait
  electoral laws in 10, 106, 262
  invasion of by Iraq 106, 129, 138, 140, 156, 254, 261, 291, 301
  Operation Desert Storm 258
  women's rights, violation in 262, 269, 276, 283

Lacey, N. 39, 59
League of Nations 15, 16, 97, 99
liberalism *see* democracy; feminist, theories of law; international law, theories of

life, right to 120, 150, 203, 233–4, 235, 316
Locke, J. 30–1
Lowe, V. 79–80
Lugones, M. 51

MacCormick, N. 164
McDougal, M. 33–4
McDougall, G. 237
MacKinnon, C. 42–3, 44, 147, 166, 259
Maine, Sir Henry 25
mainstreaming *see* gender, mainstreaming
Maldives Republic 104, 105, 107
margin of appreciation, doctrine of 215, 216
Mexico Conference *see* United Nations, conferences
militarism 160, 166, 199, 284–5
Miller, C. 15
Minow, M. 210
Mohanty, C. 53, 238
Montesquieu, C. L. 202
Morgenthau, H. 28
Mumba, F. N. M. 311
Muslim law *see* Islamic states, Muslim, *Shariah* law

Naffine, N. 129
Nairobi Conference on Women *see* United Nations, conferences
Nasreen, T. 135
nationality
  as a category of representation 185, 194–5
  of women 10, 16, 114–16, 128, 216, 317
nationalism 35, 46–7
natural law *see* international law, theories of
Nedelsky, J. 129, 132, 169
New Haven school *see* international law, theories of
New International Economic Order 36, 205
New Zealand 106, 295
non-governmental organisations 1, 124, 169, 173, 220, 321, 329